CW01164176

The Age of Secrecy

The Age of Secrecy

Jews, Christians, and the Economy of Secrets, 1400–1800

Daniel Jütte

Translated from the German by Jeremiah Riemer

Yale
UNIVERSITY PRESS
New Haven & London

Published with assistance from: the Annie Burr Lewis Fund; the foundation established in memory of Calvin Chapin of the Class of 1788, Yale College; and the foundation established in memory of Oliver Baty Cunningham of the Class of 1917, Yale College.

English translation copyright © 2015 by Yale University.
All rights reserved.
Originally published as Daniel Jütte, *Das Zeitalter des Geheimnisses,* 2nd ed., Göttingen. Copyright © 2012 by Vandenhoeck & Ruprecht GmbH & Co., KG.

This book may not be reproduced, in whole or in part, including illustrations, in any form (beyond that copying permitted by Sections 107 and 108 of the U.S. Copyright Law and except by reviewers for the public press), without written permission from the publishers.

Yale University Press books may be purchased in quantity for educational, business, or promotional use. For information, please e-mail sales.press@yale.edu (U.S. office) or sales@yaleup.co.uk (U.K. office).

Designed by
Set in Bulmer type by Westchester Book Group
Printed in the United States of America.

Library of Congress Cataloging-in-Publication Data
Jütte, Daniel, 1984- author.
[Zeitalter des Geheimnisses. English]
The age of secrecy : Jews, Christians, and the economy of secrets, 1400–1800 / Daniel Jütte ; translated from the German by Jeremiah Riemer.
pages   cm
Includes bibliographical references and index.
ISBN 978-0-300-19098-4 (hardcover : alk. paper)
1. Occultism—Europe—History. 2. Secrecy—Religious aspects—Judaism—History. 3. Secrecy—Religious aspects—Christianity—History. 4. Mystery. 5. Jewish magic—History. 6. Alchemy—Europe—History. 7. Colorni, Abraham, approximately 1530-   8. Jewish alchemists—Europe—History. I. Title.
BF1439.J88 2015
130.94—dc23
2014044267

A catalogue record for this book is available from the British Library.

This paper meets the requirements of ANSI/NISO Z39.48-1992 (Permanence of Paper).

10 9 8 7 6 5 4 3 2 1

Contents

Preface to the English Edition VII

ONE
The Age of Secrecy 1

TWO
Masters of the Arcane and Their Métiers 37

THREE
Zones of Interaction: The Case of Magic 85

FOUR
Trading in Secrets and Economic Life 94

FIVE
Abramo Colorni, Professor of Secrets 116

SIX
The Culture and Crisis of Secrecy 224

Acknowledgments 261
Notes 263
Bibliography 355
Index 415

Preface to the English Edition

Books have their own destiny, as a well-known Latin expression maintains. So do secrets. I would like to begin with the former, as this book has indeed had a somewhat unexpected destiny. I completed it shortly before its topic—secrecy—became the subject of front-page headlines amidst a major diplomatic and political imbroglio in the United States and worldwide. In 2010 and 2011, the WikiLeaks platform released hundreds of thousands of classified diplomatic and military documents, leading U.S. government officials to speak of an attack not just on America's foreign policy interests but also on the entire international community. WikiLeaks, in turn, has justified the continuing leaks by arguing that its mission is to uncover what "institutional secrecy unjustly conceals."

This book does not deal with, let alone judge, the acts of whistleblowers in our day. Surely future historians will study their deeds and motivations, and in doing so might relate their activism to a larger phenomenon, namely that of the profound distrust of secrecy in our time. "Everyone agrees that openness is a virtue in a democracy," a major U.S. newspaper recently declared. In fact, there are countries—in Scandinavia, for instance—where explicit antisecrecy policies have been established to ensure the utmost transparency in the way the government conducts its affairs. Still, politics is by no means the only domain of modern life in which we expect secrecy to be reduced to a minimum and subjected to thorough control. Openness has more generally become the mantra of our age. We assign, for example, great importance to openness in the circulation of knowledge: science is a case in point. This is also true of modern social life, not least where it takes place in the brave new digital world. By and large, secrecy is seen today as a form of antisocial or suspicious behavior.

The lay of the land was very different during the period discussed in this book, which brings us back to the destiny of secrets. This book argues that the period between the fifteenth and the eighteenth centuries was a veritable "age of secrecy." No other period in European history, neither before nor since, has shown so profound a fascination with secrecy and secret sciences. Arcane knowledge was widely considered positive knowledge, and this notion of "good secrecy" extended across all fields of life, including everyday life, the scientific and economic domains, and the political culture of the day. French philosopher René Descartes succinctly captured the essential premise underlying this phenomenon in his motto: "He who has lived well, has lived in secret." This thriving culture of secrecy was not merely a response to repression by higher authorities or the lack of freedom of expression in an age marked by bitter political, religious, and social conflicts (although such factors certainly played a role). Nor should we espouse the view that the early modern fascination with secrets constituted an intrinsically inferior or deficient mode of knowledge production bound to be obliterated by the rise of more democratic and open societies. To put it differently, early modern people were not preoccupied with secrets because they were forced to or because they were not yet "enlightened." Rather, they relished secrets because they considered true and important knowledge to be secret by definition. By the same token, few of them believed that divulging secrets was per se a good thing; in fact, the urge to reveal or the desire to know was often not the driving force behind the circulation and study of secret knowledge. Goethe was by no means alone when he described in his autobiography how as a young man studying various secret sciences he had "found more delight in these secrets than could ever be gained from their revelation."

A comprehensive history of secrecy in premodern Europe has not yet been written. This book sets out to provide a framework for such an undertaking, while also raising the question of how our own notion of secrecy has radically changed, becoming much less positive in comparison to the "age of secrecy." By offering a conceptual and methodological tool kit for the historical study of secrecy, this book will, I hope, contribute to the creation of a larger multidisciplinary field of "secrecy studies." In my exploration of the age of secrecy I have devoted special attention to the Jewish-Christian economy of secrets and its development from the Renaissance to the Enlightenment, as I believe that this phenomenon is eminently suited to illuminate the cultural significance and social function of clandestine knowledge during this period. To be sure, I do not argue that we should go back to the premodern culture of secrecy. But at the same time I hold that we should take the premodern passion for secrets seriously. In other words, if we wish to understand why people were fascinated with secrecy and how secret knowledge created distinct social, economic, and political opportunities, we must disavow a teleological narrative that depicts the history of knowledge as an inevitable march toward openness. In the same vein, we have to abandon the notion that open knowledge is inherently superior to secret knowledge.

A final word is due on editorial matters. Anyone familiar with translations from German into English knows that the task poses a myriad of challenges, similar perhaps to those encountered by the early modern alchemist in his quest for transmutation. I am fortunate to have worked with a translator who has joined forces with me toward not merely translating the original, but producing, as we hope, a readable and smooth English text. Any reader comparing the German and English editions will no doubt notice that certain liberties have been taken to that end. Still, this book is a translation, not an enlarged edition, and therefore I had to refrain from engaging with more recent publications that touch on issues related to my study in some way or another. Only in a few instances, where it could be easily integrated, have I added material that I found after the publication of the German edition, some of which was brought to my attention by reviewers. This also explains slight differences in the numbering of the notes in the German and English editions.

Italian sources with dates adhering to the old Venetian and Florentine calendars are cited according to the modern standard calendar. For the transliteration of Hebrew words I have followed, with some modifications, the rules of the most recent edition of the *Encyclopaedia Judaica* (2007). Unless indicated otherwise, all biblical quotations are taken from the King James Bible.

The Age of Secrecy

ONE

The Age of Secrecy

Secret History

> It is, therefore, entirely thinkable that public history can be clarified out of the secret history.
>
> —Johann Gottlieb Fichte, *Vorlesungen über die Freimaurerei*

When the German philosopher Johann Gottlieb Fichte (1762–1814) wrote those words, he had the history of Freemasonry in mind.[1] Fichte bequeathed anti-Semitic remarks to posterity, and he probably would have objected to having his ideas applied to Jewish history. However, that is precisely one of the goals of this book. Its point of departure is early modern Jewish history—especially the constant and varied interactions between Jewish and Christian society, which should be neither downplayed nor overemphasized. At a more general level, this book deals with the meaning and function of secrets and concealment between 1400 and 1800. One of its intentions is to use the lens of "secret history" (adapting, for a moment, Fichte's terms) to obtain a sharper picture of "public history." My topic is, in brief, the general history of knowledge in the premodern age.

What does the "public history" of the Jews in early modern Europe look like? When scholars discuss the everyday life and professional practices of early modern Jews, they usually discuss money lending, long-distance trade, medicine, peddling, and the occasional handicraft. It is particularly hard keeping track of the number of studies about Jews active in the money business. There is good reason for the abundance of such studies. After all, the money business was undoubtedly one of the most prominent and visible features of Jewish economic life well into the bourgeois era, though often at the level of small loans and pawnbroking. This book does not seek to overturn previous works on Jewish economic and cultural history in premodern Europe. Rather, it attempts to draw attention to an area of Jewish cultural history and the history of knowledge that has barely been explored. This field, whose economic significance cannot be underestimated, is the trade in secrets, or, stated in somewhat broader terms, the premodern Jewish economy of secrets.

First, a few concepts need to be clarified—especially the term "economy of secrets." As used here, "economy" picks up on recent research in the history of science in which "knowledge economy" is an umbrella term for all the different, and sometimes competing, scientific cultures of the premodern world.[2] The economy of secrets is one part of that "knowledge economy." It also reflects the commercial character of the trade in secrets. Secrets can become a commodity; this holds true for the early modern era in much the same way that it does for our own time.[3] "Economy of secrets," then, refers to all activities that involve trading, offering, negotiating, delivering, exchanging, and buying secrets. Even more broadly, it refers to any overlap between those activities and the mercantile sphere, including mercantile rhetoric, in the early modern era.

My definition of "secret" is equally broad. In early modern Europe, the secret was a sweeping concept encompassing all facets of people's lives. The cosmos was not just filled with God's miraculous signs and marked by a complex system of correspondences between all beings—the doctrine of signatures.[4] For Jews and Christians alike, the cosmos was also replete with secrets and with prohibitions on the knowledge of certain secrets.[5] According to Niklas Luhmann, "the everyday worlds of tangible and controllable meaning quickly [passed] over into that which is unknown, in need of explanation, dependent on authority; and the doctrine of religious and natural secrets fit seamlessly into this basic orientation of the familiar and unfamiliar."[6] Christians distinguished between different arcane fields. For example, there were nature's secrets (*arcana naturae*), God's secrets (*arcana Dei*), secrets of the state (*arcana imperii*), worldly secrets (*arcana mundi*), and secrets of the heart (*arcana cordis*), though these categories sometimes overlapped.[7]

The term "arcanum" in itself had different facets in early modern literature. In his monumental *Universal-Lexicon* (1732–1754), Johann Heinrich Zedler defined the arcanum as "a secret, incorporeal, and immortal thing, which cannot be recognized by man, except through experience."[8] Theological discussions and discussions of natural philosophy used this term differently. In medical texts following the tradition of Paracelsus, "arcana" denoted not just secrets in general but also specific, effective healing powers (*virtutes*) and medicines produced by alchemy. Eventually, almost all medicines whose production and ingredients were kept secret came to be viewed as arcana.[9] Moreover, we often encounter arcana in the context of guild secrets (*arcana artis*).[10]

Secretum was another term used to refer to a secret. It was frequently synonymous with arcanum in both theory and practice, but there were sometimes differences. Heidrun Kugeler has recently attempted to distinguish among the concepts *secretum, arcanum,* and *occultum* in diplomatic language and literature from the seventeenth century. According to Kugeler, we face a broad "conceptual field" where these terms referred to hidden contents as well as to techniques for both hiding and exposing those contents.[11] Things look similar in other areas of early modern life. In everyday life, however, *secretum* tended to have an even broader meaning, and it was also more deeply rooted than was arcanum. Almost any kind of knowledge could become a *secretum;* occasionally the term simply described a medical prescription or culinary recipe, or even just a trick.[12]

Moreover, *secretum* was also a philosophical category. The Aristotelian tradition distinguished between two different forms of *secreta*. One included all manifestations of occult qualities, such as natural forces whose explanation overtaxed human understanding, like magnetism. The second referred to humanmade wonders, including the secret techniques of artisans such as glassmakers.[13] Girolamo Cardano (1501–1576) provided even more definitions in his *De secretis,* first published in 1562. The famous physician and natural philosopher drew a distinction among three kinds of secrets: first, unknown phenomena that were still awaiting discovery; second, things that were known in principle but were in practice disclosed only to a small circle; and third, everyday phenomena that were widely known but whose causes remained unknown.[14]

As this outline makes clear, narrowing down the early modern concept of secrecy is an elusive task. This is especially true for the day-to-day practice of the arcane sciences. Arcane knowledge was not just a matter of secret knowledge or knowledge about secrets, as modern usage might suggest. Rather, it also encompassed knowledge about occult events that occur in nature. These occurrences were not necessarily secret—many of the processes and their repercussions were there for all to see. But their causes were secret—that is, hidden.

The broad concept of secrecy in the early modern era naturally has implications for this book. It will deal with secrets of all kinds, whether from the natural sciences, alchemy, magic, the military, or politics. The only secrets largely bypassed are those dealing with theological and spiritual matters, that is, those secrets that one could classify as the *arcana Dei* of Judaism, belonging more properly to the rabbinical theology of secrets.[15] I will also touch only briefly on the history of the dissemination and reception of Kabbalah, by both Jews and Christians. This decision may seem surprising at first glance. The dissemination of ideas derived from Jewish mysticism is no doubt a prime example of the boom in secrecy among premodern Jews. On closer examination, however, such secrets are better classified as "mysteries." This distinction between "secret" and "mystery" has conceptual importance. While the German word for secret—*Geheimnis*—combines two different meanings, English distinguishes between "secrets" and "mysteries."[16] A mystery is something not known "because it is not knowable in principle." By contrast, the reason one does not know a secret is that a person or a group of people has hidden it, even though it is "knowable in principle."[17] This book will deal with secrets of the latter kind, in fields ranging from alchemy to military affairs.

The criterion for what counts as a secret in this book is ultimately a modern one: the secrets I discuss are all "knowable in principle." As Kant already observed, these secrets differed from mysteries not least with regard to their distribution and circulation.[18] There is no doubt that the secrets of Jewish mysticism in the early modern era spread into the very capillaries of Jewish and Christian spiritual life. But—and this is important—they are seldom found in economic circulation. The spread of Jewish mysticism since the Late Middle Ages is a fascinating chapter in European intellectual history, but it hardly registers in early modern economic history. There were attempts to shape Kabbalah into a kind of "practical technology," as reflected in the distinction between theoretical Kabbalah (*Kabbala iyyunit*) and practical or magical Kabbalah (*Kabbala ma'asit*).[19] I will discuss the resulting overlap with alchemy in greater detail later. On the whole, however, I agree with Gershom Scholem in characterizing the worldview of the Kabbalists as "symbolic in the strictest sense."[20] In the popular Jewish imagination of the time, Kabbalists were often located in the sphere of the angels, while alchemists—who were perhaps the most prominent embodiment of the early modern economy of secrets—were situated in the earthly world.[21] Christians, too, regarded Kabbalists as members of a small circle preoccupied with sublime mysteries.[22]

This book is concerned with secrets that differed from mysteries not only because they were "knowable in principle," but also because they were often considered "useful knowledge" that was required in the field of technology or in the political and economic spheres.[23] It is no surprise, then, that arcana even became the foundation of a "cameralist technique for how to guide a country properly," as in the case of the alchemist and economic theoretician Johann Joachim Becher (1635–1682).[24] In fact, the countless books of secrets circulating during the early modern era were often, in substance, instruction manuals providing technical or medical know-how.[25]

Obtaining, providing, offering, and negotiating these "practical secrets" were central to premodern Jewish economic life.[26] In Italy, there were even Jewish "professors of secrets," or *professori de' secreti*. The most prominent among them was Abramo Colorni (ca. 1544–1599), on whom I focus in the fifth, and most central, chapter. There are few fields in which Colorni did not distinguish himself; he was a court engineer, mathematician, chiromancer, alchemist, weapons and powder manufacturer, cryptologist, magus, and dealer in luxury goods. Yet he was not the only

Jewish *professore de' secreti* during this era. Focusing on his largely forgotten life story is just one of many possible ways of approaching the Jewish trade in secrets. I share Anthony Grafton's view that "the public anatomy of an individual magus—or at least the dissection of the material concerning him—represents a procedure appropriate for the period under investigation."[27] Indeed, a biographical approach, though not of the genre of "heroic biography," has great potential for the history of science.[28] A critical biographical approach, especially one that is open to the methods of micro-history, can provide an opportunity to demonstrate "the multifarious dimensions that science can have within one individual protagonist," including such dimensions as "socioeconomic structures, the institutional framework, and mental hallmarks."[29]

In this sense, Colorni's life story is eminently suited to illustrating the economic and social opportunities, as well as the everyday life, of an early modern Jew operating in the economy of secrets. As Colorni's contemporaries emphasized, his varied activities can be aptly captured under the umbrella term "professor of secrets." But he was not the only member of his family to find the economy of secrets an attractive market. His son Simone (born ca. 1570), who went by the colorful byname Il Morino, gained a reputation as a purveyor of precious and mysterious objects—from unicorns to rare works of art—and was held in high esteem at the Gonzaga court in Mantua. Other relatives of Abramo Colorni were active at various courts as purveyors of sought-after goods. His father-in-law was Yeḥiel Nissim da Pisa (ca. 1493–1574), one of Italy's leading moneylenders and Kabbalists. The history of the Colorni family in the early modern era provides extensive insights into the network structures and cross-generational features that characterized the economy of secrets.

Alongside spectacular life stories like Abramo Colorni's, there were also a large number of Jews engaged in "ordinary" professions who traded in secrets. That business often provided considerable supplemental income, alongside the prospect of lucrative contracts from, and contacts with, Christian society. Offering and negotiating secrets of all kinds could also create unusual zones of contact between Jews and Christians. Both economic relevance and interfaith contact indicate how research into the trade in secrets can generate insights into key areas of early modern Jewish-Christian culture. The economy of secrets was a distinctive marketplace that opened up numerous financial and social opportunities. Historians have often assumed that the open circulation of knowledge must have held a special attraction for an oppressed minority. However, a closer look at what the economy of secrets meant for early modern Jews challenges this assumption. In the final chapter, I flesh out what this means for the historiographic debate regarding the position Jews took toward and within the "Scientific Revolution." I also elaborate on the implications for both the history of secrets in the premodern world and the history of knowledge in general.

Much of what has been said so far applies equally well to Christian suppliers of secrets. In early modern Europe, the view was widely held that the acquisition of knowledge was a hunt (*venatio*). This view created a lucrative market for *secreta,* especially at court. There were large numbers of *professori de' secreti* and others adept at secrets on the Christian side.[30] Because they formed the majority of society, the number of Christians involved in the economy of secrets was always much larger than the number of Jews. However, there were three specific characteristics of the Jewish economy of secrets that distinguished it from its Christian counterpart. The first is the widespread notion that Jews had an above-average expertise in this field. Second is the importance of the sphere of secrets for allowing Jews to forge remarkable contacts with the dominant society. And third is the fact that the activity of Jews in the economy of secrets often had a particularly complex relationship with the core areas of economic and mercantile life.

When I began my investigation, biographies like Colorni's intrigued me primarily as a point of departure to tackle questions about the place of natural science in premodern Judaism. In the course of my research, however, I found that these questions, which have been asked for a long time, bypass the sources in various ways. Instead, we need to see Colorni's life story as just one of many instances, albeit a very instructive one, of premodern Jews' engagement in secrets of all kinds. This engagement was frequently associated with, though not always solely attributable to, the notion that Jews had unique expertise in the arcane. In order to understand why the dominant society linked Jews to secrets in such a specific way, why Jews themselves were interested in secret knowledge, and what role this played in Jews' contacts with the Christian majority, I turned my attention to the general meaning and function of secrets in the premodern era. Gradually, it became clear that the topic of Jewish expertise in the arcane amounted to far more than just a footnote in the general history of knowledge. As a result, this books attempts to proceed from Jewish history to a general praxeology of secrecy in the premodern era.

Secrecy as a Historical Topic

We have already broached one of the central criteria for defining secrecy: the question of what is "knowable in principle." This describes an important feature of the secrets under discussion, but it also explains why they could become commodities in circulation and "useful knowledge." Yet it is not enough to treat secrets merely as objects. In fact, a secret cannot be artificially separated from the specific mode of social action it generates. It is often not necessary for historians to uncover the actual content of the secrets under investigation—to the extent that this content can be reconstructed in the first place. The secret itself does not offer a rich field of research so much as does the specific social interaction it creates or necessitates. In this context, historians are all well-advised to look beyond the boundaries of their own field. This is especially true because comparatively few historical studies of secrecy have been undertaken. The only significant exception is the phenomenon of secret societies, but these did not really develop until the eighteenth century, at the end of the early modern era.[31] A comprehensive account of the theory and practice of secrecy in the early modern era is still lacking.[32] However, historians can take cues from neighboring disciplines that have thought about the phenomenon of secrecy more deeply and in a more systematic way.[33] This is true of psychology, communication theory, linguistics, ethnology, and religious studies, but especially of sociology.[34]

Within the field of sociology, Georg Simmel's authoritative 1906 study "Das Geheimnis und die geheime Gesellschaft" (The Sociology of Secrecy and of Secret Societies) stands out.[35] Simmel proceeds from the general assumption that "secrecy procures enormous extension of life, because with publicity many sorts of purposes could never arrive at realization."[36] Using the example of interpersonal relations, he argues that "absolute understanding" and "psychological exhaustion . . . cripple the vitality of the relationship, and give to its continuance an appearance of utter futility."[37] Because of this, secrets are indispensable, for a secret "gives the person enshrouded by it an exceptional position . . . which is in principle quite independent of its casual content."[38] Simmel concludes, emphatically, that "secrecy in this sense—i.e., which is effective through negative or positive means of concealment—is one of the greatest accomplishments of humanity."[39] Simmel's observations have affected research to this day.[40] However, he has also been criticized for not distinguishing sharply enough between privacy and secrecy. Indeed, much of what Simmel characterizes as the "right of privacy" has less to do with secrecy than with the "state of privacy."[41] This is especially true where his study revolves around the sociology of lies, marriage, and letter-writing.

Yet Simmel's critics still have to grapple with the question of how to build a more extensive and cross-disciplinary theory of secrecy. This question has a number of answers, including the notion that a comprehensive definition of secrecy is impossible.[42] According to communication theorist Joachim Westerbarkey, a secret exists when at least one interested party is deliberately excluded from information.[43] This definition seems narrow, and it is unclear whether it can help elucidate such historical phenomena as "open secrets"—that is, secrets that are known to almost every member of society. On the other hand, Niklas Luhmann's assumption that "every precaution taken in an act of communication may be called a secret" provides a very broad definition.[44]

Scholars of communication theory have also distinguished between "simple" and "reflexive" secrets. Secrets are simple when the keeper communicates the existence of a secret but does not betray its content. This is the case with cryptography, where everyone can see the ciphertext, but only those with the key can decipher it. These secrets are distinct from "reflexive" ones, in which the very fact of secrecy is also kept secret. This is the case with steganography, where a text is encrypted but, because it is camouflaged as plaintext, appears to be readable by everyone.[45] However, defining a secret primarily by who remains excluded from confidential knowledge, and in what way, is unsatisfying to historians. Likewise, viewing secrets as strategies of deception or of withholding information misjudges the complexity of the economy of secrets. The philosopher Sissela Bok has rightly emphasized that secrets are not "bad" per se—even if they often have negative associations today.[46] According to Bok, everything can become a secret, and content cannot be used to define it. As a result, she defines a secret as "intentional concealment."[47]

The idea that secrets are intentionally concealed knowledge, alongside the idea that they are knowable in principle, provides a viable framework for analyzing the secrets treated in this book. It captures, with relative precision, the phenomenology of the secrets under discussion. At the same time, it is important to take the social and performative dimensions of secrecy into account. Analyzing the secret as an object can be only the first step toward a praxeology of secrecy. As Manfred Voigts has noted, scholars in the field of cultural studies have a special obligation "to demonstrate the basic structure within which secrecy is situated."[48] I will not discuss secrets as static objects, or even as subject matter exclusively negative in intent, but rather as specific modes of knowledge exchange and social action. Secrecy appears not as some deficient variant of open forms of knowledge but as something that gives people room to maneuver and creates zones of interaction for those involved. The secret generates its own social field and, in the specific case of the early modern era, a dynamic market.

Along these lines, we can take cues from recent social science research, in which secrets have increasingly come to be viewed as an "autonomous mode of communication" and as a form of social capital.[49] Of course, Simmel pointed out long ago that the use of secrets in interpersonal relations represents a "sociological technique," a form of social action "without which, in view of our social environment, certain purposes could not be attained."[50] For historians, it is imperative to embed the social function of the secret in its given historical context. In his studies of Freemasonry in the eighteenth century, Reinhart Koselleck made a plea to proceed precisely in this manner. "In the framework of the Absolute State," he pointed out, "the functions of the Masonic [secret] were far more important than their real or supposed content." To search for that content rather than inquire into the functions of the secret for Masonic lodges, therefore, "will mostly be in vain."[51] Richard van Dülmen has also asserted that "the 'secret' had no value as such" in the Enlightenment-minded secret order of the Illuminati in the eighteenth century "but was of functional significance instead."[52] These observations hold true for the economy of secrets as a whole.

The case of alchemy is particularly illustrative. In alchemy, a secret fulfilled different functions, and initiates had different reasons for keeping proprietary knowledge secret. Fear of the authorities was by no means the only reason why alchemists guarded their knowledge. Alchemists frequently believed their knowledge was a gift from God (*donum Dei*), and they felt a deep sense of responsibility for it.[53] Moreover, talk of secrecy in the early modern era was often a mode of staging and self-fashioning. It overlapped greatly with the business of the so-called projectors.[54] These observations lead us right into three key questions that will run throughout this book: What function did secrets and secrecy have in early modern encounters between Jews and Christians? What special room did the economy of secrets offer Jews to maneuver within Christian society that more open forms for the exchange of knowledge did not offer? And what does this mean for our understanding of the so-called Scientific Revolution, which has often been depicted as a march toward "open knowledge"?

From Medieval to Early Modern Secrecy

Historians have often argued that there was a breakthrough of "open knowledge" in the early modern era.[55] As a result, it can easily be overlooked that the popularity of secrets remained pervasive through the entire period, rooted as it was in a long tradition. As early as the twelfth century, Europeans had cultivated a lively interest in secrets that was influenced, among other things, by their reception of Islamic secret sciences—a process to which Jews made a major contribution.[56] In the early modern period, the notion of a hunt for secrets became one of the hallmarks of the knowledge economy, encompassing all strata of society. Fields of knowledge such as alchemy and Hermetism that were saturated with the aura of the secretive enjoyed wide popularity.[57] The economy of secrets flourished throughout Europe—and by no means only in secret. In contrast to universities and the emerging academies, this market was accessible to providers of all kinds; the acquisition of secrets did not necessarily depend on social status. Rather, money and information were the prevailing currencies in the economy of secrets.[58]

Consider the case of Venice. This city, for centuries the gate to the Orient, was more than just a "permanent fair" for goods and information.[59] It was also a center of production and distribution for all kinds of secrets.[60] In fact, early modern Italy saw the first appearance of the *professori de' secreti*—a profession epitomized by the nobleman, natural historian, and magus Giovan Battista Della Porta (1535–1615).[61] He even founded an Academy of Secrets (*Accademia de' Secreti*) in his hometown of Naples. Although this institution was closer to an informal salon than to an academy in today's sense, the circle around Della Porta drew people from all over Europe who were adept in secrets. This is also a reminder of the pan-European dimension of the fascination with secrets.[62] Another phenomenon that spanned all of Europe was the boom in the literature of *secreta*.[63] As early as the twelfth century, evidence exists for the formation of a specific genre of literature dealing with secrets or providing instruction about their disclosure. Yet works like the pseudo-Aristotelian *Secret of Secrets* (*Secretum secretorum*) rarely found their way into the normative canons of late medieval knowledge formed by the universities. The scholastic conception of knowledge assigned secrecy a position on the margins of *scientia*, which Aristotle had defined as a science of causes. By and large, phenomena and objects that could not be demonstrated or whose causes could not be explained by means of logic eluded *scientia* and its categories.[64] During the sixteenth century, the traditional and, in many places, normative attitude of the universities toward secrets lost its epistemic supremacy—a process to which the rise of the printing press made a major contribution.[65] Countless books claiming to divulge the most out-of-the-way secrets came on the market and were also read in academic circles, especially by those interested in natural science and natural philosophy. According to the historian

William Eamon, this process had a transformative effect on the genre itself. In Eamon's account, medieval *secreta* literature still exhibited an esoteric character, whereas the sixteenth-century books of secrets had a pronounced tendency toward openness. He dates the beginning of this process to the publication of the *Secreti del reverendo donno Alessio piemontese* (1555), a book of secrets whose author is believed to have been Girolamo Ruscelli (1500–ca. 1566). This book presented countless experiments and recipes derived from the sphere of the secret and held, according to Eamon, that it was "ethically superior" to publish secrets rather than conceal them from the unworthy masses. He claims that the epigones of Ruscelli and Della Porta adopted this position and thus the view that savants had a moral obligation to present their secrets to the public.[66] Accordingly, Eamon depicts the *professori de' secreti* as men for whom the search for secrets was "a scientific and moral crusade."[67]

It seems rash to date a general paradigm shift away from the practice of secrecy and toward the ideal of openness—in Eamon's words, a "conversion to the ethics of openness"—as early as the sixteenth century.[68] There were certainly many Jewish adepts at secrecy who, as late as the eighteenth century, had little interest in and few economic incentives for such a "conversion." Another, more general, objection to Eamon's thesis is that writing down and publishing secrets was by no means tantamount to disclosing them. Putting secrets into writing, especially during this era, is a relatively problematic criterion for claims about the "open" character of knowledge. The political philosopher Leo Strauss has rightly pointed to the art of "writing between the lines" that existed in the philosophical and esoteric tradition.[69] Commenting from the perspective of economic history, Carlo Cipolla has similarly warned against overestimating the "openness" of written sources revolving around innovations and technological know-how.[70] A case in point is the written and visual representations of a sophisticated, water-driven silk mill in the *Nuovo teatro di machine et edificii* (Padua, 1607) by the Italian engineer Vittorio Zonca. In the Piedmont, where mills of this kind were in operation, the technology was regarded as a state secret; whoever betrayed it could be subject to the death penalty. Yet the Piedmontese were not afraid of its publication. Indeed, Zonca's detailed description was of little use without the necessary expertise. Consider the case of England, where this invention was highly coveted: although Zonca's volume was available in English libraries as early as the 1620s, nobody succeeded in re-creating the machine until an Englishman had spent two years on-site in the Piedmont engaged in industrial espionage.[71] During this era, written knowledge often had to be combined with individual know-how before it could be made useful. The printed or written piece of paper is, as Cipolla puts it, "nothing more than an abstract of somebody's knowledge; it is the stepchild, not the parent of activity."[72]

This observation can be productively applied to the *secreta* literature. On its own, the publication of this literature is not necessarily evidence for an ethos of openness. Della Porta, whose *Magia naturalis* (first published in 1558) became a classic of the *secreta* literature and went through more than fifty editions in all the major European languages, still had enough secrets "in storage" after publication to yield him the handsome sum of 100,000 ducats from his princely patrons over the course of his life.[73] Cardano, too, published many of his secrets; just the same, he also remained "a veritable secret-monger."[74] By no means did publishing force early modern experts in arcana to relinquish their secrets. In this respect, printed books of secrets often had a function similar to the so-called *usus et fabrica* books at the time. These were printed instruction manuals for the manufacture of astronomical and mathematical instruments, often containing paper sheets and forms to be cut out. Only ostensibly did the dissemination of these books put the technical knowledge they contained into the hands of the public. Instruments manufactured on the basis of these texts were often inadequate for the desired task. However, they could spark buyers' interest to purchase a higher-value product. Thus, the *usus et fabrica* books did little to deprive established instrument makers of business. Instead, they generated an increasing demand for craft-manufactured instruments. Some of these books explicitly included information about local manufacturers of higher-value instruments.[75]

It is against this background that the early modern *secreta* literature needs to be seen. For one thing, such books often described secrets only vaguely, so that more was hinted at than revealed. For the other, few readers, like the well-off Italian naturalist Ulisse Aldrovandi (1522–1605), had enough leisure and means to try out every test design, recipe, or experiment from the *secreta* literature.[76] In many cases, the most reliable way to fathom and reveal secrets still required professional guidance and a performative context. The importance of oral transmission in the economy of secrets should not be underestimated, even if this phenomenon is harder for historians to grasp than are printed materials.[77]

Theatrical presentations—and theatricality in general—constituted one important element of the economy of secrets, not least among the large number of traveling charlatans.[78] Even the nobleman Della Porta—a respected playwright, among other things—held exclusive performances in his home.[79] Similarly, Leonardo Fioravanti (1518–1588)—equally well known throughout Italy as a seasoned *professore de' secreti*—reminded his readers that they could purchase the products and recipes described in his books of secrets at his house near the Church of San Luca in Venice.[80] This was a common pattern in the booklets of secrets published by charlatans—most of whom, it should be noted, were officially licensed by the authorities. Self-promotion often prevailed over the actual disclosure of secrets.[81]

As we have seen, the growing public circulation of secrets did not inevitably lead to a destabilization of the economy of secrets. Instead, publication was just one of the forms this economy assumed. As long as the secret retained its status as a relevant epistemic and cosmological category, this system remained stable. Throughout the eighteenth century, and even well into the nineteenth century, the ubiquity of charlatans and traveling *professori de' secreti* on the public squares and streets of Italy confirms that printed *secreta* literature was not capable of quenching the thirst of the broad masses for secrets.[82] In fact, it is unclear whether the broad masses were the primary target for *secreta* literature in the first place. Professors of secrets could gain income from the sale of their books, but the really lucrative business came only when publication led to a patronage relationship, especially at court.[83] To a considerable degree, the *secreta* literature functioned as a vehicle for "self-fashioning" and as an advertising strategy for their authors.[84] Even for those authors who earned their daily bread as charlatans in the market square, and who could hardly hope to rise to aristocratic patronage, publication of a secrecy booklet offered an opportunity for their own work to acquire a scholarly veneer.[85] Anyone already accepted as a true scholar, by contrast, had grounds for hoping that writing or compiling secrets might gain the attention of a wealthy patron. Throughout the early modern period, courts remained major and reliable patrons of the market for secrets.[86] Even an exponent of the "New Science" like Galileo preferred, as he was establishing contact with the Medici court, to tout the results of his scientific research as "particular secrets" (*secreti particolari*).[87] Around the same time Tommaso Campanella asserted that every true scientist (*scienziato*) was also a magus manipulating nature and its secrets.[88] Secret and open forms of knowledge interacted in complex ways during the early modern era—a fact that historians can easily miss if they are preoccupied with the question of which areas of knowledge were and were not "opened up."[89] As the humanist Giovanni Pico della Mirandola (1463-1494) noted, books containing secret knowledge could be simultaneously published and unpublished.[90] What is more, the disclosure of secrets often generated even more new secrets.

In this book, I only touch on the question of the "public" or, to put the question as it has been framed since the debate initiated by Jürgen Habermas, the controversy over when and whether such a category emerged in modern times.[91] Historians have shown that the "public" existed in various forms during the medieval and early modern periods, even if the concept as we know it today was unfamiliar at the time. There are actually good reasons for historians to speak of "publics" in the plural instead of one undivided "public."[92] But there is another reason why this book is not geared toward "proving" the emergence of a public or toward pitting that concept against the economy of secrecy: the boundaries are often blurred. As we have seen, many secrets circulated in public, or at least in a semipublic framework. This is not a contradiction in terms. Even modern industrial societies have "open secrets." The public—understood as a "communicative forum"—and *publi*cation do not clash with the economy of secrets.[93] It is true that numerous practitioners of the arcane did avoid the "light of publicity," but their reasons were often more strategic than intrinsic. Both open and secret knowledge could circulate in public; in either case, the objective was to find customers. And to circulate in public, secret knowledge did not necessarily have to be revealed.

As a result, when I discuss the tension between "secret" and "open" knowledge, I am not discussing the extent to which the knowledge in question was "public." Rather, I am interested in the way it was fashioned and presented. Secret knowledge was not necessarily hidden from the public; it differed from "open knowledge" in that the person holding it claimed to protect its contents or restrict its accessibility. This claim was expressed with different intensity, and it certainly was not automatically suspended by publication.

The "Arcanization" of Early Modern Life

Most of the early modern strategies for secrecy contradict today's ideal of science as an open form of knowledge production. Today, secrets have a negative connotation in many areas of life. It is easy to overlook that even modern science is never completely free of mechanisms geared toward secrecy.[94] Moreover, only a minority of society has the leisure, knowledge, and money to closely follow the production of scientific knowledge.[95] In contrast to early modern alchemy, however, contemporary science puts great emphasis on the open circulation of knowledge. Invoking the necessity of openness is certainly a distinctive feature of the modern concept of science, but it is also ritualized speech.[96] And establishing this ideal of openness occurred more haltingly than older, more teleological narratives in the history of science would have it.[97] In fact, the case of Jewish history can illustrate how the intellectual "paradigm shift" that supposedly characterized the Scientific Revolution was not immediate or decisive and did not lead to the spread of the New Science among all groups in society. In the case of Jews, this process was fully set in motion only when other societal parameters began to change in a massive way.[98]

The picture of the "arcanization" of early modern life becomes even more complex if one goes beyond the fields of natural science and technology and additional areas and systems of knowledge production. Indeed, the preoccupation with occult sciences continued well into the age of the

Enlightenment.[99] True, even today there continues to be considerable interest in the occult, or in what contemporary esotericists regard as occult; consider, for example, the New Age movement. However, this is no longer a reputable phenomenon outside self-styled "alternative" milieus. In fact, it has become an object of public derision that is simply not taken seriously by the scientific community. This is, of course, a major difference between the early modern era and today.

For people in the early modern era, the concept of "occult science" was not a contradiction in terms. In the seventeenth century the notion of *res natura occultae,* or an elusive hidden quality belonging to the natural world, and its associated terminology began to disappear from science's newly emerging institutions—especially from academies and learned societies.[100] But this does not mean that the notion of an everyday world rich in secrets also disappeared, let alone abruptly vanished, at the level of society as a whole.[101] The fascination with and significance of secrets remained intact across many areas of life.[102] This is especially true in the realm of private and religious everyday life, but it also holds true for other areas, like the arts. The boom in emblems, with their often enigmatic combinations of words and pictures, is just one example.[103]

Well into the eighteenth century, many believers even saw the study of nature's secrets as a genuine pathway toward a beatific vision of God.[104] Many considered magic and other divinatory practices as a way to attain a higher kind of knowledge. Books of secrets enjoyed considerable popularity both during and after the Scientific Revolution.[105] As late as 1785, the *Berliner Monatsschrift* noted the profusion of publications that had the word "secret" in their title, many of which did not necessarily have esoteric content.[106] Interest in secrets and mysteries was hardly confined to a small circle of obscurants. There was a widespread view, even in enlightened circles, that "the secret [was] absolutely the only means to improving mankind and leading it to the kingdom of virtue and enlightenment." Together with the very real need for secrecy occasioned by repression, this notion led to the establishment of Enlightenment-minded secret societies.[107] The formation and popularity of secret societies like the Freemasons, the Illuminati, and the Rosicrucians are cases in point.[108] In the realm of early modern politics and government, too, secrecy hardly eroded. Andreas Gestrich has pointed out that a history of early modern political secrecy has yet to be written.[109] This is all the more astonishing given that the idea of secrecy lies at the core of early modern political thought. Many people of the time regarded secrets as a "recognized and necessary dimension of political action," and the doctrine of the *arcana imperii* was a "centerpiece of politics."[110] The secret became "one of the most important political symbols," especially in the age of absolutism.[111] Michel Foucault has described the early modern doctrine of state arcana as an important aspect of how "governmentality" was shaped.[112] According to Foucault, "This knowledge of [the] forces [of the state] is in many cases only an instrument of government on condition of not being divulged."[113]

To be sure, the number of secrets the state believed it had to guard hardly increased during the Renaissance. There was, however, an "increasing taste for secrecy."[114] It was in this context that the concept of the *arcana imperii*, originally derived from Tacitus, became a catchphrase of political theory during the sixteenth and seventeenth centuries. For example, Arnold Clapmarius (1574–1604)—a Calvinist political theorist and the author of a widely read seventeenth-century book on statecraft, *De Arcanis Rerumpublicarum*—defined *arcana imperii* as "secret and concealed means of establishing and maintaining the state."[115] The state had to create secret structures, acquire secret knowledge, and apply secret measures in order to ensure its capacity to act. This process of the "arcanization of political action" happened all over Europe.[116]

Three major factors contributed to the rediscovery and political appropriation of the concept of arcanum, a term already known in antiquity. First of all, political arcanization was linked to the *secreta* boom in the natural sciences. Contemporary medical terminology, in which arcana played a major role, exerted an influence on political language and the idea of a functioning "body politic."[117] The second factor was even more important: the absorption of theological ideas into political theory and language. Rulers and political theorists alike drew on the significance of the secret in Christian theology to further legitimate the confidentiality of state affairs. What is more, secrecy also created a special, theologically grounded aura underscoring the ruler's closeness to God. After all, God's rule over humanity also rested on secrets like concealment of the future.[118] This idea was hardly prominent in the Middle Ages. On the contrary, the prevailing view of both theology and political thought in the Early and High Middle Ages was that God's will was "revealed" with perfect clarity in the person and actions of the ruler. Toward the end of the Middle Ages, however, Christian theologians began to think of their God as increasingly hidden (*Deus absconditus*).[119] The popularity of this idea is due, not least, to Nicholas of Cusa (1401–1464), who coined the phrase "Quia ignoro, adoro" (Because I do not know, I adore) in his *Dialogus de Deo abscondito*.[120] As the theological paradigm shifted, so too did the connotation of the secret in political discourse. Secrecy was increasingly surrounded by an aura of divinity, which explains its appeal to the (absolutist) rulers who made it a central idea for political communication.[121] Similarly, from the thirteenth century onward the idea of the church's mystical body (*corpus ecclesiae mysticum*) was increasingly applied to worldly authority, and this gradually led to the proto-absolutist concept of the state's mystical body (*corpus reipublicae mysticum*).[122] In political theory, the idea of the godliness of a prince ruling through secrets culminated in the seventeenth-century phrase "arcanum est divinum" (the arcane is divine).[123]

The third important factor contributing to the rise of government secrecy was the influence of Niccolò Machiavelli (1469–1527) and the closely related concept of raison d'état (*ratio status*).[124] This factor differed from the theological one not only because Machiavelli was often depicted as the archenemy of religion, but also because the Machiavellian and theological calls for political arcanization were driven by different motives. The theological topos of *Deus absconditus* was meant to envelope the ruler with a divine aura. By contrast, Machiavelli was more concerned with pragmatic considerations about the exercise of power. For him, the *arcana imperii* did not represent an instrument of princely self-aggrandizement as much as a "catalogue of secret practices . . . that were to secure domination over the immature people."[125] In this view, the prince also had control over the *arcana dominationis* that served to "secure the ruler against attacks from those around him."[126]

Machiavelli, then, was only one of many fathers of the political theory of the *arcana imperii*. And it would certainly be misleading to suspect only unscrupulous power politics lurking behind the secret policies of the early modern state. In fact, maintaining secrecy was also an ethical obligation for rulers and their confidants, and it was by no means regarded as inevitably immoral. In contrast to lying, which Christian doctrine forbade, the concealment of knowledge did not have an intrinsically negative connotation. The Spanish Jesuit Baltasar Gracián (1601–1658), for example, praised insincerity and dissimulation (*simulatio, dissimulatio*). He justified this kind of behavior by citing the necessity of *versatilitas*, the art of adapting.[127] In his *Art of Worldly Wisdom*, he also commended secrecy, and this tied in with his generally positive conception of secrecy on theological grounds.[128] Pragmatic considerations also came into play. In his third maxim, Gracián insisted that "it is both useless and insipid to play with your cards on the table. . . . Mix a little mystery with everything, and the very mystery arouses veneration."[129] Similarly positive views of secrecy can be found in moralistic literature from all over Europe, such as Paolo da Certaldo's fourteenth-century *Book of Good Manners* or Sebastian Brant's *The Ship of Fools* (1494).[130]

Unlike the way the concept is used today, the idea of the public clearly did not have an intrinsically positive connotation for early modern authorities. They regarded secrecy as a question of honor as well as a moral responsibility; if secrets were divulged and ended up in the wrong hands, the consequences could be disastrous for society as a whole.[131] Ironically, many saw the very writings of Machiavelli as a double-edged sword. In Niklas Luhmann's words, "One really sees what emerges when Luther and Machiavelli profane religion and politics in print and make them accessible to everyone. The results are lack of understanding, confusion, turmoil, and civil wars, since this obviously puts people out of their depth."[132]

Arcanization also played a major role in early modern authorities' economic policies. There are even explicit references to "arcanists," that is, people with technological expertise whose secrets had considerable economic use for the state. Here, arcana usually referred to instructions for manufacturing an innovative product—what we today might call "trade secrets."¹³³ The most famous example is porcelain manufacturing in the eighteenth century. In the case of white porcelain, the arcanum emerged by accident from alchemical experiments in Saxony, where it was subject to the strictest secrecy. Arcanists at the court in Dresden were paid exceedingly high salaries and lavish pensions to keep them from betraying their secrets. In order to guarantee continuing production even in case of death, the relevant knowledge was recorded in so-called arcane books. These volumes were deposited in the treasure chamber of the Green Vault in the Dresden Palace.¹³⁴ Various royal courts and governments tried to recruit these arcanists and lure them away—a pattern that is easy to find almost everywhere in early modern Europe.¹³⁵

In sum, secrecy constituted a central mode for communication between ruler and subject throughout the entire early modern period. Whoever wanted to arouse interest in "projects" at court was well-advised to emphasize their arcane character. To this day, thick bundles of files with countless secret projects have been preserved in the archives of major European courts.¹³⁶ The economy of secrets remained largely intact well into the eighteenth century. If anything, the tendency toward arcanization only increased in both political culture and private life. Even in the era of New Science, the intellectual sphere was still characterized by considerable complexity. Occult, magical, and alchemical practices continued to claim a special place all their own. The activities of Jews who traded, supplied, and delivered secrets needs to be seen precisely within this context. But there was another, more unique, factor that contributed to the Jewish trade in secrets: the idea, deeply rooted in Christian society, that there was something fundamentally "secretive" about Jews.

The Jewish "Mastery of the Arcane": Discourses and Reality

The English historian Cecil Roth (1899–1970), whose historiographic premises are now often criticized as overly rosy, was one of the first to try placing the topos of Jewish "mastery of the arcane" within a broader context. In light of the role Jews played in transmitting Greco-Arabic knowledge, Roth argued that Christians in the Middle Ages often tended to view Jews as people who preserved a certain body of philosophical texts. As humanism took shape and knowledge of Greek spread along with it, however, the Jewish services in this field became increasingly dispensable. What remained was the Christian idea "that the Jews had access to stores of recondite information." Roth was not disputing that Jews seized the opportunities that resulted from this position. Yet his overall evaluation of this development was negative: "There was thus a debasement of the currency of Jewish participation in cultural life. In place of the unostentatious translators and learned scientists of a former age, the forefront of the stage was now occupied to some extent by picturesque charlatans."[137] Here Roth clearly betrays his intellectual debt to the *Wissenschaft des Judentums* (Science of Judaism).[138] Indeed, German exponents of this influential nineteenth-century school also dismissed alchemy as "a field far removed from Jews and the Hebrew language."[139] Some scholars went so far as to claim that alchemy "was never a superstition found among the Jews."[140]

More recently, Elisheva Carlebach has examined Christian charges of excessive secrecy leveled against Jews and placed them, more decisively than Roth did, in the context of Christian theology. She identifies this accusation as a central element of Christian anti-Judaism.[141] During the Middle Ages, Christians accused Jews of excessive secrecy in almost every area of their lives.[142] Richard Sennett adds that the "Jewish body itself had . . . been thought of as a body of concealment" because of the Jewish practice of circumcision, among other reasons.[143] The fear that infection emanated from the mysterious bodies of Jews was a specter that had real, and sometimes drastic, implications for Jews in everyday life. These included spatial segregation and, in some places, a prohibition against Jews touching merchandise.[144]

Catholics were hardly the only ones to accuse Jews of secrecy. Martin Luther, too, held that the alleged *perfidia* of the Jews was concealed behind a veil of secrecy.[145] Although the related accusation of sorcery, which Luther also leveled against Jews, began to lose its clout in the early modern era, the idea that Jews were harboring secrets persisted. As Carlebach notes, the jargon of exposure was widespread in Christian polemics against Jews well into the seventeenth century. Jewish converts to Christianity who hoped to gain legitimacy or garner attention by revealing the alleged secrets of their former religion to the Christian world contributed to this discourse.[146] According to Carlebach, only after 1700 did the zeal to uncover the *nuda veritas* of Judaism gradually fade into a "delight in difference." As a case in point, she cites the writings printed about Judaism at the time. If the overwhelming number of book titles in the sixteenth century still emphasized the secret character of Judaism, the seventeenth and eighteenth centuries saw titles that—as with Johann Jacob Schudt, for example—promise a kind of ethnographic glance at the *conditio judaica* as a tableau of "curiosities."[147]

Carlebach has accurately analyzed the motives and functions of Christian accusations about Jewish secrecy. There can be no doubt that this accusation, used polemically and bolstered theologically, had no basis in reality—especially when it was linked to the phantasms of Christian anti-Judaism, such as ritual murder, desecration of the host, and poisoning of wells. However, the idea of excessive secrecy among Jews was hardly the exclusive domain of theology. One finds this prejudice even among authors who had a critical relationship to Christianity, and especially to the church. This was true, for example, of the English playwright Christopher Marlowe (1564–1593), who can hardly be called a God-fearing Christian. His blasphemous views did not stop him from drawing heavily on the traditional notion of Jews' excessive secrecy when he created the figure of Barabas in *The Jew of Malta* (ca. 1589/1590)—the very prototype of a Jewish arch villain. Over and over again in the course of the play, Barabas mentions—indeed conjures up—the need for secrecy in conversations with his slave Ithamore.[148]

It would be simplistic, however, to dismiss the discourse about a distinctive Jewish mastery of the arcane as an entirely forced characterization, especially with respect to everyday life and the economy of secrets. For one thing, there was a widespread view—among Christians and within the Jewish minority itself—that Jews were unsurpassed when it came to procuring the most out-of-the-way goods.[149] For another, in the search for a *prisca sapientia,* Christian scholars believed that hardly any path to sacred wisdom could bypass the biblical Israelites—an opinion that early modern Jewish authors often shared and even promoted, even if only on apologetic grounds.[150] For example, the physician and Kabbalist Abraham Yagel (1553–ca. 1623) assumed that Jews were predestined by God to discover the secrets of creation, and especially of nature.[151] Similar notions were present in Jewish thought from prior centuries. During the Middle Ages, rabbis were intensively preoccupied with the "secret of the Torah" (*sod ha-Torah*) and laid the cornerstone for what Moshe Idel has called a veritable "arcanization of the canonical texts."[152] In particular, between the twelfth and thirteenth centuries Jewish esotericism experienced an unprecedented boom. It would be rash to see this development as a reaction to repression, or even as a hermeneutic setback. Rather, the ideals of secrecy and arcanization fulfilled an important and stabilizing function, as Moshe Halbertal has recently argued. They enabled medieval Jews to react to the challenge posed by the different religious, philosophical, and esoteric trends with which they were increasingly confronted from outside— including astrology, Gnosticism, Aristotelianism, and Neoplatonism. The creation of esoteric doctrines allowed Jews to absorb these trends into their own intellectual cosmos without betraying the actual core of Jewish tradition.[153] Secrecy and arcanization thus became important "hermeneutic tools" granting medieval Jewish thought considerable flexibility.[154]

One outcome of this development was the rise of Kabbalah, or Jewish mysticism.[155] Jews and Christians alike often regarded Kabbalah as the key to revealing the secrets of both books God had given humankind—the holy scriptures and the book of nature.[156] This idea is featured prominently on the frontispiece of the *Kabbala denudata* (1677–1684), a milestone treatise in Christian Kabbalah. There we see Kabbalah depicted as a female figure who, with key in hand, is rushing toward the entrance of the Palace of Secrets (the "Palatium Arcanorum"), an edifice representing the totality of nature's secrets.[157] The Kabbalah quickly came to epitomize secret knowledge—even well beyond its originally Jewish context.[158] In the early modern period, this Hebrew term even entered the lexicon of various European languages, where it referred to secretive machinations and intrigues, as attested in the English word "cabal" (*Kabale* in German; *cabale* in French).[159] The early modern fascination with Kabbalah was undoubtedly a major reason why Christians thought Jews were surrounded by an aura of the arcane.

At the same time, social exclusion and discrimination occasionally turned strategies of secrecy into a very real necessity for many Jews.[160] Early modern Jewish life, especially for Sephardic Jews, was often marked by the experience of crypto-existence shaping both identity and community.[161] Even if the term "crypto-Judaism" has not always been used consistently by historians, it is clear that many *conversos* had no choice but to live their lives as Jews in secret, concealed from their Christian neighbors.[162] On the Christian side, the unrelenting persecution of this heresy by the church, and especially by the Inquisition, must have reinforced the impression that Jews were closely bound up with the realm of the secret. A typical example is the assumption that a confidant of the Este court in 1654 made about a group of Portuguese Jews expected to arrive in the duchy. In hurried anticipation of their arrival, he pointed out that the secrets of the Jews would require a great deal of skill and time to uncover.[163] In terms of economic policy, it was, of course, smarter to avoid scaring off these groups by threatening to divulge their secrets and instead to secure their trust by pledging confidentiality. Indeed, the business-savvy Medici in Tuscany cultivated a high level of confidentiality in their relationships with their Sephardic contacts, especially the crypto-Jewish ones.[164]

Even Jews who openly professed their religion were sometimes inclined to keep secrets, or at least to be discreet with respect to their economic activities and internal community affairs. This was a subject for reflection among Ashkenazi Jews—at the level of both language and literature. A story from the Yiddish *Mayse-Bukh*, first published in 1602, draws a realistic picture of the hardship Jews in Mainz experienced after the pope prohibited circumcision. According to the story, they ultimately reached an agreement with the Bishop of Mainz so that they could circumcise their children in secret (*im sod*).[165] This tale, with its happy ending, is a fictitious one; at the same time, it encapsulates real elements and collective experiences. Indeed, the Italian word *secreto*, in Hebrew transliteration, shows up in the internal documents of Italian Jewish communities.[166] The use of codes in Jews' private and business correspondences, which can be attested as early as the fifteenth century, will be treated extensively below. Yet Jews did not need strategies for keeping secrets just when they were transmitting information; the very conduct of business itself often necessitated such practices. Tellingly, Christian authorities were already exhorting Jewish moneylenders, entrepreneurs, and traders to conduct their business in the local language, not in Hebrew, long before this became a precondition for "emancipation" in the nineteenth century.

For Jewish moneylenders, discretion usually sufficed.[167] But Jews who dealt in precious stones and jewelers often depended on absolute confidentiality to conduct their business.[168] For example, Jews were officially prohibited from dealing in or manufacturing precious stones in Venetian territory for centuries.[169] As a consequence, secrecy was a necessity in this trade. This applied even to Salomone di Vita Levi, the most important supplier of precious stones for the Gonzaga family. Levi was also involved in the business of fabricating gold, silver, and jewels. He cultivated contacts with Italy's most respected goldsmiths and merchants.[170] Still, even he had to place great value on secrecy in his business relations. Working out of Venice in 1575, he transacted a deal with the Duke of Mantua in a way that was "most secret" ("secretisimamente" [sic]).[171] Likewise, the same ducal court characterized its purchases of precious stones from the Jewish jeweler David Cervi as a secret transaction ("com'era segretto questo negotio").[172] In the 1590s, Cervi himself remarked to a Mantuan court official that any deals in jewels and precious stones had to be transacted in a secret manner ("in motto di segretezza").[173] In 1612, a group of Portuguese Jews from Venice, preparing for a jewelry deal with the court in Mantua, informed the duke in equally explicit terms that they appreciated keeping these business relations secret.[174]

Jewelers were not, however, the only group in Jewish society that required discretion and confidentiality. In some occupations—for example, in the cattle trade—elaborate secret languages developed among Jews in the early modern era. Christians frequently harbored unwarranted suspicions that malicious intentions were lurking behind the argot of Jewish traders. In reality, disguising conversations by inventing or combining languages actually often took on playful guises among early modern Jews, especially in a familial or intracommunity context. The poet and scholar Dan Pagis deserves credit for having rediscovered, in the 1980s, a long-forgotten Hebrew literary genre that enjoyed great popularity for almost two hundred years—especially among Italian Jews and Sephardic Jews in the Netherlands—from the seventeenth century onward. It consisted of riddle poems featuring an enigmatic image (a *tzurat ha-ḥida* in Hebrew, or *figura dell'enigma* in Italian) along with a complicated Hebrew text; the verses were often further complicated by the insertion of Italian and Spanish words. This highly elaborate genre was unique to early modern Jewish culture, even if one can speculate about influences derived from Christian baroque verse, especially from the concept of *argutia,* and from emblem literature. In the Jewish communities of Italy and the Netherlands, there were veritable competitions, for example at weddings, where contestants tried their hands at deciphering these multilingual riddle poems, many of which are hard to interpret even today.[175]

However, not only Jews made use of Hebrew in order to hide messages and conversations. Words borrowed from Hebrew played an important role in the argot of deviant social groups that outsiders found hard to understand. This was especially true for the argot of beggars and thieves—as well as for underworld slang, in which almost 20 percent of the words were taken from Hebrew, according to modern estimates.[176] Such linguistic phenomena certainly contributed to the belief in a specifically Jewish mastery of the arcane. This is also true with regard to the disproportionate multilingualism of many Jews. A Frenchman traveling in the Levant in the sixteenth century attributed what he saw as the outstanding position of Jewish physicians in the Ottoman Empire to their command of various languages, including Greek and Arabic, since these were indispensable to the study of the medical arts, natural philosophy, and astrology.[177] More than anything else, however, the command of Hebrew contributed to the view of a distinctively Jewish mastery of the arcane. Hebrew's special status as the most mystical of languages was summed up by seventeenth-century English clergyman Barten Holyday when he spoke of "the nimble French, majestike Spanish, courtly Italian, masculine Dutch, happily-compounding Greeke, *mysticall Hebrew,* and physicall Arabicke."[178]

Belief that the Hebrew language possessed a profoundly occult dimension was widespread. This had to do, in the first place, with the outward appearance of the language. Any consonantal script in which the vowels were, so to speak, concealed was regarded as a highly favorable medium for disguising secrets. But this was especially true for Hebrew. This attitude is vividly captured in the *Mirror of Alchimy,* a popular treatise attributed to Roger Bacon: "Some have hidden their secretes by their maners of writing, as namely by consonants only: so that no man can reade them, without he knowe the signification of the words . . . and therefore there is a great concealing with them, but especially with the Iewes."[179] In the same vein, Christian language scholars published entire books that promised to "reveal the arcanum of punctuation marks" (*arcanum punctationis*).[180] No less important for the notion of Hebrew's occult potential was the rabbinical idea of the fourfold meaning of the holy scriptures. The Jewish tradition distinguishes among four ways of interpreting the scriptures: *peshat,* or the simple meaning; *remez,* or the allegorical meaning; *derash,* or the rabbinic-homiletic interpretation; and *sod,* or the secret, mystical meaning. (These were traditionally referred to with the acronym PaRDeS, from the initial letters of the four words in Hebrew.) In Christian biblical exegesis, there was also a notion of a fourfold scriptural meaning. However, the Christian tradition lacked an equivalent for the category of an explicitly secret sense of scripture (*sod*). This was one important reason why Judaism exercised such fascination over numerous Christian Hebraists and Kabbalists. Giovanni Pico della Mirandola, who assumed that there were more than four levels of scriptural meaning, was one of the scholars who attempted to explore the hidden dimension of the biblical text.[181] Under the influence of his preoccupation with Kabbalah, Pico went so far as to claim that all wisdom—of both a divine and a human nature—was contained in the Five Books of Moses, arguing that this knowledge was concealed within the order of Hebrew letters in the holy scriptures. Along these lines, Pico promoted a kind of combinatorial exegesis in which, taking into account relevant Jewish teachings, the letters of the holy scriptures were to be reordered and commuted. In this way it would be possible to reveal the "secrets of all the liberal arts" ("secreta omnium liberalium disciplinarium").[182]

Johannes Reuchlin (1455–1522), who made crucial contributions to the reception of Kabbalah and rabbinical literature in Christian circles, likewise believed in the secret potential of the Hebrew language. The ideas shaped by Pico and Reuchlin soon became widely held expert opinions.[183] In 1524, when the Cambridge Hebraist Robert Wakefield (d. 1537) published an emphatic plea for learning the Hebrew language, he did not fail to point out that it concealed its treasures and tended to safeguard its secrets.[184] And, of course, knowledge of Hebrew was an important key not only for access to the holy scriptures, but also for exploring the holy sites themselves. Even pilgrims from the aristocracy and clergy availed themselves of Jewish guides as they set out to discover the secrets of the Holy Land.[185]

Although the number of Christians who learned Hebrew increased starting in the sixteenth century, this hardly dispelled the idea that the language had an arcane dimension. As late as the end of the eighteenth century, biblical Hebrew still formed a central element in the "sought-after new aesthetics of darkness and secrecy," as promoted by writers like Johann Georg Hamann and Johann Gottfried Herder, especially in the latter's myth-saturated writings on the Old Testament.[186] Yet it was not just scholars who were intrigued by the supposedly occult dimension of the Hebrew language. The same fascination existed in popular culture as well. A case in point is the story of three Jewish converts from Padua. During the 1580s, they quickly succeeded in gaining a foothold in the milieu of Venetian charlatans, where there was no lack of competition, and earning money by speaking Hebrew most of the time before a greatly impressed audience.[187]

It would be rash to assume that the discourses and polemics of theologians, Kabbalists, and Hebraists were solely responsible for the Christian notion of a special Jewish expertise in the economy of secrets. As we have seen, the idea of Jewish proficiency in the arcane sometimes was bolstered by real-life impressions. Pre-Christian and extra-Christian traditions also contributed to the idea that Jews had a specific mastery of the secret. This is salient in the case of alchemy, a field associated with Jews as early as antiquity.[188] As Christian alchemists since the Late Middle Ages began to trace back their arts—for the sake of legitimation, among other reasons—to biblical figures such as Adam, Tubal-Cain, Moses, and Solomon, the assumption spread that Jews were experts in this field.[189] The idea that Jews had brought knowledge about alchemy to Europe from the Islamic world was another contributory factor.[190]

Some Christian alchemists even assumed that real mastery in alchemy was impossible without consulting Jewish sources. This partly accounts for the growing interest Christians had in Kabbalah.[191] The hopes Christian alchemists associated with the study of Kabbalah, or with the texts that circulated under that label, were not entirely farfetched. This was particularly true for so-called practical Kabbalah. While it is unfortunate that academic scholarship about practical Kabbalah and its intersection with alchemy persists "only at the extreme margin of modern research," as Moshe Idel puts it, at least we do know there were Jewish Kabbalists, such as the famous Ḥayyim Vital, who were deeply preoccupied with alchemy and related fields.[192] In the first quarter of the seventeenth century, Vital even composed a handwritten book of secrets in Hebrew, titled *Kabbala ma'asit ve-Alkimiyya* (Practical Kabbalah and Alchemy), in which he gathered secrets from magic, medicine, technology, metallurgy, and chemistry.[193] However, points of contact and affinities with alchemy also existed in "theoretical Kabbalah" (*Kabbala iyyunit*).[194]

It is unclear to what extent the majority of those Christian naturalists and alchemists who, like Paracelsus, either recommended the study of Kabbalah or regarded it as necessary had actually studied the writings of Jewish mysticism in depth.[195] But the mere notion, no matter how vague, that alchemical knowledge was present or hidden in Kabbalistic writings was enough to attribute a distinctive expertise in alchemy to Jews. Moreover, the idea of Hebrew's occult qualities and magical potential left an imprint on the language of alchemy: alchemical discourse drew on important "power words" taken from Hebrew, including the widely used and often distorted term "Kabbalah" itself. It is no exaggeration to say that basic knowledge of Hebrew was just as important for the alchemist and the magus as Latin was for the trained physician.[196] These factors led to a major boom in alchemical writings purportedly penned by Jewish authors.[197]

Jews were by no means immune to believing in these kinds of attributions. Some Jewish circles even claimed that Maimonides, of all people, had written a treatise on alchemy.[198]

The case of alchemy makes it clear that the idea that Jews commanded a special mastery of the arcane was not rooted solely in theological anti-Judaism. Rather, it tied in with a wide range of extratheological sources and fictions, including some that were Jewish. Moreover, the accusation of excessive secrecy should not make us overlook the fact that some Jews were willing to meet Christians' demands for secrets of all kinds. These interactions between Jews and Christians are a key subject of the present book. No social group was credited with greater talents in the economy of secrets than were Jews. It is true that contemporaries also attributed considerable secret knowledge to a much larger social group—namely, women.[199] As in the case of Jews, this resulted in opportunities and professional niches for women who were adept at secrecy. Yet the content of this female secret knowledge—and this makes it much different from the Jewish situation—was significantly shaped by the gendered expectations of male customers. Women's secret knowledge was considered particularly credible where it was related to the mysterious female body.[200] There was, to be sure, no lack of women in the economy of secrets, but actual economic opportunities for female participants were relatively limited. Various roles, from midwife to herbalist and wise woman to faith healer, existed for women in the economy of secrets. Yet very few of these women, such as a small number of highly paid midwives at court, were able to advance from the low social position to which a patriarchal society assigned them.

By contrast, it seemed more likely, even if only in the Christian imagination, that Jewish adepts at secrets would use their knowledge as a means of overcoming almost any kind of social barrier. A striking example is the figure of Iachelino in Ariosto's now-obscure comedy *Il negromante* (1510).[201] The titular nigromancer is a Jew who, as the plot unfolds, proves to be a *professore de' secreti* much in demand in elite circles of Christian society.[202] The list of Iachelino's talents is long, including philosophy, alchemy, medicine, astrology, magic, and spirit-conjuring.[203] What is more, the Jewish magus boasts that he knows the secret of how to become invisible, make the earth quake, and turn humans into animals. Yet in Renaissance Cremona, where this comedy takes place, he hardly needs these skills, as the job entrusted to him is more prosaic: he is asked to intervene by supernatural means in a complicated romantic drama that revolves around unrequited love, impotence, and a paternal marriage strategy. Iachelino, however, seeks advantage by devious means, and this ultimately proves his undoing. In the end, the nigromancer has to leave town in a hurry.

In his comedy, Ariosto caricatures the naïveté of those Christians who, before disavowing Iachelino, enabled him to earn money by swindling. The Jew, in turn, is predestined for the role of magus simply by virtue of his religion. It doesn't matter that Iachelino, expelled from Spain, actually denies his Judaism.[204] The figure of the Jewish magus, depicted with little sympathy and considerable prejudice, was certainly credible in the eyes of Christian contemporaries—as attested by the comedy's eventful performance history. It is said that the premiere, ordered by Pope Leo X on the occasion of Carnival in 1520, was canceled because the pontiff feared that the fictitious Iachelino might be associated with his personal physician, Bonetto de Latis (Bonet de Lattes, born ca. 1450). This Jewish physician had already served Alexander VI and Julius II and had also acquired a reputation as an astrologer.[205] To what extent the figure of the nigromancer was modeled on Bonetto de Latis is a question that still requires more research.[206] At any rate, Ariosto's comedy captures reality insofar as it depicts the opportunities for upward mobility that the economy of secrets offered a Jew who, like Iachelino, was impecunious and homeless, in need of a professional niche, and almost illiterate to boot. At the same time, however, the play also highlights the risks associated with this profession.

These risks will be discussed in greater detail below. Here it suffices to say that dangers could ensue even if the alleged expertise in arcana was limited to a specific field like alchemy. While involvement with alchemy was not punishable from a legal standpoint, authorities could quickly find pretexts for intervention. For the church, in particular, alchemy's proximity to magic, deception, or counterfeiting was a suspicion hanging in the air.[207] Jews' real or imagined alchemical knowledge was grist for the mill to those making the case for expelling Jews for the benefit of Christian society. In

1519, shortly after the expulsion of the Jews from Regensburg, a local Christian chronicler was pleased to assert that the houses of the former Jewish quarter were discovered to be harboring underground smelting furnaces in which Jews had experimented with alchemy; in reality, these were more likely conventional ovens used, among other things, to make matzo.[208] In extreme cases, the prestige Jews enjoyed in the field of alchemy even led to the ludicrous theory that gold could be produced from a Jewish body.[209] Moreover, not every ruler or every court was necessarily receptive to secrets from Jews—especially if black magic were thought to be in play. Luther evinced schadenfreude in reporting the story of a Jew who supposedly confided a secret about so-called *Festmachen*—the magical practice of rendering somebody invulnerable—to Duke Albert of Saxony (1443–1500). The "Jew offered to sell him a talisman, covered with strange characters, which he said effectually protected the wearer against any sword or dagger thrust." Yet the duke came up with the idea of trying out this method on the Jew himself, and "putting the talisman round the fellow's neck, he drew his sword and passed it through his body."[210] Generally speaking, the situation could become dangerous for Jewish, and even Christian, adepts at secrets when the accusation of sorcery and magic was leveled against them. This could lead to an Inquisition trial and, in the worst case, to burning at the stake.[211]

On the whole, though, the considerable opportunities that the economy of secrets offered Jews outweighed the dangers. Here, too, alchemy—the secret science par excellence and a key area of the early modern economy of secrets—is a case in point.[212] Jews were not the only group for whom the practice of alchemy, and the market for secrets overall, provided a notable economic niche, but they were the most prominent. Unlike the operation of a university, alchemy was only barely institutionalized. For this reason, it was rich in opportunities for members of all social classes, from court ladies to priests to adventurers.[213] Consider the career of Marco Bragadino (ca. 1545–1591) in late-sixteenth-century Venice: this completely unknown and impecunious young Cypriot rose to become one of the most sought-after alchemists of his time, which also led him into the highest political circles. The engagement that took him to Venice was an affair of state of such dimensions that, out of fear that the alchemist might be kidnapped during his journey to the Serenissima, several infantry companies and artillery units accompanied Bradagino's convoy.[214] Bragadino's arrival in the city of lagoons led to such a boom in alchemy there that, after a short time, books on the subject could no longer be found in the entire city.[215]

Unlike universities and guilds, the world of alchemy offered numerous points of entry. The path to alchemy did not depend on birth or social background; what counted was experience, talent, and credibility. Social background tended to be negligible, not least because the practice of alchemy offered considerable scope for adepts' "self-construction."[216] Alchemy—and this is true for most of the occult sciences—often allowed its adepts to overcome considerable social and geographic barriers.[217] Some historians have argued that it even served as a "language of mediation" that helped transcend differences among various religious denominations at courts like that of Rudolf II in Prague.[218] Along these lines, William R. Newman argues that alchemy formed a "natural locus for unorthodox religious speculation at the height of the massive confessional upheaval of early modern Europe," which in turn was one of the major reasons for the sixteenth-century boom in alchemy.[219]

It should come as no surprise, then, that the economy of secrets in general—and alchemy in particular—proved especially attractive for Jews. There were many more Jews in the field of alchemy than scholarship has previously assumed, and the same holds true for magic and other secret sciences. In contrast to the *accusation* of excessive secrecy, the real *practice* of trading in secrets among early modern Jews has yet to be adequately researched. A systematic, or even comprehensive, study is not available. Admittedly, historians have to proceed with caution; the association between Jews and the economy of secrets was so pronounced in early modernity that even Christian writers of *secreta* literature occasionally picked up a reputation for being Jews. This happened posthumously with the late medieval physician and philosopher Guglielmo Varignana (d. 1330), the scion of a respected family of scholars from Bologna. In 1519, his manuscript *Secreta sublimia ad varios curandos morbos* was published for the first time and quickly achieved great popularity. Soon enough, the idea spread that the author was Jewish.[220] Varignana was not an isolated case. There were even claims that Aristotle was Jewish, owing to his (baseless) reputation as the author of the highly popular *Secret of Secrets* (*Secretum secretorum*).[221]

Having set the context for Jewish participation in the economy of secrets, we can now turn to the question of how this range of arcane activities took shape in reality. I cannot presume to cover the whole range of these activities; however, I hope to establish a number of gateways into this phenomenon that will allow us to begin to understand it—among them alchemy, medicine, espionage, cryptography, technology, and finally the trade in unicorns.

TWO

Masters of the Arcane and Their Métiers

Alchemy

As a historical phenomenon, alchemy is an object of fascination even today. Often, however, the presuppositions that underlie this fascination are wrong or simplistic. In early modern Europe, alchemy was more than just striving for the "philosopher's stone" and making gold—so-called transmutation. Even though there were fraudulent practitioners, we cannot equate alchemy with deceit on the whole. Scholars have observed that alchemy was not a natural science, although it was certainly a science of nature.[1] It was multifaceted and had many branches, including medical and mythical-Christological ones. This is why some scholars have even suggested that we should speak of several premodern *alchemies* rather than just one alchemy.[2] It is only against this background that we can explore the roles and opportunities that alchemy offered Jews.

    Jewish alchemists can be attested in Europe for the entire early modern era, and even as early as the Late Middle Ages. There is also a remarkable body of Hebrew literature on alchemy, especially since the Renaissance. However, as this facet of Jews' involvement with alchemy is relatively well-researched, it will not be my focus.[3] Rather, I will concentrate on Jewish alchemists' concrete actions, their motives, and the opportunities they had in everyday life—topics that have largely been overlooked. One exception is a study by folklorist Raphael Patai. Unfortunately, it has substantive flaws and can be used only with reservations.[4] Moreover, Patai's attention was primarily focused on Sephardic Jews. They did, indeed, have a long-standing interest in alchemy. As early as the mid-fourteenth century, for example, we find a Jewish physician and astrologer by the name of Menaḥem (Magister Menaym Judaeus) at the court of King Peter IV of Aragon (r. 1336–1387) dealing with alchemy.[5] A few decades later, in 1396, a Jew named Caracosa (Saracosa) Samuel from Perpignan received a royal privilege to carry out his alchemical experiments throughout the same kingdom. King John I explicitly ordered authorities not to hinder this Jew's alchemical ventures in any way.[6] We have no record of what this Caracosa Samuel intended to do or what he accomplished, but he was certainly not a swindler passing through Aragon. Rather, he lived in the town of Perpignan for more than a quarter of a century. There, he was well-respected in both Jewish and Christian circles. In 1367 he held a high position in the local Jewish community, and a few years later he was summoned to Barcelona by King Peter IV in order to provide information as a legal expert.[7] Magister Menaḥem and Caracosa Samuel were not the only Jewish arcanists in medieval Spain. In 1384, when the king of Aragon issued a decree allowing three Christians to practice alchemy in what is today the city of Montblanc, he tellingly allowed them to collaborate, as needed, with Christians and with Jews and Saracens.[8]

Comparable examples of Ashkenazic Jews active in alchemy are attested going back to the Late Middle Ages, especially in the Holy Roman Empire.[9] To what extent this phenomenon might reach back even as far as the High Middle Ages is a question that remains difficult to answer. In any event, around 1060 the chronicler Adam of Bremen mentioned a fraudulent Jewish alchemist associated with Archbishop Adalbert of Hamburg (ca. 1000–1072). According to the chronicler, this alchemist claimed to have acquired his knowledge of alchemy during a trip to Byzantium.[10] One of the earliest and most reliable pieces of evidence dates from the 1420s, when a Jew named Salman (Salomon) Teublein enjoyed a great reputation at the court of the Landgrave of Leuchtenberg, in the vicinity of Passau.[11] Although the territory of the landgrave was relatively small, the court was an important center of alchemical activities in the early fifteenth century. One of the oldest alchemical works written in the German language, the *Alchymey teuczsch* (1426), probably originated within its environs.[12] This codex also contains crucial evidence for Salman Teublein's secret work. It begins with a detailed description of how the Jew, his wife, and his servants enjoyed the same privileges in the landgraviate as did other Jews in the neighboring cities of Regensburg and Straubing—holding Jewish religious services, teaching school, and lending money within the territory. Yet the ensuing clauses elevate this document, which at first looks like the summary of a traditional letter of protection, to a secretive level by explicitly stating that Teublein is not obligated to communicate his arts to anyone. He could, of course, leave the landgrave's service, in which case he would be required to reveal three of his best secrets.[13] In return, the landgrave commits himself to passing on these secrets only to his own offspring.[14]

The detailed contractual regulations on divulging and concealing Teublein's "arts" elucidate how these secrets constituted an asset for the Jew in his agreement with the landgrave. The text reveals little about the actual content of Teublein's secrets. They were probably alchemical or magical in nature; indeed, the agreement was copied in an alchemical codex. Scholars have conjectured that Teublein's effort to keep his knowledge to himself not only expressed his wish "to protect the trade secrets by which he earned a living, but also the sense of ethical responsibility that suffused many late medieval and early modern alchemists."[15] The reference to an ethos of secrecy among alchemists is certainly correct. To some extent, it recalls the Jewish tradition in which only an adult man may study mystical writings, and then only with extreme conscientiousness.[16] In Teublein's specific case, however, secrecy might also be linked with his social position as a Jew. He knew that suggestive talk about strictly confidential arts would elicit the landgrave's attention. Sources that have come to light only recently corroborate this hunch, indicating that Teublein is apparently one and the same with a certain "Salman of Hals" who, on account of this secret knowledge, enjoyed the patronage of Frederick IV of Tyrol in the 1410s. The offer to divulge an unspecified arcane art allowed Salman to persuade this ruler to release an incarcerated Nuremberg Jew after repeated pleas for clemency and offers of ransom money by the family and Jewish community had been rejected.[17] The contact Teublein established with various princely courts presents us with a pattern that, as we will see, continued to exist well into the eighteenth century. In a society marked by the

Christian notion of Jews being adept at secrets, offering such knowledge helped to create channels of communication and exchange between these two groups. The secrets in question did not necessarily have to be revealed, as was the case with Teublein, or even actually exist.

There is further evidence of Jewish involvement in the business of alchemy in the fifteenth century. Around 1455, a Jewish alchemist by the name of Michael was employed in the service of the Landgrave of Kassel.[18] At the same time, the Jewish physician Seligmann was experimenting with methods of transmutation on behalf of the Austrian Archduke Sigismund.[19] A few years earlier, the beadle of the Nuremberg Jewish community tried his luck at making gold, though without a noble patron and the protection that offered. In 1440 he was arrested "on account of dangerous alchemy" and "branded on the forehead" at the behest of the city authorities.[20] Apparently, however, he was not the only alchemical practitioner among the ranks of Nuremberg's Jews.[21]

The phenomenon of Jewish alchemists proved to be geographically diverse, and Europe's network of princely courts formed a polycentric infrastructure that supported both Christian and Jewish alchemists. As early as the thirteenth century, Jacob Anatoli (ca. 1194–1256), a Jewish translator from France who was also a follower of Maimonides, is believed to have been involved in alchemy on behalf of Emperor Frederick II in Naples.[22] In early modern Europe, Jews practiced alchemy at a number of important courts, including Dresden, Stuttgart, and especially Prague. At the Prague court of Emperor Rudolf II, a Jew by the name of Mardochaeus de Nelle even held the office of alchemical chronicler, recording in verse the experiments conducted at court.[23] Recently, historian Rotraud Ries has noted—accurately, if rather incidentally—that the spectrum of activities available to Jews at early modern courts ranged from house tutor and head of the court kitchen all the way to military expert and even "alchemical advisor."[24] On the whole, though, she assigns Jewish alchemists an "exceptional position" within the Jewish occupational structure.[25] This assessment may be too guarded. After all, Jews also acted as alchemists outside the courts. In Hildesheim in the 1570s, for example, the Jew Aaron Goldschmidt charged a high fee for instructing Christian burghers in the art of transmutation.[26] Ultimately, Goldschmidt was invited to the ducal court in nearby Wolfenbüttel, presumably at the initiative of Christian subjects.[27] During the same period in nearby Hanover, the respected metallurgical expert and senior mining official Lazarus Ercker learned from a Jew named Gottschalck the secret of how to raise bad gold to the same level of quality as a ducat.[28] In his *Aureum vellus* (first published in 1598/1599), the alchemist Salomon Trismosin—whose work was widely read in the early modern period—recounted his travels through Italy as a young man in the 1470s with an Italian merchant and a German-speaking Jewish alchemist who formed an entrepreneurial team.[29]

It would be rash to conclude that only impoverished Ashkenazic Jews who set their hopes for quick riches on the philosopher's stone were involved in transmutational alchemy in the Holy Roman Empire. There certainly were such cases; however, alchemy was also popular in the Sephardic communities in German lands—in other words, within a group that formed part of the Jewish economic elite. Sephardic physicians were among alchemy's most prominent exponents.[30] Even the extraordinarily wealthy Portuguese merchant Manoel Texeira (1631-1705) did not shy away from establishing contacts with an Italian transmutation alchemist on behalf of his patroness Christina of Sweden, for whom he served as financial agent and representative in Hamburg.[31] The Swedish queen, who was fascinated with mysticism and the occult, got in touch with the contact Texeira had arranged for her to meet during a visit to Hamburg in 1667. Texeira also supplied her with information about a secret elixir, presumably alchemical in nature.[32] His willingness to provide these arcane services might simply have been due to the exigencies of his patronage relationship, but this explanation seems too narrow. Texeira was not the only Sephardic Jew in Hamburg at that time who hoped alchemy would produce tangible results. As early as the 1630s, respected Hamburg Sephardim had been talking in emphatic terms about alchemy's potential. One of them was Jacob Rosales (ca. 1588-1662), the Spanish king's resident agent in the city.[33] Rosales was a respected physician, astronomer, and astrologer. Born in Lisbon as the son of crypto-Jews, he studied medicine, physics, astronomy, and mathematics. He stayed in Rome for several weeks after being reported to the Inquisition

(1624). There he lived in close proximity to Galileo, who called him a "very admired and extremely learned man" and "first among astrologers."[34] Starting in the 1630s, Rosales resided as a physician in Hamburg, where he was held in high esteem as personal physician to numerous aristocrats and was even awarded the title of Imperial Count Palatine (*comitiva minor*) by Emperor Ferdinand III.[35] Whether his aristocratic patients availed themselves of his alchemical experiments is an open question. In any event, we know that Rosales praised alchemy several times in his writings and published the first known treatise on this subject in Portuguese—*Anotaçam crisopeia*, or *On the Art of Making Gold*.[36]

The works of the Sephardic physician Binyamin Mussafia (1606–1675) were even better known. He also served as an *Avisenschreiber* (agent and writer of dispatches) for the nearby court at Gottorp.[37] Mussafia's position was firmly rooted in the economy of secrets: the job of an *Avisenschreiber* was to collect information at the place of his deployment and transmit it as soon as possible to his courtly patrons; not infrequently, this activity overlapped with spying. In general, the entire courtly system for collecting information through so-called agents was marked by secrecy. As a rule, the courts did not reveal the names of their correspondents; conversely, *Avisenschreiber* avoided signing their reports.[38] Although the official title was simply "court Jew," Mussafia's position would have made him well-accustomed to dealing with secrets of all sorts. He had studied medicine in Padua and was also a versatile and multilingual writer, displaying traits of a veritable polyhistor. From Hamburg, he corresponded with Christian diplomats and Portuguese scholars about alchemy and astronomy. In 1638 he published in Hamburg *Mezahab Epistola*—a paean to alchemy that went through numerous reprints. It details his thesis that the Bible had already presaged Jewish knowledge of alchemy.[39] Mussafia based this theory on his work's titular character, the biblical figure of Me-zahab (Gen 36:39; 1 Chron 1:50), whose name literally means "gold water." Mussafia's work is virtually unknown today, though is more familiar via excerpts reprinted in the *Jüdische Merckwürdigkeiten* compiled by Johann Jacob Schudt in 1714.[40] However, the extensive commentary found in a 1694 treatise written by

Johann Ludwig Hannemann testifies to the prominent reception of *Mezahab Epistola* among contemporaries.[41]

So far our discussion has focused on Jewish communities in German-speaking and Iberian Europe. But the phenomenon of Jewish alchemists was hardly confined to those places. Examples can also be found in Eastern Europe and the Ottoman Empire, and the need for research is particularly salient in these areas. A Jew named Zacharias, who founded a Jewish-Christian sect in Novgorod around 1470, was supposedly well-versed in alchemy.[42] Another Jewish alchemist by the name of Mordecai lived in the Jewish community of mid-sixteenth-century Cracow.[43] Early modern Jews' considerable mobility contributed to the dissemination of alchemical knowledge from southern and Central Europe to Eastern Europe. For example, the respected physician Joseph Salomon Delmedigo (1591–1655)—an adept at alchemy who grew up in Crete and was educated in Italy—worked in Poland and Lithuania for several years.[44] In the seventeenth-century Ottoman Empire, Jewish producers of chemicals and alchemical substances even had their own guild.[45] In Damascus shortly after 1600, the distinguished Kabbalist Ḥayyim Vital wrote his treatise *Practical Kabbalah and Alchemy*.[46] When David Reuveni—the adventurer whom some Jewish contemporaries viewed as the Messiah—approached the powerful Jewish mint owner Abraham Castro in Egypt in the 1520s to offer him a secret (*sod*), alchemy was probably in play.[47]

Alchemy flourished among Jews in Italy more than in any other country. Several Hebrew-language alchemical manuscripts from early modern Italy testify to this. The Mantuan physician Abraham Portaleone had his partly alchemical work *De auro dialogi tres* printed in 1584.[48] We do not yet have a systematic exploration of this body of texts, even if preliminary studies are available.[49] However, it is clear that this corpus of recorded knowledge amounts to just a small portion of the spectrum of alchemical activity among Italy's Jews. Fascination with alchemical experiments is evident in the everyday lives of Italian Jews throughout the entire early modern period.[50] We can find examples reaching as far back as the middle of the fifteenth century. Take the case of Abraham Foa, a

Jewish physician famous well beyond his hometown of Cuneo. Foa, whose medical practice included such prominent patients as the Duke of Milan and the Margravine of Saluzzo, headed the local Jewish community for a while.[51] His career does not seem to have been hindered by the fine of 60 florins imposed on him earlier for alchemical experiments.[52] Around the same time, another Jewish physician, Perret Symuel, also enjoyed a distinguished reputation in northern Italy and the Alpine region. It was even thought that he headed a school of alchemists, and we know he had both Jewish and Christian confidants. His specialty was reportedly producing silver.[53]

The best-known case of all, however, is that of Leon Modena (1571–1648). Not only did this Venetian rabbi, who was also respected among Christians, occasionally deal with alchemy, but his son Mordecai, who was a far more zealous adept, even lost his life by breathing in poisonous fumes during an experiment.[54] A friend of Modena—the physician and later Roman rabbi Abraham di Cammeo—also invested a great deal of time and money in alchemy.[55] Modena's son was by no means the only early modern Jew who was willing to take great risks for alchemy. These risks were usually financial in nature. For example, in 1569 a Venetian Jew placed his trust in an alchemist by the name of Timolione who had caused a stir in the Serenissima with his promises to produce saltpeter. Timolione borrowed considerable sums of money from the Jew. Of course, the money never resurfaced after the alchemist's sudden disappearance.[56] In Poland, too, Jewish merchants in the late sixteenth century were said to have to been gullible about placing their trust in the famous alchemist Michael Sendivogius.[57] Several decades later, Leon Modena related a story about his uncle Shemaia, a Jewish moneylender from the city of Modena who got carried away in his enthusiasm for an experiment performed by a Christian alchemist meant to increase his riches considerably. To this end Shemaia collected all his silver and gold in a room where he awaited the miraculous increase of his precious metals. Instead, the alchemist ended up killing him and stealing his worldly possessions.[58]

Hopes of quick riches also led the Italian Jew Abraham Segre, from Savigliano, in the Piedmont, to conduct alchemical experiments. He was eventually arrested in Genoa in 1608 after he introduced gold coins that had a higher share of gold than was allowed in the republic. Manipulating coins was a serious crime in Genoa, especially since it was rare for such manipulations to lead to an actual increase in the currency's value. The fact that Segre had managed to enhance the money's value was probably the reason why the death penalty hanging over his head was averted. He was able to persuade the republic's authorities that increasing the coins' gold content had been his intention from the outset. He claimed that a German Jew had revealed this secret to him—a secret presumably taken from the field of transmutational alchemy. He carried out the actual "alchemical operation" (*operazione alchimistica*) in a village near Genoa. The authorities required Segre to atone for this foolishness on the galleys of the republic.[59] By contrast, in 1629 the Jew Isach Buzalini from Verona aroused a more positive interest on the part of the Republic of Genoa by offering the authorities a written secret, apparently alchemically inspired, for a method meant to keep weapons from rusting.[60]

The cases described here might create the impression that Jews were chiefly pursuing transmutation. However, there were other branches of alchemy that had nothing to do with producing gold, such as iatrochemistry (medical alchemy).[61] There were also trades and crafts that routinely drew on alchemical knowledge, as in the manufacture of powder and glass or in metallurgy. As will become apparent, early modern Jews were active in all three fields. In fact, they were even regarded as particularly competent. In professions like these, knowledge of so-called practical alchemy was indispensable. This kind of knowledge was also useful in dyeing, which Jews in many places throughout Italy practiced widely.[62] The art of dyeing required a "distinctive chemical knowledge" as well as familiarity with alchemical manufacturing methods and procedures. The literature on dyeing frequently employed a specialized alchemical terminology.[63] However, it would be ahistorical to speak of a "chemical industry," or even posit an artificial distinction between "chemistry" and "alchemy," for this period. This kind of categorization does not correspond to early modern concepts. As late as the seventeenth century, a sharp distinction between alchemy and chemistry still did not exist.[64]

An instructive example of this entanglement comes from Venice. There, the Jewish Sarfatti family started producing chemical substances in the 1630s, partly based on the use of alchemical formulas. They maintained this business for almost 150 years. This case vividly illustrates how secrets functioned as economic assets that could also appeal to authorities' economic policy interests. In May of 1630, a Sephardic Jew by the name of Nacaman Sarfatti petitioned the Republic of Venice with an offer of his "secret" (*secretto*), singling out his skills in "matters of alchemy and commerce."[65] Here, "alchemy" meant practical alchemy more than it indicated transmutational alchemy. One month after examining the petition, both the republic's legal counselors and the Cinque Savi alla Mercanzia—the five members of the city's board of trade—concluded that the plan was worth a try.[66] The privilege granted to Nacaman by the Senate details the substances that he was meant to manufacture. These were mercury compounds, including the sublimate mercuric chloride and mercury sulfide (cinnabar)—two chemicals that were much in demand at the time, for both commercial and alchemical purposes.[67] In addition, he was to produce a few alchemical substances that were not explicitly named ("simile materie d'Alchimia").[68]

It must be emphasized that Nacaman was neither an adventurer nor a charlatan. In fact, he was well-respected in the Venetian Jewish community, where he served as one of the five members of the powerful commission entrusted with allocating housing in the so-called Ghetto Novissimo.[69] By 1665 he had even risen to become the representative of Levantine Jews ("Massaro della Nazion ebrea levantina"). As a private person, Nacaman was able to afford having costly decorative work completed in his home by prestigious Christian artisans.[70] There is therefore little reason to assume that his chemical undertakings were some kind of esoteric experiment. Even in the initial privilege granted to him, the authorities explicitly spoke of his "business" and ordered that its progress should not be impeded under any circumstances ("che non sia perturbato ne impedito il progresso").[71] Indeed, Nacaman must have obtained some favorable results fairly quickly. Almost thirty years later, he was still pursuing his activities in the Serenissima, and his (al)chemical secrets continued to be at the core of his success. Tellingly, for more than a quarter century after Nacaman was originally granted his privilege, the Christian authorities were still referring to the entrepreneur's "secret" ("secretto che possiede Nacaman Giuda hebreo Levantino").[72] The business had to be officially conducted under the name of a Christian merchant; apparently, only Nacaman and his sons were initiated into the company's trade secrets. This may have aroused suspicion on the part of the Ufficiali al Cattaver, the officials in charge of monitoring the ghetto. In the late 1650s they revoked Nacaman's license without any explanation, along with the special permit that allowed him and his family to live, if necessary, day and night in the production facilities outside the ghetto.[73] Nacaman immediately raised objections against this decision. He pointed out that his production required a great deal of space simply to accommodate the ovens and equipment required; he also argued that the heightened fire hazard made it necessary to operate the manufacturing sites outside the ghetto.[74] These arguments persuaded the Senate, which expressly reaffirmed that the privilege would continue to be valid and would even be extended.[75] The decision to permit Nacaman to continue working all day and even overnight outside the ghetto illustrates the importance attributed to his secrets by the Venetian Senate. At that time this was a rare privilege granted only to a small minority of ghetto inhabitants, especially when it involved permission to leave the Jewish quarter at night.[76]

Nacaman Sarfatti was able to continue his previous occupation, even after the dispute with the Ufficiali al Cattaver. He also retained his instinct about the Venetian authorities' continued interest in lucrative secrets. In 1662 he approached the doge with a petition as vague as it was secretive, in which he made a business proposal promising significant improvements in the republic's finances. Upon closer investigation by the city's officials, he revealed that he wanted to devote himself to Venice's lead-making industry, claiming that its potential had not been fully exhausted yet. Nacaman mentioned an interested party who was prepared to pay 22,500 ducats for a privilege designed to last ten years.[77] The authorities immediately followed up on the offer. In the end, they granted the privilege to a certain Abram Sarfatti—presumably a relative of the entrepreneur. In addition, Nacaman made sure his secretive chemicals production remained in the hands of his family. As late as 1753, almost a century later, members of the Sarfatti family were still active in the "chemical industry" of Venice and allowed to live outside the ghetto.[78]

Apparently, the family also tried to expand its undertakings beyond the territory of the republic. In 1697 Abram Scarfatti [sic] established a manufacturing site for mercuric chloride and a series of additional, not otherwise specified mercury compounds in Finale, a town then under the rule of the House of Este.[79] This entrepreneur may have been identical with that Abram from the Venetian Sarfatti family who had established a foothold in the lead-making industry of the Serenissima during the 1660s. He may also have been the one who, in 1673, received a privilege in Tuscany to produce mercury compounds, including mercuric chloride.[80] In the Tuscan sources, the name appears as Nataniel Zalfaldi—perhaps a corrupted version of "Sarfatti." At any rate, it is clear that around 1700 the Venetian Sarfatti family moved its chemical workshop to Trieste for several years.[81] This prompted the Serenissima to offer the family considerable incentives to return to the city: the republic offered the family a number of materials necessary for its business, such as saltpeter, as well as state subsidies. Indeed, the authorities continued to regard the Sarfattis as guardians of important secrets in the production of chemicals that were indispensable in medicine, gold work, and military matters.[82] Even occasional irregularities in the use of state subsidies apparently did not have a negative effect over the long run. The Sarfatti family's business continued until the fall of the republic in 1797. In the 1760s, the family had some twenty-eight ovens for producing different mercury compounds and even recorded exports of chemicals to Genoa and the Ottoman Empire. In the 1770s the family attempted to expand and take up the production of tartrates.[83] What became of the Sarfatti family and its production after the fall of the Venetian republic requires further research. It is possible that a cut in subsidies put the company in a precarious position. In any event, no documents have come to light indicating that, after this period, the Sarfatti family continued these successful activities at the intersection of secret knowledge and innovative entrepreneurial spirit in which it had been engaged for two centuries.

Medical Arcana

Our survey of alchemy supports Raphael Patai's argument that it was a "favorite and high-prestige occupation" for medieval and early modern Jews.[84] But we can extend Patai's thesis well beyond alchemy and its secrets; in fact, we can apply it to the entire spectrum of the economy of secrets. For example, there was a considerable demand for medical secrets kept by Jews. During this era, a physician's reputation was often based on his supposed knowledge of arcana.[85] In the tradition of Paracelsus, in particular, a "pharmaceutical arcanology" had emerged starting in the sixteenth century.[86] Among the Paracelsists, the term "arcanum" included medicines (*materia medica*) produced in an (al)chemical fashion—so-called iatrochemistry.[87] Paracelsus himself had called upon the ideal physician to "make arcana and direct them against the diseases."[88] Soon enough the use of the term had become inflated. As late as the eighteenth century, there were complaints that "anyone [can] claim his medicines to be arcana if he will only keep quiet about the ingredientia and the modum praeparandi."[89] The widespread notion that medical secrets had value and utility proved advantageous to Jewish physicians, especially in a society where the Christian majority ascribed special competence to Jews in the economy of secrets and alchemy. Many Christians saw Jewish physicians as shrouded in a "nimbus of the mysterious."[90] In Goethe's words, "And all herbs and stones the Jew is especially versed in."[91]

As early as 1509, we find in Venice a Jew by the name of Abraham Lunardi who prided himself on his mysterious talent (*ingegno*) for devising methods to keep the Venetian lagoon clean and preventing plague.[92] In the first half of the seventeenth century, Venice was also home to the famous rabbi Leon Modena, who earned extra income by offering instruction in medical arcana as well as by selling amulets and prescription books containing secret medical nostrums.[93] The Jewish physician Salomo Ashkenazi (ca. 1520–1602), who rose to become one of the most powerful confidants of the Ottoman sultan, transmitted secret messages to Italy on occasion. Alongside his diplomatic activities, however, he also continued to run a medical practice in which nostrums and *secreta* played an important role.[94] During their travels to the Levant, Venetian merchants often secured the services of Jews from the Balkans. On these occasions, they usually made a point of acquiring medical secrets and prescriptions. For example, in 1567 a Venetian merchant traveled with a Jew named Aaron who guided him across the Balkans to Constantinople and revealed a number of secrets en route—including secrets from herbal medicine.[95] Sometime later, Johann Jacob Schudt mentioned a Jewish physician who "bragged that he had a peculiar arcanum against the plague also sold one dear to a nobleman."[96] Patients often pinned high expectations, and even their final hopes, on Jewish physicians who had mastery of arcane knowledge. In the 1590s the famous Fugger merchant family hired a Jewish healer from the vicinity of Augsburg after a series of Christian physicians had failed to treat a mysterious case of illness in the family. The family patriarch, Hans Fugger, was pleased with the Jew's therapeutic approach, in which secrets apparently played an important role. The otherwise laconic sources reveal, at least, that the medical ingredients administered by the Jewish healer could not be obtained in pharmacies at that time.[97]

The Jewish physicians' secrets often found their way into the *secreta* literature, including unpublished books of secrets, or "Kunstbüchlein," as they were called in German. For example, the *Libro di Segreti d'arti diverse*, a thick sixteenth-century volume that remained in manuscript form and is stored today in the Marciana Library in Venice, contains remedies and prescriptions directly attributed to Jewish physicians.[98] Apart from medical *secreta*, these include recipes such as a secret for producing white soap from black.[99] Indeed, refined ointments and cosmetics were among the *secreta* whose recipes were commonly passed down in early modern books of secrets. Here there was a tradition of ascribing particular expertise to women. As a result, this sector of the economy of secrets also provided opportunities for Jewish women, such as the Roman Jewess named Anna who delivered facial ointments and cosmetics to Caterina Sforza around 1500.[100] In sixteenth-century Tuscany there is evidence that Jews produced and dealt in cosmetics and perfumes.[101] In the Duchy of Mantua in 1590, a Jew by the name of Manuele Ongaro imported precious ointments enriched with musk and amber. He even received an exclusive privilege from the Gonzaga family to manufacture and sell these products.[102] In 1570s Imola, a Jew named Gioseffo produced aphrodisiacs that enjoyed great popularity among Christian clients, even though some rather unappetizing ingredients were involved. These products were in demand even among clergymen.[103]

Jewish physicians and healers had more than just medical secrets on offer. In fact, their interests and the services they offered were extremely broad. Even medicine and moneylending were not mutually exclusive.[104] Jewish physicians' preoccupation with Jewish mysticism was also much more widespread than is frequently assumed.[105] It often extended well beyond a fascination with Kabbalah to include a wide range of other arcana and occult traditions. Jewish historiography and the history of science often portray Jewish medical professionals as a rational, academically trained elite; this image, however, appears to be overdrawn and is, in any event, a nineteenth-century construct that does not reflect how complex the activities of many early modern Jewish physicians really were.[106] In late-seventeenth-century Venice, for example, the Jewish physician Israel Conegliano earned a considerable portion of his living by delivering "curious books," especially magical works, to customers throughout Europe.[107] Renowned sixteenth-century *professore de' secreti* Leonardo Fioravanti praised a Venetian Jewish physician by the name of Davide Calonimos who had distinguished himself as a collector of a wide variety of arcana. Unfortunately, it is not exactly clear what secrets Fioravanti received from his Jewish friend (his "cordialissimo amico").[108]

There were also Jewish physicians—and rabbis, by the way—who rose to prominence in the field of astrology, not only in theory but also in practice.[109] Here, too, they could rely on a rich body of Jewish literature.[110] In the early sixteenth century, high-level representatives of the Venetian government, including the doge himself, enlisted the astrological expertise of the Jewish physician Marco Challo.[111] The physician Leon Abravanel worked in Naples at the same time. His talents were not limited to making predictions; in Constantinople in 1500, he also offered the Venetians the opportunity to acquire sensitive political information by way of his contacts with the sultan's astrologer.[112]

Another kind of secret activity that was neither magical nor alchemical in nature deserves fuller treatment—the production and sale of poisons and antidotes. This topic presents challenges for historians. It would, of course, be absurd to connect the material presented here with the accusation of well poisoning that Christians often leveled against Jews.[113] To begin with, Christian accusations that Jews poisoned wells predate documented cases of Jews engaging in the production or trade of poisons in Europe. I am not aware of a single credible case of Jewish trade in poisons before 1400. We generally have to be cautious of Christian claims that Jews prepared poisons even if these claims are not connected to the charge of poisoning wells.[114]

In fact, well poisoning was a phantasm of Christian anti-Judaism. When Christians accused Jews of making poisons, it was often related less to some specific scenario arousing anxieties and more to deliberate defamation. Recently, scholars have also pointed out that the charge of well poisoning was only rarely the initial trigger for "spontaneous" pogroms against local Jews, even during the plague years of the fourteenth century; instead, this accusation tended to justify pogroms that had already been carefully planned by the authorities.[115] The poisoning accusation itself was not a product of the plague years, with all its attendant fears, but rather something we find as early as the twelfth century. Neither was the range of allegations about Jewish poison attacks confined to wells.[116] In any case, as the idea of Jews as well poisoners became increasingly prominent in the collective imagination, especially after the devastating waves of plague during the fourteenth century, a distinctive demand for Jewish poisons also began to emerge. Some Jewish physicians and naturalists were ready to comply by offering their services. Of course, a criminal intent was not automatically present in every case where the sources mention poisons. Terms like "venenum" could, for example, just as easily have designated abortifacients. Also, where poisons were involved, antidotes were usually not far away. As we will see shortly, a number of prominent early modern Jewish physicians were indeed knowledgeable about one substance that many contemporaries regarded as an unsurpassed antidote—the horn of the legendary unicorn.[117]

Jewish trade in poisons cannot be separated from Christian demand. In early modern Europe, demand was greatest in Italy and, more specifically, in Venice. As contemporaries were already aware, Venetian authorities in particular did not shy away from using poison to murder political opponents.[118] Such attacks are attested as early as the fifteenth century, but they became more frequent in the sixteenth century. They also gained additional legitimacy from the theory of secrets of state. This doctrine placed secret, and often morally reprehensible, methods in the hands of political authorities—especially in situations where the state faced dangerous threats. In 1450, the Venetian Council of Ten received a recommendation on behalf of a Jew who was said to be very seasoned in the science of poisons ("qui dicitur doctissimus in hac scientia venenosa").[119] Between 1450 and 1474 alone, the Council of Ten ordered ten poison attacks, including multiple attempts on the life of Francesco Sforza in Milan and the Ottoman sultan Mehmed II. Two Jews were among the hired assassins, a group that included several Italians, a Croat, a Pole, and a Catalan.[120] In 1471, Jacopo da Gaeta (Ya'qūb Pasha)—a Jew who had converted to Islam and become Sultan Mehmed II's personal physician—offered to kill the conqueror of Constantinople, hated throughout Christian Europe, on behalf of the Venetians. As a reward, he asked Venice for a one-time payment, a tax exemption, and Venetian citizenship. He never carried out the plans, and it is unclear how serious he was about the offer.[121] For the Venetian authorities, however, he was credible.[122] Several years later, around 1475, the Jewish moneylender Salomon of Piove offered to send a Jewish physician by the name of Valchus ("magister valchus") to Constantinople in order to poison Sultan Mehmed II on behalf of the Republic of Venice. When Salomon died unexpectedly, his son took up the plan. In return for carrying out the attack, Salomoncinus asked Venice to allow him and his descendants to trade freely in the Serenissima and to establish five banks.[123] It is not possible to say why this project failed. Valchus, the physician entrusted with the assassination, got as far as the Ottoman court. However, the already ailing sultan still lived on for four more years.[124] By contrast, an unnamed "Jewish doctor" ("medico Giudeo") did manage to carry out a poisoning commissioned by the authorities of the Serenissima in 1545. Secrecy was of the highest priority in this assassination, and so the Council of Ten made a point of ordering that the name of the Jewish poison expert remain concealed. Hence, the sources speak in a rather laconic way of "a person whom one could trust" ("una persona, a chi si può prestar fede").[125] We also have only sparse information about another project involving a Jew named Zacuti, who promised the Venetians that he could use poison to get rid of a traitor in Constantinople in 1654.[126] In the late 1590s, apparently without any concrete assassination plans in mind, Abramo Colorni presented Venetian authorities and the Duke of Modena with a proposal as martial as it was risky: he promised to deliver weapons using poisonous substances (and a matching antidote) that could be used to kill large crowds—including, of all people, the flock of parishioners assembled in a church—at one stroke.[127]

Jews' alleged expertise at producing poisons was much in demand in Venice even apart from concrete assassination plans. In 1601, authorities summoned the convert Domenico Gerosolimitano from Mantua to come to the city in order to present a book in Hebrew about poisons.[128] The idea of special Jewish expertise in this field was probably also bolstered by the fact that several poisons are mentioned in the Bible and that both the holy scriptures and later Jewish writings had a nuanced Hebrew terminology for poisons.[129] Jews' extensive trade contacts also strengthened their association with poisons. During the Late Middle Ages, there was a widespread view that the most dangerous poisons were produced in faraway countries. Against this background, Jewish traders and travelers could easily become a target for accusations and suspicions.[130] In Strasbourg in the plague year 1348, for example, accusations spread that a certain "Frau Guothild, the Jewess, crossed the ocean and brought a load full of poison along with her."[131] Last but not least, Jews' familiarity with Islamic sciences fueled the assumption that they had special theoretical knowledge about poisons. In principle, this suspicion was not entirely farfetched. For example, an alchemical anthology written around 1600 in Hebrew and now preserved at the State Library in Berlin shows that some early modern Jews clearly knew about the Arabic-language Book of Poisons by Jābir ibn Ḥayyān (late ninth century), which was overwhelmingly based on Greek sources, even though it is regarded as the "most comprehensive Arab-language account in this field."[132] In the late twelfth century, the famous Jewish rabbi and physician Maimonides wrote a treatise on poisons and antidotes in Arabic that became known in Christian Europe under the title *Tractatus de venenis*.[133] A book of secrets by the important Italian Kabbalist Ḥayyim Vital, composed in the Ottoman Empire shortly after 1600, likewise cites prescriptions for making deadly poisons and corresponding antidotes.[134]

In Venice, Jews' reputation as experts in poisons was strengthened by the fact that one generation after another of the Jewish Sarfatti family had been producing sublimate mercuric chloride—one of the chemical substances favored by the Venetian authorities as a poison.[135] As we have seen, the Sarfattis also produced cinnabar, which was often used as a poison in the early modern era.[136] In Tuscany and the Duchy of Modena, too, Jewish entrepreneurs held franchises for the production of mercuric chloride starting in the late seventeenth century.[137] Of course, this does not imply that the chemicals these Jews produced were necessarily used as poisons in practice. In the eyes of the authorities, however, Jews were associated with these substances.

With the erosion of Venetian influence in the early modern Mediterranean, the Serenissima was increasingly willing to use poison to damage the Ottoman Empire. Even premodern forms of chemical and biological warfare were tested, and not just by the Venetians. The Duke of Mantua, who in 1601 led an offensive with imperial troops against the Ottoman fortress of Canissa (today Nagykanizsa in Hungary), ordered his alchemists to produce poisonous projectiles.[138] Admittedly, these kinds of warfare techniques had been described for centuries. Before the sixteenth century, however, they were either rarely used, as in the infamous siege of Kaffa, or simply remained audacious theory, as in the case of Leonardo da Vinci's ideas for developing biological weapons in the form of projectiles.[139] Starting in the 1570s, however, one can observe greater efforts by both Venetians and Turks to put biological warfare into practice, as in the attempt to gain strategic advantage by poisoning enemy waters.[140] For Jews, this kind of development was potentially dangerous. Reports circulated of wells poisoned by Jews on behalf of the Turks, as in a 1615 dispatch from Constantinople that mentioned actions of this kind planned for Malta.[141] When the Ottomans actually applied these methods of warfare, especially in the Balkans, it was clear that Christians would accuse local Jews of complicity.[142] It could well have been fear of such accusations that prompted a Jew from Ragusa to write a letter informing the Venetian Council of Ten about well poisonings the Turks allegedly planned in the vicinity of several Venetian strongholds in Dalmatia in 1570.[143]

There were also Jews who offered, either out of loyalty to the Venetian cause or simply because it made good business sense, to help the Serenissima plan biological and chemical warfare. In 1654, for example, a Jewish physician named Michel Angelo Salomon offered the republic a plague-contaminated poison meant to soak clothes and textiles that had been manufactured for export into the Ottoman Empire.[144] This physician may be identical with Salomone da Zara, who established contact with the Venetian *provveditore generale* (governor-general) in Dalmatia in 1650 and offered a poison that purportedly contained the "quintessence of the plague."[145] The governor-general, who had previously undertaken repeated efforts at using poisons in the war over Candia (Crete), reacted positively to the Jewish physician's suggestion but ultimately had to give up on the project in 1652 after several attempts at implementation. What proved most decisive was the Venetians' fear that the plague might infect their own ranks. Whether Salomone ever received the yearly wage of 300 ducats promised him is, accordingly, doubtful.

Cryptography

Cryptography is a prime example of a field in which the early modern theory of state arcana fostered previously unknown forms of secrecy. In medieval letters, it was relatively rare for correspondents to use methods of encryption.[146] In Italy, interest in ciphers intensified around the middle of the fourteenth century.[147] Another, later, factor was Machiavelli's writings, which touched on the usefulness of secrecy for the prince and were often cited, though not always uncritically, by theoreticians of *arcana imperii*.[148]

Above all, however, the emergence in the middle of the fifteenth century of a permanent ambassadorial system and of diplomacy, which was regarded as an "art of secrecy," encouraged this development.[149] Scholars have thoroughly researched the rise of cryptography and, in particular, the contributions made by the Italian humanist Leon Battista Alberti and the German abbot Johannes Trithemius.[150] By contrast, the fact that the boom in cryptography also brought Jews into the arena, both in theory and in practice, has been largely overlooked.

We know that Jews were encrypting letters before the sixteenth century. Already in the Middle Ages, and especially during the Renaissance, letter-writing played a special role for Jews.[151] Letters were a crucial means of communication among a minority group whose members were dispersed across numerous lands. The ability to read and write was traditionally accorded great significance in Judaism. Knowledge was also a religious category, and whoever could write was in a position to pass on this precious commodity to interested parties across great distances.[152] Jews also communicated knowledge about political developments and business affairs in letters. Of course, sending a letter meant that the knowledge it contained—whether religious or business-related—was literally no longer in one's own hands. This was also true of family correspondence, as reflected in a private letter written in 1619 by the Jew Zachariah to his sister Bela in Vienna. Zachariah discusses the importance of the encryption key: "Otherwise, dear sister, know that I have lost the [secret] language [in the original: *dos loshn*] . . . so make sure to have someone send me back the [secret] language, for one cannot have everything written in German going out by mail."[153] We do not know what encryption methods Zachariah employed. Among Italian Jews, at any rate, different methods for encrypting messages had been in circulation since the beginning of the Renaissance.[154]

The first published works by Jews about cryptography date back to the sixteenth century. With his *Scotographia* (Prague, 1593), a book discussed in greater detail in Chapter 5, Abramo Colorni even produced one of the sixteenth century's major cryptographic works. Rabbis, too, engaged in cryptography. This was the case, for example, with Abraham Menaḥem Porto (1520–after 1594), who later became a noted rabbi in Verona.[155] In 1555, his cryptographic treatise *Zafnat Paneaḥ* was published in Italy. As the author admitted, it was based, in part, on the method of a Christian author.[156] The famous Italian rabbi Samuel Archevolti (ca. 1530–1611) had far more ambitious aspirations. The thirtieth chapter of his Hebrew grammar, *Arugat ha-Bosem* (Venice, 1602; reprinted Amsterdam, 1730), discusses eighteen different cryptographic methods, for which Archevolti also proposes a concise Hebrew terminology. In addition to recipes for secret inks and other instructions for "invisible writing," Archevolti gave procedures for coding using figurative signs, letters, and numbers. In addition, he situated the origins of contemporary cryptography in the Talmud.[157]

Acting as an agent of the Serenissima around 1570, the Sephardic merchant Ḥayyim Saruk developed his own idiosyncratic, handwritten code book, of which more will be said below.[158] The Kabbalist Ḥayyim Vital dealt with invisible ink in his book of secrets, composed after 1610.[159] In *Shiltei ha-Gibborim* (1612) by the Mantuan physician Abraham Portaleone, too, three methods are presented for transmitting important messages during wartime. They include instructions for how to inscribe articles of clothing with fruit juice and how to make the message reappear by heating.[160] Even if these kinds of experiments might look amateurish from today's perspective, to many contemporaries they seemed highly promising.[161] Indeed, even the Venetian *Bailo* (consul) in Constantinople "enciphered" his dispatches to the Serenissima with lemon juice during the Ottoman-Venetian War of 1570.[162] A few decades earlier (1525), the Venetian Council of Ten honored a Jew named Marco Rafael who had offered the republic a "method for secret writing" ("modo de scriver occulto"). It was also based on special secret ink that could be made visible only by applying a "certain liquid."[163] There was no shortage of such formulas at the time, but this secret ink must have been especially compelling in the Venetians' eyes, as the republic granted the Jewish inventor a pension for several years.[164] Apparently, he even obtained a post in the Serenissima's encryption office. In addition, he worked as "Praeceptor" of the Hebrew language. In this way, the Italian military engineer Mario Savorgnano learned Hebrew with Rafael.[165] Venice was not, however, the only place where Rafael's services were sought after. Toward the end of the 1520s, King Henry VIII of England succeeded in luring him away to London. The appointment in England must have been the decisive factor behind Rafael's conversion to Christianity.[166] From then on, English sources occasionally referred to him as a "Jewish renegade." There was hardly any place for unbaptized Jews at the court of Henry VIII, which does not mean, however, that the king rejected Jewish (secret) knowledge. To the contrary, Rafael and Jacob Mantino—a noted Jewish physician living in Venice—were given an explosive assignment by the English court; they were to submit an expert report, as positive as possible, from a Jewish perspective on the legitimacy of Henry VIII's infamous divorce from his first wife.[167] Rafael seems to have completed this assignment to the court's utter satisfaction.[168] Accordingly, "Dom. Marco Raphael" enjoyed a privileged position at court. For example, he was entrusted with diplomatic negotiations and continued to maintain contacts with the Serenissima as well as with foreign ambassadors at the English court. He even arranged for two royal councilors to serve as guides through Henry VIII's palaces and collections during a visit to London by Mario Savorgnano, his former Hebrew student.[169]

Today it is hard to fully fathom how Jews like Marco Rafael made their secret inks. It is true that the Talmud had already mentioned the production of invisible inks, but this does not mean that Jews had a special set of skills.[170] In reality, the experiments of Jews like Rafael were probably quite similar to the procedures developed by Christian scholars such as Georgius Agricola, Cardano, and Della Porta.[171] Even Colorni's ambitious cryptographic system did not lack competition; a contemporary buyer would not have had much difficulty finding equally elaborate treatises authored by Christian writers. Yet some evidence indicates that many Christians believed that Jews were particularly competent in cryptography. The priests of the biblical temple and the authorities of the Talmud were stylized by both Christians and Jews as guardians of cryptographic knowledge.[172] Christian reception of the Kabbalah and, in particular, of the methods of gematria proved no less important.[173] Many early modern Christian scholars were fascinated by Kabbalists' intensive preoccupation with the commutation of letters and with "numerological secrets."[174] It is no accident that somebody like the French diplomat and mathematician Blaise de

Vigenère (1523–1596) was not only an eminent author of works on cryptography, but also a prominent Christian Kabbalist.[175] On the Christian side, there was a widespread view that Hebrew script had an intrinsically occult dimension and, as a result, also qualified as a universal language—an idea that intrigued scholars throughout almost all of Europe during the seventeenth century and was often inseparable from cryptographic theories.[176]

To summarize, Christians credited Jews with a special talent for cryptography, not least on the basis of their familiarity with the Hebrew language and their purported knowledge of its occult potential. This reputation was bolstered by the notable role Jews played as spies throughout this entire era. Cryptographic knowledge was, understandably, quite useful for the practice of espionage. Indeed, Levantine Jews who operated abroad as spies for Venice and Spain often wrote up their dispatches and reports in code.[177] Inside Italy, as well, Jews were often employed as spies and collectors of information between rival courts. In those cases, too, they were frequently outfitted with encryption keys.[178]

Spying and Procuring Information

Christian authorities' growing willingness to employ Jews as spies and procurers of information certainly had to do with the general boom in secrecy that resulted from the rise of the theory of state arcana. Irrespective of actual evidence for Jewish espionage activities, however, the figure of the Jewish spy was also a deeply rooted stereotype that has lived on in modern anti-Semitism.[179] Tellingly, certain early modern argots, including the thieves' cant Rotwelsch and the itinerants' language Yeniche, often designate the act of spying on someone (as a prelude to some criminal act) by using the Hebrew-derived term (*aus*)*baldowern*. This term means to "scout out" in German slang, and it comes from the Hebrew *ba'al davar*.[180] Jewish spies, whether real or imagined, fired Christians' imaginations. For this reason, it was worth it simply from a commercial point of view for the English publisher of *Lettres juives* (1735–1737), by the philosopher Jean-Baptiste de Boyer d'Argens, to give this book the suggestive title *The Jewish*

Spy, even though it was not a work revealing the hidden world of espionage, but rather a relatively philosemitic Enlightenment treatise in the form of a fictitious exchange of letters between two Jewish correspondents.[181] The sensationalist title does not seem to have harmed demand for the book. On the contrary, *The Jewish Spy* went through several editions in England within just a few years.[182]

The phantasms about Jewish spies should not make us overlook the fact that there were certain situations in which Christian authorities had good reasons for entrusting Jews with espionage. By no means was procuring secret information a job only for professional diplomats.[183] It could also be carried out by merchants, and this was especially true for Jewish merchants in the Mediterranean region, whose activities as spies are attested throughout this period.[184] The frequent business trips they took in their full-time profession as merchants had them traveling constantly between Italy, the Balkans, and the Ottoman Empire, which put them in an ideal position to collect and transmit timely, up-to-date information.

Indeed, many of the so-called Jewish consuls of the Levantine and Ponentine "nation" were involved in espionage, often for the Republic of Venice.[185] In Bohemia, authorities recruited the Jewish physician Feifel as a procurer of information as early as the fifteenth century. In 1417, King Wenceslas exempted him from all specifically Jewish taxes. The king valued this "itinerant man and surgeon from the holy city of Jerusalem" for his "loyal service in medicine as well as clandestine intelligence" ("getrewen dinst in ercztnei und auch heimliche botschaft").[186] In the sixteenth century, the Habsburgs, too, knew quite well that one "inevitably has to keep such people in Buda, Belgrade, and Sofia by way of whom good, reliable reports often arrive."[187] Jews were also spies for the Ottoman Empire, though contemporary Christians greatly exaggerated the extent of their activities.[188] And, to be sure, the methods of Jewish information procurers were not by default more original or efficient than those of their Christian colleagues. In 1617, for example, a Polish Jew named Giacob Levi informed the Venetian authorities that the simplest, if rather unimaginative, way to obtain information from Trieste was to send an informant clothed in rags. The informant would then go to the market square and the most popular taverns and act as if he were begging. These, Levi explained, were the easiest places to discover what was happening in a city.[189]

Certainly more imagination than reality was at work in 1785 when the tried and tested Venetian spy Giovanni Cattaneo claimed that Jews were "the best race for spies."[190] Cattaneo's exaggerated views may, however, reflect that the Serenissima regularly employed Jews as informers during the early modern era, even within Venetian society.[191] And spying was not the only job European Jews took on in the field of secret intelligence. Consider the case of the anonymous Jew who worked for the "Secret Expedition" (*Geheime Expedition*) of Count Heinrich von Brühl in the 1740s. The "Expedition" was an intelligence service, equally efficient and unscrupulous, run by this powerful Saxon prime minster. The Jewish employee was entrusted with counterfeiting seals used in the interception of letters.[192]

It is impossible to generalize about what motivated Jews to become spies or procurers of sensitive information. By and large, economic incentives probably outweighed political motives.[193] According to the historian Paolo Preto, Venetian Jews' remarkable willingness to work as spies and information procurers for the Serenissima stemmed from the fear of possible repression if they refused. In other words, it was a result of intimidation and preemptive obedience. But this explanation is not fully convincing, and it certainly does not apply to the majority of Jewish spies and information procurers.[194] In fact, the pathway to spying in the early modern era was often a gradual one.[195] Jews' work as agents and dispatch writers—a phenomenon attested throughout Europe—occasionally overlapped with the practice of spying.[196] In a similar vein, court Jews could use their far-flung trade and communication networks to procure sensitive information and work as agents.[197]

In general, it makes sense to view early modern espionage and the procurement of sensitive information less as the result of carrying out orders from the top down and more as a relatively flexible system for circulating information in which secrets were exchanged as part of a quid pro quo of services. For example, in 1415 a Jew from Innsbruck named Salman von Hals (probably identical with the aforementioned Salman Teublein) was able to secure the release of another Jew from prison by revealing an unspecified "art" to Duke Frederick IV of Tyrol.[198] David Mavrogonato, a merchant residing in Crete who did some major spying for the Venetians in the Ottoman Empire during the second half of the fifteenth century, did not receive just honoraria and personal privileges in return; he was also able to negotiate assurances for the Jewish community on the island where he lived.[199] In 1562, the Jew Manuello Dellavolta, a subject of the Este dukes, reminded the governor of Reggio about the information he had provided in a recent military conflict and asked for a letter of safe conduct in return.[200] This brings to mind the case of the Viennese Court Jew Lebl Höschl (d. 1681), who, like all Jews in Vienna, was expelled from the city in 1670. Höschl resettled in Buda and started a brisk business in secret information. His valuable reports about Ottoman internal affairs gained him one of the first licenses for trade visits to Vienna granted to a Jew after the community's expulsion from the city. Interestingly, the dispatches he wrote to the imperial war council were encrypted in Hebrew and Yiddish. It must be assumed that Habsburg authorities had staff on their payroll, undoubtedly either Jews or converts, who could decipher messages composed in these languages.[201]

In Venice, it was not only the authorities who availed themselves of the services of Jews when it came to sensitive issues and the procurement of information. Numerous accounts written by travelers to the city emphasize how the Venetian upper class sought the services of Jews for keeping and preserving secrets. The anonymous author of an account titled *Relatione della città e republica di Venetia* (1672) was one of the first to describe this phenomenon in greater detail. Claiming that Jews characteristically knew how to handle secrets ("essendo proprio dell'Ebreo d'esser segreto"), he went on to note that the *nobili* in the city would often entrust Jews with a variety of tasks requiring discretion and confidentiality.[202] A few years later, the Jewish convert Giulio Morosini, whose writings should generally be treated with a certain degree of skepticism, wrote that there was enough trust between Jewish merchants and Christian nobles so that the latter sometimes let Jews keep the keys to their houses.[203] During the same period, the French traveler Limojon de Saint-Didier described how Jews in the Serenissima were "esteem'd to be Men of Secrecy, so this good Quality gets them many Protectors among the Nobility, who have divers ways of employing them."[204] A few years later, the English traveler John Clenche confirmed this impression and claimed that "these [Jews] for their reputed secrecy are very much cherished by the nobility, there not being one but has his Jew for his confident, nor Jew without his protector."[205] Exactly what jobs a *confidente* performed is a detail on which the travelers were regrettably silent. Some years later, in 1688, the Frenchman Maximilian Misson was able to report only that the Jews "are generally a Sort of People that never refuse any Kind of Employment, and are made Use of on several Occasions; especially by the Nobles, who are very great Support to them."[206] And in the early eighteenth century, Johann Jacob Schudt reported that "in Venice every noble family [has] their Jew as trusted confident in whom the most secret affairs of the families are confided."[207]

It is difficult to discern where reality blends into fantasy in such accounts. In the case of Venice, at least, there seems to be a core of truth. Close ties between Jews and the Venetian *nobili* did lead to a judicial scandal resulting in several death sentences in the 1630s. A number of Jews and *nobili* were found guilty of scheming together on machinations that included the payment of bribes.[208] We also know that—much to the annoyance of the authorities, and especially the Inquisitors—Jews in the ghetto routinely formed small groups that exchanged up-to-date, and often sensitive, information among their members. Such forms of gathering were also common among Christians at the time, to be sure. Filippo de Vivo has surmised that they served the purpose of quenching one's curiosity in an era before mass media. Still, these groups were often perceived as more than just a type of early modern sociability. After all, even their members called them *bozzoli*—a reference to the Italian word for a silkworm cocoon. Clearly, these "cocoons" of information exchange sometimes aroused suspicion among outsiders, whether or not this was justified.[209]

It is in the nature of the business that we do not know precisely what these Jewish *confidenti*—mentioned by so many travelers to Venice—did. They were, as the very term suggests, sworn to secrecy. In Venice, the term *confidente* was also frequently applied to spies and informers for the republic, though this was nothing short of a euphemism: one's own people were designated *confidenti,* but those procuring information for the enemy were, as a rule, called spies.[210] Interestingly, the word *confidente* can also be found in internal Jewish contexts. For example, northern Italy's Jewish communities appointed official *deputati confidenti,* or just *confidenti,* mostly totaling three and almost always including the local rabbi.[211] These officials conducted discreet talks with members of the community about their tax burdens and their willingness to donate money. Such inquiries required knowledge about the financial situation of each community member, which further reinforced the need for secrecy. Disclosing negative details about community members' financial circumstances could do serious damage to their businesses and reputations, especially those who operated in the financial sector. While tax assessors in Jewish communities in Central Europe were not called *confidenti,* they were also encouraged to keep secrets. As one contemporary translation of a rabbinical edict (1603) explains, "[T]hose ordered to make such an assessment on site should keep each such assessment secret to the utmost extent possible and not reveal it."[212]

Military and Civilian Technology

The technological sector in early modern Europe was much more closely connected to the economy of secrets than one might at first suspect. The advent of patents during this period does not contradict this observation. As Mario Biagioli has persuasively argued, early modern patents of technologies served more to grant certain privileges to inventors than to protect their intellectual property. The primary reason for granting patents was to establish manufactories, produce machines (in the early modern sense of the word), and transfer technology along with trained and specialized workers across geographic and political boundaries.[213] Early modern patents were not a contract between inventor and society. Today, technology patents are publicly accessible because of the guarantees afforded by official patent protections. However, early patents were not a form of public knowledge in the first place.[214] In most cases, patents were not even printed—even in major hubs of intellectual and technological activity, such as Venice.

Instead, they were simply issued by the Senate on behalf of inventors in the name of the doge.[215] Inventors who were granted a patent did not have to divulge their secrets, or even make them public. In fact, patents could make knowledge of an invention even more inaccessible than if its original secrecy had simply been maintained.[216]

Throughout the early modern period, strict secrecy remained a prime concern for many inventors and engineers.[217] This was also true for the period before the advent of patents—especially with regard to the engineering profession, which started to take shape in the twelfth century and was often associated with the figure of the magus.[218] Some engineers even fashioned their claim to mastery of nature and omnipotence in a rhetoric that recalled the posture and language of the magus.[219] As Penelope Gouk notes, "the Renaissance philosopher-engineer, skilled in all aspects of the Vitruvian arts such as military technology, architecture, and garden and theatre design, came to be widely regarded as a natural magician par excellence."[220] In the eyes of contemporaries, the eponymous *ingenio* empowered the engineer to master and manipulate nature as profoundly as only a magus could.[221] In addition, military engineers such as the famous Mariano di Jacopo from Siena—more commonly known as Taccola (1382–ca. 1453)— saw service in the role of augurs for their rulers as one of their duties. An augur's job included tasks such as using astrology to pick the most favorable time for launching a war.[222] Undoubtedly, the figure of the engineer was firmly entrenched in the economy of secrets.

We have to look at Jewish activities in the early modern technology sector against this background. It would be misleading to subsume the phenomenon of Jews active in the field of technology under a narrative that idealizes a Jewish "contribution" to science and technology. Rather, we need to embed the technological activities of early modern Jews in the larger social context of the economy of secrets. Technological knowledge was highly confidential, both because intellectual property lacked effective protection and because it was inherently linked to state secrets. The technological knowledge of engineers, architects, and inventors was closely tied to early modern state formation; in fact, it was largely generated by government demands in the first place.[223] It served the immediate purpose of stabilizing, expanding, and aggrandizing the state's rule. For that reason alone, it was often far from openly available. Engineers, fortification architects, and inventors alike knew how to make the most of their talents in their dealings with political authorities and royal courts, and their kind of expertise belonged to the phenomenon Michel Foucault has aptly called "knowledge-power."[224]

Naturally, these observations apply to Jewish technology adepts, engineers, and inventors as well. Their strategies for keeping secrets cannot be overlooked, as noted by Shlomo Simonsohn, one of the few historians who has drawn attention, if only in passing, to the considerable number of Jewish inventors and engineers in early modern Italy.[225] A case in point is Venice, where Jews' importance in the development and transfer of technology is quantitatively measurable: of those "nations" that obtained patents (*brevetti*) in the republic between 1478 and 1788, Jews were awarded at least twenty-seven. This puts them in third place behind the French, with fifty-seven, and the Germans, who had forty-four.[226] Historical research on this phenomenon has been haphazard, at best. Thus far, there are no systematic studies on Jewish engineers and inventors in the late medieval and early modern eras. For the same reason, we still know very little about how Jewish engineers and technology adepts were trained and what kinds of job opportunities they had within the Jewish community. One scholar has speculated that the Jewish engineers' expertise derived from complex religious rules about the construction of ritual baths.[227] It seems far more likely, however, that Jews' experience in mining and minting might have played a role. We know that Jews constructed and operated mines in Italy and the Holy Roman Empire as early as the middle of the fifteenth century; this is documented for the Ottoman Empire as well.[228] Moreover, the growing employment opportunities and patronage structures for engineers at royal courts and in larger cities encouraged Jews to enter this field. The absence of any guildlike organization in this profession was an added advantage. Finally, the associations between the engineer and the figure of the magus might have lent particular prestige or credibility to Jews. As we will see, however, this could also turn into a risk.

As early as the Late Middle Ages, there is evidence that Jews were in demand as experts on technological matters in German lands.[229] Sources mention Ashkenazi Jews as builders of mills on several occasions in the late fifteenth century.[230] In 1431, the Nuremberg Council employed a Jewish expert on canalization; this may have been Josep von Ulm, a Jewish engineer and skilled fountain designer who died in Stuttgart in 1462.[231] In 1429, the Jew Salman the Mining Master (*Bergmeister*) and his Christian business partner, the Count of Veldenz, received a privilege allowing them to "mine all ore they can discover and find" in a designated area near Trier. Salman's technical expertise must have been considerable: it was he who detected the ore deposits in the first place, and for centuries this site was still known as the "Jewish shaft."[232] Around the same time, a Nuremberg patrician sent a Jewish engineer named Sammel von Kassel to Goslar to work on mining business.[233] The sources are even more detailed for Italy. As early as the mid-fifteenth century, the Venetian Senate employed a Jewish engineer named Salomone who specialized in hydraulic constructions, which were naturally always in demand in the city of lagoons. In addition, "maestro Salomon the Jew" was commissioned to have taken care of the project for diverting the Brenta River toward Chioggia.[234] Sixteenth-century Venetian writers also mention Jewish expertise on the Venetian lagoon's development and public sanitation.[235] In 1554, the Jew Graziadio Mantino was granted a permit for introducing a method to desalinate seawater in the Serenissima.[236]

In the 1630s, the Jewish entrepreneur Daniel Israel Perez received a patent from the Venetian government for using a portable device to drain swamps and bogs.[237] This episode testifies not only to Jews' ongoing activity as engineers, but also to the undiminished need for confidentiality. Only a few months after the patent was granted, Perez approached the authorities again to request special protection for his device, which had to be built outside of the city for reasons of space and could therefore be viewed by far too many curious onlookers.[238] The Senate complied with his request, especially since keeping the enterprise secret was also in the interest of the republic.[239] Only weeks after the patent application was submitted, the *Provveditori all'Arsenal* even recommended to the doge that Perez's device for pumping water and mud be used in the arsenal. Thus, the Jewish inventor was able to assume his work in the arsenal, a site normally off-limits, not just to Jews but also to most ordinary citizens.[240] Nothing else is known about the success of the project and the further fortunes of its inventor, but it is a testament to the fundamental seriousness of this enterprise that its inventor, Perez, was also granted a license to introduce water-driven milling machines and pump systems in Dalmatia.[241] Around the same time, "Dottor Daniele Israele Perez hebreo" received a privilege to introduce his irrigation and pump machines in the Duchy of Mantua.[242]

Christians in Venice and its territories were not the only ones who sought the services of Jewish engineers. Jewish "masters of the mechanical arts" ("maestri de arte mechanica") were also found in southern Italy.[243] In 1444, the Marquis of Ferrara, Leonello d'Este, hired the aforementioned Jewish engineer Salomon ("nostro Inzignero Magistro Salomone Iudio").[244] In the late sixteenth century, a certain Josef Levi received an official commission from the ducal chamber to work on fortifications and ramparts in the territory.[245] In Milan in 1437, and before that, in Ferrara, a Jew named Isaac of Noyon, also known as "Magister Achino," offered his services for the construction of a bridge across the Po.[246] Authorities entrusted the Jewish military engineer Abramo da Cremona, who enjoyed the confidence of Francesco Sforza (1401–1466), with the manufacture and installation of military equipment for fortifications in Cremona and Matignano.[247] A Jewish engineer ("ducalis ingeniarius") named Simon (Samuel) was also in service to the Duke of Milan during the 1450s.[248] In all likelihood, this Simon is different from the Jewish engineer Simone Bettini, for whom there is a record from 1486 and who also applied for commissions from the House of Este.[249] In Gonzaga-ruled Mantua in 1592, a Jew named Daniel Pasciuto, who was known by the colorful nickname "The Prophet," received a twenty-five-year patent for a mechanical invention he made to load and unload ships.[250] Likewise, the Margrave of Monferrat employed a Jewish engineer ("Luppo ebreo inginero") as early as the 1470s.[251]

The case of Abramo Colorni, the court engineer at Ferrara, is especially noteworthy. The harquebus he invented was said to have allowed multiple firings without reloading, and Colorni was certainly not the only Jewish engineer well-versed in military technology. This highlights the need to revise a notion still widespread in the study of Jewish history—that early modern Jews did not carry or use any weapons, much less manufacture them and offer them for sale. Moses Ginsburger tentatively explored this topic in 1929, but his exploration remained confined to what he saw as a list of curious exceptions.[252] More recently, David Biale has questioned narratives about the defenselessness of early modern Jews, which are largely based on normative documents like prohibitions on carrying weapons.[253] Other recent attempts to arrive at a more differentiated perspective on the topic of Jews and weapons have likewise dealt primarily with how they were carried on a day-to-day basis.[254] The question of weapons production is almost always missing from these treatments. It is not, however, a farfetched question. Even though professions like master gunsmith were generally organized in guilds, there were still niches for Jews outside the Christian guilds. In Frankfurt am Main in the 1450s, the city council expressed interest in the services of an unnamed Jewish demolitions expert and his "foreign art." This engineer, with whom the city had established contacts through the mediation of a local Jew, advertised that his products were, among other things, capable of crushing towers.[255] In 1486, the Göttingen city council bought a gun manufactured by a Jewish gunsmith named Moyses from Mühlhausen.[256]

Jewish engineers and technology adepts from German-speaking Europe also exported their know-how across the Alps. This was the case, for example, with the Jewish physician and engineer (*inzignero*) Abralino de Colonia, whose family had a Rhenish background.[257] Abralino first approached the Duke of Milan in 1442 and presented him with various projects as ambitious as they were secret ("inzegni secreto").[258] These included erecting a bridge, building a cannon (*bombarde*) meant to enable several shots simultaneously, constructing a machine to assault fortifications, producing powder, and a number of other military technology projects. The proposals were apparently persuasive, and the duke invited the Ashkenazi military engineer to his court.

We gain an even fuller picture of the activities of Jewish bombard makers, military engineers, and master gunsmiths if we look beyond the Holy Roman Empire and northern Italy. In Poland, there is evidence of Jews as master gunsmiths since the sixteenth century, at the latest.[259] In Rome, the

Descriptio urbis from 1526/1527 listed a Jewish master gunsmith. There could well have been others; this list indicates a profession for only a quarter of the 1,750 Jews who lived in the city.[260] Jews' involvement with military technology was particularly conspicuous, until the great waves of expulsion, in the Iberian sphere of influence. At the court of Navarra around 1430, a Jew named Samuel Ravatoso was in charge of the king's artillery.[261] There are additional examples from Spanish Sicily. In the 1420s, the Viceroy of Sicily commissioned the Jewish smith "Magister Siminto" to refit cannons so they could be used on the high seas ("pro aptando tres bonbardas castri ad marem").[262] Shortly thereafter, in 1441, a Jew from Messina named Abraham de Ragusa worked as an artillery expert (*balistarius*) in the service of King Alfonso of Aragon and Sicily.[263] The case of Gauyu (Gaiuczu) Conti in Catania a few decades later is especially noteworthy. The authorities in this Sicilian city apparently employed him as a military engineer, gunpowder producer, and defense expert for almost a quarter century starting in the 1460s.[264] After Conti either retired or died, another Jew held this office.[265] That successor was Gauyu (Gaudiu) lu Presti, whose reputation must have been just as great. The viceroy not only exempted him from all taxes, but also entrusted him with organizing fireworks for the festival of the city's saints![266]

There were also instances of Jewish armorers in this era. One was Salomone da Sesso (1465–1519), who eventually converted to Christianity and assumed the name Ercole de' Fideli. The sword he forged for Cesare Borgia became famous.[267] Overall, however, the number of Jewish master gunsmiths and bombard makers is particularly striking. A major reason why Jews were active in producing firearms was probably that métier's connection to the production of saltpeter and gunpowder, a field in which, as we will see, Jews were active through the entire period and in which Abramo Colorni would later acquire considerable renown.[268] Some early modern Jewish authors even claimed that ancient Jews had been in possession of military technology, thereby fashioning the Bible into a veritable "handbook for the art of war."[269] Among Christians, too, the notion that Moses had invented various types of military equipment in Egypt was widespread.[270] The belief, shared by both Christians and Muslims, that Jews played an important role in the transfer of technology, especially military technology, also bolstered the credibility of Jewish weapons producers. This was a rather distorted belief, but it did play a role in the granting of commissions. Ottoman authorities made one such commission to an unspecified group of Jews in 1552 who the Turks believed had exceptional competence in weapons technology. The authorities ordered them to manufacture harquebuses in Syria. From the correspondence with the sultan's court in Constantinople, however, it is clear that these Jews were overtaxed by the assignment.[271]

Less technical knowledge was needed for selling weapons or military technology. Here, too, there is no lack of examples. They extend from the continent-wide dealings of Sephardic merchants to small daily transactions documented as early as the first half of the early fifteenth century.[272] Royal courts and governing authorities were the most important customers for the weapons—and also, occasionally, armor—supplied by Jewish merchants. This is true for German lands in particular. In 1537, in what is today Lower Saxony, two Jews offered to sell a nobleman in Moritzberg a secret iron device that, they said, was not to be shown to any other person. Here, once again, secrecy enjoyed the highest priority. The relevant sources are correspondingly terse—which is unfortunate for historians.[273] There is also evidence that Jews in Lower Saxony occupied a dominant position when trading in metals, weapons, ammunition, and the chemicals used for manufacturing munitions.[274] In the Electorate of Saxony during the middle of the sixteenth century, Jews offered for sale a device for throwing fire as well as parts for various sorts of firearms.[275] In 1569, the Margrave of Baden purchased armaments from the Jew Jacob of Pforzheim.[276] There are also instances of city magistrates acting as buyers, as in Hildesheim in 1441, when the city magistrate bought harquebuses from the Jew Samuel.[277]

We know that Jews made large-scale weapons deliveries to troops even before the sixteenth century.[278] In the seventeenth century, however, these kinds of activities became much more prominent. The historian Selma Stern cited the growing importance of standing armies as a major reason for the emergence of what she called "Jewish war commissaries."[279] By contrast, Jonathan Israel has argued that the Thirty Years War (1618–1648) was the pivotal event.[280] According to Israel, the enormous demand from all sides for gunpowder and weapons provided previously unknown opportunities for Jewish army suppliers, who operated between the denominational frontlines of this war between Christians. He dates Jewish army suppliers' heyday from around 1700. A case in point is the life of Samuel Oppenheimer (1630–1703), who is regarded today as one of the most important representatives of court Jewry during that era.[281] Oppenheimer started his career as a "war factor" in the service of the Habsburgs. He acquired renown in 1683, when he supplied imperial troops fighting the Turks not only with urgently required provisions, but also with "handgrenades, gunpowder, pistols, and carbines sent on ships and rafts down the Danube and by means of wagons and horses on the roads."[282] Oppenheimer worked for the emperor, yet we also find comparable cases among the various territorial rulers of the empire starting in the seventeenth century. Admittedly, working for these rulers did not always involve the large quantities and sums that Oppenheimer worked with. Still, what most Jewish suppliers had in common, and what gave them an edge, was that they managed their operations—which were often geographically quite extensive—in a particularly efficient way by keeping a tight rein on subcontracting suppliers and agents.[283]

Jewish inventors and engineers were not, to be sure, restricted to the field of military technology. Detailed sources from the end of the sixteenth century document a project by the inventor Mendel Isaak, a Jew from Cracow, to build a bridge across the Danube at Vienna.[284] Little is known about Mendel's background; presumably, he is identical with a contemporary by the name of Mendel Sax who served as head of Cracow's Jewish community.[285] According to his own testimony, Mendel Isaak had already built bridges and pontoons for the Polish king Stephan Báthory before approaching Emperor Rudolf II in 1589.[286] The Imperial Court Chamber was not averse to the project, which promised a much-needed piece of infrastructure for the city of Vienna. After the inventor was "questioned more extensively orally" the same year, the Court Chamber came to the conclusion that "one must take it that he [is] not inexperienced in such matters."[287] Mendel then summarized his project in greater detail and presented the emperor with a proposal for what he called a stable (*gesenkte*) bridge, costing 30,000 thalers, whose structural form he demonstrated with a model. A pontoon bridge resting on floating parts was also considered.[288]

Mendel's core expertise as an engineer lay in the civilian field. Yet he, too, insisted on secrecy and did not disclose his plans to the Viennese authorities, let alone the wider public. Rather, he conducted negotiations only with the emperor's inner circle, and he addressed his petitions directly to Rudolf II. None of this aroused any mistrust, as it was well-known at court that Mendel knew something about secrets. Indeed, in the recent conflict between Poland and the Habsburgs (1588/1589), Mendel had played an important role as courier and spy. The Habsburgs even entrusted him with the job of emissary for negotiating a marriage of state.[289]

In contrast to the numerous projects that were proposed to the court in Prague at the time and often barely withstood initial scrutiny, Mendel's bridge project proved capable of persuading the Habsburgs. Emperor Rudolf II himself expressed an interest, but the commissaries he entrusted with this matter delayed their decision, and the negotiations between Mendel and the court dragged on for more than two years. Ultimately, the costly project petered out—a demise to which the outbreak of the so-called Long War between the Habsburgs and the Ottomans (1593) presumably contributed.[290] Whether news of this setback spread in Jewish circles cannot be determined; we do know, however, that Mendel Isaak and his projects were apparently not as unusual among contemporary Jews as one might think. Around the same time, a certain Leobel Mirowitz, who is referred to as a "court Jew" in the sources, and his Christian business partner applied to the emperor for permission to improve navigation by building canals on rivers in the Holy Roman Empire, including the Elbe. This project's implementation would have required considerable technological know-how and significant expenditures, and it is unclear whether it was seriously contemplated at court.[291] On the Spanish side of the Habsburg family, King Philip II of Spain expressed interest in a secret for desalinating ocean water that was being offered by a Lombard Jew—at the same time that the king was in the middle of ordering the expulsion of the Jews from Spanish Lombardy in the 1590s.[292] During the same period, officials at the Spanish court became interested in the hydraulic inventions of a certain Kalonimos from Lodi, whom the king had granted a privilege.[293] This Kalonimos was actually identical with the Jew Clemente Pavia from Lodi, who in 1595 received a privilege from the Duke of Mantua for an invention he made to irrigate fields.[294] He was an ordained rabbi, moneylender, and inventor.[295] Two of his brothers also devoted their efforts to developing and marketing technical innovations. The brother Sansone Pavia had, for example, invented a method for cleaning rice in 1588. However, the three brothers achieved fame mostly because of the aforementioned "invenzione delle acque," which revolved around a new kind of water pump. Detailed technical drawings of the pump still exist, and there is much to indicate that it actually worked. We know that in Lombardy, where the invention had been patented in 1594, Christian customers, including one nobleman, bought this pump to irrigate their own estates.[296]

In addition, a large share of the technologies and inventions that Jews patented concerned the textile industry.[297] Jews also patented chemical processes.[298] For example, in 1608 the Piedmontese Jews Fortunio Lattis and Isac Grechetto were granted a privilege in Tuscany allowing them to extract various mineral salts from swampland and manufacture vitriol.[299] In 1515, Cardinal Giulio de' Medici informed his cousin Lorenzo in Florence about a group of Jews who had come to Rome bringing "secret methods" for producing saltpeter and vitriol ("certi giudei maestri di salnitri, e' quali hanno certi nuovi modi secreti, molto belli et varii").[300] The cardinal attributed great significance to the matter, hoping these secrets would bring considerable economic advantages.[301] He recommended inviting these (presumably Sephardic) Jews to Pisa, where they could then furnish proof of their skills.[302] In Venice, as we have seen, the Jewish Sarfatti family held the privilege to produce mercuric chloride and a number of other chemical substances over several generations, on the basis of special secrets.

To be sure, Jews also put forward some rather dubious technological secrets. During the severe hunger crisis of 1590, for example, three Jews sent letters to the Venetian authorities offering fantastic secrets to increase the supply of flour. A certain Salamon Navarro made the first attempt. His "marvelous secret" ("secreto mirabile") promised to increase the supply of flour by 25 percent. Navarro left no doubt that he was thoroughly acquainted with the field of arcana and had already traveled the world in search of lucrative secrets.[303] This was a rhetorical commonplace at the time, and Navarro was not without competition by any means.[304] Just a few weeks later, one Salomon da Bassano was praising a special and no less secret type of flour that he also claimed would lead to an enormous spike in the supply of bread.[305] Around the same time, another Jew named Simon di Roman arrived on the scene offering the Serenissima a secret for increasing the supply of bread by 50 percent.[306] While his competitors merely asked for a gratification of 500 ducats and a privilege in return for their secret knowledge, Simon di Roman went further. In fact, in his case the fluid boundary between the trade in secrets and traditional forms of Jewish economic life is especially clear: Simon was less interested in getting a one-time fee for his secret than in obtaining permission to operate three broker and agent businesses in Venice.[307]

At this time, the Venetian authorities were feverishly searching for a way out of the hunger crisis. They even entered into negotiations with the Cypriot alchemist Marco Bragadino—who came, both socially and geographically, from the periphery of Venetian territory—about fantastic grain deliveries from Bavaria.[308] Against this background, it can come as no surprise that the Venetian authorities also took Jewish inventors' secretive offers seriously. As the historian Piero Camporesi has shown, hunger— and in particular the shortage of bread—was one of the most urgent problems of the early modern period.[309] Around the same time, the noted professor of secrets Giovan Battista Della Porta incorporated secrets about the making of bread into the expanded edition of his *Magia naturalis*.[310] The Venetian Senate was even prepared to grant a monthly pension of 100 ducats to the person who could deliver an easy remedy against the famine. However, the *Provveditori alla biave*—the officials overseeing the grain market—linked this reward to three conditions. First, the secret had to be previously unknown and undescribed. Second, it had to be fully "revealed" (*palesato*) to the authorities. And third, a physician had to declare it completely safe on health grounds.[311] Whether the three inventive Jews were in a position to meet these conditions can no longer be ascertained. This is also true for the four Christian petitioners who approached the

Venetian authorities on the same matter.[312] Interestingly, though, some of the Christians opted for anonymity. But the Jewish petitioners, without exception, revealed both their names and their religion. Emphasizing their Jewish background might actually have enhanced their credibility; it took little imagination for Christians to ascribe a priori this kind of secret knowledge, bordering on the magical, to Jews.

Such dubious inventions certainly did not shatter the widespread belief that Jews had considerable expertise in the development and transfer of technology. As we have seen, this impression was not entirely unfounded. The notion that Jews had a special kind of technological expertise even facilitated their resettlement in sixteenth-century Italy. In the 1590s, Grand Duke Ferdinando of Tuscany was hoping that his invitation to Levantine merchants would not only lead to an increase in trade with the Levant, but also bring technological know-how into his territory.[313] In Italy, it was Sephardic Jews who enjoyed a reputation for being able to procure technological knowledge, and there is evidence that this assumption corresponded to reality.[314] In the middle of the seventeenth century, the Duke of Savoy invited Iberian Jews to move to his state—especially in their capacity as "inventors."[315] Technical knowledge among early modern Jews was, of course, not just restricted to a small group of professional engineers. For example, an Italian Jew in the late sixteenth century writing about a (presumably Christian) wedding that featured lavish water games and machines displayed considerable interest in the mechanics operating these attractions.[316] The Jewish physician Joseph Salomon Delmedigo also delved into the subject of hydraulic machines in his discussion of the contributions made by engineers.[317]

One of the most important English plays of the late sixteenth century, Christopher Marlowe's *The Jew of Malta* (ca. 1589/1590), reminds us, however, that Jewish engineers could also be linked to allegations bordering on the absurd. More specifically, they were sometimes accused of maliciously using their technological knowledge against Christians. In Marlowe's play, the fanatical Jewish main character Barabas is an engineer by profession.[318] In their discussion of this play, literary scholars have pointed to elements of traditional medieval anti-Judaism.[319] However, no scholar has addressed the question of why Marlowe presented the Jewish protagonist as an engineer. This decision on Marlowe's part can hardly be attributed to the influence of medieval anti-Jewish literature. Rather, it has to be seen against the background of sixteenth-century discourses about the role of Jews in early modern technology transfer.[320] Indeed, in Marlowe's era, some Christian authors claimed that Sephardic Jews had betrayed sensitive details about European weapons technology and military secrets to the Turkish archenemy when they settled in the Ottoman Empire. One influential source of such anti-Jewish rhetoric was the treatise *Quatre premiers livres des navigations* by the French court geographer Nicolas de Nicolay (1517–1583), in which the author leveled precisely this accusation.[321] It was published many times and translated into all the major European languages. Jewish authors in the sixteenth century also put forward similar assertions, although for motives entirely different from Nicolay's. Writers such as Eliya Capsali and Joseph ha-Cohen were eager to enhance their religion's reputation by asserting that Jews ignominiously expelled from Spain were "such expert workers in the manufacture of cannons, bows, and crude shooting engines, swords, shields, and spears."[322]

Some later historians credited Nicolay's assertions all too uncritically.[323] However, recent scholarship has shown that his account is, by and large, not tenable.[324] A large-scale transfer of military technology by Sephardic Jews never happened. This does not imply, however, that Nicolay's accusations were motivated only by his obvious anti-Judaism.[325] By putting the blame on Sephardic Jews, Christian authors like Nicolay were implicitly touching on, and diverting attention from, the delicate issue of Christian deserters in the Ottoman Empire. Moreover, accusations like these gave French authors such as Nicolay a welcome opportunity to level criticism at France's perennial rival, Spain, whose policy of expelling the Jews had caused the alleged transfer of technology in the first place.[326]

It is certainly true that Ottoman sultans engaged the services of military experts from other countries, including Jews and Christian renegades, during the sixteenth century.[327] Thus, we find evidence of Jewish smiths and metallurgists in the central artillery foundry (Tophane-i Amire) in Constantinople. Among those working in this foundry in the 1510s, for example, were thirteen Jewish and seven originally Christian specialists. With an estimated total of sixty workers on the staff of the Tophane-i Amire, the share of Jews comes to around 20 percent.[328] In 1517/1518, Jewish workers also helped produce twenty-one large cannons, several meters long, for the sultan.[329] However, it is doubtful that Nicolay knew about any of these things. In the Ottoman Empire, as in Europe, weapons production was subject to strict secrecy. In Constantinople, too, the requisite metallurgical and military knowledge was passed on only from master to pupil.[330]

It is more likely that accusations such as those made by Nicolay picked up on reports of Jews as purveyors of textiles for the Janissaries, the Ottoman troops feared throughout Europe. These provisions, hardly surprising given Jews' dominant position in the Ottoman textile industry, may have led to the impression on the part of European travelers that Jews were operating as suppliers to the Turkish army on a grand scale and in a technological capacity.[331] The spectacular emergence of the adventurer David Reuveni in Europe during the 1520s must have further fueled such rumors. Reuveni, whose background remains unclear to this day, aroused great attention by asserting that he had come to Europe in order to procure weapons and recruit military experts in his capacity as minister of war to the Jewish king of the desert kingdom of Ḥabor.[332]

The Unicorn and the Secrets of Nature

Our survey of Jewish involvement in the early modern economy of secrets would be incomplete without an excursus focusing on the role of Jews as purveyors, dealers, and connoisseurs of the object that contemporaries believed to be one of the most coveted secrets of nature—the legendary unicorn. The Italian scholar Andrea Bacci was not exaggerating in his 1573 treatise *L'alicorno* when he called the unicorn the epitome of nature's secrets.[333] Bacci even claimed that no previous era had displayed such a fascination with this rare animal as did his own epoch.[334] Being able to possess the horn (*alicorno* in Italian) of this legendary animal (*unicorno*) was considered the crowning achievement of every princely or private cabinet of curiosities.[335] Yet it was not just the rarity of the unicorn horn that made it a coveted object among collectors all over Europe. Rather, its purported magical properties were what contributed so much to its demand.[336] The horn was regarded as an extremely precious medicine, especially as an antidote that would never fail.[337] It was also processed into talismans.[338]

Only a few princes and private collectors were able to get hold of an entire horn. Therefore, it is hardly surprising that, among the thousands of objects described in the inventory of Emperor Rudolf II's cabinet of curiosities we find, under the category "all manner of delightful horns and bones," "one unicorn, entire length" right at the top of the list.[339] The Republic of Venice even collared three such horns—some under politically delicate circumstances—and stored them in the state treasury.[340] The Gonzaga family kept its unicorn horn in the ducal treasure chamber, and it was frequently mentioned in travel accounts.[341] Enormous sums were paid for the purported horns. As early as the time of Pope Clemens VII, a horn sold for 27,000 ducats. In 1611, the Venetian Senate even offered to acquire the horn from the collection of August I of Saxony for the spectacular sum of 100,000 florins, though to no avail.[342] It was easier to buy smaller quantities of the horn, though this, too, came at a price. In the early modern era, even *alicorno* that was pulverized or offered in pieces sold for sums ten times higher than gold.[343] This hardly put a dent in the demand. The court of Mantua, for example, believed that even exorbitant prices were justified when it came to that cure-all—as opposed to, say, jewels. As a court official argued in 1591, unicorn horn could be life-saving, whereas precious stones merely pleased the eye.[344]

Of course, the animal for which such incredible sums were paid did not exist back then anymore than it does today. This raises the question of what the much-admired horns in those cabinets of curiosities really were. Scholars assume that most of the unicorn horns circulating in Europe actually came from narwhals, and more rarely from elephants.[345] The fact that most of these prestige objects had come to Europe from Asia did not arouse mistrust among princely collectors or in learned circles. Since ancient times, Asia—and especially India—had been regarded as the rare animal's natural habitat.[346] Because of Jews' purported knowledge about the Orient and their trade relations reaching as far as India, it is hardly surprising that Christians regarded them as unicorn experts. Courts often turned to Jews to unveil "secrets of the Levant."[347] Indeed, we know of Jews from this period who supplied exotic animals from the Levant and northern Africa. For example, in the late sixteenth century the court of Mantua commissioned the Jewish jeweler David Cervi to procure lynxes from the Orient.[348] In 1662, a Jew named Angelo (Mordechai Baruch) Lima—acting on behalf of the Bey of Tripoli, in what is today Libya—delivered a number of live exotic animals to the Grand Duke of Tuscany, including a lion, four antelopes, and seven apes (*maimoni* in Italian, presumably long-tailed monkeys).[349] It seems this Jewish purveyor belonged to the Lima family—a dynasty of noted merchants and consuls.[350]

No less a personality than the powerful Sephardic merchant Salomon Abenaes (1520–1603) presented the Tuscan Grand Duke Cosimo I with a goblet made from unicorn, which he claimed to have received from the king of Narsinghgarh in India.[351] This rare gift was more than just a precious item; physicians had regarded drinking out of such a goblet as a miraculous cure-all since ancient times.[352] Today, we might be justifiably skeptical about both the curative powers of such receptacles and the material from which they were made, but this should not make us overlook that the goblet's Indian provenance was highly credible in the eyes of contemporaries. The Indian connection was even more plausible because Abenaes—who had been born into a Portuguese *converso* family under the name Alvaro Mendes and officially returned to the Jewish faith in 1585 in the Ottoman Empire—had indeed earned a fortune mining diamonds in the Indian principality of Narsinghgarh.[353] His wealth was already legendary during his lifetime; he was said, for example, to have paid the Ottoman sultan 30,000 florins for the privilege of a kiss on the hand.[354] Abenaes was one of the most powerful Jews at the Ottoman court, and he was even appointed Duke of Mytilene, in the Aegean. He also became one of the most important architects of political rapprochement between England and the Ottoman Empire in the late sixteenth century. Tellingly, he was the first person to deliver the news of the Spanish Armada's defeat to the Ottoman Empire in 1588.[355]

The expertise attributed to Jews, especially to well-networked merchants like Abenaes, went well beyond the ability to acquire the coveted horn. In fact, Christians attributed special knowledge about the rare animal to them. Jews were given explicit credit in the medical literature for this kind of expertise.[356] And the patristic literature sometimes compared the unicorn to the Jews, since the latter believed only in one God and claimed to be unique.[357] Moreover, Christian scholars noted that the Hebrew Bible mentions an animal called *re'em*, which, in accordance with Jewish commentators, they often identified as a unicorn.[358] According to a postbiblical legend, the tribe of Manasseh had crossed the desert carrying a banner depicting a unicorn.[359] For Christians, the Jews' knowledge of the unicorn's secret existence was most ancient. In Bacci's book about the unicorn, one finds detailed discussions about the animal in the Chaldean and Hebrew languages and literature.[360] It is interesting to note that one contemporary reader, whose name is unfortunately not recorded in the copy today preserved in Harvard University's Houghton Library, made a point of highlighting only those passages in Bacci's treatise that dealt with the unicorn in Judaism (and especially in the *Sefer Yosippon*).[361]

Contemporary readers, especially Jewish ones, could also turn to the Talmud in order to learn more about the wondrous animal.[362] Numerous illuminated Hebrew manuscripts from the medieval period included pictorial representations of the unicorn. Such depictions were also popular in Hebrew bestiaries from Ashkenazi Europe, which included the motif of the hunt for the defenseless unicorn.[363] The latter depictions display similarities to Christian iconography, where this motif typically symbolizes the passion of Christ. In Jewish manuscripts, the use of such a theologically charged motif implied an iconographic inversion whereby the unicorn became a symbol for the Jewish history of suffering. This does not exclude the possibility that the unicorn, a common motif in Jewish iconography well into the nineteenth century, also functioned as a symbol for the messianic age.[364] Its popularity in Jewish lore might explain why two houses in Frankfurt's Judengasse—the Haus zum Einhorn and the Haus zum Goldnen Einhorn—were named after unicorns as early as the sixteenth century.[365]

A number of prominent Jewish authors from the sixteenth and seventeenth centuries dealt with the legendary animal in their writings. The noted Jewish physician David de Pomis described the unicorn in a medical context and presented an elaborate procedure for distinguishing between genuine and fake *alicorno* medications.[366] His renowned colleagues Amatus Lusitanus, Abraham Portaleone, and Isaac Cardoso also wrote about the mysterious animal.[367] Even rabbinic authorities attended to the unicorn and its abilities. Rabbi Moses Trani, who lived in the Ottoman Empire during the sixteenth century, pointed to the utility of unicorn goblets for preventing illnesses in a responsum that soon also circulated throughout Italy.[368] Particularly noteworthy is the detailed treatment that the physician and Kabbalist Abraham Yagel devoted to the unicorn in his unpublished treatise *Beit Ya'ar ha-Levanon*. He, too, identified the animal with the ambiguous biblical *re'em,* by which he imagined both the unicorn and the rhinoceros. Yagel's thorough discussion of the subject might have been related to the interests of his patron, the wealthy Jewish moneylender Salomon Fano from Lugo.[369] It is possible that Fano was searching for information about the exotic animal that had economic use. Indeed, one did not have to be a physician in order to earn money from the trade in *alicorno*. For example, the Jewish art and gunpowder dealer Simone Colorni, son of Abramo Colorni, listed unicorn-based medications in his range of product offerings. When the Gonzaga agent at the Imperial Court in Prague collapsed as a result of exhaustion caused by his official duties in 1608, immediate administration of Colorni's *alicorno* powder was said to have saved his life.[370]

Yagel's remarks about the curative uses of the horn were presumably based on comparable observations made in his own medical practice. In his treatise, he dealt extensively with the horn's use as an antidote and, depending on how it was applied, as a poison. He also described the therapeutic utility of the unicorn's blood, teeth, skin, and hooves. For Yagel, however, the unicorn was not just important from a medical perspective; he also elevated the animal, ennobled as it was by virtue of being mentioned in the Bible, into a symbol of the greatness and majesty of the Jewish people.[371] Yagel was not the only Jewish contemporary to assume that the sixteenth century had ushered in an era offering unprecedented opportunities to investigate the secrets of nature, embodied par excellence by the unicorn. In this context, Jewish literature, and especially the Torah, was seen as a God-given resource for knowledge and as a body of secrets fully accessible only to Jews. To investigate the secrets of nature—proceeding from the Torah—also meant to magnify the glory of God.[372] Thus, with his remarks on the unicorn, Yagel was also contributing to the theological legitimization of Jews' remarkable engagement with the early modern economy of secrets.

THREE

Zones of Interaction: The Case of Magic

THE RANGE OF JEWISH SERVICES and activities in the economy of secrets was wide. But one thing obviously missing from the discussion thus far has been magic. Unlike the case with alchemy or technological knowledge, the importance of magic in early modern Jewish thought does not require detailed elaboration. A number of studies have dealt with how premodern Jews conceived of magic.[1] It has also been shown that magic represented a real, and sometimes even prominent, phenomenon in the everyday life of Jews—and, of course, Christians—throughout this period. However, magic was not just on the fringes of the Jewish community, as some scholars have asserted.[2] In fact, members of the Jewish economic and intellectual elite engaged in magic, which some of them even praised as the noblest of human arts.[3] For example, Yoḥanan Alemanno, Giovanni Pico della Mirandola's Jewish teacher of Hebrew, considered magic the highest form of human activity; he even wanted it integrated into the curriculum of studies.[4] In the eyes of their Christian contemporaries, Jews were indisputably competent in the field of magic.[5] The association between Jews and magic proved stubbornly persistent even in countries where Jews no longer lived.[6] Christians regarded them as "natural guardians of magical knowledge," and Renaissance intellectuals such as Pico, taking a profound interest in the secrets of the Jews, helped to amplify and, to a certain extent, ennoble the Christian image of Jewish magic.[7]

The motives behind early modern Jews' fascination with magic were, on the whole, no different from those of Christians.[8] Early modern society was confronted with imponderables and risks to a far greater extent than our own. Because of this, magic enticed Jews and Christians alike with the prospect of being able to help them overcome or avoid dangerous situations.[9] Many early modern people saw magic, especially in the variant of *magia naturalis,* not as an esoteric practice but as a tried and tested technology for solving everyday problems.[10] Yet this functionalist explanation of magic, which goes back to the anthropologist Bronisław Malinowski, cannot fully explain the Jewish interest in magic.[11] Magic was not just a way of coping with specific everyday challenges; for Jews, it sometimes also offered an idealized substitute for the kind of direct political action largely closed off to them. There was a widespread view among Jews that magic was a way to fight against Christian anti-Judaism—or even against Christianity itself.[12] Among Jews, messianic martyrs such as the Portuguese Jew Salomon Molcho (ca. 1500–1532) or the false messiah Shabbetai Zevi (1626–1676) were often associated with magical skills that allowed them to defy the oppression and humiliation Jews suffered at the hands of Christians.[13] In the same vein, Jews were also fascinated by "miracle rabbis" and magical golems.[14] Many Christians, in turn, firmly believed Jews would use magic to achieve political goals. For example, the Annals of Hirsau, which appeared in print in the early modern era, record that in 1059 the Jews of Trier prevented their expulsion from that city by means of sorcery.[15]

Magic is a prime example of how the economy of secrets functioned and what made it attractive. In particular, magic created zones of contact between the Christian majority and the Jewish minority in important ways.[16] As we shall see, the practice of magic often created niches for intense and trusting contact between Jews and Christians. Officially, these interactions were of course not supposed to exist. In the introduction to Judaism he wrote for Christian readers, Venetian rabbi Leon Modena—who dealt in alchemy himself and who earned extra income by selling books of secrets—wrote that Jews "account it a very great sin, to give any Credit to, or have any Faith in any Kind of Divination whatsoever, or to Judiciary Astrology, Geomancy, Chiromancy, or to any Fortunetellers, or the like. Much more do they abhor the Practice of any Necromancy, or receiving Answers from the Dead, Magick, Witchcraft, Conjuration of Devils, or of Angels, and the like."[17]

Certainly, Christian authorities and the church did not tolerate Jewish magic. Clerical and secular polemics against Jewish sorcery are abundant. In 1598, for example, Jews in Rome were expressly forbidden "to practice magic and witchcraft" for Christians and "to tell their fortunes," and such mundane activities as singing, dancing, and playing musical instruments were also banned.[18] Admittedly, it was harder for the church to proceed against Jewish magic outside the Papal States. As long as they were not judaizing, Jews could not be subjected to clerical jurisdiction. Only gradually did the view emerge that the church could also intervene in cases of blasphemy and magic by Jews, especially when Christians were affected.[19] However, as the records of Italian inquisitors reveal, it was often pointless to try to fight magical practices that brought Jews and Christians together. There is even visual evidence confirming how futile this was: the Italian painter Pietro della Vecchia (ca. 1602–1678) created genre paintings in which Jews can be seen performing occult arts before attentive Christian audiences.[20]

Magic, like alchemy, allowed Jews to adopt a position superior to Christians—as when a Jewish alchemist became a much-sought-after master supervising Christian practitioners.[21] However, the interpersonal contacts generated by magic and alchemy did not always make for a vertical hierarchy between master and client. In fact, not only did magic break down geographical boundaries and social distinctions within Christian society, but it also brought Jews and Christians together, often on equal terms.[22] This led to constellations that would have been impossible otherwise. Consider the case of the noted Venetian mathematician, humanist, and nobleman Francesco Barozzi (1537–1604), who fostered a passion for the occult and devoted himself to experiments with animal blood, magical texts, and conjuring spirits. In the 1580s, Barozzi maintained intensive contacts with a Jewish boy in the Venetian ghetto, even employing him as a part-time assistant and idea generator. The boy became indispensable—not least of all because he communicated with a spirit (*ingenio*) on Barozzi's behalf. This collaboration ended only, and precipitously, when Barozzi's activities began to attract the attention of the Inquisition. He was arrested and sent to jail for several months.[23]

That same year, another case that is equally instructive took place in Venice. During her interrogation by the Inquisition, the Christian widow

Valeria Brugnaleschi gave a detailed depiction of her life. For several years she had worked in a school for Jewish girls in the ghetto. Later, she moved into the segregated Jewish quarter for good. Her attitude toward Judaism became increasingly positive, and she started to reject certain doctrines of the church. Brugnaleschi moved back out of the ghetto at an advanced age to live with her daughter; however, she did not break off her contacts there. Instead, she invited a Jew into her home, where he augured her future and conducted a number of magical rituals. When the Inquisition uncovered these activities, the widow and her daughter were publicly whipped and banned from the city for several years.[24] But even harsh punishments like these could not keep Jews and Christians from conducting magical rituals together within the confines of their own homes. During a campaign against Jewish books in Reggio in 1631, the bishop complained that Jews were protected by several influential people ("persone grandi"), which led to all kinds of "sorcery" in the city.[25] The historian Federico Barbierato has also described a fascinating Venetian case from the same time in which several Jews and Christians were even meeting regularly for magical rituals.[26]

The Venetian ghetto was surrounded by walls and water, with guards posted at its gates—making it quite literally a kind of island in the middle of the urban space. Officially, entry and exit were allowed only by day and only under strict conditions. It remained that way until 1797. Thus, the sociologist Richard Sennett has described the Venetian ghetto as a site where the segregation of minorities in modern times was already anticipated. In Sennett's view the Venetian ghetto was an "urban condom" that prevented exchanges between Jews and Christians.[27] The cases presented here, however, do not support this view. In fact, the Venetian ghetto functioned, against the intention of the authorities, as one of Europe's most important marketplaces for occult, magical, and chemical information through the eighteenth century.[28] Stories about Jewish sorcerers from Venice even spread into German superstitions and the storehouse of fairy tales.[29] Christians, especially travelers, deliberately went into the ghetto in order to acquire arcana and magical knowledge there.[30] Even the Jewish cemetery on the Lido repeatedly became the scene of magic rituals performed by Christians. Magical qualities were attributed to herbs collected there.[31]

Against this background, it is hardly surprising that some inhabitants of the ghetto chose to specialize in the sale or provision of occult knowledge. In the 1590s a white-bearded Jew named Caliman demonstrated magic tricks with playing cards in the houses of Venetian aristocrats and earned extra income selling aphrodisiacs.[32] In 1686 a Venetian Jew named Joel Abram Coniano was arrested by the Inquisition because he had sold Christians books by Trithemius, Agrippa, and Pseudo-Albertus Magnus.[33] One could also obtain books of secrets from Leon Modena, the famous rabbi of the Venetian ghetto. In his autobiography, the rabbi candidly listed trade in arcana and the sale of related books as two of the twenty-six pursuits he practiced during his lifetime.[34]

Modena was hardly an exception. Evidence suggests that there were other ordained rabbis from whom Christians could gain an introduction to the secrets of chemical experiments. In the 1650s, for example, a rabbi named Isaac at the ghetto's Italian synagogue was said to have earned extra income with alchemical and occult activities, such as offering to track down thieves using magic.[35] Works by, or thought to be by, Pietro d'Abano and Ramon Llull were also easy to obtain in the ghetto.[36] However, among the wide range of magical services on offer in Italian ghettos, the ones that flourished most were transactions involving the notorious *Clavicula Salomonis,* a compendium of magical practices. Business was especially brisk in Venice.[37]

As early as the fifteenth century, Jewish writers were earning extra income by compiling medical, Kabbalistic, and magical secrets.[38] Much of what has been said here about the ghetto in Venice can also be applied to other places in Italy and German lands.[39] One need only think of Goethe's description of the Judengasse in the imperial city of Frankfurt. Growing up in Frankfurt, Goethe was fascinated by this segregated Jewish neighborhood, which he frequently "ventured into" full of curiosity.[40] As early as 1488 two members of the Frankfurt city council had made their way into the Judengasse in order to view the "outlandish arts and monsters" of one of the residents there.[41]

But did Jews also use magical services provided by Christians? This question still requires extensive research.[42] The material available thus far does strongly indicate that there was no lack of Jews who were active consumers of Christian magic. The reception of Agrippa among Kabbalists is worth mentioning in this regard.[43] We also know of many Jewish physicians well-versed in the *ars magica* of the Christian world.[44] Christian *secreta* literature and Hermetic writings were likewise given a lively reception by Jewish authors.[45] We can adduce further examples from the study of everyday Jewish life. In Venice, for instance, Jewish merchants were among the customers of a magician named Maddalena the Greek, who had specialized in the treatment of lithiasis and syphilis, as well as in a variety of magical practices.[46] Outside the Serenissima, too, one can find Christian sorceresses whose services were enlisted by Jews. The case of the sorceress Giacomoa la Mantilara is especially noteworthy. She worked in the small town of Bondeno in Emilia-Romagna around 1600 and attracted both Christians and Jews from the surrounding area.[47]

The cases presented here illustrate the existence of Jewish-Christian zones of interaction and afford insight into a multifaceted culture of collaboration between Jews and Christians in the field of magic. Not only was the practice of magic a reality in many places, despite being officially fought by both Christian and Jewish authorities; it also generated a socially and economically significant, if risky, sphere of contact between members of the two faiths.

We can observe similar forms of interaction created by secret knowledge in fields such as Kabbalah, alchemy, and astrology.[48] Consider young Tommaso Campanella (1568–1639), who owed his initial instruction in astrology and the occult sciences, including magic, to a Jewish rabbi nearly the same age named Abraham, with whom he cultivated a friendship. Abraham predicted an extraordinary fate for the young Dominican monk that proved not far off the mark. Understandably, there has been a lot of speculation about the influence this friendship had on Campanella's later mystical, utopian thinking. Even Campanella's contemporaries, especially his superiors in the Dominican order, were aware of his friendship with Abraham. In fact, it may have been a major reason why Campanella left his home in Calabria—with Abraham by his side, according to some accounts.[49] Several years later in Venice, Mordecai Modena, son of the rabbi Leon Modena, conducted alchemical experiments together with, of all people, a Catholic priest. The young Modena had found special rooms in the ghetto for his experiments, which by 1617 would cost him his life.[50] In 1596 secret knowledge enriched by prophetic rhetoric was what allowed a Jew named Abraham Sasson to appear before the Este court on various occasions with the unusual title of "minimo teologo hebreo." He undergirded the credibility of his prognostications, which focused on the progress of the wars with the Turks, by inserting Hebrew words and citations.[51] In Florence at the beginning of the seventeenth century, the Tuscan Jew Benedetto Blanis, who displayed great expertise in the field of arcana, obtained a prestigious post in the court of the Medicis. Not only did Blanis organize the Medici library and supply it with arcane writings, but he also maintained contacts with scholars from a wide range of secret sciences at court.[52]

We can extend these observations about the Jewish-Christian contact zones generated by magic and alchemy to the entire economy of secrets. One telling episode comes from the life of Prague's Rabbi Judah Loew ben Bezalel (ca. 1525–1609), also known as the Maharal and as the purported creator of the golem. In 1592 the Maharal is said to have had a nocturnal meeting with Emperor Rudolf II on Prague's Charles Bridge—an event shrouded in secrecy to this day. Historians have occasionally depicted the Maharal as a Jewish humanist; however, the extant sources give no indication whether or not the emperor sought him out because of his scientific, "humanist" interests.[53] There is also nothing to indicate that the meeting took place in the spirit of that tolerant religious attitude often attributed to Rudolf II. Instead, what emerged from a contemporary report left behind by the Maharal's son-in-law was merely that the emperor arranged the encounter with the "High Rabbi of Prague" in order to exchange secrets.[54] Another contemporary chronicler and student of the Maharal even stressed how the emperor and the rabbi spoke on equal terms—"as a man speaketh unto his friend" (Exod 33:11).[55] The encounter between rabbi and king is a particularly vivid example of how secrets created a remarkable zone of interaction between Christian and Jew in early modern Europe.

Alleged, or even just putative, knowledge of secrets could arouse the interest of elites and quickly lead Jews into the highest social circles. In 1603, for example, Emperor Rudolf II's brother, Archduke Maximilian, sent a handwritten letter to a secretive Jew from Jerusalem who did "not want to reveal [himself] to everybody." No one knows what became of this encounter. However, in light of the archduke's demonstrable interest in the occult, there is reason to believe that alchemy was involved.[56] By contrast, the story of David Reuveni is much better documented. In the Europe of the 1520s, his mysterious appearance as a Jewish emissary from the desert caused a sensation. He even won attention from leading rulers, including the pope and the king of Portugal, not least owing to the abundant talk about secrets (*sodot*) surrounding his arrival. Indeed, secrets were central to Reuveni's self-fashioning—even within Jewish circles.[57]

The cases mentioned here, especially the image of the emperor and the rabbi exchanging secrets on the Charles Bridge, tie in with Barbara Stollberg-Rilinger's observation about premodern political-social culture, where "the secret did not hinder communication but rather organized, structured, even enabled it by establishing boundaries around spaces of communication and action."[58] But these boundaries were not static; rather, secrets facilitated boundary-crossing and generated dynamic zones of contact.

The culture of secrecy even provides clues to something that is usually hard to detect in early modern Christian-Jewish relations: irony. Consider the handwritten code book used by the Sephardic merchant Ḥayyim Saruk from Thessaloniki, which he compiled in 1570. In that year the Venetian Council of Ten dispatched Saruk as an agent to the Ottoman Empire, from whence Saruk was to provide information about the Turks and their military operations. For this delicate mission, Saruk and the council agreed to use a then-popular encoding method called "in parabula" that allowed for a high degree of customization.[59] Still extant today, Saruk's nearly twenty-page notebook records all the sensitive words—especially for people, places, weapons, and goods—that he would use in letters supposedly addressed to his family (although actually meant for Venetian officials). Saruk substituted inconspicuous code words for these terms. When Venetian officials intercepted the letters, they used the key he developed to reveal the hidden information. Presumably, the Venetian authorities had provided the list of terms; however, they left the choice of code words up to their Jewish agent. With a fine sense of irony, Saruk turned "tribute payments" into "alms" (*limosina per poveretti*) and the "pope" into, of all people, a "rabbi" (*rav*).[60]

Let us conclude with another episode from the economy of secrets that casts additional light on this culture of waggishness, as it has been described by Michael Bakhtin in other early modern contexts.[61] The case in question is an encounter between a Jewish magus and Johann Weichard Valvasor (1641–1693), a Carniolan nobleman who later became a member of the Royal Society of London. In certain respects, this incident resembled a commedia dell'arte. It took place in 1679.[62] At that time, Valvasor was staying in Venice. He met a Jew in the ghetto with a "magical mirror that was made only of glass." The Jew was explicit about extolling this "secretum." If one buried the mirror for three days and then dug it up again to the accompaniment of magical incantations, the Jew claimed, "whoever then peered in would die a sudden death." Valvasor was impressed by this "death-mirror" and requested a demonstration of additional tricks. The Jew covered the mirror and asked exactly what is was the noble customer wanted to see. Valvasor secretly wished to see his Wagensberg Castle, but he "jokingly" uttered a meaningless sentence "in Carniolan so that the Jew would not understand." After Valvasor had spoken the words "Zherna farba Kos Iove" (meaning "black color/ram's testicles"), nothing happened: "When he thereupon opened the mirror, there was nothing in there for me to see." The Jew asked Valvasor to no longer "stray but rather to request a certain sight." In response, Valvasor asked—again in Carniolan—to see his castle: "As soon as he removed the curtain I beheld thereon my Castle Wagensberg in the mirror [as if it were] quite real." The same man who had been inclined to make jokes only minutes before became timorous, suspected a work of the devil, and rejected the Jew's offer of another try.[63]

FOUR

Trading in Secrets and Economic Life

THE SIGNIFICANCE OF THE ECONOMY of secrets for a cultural history of early modern Jewry is hard to overestimate. At the same time, it is important to emphasize the economic-mercantile dimension of the phenomenon. For instance, at the time, alchemy was widely regarded as a technology that provided effective methods for solving economic challenges.[1] Rulers of smaller territories even hoped to use it to gain advantages over the great powers that dominated Europe.[2] Alchemy lured rulers, especially those who had absolutist pretensions or saw themselves in the role of "princely entrepreneur," with the bold promise of a massive improvement in their public finances, above all via the successful transmutation of base metals into coveted gold.[3]

But alchemy was not the only form of arcane knowledge that influenced early modern political and economic thought; magic also offered entrepreneurial potential.[4] The historian Lyndal Roper has argued that "the overlap between the mental worlds of early capitalism (which we assume to have been rational) and sorcery" was greater than commonly assumed.[5] Even key political and dynastic decisions were sometimes made by recourse to occult knowledge, as derived (for example) from astrology.[6]

Not just royal courts were fascinated with the idea that they could miraculously increase their capital by transmutation. Well into the eighteenth century, both ordinary citizens and affluent merchants also experimented with alchemy, which offered them the prospect of gaining contacts with and commissions from the highest aristocratic circles.[7] Although there certainly were opportunities for astute swindlers, many practitioners continued to believe in the promise of alchemy with a faith that was as hopeful as it was unshakable. A characteristic case is that of the successful Leipzig silk and jewel merchant Heinrich Cramer von Clausburg, who conducted intensive negotiations—lacking in any deceitful intentions—with the Saxon elector about selling the philosopher's stone and divulging a number of alchemical formulas.[8] Beyond projects like this, which aimed at immediate and spectacular success, there are also examples of a more systematic and comprehensive entanglement of the alchemical and economic spheres. One such example is the case of the alchemist and economic theoretician Johann Joachim Becher, who worked for the Viennese court during the second half of the seventeenth century.[9] Becher was not the only contemporary who believed in an intrinsic affinity between the language of alchemy and the economic agenda of early mercantilism. Indeed, expertise in practical alchemy was often indispensable in a range of economic sectors critical to the development of the early modern state—fields such as mining, metallurgy, and the manufacture of gunpowder.

We have to see the complex interconnections between Jewish economic life and the early modern economy of secrets against this backdrop. The mere fact that renowned court Jews displayed strong Kabbalistic interests casts doubt on the idea that the early modern Jewish economic elite was thoroughly committed to a purely rational way of thinking.[10] Functionalist explanations, such as attributing Jews' extensive alchemical activities solely to medical interests, are not sufficient. Such explanations neglect the considerable economic incentives offered by the economy of secrets.[11] Numerous sources indicate that the trade in secrets was often interwoven with early modern Jews' mercantile and financial activities in close and complex ways. In this respect, Jewish secrecy mavens, and alchemists in particular, are no different from Jewish physicians, some of whom commonly engaged in entrepreneurial, and occasionally also political, activity.[12]

A salient example is the life story of the Jewish mint-master Lippold, who rose to become treasurer of the chamber for the Brandenburg Elector Joachim II (r. 1535–1571). Lippold first made a name for himself with deliveries of silver to the court, which were connected to his work as master of the mint. The office of moneyer, which numerous court Jews held during that period, could hardly be practiced without knowledge of metallurgy—knowledge that could not be neatly separated from alchemy.[13] This could have reinforced the impression that Jews, who had extensive dealings in the money and metals trades as well as in coinage, were predestined for the practice of alchemy.[14] In Lippold's account books, we find entries that show he purchased alchemical instruments for the elector.[15] It is unclear to what extent Lippold was involved in alchemical activities of his own free will. His later confession that he had a magic book in his house containing "quite a few pieces on alchemy" must be treated with caution, as it was extorted from him under torture after the elector's death and played a part in his own death sentence, which was carried out in gruesome fashion in 1573.[16]

It is possible that Lippold had little choice but to deliver the alchemical instruments and materials to the elector, who was a passionate alchemist. In any case, much greater self-initiative was at play a few years later in the Duchy of Savoy, where another Jew provided alchemical and occult knowledge to a court. The figure at the center of these events was one of the most renowned and economically powerful Jews of northern Italy, the moneylender Vitale Sacerdote.[17] A resident of Alessandria, he was held in high esteem by both the Christian authorities in Spanish-ruled Lombardy and his Jewish coreligionists, for whom he functioned as community leader. He was accorded respect not only for his economic position, but also for his competence in dealing with a wide variety of secrets. In the 1560s—that is, before the expulsion of most Jews from Spanish Lombardy—Sacerdote had undertaken secret missions ("commissione secreta") for the Spanish authorities on various occasions, sometimes even on command from the highest authority, Philip II himself.[18] In the 1560s, Sacerdote was sent to the Holy Roman Empire and to Switzerland, and between 1569 and 1570 he carried out a mission in the Piedmont.[19] In 1572 he discreetly represented the interests of his exiled Jewish coreligionists in the Duchy of Savoy. In this connection, Sacerdote was able to win over the Duke of Savoy to the idea of a free port in the vicinity of Nice to which Sephardic merchants would be invited.[20] In exchange for being granted economic privileges and a wide degree of religious freedom, the Jews were to expand the site into a major trade hub that would hit archenemy Venice in a much more damaging way than would have been possible with military undertakings.[21] That same year, the duke issued an invitation to the Jewish merchants. Even if the settlement plans did collapse shortly afterward owing to resistance from Spain and the pope, the charter issued in connection with the project marked a milestone in the history of Sephardic settlement in Italy and had some influence on the composition of the famous Livornina—the privileges of Livorno—barely two decades later.

Sacerdote was no doubt one of the most important advisors behind the scenes of the Savoyard duke's policy toward Jews. However, his reputation at court was not just due to his economic position. Sacerdote had also won the favor of the duke by delivering alchemical formulas and exotic objects on various occasions. Sacerdote was even said to have brought a rhinoceros to Savoy for the ducal menagerie.[22] In addition to procuring such *secreta naturae*, he supplied clues about hidden precious metal deposits and offered weapons for sale.[23]

Sacerdote offers an impressive illustration of how, even for an affluent moneylender, trading in secrets represented a tangible asset for establishing and fostering contacts with the authorities—and especially with royal courts. His son, Simone, remained true to his father's policy. He was one of the last Jews who managed to stay in touch with Philip II after the Spanish crown's final decision to expel the Jews from Spanish Lombardy. His longstanding services in the field of espionage and in exposing foreign spies were explicitly acknowledged at the Spanish court, which also valued his talent for communicating and trading in technological secrets.[24] In 1591, for example, he revealed to the Spanish crown a device for desalinating ocean water invented by a Jewish coreligionist.[25]

Significant political relevance was attributed to these kinds of technological projects. Take, for example, the case of the Pavia brothers from Lodi. These three Jewish inventors, who shared a secret with the Spanish crown in the 1590s about a pump-driven invention, were among the few Jews who managed to evade expulsion from Spanish Lombardy.[26] In this family, too, the boundaries between knowledge about (technological) secrets and the economic sphere were fluid. At least one of the brothers was active as a money trader. In 1604, the three made a joint offer to build a new machine, not described in any greater detail, that might prove useful to the city of Lodi; they linked this project with a proposal to open a money-lending business.[27]

Secrets could represent a strong currency in dealings with the authorities and rulers. This, at least, was no secret in the Prague of Emperor Rudolf II—a ruler fascinated with all manner of arcana. Indeed, Jews in Prague did not hesitate to give the emperor secret objects as presents. For example, the "Prague Ḥoshen"—a breastplate much discussed in art history that is adorned with magical formulas and angels—was probably a gift from Mordechai Meyzl, the wealthiest and presumably most influential Jew in Prague at the time.[28] Meyzl also supplied the emperor with a rare "sophierstain" ("sapphire stone") for the handsome sum of nearly 3,000 gulden.[29] Within the orbit of medium-sized courts such as Mantua's, too, occult activities frequently dovetailed with mercantile practices among Jews. This was the case with Levi di Vita, one of the leading jewel suppliers for the Gonzaga court. He called himself a Jewish jeweler ("hebreo gioiellero"), but he also communicated secrets to the court, thereby gaining the Gonzaga family's favor and attention. Writing from Prague in 1604, for example, he offered his services for the purchase of a chemical secret ("secreto vero, reale, per distinger l'oro et ridurlo in olio").[30] Just a year later he was offering an alchemical treatise meant as a guide to transmutation. However, it remains unclear whether the wary owner of the codex, no less than Emperor Rudolf II himself, would have approved the sale.[31]

Another supplier of precious stones used by the court in Mantua, David Cervi, knew of secrets whose divulgence earned him the favor of the court. In 1591, Cervi arranged for the court to hire a German engineer who had many secrets in military technology and gunpowder production ("molti secreti per conto di polvere"), including artillery devices that were said to be all-destructive.[32] In Venice, the respected physician David de Pomis—later elevated by historians into a "noble idealist" or the "greatest Jewish physician in sixteenth-century Italy"—was not just devoting himself to the noble study of medicine; he was also an expert in alchemy.[33] When he felt he was too old to accept an invitation to Pisa from Grand Duke Ferdinando I in 1593, he sent the prince a formula for producing *aurum potabile* (po-table gold) that he had apparently been testing for several years.[34] De Pomis also supplied the Gonzaga family with rare, precious objects.[35]

Such trade in secrets was not necessarily limited to individuals; it could also be conducted on a larger scale. For example, a seventeenth-century Jewish trading company established in Casale Monferrato specialized in financial transactions and army deliveries. In addition to dealing in credits and military consumer goods, the company stocked chemical substances such as manganese and powder made from the Spanish fly (cantharides).[36] While manganese would have been used in glass production—a process guarded like a state secret in many places—the cantharides was used as a poison, an aphrodisiac, and a treatment for impotence.[37] Both materials were shrouded in an aura of secrecy, since they were difficult to procure. Jewish entrepreneurs sometimes explicitly invoked this aura of secrecy even when their business or the project in question did not really require it. For example, the Jewish banker Iseppe Prospero Levi from Mantua insisted on a "secret audience" ("audienza secreta") when, in the 1650s, he submitted to the emperor various sensible proposals for increasing state revenues, including toll hikes and surcharges on different foodstuffs—oil, fish, and grain.[38] The Roman Jew Salomon Gionattavo probably had similar proposals in mind when, in 1609, he offered the Duke of Modena a "secret" for improving the state's public finances. Exactly what this secret entailed is not, however, revealed in the surviving letters.[39]

One case that illustrates this entanglement between a mercantile agenda and the economy of secrets in a particularly vivid way is the career of the Jewish entrepreneur and inventor Maggino di Gabrielli.[40] Born in 1561 in Padua, he was still in his twenties when he received patents for various inventions in the Rome of Pope Sixtus V. Maggino was regarded as an expert in the field of glass and silk manufacturing. He was also masterful at striking a balance between secrecy and public self-fashioning.[41] Maggino's activities in the glass industry placed him in a branch of commercial life profoundly marked by secrecy—a branch that also overlapped with practical alchemy.[42] Knowledge about the techniques and materials used in glass manufacturing were guarded like state secrets in early modern Europe, and punishments for divulging such arcana were correspondingly draconian.

The printed text of the papal privilege for glass manufacturing granted to Maggino in 1588 and posted throughout Rome therefore raises more questions than it answers with regard to its technical execution.[43] The inventor himself spoke of a "very noble secret" ("secreto molto nobile").[44] It was, nonetheless, a serious enterprise on the part of the Jewish inventor, who would soon rise to become one of the leading glass suppliers for a series of prestigious buildings for the pope, including the Lateran Palace.[45] A few years later Maggino was even specializing in manufacturing glass pearls for the rosaries of the Catholic faithful.[46]

In the field of silk manufacturing, too, it was important for Maggino to find the right balance between keeping his technological knowledge a secret and divulging it. In his 1588 treatise *Dialoghi sopra l'utili sue inventioni circa la seta,* he introduced the method he had discovered for sericulture, providing a description both detailed and replete with vague allusions.[47] The high-quality illustrations show the Jewish inventor as he presented his method to an astonished audience in theatrically staged courtly settings that invoked associations with the appearance of a magus.[48] Maggino's claim that he was ridding himself of a burden by publishing his secrets should be evaluated just as cautiously as his assertion that he was divulging his secrets in order to make the world a better place.[49] In both cases these are typical topoi of the *secreta* literature. Maggino's work was, to be sure, conceived as a how-to manual, but the text and illustrations leave something to be desired in the way of clarity. One wonders, in fact, whether the *Dialoghi* served the purpose of divulging the author's secrets in the first place or whether the treatise represented a lavishly produced self-advertisement. In fact, anybody who wanted to actually use the Jewish inventor's technology still had to acquire the requisite utensils and instruments from merchants appointed by Maggino.

Maggino's treatise, like the *usus et fabrica* books mentioned earlier, illustrates how an announcement about the intention to reveal secrets could help garner attention and generate demand. After the death of the pope in 1590, there was no possibility for Maggino to remain in Rome. However, his competence in dealing with secrets proved to be an asset. The Medici entrusted him with carrying out a delicate political mission to the Levant and, in 1591, appointed him as consul for the Jews of Pisa and Livorno. After just a few years, Maggino's remarkable career as consul in those two cities foundered over differences with the local Jewish communities, whereupon he decided to found a Levantine trade company in the Holy Roman Empire. He established subsidiaries in Lorraine, Electoral Trier, and Württemberg. This ambitious project was impossible to achieve without patronage and privileges granted by the powerful territorial rulers in these parts of the Holy Roman Empire, who often pursued proto-absolutist policies. Maggino knew that the Duke of Württemberg was a man passionately devoted to alchemy, and this was one reason why the Jewish entrepreneur tried to gain his goodwill by offering him secrets, including help in recruiting an alchemist knowledgeable about making gold.[50] Since Maggino was also eager to resume the manufacture of Venetian glass and mirrors in Württemberg, he praised his own plans in a way that clearly recalled a kind of speech widely used by alchemists, fashioning his knowledge as a gift of God (*donum Dei*).[51] One of the men who apparently helped Maggino and his Jewish trading company set up contacts with the Duke of Württemberg was the only Jew then working at the court in Stuttgart—the alchemist Abramo Colorni.[52]

The examples presented thus far have mainly illustrated the importance of secrets in relations between Jews and courts. Yet trading in secrets was also a lucrative business for poorer Jews, as well as for those not even in the orbit of a court. Consider the case of the Italian Jew Isaac Sanguineti.[53] In the duchy of the Este during the early seventeenth century, Sanguineti earned extra income by conveying magic secrets ("secreti magici") and esoteric works such as the notorious *Clavicula Salomonis*. One of his specialties was supposedly conjuring up the spirit of Lilith. Although the Inquisition arrested Sanguineti several times between 1598 and 1621, he still remained loyal to his "profession" over the years.[54] His persistence does not imply that the Inquisition was an insufficient deterrent or imposed lax punishments. In a trial against Sanguineti, one Jewish witness testified that he and his coreligionists were indeed afraid of the

Inquisition.⁵⁵ Rather, Sanguineti's ongoing activities suggest that trading in secrets and practicing magic, even if at a modest level, were good enough business for Sanguineti to risk possible punishment.

The economy of secrets, and in particular the business of alchemy and the occult, also provided Jewish converts with opportunities for earning income and making a name for themselves. In the eyes of many Christians, converts did not lose their mastery of the arcane by renouncing their Jewish faith. Jewish converts who earned their living as traveling charlatans and assumed new, Christian names still invoked their Jewish background or even tried to impress their audiences with presentations in Hebrew. Some of these neophytes even fashioned their products accordingly—for instance, by praising a certain elixir as a "vital balsam made by the converted Jew" ("Balsamo vitale dell'ebreo fatto christiano"). The church condemned such practices (though to little avail) because it was obvious that these converts were still capitalizing on the nimbus surrounding Jewish mastery of the arcane.⁵⁶

Giovanni Battista Isacchi from Reggio was likely a converted Jew.⁵⁷ In 1579 he published a treatise promising to reveal his technological inventions ("inventioni") and various secrets ("varij secreti & utili avisi"), which were overwhelmingly military in nature.⁵⁸ Although the volume included illustrations, a great deal was hinted at rather than explained. As in the printed *secreta* literature in general, the main purpose of Isacchi's book was less to provide a hands-on instruction manual than to initiate new patronage relationships or render thanks for existing ones. According to his book, Isacchi enjoyed the confidence of a number of illustrious noble patrons and courtiers; every secret presented in this volume has its own dedicatee. Isacchi's presumably Jewish background likely bolstered the confidence these Christian patrons placed in his knowledge of the arcane.

We get a similar impression from the life story of the convert Josias Markus (1527–1599), who was appointed to a government position in Weimar right after graduation from the University of Wittenberg.⁵⁹ Soon after, he rose to the position of vice chancellor in the Duchy of Braunschweig-Wolfenbüttel. He owed this promotion to the initiative of the fraudulent alchemist Philipp Sömmering, who had gained the favor of the duke in the 1570s. It is no longer possible to reconstruct the extent to which Markus was actually involved in the alchemical activities of the Sömmering circle; yet there must have been some foundation of trust between the vice chancellor and the alchemist. The agreement they struck was advantageous to both of them. For the alchemist's part, he initiated a major shakeup in the government, using the opportunity to shut out some of his harshest critics at court. For Markus, an opportunity for a career leap opened up in Wolfenbüttel that would otherwise have remained blocked to him, especially since those around him continued to associate him with Judaism. This background is hinted at in the "slanderous verses" ("Famosreimen") that the circle of alchemists around Sömmering composed offhandedly and that were confiscated after his arrest. They describe the dismissals Sömmering initiated at court as follows:

> Those who took their place were people
> Who usually would dodge any service,
> Companions of Jews and the like,
> And there's no vice they would avoid.[60]

These lines were an undisguised allusion to the convert Markus, as Sömmering himself later admitted under interrogation. This stanza was supposedly composed by three of Sömmering's partners. The object of their derision was hardly in any position to reciprocate. Admittedly, Markus did escape Sömmering's fate—a gruesome public execution. But as soon as the powerful alchemist was arrested, the vice chancellor's political downfall was also sealed.

This episode highlights the risks that could imperil both converts and Jews who tied their political and economic fates too closely to the success of alchemical enterprises or who were associated with fraudulent alchemy. Many clerics and humanists saw alchemy as an annoyance, if not a dangerous vice that led to hubris and deceit. In his *Inferno,* Dante banished alchemists to the nether regions of hell, alongside counterfeiters.[61] This kind of polemic against alchemy was often just a pretext for leveling more general critiques against undesirable political and economic developments. The figure of the deceitful alchemist, which has significantly shaped today's ideas about alchemy, is to a significant extent a construct of these polemics.[62]

The situation of Jewish alchemists could no doubt become precarious very quickly. The close ties between Jews' economic and alchemical activities served as a point of departure for Christian phantasms. For instance, Martin Luther warned against (court) Jews and alchemists in the same breath.[63] In a letter to the Elector of Brandenburg, he pointed out that serious vigilance had to be maintained toward both groups, as their activities at court would only lead to "perfidy" and "deception."[64] It is unclear whether this was as an explicit warning against Jewish alchemists at the court of Brandenburg.[65] At any rate, the figure of the Jew and of the alchemist did coincide for Luther, and his warning against both groups belonged in the same political context. For Luther, alchemy was one facet in a larger spectrum of earthly depravity and deceitful activity that he associated, especially in his later years, with Jews and their (economic) influence. In other words, Luther's tirade against the Jews at the Brandenburg court was not just rooted in the theological motifs that played such an important role in his notorious anti-Judaism.[66] As we will see, linking anti-Judaism with a critique of alchemy was an independent and widespread discourse.

It is true that the alchemical activities of early modern Jews often intersected with minting and upgrading coins, or with metallurgy in general. This was not a specifically Jewish phenomenon, however, but had to do with the nature of metallurgy at the time. During this era, the boundaries between metallurgy, coinage, and alchemical knowledge were fluid.[67] What is more, coinage was regarded as a crucial state secret, and the ability to handle and keep secrets was therefore indispensable.[68] Likewise, expertise in metals was imperative for anyone holding the office of moneyer (master of the mint), a position entrusted to numerous court Jews during the early modern era.[69] This kind of knowledge was never restricted just to Christian artisans or guilds. Rather, we have evidence of Jews engaged in metallurgy in Christian Europe as early as the Middle Ages.[70] In the early modern Holy Roman Empire, Jews were even foundry managers.[71] In addition, trade in iron, copper, and scrap metal was an integral part of premodern

Jewish economic life.[72] And so-called Münzjuden—Jewish mint-masters—played an important role in connection with gold and silver deliveries.[73]

The specific role Jews played in trading and processing metals explains the alchemical interests that many of them maintained. At the same time, it gave Christians a springboard for sweeping generalizations about and polemics against Jews. Christian anti-Judaism and its exponents turned the fluid boundary between metallurgical and alchemical knowledge into something negative and stylized it as a significant peril. This was especially true when suspicions arose about counterfeiting. Coinage was a critically important sector for the functioning of the state—a great concern for Luther. Jews, in particular, were perceived as a threat to monetary stability and subjected to the accusation that "everywhere where gold and money is to be made they are present and they have also been interfering in making gold and alchemy."[74] This led to a more general analogy between the deceitful alchemist who intervenes in the system of elements and the evil court Jew or moneyer who attempts to manipulate the circulation of precious metals and coins. Throughout the early modern period, the accusation of currency manipulation was leveled against both court Jews in general and Jewish moneyers in particular.[75] And while it is true that some court Jews were involved in debasing and manipulating precious metals and coins, their princely employers often explicitly approved, or even imposed, this kind of criminal activity.[76]

To be sure, some Jewish moneyers acted on their own initiative. However, this was often less out of interest in depreciating metals and more out of eagerness to increase the value of the metals they were processing—a goal to which alchemy undoubtedly lent itself. In the late sixteenth century, for example, a northern German Jew named Gottschalk offered to use his knowledge of alchemy to improve the business of coinage. Gottschalk was not a traveling charlatan; in fact, he came from an influential Jewish family with expertise in the field of minting.[77] His father Phibes from Hanover had leased the monopoly on coinage in Wunstorf and was involved in risky monetary transactions with Christian partners, including the Duke of Calenberg. Gottschalk inherited his father's debts upon the latter's death in 1579 or 1580, and this might have been an incentive for him to intensify his involvement with alchemy and its promise of miraculous transmutation.[78] Only a few years before, he had instructed the Christian mining official Lazarus Ercker in the art of turning bad gold into ducats of the highest quality.[79] His aim was clearly improving coins, not debasing them. Although these experiments were bound to fail from today's perspective, it is clear that Gottschalk had solid expertise in metallurgy and chemistry. In 1582 Julius, the Duke of Braunschweig-Wolfenbüttel, hired him to conduct negotiations on the sale of lead, vitriol, and sulfur. Presumably, it was in this context that Gottschalk also transacted business revolving around weapons, ammunition, saltpeter, and chemicals.[80] Gottschalk relocated to Prague only when his financial troubles became too severe.[81] There, too, his metallurgical and alchemical knowledge quickly allowed him to become a sought-after expert. This time he was in the service of the aristocratic Rosenberg family, whose best-known representative, Peter Wok von Rosenberg (1539–1611), was himself a major practitioner of alchemy.[82]

In 1606, at a castle in the Electorate of Trier, a Jewish moneylender and merchant named Feivelmann conducted alchemical experiments in connection with a commission he had received to mint coins. Feivelmann had enlisted Christian fellow practitioners, including the castle's burgrave himself. When the experiments came to a halt for unknown reasons, the partners feuded. Their dispute was ultimately brought to court. Interestingly, however, the only issue discussed before the judge was repayment of sums one of the Christian partners had invested in the experiments; the experiments themselves were not a bone of contention.[83] When alchemy and minting were joined in a real or imaginary marriage, it did not always end this well. In 1572, for example, two Jews in Marburg were reported to the authorities and subjected to an interrogation under torture because of their apparent involvement in the machinations of a group of alchemists and counterfeiters.[84]

This brings us back to the question of the risks the entanglement of alchemy, metallurgy, and coinage posed to Jews. A particularly vivid case is the rise and fall of Joseph Süß Oppenheimer (1698–1738), perhaps the best-known German court Jew of this period.[85] The story that is of interest here began in the landgraviate of Hesse-Darmstadt, which had been suffering from a disastrous financial situation. The incompetence of the ruling landgrave, Ernst Ludwig (r. 1678–1739), in coping with financial problems was obvious. In the 1720s, the royal cabinet treasury's debts alone amounted to 2 million gulden.[86] The landgrave, like numerous rulers before him, looked to alchemists, from whom he expected a miraculous production of great quantities of gold, for his salvation. As one historian has put it, he would stop at nothing to "live in princely luxury and stay clear of afflictions and shortages."[87] Even some of the landgrave's confidants got involved in these alchemical ambitions. However, a faction at court was opposed to the experiments. As early as 1728, the privy council used unusually severe language in asking the landgrave "to reject completely, above all, the alchemical laboratory operators, who corrode everything around them like secret fire and coal" and, in addition, not to receive treasure-seekers at court any longer.[88] In this context, some of the landgrave's Jewish financiers were explicitly linked to the alchemical experiments at court.[89]

It is no longer possible to reconstruct whether these accusations against the court Jews were accurate. As we have seen in this chapter, it was not at all uncommon during this period for members of the Jewish—and also, of course, of the Christian—economic elite to be involved in these kinds of arcane undertakings. Irrespective of how true the accusations were, the case of Hesse-Darmstadt provides a highly instructive look into the mechanisms behind the idea of court Jews as alchemists. This is where Oppenheimer comes into play. In 1732 the landgrave began to launch his project "to establish a gold coin manufactory" (a "Gold-Müntz-Fabrique").[90] This seemingly unsuspicious designation concealed the enterprise of minting coins that would have a lower precious metal content than prescribed by imperial law. Some of the leading territories of the Holy Roman Empire, including Electoral Bavaria and Württemberg, had already brought coins like this into circulation. Together with a Christian councilor of the landgrave, Oppenheimer promoted the project.[91] They encountered few scruples from the landgrave, and the new mint began operations in September 1733.[92]

This was, without question, a dangerous project. Any kind of coinage manipulation was prohibited by imperial law and could ultimately lead to the territorial ruler losing minting privileges. It is not surprising that those involved made great efforts to keep the entire enterprise as secret as possible. To begin with, the large-scale procurement of gold for the debased coins, procurements for which Oppenheimer was partially responsible, had to be transacted discreetly. By the same token, the general population had to be prevented from getting suspicious about the illegal character of the coinage. These preconditions quite literally left an imprint on the look of the Ernest d'Or, the coin brought into circulation in 1733. The gold coin's head had a conventional appearance, showing a portrait of the landgrave Ernst Ludwig. On the tails side, however, was a Latin inscription that said "OCCULTA PATEBVNT" (meaning, "secrets will become accessible").[93] This allusive line was intended to let the public believe that the gold used for the minting of the coins had been enhanced by alchemical means.[94] In the long run, however, the manipulations could not be concealed, and by 1737 the coinage had to be stopped under imperial pressure. Although every effort was made to hush up the events—the relevant archival files were even sealed—we do know that some subjects were nonetheless in the picture about the undertaking. A judicial investigation of the events dragged on for years, and injured parties and their descendants were still seeking compensation at courts of law almost a century (!) later.[95]

For Oppenheimer, the affair might have turned out more favorably if the whole truth had been disclosed at the time. It would have become clear that in reality the procurement of the gold, for which Oppenheimer was held responsible, had nothing to do with alchemy, as the inscription on the coin suggested. Instead, the association with alchemy stuck to him. Soon enough, he was invited to Stuttgart by Duke Karl Alexander of Württemberg (r. 1733–1737). In Württemberg, too, Oppenheimer began to work in the mint as its de facto director. Here again the monetary standard was manipulated, even if the undertaking proved only minimally profitable for Oppenheimer.[96] What is more, despite the formidable opposition of the ducal councilors, the Jewish "Fiscal Privy Councilor" undertook numerous attempts at reforming the territory's economy and increasing ducal revenues. Scholars have exhaustively researched these measures and, to some extent, judged them positively. However, they have not sufficiently emphasized that the court Jew's expertise was also based on his knowledge of secrets and his capacity for concealment. Oppenheimer himself explicitly talked about the "secrets of coinage" ("Geheimnisse der Münz").[97] The correspondence between him and the duke is characterized by great trust and a remarkably friendly tone; there is also repeated talk of secrets and secretive matters. In the 1730s, for example, the Württembergian duke ("Thy gracious Carl Alexander") wrote Oppenheimer a letter written in his own hand: "Thou must also not stay away too long, for I want to confide to thee something that I cannot write down, and thou wilt be splendidly surprised; do not show this letter to anyone, whoever it may be."[98] There is reason to believe that the duke was alluding here to a deal in precious stones. Discretion and secrecy were always virtues when it came to the numerous commissions Oppenheimer received for procuring jewels, especially since the duke's passion for precious stones was connected to his interest in alchemy and astrology.[99] Quite apart from this, rumors flourished about Oppenheimer's alleged occult and Kabbalistic arts. As Selma Stern has noted, public opinion was rife with talk "about a horoscope that he had used to prophecy the Württembergian ducal crown to Prince Karl Alexander; it attributed his domineering position to his magical arts and the duke's steadfast love for the Jew to a Kabbalistic secret."[100]

When the duke died unexpectedly in 1737, Oppenheimer found himself at the mercy of his opponents at court. Just a year later, he was publicly executed at an iron gallows outside the gates of Stuttgart. The trial and execution, which historians today view as a case of judicial murder, have been thoroughly researched.[101] Yet one question has not been discussed at all: Why did Oppenheimer die on Stuttgart's iron gallows, which at twelve meters was the highest gallows in the entire Holy Roman Empire? This question can be answered only in the context of the analogy commonly drawn between court Jews and alchemists. This is also why a number of contemporary depictions showing Oppenheimer's execution mention the events leading to the iron gallows' erection and first use almost 150 years earlier—namely, the gruesome execution of the alchemist Jörg Honauer, who was put to death in 1597 because of an unkept promise to produce several thousand gold ducats for the Duke of Württemberg by way of transmutation from iron. The gallows, which weighed more than a ton, were manufactured from the very iron the duke had ordered to Stuttgart in large quantities for Honauer's experiments.[102] On the day of the execution, the Württembergian duke rendered a preliminary "act of mercy" to the condemned alchemist by ordering that only some of his fingers, rather than his entire right hand, be chopped off. Honauer, cynically clothed in a golden robe, was then hanged on the gallows, where he, in the words of a contemporary, "languished in great torment and . . . died."[103]

It was no accident that Joseph Süß Oppenheimer was hanged on the same gallows in 1738 while twenty thousand spectators watched. The execution deliberately established a typological analogy that has been overlooked thus far.[104] Oppenheimer was likened to a deceitful alchemist manipulating the monetary system and the circulation of precious metals. Although he was officially condemned to death because of "only" high treason, the judges had also been deliberating about a sentence of counterfeiting down to the very end of the trial.[105] Irrespective of the legal minutiae, numerous pamphlets and leaflets made a point of drawing an analogy between the court Jew and the court alchemist based on their common manner of execution.[106] A text cartouche of an anonymously illustrated leaflet from 1738 on which the stations of Oppenheimer's path to the gallows are depicted, along with a larger picture of the execution itself, says: "[This is] the iron gallows on which he was hanged and enclosed in the cage. This gallows was built Anno 1597 for someone posing as a maker of gold who was an arch-swindler who was also hanged thereupon on the 12th of April of said year."[107] In other leaflets, the court Jew was even more explicitly equated with the court alchemist; an anonymous leaflet from 1738 shows a gallows flanked on the left by a portrait of the one and on the right by a portrait of the other.[108]

Oppenheimer and Honauer's highly unusual executions were alike down to the last detail. Although illustrations from the late sixteenth century do not show Honauer in a cage at the gallows, as Oppenheimer was later depicted, a contemporary witness said Honauer was "surrounded by a grated iron casing or cage" to ensure that the alchemist would "hang for a long time and not be consumed by the ravens."[109] There is strong evidence indicating that the judges had the case of the sixteenth-century court alchemist in mind as they deliberated on how to execute Oppenheimer. For example, we know they carefully looked into different methods of execution and rejected the options of having him quartered, burned alive, or executed by sword.[110]

It is clear, then, that the similarities between Oppenheimer's and Honauer's executions were no mere accident. The parallels are even more striking when one considers that the iron gallows had hardly been used during the nearly 150 years between the two events. In fact, before Oppenheimer's execution, this gallows was used exclusively to end the lives of ducal alchemists. Records of the special tribunal presiding over the case in 1738 make clear that the judges saw Oppenheimer in this very tradition. We find a plea for execution using the iron gallows on the grounds that "there are older examples of similar pestibus et turbatoribus Reipublicae nostrae [those who plague and disturb our republic], e.g. that of Petrus Mundanus in the year 1601 and of the Alchemist Mühlenfels in the year 1604, *thus the iron gallows was not created without a certain purpose.*"[111]

The execution of "Jud Süß," as he was called, attracted enormous attention among contemporaries, and a flood of publications and leaflets appeared on the subject throughout Europe during the eighteenth century.[112] This underscores how widespread the analogy, already present in Luther's writings, between court Jew and alchemist really was. Indeed, it was not just contemporaries of Oppenheimer's execution who perceived this analogy. As late as the end of the eighteenth century, the German historian Friedrich Wilhelm Moser invoked this discourse, drawing an explicit parallel between the court factor "Jud Süß" and the sixteenth-century "Cabinet Jew"—a reference to the Württembergian court alchemist Abramo Colorni, whom we will encounter in greater detail shortly.[113]

A final example of the entanglement between arcane and mercantile agendas is the story of the Wahls, a family of eighteenth-century German court Jews. It highlights the manifold ways in which the phenomenon of court Jewry intersected with the economy of secrets, and why Christians often linked the Jewish economic elite with alchemy. It is no exaggeration to say that trading in arcana and expertise in alchemy paved the way for the Jew Herz Wahl Dessauer to the court of Christian IV of Palatinate-Zweibrücken (r. 1740–1775).[114] The count palatine had first established contact with the Jewish entrepreneur in 1761, hoping to obtain an "arcanum" for making gold. To encourage him to reveal the secret, the count promised to reward Wahl with the exceedingly high sum of 120,000 gulden and to appoint him to a position at court. Was this just a bizarre episode and Herz Wahl merely a cunning swindler?

A closer look at the source makes it clear that Wahl was no Jewish fortune hunter or a traveling con man. He had begun his career as an agent for the court of Hesse-Darmstadt. As far as his family background was concerned, some evidence even indicates that he was an uncle of Moses Mendelssohn. He lived the life of an observant Jew. Even after his appointment as a court Jew, he rested from work and service on Jewish holidays. "As a Jew I wish to remain a Jew in my lowly humility," he wrote in a letter to his princely patron.[115] Wahl and his son were certainly not some dubious parvenus who looked with indifference on the fate of their coreligionists. Instead, they occasionally used their prominent positions and political influence to obtain improvements for the Jews in the principality.

For his part, the count palatine was neither a naïve dreamer nor a patsy for easy swindles. Rather, Christian IV, a well-versed practitioner of alchemy, embodied the "prototype of the enlightened ruler" and was "without a doubt the most important prince of Zweibrücken in the eighteenth century."[116] One of his priorities was reforming and boosting the territory's economy. This was one of the reasons why the count sought the consulting services of a court Jew; even more important, however, was Wahl's expertise in alchemy. At the time, this was clearly not a paradox. Many of Wahl's alchemical projects and arcana had an eminently economic dimension. What is more, his experiments delivered on what they promised.

The original "arcanum" for making gold apparently did prove promising. We do not know how this happened, but it would be rash to suspect fraud. Rather, as historians of science have pointed out, the perceived "success" of a transmutation experiment could be due to gold residues, which were not identifiable at that time, in the raw material.[117] In any event, after Wahl was able to produce some samples testifying to his abilities, the count palatine rewarded him with handsome sums of money and granted him far-reaching privileges. In addition to his title and salary, he was exempted from having to pay protection money and the body tax (*Leibzoll*) usually imposed on Jews, and he was also granted freedom of movement, freedom to practice his religion, preferential treatment in court business, and a privileged legal status.

Although we can no longer reconstruct whatever wondrous methods Wahl used to produce the gold, we do know that he was seriously interested in the idea of the philosopher's stone. As Dieter Blinn has noted, "preoccupation with the production, augmentation, and transmutation of precious metals by alchemical methods" was a common thread that ran through the Wahl family business.[118] Many questions also surround Wahl's attempts to obtain gold from Rhine River sand. His reputation in this field spread all the way to the Elector of Mainz, who granted him a permit and a commission to build a gold panning apparatus of his own invention on the banks of the river. We cannot rule out alchemy's involvement in these undertakings, but here again, that does not necessarily make them dubious. In fact, Wahl's efforts recall alchemist and economic theoretician Johann Joachim Becher's attempts during the 1670s to obtain gold by smelting sea sand, a project in which his famous contemporary Gottfried Wilhelm Leibniz also showed a keen interest.[119]

Wahl's experimental ambition was not restricted to mastering the art of transmutation. He also engaged in metallurgical experiments revolving around ore, gravel, and silver. In Homburg, which had a Jewish community, the count palatine built a laboratory within an existing government building especially for the court Jew's experiments. Unfortunately, not much time remained for Herz Wahl to use the premises; he died in 1764. After his death, the office and title of agent for the court of Palatinate-Zweibrücken transferred seamlessly to his son Saul, who shared his father's fascination with alchemy. Saul Wahl initially experimented in the same government building in Homburg that his father had used. Following his move to Zweibrücken in 1770, however, a new laboratory was built for him in the capital. In Zweibrücken, he was not the only alchemist in service to the duke. Christian IV generously promoted alchemy at his court, and the skilled

Jewish practitioner was soon attracting jealousy and rejection, particularly among competing Christian alchemists. Saul defended himself by highlighting his reputation and preeminence. Exhibiting a certain degree of self-assuredness, he furnished his letters to the count with a special seal and remarked mysteriously, "So long as I may wield this seal as a Rosicrucian initiate, I will be confident that I am also a chymist."[120]

What Saul really meant by this Rosicrucian affiliation remains his secret. We do at least know that he maintained contacts with alchemists in France and with Masonic circles. But grand theorizing and ceremony were, by and large, not his hallmark. He recommended himself to the count palatine more as a practical expert and as a man "who has made commerce his profession and has learned that commerce cannot be achieved with the quill alone."[121] He seldom lost sight of the commercial implications of his alchemical activities and dealings in arcana. His secret knowledge was closely tied to his economic agenda. The metallurgical experiments he undertook, for example, were impossible to separate from his role as a coin dealer, his monopoly on the silver trade, and his obligation to supply the princely mint with this precious metal.

Saul's entrepreneurial ambition extended to include fields that had either little or nothing in common with alchemy. The court Jew shared his patron's view that the entire economic system of the territory needed to be reformed and reshaped in accordance with cameralist principles. He gave the count palatine suggestions on manufactories for textiles, tobacco factories, iron works, ceramic manufactories, and even the fabrication of pipes. He looked into establishing a pawn office and a lottery. Some of these projects were apparently realized. A farm for cultivating pearls even became particularly successful. His chemical experiments for the production of dyes also yielded promising results, and he obtained a monopoly on the dye he produced. Saul also continued to experiment with enhanced cultivation methods and fertilizer, especially for barley, flax, and hemp.

There is no reason to make categorical distinctions between Saul Wahl's arcane agenda and his "serious" mercantile one. In fact, it is telling that the court Jew presented the quintessence of his economic policy goals to the count palatine in the form of a list enumerating various "arcana," a label that encompassed almost a hundred different projects, including ones from the fields of economy, the cameralist sciences (*Kameralia*), and public order (*Policey*). Saul saw himself as an entrepreneur who traded in secrets, even if these assumed a wide variety of forms and involved quite different fields. Talk about these secrets was much more than a clever advertising strategy; it was also an indispensable feature of Saul's business model. In the face of court intrigue and obstruction coming from the ranks of the Zweibrücken government, the procurement of secrets, be they fictitious or real, was crucial for Saul's efforts to remain in favor with the count, who stood firmly in a princely tradition that emphasized the importance of arcana for the ruler's ability to govern. Like his father before him, Saul strongly believed in the utility of arcana and the legitimacy of the economy of secrets. He even clung to this business model long after he had already fallen out of favor with the court. With Count Christian IV's sudden death in 1775, Saul's downfall was sealed—as was the case with so many court Jews in the early modern era upon the death of their aristocratic patrons. Saul's nearly decade-long career came to an abrupt end when the former court favorite was denounced and expelled. He settled with his family in the nearby town of Pirmasens, where he died, impoverished, in 1791. But even after his downfall, he still hoped to make his fortune, or at least to find a niche for himself, in the economy of secrets. He made an effort to interest the new count palatine in a range of arcane and (al)chemical projects, including "a great science for erasing writings from paper" without damaging the paper itself.[122] The new prince, however, reacted coldly.

The case of the Wahl family has led us to a point just short of the threshold to the nineteenth century. The era of the economy of secrets had not come to a complete end quite yet. In the next chapter we return to that era's heyday, the sixteenth century, and use a spectacular life story to get a fuller picture of the inner workings and driving forces behind the economy of secrets. The concluding chapter tackles the question of what course this economy took after 1800 and what its ultimate decline meant for the overall societal status of secrecy.

FIVE

Abramo Colorni, Professor of Secrets

In Search of Abramo Colorni

When historians engage in biographical research, they often claim that their protagonist has wrongly fallen into oblivion. The subject of this chapter, Abramo Colorni, has indeed fallen into almost complete oblivion. In major works on early modern Jewish history, he appears as infrequently as he can be found in the relevant literature on the history of science. In the case of Colorni, however, it is less a question of whether or not this neglect has been just. In fact, it is not at all surprising that Colorni has hardly aroused the interest of historians so far. For it is impossible to sever his biography from the context of Jewish history, and this is precisely what poses a substantial problem. Colorni's career evades classification into the traditional, and persistently influential, interpretations of early modern Jewish history. It eludes well-worn narratives and clichéd dichotomies such as "integration" versus "exclusion." Colorni was also no forerunner of the Haskalah, or Jewish Enlightenment. Nor was he attempting to reform, much less leave behind, the Jewish world, in which he was deeply embedded. At the same time, his biography cannot be understood solely in a Jewish context.

One may put this to the test: Colorni was a devout Jew who served at the court of the most important Christian rulers of his time; he was friends with a Catholic cleric while at the same time offering explosive devices for sale with which an entire crowd of churchgoers could be killed in a single blow; he quoted freely from the church fathers and yet resisted all invitations to be baptized; he would cause a public sensation yet was also firmly embedded in the economy of secrets. How, then, should one approach the life of a man who, in the course of his career, made his mark as an engineer, mathematician, chiromancer, cryptographer, alchemist, inventor, magus, and merchant—to name just a few of his professions? The answers given by those few historians who have dealt with Colorni have frequently oscillated between two extremes: he is portrayed as either a "charlatan" or a "Jewish Leonardo." We will return later in this chapter to these kinds of judgments—and the historiographic questions they raise. For now, the aim is more modest: to analyze Colorni's biography layer by layer. This requires attending to both its Jewish and its Christian contexts. Seen from this angle, Colorni's biography allows us to explore the concrete opportunities and challenges facing Jews who were active in the economy of secrets. At a few places, I try to ascertain what may have been hidden behind the secrets that Colorni offered for sale. But primarily I focus on the question of how he drew attention to his secrets and, by extension, to himself

Secret Projects, Public Fame: Years of Apprenticeship

Abramo Colorni was born around 1544, presumably in Mantua.[1] He came from a Jewish family that apparently had German roots, was known to have been in Italy since 1477, and whose descendants still live in Mantua today.[2] His father Salomone, who was engaged in silk manufacturing, was among the most prominent Jews in the Duchy of Gonzaga.[3] In 1563 he was one of the members of a Jewish delegation that attempted to prevent the Council of Trent from burning Hebrew books.[4] His son Abramo came from his first marriage to a woman named Gentile. Following her death, Salomone married a widow named Diamante.[5]

We know little about when and how Abramo Colorni developed the diverse interests and skills that would lead him to professional success. What has come down to us is that he was already preoccupied with the mechanical arts as a child.[6] We also know he received a versatile education from his parents.[7] Colorni is even said to have mastered fencing. It is entirely possible that he learned how to use a sword and dagger in Jewish circles. Officially, it is true, Jews were frequently prohibited from carrying weapons. Nonetheless, there were Jewish fencers during this era who jousted both professionally and for show, even if this is little known today.[8] At any rate, evidence indicates that Colorni received part of his practical and intellectual training from non-Jewish teachers. Indeed, as Rabbi Leon Modena noted a few decades later, some "quick-witted" Jews at the time went beyond the study of Torah and Talmud, "apply[ing] themselves to the study of any other science." Perhaps one of the cases Modena had in mind was his famous contemporary Colorni.[9]

There is no comprehensive biography of Colorni. Many questions about his life, including many relating to his education and training, would be easier to answer if we could find the biography that the Catholic cleric Tomaso Garzoni wrote in the 1580s. Since the manuscript for this biography, which was apparently never published, is presently missing, pivotal questions regarding Colorni's youth remain open. We also have a fuzzy picture of his outward appearance. No pictorial representation has been preserved, and it is hardly possible to draw conclusions about his appearance from the few written sources that have come down to us. We are more likely to get an idea of his language skills. Italian was his mother tongue. He was a connoisseur of Italian literature, weaving quotations from Dante's *Divine Comedy* into his writings, and an admirer of the "divine Ariosto" (as he called the poet).[10] Colorni was no doubt deeply rooted in Italian life. Even at the imperial court in Prague, he could not do without Italian cuisine.[11]

All of Colorni's surviving works and letters are written in Italian. However, he was also well-versed in Hebrew. This emerges from the list in which he, like all Mantuan Jews, had to catalogue the books in his house by order of the Inquisition in 1595.[12] Since this inventory can no longer be found today, we must rely on a second booklist from 1605 that still exists in the archives.[13] Admittedly, Colorni was already dead for six years when the Inquisition decided to scrutinize the book holdings of Mantua's Jews again. Yet we may safely assume that the numerous books found in 1605 in the possession of his only son were volumes from Abramo's estate. This list was primarily made up of Jewish literature in Hebrew, both religious and secular.

Colorni was apparently proficient in Latin, and he even succeeded in having one of his works published in that language. It remains an open question as to whether he mastered Greek. In any event, he had no trouble becoming acquainted with the great works of the ancient Greco-Roman authors and even the writings of a few church fathers and Christian theologians.[14] We cannot know for sure whether Colorni also had a working knowledge of German. As an adult, however, he certainly had the opportunity to learn German and perhaps even Czech during his nearly nine-year stay in Prague. Some of the passages from his *Scotographia*, which he wrote and had published in Prague, indicate as much, as does this cryptographic work's stated aspiration to assist letter writers using German and Czech.[15]

In addition to nearly twenty-five letters by Colorni, some unpublished, that have come down to us, his books are the most important sources for biographical information about him. Three of at least six of his treatises have been preserved. There is a treatise about the art of engineering (*Euthimetria*), a book on chiromancy (*Chirofisionomia*), and a treatise on cryptography (*Scotographia*), which is the only one that appeared in print. All the treatises mentioned here deserve careful scrutiny; however, to date Colorni's works have not been closely investigated. Here my main objective is to situate Colorni's works in a biographical context and examine them as part of his self-fashioning as a *professore de' secreti*.[16] There is still much to say about the wealth of technical details these works contain, be they from the field of astrology (as in the *Chirofisionomia*) or of engineering (as in the *Euthimetria*).[17]

Two cities were critically important for Abramo Colorni's apprenticeship years: his hometown of Mantua and his subsequent place of employment, Ferrara. He would return repeatedly to these two places throughout his life, and for decades he provided loyal service to the dynastic families that ruled them—the Gonzaga in Mantua and the Este in Ferrara. Even if tensions and rivalries between these two dynasties came to light from time to time, their commonalities, especially owing to a skillful marriage policy, could not be overlooked. This also held true with respect to their policies toward Jews.[18] For both the Gonzaga and the Este families, those policies were marked by pragmatism and relative "tolerance" throughout the second half of the sixteenth century.[19] To be sure, there were arbitrary measures and symbolic gestures of intimidation as part of the Counter-Reformation, but on the whole, living conditions for Jews like Colorni were favorable in these duchies. In both capitals, Jews were isolated into ghettos only after the turn of the seventeenth century: 1612 in Mantua and 1624 in Ferrara (which had, by then, reverted to the Papal States).

In the late sixteenth century, Jewish subjects in both cities enjoyed considerable economic freedom. In Mantua, for example, the Gonzaga dukes' relatively pragmatic Jewish policy, which came to an end only during the last years of the reign of Vincenzo Gonzaga, enabled Jews to engage in businesses well beyond finance and trade.[20] Nearly three thousand Jews lived in the duchy around 1600. In Colorni's time, Mantua had a flourishing Jewish life. The city benefited from this: the famous musician and composer Salamone Rossi and the theater director and author Leone de' Sommi had places at court alongside numerous Jewish suppliers.[21] Sommi came from the distinguished Portaleone family, whose members made a reputation for themselves well beyond the city limits of Mantua, chiefly as physicians. In the 1560s, there were even plans for the construction of a Jewish college that would have taught secular subjects, among other things.[22] Colorni knew one of this project's initiators, Rabbi David Provenzali (b. 1506).[23] In addition, Mantua was a center of Kabbalist activities.[24]

In the neighboring Duchy of Este, a similar climate of relative open-mindedness prevailed. Under the rule of the Este, Jews expelled from Spain, including so-called Marranos, had been settling in the duchy. The authorities occasionally took action against the Marranos under papal pressure, but on the whole, Ferrara remained one of Italy's most vibrant Jewish communities, with up to ten synagogues. More than two thousand Jews lived in the duchy during the late sixteenth century.

In the rural areas and smaller towns of the Gonzaga and Este territories, too, there were Jewish settlements of note that are still called to mind by the places of publication mentioned on the frontispieces of Hebrew books from this era. In smaller towns like these, Jews were often in charge of money and credit transactions. Yet we also find Jews who traded in the region's natural products—products the Po Delta remains rich in to this day.[25] That mighty river greatly affected the region's rhythm of life and economy. It also posed serious problems like flooding and silting up. The dukes of Este, in particular, had long been confronted by the problem of how to govern a territory whose natural shape was continuously changing and that was literally in a state of flux. This was a major reason why there was a steady demand for engineers at the Este court.[26] Countless engineers and master builders were employed at the courts of Mantua and Ferrara during the early modern era.[27] Some of them achieved great fame in their lifetimes, including Leon Battista Alberti (1404-1472) and Giovanni Battista Aleotti (1546-1636).

Engineering was particularly attractive to Jews like Colorni because the course of training was not strictly prescribed, and it did not necessarily lead through the universities. Instead, court patronage played an important part. In the preceding chapters, we have encountered Jews who were active as civil or military engineers going back to the Late Middle Ages. Colorni also chose this path; however, none of his surviving letters or writings say anything about the place and manner of his training. At the very least there are some indications that, from the outset, he sought a general education that was as broad as possible. In his *Chirofisionomia* he mentions that he attended anatomy lectures given by the Christian professor of medicine Antonio Maria Parolini (d. 1588) as a young man at the University of Ferrara.[28] Parolini, who taught at the university for almost three decades (1559-1587), had achieved fame as the author of a treatise on the plague; in addition to holding a professorship, he served as *protomedico* (chief public health officer) for the entire territory.[29]

It was presumably from Parolini that Colorni acquired the substantial stock of medical knowledge that later left its mark on some of his own works and projects.[30] Indeed, Colorni was later called a "most renowned physician and philosopher."[31] Whether he actually completed a proper course of medical study or initially aspired to practice medicine as a profession is unclear. There were certainly no insurmountable hurdles preventing a Jew from completing the study of medicine in the Ferrara of Colorni's youth. While nearby Padua was the most prominent Italian university where Jews could study without major restrictions, even if they were confined to medicine, about a dozen Jewish students also completed medical studies in Ferrara during the second half of the sixteenth century.[32] The university was not officially responsible for awarding these doctoral degrees. Instead, titles were granted by an outside committee formed for this purpose and made up of a handful of university instructors. This granting of degrees to Jews had been situated in a legal gray zone from the outset and, since the Council of Trent at the latest, openly contradicted the church's legal opinion. Yet it was possible to maintain this practice until the 1580s, and it was still in effect at the time of Colorni's studies, which probably happened in the late 1560s. In any event, Colorni would have been able to count on support from Parolini for a doctorate. Parolini was a frequent member of the special commission on awarding doctoral degrees to Jewish students.[33] He seems to have been relatively open to Jewish students in general. Take, for example, the Jewish naturalist Rafael Mirami, who must have attended the university in Ferrara at about the same time as Colorni, who also studied under Parolini, and who worked as a physician in Ferrara during the 1580s. Mirami was full of praise for Parolini, even if it remains unclear whether the Jewish student actually received a doctorate in Ferrara.[34] In any event, Parolini encouraged Mirami to do research in mathematics as well.[35]

Colorni must have been enticed by the prospect of exploring different areas of knowledge and venturing beyond the academic curriculum. The university at Ferrara offered instruction in a variety of subjects that would have been of interest to him, such as the young disciplines of botany and natural history. Ferrara was one of the first universities in Italy with a professorship in natural history. A circle of researchers and collectors who shared a strong interest in the secrets of nature emerged around this field.[36] As early as the middle of the sixteenth century, the famous Sephardic physician Amatus Lusitanus (1511–1568) had recommended that anybody interested in studying botany and medicine move to Ferrara.[37] Lusitanus knew whereof he spoke: he had, after all, lived as a crypto-Jew from 1540 through 1547 in Ferrara, where he also occasionally taught at the university. (Only later, in the Ottoman Empire, would he officially return to Judaism.) Maybe Colorni had the words of this renowned coreligionist in the back of his mind when he arrived at the University of Ferrara. Perhaps he also knew that Gaspare Gabrieli, the first professor of medical botany in Ferrara, had forcefully announced in 1543 that the history of nature deserved to be studied by people from all social strata.[38] But Ferrara was not animated solely by noble intellectual ideals. The university offered its students a number of concrete opportunities for establishing social contacts with the world of the court. If Colorni attended lectures on natural philosophy, he would have inevitably encountered Antonio Montecatini, the most prominent professor in this subject. Montecatini, who taught at Ferrara for almost four decades (1563–1599) and was one of the best-paid professors at the university, maintained excellent contacts at the Este court. The duke employed him as an advisor, appointed him to be a temporary ambassador, and entrusted him with delicate political missions.[39] Having contact, or even a patronage relationship, with a personality like Montecatini was a promising prospect. It is noteworthy that Rafael Mirami later dedicated his only published book to Antonio Montecatini.[40]

While Mirami opted for a career as a physician, Colorni apparently saw his future at court from the start. This assumption is supported by the earliest extant source on Colorni. The document in question, which previous research on Colorni has overlooked, is a letter of Colorni to Francesco Gonzaga (1519–1577), the Count of Novellara, written sometime during or before 1572.[41] It is a crucial document for a number of reasons. First, it makes clear that Colorni was being promoted by the Gonzaga family—more precisely, by the family's branch line in Novellara—as early as the 1570s. That is several years before he officially entered into the service of the Este.[42] Second, it shows that the young Colorni already enjoyed a reputation well beyond the borders of Mantua. The letter specifically mentions commissions awarded by the Duke of Nevers, another offshoot of the Gonzaga family. The letter may be found today in Florence, where it arrived in 1572 along with a letter of recommendation from the duke to the Medici.[43] But the third reason for the document's relevance is the most important here, as it concerns the way Colorni depicted himself. Then barely thirty years old,

Colorni presents himself as a seasoned engineer and inventor designing an agenda of ambitious projects at the request of his noble patron. His letter, which is organized around nine points, then lists his services and inventions: the manufacturing of weapons (including guns with "many shots"), "experimentation" with artillery technology, construction of war machines (previously demonstrated in model form) and of bridges spanning rivers and moats, the manufacture of ladders for scaling ramparts, the design of an apparatus for digging canals, and an invention for simplifying certain mechanical tasks. Colorni also mentions a water clock and a crane apparatus for lifting water and heavy weights.

This catalogue recalls, and not only from a formal perspective, a letter that Leonardo da Vinci sent to Lodovico Sforza a century earlier, in which Leonardo dangled the prospect of different "secrets" before his patron. The documents are also similar in substance. Leonardo, too, talked about bridges, artillery, siege ladders, and machines that could be used to conquer any conceivable fortress.[44] While Colorni was almost certainly not acquainted with Leonardo's letter, the similarities provide evidence of how much the up-and-coming Jew from Mantua had already mastered the rhetoric of a professional engineer's self-presentation. His 1572 catalogue shows Colorni as a full-fledged engineer in the Renaissance tradition; expertise in building, refining, and inventing military equipment was among the core skills of numerous Italian Renaissance engineers.[45] In fact, it was this kind of knowledge that procured commissions and appointments for Italian engineers throughout Europe.[46]

While military know-how was an important aspect of engineering in Renaissance Italy, it was not its only characteristic. The image of the engineer was multifaceted, ranging from magus to artist. "Like the magus, the engineer was another figure of great power and one frequently situated at the center of bitter controversies," as Anthony Grafton has put it.[47] Some engineers did indeed share with magi an enthusiasm for daring, seemingly supernatural projects. Engineers who distinguished themselves as solid specialists did not usually gain major recognition. It went instead to the all-around talents and suppliers of wonders who did not scrimp on special effects. Citing the case of Leonardo, Grafton has noted that "for the Renaissance artist, painting did not necessarily count as a higher or more important skill than the invention of military vehicles that moved along on their own, or the manufacture of cannons that did not shatter."[48] Colorni was familiar with the works of famous Christian engineers of the Renaissance. For example, the writings of Alberti and Tartaglia obviously inspired him.[49] He would also have been well-acquainted with the inventions of Taccola—the "Archimedes of Siena"—as well as those of the German engineer Conrad Kyeser.[50]

From the letter Colorni sent to the Count of Novellara, it is clear that the court at Ferrara was not the first place where the Jewish engineer worked.[51] We can also correct the older view that Colorni first arrived in Ferrara in 1579, following the marriage of the Duke of Ferrara, Alfonso II d'Este (r. 1559–1597), to Margherita Gonzaga. From an unpublished letter Colorni wrote at a later time, we can infer that he entered into service at the House of Este as early as 1576.[52] The then-reigning Duke Alfonso II was a prince entirely in the tradition of the Italian Renaissance. His contemporaries regarded him as ambitious and pomp-loving, learned and haughty.[53] Today, scholars remember Alfonso, whose court comprised almost five hundred people, as the patron of the poet Torquato Tasso, who spent several years in Ferrara.[54] On the whole, the court of Ferrara under Alfonso could look back at decades of artistic and intellectual flourishing.[55] However, Alfonso was also the last duke under whom the luster of the Este court continued.

As of 1582 at the very latest, Colorni held the official title of ducal engineer ("Ingegniero del Serenissimo di Ferrara").[56] But what assignments were entrusted to him at the court of the Este? It has been speculated that Colorni collaborated on the design of the Palazzo della Mesola that the duke ordered built at that time. Within range of the palace, the duke planned to establish a new town dedicated to international trade, and he had related plans to include Jewish merchants among the settlers. But except for the construction of the palace, which still stands today, these daring projects were never realized. While it is conceivable that Colorni was involved in the Mesola project, there were probably other reasons for the duke's interest in him.[57] To begin with, Alfonso was intensively involved in alchemy—a field in which Colorni also displayed considerable knowledge.[58] Furthermore, it is possible that the duke hired Colorni to work on the court's lavish theatrical productions, especially in light of what he knew about machine technology and stage effects. In Colorni's native city of Mantua during the sixteenth century, there was in fact a tradition of entrusting members of the Jewish community with organizing theatrical productions at court—all the way down to supplying the actors and designing the artwork. At least one of Colorni's cousins worked on these theatrical productions.[59] It is not farfetched to suspect that this was also true of Colorni himself.

Colorni also enjoyed a reputation as an antiquities dealer.[60] At the time, the term *antiquario* often designated more than just a dealer in antique objects. In those days, many antiquarians were also responsible for the "archaeological" excavations that were a requisite part of the business.[61] This may have given Colorni opportunities to test some of the hoisting apparatuses and excavation machines attributed to him. Whatever methods he used to obtain antique relics, he was said to have maintained an entire studio in Ferrara filled with precious objects and to have distinguished himself as the author of a treatise (now lost) on antiquities.[62] It is easy to imagine the Este resorting to Colorni's services as an antiquarian, especially since numerous members of the ducal family harbored a passion for collecting statues, busts, coins, and medallions—even prompting some wits to speak mockingly of the "antique disease" afflicting the Este family.[63]

Engineers were in greater demand than usual in Ferrara during those years because of an event as extraordinary as it was unforeseeable—the 1570 earthquake that caused massive damage in the duchy. We even have a number of reports written by Jews in Hebrew describing this natural catastrophe.[64] It is quite possible that Colorni witnessed the earthquake, since his wife's family lived in Ferrara at the time. In any event, his expertise as an engineer might have been as much in demand when it came to clearing away the rubble as it would have been for rebuilding, which would continue for years. Here, too, Colorni's crane constructions and hoisting machines could have been put to the test.

Colorni's knowledge in the military field must have been especially sought-after in Ferrara. In the second edition of his *Piazza universale*, published in 1587, the writer Tomaso Garzoni was full of praise for the military inventions that Colorni designed. These included weapons, scaffolding for cleaning deep fosses, ladders with which one could reach "up to the Tower of Babel," and communication trenches with which entire regiments could be safely evacuated. Colorni also invented lightweight boats, equipment for lifting water and heavy weights up high, and apparatuses to help turn mill wheels.[65] Above all, Garzoni admired the harquebuses Colorni developed—guns that, once loaded, were able to fire several shots one after another from a single barrel.[66] In the twentieth century, this invention has occasionally earned Colorni a dubious distinction as the father of the modern machine gun.[67] Irrespective of what one thinks about such labels, the question of what to make of this invention remains. Garzoni hardly seems to have been exaggerating in his account, and this is confirmed by contemporary sources relating how Duke Alfonso showed the pope a collection of such harquebuses and muskets.[68] Colorni himself boasted about this invention.[69] Recently, additional evidence has emerged indicating that Colorni's designs for handguns were realized.[70]

Colorni's project was not unusual for the times. Even multibarreled firearms were known around 1600, though most of them were not very practical.[71] Conrad Kyeser had discussed these kinds of weapons in his 1405 treatise *Bellifortis*, which also included some designs for a rocket that are puzzling today.[72] Several decades later, Leonardo da Vinci made sketches of guns intended to shoot from multiple barrels.[73] In Colorni's own lifetime, the engineer Giovanni Battista Isacchi from Reggio (see Chapter 4) also dealt with these kinds of inventions.[74] Colorni was taking on a project that had been stoking the ambition of several engineers and master gunsmiths. Here the great challenge was not so much the theoretical construction of such a gun; much more critical was guaranteeing the weapon's fitness in battle and minimizing the danger of explosion. As early as the middle of the sixteenth century, battlefield experiments were conducted with so-called scatter tubes—*Streurohre* in German—that could shoot several bullets out of a single barrel. But the *Buch von kaiserlichen Kriegsrechten* (Book of Imperial Rules of War, 1552) gives a vivid account of the deficiencies and limitations of these weapons. In theory, one loaded "such guns . . . with many handgun bullets, about twelve or fifteen at once, and this way they will be conveniently used in a garrison against storming troops, particularly in defensive casemates." Yet in practice, "one cannot use it [for shooting] long-distance; but at short distances it scatters [shots] and does great damage."[75] The danger of "collateral damage" would not, however, have prevented the Duke of Ferrara from investing in the development of these weapons. Alfonso II was an out-and-out connoisseur of weapons, even though he lacked opportunities to wage war and test his military arsenal in practice. He summoned leading metallurgists, armorers, and engineers to his court; commissioned newfangled guns; and experimented with innovative battle formations.[76] Some of the weapons developed under Alfonso since the 1560s, especially muskets, proved profitable as exports and were purchased by such powerful customers as the Venetians and the emperor.[77]

The duke's endeavors in the military field were more than just a matter of princely connoisseurship and commercial ambitions. They were also to become, especially during the last years of Alfonso's life, part of his feverish efforts to preserve his dynasty. By the 1590s at the latest, it was apparent that even Alfonso's third marriage would not produce the male heir he so urgently needed. He had no choice but to persuade the pope to enfeoff Ferrara to his (illegitimate) cousin Cesare d'Este (1552–1628); by contrast, enfeoffment with Modena and Reggio, together with a few smaller territories, depended on the emperor. On the latter question, at least, Alfonso was able get Emperor Rudolf II on his side in 1594 in return for substantial payments. By contrast, neither the duke's money nor his words were sufficient to put enough pressure on the pope with regard to the enfeoffment of Ferrara. Alfonso repeatedly tried to gain the emperor's support on this issue by offering troops and leadership in a campaign against the Turks. Still, these negotiations proved tough, and they ultimately faltered. In 1596 the duke resumed negotiations with the imperial court via an emissary and offered the emperor a previously unknown weapons technology. Rudolf II expressed interest, but the duke told him to swear to complete confidentiality about this technology.[78] As a result, the sources we have are extremely laconic. Apparently, the technology involved harquebuses or muskets that were "characterized by a rate of fire three to four times higher than usual and also more reliable in utilization."[79] The weapons also had a previously unknown type of matchlock that allowed cavalry to use them.[80] Whether Colorni—an engineer for the duke, first in Ferrara and later at the imperial court—was secretly involved in this project remains unclear, but it seems likely. Colorni's fascination with weapons development and military equipment persisted until the end of his life. Only a short time before the death of Alfonso II in 1597, he promised the duke new military inventions.[81] Colorni even tried to expand his product range in the 1590s by conducting experiments with "chemical" weapons based on poisonous substances.[82]

In light of the wide range of services Colorni had to offer, it is no wonder that he attracted interest from different courts. In 1581, "Messer Abraam" stayed at the court of the Duke of Savoy-Nemours, near Turin, at the recommendation of the Este. This court had an explicit interest in Colorni's "secrets."[83] We have already seen how, as early as 1572, Count Francesco Gonzaga was unstinting in his praise for Colorni in communications with the Medici, calling him "such a beautiful mind."[84] In 1584, Spanish Lombardy also showed interest in Colorni's projects for "miraculous things." Unfortunately, the sources there do not say what these projects in Milan were about or what became of them.[85]

In Venice during the 1580s, Colorni was even allowed to wear a black hat instead of the otherwise obligatory Jewish yellow hat. In addition, he was granted the privilege—seldom granted to Jews in the Serenissima—of residing outside the ghetto.[86] Such special permits were almost exclusively granted for health reasons or to physicians who had been called to the houses of Christian patients.[87] Colorni's special permit testifies to the reputation he enjoyed among Venetian authorities—a high esteem possibly amplified by a letter of recommendation from the Ferrarese court. Colorni was certainly no stranger to the Venetian authorities in the late sixteenth century. Starting in the 1580s, he approached the Serenissima several times with various projects. These proposals largely revolved around military technology and cryptography.[88] Again, we can no longer reconstruct what exactly became of these projects; however, we know the Venetians appreciated

Colorni's competence in dealing with secrets.[89] His exemption from the humiliating dress codes and residential regulations imposed on Jews needs to be seen against this backdrop. Several decades later, authorities granted another Jew who was firmly rooted in the economy of secrets a special exemption—the chemical producer Nacaman Sarfatti, in whose *secreti* the Serenissima likewise saw a great deal of promise.

In any event, Colorni enjoyed a great reputation at the courts of Mantua and Ferrara. Poems praising him have come down to us from the pens of local Christian contemporaries, such as the acclaimed Christian writer Alessandro Tassoni (1565–1635).[90] Colorni's greatest panegyrist and admirer, however, was the cleric Tomaso Garzoni (1549–1589), mentioned above. A sonnet addressed to Colorni in the *Piazza universale* testifies to this, as does a longer letter to the Jewish engineer prefacing that work.[91] Not much is known about Garzoni's life. The canon from Bagnacavallo, a small town near Ferrara, has been remembered mostly as a polyhistor. His major work, the *Piazza universale,* was an encyclopedia of the late-sixteenth-century professional world.[92] The work first appeared in 1585, and it included the poem to Colorni starting with the second edition in 1587. In line with the imagery of its title, this weighty, yet often entertaining, volume presented a "universal" tableau of society at the time. It discussed, to name just a few examples, clerics and prostitutes as well as artisans and thieves. This kind of compendium was unprecedented. It is not surprising that the *Piazza* became a "best seller" throughout Europe within just a few years. For Italy alone, we find more than twenty editions through the seventeenth century.[93] In German-speaking Europe, the *Piazza* turned out to be one of the era's most popular Italian books.[94] In the seventeenth century, some schools even used it as a primer.[95] Not all the posthumous editions and translations included the poem to Colorni, since some publishers and translators cut out all personal statements by Garzoni.[96] Yet older editions continued to circulate, and along with them the preface praising Colorni. We should not underestimate the effect of Garzoni's panegyric on Colorni's reputation. As late as the middle of the seventeenth century, authors were still referring to Garzoni's paean in their own accounts of Colorni.

Colorni's name was among the most famous in Italy, wrote Garzoni, full of enthusiasm for his Jewish contemporary.[97] What prompted a Catholic cleric to pen such praise for a Jew during the Counter-Reformation? We cannot answer this question with complete certainty; however, it was reasonable to open a synopsis of the professional world with a tribute to a Jewish contemporary who was a universalist par excellence. Garzoni's praise for "maestro Abramo carissimo" also had a deeper meaning.[98] An open invitation for Colorni to convert to Christianity is a leitmotif running through the entire preface.[99] It is possible that Garzoni intended this prominently placed attempt at conversion as a counterweight to other passages of his book that were theologically questionable.[100] At the same time, it would be an exaggeration to suspect only rhetorical calculation lurking behind Garzoni's accolade. There is much to indicate that a bond of friendship existed between the cleric and the Jew. Garzoni's contact with Colorni might have sprung from his cautious and ambivalent interest in Kabbalah.[101] Letters between Colorni and Garzoni do indeed exist. One from the cleric even ends with the valediction "I kiss your hand" ("le bascio la mano")—highly unusual when addressed to Jews.[102] In the *Piazza,* too, Garzoni wrote explicitly about his "affection" ("affettione") for Colorni.[103] Garzoni is even supposed to have composed a biography of Colorni, though it was never published and no manuscript has survived.[104] Still, the *Piazza* is not the only source about Colorni in Garzoni's œuvre. In his *La sinagoga de gl'ignoranti* (1589), he announced that he would soon describe Colorni's magical skills in greater detail.[105] The book he had in mind was the *Serraglio de gli stupori del mondo* (1613), a comprehensive and posthumously published treatise on the world of miracles and magic, in which Garzoni dedicated another flattering section to Colorni.

But what kind of reputation did Colorni have among his Jewish contemporaries? Rafael Mirami obviously had high esteem for him, whom he called a "rare engineer of our age."[106] Mirami was not alone in his esteem, as we will see further below. In this context, it is also instructive to reconstruct Colorni's family ties. For a long time, scholars assumed that the earliest account of Colorni's marriage to a certain Violante dated from 1577.[107]

Two children came from this marriage. One of them, Simone, has left behind a number of traces in the archives, whereas we have only fragmentary knowledge of the daughter named Colomba. She married a moneylender named Gabriele Fattorino, who died young. Colomba survived her husband with four small children and apparently lived later for a while in her parents' house.[108]

Older studies had nothing to say about the background of Colorni's wife; the relevant documents from Mantua are likewise silent on the subject. The critical piece of the mosaic in this case comes from Tuscan documents indicating that Violante was one of the daughters of the prominent moneylender and renowned scholar Vitale (Yeḥiel) Nissim da Pisa. In the mid-1560s, with a relatively modest dowry of 300 scudi, she was sent to Mantua to be married to "Abramo di Salomone Colorni."[109] The groom can only be our engineer, Abramo Colorni.[110]

Although the Tuscan sources have little to add about his wife, we do know more about Colorni's illustrious father-in-law, Yeḥiel Nissim da Pisa. To this day, he is known as the author of a treatise on the moneylending business. The affluent Yeḥiel also distinguished himself as a well-rounded and learned scholar who wrote works on numerous subjects throughout his life.[111] Above all, he devoted himself to religious and Kabbalistic questions, often sharply criticizing philosophical positions and their exponents. The hospitality he extended to David Reuveni, the mysterious Jewish emissary from the desert of Ḥabor, in Tuscany during the 1520s is well-documented.[112] From a financial point of view, a member of the Colorni family would have been, as the pecuniary terms of the marriage make clear, a rather middling match for the da Pisa family.[113] Does this mean that Abramo Colorni's prestige was the determining factor in the marriage decision? We have seen how, shortly afterwards, Colorni's reputation extended all the way to the court of the Medici. It is also possible that the Kabbalist Yeḥiel Nissim da Pisa was fascinated by Colorni's versatile talents in the economy of secrets. There was in all likelihood a link between Colorni's contacts in Ferrara and the last years of Yeḥiel's life; the latter had left Tuscany toward the end of the 1560s because of harsher laws affecting Jewish moneylenders and spent the rest of his life in Ferrara, where he died in 1574.

The relationship, sealed by marriage, between one of Tuscany's wealthiest Jewish families and the Colornis from Mantua deserves closer investigation, as does the question of how much intellectual influence Yeḥiel Nissim da Pisa exerted on the young Abramo Colorni. One can certainly assume that Colorni was acquainted with his father-in-law's impressive library.[114] At any rate, these family ties to Tuscany explain why Colorni repeatedly spent longer periods of time in Florence, at least during the 1570s. Colorni's erudition and expertise, however, were not just put to use making friends within the Tuscan Jewish community. Consider a dispute that occurred in 1575 in the Florence ghetto, established just a few years earlier.[115] At that time, residents were constructing a bathhouse in the ghetto that was also intended to serve as a mikveh.[116] Colorni criticized the way they were executing this building project, undoubtedly from his perspective as an engineer. This enraged the head of the community, Giuseppe Ursi (Iosef d'Orso Tedesco). The disagreement escalated into a heated dispute conducted under the watch of the ghetto's inhabitants. In the course of this dispute, Colorni called Ursi a "disgraceful man and a sodomite who has slept with his own daughter." This prompted Ursi to have Colorni arrested and brought to trial. In October 1575, the judges decided that Colorni should be banished from Florence for a year. On closer examination, however, the question of guilt was apparently not as clear-cut as Colorni's swear words made it sound. As early as January 1576, the ban against him was rescinded. Now Colorni himself turned to the court and accused Ursi and his supporters of putting all sorts of hindrances in his way. We do not know the outcome of the case. It is undeniable that Colorni's extremely scurrilous insults contributed to the conflict's escalation. The actual cause of the dispute, however, was more likely Ursi's inability to deal with the substance of Colorni's critique of the construction work. It would not have been Ursi's only character flaw: he is suspected of having stolen from the coffers of the Jewish community in Perugia a few years earlier.[117]

In the long run, the dispute did not damage Colorni's reputation, among both Jews and Christians. As we will see, the fact that he had to spend some time in jail would even turn to his advantage later.

Counting (on) Secrets: Mathematics, Mechanics, and the Art of Measuring

Colorni's reputation had already spread throughout Italy at an early stage of his career. How was this possible? One explanation is that Colorni was indeed capable of realizing some of the machines and inventions he was offering on paper. As early as 1572, Francesco Gonzaga had highlighted the functionality and practical utility of some of Colorni's inventions in a letter to the Medici. He was referring specifically to weapons and bridge constructions.[118] There is further evidence that some of the elaborate stabbing weapons Colorni devised were actually manufactured.[119] By contrast, information about his war machines is more scarce. The machines Colorni invented for peaceful purposes were less ambitious and therefore easier to produce. For example, he designed comfortable vehicles for the gout-plagued Duke of Savoy-Nemours, possibly similar to today's wheelchair.[120] Colorni was not one of those early modern inventors whose machines existed solely in magnificent folio volumes. Such "machine books" formed a popular early modern genre.[121] They displayed the most exciting inventions and military equipment in great detail, yet they were rarely concerned with these devices' practicality.[122] Colorni was no doubt a "projector" and "machine master" in an early modern sense, but he also acquired enough technical know-how early in his career so that he was able to realize some of his projects.

This may be one reason why a certain sense for what can be achieved characterized Colorni's book about machines, the *Euthimetria*, written in the 1580s and still largely unexplored by scholars.[123] Colorni was certainly a child of his time when he rhapsodized in the book's introduction about "marvelous machines," buildings, and instruments. At the same time, he states that such projects are bound to remain just fantasies on paper without a profound knowledge of mathematics. Colorni feared that handicrafts and arts, especially the "most noble professions" of engineer and machine maker, would be worthless if they were to dispense with a grounding in mathematics.[124] To a certain extent, such topoi belonged to a pervasive rhetoric. Colorni's plea aligned him with those calling for a more intensive mathematicization of the engineering profession. A few decades later, for example, the German fortress-builder Johann Faulhaber (1580–1635), in his book *Ingenieurs Schul* (1633), defined the ideal engineer as "a fortress builder and military master architect who has keen talent [*Ingenium*] as well as complete experience in arithmetic, also lengthy practical experience in geometry, mathematics, and mechanics as well as theoretical knowledge in artillery and gunsmith work."[125] All of this evidently applies to Colorni, even if it never led him to give up playing the role of magus.

In Colorni's *Euthimetria*, mathematics is a leitmotif running through the entire treatise. It is invoked less as a matter of theory, which Colorni had presumably already addressed in his now-lost *Tavole mathematiche*, than as a matter of practical utility.[126] Almost all of the inventions Colorni introduces in the *Euthimetria* revolve around questions of how reality can be apprehended mathematically, and specifically about measurement. The very title of the work arouses associations with mathematics. Colorni did not present his knowledge about machines in the popular form of a *theatrum;* by picking the title *Euthimetria*, he opted for a term occasionally used in early modern Europe to designate the science of straight lines.[127] In this respect, Colorni's treatise overlapped thematically with Girolamo Cardano's *Operatione della linea*, which was still unpublished at the time.[128] Throughout his treatise, Colorni copiously describes various instruments for measurement and develops a technique for measuring distances by using mirrors.[129] In addition, he takes up a project that had already preoccupied Vitruvius and Alberti—namely, how to construct a mechanical device that measures the distance covered by a traveling coach.[130] Constructing an odometer like this required a thorough knowledge of mechanics.[131] Colorni could evidently lay claim to this kind of knowledge and was capable of realizing his project, as we know from his contemporary Alessandro Tassoni. A native of Modena, Tassoni acquired considerable prestige as a writer, diplomat, and secretary to various princes and cardinals. He must have known about Colorni through his connections to the House of Este. In any event, in his oft-reprinted *Pensieri* (1612), Tassoni provided a credible account of how Colorni designed coaches with odometers.[132]

The only surviving manuscript of Colorni's *Euthimetria* is located today in the ducal library of Wolfenbüttel, in northern Germany.[133] This copy, whose provenance has not been established, is probably Colorni's autograph. It is a provisional and fragmentary version, replete with numerous additions and deletions but not yet ready for print as fair copy. The author was still experimenting with the chapter divisions, and this version's 215 pages are also missing some of the copperplate engravings that were meant to be added as illustrations. It remains unclear why the *Euthimetria* was never published. In 1580, Colorni obtained a privilege from the Gonzaga duke allowing him to print the work.[134] More than a decade later, the Medici also granted him a comparable permit for Tuscany.[135] The *Euthimetria*, of which a Latin edition must also have existed, would have been a valuable contribution to the market for printed books about machines.[136] More specifically, there was a tangible demand for the various measuring instruments Colorni presented in his book—whether that demand came from fields such as navigation or cartography.[137] The section on measuring with mirrors could also count on many interested readers in an era fascinated by the technical utility of products from the glass industry.[138] Tellingly, the naturalist and philosopher Giovanni Battista Hodierna (1597–1660), who several decades later would even rhapsodize about his time as a "crystalline century," knew of Colorni's work.[139] What is more, passages from the *Euthimetria* dealing with glass overlapped conspicuously with accounts of the experiments that Galileo, Giovan Battista Della Porta, and Thomas Digges were conducting around the same time with lenses and mirrors—research that ultimately contributed to the invention of the telescope. In fact, it is entirely possible that Galileo was acquainted with Colorni's treatise.[140]

Unlike the *Euthimetria*, the other treatise Colorni wrote at the same time, *Tavole mathematiche*, is now lost.[141] It may be the same as a treatise referred to as *Arithmetica* when an edition of Colorni's collected works was prepared in the 1590s. Unfortunately, too little is known about the content of this *Arithmetica*, other than that Colorni made an effort to have it printed in Prague. All we know is that it contained different arithmetic "rules" and an introduction to the Jewish calendar.[142] Also lost is a manuscript in which Colorni discussed various instruments with a wide range of applications—from measurement technology, to methods for determining perspective, to astrology and clocks.[143] In fact, only one contemporary source mentions this work. We do not know its title, even though it was meant to be printed in Venice during the 1590s in Latin and Italian.[144]

It could be argued that Colorni's failed attempts to get both the *Euthimetria* and his additional writings on mathematics and the art of engineering published prompted him to turn away from the "exact sciences" and devote himself to more "esoteric" fields.[145] But things are probably not quite that simple. Colorni's life story is not one of a "decline" from science to charlatanry. Both terms are misleading in this context. The one golden thread running through Colorni's life story is his expertise in the economy of secrets. The engineering profession was closely associated with the business of arcana, and Colorni's talk of mathematics does not belie that link. While the reference to mathematics helped him to underscore the practical feasibility of his own projects and inventions, this does not imply that Colorni's knowledge was characterized by openness. During this period mathematics was not necessarily an open science to begin with. Even its subjects were sometimes shrouded in secrecy.[146] Girolamo Cardano—himself an accomplished sixteenth-century mathematician—had already talked about the "secrets of geometry and arithmetic."[147] And while "lines," "numbers," and "proportions" could be measured by anyone at the surface, Colorni noted that the rules underlying them all were secret ("secreto").[148]

Of course, Colorni claimed to be acquainted with these secret rules. There was surely a quantum of rhetoric at play here. Yet Colorni was not the era's only mathematician to apply strategies like this as a way of highlighting and enhancing the value of his own knowledge. In the first place, this had to do with mathematics' relatively low social prestige in early modern Europe. Many mathematicians had to work part time in professions like land surveying in order to earn a living.[149] In sixteenth-century England, and not only there, mathematicians were sometimes even associated with the activities of criminals and heretics.[150] In his early-eighteenth-century autobiography, the English mathematician John Wallis recalled how his discipline was "scarce looked on as academical studies, but rather mechanical—as the business of traders, merchants, seamen, carpenters, surveyors of lands and the like."[151] Because of this, the military sector offered mathematicians some of the best opportunities for prestige and making a decent living.[152]

Historians of science have argued that the manner and language in which so many early modern mathematicians presented their knowledge were partly responsible for the association of mathematics with magic. Indeed, many mathematicians tried to use spectacular claims about their discipline as a way of winning over a public that often lacked the most basic knowledge.[153] Yet the necessity of drawing attention to their subject was not the only reason mathematicians marketed their knowledge as exclusive or arcane. In practice, mathematics often had a close and reciprocal relationship with astrology. Moreover, mathematical knowledge could be turned into a fruitful tool for religious and mystical aims, including how to calculate when Judgment Day would arrive.[154] A number of contemporaries even believed in an intrinsic connection between mathematics and the cosmos of secrecy. A well-known example is the Englishman John Dee (1527–1608), who resided at the Prague court during the 1580s—a stay that overlapped with Colorni's time there. Dee was a noted mathematician, astrologer, and magus. For a time, he was also an advisor to Queen Elizabeth I. He was regarded as the "arch-magus" of England. In Dee's intellectual cosmos, the boundaries between solid mathematical expertise and expertise in the occult were fluid.[155] Moreover, there was no lack of ordinary people during this era who regarded knowledge of numbers as supernatural and replete with secrets, associated in their minds as it was with scholastic hair-splitting and the mystical teachings of Kabbalah.[156]

The range of meanings attached to the word "mathematics" in the early modern era was much broader than it is today. Along with the traditional disciplines of arithmetic and geometry, it encompassed a number of arts and methods, including some that were occult. Their common denominator was reference to numbers and geometric forms. For an important mathematician such as Dee, this range extended from music and astrology, to the manufacture of water pumps, to the creation of wondrous "machines." Some contemporaries even suspected that mathematics could make it possible for someone to fly through the air or walk across water.[157]

Clearly, mathematicians' position in the knowledge economy of early modern Europe was ambivalent. It oscillated between academic ambitions and ties to the economy of secrets.[158] This tension is also apparent in Colorni's *Euthimetria*. While some of the knowledge it presents could certainly be applied in practice, it is not a simple how-to manual. This tension is typical of works by major early modern mathematicians and engineers.[159] For example, Leonardo da Vinci marketed his mechanical inventions as secrets, at times even using a kind of secret writing. There is no contradiction between Colorni's profound mathematical knowledge and his continuous activity as a *professore de' secreti*. It would be inaccurate to maintain that he was a mathematician who later "deteriorated" into a professor of secrets. For Colorni and many of his sixteenth-century contemporaries, the two professions were compatible. As far as Colorni was concerned, mathematics remained one kind of expertise among many in his diverse repertoire of abilities and skills within the economy of secrets.[160] This attitude fit the expectations of his colleagues and clients. At the Gonzaga and Este courts, Colorni the mathematician would hardly have encountered accusations of black magic. But what about outside the world of the court? After all, even a reputable English mathematician complained that he had been accused of practicing magic when he attempted to measure the height of a rural church tower as late as the middle of the seventeenth century.[161] We have no evidence that Este officials exempted Colorni from wearing the obligatory Jewish badge. Thus, it is easy enough to imagine that he drew even more suspicious stares from the general population when, outfitted with his instruments, he conducted public experiments in the countryside to measure distances and building heights. Even in a city like Ferrara, Colorni must have attracted considerable attention when he, a Jew, experimented with measuring techniques from, of all places, the cathedral bell tower.[162]

Divination and Distinction

Colorni was clearly not a humanistic scholar seeking to spend most of his days in the isolation of his study or in the library. The court was his field of activity—his stage. A number of details, including his polished letters to princes and his fencing skills, illustrate Colorni's familiarity with the world of the court and its social conventions. It was common for Colorni's patrons to take him along on journeys or short stays outside the royal residence. Around 1586, he was staying in the castle at Marmirolo, where the Duke of Mantua, Vincenzo Gonzaga, occasionally spent time relaxing and entertaining himself. The duke sometimes invited Jews as guests or ordered Jewish court musicians to play for him;[163] Jews sometimes even participated in gambling activities at his court.[164]

Unfortunately, we do not know why Colorni was staying in Marmirolo at that time; the Este may have loaned him out as an engineer in order to supervise the palace's renovation. It was common for experts and scholars in princely service to participate—or be required to participate—in the court's banquets and entertainments. Even Colorni's contemporary, Galileo, was not able to rid himself of such obligations at the court of the Medici. As Mario Biagioli has shown, such events certainly entailed risks for scholars and experts like Galileo. Someone might spontaneously ask them to answer a difficult question or provide information that they were not able to grant straightaway. In such a situation, scholars could not just withdraw if they were worried about maintaining their patronage relationship. Biagioli has called these kinds of situations "dangerous performances."[165] It is in this very specific framework of courtly patronage that he sees one of the reasons why even a man like Galileo, a court mathematician who is often put on a pedestal today as a hero of science, displays a "lack of system" on closer examination.[166]

Colorni also found himself in a tight spot when Duke Vincenzo Gonzaga summoned him to make a written statement about palm reading while visiting Marmirolo.[167] Earlier, Colorni had apparently presented some knowledge of chiromancy in jest that produced astonishment in court society.[168] The day ended with a ducal commission to write a compendium about chiromancy and the related subject of physiognomy. Later, in the preface to his *Chirofisionomia,* Colorni left behind a vivid retrospective on these events in Marmirolo from which we can infer that this assignment was not exactly a welcome one. However, there was no way for him to avoid carrying it out. Alluding to his own first name, Colorni even compared himself to the biblical patriarch Abraham, who submitted to God's will even when called upon to sacrifice his own son.[169]

There were a number of reasons why Colorni found the ducal assignment unwelcome. First, it must have kept him from more important projects of his own design, as well as from his duties as court engineer. Moreover, chiromancy harbored substantial dangers. Palmists who wanted to look credible had to do more than just draw positive conclusions from reading lines on the palm of a hand. However, they could quickly come to feel the wrath of their patrons if they made predictions that were too unpleasant. It was common for angry princes to inflict draconian punishments on their palmists.[170] Presumably, however, the most important reason for Colorni's caution was fear of being associated with a field populated by many charlatans and only recently forbidden outright by the "Iron Pope" Sixtus V (r. 1585–1590). In his *Constitutio contra exercentes astrologiae iudiciariae artem* and in the papal bull *Coeli et terrae creator* (1586), the pope declared war on a number of divinatory practices.[171] This soon led to the public punishment of practitioners, even outside the Papal States.[172] It is telling that Colorni emphasized how he had been involved with chiromancy only during his youth—in other words, at a time when writings on the subject had not yet been banned—and said that it stood outside his professional expertise ("materie lontane dalla mia professione").[173] In reality, however, he did not shy away from undertaking such demonstrations at court. There is evidence that, contrary to all protestations, Colorni privately continued his involvement with such "arts" even as an adult. His hesitation about composing a treatise on the subject did not have to do with any general skepticism but rather with the question of how such a topic could be presented in an unsuspicious manner. As far as the latter was concerned, Colorni's concerns were thoroughly justified. Indeed, he did not prove successful at devising a harmless chiromancy.

Colorni prefixed his work, whose first draft has to be dated to 1586/1587, with an exchange of letters between him and Tomaso Garzoni.[174] Not only was Garzoni Colorni's interlocutor and admirer, but as a Catholic priest he was also invested with clerical authority. Colorni certainly expected this association to lend his work legitimacy. In a letter refashioned into a preface, Garzoni strongly praised Colorni's treatise and certified its conformity with the doctrines of theology and philosophy. In his *Piazza universale,* too, Garzoni explicitly lauded the Jewish author's commitment to opposing "superstition" in physiognomy and chiromancy.[175] In return, Garzoni took the liberty of asking the Jewish author—in the preface to the *Chirofisionomia,* as he did in his *Piazza*—to convert in hopes of leading him down the "path of salvation."[176] However, not every Catholic cleric was convinced of Garzoni's arguments in favor of the *Chirofisionomia.* The Bishop of Ascoli Satriano (in Apulia), who came across Colorni's *Chirofisionomia* a few years later, expressed his reservations about the treatise to Duke Vincenzo in Mantua.[177]

Sanctions against chiromancy were the church's reaction to a common belief, especially widespread in Italy, in the utility of such divinatory practices, which experienced a boom in the sixteenth and seventeenth centuries.[178] Numerous publications and manuscripts about physiognomy and chiromancy circulated at the time. There was hardly anything new about this interest in knowledge promising to read people's character or predict their future on the basis of their physical features; in fact, the history of such arts reaches back into ancient times. Many Europeans cited biblical passages about the importance of bodily signs for selecting priests as an example of physiognomy's antiquity. But, of course, in the day-to-day practice of physiognomy, early modern people were much less interested in this past than in the future. They hoped to read the future in hands (chiromancy), in foreheads (metoposcopy), and in the body's physique or in the face (physiognomy). This is where the problem really started for the Catholic Church.

The information early modern people hoped to get from these kinds of arts was often quite concrete. From some of the notes they scribbled in the margins of books on this subject, we know that many of the people who bought such treatises were searching for predictions about their own fertility or that of a spouse.[179] At other times, the marginalia explicitly indicate names of acquaintances and relatives—their physical features suddenly appeared to the reader in a new light.[180] A considerable amount of superstition was involved in this field, but this does not mean these arts were prevalent among only the lower classes. On the contrary: in the late sixteenth century, quite a few scholars argued in favor of physiognomy and related arts. What is more, these arts' practical utility and theoretical coherence were often bolstered by complex references to disciplines like astrology.[181] As the historian Keith Thomas has noted, "lore of this kind was taken seriously by many Renaissance intellectuals, however debased its practice at the village level may have been."[182]

Indeed, the fascination with physiognomy and chiromancy was a preoccupation that ran through all strata of society—and so, of course, it can also be found among contemporary Jews.[183] It is a myth to think that Jews had always avoided divination, especially during this era. But it is a myth with far-reaching implications. For example, Walter Benjamin explained his idea about a particular Jewish consciousness of time and history with this incorrect claim: "We know that the Jews were prohibited from investigating the future. The Torah and the prayers instruct them in remembrance, however. This stripped the future of its magic, to which all those succumb who turn to the soothsayers for enlightenment."[184] The historical record suggests quite the opposite.[185] A great deal of evidence indicates that early modern Jews were well-acquainted with the physiognomic, and more generally the divinatory, literature of the time.[186] Many Christians even regarded chiromancy (Ḥokhmat ha-Yad) and metoposcopy (Ḥokhmat ha-Partzuf) as activities frequently practiced by Jews (and by gypsies).[187] For example, a painting by the seventeenth-century Italian artist Pietro della Vecchia shows a Jewish palm reader offering his services in front of astonished onlookers.[188] A similar sight presumably presented itself to the Catholic clerics who, during a canonical visitation in Cremona in 1575, found out about a popular Jewish palm reader who was predicting the future for Christians and offering his services as an astrologer, even though he knew this was forbidden.[189] There was also great interest in these "arts" within the Jewish community. Early Jewish mystics regarded chiromancy and physiognomy both as objects of secret knowledge and as criteria "for the admission of novices."[190] The *Zohar,* compiled during the Middle Ages, includes detailed sections on physiognomy and chiromancy.[191] In Colorni's lifetime, these arts enjoyed considerable popularity within Kabbalah—especially among the followers of the famous Kabbalist Isaac Luria (1534–1572), who is said to have mastered them.[192] Rabbi Leon Modena also resorted to the art of palm reading on occasion.[193] His Jewish contemporary Joseph Salomon Delmedigo—a renowned physician and a student of Galileo—was just as fascinated by physiognomy and chiromancy.[194] In the late eighteenth century, the Sephardic merchant David Attias from Livorno published a tractate on physiognomy as part of a book he wrote in Ladino, *La Güerta de Oro* (1778).[195]

Colorni also believed in the utility of chiromancy, even if he was less inclined to comment on it in writing. However, commissions of this kind were the order of the day within the structures of patronage. Colorni's much better-known contemporary, Galileo, also had to accept this fact at the court of the Medici. But that does not mean we should view the works that emerged from such courtly commissions simply as tedious compulsory exercises. A skilled courtier, and this was a group that included both Galileo and Colorni, could always use such tasks for adroit self-fashioning.[196] Colorni, for one, used the opportunity to distinguish himself once more as a well-versed *professore de' secreti* and to emphasize that he should not be lumped together with charlatans.

Before we return to this point, we have to take a closer look at the contents of the work.[197] Indeed, it has hardly been studied to date.[198] Colorni divided the *Chirofisionomia* into three books. The neologism in the title seems to imply that the book also deals with physiognomy; however, this is not the case. For Colorni, "Chirofisionomia" functions as an overarching concept for the science of hand signs ("scientia della mano").[199] To the best of my knowledge, this neologism occurs only in Della Porta's almost identically titled, posthumous work *Della Chirofisonomia*.[200] Much evidence indicates that Colorni's work circulated outside the court of Mantua during the sixteenth century, even reaching the imperial court in Prague.[201] It could even have gotten as far as Naples and landed in the hands of Della Porta, who only a few years later committed his own treatise to paper. However, in his correspondence from that time, Della Porta did not use the term "Chirofis[i]onomia" to designate his own work; instead, he used the working titles *Chironomia* and *Chiromantia*.[202] His work received the title *Chirofisonomia* only when it was published posthumously in 1677.[203] In the relevant literature, only Colorni's unpublished manuscript from the 1580s could have served as a model for this unusual title. It is unclear how Della Porta's editor learned about Colorni's work almost a century later, but, as we shall see, it certainly has to be more than sheer coincidence.

Although Colorni's *Chirofisionomia* was never published, there were proposals to do so shortly after it was written.[204] At the beginning of the 1590s, Colorni even made an effort to publish the treatise in Prague as part of an edition of his collected works. This plan failed, but several contemporary copies made the rounds, of which only two are preserved today. Although these copies contain numerous pen-and-ink drawings of palms and their lines, it is not always easy for a reader to follow them today. Much like chiromancy itself, some of the treatise's central tenets make sense only when the reader is acquainted with and willing to accept their underlying and complex astrological premises. Even in the third book, which introduces the "chirometro," an instrument Colorni designed to measure the hand, some passages are relatively opaque. It remains unclear whether the duke to whom the book was dedicated, Vincenzo Gonzaga, was able to draw the kind of insight from the subject that he had been expecting. A few passages do indicate that Colorni had not lost sight of his noble patron's predilections and interests. For example, there is a chapter on the causes of impotence—an affliction that plagued the duke and even resulted in some politically embarrassing situations.[205]

The *Chirofisionomia* is remarkable today because, among all of Colorni's surviving works, it provides the best insight into his intellectual cosmos. Although Colorni uses the dedication to flirt with notions that he is not really competent in this field, the *Chirofisionomia* presents itself as a demonstration of expertise by a well-versed *professore de' secreti* with encyclopedic knowledge. The lengthy subtitle explicitly announces that the author is going to furnish proof of his knowledge in fields as different as theology, philosophy, and medicine. This claim is underpinned in the work itself by quotations from a wide variety of sources. The range extends from the luminaries of ancient medicine (Hippocrates and Galen) and philosophy (Aristotle and Plato), to the pseudo-Aristotelian *Secretum secretorum*, all the way to the Renaissance authors Ficino and Ariosto. Colorni also cites

Solon, Vegetius, Marcus Terentius Varro, and Avicenna. It is particularly striking how familiar the Jewish author is with Christian theology. He refers to Augustine's *De Civitate Dei,* Thomas Aquinas's *Summa contra Gentiles,* and the writings of Isidore of Seville. This kind of acquaintance with Christian theology was unusual for a Jew in the sixteenth century, even if one takes into account that some Jewish intellectuals in fifteenth- and sixteenth-century Italy were quite open-minded readers of Christian literature.[206] This is not to say that Colorni's case was entirely unprecedented. For example, we have evidence that an important Jewish scholar of this period, Azariah de' Rossi (ca. 1511–1578), referred to Augustine during a controversy triggered by his *Me'or 'Enayim* in 1573.[207] However, placing Colorni in de' Rossi's intellectual company might come as a surprise to historians who have dismissed Colorni as a charlatan.

How Colorni became acquainted with Christian literature is an open question for now. He could have asked his clerical friend Garzoni for advice in this field. However, it is also possible that Colorni was keeping in touch with one of the most famous theologians of his time, the Venetian Paolo Sarpi (1552–1623). In the late 1560s and early 1570s, Sarpi spent several years working and studying in Mantua. During this period, he also learned Hebrew from local Jews.[208] Sarpi, who would later challenge papal authority in his capacity as advisor to the Venetian republic and made no secret of his sympathy for the Protestant cause, was relatively open toward Jews. We even have evidence of his friendly acquaintance with the Venetian rabbi Leon Modena.[209] Contact between Sarpi and Colorni could have arisen not only from the years when they were both in Mantua, but also from Sarpi's acute interest in questions of optics, and especially in the practical application of mirrors.[210] In the latter field, Colorni was regarded at the time as a leading mind.

But let us return to the question of what sources Colorni uses in the *Chirofisionomia*. He does not cite any Jewish sources except for the Hebrew Bible. Although Maimonides is mentioned ("Rabi Moisè d'egitto"), it is in his capacity as a medical authority. Colorni also makes scattered references to the Jewish physician and writer Leone Ebreo (Yehuda Abravanel, ca. 1460–1521) and his *Dialoghi d'amore* (first published 1535), but these too have less to do with the author's Judaism than with Colorni's esteem for this work as a standard text of Platonic Renaissance philosophy. By contrast, whenever Colorni consults the Bible in order to undergird his arguments, he presents views that indicate a familiarity with Kabbalah. Take his interpretation of the prophet Isaiah as one of the first physiognomists: here Colorni invokes a biblical verse meant to prove that the prophet could see people's sins in their faces.[211] This view was in line with interpretations of the very same verse from Isaiah found in Jewish mysticism as early as the third century CE.[212]

Despite the wealth of authors cited in the *Chirofisionomia*, Colorni revealed clear preferences identifying himself as a follower of ancient medical doctrines. His ideas about the human body and medicine were strongly influenced by those of Aristotle and Galen. Specifically, he praised Aristotle's *Physiognomonica*—actually a pseudo-Aristotelian writing—as a standard work of unsurpassed truth and judiciousness.[213] When it came to interpreting the stars, Colorni regarded Ptolemy as the "prince of astrologers" and a "true observer" of celestial phenomena.[214] Ancient natural philosophy and astrology are two key points of reference in the *Chirofisionomia*. Astrological arguments run through the entire work. Like many of his Christian contemporaries, Colorni assumed chiromancy could have no predictive value without astrology. The shapes of sectors and lines on the palm, varying from one person to another, were always the outcome of influences that specific planetary constellations had on the individual.[215] Ultimately responsible for all this was the will of God. The Creator had endowed each human being with certain outward signs, even if they were not always immediately visible. In Colorni's view, these signs made it possible to determine the role that each individual was capable of assuming in society. He argued that Plato's notion of the ideal state could be realized only if it were possible to ascertain without any doubt who was properly equipped to bear arms, to safeguard the laws, and to practice the arts and handicrafts. In this regard, interpreting the body's external aspects, and especially the hand's, could prove particularly useful.[216] Here Colorni was obviously building on the ancient discourse about the ideal state, an idea that preoccupied many other scholars during the sixteenth century. For contemporaries, Colorni's references to Plato were neither abstruse nor anachronistic. His concept of an ideal commonwealth, a design informed by biological determinism, resembles the ideas that Tommaso Campanella propagated—a few years after Colorni—in his utopian *The City of the Sun*. Around 1600, another contemporary, the Jewish physician Abraham Portaleone, also investigated the question of what "significance a bodily limb deviating from its form or normal condition has for one's mental disposition."[217] For Portaleone, who knew the relevant literature on physiognomy very well, the starting point was Leviticus (chapter 21), with its passages about priests' bodily features.[218]

Colorni obviously grants the learned chiromancer great social responsibility. For this reason, he urges diligence and warns against hasty conclusions. It is not enough to base an assessment on one or two features of the hand. Rather, insights from philosophy, medicine, and astrology have to be taken into consideration.[219] According to Colorni, there is a fundamental difference between a "natural" and a "false" chiromancy. He claimed to have learned as a young man how to distinguish between the features of the "good natural physiognomist" and the hallmarks of the art's fraudulent exponents.[220] He associated the latter with popular authors such as Tricasso, Cocles, and Pseudo-Geber, whose works Colorni felt were replete with superstition and rightly banned. (Here Colorni was explicitly referring to the Catholic Church's *Index librorum prohibitorum*.)[221] Colorni rejected any predictions, either from hand lines or from astrology itself, that could be construed as too concrete or trivial. Questions like somebody's time of birth, a woman's virginity, the birth of a "monster," or the chances of becoming rich through an inheritance could not be answered. Yet Colorni admitted that astrology and physiognomy are suitable methods for predicting the future in ways that are "real and permissible."[222]

As its rather verbose subtitle underscores, the *Chirofisionomia* is both a diatribe against superstition and a plea for a learned and systematic chiromancy. To be sure, this does not make it a critique of the economy of secrets. Writing about chiromancy and physiognomy in the sixteenth century almost inevitably meant making a contribution to the corpus of *secreta* literature.[223] Today, the relevance of Colorni's long-winded work does not rest primarily on its "technical" elaborations. Rather, it demands attention as a Jewish author's attempt to claim for himself the role of a "learned" *professore de' secreti*. By contrast, Colorni's Judaism was largely irrelevant to the treatise's argument. There was also no need for him to demonstrate that he was acquainted with the secrets of nature in great detail—a claim for which referring to his Judaism would have been useful. In fact, he did not need to demonstrate his personal expertise in the economy of secrets at all, as these credentials were what led to this work's commission in the first place.

Colorni was able to use the *Chirofisionomia* as a way of defining his role in the economy of secrets more precisely. He sketches a picture of himself as a learned professor of secrets who connects his claim to being "scientific" with the (partial) divulgence of his secrets. Colorni argued he was obligated to defend physiognomy, chiromancy, and astrology against those "unworthy subjects" that merely promoted superstition and did not merit the title of a "scientiato."[224] Ironically, modern readers might find the *Chirofisionomia* to be just as "unscientific" and esoteric as the doctrines of a Tricasso or Cocles, two authors whom Colorni criticized so strongly.[225] It is mostly Colorni's attitude and rhetoric that distinguish him from such authors.

In the sixteenth century, and well into the era of Johann Caspar Lavater, Della Porta was one of the most prominent exponents of this type of learned physiognomy. He propagated a "scientifically" inspired and systematized physiognomy in a series of writings that took into account all the features of the human body, down to the navel, while also relying on analogies to the animal kingdom.[226] Like Colorni, Della Porta vigorously opposed charlatans distorting and abusing what he regarded as a noble art. Both authors harshly rejected these alleged fraudsters' deceitful practices, which Della Porto blamed on superstition among the lower orders of society. Characteristically, Della Porta was unsparing in his criticism of the very same chiromancy textbook authors from whom Colorni tried to distance himself. We do not know how Colorni's work came to the attention of the publisher of Della Porta's *Chirofisonomia* in the late seventeenth century. Borrowing the neologism from Colorni's treatise was certainly a suitable way of disassociating Della Porta's book from the term "chiromancy," which was too strongly associated with the conduct of fraudulent chiromancers in the publisher's eyes.[227] But Della Porta, the aristocratic Catholic from Naples, and Colorni, the Jewish *professore de' secreti* from Mantua, also shared the goal of making physiognomy in general and chiromancy in particular more scientific. Their English contemporary Francis Bacon (1561–1626) was also open to a learned kind of physiognomy.[228] References to ancient authorities constituted a frequent topos in this kind of defense.[229] By the same token, Colorni's criticism of ordinary practitioners' deficient or completely lacking scientific skills allowed him to showcase his self-image as a serious and learned researcher into nature's secrets. It also helped him underscore his knowledge in the fields of "theology, philosophy, and medicine," as indicated in his manuscript's subtitle.

A final commonality between Colorni and Della Porta was the fate of their respective works. While both authors made no secret of their contempt for traveling chiromancers and instead tried to apply the veneer of learned "scientia" to themselves—Della Porta even wrote in Latin—they were both skating on thin ice. The Inquisition could easily deem their avowals insufficient. In Colorni's case, it is evident that he did not entirely discard chiromancy's astrological-divinatory foundations. The Catholic Church's stance, however, was quite clear in this respect: any astrologically inspired chiromancy was forbidden.[230] As a result, Colorni would have gotten into trouble with the Inquisition if he had published his *Chirofisionomia* in Italy.[231] It is certainly no coincidence that the work was supposed to be published in Prague in the early 1590s under Rudolf II—a ruler deeply fascinated by these arts.

For his part, Della Porta had already attracted the suspicion of the Inquisition because of his earlier writings on physiognomy, among other things, and he was able to assuage the church's suspicions only by making textual revisions. When, around 1600, he set about writing his work on chiromancy, he had these experiences in mind. He knew that the only chiromancy acceptable to the church was one that did not aspire to be anything more than descriptive.[232] In different stages of his revisions, Della Porta attempted to delete as many of his initial references to astrology as possible. He replaced these with stronger references to the Aristotelian tradition and to humoral medicine.[233] Yet he did not succeed in doing this completely, which may help explain why his treatise remained unpublished during his lifetime. In the Italian edition that came out more than half a century after his death, problematic passages were largely removed by an editor's cuts. Only in this way did the posthumous publication become a frequently cited example of a descriptive chiromancy based on "natural principles."[234]

In principle, both Colorni and Della Porta believed in the legitimacy of divinatory practices, as well as in the possibilities of a natural magic. Colorni explicitly wanted to establish these arts as "scienza" resting on a solid foundation.[235] An important building block for this was mathematics; one should not forget that the *Chirofisionomia* includes detailed instructions on how to build an instrument for making precise measurements of the hand. Colorni had formulated a similar view a few years earlier in his *Euthimetria* when he laid out his vision of a natural magic that would amount to little more than a "fume" unless founded on a thorough knowledge of proportions, numbers, and weights.[236] This claim to seriousness was a common theme in the scholarly discourse of the time about *magia naturalis* and its legitimacy. But from a Christian, and especially a Jewish, perspective, Colorni's talk about proportions, numbers, and weights was also a thinly veiled allusion to the famous verse from the apocryphal Book of Wisdom, ascribed to King Solomon, that says God "hast ordered all things in measure and number and weight."[237] This verse played a major role in the formation of theological and artistic thinking about the concept of order in Christian Europe.[238] For Jewish contemporaries, however, this might not have exhausted the associations linked with this verse, and this brings us back to the question of whether Colorni's self-fashioning also included elements that were distinctively Jewish. It is true that Colorni was acquainted with and frequently cited the great Greco-Roman authorities of antiquity—especially Aristotle and Vitruvius. He was clearly also familiar with Neoplatonism and the phenomenon that would later come to be called the "Hermetic tradition." But was he placing himself first and foremost in the tradition of these ancient authorities, or even of Hermes Trismegistos, when he designed those daring devices that predicted the future and dazzled his audience with "natural magic"? Probably not. It is more likely that he was placing himself in the tradition of Solomon.

The Magus and His Cosmos

What was at the core of Colorni's reputation, which he had already acquired early on in his career? We have tried to answer this question from different angles, but there is one important piece still eluding our view. Let us therefore return to Tomaso Garzoni, to whom we are indebted for the most complete contemporary portrait of Colorni. Garzoni was lavish in his praise for Colorni's achievements as an engineer, inventor, and mathematician. Yet his admiration for Colorni the magus was no less emphatic. In the *Piazza universale,* Garzoni gives a comprehensive account of Colorni's magical talents and miraculous feats.[239] Garzoni's fascination with Colorni's magical skills persisted even after the publication of the *Piazza*. Shortly before his death, he decided to write an encyclopedia of magic and the miraculous.[240] This time, however, neither a theater stage nor a piazza served as the allegorical scene for his work. Rather, Garzoni pictured the world of magic and the miraculous as a "seraglio," as an imposing palace with countless rooms and winding hallways. In this building there was also a "magical apartment," and this is where Garzoni mentioned Colorni. This put him in illustrious company, well in line with Garzoni's earlier remark that Colorni deserved a place in the circle of Plato, Plotinus, Roger Bacon, and Pietro d'Abano, to name just a few.[241]

Garzoni recalled how Colorni had changed nuts into jewels and pearls in front of astonished onlookers.[242] Various card tricks were also part of Colorni's basic repertoire at all his demonstrations.[243] Garzoni had witnessed such demonstrations himself, and he depicted how Colorni once used these kinds of feats to astound a young Spaniard and a prelate in Ferrara.[244] At Colorni's behest, painted animals were said to have begun flying, and gold chains supposedly morphed into live snakes.[245]

We do not know whether Colorni also performed his feats in Jewish circles, but it is entirely possible that he did. In the Jewish world in which Colorni grew up, there was a considerable fascination with magic. The physician and scholar Abraham Yagel, a contemporary of Colorni's, openly admitted his admiration for the magical potential of playing cards—something Colorni had mastered with virtuosity.[246] While it was well-known that the

Bible strongly condemned magic, the rabbinic tradition had taken a more differentiated approach analogous to the Christian distinction between black and white magic.[247] Magicians started to commit a crime, according to this widespread view, only when they inflicted physical damage. Deceiving the eye was not in itself enough to constitute magic.[248] Accordingly, sanctions against prestidigitators were unusual in Judaism.[249]

With the spread of Kabbalah during the early modern period, the role of magic in Jewish life and thought took on an entirely new dimension. Jewish natural philosophers and Kabbalists like Yoḥanan Alemanno and Abraham Yagel advocated the "noble discipline" of magic and assumed they could gain instruction about it from studying the writings of Judaism.[250] Colorni's father-in-law, Yeḥiel Nissim da Pisa, was also greatly interested in the practice of magic.[251] In German-speaking and Eastern Europe, in particular, numerous "miracle rabbis" were at work.[252] What Keith Thomas has said in his classic study about the relationship between religion and magic among early modern Christians can be applied to early modern Jewry, too: magic and religion were not two contradictory or irreconcilable systems of knowledge. Magical components were preserved in religion, and the practice of magic exhibited religious characteristics.[253]

But let us dwell for a moment on a simple question concerning Colorni's magic craft. Where had he actually learned his feats, which must have required great virtuosity? There were certainly opportunities aplenty, for the late sixteenth century was a heyday for magic tricks like these.[254] For example, Jean Prévost issued his *La Première Partie des subtiles et plaisantes inventions* in Lyons in 1584—a publication that has been called the first "do-it-yourself" book for magic tricks.[255] It is not plausible, however, that Colorni drew his magic repertoire primarily, or even exclusively, from studying books. It makes more sense to assume he had concrete opportunities to attend live demonstrations of magic tricks as a young man, especially at the courts of the Gonzaga and the Este. One possible candidate for the role of Colorni's mentor is his contemporary Girolamo Scotto (Hieronymus Scotus), who had caused a stir in Italy in the 1570s with his card tricks. Evidence indicates that Colorni knew about and was inspired by additional feats that Scotto performed.[256]

Scotto was one of the most mysterious figures in the history of early modern magic. His biographical data remain unknown, and he went by different names.[257] At the end of his life, this magus, who was most likely born in Piacenza, could look back on a Europe-wide career that had led him from the royal courts of Italy into the services of the Margrave of Ansbach, the Bishop of Würzburg, and the Archbishop of Cologne. Scotto owed these appointments not least to his talents as a diplomat. Following an admittedly not very diplomatic adultery with the wife of a German prince, Scotto's situation became precarious. Whether he knew how to make himself invisible in this situation—an ability that many contemporaries presumed he had—is rather questionable. He is said to have spent his final years as a marauding imperial field colonel.

Several constellations would have enabled Scotto and Colorni to cross paths. Colorni could have encountered Scotto as early as the 1570s in Italy. This was how Marco Bragadino, an alchemist who later became a legend in his own right, met his master Scotto.[258] At that time, Scotto performed at various Italian courts, as well as in Venice. In 1574, for example, he is mentioned in the correspondence of the court at Novellara—the very same side branch of the Gonzaga family that was promoting Colorni at the time.[259] It is also possible that the two men met during Colorni's years in Prague. At this time Scotto was indeed periodically residing at the imperial court, where he garnered great attention with his magic and his bombastic behavior.

Scotto may have been one of Colorni's mentors, even if not the only one. Ultimately, however, the question of who initiated Colorni into the craft of magic is likely to remain open. By contrast, it is easier to address the central question of how Colorni understood magic and the role of the magus. We have seen how he made an effort to distinguish himself as a learned *professore de' secreti,* how he propagated a systematic and scientific *magia naturalis* while attacking "superstition." How do these attitudes fit in with a Colorni who conjured up precious stones in full view of astonished onlookers and knew how to guess what was on the face of a concealed playing card? This is a contradiction only at first glance. After all, we find the same phenomenon in the case of Della Porta, the very prototype of the learned professor of secrets. Indeed, some of the tricks with which Colorni caused a stir hark back to the common repertoire of the *magia naturalis,* as popularized by Della Porta's eponymous treatise from the 1550s. If one takes as a yardstick the definition of *magia naturalis* that was coined around the middle of the seventeenth century by Caspar Schott (1608–1666)—a Jesuit and admirer of Athanasius Kircher—then Colorni was an exemplary exponent of it. According to this view, natural magic was the "perfection of natural wisdom and pinnacle of the secret sciences" as well as the "capacity to accomplish miraculous and unusual things in a secret fashion."[260]

But where exactly was the borderline for contemporaries between legitimate *magia naturalis* and black magic? Explicit renunciation of sorcery, as well as of attempts to conjure up the devil and his ilk, was an important factor.[261] Nonetheless, it is impossible to give a general answer to this question. Even in the seventeenth century, rather harmless feats of the kind Colorni willingly performed could easily arouse suspicion. Occasionally, just performing sleight-of-hand tricks could lead to excommunication by the church.[262] In the Christian world, the legitimacy of the magus ultimately depended on the kind of rhetoric he used. For example, Scotto was widely regarded as an exponent of black magic, while Della Porta did not have this reputation. Like his fifteenth-century predecessor Marsilio Ficino, Della Porta and his followers made an effort to present their own interests in magic as part of an overall concern with the secrets of nature, a kind of research into nature's hidden potentials and a "science" in its own right.[263] The art of prudent self-fashioning was among the many talents that the practitioner of a learned *magia naturalis* needed to master.

By the same token, Colorni emphasized that his feats were a matter of natural magic. Perhaps this was the reason he agreed to grant his Christian admirer Garzoni a look behind the scenes. Garzoni was proud to report that the Jewish magus had revealed to him, under the seal of confidentiality, the natural secrets behind some of his tricks.[264] In the *Piazza universale,* Garzoni had already announced that Colorni's magic was "purely natural."[265] Now he reaffirmed that Colorni had always remained true to the principles of so-called white magic while performing these feats. What is more, Colorni could be included among those thoroughly steeped in the knowledge of *magia naturalis*.[266]

Such an assessment from Garzoni's pen must have been most welcome to Colorni, and he may even have asked for the endorsement. An attestation printed in black and white by a Catholic cleric saying that these feats were not a matter of black magic could protect Colorni against many an inconvenience, not least against trouble from the Inquisition. As a Jew appearing before Christian audiences, Colorni had good reason to avoid being associated with black magic. Christians frequently believed that Jews possessed magical skills by definition.[267] A brief glance into Colorni's own time illustrates how quickly concrete accusations could arise. In 1599, for example, two Jews in Vienna were accused of causing a thousand head of cattle to perish by magic.[268] Just a short time later in France, a renowned Jewish court physician of Portuguese extraction, Eliahu Montalto (d. 1616), was accused of magic and sorcery.[269] And a year after Colorni's death, some of his very first promoters—the ducal Gonzaga family—joined hundreds of spectators in Mantua as they gathered around the stake on which an aged Jewish woman was burned alive owing to an accusation of witchcraft.[270]

Whether he liked it or not, Colorni could not avoid Christians attributing a special competence in magic to him as a Jew. In the late 1580s, the Duke of Mantua commissioned him to translate into Italian the *Clavicula Salomonis*, a text then shrouded in secrets and suspicions. The *Clavicula Salomonis* was a corpus of "nigromantic-astro-magical works" attributed to King Solomon.[271] Viewed objectively, this work should more properly be discussed in the plural, as the *Claviculae Salomonis*, since the differences between the treatises circulating under this title are considerable.[272] In public libraries in North America and Europe alone, we know today of 122 Latin manuscripts titled *Clavicula Salomonis;* the number would be considerably larger if manuscripts surviving in archives were added.[273] The first extant Latin manuscripts date back to the early fourteenth century, and this corpus grew significantly during the sixteenth century.[274] We have to draw a distinction between these Latin editions and the Greek manuscripts of the *Clavicula,* which are late Byzantine versions from the fifteenth century.

Medieval manuscripts of the *Clavicula* are as good as nonextant. Most of them likely fell victim to the destructive frenzy of the authorities—especially the church, which regarded the work as extremely dangerous.[275] Tales about the abuse of the *Clavicula* circulated early. One legend recounts a Jewish sorcerer named Aaron who was said to have worked as an advisor to the Byzantine emperor and commanded entire legions of evil spirits.[276] It should come as no surprise to learn that well-known preachers such as Bernardino da Siena expressly denounced the *Clavicula* and those who studied it.[277] Of course, such warnings hardly spoiled the work's popularity. In early modern Venice, for example, the *Clavicula* was apparently the most coveted magic book—and the one that led to the most interrogations by the Inquisition.[278] In the highest aristocratic circles, too, there was a Europe-wide interest in the work.[279] Unsurprisingly, the *Clavicula* appears in the very first version of the Catholic Church's *Index librorum prohibitorum.*[280] Yet the prohibition's effect was limited. Even the Enlightenment could barely harm this work's popularity. True, Georg von Welling rendered a harsh verdict in his *Opus mago-cabbalisticum et theologicum* (1708–1721), a work that also interested Goethe, with Welling castigating "these kinds of devilish writings and books, not least of which is the so-called Claviculae [*sic*] Salomonis."[281] Voltaire likewise mocked the *Clavicula.*[282] Yet the book actually experienced a boom during the eighteenth century, especially in France.[283]

If there ever was an urtext of the *Clavicula,* it was likely written in Greek in late antiquity.[284] Certain ritual and parareligious elements of the *Clavicula* also indicate influences from Jewish magic in the era of Hellenism and late antiquity.[285] Chapters from the Hebrew magic book *Sefer Raziel* also found their way into versions of the *Clavicula.*[286] But the *Clavicula* is not an unadulterated testimonial to Jewish magic from these eras. Rather, the work was also shaped by ideas from Hermetic magic—especially in its astrological parts.[287] Throughout the Middle Ages, elements of magical literature mined from Byzantine, Arabic, and Latin sources were deposited, one layer after another, on different versions of the *Clavicula*.[288] Well into the twentieth century, however, it was assumed that an original Hebrew version of the work must have existed. This tied in with the idea that a text whose authorship was attributed to the biblical King Solomon must have originally been written in Hebrew.[289] On the title pages of numerous early modern Italian and French versions of *Clavicula* manuscripts, we find a statement saying that the text was originally written in Hebrew, under the title *Mafteach Shelomo*, and only later translated into Italian.[290] This translation has been associated with Abramo Colorni since the end of the sixteenth century.

In reality, the process of transmitting the text almost certainly ran in the opposite direction. Today, the earliest extant Hebrew manuscripts of the *Clavicula* date back to the seventeenth century and were actually translated either from Italian or Latin.[291] Still, the dissemination of Colorni's "translation" starting in the 1590s marks a turning point in the history of the *Clavicula*'s influence.[292] This version in particular, enveloped as it was by the aura of a translation from the Hebrew original (and by a Jew at that), was coveted well beyond Italy.[293] We cannot rule out the possibility that Colorni really did base his Italian translation on a Hebrew version that is missing today.[294] However, no such prototype has been discovered, and it is likely that such a version in itself would still have been a translation from Latin. We actually know that a relatively old Latin copy of the *Clavicula* existed in the Gonzaga library in Mantua as early as 1407.[295] It is possible that, almost two centuries later, this copy aroused the interest of Duke Vincenzo I and led him to commission Colorni to locate an even older Hebrew (ur)text and translate it into Italian. Some scholars have claimed that the translation project was ultimately a combination of the "Duke of Mantua's typically Renaissance desire for a (Hebrew) urtext with philological charlatanry on the part of Abramo Colorni."[296] But this is easier to assert than to prove. To begin with, it is entirely possible that Colorni, just like his contemporaries and his ducal patron, was convinced that an original Hebrew version did exist. Moreover, we cannot say anything about the quality of the text that Colorni produced, since none of the extant Italian manuscripts can be identified as an original copy of his "translation." The many copies circulating under his name do not permit us to make any conclusive statements about the philological qualities of his work. For example, there are obvious differences between all three seventeenth- and eighteenth-century French manuscripts of the *Clavicula Salomonis* that are located today in the British Library, all of which claim to be based on the translation attributed to Colorni.[297]

The question remains as to why Colorni accepted a ducal assignment that was bound to channel him into the waters of black magic. As with his *Chirofisionomia,* the explanation probably lies in the exigencies of the patronage relationship that Colorni had established with Vincenzo Gonzaga— and which he was interested in deepening even further. This entailed jobs that Colorni could probably not refuse, even if he wanted to. He may also have seen an opportunity in the assignment. The historian Richard Kieckhefer has argued that Jews did not adopt Solomonic magic literature primarily owing to an interest in black magic. Rather, he sees a larger "quest of knowledge through magical means" as a decisive reason for the preoccupation with this corpus of texts.[298] Colorni never claimed that he wanted to achieve his aims by way of black magic. This does not exclude the possibility that he used the *Clavicula Salomonis* as a source of ideas for feats that he could incorporate into his "repertoire" as professor of secrets. This likely held true for the secret of *disprigionare* (escape)—a secret to which Colorni would later turn in a politically explosive situation.

Above all, translating the *Clavicula* opened up an opportunity for Colorni to have the glory of the venerable Solomonic tradition shine on him. This was beneficial to him at the courts of both Mantua and Ferrara, where interest in Solomonic magic literature was lively.[299] Being associated with the legendary biblical king allowed a Jew to claim a distinctive role for himself in the economy of secrets. Indeed, the *Clavicula* was a book that elevated King Solomon to the status of magus and even stylized him into a kind of Jewish Hermes Trismegistos.[300] This ties in with the observation that the Hermetic elements of the work are less pronounced in the Colorni versions of *Clavicula* manuscripts.[301]

Colorni was not alone among his Jewish and Christian contemporaries in his fascination with the biblical King Solomon. Many contemporary Jews regarded the wise king who had built the temple and was credited with supernatural powers as a shining light whose knowledge, including in the field of natural science, was older than everything derived from heathen and Christian authorities.[302] Invoking various biblical passages, some Christians and Jews even maintained that the king had mastered the secrets of alchemy and physiognomy.[303] No less eminent was Solomon's authority as a magician, even beyond the *Clavicula Salomonis* literature.[304] Some Jews maintained that Solomon had written a "Book of the Secrets of Nature."[305] The notion that Solomon was well-versed in secrets was also widespread in popular Jewish literature. The frequently published and widely read *Mayse-Bukh* (first published in Basel in 1602) includes a story in which King Solomon gives one of his students three pearls of wisdom to take along on life's journey. The third is the advice never to reveal his own secrets to a woman. Years later, the student fails to take this piece of wisdom to heart, which nearly results in his being condemned to death. Only an appeal for clemency with King Solomon brings about a turn of events and an acquittal, whereupon the wise king once again urges caution in dealing with secrets—even within one's own family.[306]

For Jews, tracing their own scientific and magical activities back to King Solomon meant ennobling such activities and protecting them against Christian polemics.[307] What is more, the appeal to Solomon allowed Jews to claim for themselves a genuinely Jewish *prisca sapientia*. Next to the wise king, even a figure like Hermes Trismegistos would seem a mere epigone. Colorni, too, employed the aura associated with the Solomonic tradition. It allowed him to combine and harmonize the roles of Jew, scholar, engineer, alchemist, and magus. The result was his self-fashioning as a Jewish *professore de' secreti* who, like King Solomon of old, strove to know all of nature's secrets. Situating himself in this way did not just lend Colorni legitimacy within the Jewish community. In relations with the outside world, it was no less advantageous to evoke associations with the Solomonic tradition. Solomon's reputation as one of the greatest secrecy adepts of all times was undisputed among Christians. As late as the eighteenth century, the biblical verses about those for whom "the secret of the Lord is with them" were chiefly regarded as a reference to Solomon.[308] In England, for example, outright admiration for the biblical king was widespread in Puritan circles, which elevated Solomon into a model for the scholarly exploration of nature and its secrets.[309] Recall that Francis Bacon, in his widely read social-scientific utopia *New Atlantis,* called the central institution of the island state "Salomon's House."[310] To be sure, in Bacon's narrative this name actually stems from a fictitious character, the island king Solamona. That notwithstanding, Salomon's House is clearly meant to be associated with the biblical king.[311] Bacon was not the only early modern Christian who regarded Solomon as a king whose empire and riches rested on his technological and scientific expertise.[312] In early modern times, the temple of Solomon became both a powerful metaphor in itself and an idealized site for the pursuit of knowledge as universal as it was arcane.[313] In fact, Colorni opened his *Scotographia* with a comparison between the Rudolphine imperial court and the Solomonic temple. In Colorni's eyes, the Habsburg emperor—so often described by contemporaries as the "German Hermes Trismegistos"—became an heir to King Solomon, and, by extension, Colorni became a collaborator in the project of recovering Solomonic wisdom.[314] No less revealing is the way in which Colorni singles out a proverb by Solomon as one way to demonstrate his cryptographic method. As we will see, this proverb praises those who know how to keep a secret—which reveals much about Colorni's ideal image of a Solomonic *professore de' secreti.*

"Arcana imperii," "Imperium arcanorum": The Imperial Court of Rudolf II

The year 1588 was a watershed in Colorni's life. It marks the start of his almost decade-long activity in the power center of the Holy Roman Empire. Throughout all those years, Colorni's work north of the Alps was, as we shall see, closely tied in with the political and military events of the time. Indeed, his original appointment came at a moment of crisis for the House of Habsburg. In the dispute over the Polish crown, the Swedish Prince Sigismund Vasa defeated and arrested the Habsburg Archduke Maximilian—who was a brother of Emperor Rudolf II—in 1588. The archduke's capture was a hard blow, both politically and personally, to the fickle emperor.

Indeed, these events "greatly troubled the mind of the Emperor," as an informant at the English court reported at the time.[315] Only later would it emerge that the fate of the archduke was not as dramatic as had been feared. Maximilian had hardly been put into irons by the Polish troops allied with Sigismund Vasa. Instead, he was placed under house arrest in a rural area, where he was able to move about freely on the grounds and practice the "Waidwerk," or art of hunting. He was even allowed to celebrate carnival during his captivity.[316]

Meanwhile, in the Holy Roman Empire, feverish efforts were under way to free the archduke from captivity. The emperor requested assistance from various European princes, including the Duke of Ferrara.[317] The emperor wanted to see the archduke freed as quickly as possible, but he also preferred it to be done peacefully. A courtier from Ferrara finally realized that Duke Alfonso had a Jew in his service who could be entrusted with this difficult task. The idea was not entirely farfetched. Colorni enjoyed the reputation of being able to break out of any prison.[318] Garzoni had already mentioned Colorni's special talent in a colorful passage of his *Piazza universale,* which would certainly have helped spread this reputation.[319] Colorni himself claimed he had the talent of *disprigionare.*[320] He might have picked up this idea during his translation of the *Clavicula Salomonis*. Indeed, contemporary manuscripts of this work, including later Hebrew editions, contain magical instructions for breaking out of prison.[321] One repeatedly encounters similar instructions in the Jewish and Christian magical literature of the time.[322] In any event, Colorni's contemporaries took his claim seriously. Proudly anticipating the emperor's gratitude, the court of Ferrara began preparations for the Jewish court engineer's mission "in all secrecy" ("con ogni segretezza"). As a precaution, Colorni was even instructed to avoid contact with Polish merchants. He arrived in Prague in May 1588.[323]

The nearly nine years that Colorni would spend at the imperial court in Prague are among the least well-known chapters of his life. The main sources we have from modern publications dealing with the Rudolphine court are silent about Colorni; he is also almost entirely absent from historical studies on this subject.[324] Conversely, none of the historians who have dealt with Colorni have ever consulted sources from the Habsburg archives. This is all the more surprising because, in many respects, Colorni reached the pinnacle of his career during his time in Prague. What is more, he soon rose to become one of the emperor's favorites among the numerous alchemists and arcanists on the Hradčany. Colorni's absence from the imperial court's staff lists has little significance. After all, most of Rudolf's nearly fifty alchemists are missing from these lists, since their work was financed out of the emperor's private funds.[325] By contrast, there is no lack of archival sources about Colorni in the files of the imperial court chamber, and these sources allow us to construct a much fuller picture of the Prague years.[326] A number of previously unknown original letters that Colorni sent from Prague have also surfaced in Italian archives. In these letters, Colorni occasionally complained about being separated from his family, which had remained behind in Italy. But it is also clear that he fully understood how to value the career opportunities and the room for maneuver that the imperial court afforded him.

At that time, the court of Rudolf II constituted a unique intellectual and artistic cosmos.[327] Around 1600, no fewer than 124 artists and artisans were on the court payroll, including the famous painters Giuseppe Arcimboldo and Hans von Aachen. Overall, the imperial court comprised almost a thousand people.[328] At that time, Prague was also a center for secret arts and sciences of all kinds. Emperor Rudolf II (r. 1552–1612) initiated and actively promoted this development.[329] There were also generous patrons of the occult sciences among the Bohemian aristocracy, including Peter Wok von Rosenberg (1539–1611), who employed numerous alchemists and compiled a widely known collection of curiosa.[330] Yet the attraction that the court of Rudolf II exerted on arcanists and natural scientists throughout Europe remained unsurpassed. The passion that the melancholic and eccentric emperor harbored for the occult sciences, and especially for alchemy, was widely known among his contemporaries.

Older scholarship regarded this passion as a character weakness and the activities at the court in Prague as a wrong track in the history of science.[331] Today, historians tend to view the research and experiments undertaken at the court as an expression of the emperor's politically connoted striving for universal knowledge and for the establishment of an ideal society. The overlap between politics, art, and the occult was highly fluid under Rudolf's rule.[332] As Pamela Smith has shown, alchemy in particular played the role of a "language of mediation" at the imperial court.[333] In the practice and rhetoric of alchemy, tensions between practitioners with different confessional backgrounds were often neutralized. In general, denominational factors faded into the background in light of Rudolf's ambitious and wide-ranging thirst for knowledge. Although the highest offices at court were primarily staffed by Catholics, the circle of scholars, artists, and artisans there formed a denominationally heterogeneous society.[334]

Many of the most famous alchemists, astrologers, and magi of the time stayed for shorter or longer periods at Prague Castle, where they sought to gain the emperor's patronage. Especially well-known to this day are the visits of the English mathematician and magus John Dee, who spent time at the imperial court in the mid-1580s together with the fraudulent alchemist Edward Kelley. The Hermetic philosopher Giordano Bruno also presented himself at Rudolf's court. Michael Maier (1569–1622), Oswald Croll (1560–1609), and Michael Sendivogius (1566–1636)—some of the most prominent alchemists of the late sixteenth century—likewise came to Prague. Noted Christian Kabbalists contributed to the interest in Hebrew mysticism at court.[335] Finally, distinguished naturalists, some of whom are today portrayed as pioneers of modern natural science, also worked for Rudolf II. The most famous were Tycho Brahe (1546–1601) and Johannes Kepler (1571–1630). Brahe stayed in Prague from 1599 until his death, and Kepler held the post of court mathematician from 1600 to 1612. Kepler could not have gotten to know Colorni in Prague, since the Jewish alchemist had already left the court in 1597. But we cannot rule out the possibility that Kepler was acquainted with Colorni's name, even if this was more likely in connection with Colorni's later relocation to Württemberg, Kepler's homeland.[336]

Colorni's first weeks in Prague were arduous and frustrating. The emperor let several weeks go by before he received Colorni. In the meantime, Colorni—who must have realized how momentous and daring his claim was, and whose family back in Mantua was getting short on money—fell gravely ill.[337] His arrival in Prague also caused more of a stir than the secrecy-minded diplomats at the imperial court thought proper.[338] Not until July 1588 did Colorni finally get an audience with Rudolf II. To the amazement of the emperor's courtiers, it lasted almost three hours. During this conversation, Colorni succeeded in performing perhaps his greatest feat: instead of presenting Rudolf with his would-be—yet in practice hardly feasible—plan to liberate the archduke, Colorni began telling the emperor stories on subjects ranging from gambling to the manufacture of harquebuses. These stories did not miss their mark with the emperor, whose fascination with the arcane and miraculous was almost unlimited. A consternated Ferrarese ambassador reported back to Italy that the conversation revolved "around games, harquebuses, and such things," without a word being spoken about the rescue mission ("senza parlar punto dello sprigionare").[339] Nonetheless, the emperor took a fancy to the Italian Jew's promises ("mostra di haver gusto della persona"). He kept Colorni at his court for almost nine years.[340]

Colorni had apparently done his best to divert attention from the real reason for his deployment to Prague. Here, he benefited from the course of time. There were indications that the negotiations between the imperial and Polish side would lead to the archduke's peaceful release. This goal was finally reached with the so-called Pacification Treaty in early 1589. Sending Colorni behind enemy lines would have entailed an unnecessary risk for negotiations in the summer of 1588, even if it is entirely conceivable that the emperor fundamentally believed in Colorni's reputation as a *disprigionatore*. In any event, the decision against executing this plan had nothing to do with Colorni's Jewish background. In fact, the Habsburgs were hardly hesitant about involving Jews in their military and political-diplomatic operations if necessary. Tellingly, it was actually a Polish Jew—who, like Colorni, had made a name for himself as an engineer—who took part in the negotiations to release the archduke.[341]

Colorni had every reason to be pleased about the turn of events and about the emperor's goodwill.[342] By August 1588, the emperor had gone ahead and allocated a rent-free house to Colorni.[343] In this "comfortable house," apparently in Prague's Old Town, Colorni's physical well-being was also provided for. A contented Colorni wrote home that an Italian-speaking Jewish couple had been assigned to him, among other reasons to provide him with Italian cuisine. A guard was also seconded so that this Jew living in a prominent and privileged position would not be harassed.[344]

The multitalented newcomer from Ferrara was able to offer the emperor a variety of services. Buying jewelry was apparently one of these. We know that Rudolf raised several thousand thalers "to pay for the Oriental diamond purchased by Abraham the Jew."[345] The expensive precious stone was one in a series of "wares purchased in Venice [by Abraham]." Ironically, the emperor wanted to pay for these goods by collecting fines from prominent Jews in the empire. The supposition that a Jew named in the sources as "Abraham" was Colorni is bolstered by Italian documents from the time showing that Colorni's son Simone was actually staying in Venice during the late 1580s in connection with jewelry purchases.[346]

However, what the emperor wanted above all was a steady stream of new inventions and feats. At first, discoveries in mathematics and practical applications for mirrors aroused the emperor's enthusiasm. Then his interest shifted to questions of weapons production. Finally, Colorni's audiences with the emperor revolved around all manner of card games and magic tricks again. The ruler also enjoyed Colorni's writings and a sundial he constructed.[347] Colorni even designed a little box with mirrors in which living or dead family members could supposedly be seen. Did this cross the line to charlatanism, or even to bogus claims? In order to answer this question, we need to investigate what this magic mirror could possibly have been all about. Some evidence indicates that it had to do with effects created either by a distorting mirror or by anamorphoses that were then straightened out using a cylindrical mirror. Mirrors like this also could be found, for example, in the "curiosity cabinet" completed in 1631 for the Swedish King Gustavus Adolphus.[348] In the literature from the field of *magia naturalis*, instructions on how to produce or use these kinds of mirrors enjoyed great popularity.[349] Ultimately, though, it remains an elusive task for the historian to reconstruct the technique Colorni used to provide Rudolf II with supernatural "insights." In any case, and this is the crucial point, the emperor, and perhaps the inventor himself, believed in what they thought they were seeing. In this regard, evidence was created not only by what one could actually see in the mirror, but also by invoking the long tradition of occult literature.[350] There was a widespread view at the time that magic mirrors had already existed in antiquity, and even in biblical times.[351] In the sixteenth century, there were different theories about mirrors and their magical properties. In particular, the Paracelsian and pseudo-Paracelsian literature was a rich resource for addressing questions such as how to see events at great distances, in both a spatial and a temporal sense.[352] Looking into a magic mirror was an act overlaid with certain associations and expectations. This included the idea that Jews were especially well-suited to handle magic mirrors. Even after 1700, a legend reaching back into the Late Middle Ages was still being passed down about one Rabbi Simeon of Mainz, whose house contained mirrors "in which he could see everything that had happened and was still to happen."[353] In the ghetto of Venice, as elsewhere, some Jews even earned their keep by peddling various arts involving magic mirrors. As we have seen, the aristocratic traveler Johann Weichard Valvasor has left us a vivid description of his consultation with a "magical mirror that was made only of glass" around 1679 in the Venetian ghetto.[354]

It is important to keep such traditions in mind in order to provide a context for the kind of feats Colorni performed—feats that today would merely be derided as some kind of magical mystery show using special effects. In any case, the emperor is said to have "highly" enjoyed Colorni's diverse inventions.[355] He thanked the Duke of Ferrara personally for the "delight" afforded by Colorni's stay at the court.[356] In Ferrara, these words must have been received with great satisfaction, and the court there must have also attached political hopes to Rudolf's gratitude. Indeed, it would be shortsighted to view Colorni's dispatch to Prague solely in connection with the fate of the archduke. While the Duke of Ferrara probably believed in Colorni's ability to liberate the emperor's brother from captivity, dispatching the Jewish courtier was no mere altruistic gesture. Substantial political motives were certainly in play. To begin with, it was advantageous for Alfonso II to have an additional liaison at the imperial court. At that time the Duke of Ferrara entertained ambitious plans well beyond the horizon of his territory. He was, for instance, preparing a candidacy for the Polish crown.[357] Quite apart from such political adventures, it had become a matter of great political importance for the Duke of Ferrara to maintain good contacts with the empire, and especially with the emperor. It was increasingly apparent that even Alfonso's third marriage was going to leave him childless and thus without a natural heir. Although a hereditary regulation in favor of his illegitimate cousin Don Cesare d'Este was legally possible and dynastically acceptable in Ferrara, this kind of solution did not meet with Rome's approval. The pope openly threatened to have Ferrara revert to the Papal States should Alfonso die without a natural male heir. This is what eventually happened upon Alfonso's death in 1597. Just a year later, it led to the breakup of the Este territory.

In the 1580s and early 1590s, however, the duchy's fate was still open. At the court of Ferrara, there were feverish efforts to get the emperor on Alfonso's side and thereby weaken the pope's argument. Substantial sums of money and high-ranking emissaries went from Ferrara to Prague.[358] Ferrara even offered to disclose secret weapons technologies to the emperor.[359] Every year the emperor and the archduke also received deliveries from Ferrara containing luxurious or hard-to-find gifts, including rare plants and exotic spices.[360] These efforts by Alfonso, who began to wear only black clothes during the last years of his life, were well-known in political circles throughout Europe.[361]

Sending Colorni to Prague, then, was a clever move on the part of the duke, especially since there was talk of resuming negotiations about the enfeoffment of Modena and Reggio at that very moment.[362] Although Colorni never held an official position at the imperial court, he did gain Rudolf's trust within a short period of time. For the court in Ferrara, this was all the more important in light of the major problems the duke's emissaries in Prague repeatedly faced just trying to establish contact with the melancholy and reclusive emperor. The case of the Ferrarese emissary Count Guido Calcagnino—who complained about how hard it was for him, a nobleman, to gain admission to see the emperor during a 1592 mission to Prague—is telling.[363] Colorni's proximity to the emperor gave the court in Ferrara a promising contact who could represent Alfonso's interests. This helps explain why Colorni remained on the payroll of the Ferrarese court, imperial honoraria aside.

The Gonzaga family in Mantua, which had its own political reasons for wanting to secure the emperor's goodwill, must also have hoped to get information from its former courtier. Vincenzo Gonzaga was involved in a bitter territorial dispute about the town of Castel Goffredo and sought the emperor's intervention on his side. From August through October 1595, the duke even stayed in Prague with a large delegation, including his famous court conductor Claudio Monteverdi.[364] Vincenzo's attempts to deepen relations with the imperial court dovetailed with Colorni's growing wish, since the mid-1590s, to return eventually to service for the Gonzaga family, which meant obtaining favor with the court in Mantua. Indeed, the correspondence between the Gonzaga ambassador in Prague and the court in Mantua contains repeated references to and original letters from Colorni.[365] In short, Colorni was a promising contact both for his employer in Ferrara and for his former patrons, the Gonzaga family. He profited not only from his proximity to the emperor, but also from his contacts with Rudolf's closest circle. Colorni was well-networked at the court in Prague. In a way, this tied in with a prevalent expectation among Christians that Jews had a natural talent for the role of liaison and confidant. Royal courts on both sides of the Alps often sought Jews' services in situations that required discretion or even secrecy. It is no accident that Vincenzo Gonzaga appointed his Jewish court actor Leone de' Sommi to be one of three agents entrusted, under strictest confidence, with sounding out the duke's chances regarding his candidacy for the Polish crown.[366]

Quite apart from such general notions regarding Jews and their mastery of secrets, the question of whom exactly Colorni got to know at court in Prague remains. Most important, of course, was his closeness to the emperor himself. The outbreak of the Long Turkish War in 1593, which required the emperor to devote more time to military and political obligations, might have affected Colorni's proximity to Rudolf II.[367] Even at this time, however, Colorni could fall back on his contacts with people from the ruler's closest circle. The Venetian ambassador, who usually observed the alchemical and occult activities at the imperial court rather skeptically, was favorably inclined toward Colorni and reported home that he was highly esteemed at court ("molto estimato qui in Corte").[368] According to these letters, Colorni cultivated contacts with the court chamberlain Wolfgang Rumpf—then the emperor's most influential councilor—as well as with an unnamed personal physician at the imperial court.[369] The latter must have been either Moses Lucerna—a Jewish physician who had also grown up in Mantua—or the Christian historiographer and physician Claudius Ancantherus.[370] For his part, Ancantherus composed introductory poems for Colorni's *Chirofisionomia*.[371] Colorni's letters from Prague also repeatedly make mention of his excellent contacts with the Italian ambassadors.[372] Later, Colorni even spoke of "all the friends" that he had left behind after his departure from Prague.[373]

But how did things stand regarding Colorni's relations with the Prague Jewish community? Astonishingly, he has so far remained almost unmentioned in the numerous historical studies of early modern Prague's Jewish community. Nothing is known about his contacts with the community, which was then a major cultural center for Central European Jewry. At this time, roughly three thousand Jews lived in the city, making it the largest Jewish community in the Holy Roman Empire. During the first decade of Rudolf's rule, the economic situation of Jews in Prague and Bohemia had generally improved. The emperor granted Jews permission to practice a number of crafts, including the professions of goldsmith, silversmith, and jeweler.[374] Colorni's time in Prague fell into the first half of Rudolf's reign that historians sometimes call the "Golden Age" of Prague Jewry.[375] However, relations between the emperor and the Jewish community would soon rupture after he confiscated the estate of the recently deceased court Jew Mordechai Meyzl (1528–1601); the alleged Frankfurt "rabbinical conspiracy" of 1603 led to further acts of repression.[376]

Meyzl was an Ashkenazic Jew who distinguished himself both as a banker and as an art supplier to Rudolf II. He held a leading economic position within the Bohemian Jewish community during Colorni's years in Prague. As we have seen, there is some evidence that Meyzl was involved in delivering the so-called Prague Ḥoshen, a valuable amulet with magical inscriptions, to the emperor.[377] To this day, the synagogue in Prague named after Meyzl recalls this versatile court Jew, who also made a name for himself as a patron on behalf of Jewish causes. In the late sixteenth century, there were also a number of Italian Jews staying in the Bohemian capital. Most were merchants who made their money trading in spices, luxury goods, and precious metals.[378] The best-known were the brothers Jacob and Samuel Bassevi. They had been living in Bohemia since the 1590s, and over the years they would make a fortune as wholesale merchants. During the Thirty Years War, Jacob became involved in the coin business and was ultimately ennobled in the 1620s by Emperor Ferdinand II, after which he went by the name Jacob von Treuenberg.[379]

Among the spiritual heads of the Jewish community in late-sixteenth-century Prague was the famous Maharal, or "High Rabbi" Judah Loew ben Bezalel—the purported creator of the legendary golem (see Chapter 3).[380] It is possible that there were contacts between the Maharal and Colorni. Both Rabbi Loew and his student David Gans (1541–1613), who made a name as a chronicler and astronomer, were quite open to research in the natural sciences and astronomy as a supplement to rabbinical training.[381] In February 1592, there was even a legendary, secret conversation between Rabbi Loew and Emperor Rudolf. It is tempting to speculate about whether Colorni had a hand in bringing about this encounter.[382] The "High Rabbi of Prague" followed discussions about the Copernican revolution, though he and Gans ultimately rejected the new theory as incompatible with the Bible. In the eyes of the Maharal and his circle, science was acceptable and welcome as long as it did not question the foundations of holy scripture. Despite all his fascination with practical sciences such as medicine and astrology, he could not accept them as the "ultimate explanation of the cosmos."[383] Loew likened human explorations of earthly phenomena to ascending a ladder ultimately leading to the comprehensive wisdom of the Torah.

Colorni, whose house in Prague's Old Town was apparently outside the Jewish quarter, did not necessarily need to establish contacts with the Prague Jewish community in order to encounter coreligionists daily.[384] Indeed, he was not the only Jew at the imperial court. What is more, some members of the court either had Jewish ancestors or had converted to Christianity.[385] This was the case with the ambassador from Ferrara,

Ascanio Giraldini, who was an important interlocutor for Colorni, especially during his first few months at the imperial court. Giraldini was a rabbi's son who converted to Christianity as a young man but whose Jewish background remained known in court circles.[386] The courtier Philipp Lang, who rose rapidly after 1603 to become the Emperor's *Kammerdiener*, and thus one of the most powerful men at the court in Prague, was also believed to be a convert, even if that belief was groundless. Lang was demonstrably involved in alchemical and magical activities at court. Following his downfall, others accused him of having tinkered with the *Sigillum Salomonis*, a magic book, as well as with obscure notes written in Hebrew.[387]

By contrast, Prague native Joachim Gans (Gaunse)—a Jewish metallurgist and mining engineer, who was not related to David Gans—resisted conversion. Joachim emigrated to England in the early 1580s after the Society of Mines Royal there recruited him. In England, he soon acquired the reputation of an esteemed "Minerall man." In 1585, he joined a two-year expedition to North America under the leadership of Sir Walter Raleigh. Gans was among the first settlers in the North American colony of Roanoke, located in modern-day North Carolina, where he surveyed mineral deposits.[388] While Colorni is unlikely to have met him in Prague, Gans's case underscores the fact that Jewish employment at the imperial court was not out of the ordinary. In the mid-1580s, John Dee even wrote in his diaries about the influence of some unnamed Jews on Emperor Rudolf II.[389]

At the Prague court, there were indeed Jews in positions surrounded by a distinctly arcane aura. Colorni's contemporary Mardochaeus de Nelle—an alchemist whose background and career remain mysterious to this day—is particularly noteworthy. Very little is known about this man who worked as a chronicler and panegyrist of alchemical experiments.[390] To complicate matters, his name has circulated in different variations, including "Martinus de Delle," "Mardochaeus de Delle," "Mordechai de Nello," or just plain "de Nelle."[391] The form "Delle" might have been a misspelling that got into circulation owing to a copyist's error. By contrast, the name "Nelle" seems more plausible, as it is occasionally attested among Italian Jews and derives either from "Netanel" or "Leonello," which would correspond to the Hebrew Aryeh.[392] The question of naming is not, however, the only enigma in his biography. Historian of alchemy Joachim Telle has rightly called Nelle a "Rabbi and alchemical author largely shrouded in darkness."[393] Nelle's laudatory poems about the fate of famous alchemists exist only as fragmentary copies.[394] His poetry also includes panegyrics to alchemists from earlier times. Thus, Nelle praises his role model Paracelsus as a connoisseur "of hidden, High, and Secret Matters / Making one's Heart jump for Joy."[395]

In addition, several treatises on alchemy were attributed to Nelle, probably accurately, after he died. Examples include a commentary on Paracelsus, a "Discourse on Universal Things," a *Schmelzkunst* (book on the art of smelting), a work called *Philosophische Meditationen* (a book of philosophical meditations), and an instruction manual on how to carry out a chemical sublimation.[396] Some seventeenth- and eighteenth-century works assert that Nelle was born in Vitri [*sic*], near Milan.[397] We cannot know whether this claim is true; the same goes for the assertion that he was a Polish Jew.[398] Speculation about his conversion is almost certainly unfounded.[399] It is less clear whether Nelle is identical with a Jew named "Martino l'Italien" who occasionally appears in Prague's customs records from the 1590s.[400] We can, however, clearly refute the eighteenth-century view that Nelle was a *Kammerdiener* of Rudolf II.[401] Like most of the emperor's alchemists, Nelle does not even appear on the court staff lists, and his salary must have come out of the emperor's private coffers.

To what extent was Nelle involved in the alchemical experiments he celebrated in his poetry? In an alchemical manuscript written after 1600, a highly suggestive remark about Nelle indicates that "this Jew was not a child when it came to chemistry."[402] It seems likely that Nelle, whose son was also involved in alchemy, was a seasoned alchemist.[403] The earliest extant source on Nelle—a description of the mine in Silesian Reichenstein (Złoty Stok) from 1567—even refers to him as a "smelter" who "extracted the ore using lye, the process for which he took from Theophrastus Paracelsus' elements, having also written a special commentary on this."[404] These activities in Reichenstein might be linked to the patronage of the Rosenbergs, an aristocratic Bohemian family that was deeply involved in the business of alchemy and operated a mine and several laboratories.[405] In 1573, Nelle's presence is recorded in Cracow.[406] Ultimately, his path took him to the court of August I of Saxony, where he apparently persuaded the ruler to learn Hebrew.[407] A manuscript has been preserved from this Dresden period that seems to be the only extant autograph of a Nelle treatise. It dates from the 1570s or 1580s and bears the title, added later, "Prophecy of a Jew from the Times of the Elector August, to which the latter has added comments in the margins."[408] In this work, the author styles himself "I, Mardochaeus de Nelle, Rabbi." The treatise is divided into two parts. The first is made up of the actual prophecy, which is followed by an alchemical writing about red silver ore (pyrargyrite). The prophecy was composed especially for the Elector August I (r. 1553–1586), who was keenly interested in the occult sciences and alchemy. The prognostication, which drew on biblical images and concepts, contains annotations indicating the elector's approval. He noted that he found the work truthful and had spent a total of forty-one weeks studying the treatise.

As this survey demonstrates, Colorni was not the only Jew who conducted experiments at the imperial court. This was also no secret to contemporaries, especially those who were well-informed about courtly life in Prague. Consider the novel *Euphormionis Lusinini Satyricon,* which the contemporary Scottish writer John Barclay (1582–1621) published between 1605 and 1607.[409] This Latin-language satire became one of the most popular novels of the early seventeenth century, with almost fifty editions well into the eighteenth century.[410] Although Barclay drew on classical models, especially the *Satyricon* of Petronius, many of the themes and motifs for his satire came directly from his own times.[411] Barclay was a Catholic who had traveled extensively throughout Europe, getting his education and training in France, Italy, and England; he was also knowledgeable about contemporary Prague. Indeed, his book, which deals with the fictitious first-person narrator Euphormio's apprenticeship and journeyman years, is also a roman à clef about the court of Rudolf II, who was still in power at the time. In one chapter, Euphormio describes a visit to the court of the king of Thebes, named Aquilius. Contemporaries understood that the Thebans stood for the Germans and that the fictitious ruler Aquilius was no other than Rudolf II.[412] Not only did the reality of the Rudolphine court inform Barclay's depiction of Aquilius, but his depiction also ended up contributing to the many legends and myths surrounding Rudolf II.[413] In the novel, the emperor appears as a loner completely engrossed in a world of fancy.[414] Even the courtiers are unable to make any inroads with him. Only artists and alchemists gain access to the ruler. Owing to the mediation of a highly placed courtier named Trifartitus, the first-person narrator finally succeeds in getting through to Aquilius and his "secrets."[415] The private chambers in which Aquilius spends most of his time are filled with wondrous objects, globes, and (mostly erotic) paintings. When the ruler is not lingering in these rooms, he is spending his time in the alchemical laboratories he has installed.[416] There, numerous alchemists are busy with ovens, vessels, and experimental devices. In this bewildering setting, though, one person stands out. It is, of all people, a Jew ("Hebraeus"). As the visitor learns, this Jew—dressed in a lavish garment—turns out to be the superintendent of all experimental activities at court and one of the king's most powerful confidants.[417]

Is this Hebraeus a portrait of Colorni or Nelle? It is entirely possible, and a modern editor of the *Satyricon* has indeed suspected that this character must have been based on a real Jewish alchemist or advisor to Rudolf II.[418] On closer examination, however, the figure of Hebraeus is hard to identify with any single historical model. The so-called keys to the work—concordances printed in the seventeenth century where readers attempted to match the numerous protagonists with real-life historical models—reinforce this impression. Hebraeus is associated with names like Mersel, Wenzel, and Senc. This points to a variety of real-life inspirations for this character in the novel.[419] As the name "Mersel" suggests, for example, Hebraeus could well have been modeled on the Rudolphine court Jew Meyzl, mentioned above. The character also bears a resemblance to the imperial *Kammerdiener* Philipp Lang, who was suspected of having been a baptized Jew.[420] It is likely, then, that features of several different real-life people, including Colorni, informed Barclay's portrait of Hebraeus. At any rate, Barclay was not the only contemporary who believed that Jews held considerable influence over the fickle emperor. A general rumor at the time asserted that "in addition to the Roman Emperor, the king of the Jews rules over the German empire."[421]

In light of such perceptions, Colorni was surely aware of the risks that threatened a Jew who tied his fortunes too closely to the emperor's goodwill. Intrigues were no rarity at the court; Rudolf's reign witnessed the downfall of various favorites who had previously experienced a meteoric rise to the top. The air was thin at the political heights Colorni had reached in Prague. The "Italian Jew" who had obtained the emperor's favor undoubtedly had enviers and enemies. Indeed, in 1589, Colorni was caught up in a maelstrom of events that would lead to a scandal on the Hradčany and make waves at several great courts of Europe. This episode has been described in older historical accounts as the "Lorraine Address to Sixtus V." But to this day, Colorni's role in the affair has been completely overlooked.

The events were triggered by a detailed letter from an emissary of the Duke of Lorraine to Pope Sixtus V. The document was leaked to the emperor, who reacted with outrage—and it is easy to see why. The "address" contained serious accusations against the emperor and the House of Habsburg.[422] Above all, it accused the Habsburgs of operating against the pope's interests. The "slanderous libel" culminated in a request for the pope to transfer rule over the Holy Roman Empire to the Duke of Lorraine. The letter explicitly cited Rudolf's weakness of character as a reason. Moreover, it accused the emperor of failing to show respect for the Catholic faith, granting protection to heretics, and almost never attending confession. In addition, he was said to have discredited himself by his excessive preoccupation with women and magic—as well as his dealings with a Jewish magician.[423] The latter was an unmistakable reference to Colorni. This was not lost on a Mantuan diplomat who summarized the "Lorraine Address" for his patrons, the Gonzaga. According to his paraphrase of this passage, no day went by without the emperor spending many hours with the Jew from Ferrara, who was a "doctor of magic."[424] This could only have meant one person—Colorni.

The enraged emperor had many of his councilors and courtiers interrogated as part of his investigations into the authorship of this infamous writing. In the course of the probe, it emerged that the letter was a forgery intended to sow discord between the emperor and the Catholic princes, especially the Duke of Lorraine.[425] The forger, who could not be apprehended, nearly succeeded. Even after the mystery of the affair was solved, the situation remained unclear. Months later, the dukes of Lorraine and Bavaria apologized for the infelicities of which they were not guilty.[426] It seems that the affair surrounding the "Lorraine Address" was also one reason why relations between Emperor Rudolf II and Pope Sixtus V soured.[427] Colorni himself apparently emerged from the affair unscathed; at least, there is nothing to indicate that his reputation suffered under the pressure of these events. He continued to have the emperor's backing for a project that he was about to tackle, and for which he would receive a privilege from Rudolf II: the *Scotographia,* Colorni's only treatise to find its way into print.

Conveying Secrets

Published in Prague in 1593 by the printer Johann Schumann (Jan Šuman), the *Scotographia* was an unusual work.[428] To begin with, it was written in Italian but published in Bohemia. The quarto's unconventional horizontal format was also striking. Upon opening the lavishly designed volume, most readers would have first marveled at dozens of pages with cryptic rows of numbers and letters. The Greek title itself was enigmatic. *Scotographia* means "dark treatise."

The author's name and religion were apparent at first glance. "Abram Colorni, Mantuan Jew" say the letters on the title page. As we have already seen, Colorni was not the only Jew preoccupied with message encryption—especially in Italy, where cryptographic treatises were much in demand. A wealth of publications like this found their way onto the market in the sixteenth century. Thus, Colorni had grounds for speculating on the success of his *Scotographia* and for putting his ambition to work on the book. He dedicated his treatise to no less a figure than Emperor Rudolf II. This suggests that the emperor was already acquainted with the work, at least in its outlines, before it was printed. Moreover, Colorni undertook a major effort to obtain the privileges necessary for the book's distribution in the leading Italian territories, including Mantua, Venice, and

Florence.[429] In addition to the quarto edition, a smaller, handy pocket edition was printed in duodecimo format.[430]

So far, there is no comprehensive study of the *Scotographia;* the treatise is also missing from most of the modern literature on the history of cryptography.[431] This absence is all the more striking given the fact that it was still being read well into the eighteenth century. As early as the 1620s, the learned Duke August of Braunschweig-Lüneburg devoted almost sixty pages of his own famous treatise on cryptography—written under the pseudonym Gustavus Selenus—to a detailed account of the *Scotographia*.[432] Only Abbot Trithemius, the fifteenth-century author of an "authoritative compendium in this field," received more space in Selenus's treatise.[433] Furthermore, the duke left no doubts about his praise for Colorni's *Scotographia*.[434] But Colorni's work was not just read in German-speaking Europe, and not only by aristocratic bibliophiles like August of Braunschweig-Lüneburg. This is evident from the duke's expression of gratitude toward the Scotsman Thomas Seghetus (ca. 1569–1627). It was this poet—who was well-networked in the Republic of Letters and was a student of Justus Lipsius, as well as a confidant of Galileo and Kepler—who had introduced the duke to Colorni's work in the first place.[435] Even a century after this episode, Johann Heinrich Zedler's monumental *Universal-Lexicon* explicitly mentions Colorni as the author of the *Scotographia*.[436]

Aristocratic circles were certainly one of the target audiences for the *Scotographia*. At the very outset, Colorni emphasized that the method he had developed was particularly useful to the "agents of princes."[437] He was well aware of the need for subjecting *arcana imperii* to strict confidentiality.[438] His aristocratic employers in Mantua and Ferrara needed little persuading on this point.[439] In the Holy Roman Empire, by contrast, royal courts were lagging behind in matters of cryptography. The Italian Matteo Argenti, who served as cipher secretary for five popes from 1591 to 1605, commented sarcastically that the Germans would rather burn encoded letters they intercepted than attempt to decipher them.[440] It seems that Colorni had this problem on his mind. His *Scotographia* includes not only instructions for decoding, but also a chapter on crypto-analysis, or code-breaking—excluding, of course, Colorni's own code.[441] Even at the court of the emperor, to whom the work was dedicated, there was still a fair amount to be learned about crypto-analysis.[442] But Colorni set himself an even more ambitious goal—to create a universal method that would allow correspondents throughout Europe to write in code.[443] This was one reason why Colorni included Latin letters in his cryptographic system that were almost never used in Italian, such as *K, W, X,* and *Y*.[444] This was a prudent decision. The papal cipher secretary had begun to develop cryptographic methods incorporating these letters around the same time.[445] Colorni even contemplated the application of his own method to non-European languages.[446]

Admittedly, such promising declarations were not compelling enough for prospective buyers. The author had to dispel a general reservation held by potential buyers of cryptographic literature. Like a great deal of the printed cryptographic literature from this era, the *Scotographia* was marked by a hermeneutic contradiction: making an encryption method public undermines the claim that it cannot be deciphered by a third party. If a printed cryptographic work was going to appeal to a broad buying public, its author first needed to answer the question of how it could be safely individualized.[447]

Colorni's answer to this problem is best demonstrated using the same concrete example he chose to illustrate it.[448] The plaintext is Ps 119:3 (Vulgate). Colorni encrypted the Latin words "Quid detur tibi, aut apponatur tibi, ad linguam dolosam" (What shall be given unto thee? Or what shall be done unto thee, thou false tongue?) into TSXGFY GHTPXA SKGHIN MIB MBSIMHSSC SKGHIN MZQ XKFFLTWPL GWYIXGWPL. To get this result, he first cut the words of the verse into groups of three letters each. This was not unusual in sixteenth-century cryptography; it resembles, for example, the method developed by Cardano.[449] In the case at hand, this means that the first unit to be encrypted is the letter group "Qui." In the nearly fifty-page appendix to the *Scotographia,* all possible combinations of three letters are listed in tabular form. The letter writer needs to look up the charts containing those trios that begin with the letter *Q.* There are twenty-four such charts—one for every letter of the alphabet (keeping in mind that $I = J$ and $V = U$). In order to individualize the encoding method, the correspondents would have agreed that each of the initial letters to which a chart page is dedicated will, for internal uses, be replaced by one of the remaining twenty-three letters of the alphabet. Thus, for instance, the letter *Q* will be replaced by the (arbitrarily chosen) letter *T*. In the correspondents' copies of the *Scotographia*, these substitutions are then flagged using scraps of paper stuck to the relevant chart pages.[450]

In our example, the cipher for the unit "Qui" will therefore always begin with the letter *T*. It is augmented by the letters *S* and *X*, which are part of that system of letters (highlighted typographically in print) from which it is possible to ascertain, as in a kind of coordinate system, the respective place of a given triplet of letters in the charts. From "Qui" we therefore get *TSX*, and so on, though this is apparent only to the correspondents, who have previously agreed on a shared key (*registro*) to use in making substitutions for the initial letters.[451] Colorni's *Scotographia* also allows correspondents to employ a similar method based on groups of numbers.[452] He demonstrates this by using one of Solomon's sayings (Prov 10:14) as an example: "Sapientes abscondunt scientiam, os autem stulti confusione proximum est" (Wise men lay up knowledge: but the mouth of the foolish is near destruction).[453]

By Colorni's own account, his method was watertight.[454] Indeed, it is a polyalphabetic method—a system in which each letter is never, or only rarely, replaced in the same manner. A complex polyalphabetic secret writing could not have been deciphered by contemporary code breakers unless they knew what key the correspondents had agreed on. Such polyalphabetic systems started to gain currency only in the fifteenth century. However, Colorni knew that the method he had developed was demanding and time-consuming. He therefore recommended using it primarily for transmitting information that required the utmost secrecy on political or military grounds. For merchants, traders, and all others who had a high volume of correspondence for professional reasons, the *Scotographia* offered a number of additional, less elaborate methods.[455] To this end, the work included an appendix with two cryptographic squares (*quadrato*) and two cryptographic disks (*ruota*). The disks suggest that Colorni was familiar with the cryptography of Leon Battista Alberti, who had popularized this technique in the fifteenth century.[456] Colorni had clearly also taken cues from the relevant cryptographic works of Trithemius (*Polygraphiae libri sex*, 1518), Della Porta (*De furtivis literarum notis*, Naples 1563), and Cardano (sections from *De subtilitate*, 1550, as well as from *De rerum varietate*, 1557).

The *Scotographia* shows that Colorni was well-acquainted with the full range of contemporary cryptographic literature. Even the title is probably an allusion to one of the most famous and puzzling works about cryptography from that era, namely the *Steganographia* by Abbot Johannes Trithemius (1462–1516). For decades, this work circulated only in the form of manuscript copies before it was finally printed in 1606, just a few years after the publication of Colorni's *Scotographia*. Since then, numerous historians have studied the treatise, which contains a number of coherent cryptographic methods, though under the veil of murky language. The *Steganographia* was also a storehouse of curious ideas, such as the assertion that two friends could send each other secret messages across any distance without help from any additional tools.[457] Similarly bold theories about encryption circulated among Trithemius's followers. Thus, we find ideas about how to transmit secret messages using moonbeams or mirrors.[458] Following up on an idea introduced by Della Porta, some early modern cryptographers thought a mutual injection of blood created a secret mode of communication between a message's sender and its receiver.[459] By contrast, the distinction between transmission by immersing the writing surface in a liquid (*genus hyphasmaticum*) and by using an invisible ink that could be made visible only through chemical processes (*genus aleoticum*) was much more sensible.[460]

Colorni was relatively open to the use of such secret inks, and his *Scotographia* mentions various formulas for producing them. Here he might have been influenced by Della Porta, who included similar instructions in his widely circulated *Magia naturalis*.[461] Colorni's Jewish contemporary Abraham Portaleone described how to heat articles of clothing inscribed with fruit juice so that the message written on them would become visible. He also looked into a method that used the milklike juice of figs to write on the body of a messenger a note that could later be made visible by applying crushed charcoal.[462] Portaleone's remarks give some indication of what Colorni must have had in mind around 1597, when, in a "special secret" presented to the Duke of Württemberg, he praised the merits of an encoding procedure in which the messenger would deliver a secret message that would remain outwardly invisible even if the messenger were to be captured by enemy forces and undressed.[463] The foreword to the *Scotographia* suggests that Colorni was also familiar with archaic methods said to have been used to transmit secret messages in antiquity.[464] These included writing on the scalp of a shaven slave whose hair would grow back and literally cover up the words.[465] Colorni also displayed familiarity with a method for encryption by means of musical notation.[466] True, he did not hide his skepticism about some of these methods. In line with some of his earlier works, he reiterated that a large part of his discussion rested on a mathematical foundation.[467] Colorni even presented calculations in order to demonstrate the impossibility of breaking the encoding method he had invented.

But why did Colorni choose a title that was bound to prompt associations with the *Steganographia* by Trithemius, a work strongly surrounded by a magical aura?[468] Colorni's decision was probably more than just an attempt to come up with an eye-catching title. In fact, as Gerhard Strasser has noted, the "combination of an often surprisingly advanced cryptography with *magia naturalis*" was by no means rare in the sixteenth century.[469] The artful title captures this complexity. On one hand, Colorni's polyalphabetic method could justifiably claim to be a serious "science" based on logical and mathematical principles, as his work's subtitle explicitly stated. On the other hand, there were allusions linking the work and its author with the economy of secrets. For example, the Italian verb *cavare* that Colorni occasionally uses to describe the process of encoding also played an important part in sixteenth-century alchemical and metallurgical discourses, where it denotes sublimation—that is, the vaporization of materials.[470] This suggests that Colorni saw the process of encoding as a kind of alchemy of words—or, at least, as analogous to the chemical process of sublimation. By using such metaphors, Colorni may have been attempting to ignite alchemists' interest in his work. Encoding formulas and technical secrets was very common among this group.[471] But playing with alchemical catchwords could also arouse the popular notion that Jews, and especially Kabbalists, had mastered an "alchemy of words."[472] This leads to the question of how Colorni's *Scotographia* deals with the Jewish tradition. As we have seen, Christians commonly ascribed expertise in the field of cryptography to Jews, especially since they often suspected connections between cryptographic knowledge and the Kabbalistic methods of gematria.[473] Della Porta, for one, maintained that the Jews had developed methods to keep their writings secret as early as biblical times.[474] Abraham Portaleone devoted considerable attention to cryptography in his encyclopedia, which also celebrated the ancient Israelites' scientific achievements.

Several passages in Colorni's *Scotographia* explicitly mention the author's Jewish background—and not only when this reference was obligatory, as on the title page. He addresses his knowledge of Hebrew in the very first chapter.[475] And Prov 25:2—a line attributed to Solomon—is prefixed to the book as a kind of motto: "Gloria Dei est celare verbum, & gloria regum investigare sermonem" (It is the glory of God to conceal a matter; to search out a matter is the glory of kings).[476] Colorni used verses from only Psalms and Proverbs to demonstrate his cryptographic method—especially verses revolving around the necessity of keeping secrets. This is all the more striking because Italian authors of cryptographic treatises during this era frequently used verses from Petrarch, Dante, or Vergil as plaintext to illustrate their respective methods.[477] Sometimes cryptographers also chose sentences that would make readers raise their eyebrows. For example, Della Porta demonstrated his method by using the rather lewd, and certainly encryption-worthy, sentence "Puellam hodie amatam defloravi" (Today I deflowered the beloved girl).[478] No less curious was Trithemius's so-called Ave Maria Method, in which Christian prayers served as camouflage for the encrypted text.[479]

Authors of early modern cryptographies were clearly deliberate about the way they chose their plaintext sample sentences—intending either to underscore how well-read and pious they were or to amuse the reader with witty and even indecent sentences. Thus, Colorni's decision to illustrate his own method using allusive verses from the Hebrew Bible, and especially from Solomon's proverbs, deserves attention. This becomes even more salient when one compares Colorni's treatise with the one composed by his contemporary, Rabbi Samuel Archevolti (ca. 1530–1611). Ten years after the *Scotographia,* Archevolti provided a copious introduction to different methods of cryptography within the framework of his Hebrew grammar *Arugat ha-Bosem* (Venice, 1602). Archevolti, who located the origins of cryptography in the Talmud, incorporated explicit allusions and references to the Hebrew Bible. Not only did he use biblical verses as plaintext, but like Colorni, he derived cryptography's legitimacy from holy scripture. In the biblical wisdom literature he saw nothing short of a summons to encode knowledge.[480] There is, however, one important difference between Colorni's and Archevolti's cryptographic discussions: Colorni was writing for a Christian audience, whereas Archevolti was writing for a Jewish one. For Colorni's Christian readers, his prominent use of quotations from the Hebrew Bible in a cryptographic work was more unusual than it would have been for readers of Hebrew literature. For Archevolti, who was writing in Hebrew, it was natural to use biblical lines; by contrast, Colorni could have chosen from a range of other options. His decision to use Hebrew Bible verses might in itself be a kind of encoded message; for the historian, at any rate, it provides a key to "deciphering" the intellectual role and Solomonic tradition in which Colorni saw himself.

Explosive Knowledge

In the spring of 1591, news spread through royal courts all across Europe concerning an accident that happened to Emperor Rudolf II during an alchemical experiment. Apparently, he had attempted to produce explosive materials and had singed his beard and eyebrows and sustained burns on his face.[481]

Despite such dangers, the emperor was not alone in his interest in explosive materials. The extraction of saltpeter, which was indispensable for the manufacture of gunpowder, was a focus of activity at the Prague court in the field of so-called practical alchemy. There were even experiments using advanced crystallization ovens.[482] With the outbreak of the Long Turkish War in 1593, these experiments assumed even greater importance.[483] For Colorni, who had already gained experience in these matters during his time in Italy and had just published his *Scotographia,* 1593 opened up a promising field of activity. He was hardly the only early modern Jew to gain renown in this field: the phenomenon of Jewish saltpeter manufacturers and merchants is a multifaceted aspect of early modern Jewish history—one largely unexplored until now. We cannot explain it exclusively in terms of economic and social history. Rather, we need to clarify why so many contemporaries attributed to Jews a distinctive expertise in the manufacture of saltpeter and gunpowder in the first place. To what extent did Jews really have specific knowledge about extracting saltpeter? To answer this question, it is important to consider the historical development of the saltpeter industry in Europe. It is only in this context that the role of early modern Jews in the saltpeter business can be adequately described.

The term "saltpeter," which originally meant "rock salt," is a popular designation for different nitrates that is common to this day. Naturally extracted saltpeter, however, plays almost no role in commercial and industrial life today. It has largely been replaced by synthetically created saltpeter. Early modern professions like the "saltpeter man" (in German, "Salitterer" or "Salpeterer") are also extinct. The very existence of such professions indicates the importance saltpeter held in the premodern economic world.[484] At the time, saltpeter was used in fertilizers, food preservation, fungicides, textile manufacturing, metallurgy, and mining, to name just a few applications.[485] Alchemists likewise employed saltpeter for a variety of purposes, though they did not always use the term consistently.[486] Alchemists' knowledge about saltpeter also played a role in gunpowder production.[487] Indeed, saltpeter's primary importance was military. The ideal mixture for gunpowder was 75 percent saltpeter, 15 percent carbon, and 10 percent sulfur.[488] These proportions make it clear why saltpeter was indispensable for early modern rulers' military ambitions. Accordingly, the authorities took a keen interest in its production. Gunpowder manufacturing, or even maintaining an autarkic supply situation, was a matter of military survival to many rulers. Tellingly, the bellicose early modern era regarded gunpowder as one of humanity's three most important inventions, along with book printing and the compass.[489]

Europe learned of gunpowder, a Chinese invention, in the thirteenth century, although it did not play a part in weapons technology right away. With the spread of firearms in the fourteenth century, however, gunpowder soon took on a prominent role. It was not just growing military demand that led to higher prices for saltpeter, however; well into the fifteenth century, overdependence on imports—which primarily came from India, where natural deposits were extensive—was also to blame.[490] Only gradually did Europeans develop enough know-how to manufacture "artificial saltpeter." This reduced their import dependence and helped lower prices for this coveted resource.[491] The large-scale operation of so-called saltpeter farms was a critical factor here. Landfills made up of nitrous substances—such as refuse from plants and animals, as well as excrement—were laid out, and these were mixed and repeatedly moistened with clay or ashes. Turning and moistening the landfill accelerated the natural weathering process through which the organically bound nitrogen oxidized and turned into nitrate. The raw saltpeter that formed an outer layer facing the air could then be skimmed off. Through boiling and repeated recrystallization, this was purified into pure saltpeter so that it could be used to manufacture gunpowder. In addition to this form of saltpeter production, there was also the business of the "saltpeter men," who, often at the behest of the authorities, were on the lookout in stables and private homes for saltpeter that had naturally formed on walls and under boards (so-called wall saltpeter). Such searches of entire houses in order to find an inconspicuous material led many residents to view the saltpeter men as intruders both unwelcome and suspicious, who would not even stop at searching foundation walls and graves.[492] An aura of the mysterious adhered to the entire business of producing gunpowder. In early modern Europe, the notion was widespread that "the Devil must have something to do with the inexplicable driving force and explosive power of gunpowder."[493] Some even leveled accusations of witchcraft.

Saltpeter itself was shrouded in mystery throughout the entire early modern period. In the first place, this had something to do with its importance for alchemy.[494] Numerous alchemists were fascinated by saltpeter because of its various properties and possible uses. Some of them even believed that there were explicit references to its importance in the Hermetic literature.[495] Others suspected that saltpeter could provide a key to the successful transmutation of gold. The puzzling natural growth of saltpeter—as well as its role, not fully understood, in the devastating effect of gunpowder—contributed to the arcane nimbus surrounding it.[496] However, saltpeter's importance for alchemy is not the only reason why its production formed part of the economy of secrets. Its military uses also required confidentiality. As a result, many early modern descriptions of saltpeter manufacture are strikingly vague.[497] People commonly referred to this process as a secret well into the eighteenth century. Authorities were strongly concerned about possible breaches of confidentiality. In some places, the authorities even made sure that saltpeter boilers were sworn to secrecy.[498]

In light of the prominent role Jews played in the economy of secrets, both in reality and in the public imagination, it is not surprising that many Christians felt they had special competence in saltpeter production and munitions manufacturing. Consider the emphatic letters of recommendation from 1515 in which Cardinal Giulio de' Medici told his cousin Lorenzo de' Medici about the arrival of a group of Jews who had offered to reveal a variety of "very beautiful and diverse secrets" about saltpeter production.[499] The case of Moses Israel from Thessaloniki—an enigmatic person to begin with—is also instructive. He shuttled back and forth between the Ottoman Empire and Italy and converted three times (!) in the 1620s and 1630s before the Venetian Inquisition sentenced him to seven years' imprisonment as a galley slave.[500] The first time he converted, he was granted permission to manufacture gunpowder; apparently, his Christian patrons expected some concrete advantages from employing a Jew in this field. Such expectations persisted as late as the eighteenth century, as indicated by a manuscript first published in 1735—though some parts of it are apparently much older—with the title *Uraltes Chymisches Werck* (Ancient Chemical Work). The publisher, Julius Gervasius, issued the work as the legacy of an obviously fictitious rabbi by the name of Abraham Eleazar.[501] It dealt extensively with the process of heating saltpeter, which (we now realize) produces oxygen. One historian of science has even claimed "to have found in Eleazar one of the early discoverers of oxygen."[502] Such claims aside, it is noteworthy that a book in which experiments with saltpeter play such a prominent role was attributed to a Jewish author as late as the eighteenth century.

Additional factors lent further support to the idea that Jews had a particular competence in this field. Christians frequently attributed knowledge about supernatural, even diabolical, matters to Jews. But this idea of a distinctive Jewish expertise also tied in with a series of biblical verses. For example, in Jer 2:22 it says, "For though thou wash thee with nitre, and take thee much soap, yet thine iniquity is marked before me, saith the Lord God." In the Hebrew original, the word "nitre" is "neter," which both Jewish and Christian interpreters linked to saltpeter.[503] In the late seventeenth century, the Christian naturalist Johann Ludwig Hannemann, a professor in Kiel, identified another passage that seemed to prove that Jews were already acquainted with saltpeter and gunpowder in biblical times. Deuteronomy 29:23 says, "And that the whole land thereof is brimstone, and salt, and burning, that it is not sown, nor beareth, nor any grass groweth therein, like the overthrow of Sodom, and Gomorrah, Admah, and Zeboim, which the Lord overthrew in his anger, and in his wrath."[504] Jews also advanced interpretations similar to Hannemann's. In fact, the idea that the ancient Israelites had a highly developed stock of military knowledge and firearms was especially popular with Jewish authors.[505] Binyamin Mussafia (see Chapter 2)—a Sephardic doctor from Hamburg and personal physician to the Danish King Christian IV—even saw the ancient Jews as the inventors of gunpowder.[506] The Christian author Johann Jacob Schudt also assumed Jews knew about saltpeter in biblical times, although he could not resist linking this observation with a reference to the *foetor judaicus* (the "Jewish stench"). "In old times," according to Schudt, Jews "must have paid more attention to cleanliness, for they cultivated the habit of using saltpeter lye to wash and meticulously remove all dirt and refuse, as Jeremiah gives us to understand."[507] Schudt's remarks point to another ambiguous feature of saltpeter: turned into lye, it could be used for hygienic purposes, whereas in the original production process unpleasant odors were the order of the day. What is more, copious fecal matter, urine, and liquid manure were used to produce saltpeter. Given the ammonium content of these kinds of excrement, the resulting smells were certainly hard to take.[508] This could be one reason why a giant "saltpeter hill" was placed in close proximity to the Jewish residential area in Prague as a way of humiliating Jews; it also helps explain why the Frankfurt city council, unfazed by the Jewish community's protest, insisted on setting up a gunpowder mill at the Jewish cemetery in 1519.[509] There are further examples that make explicit the link between Jews' alleged stench and the smells of saltpeter. A broadsheet from 1750 showing how the Prague saltpeter hill "burnt without damage and how the Jews extinguished it" also depicts a Christian who is spitefully telling a Jew, "The hill stinks like you of rubbish, dirt, and shards, as befits everything foul, to your own wrack and ruin, for all you acquire is from falseness and deceit."[510]

The unpleasant odors associated with saltpeter also affected the social status of saltpeter men and boilers. In early modern Europe, the extraction of and search for saltpeter were poorly tolerated and often physically demanding activities that required a high degree of mobility.[511] The men who boiled saltpeter were not, for the most part, organized into guilds; instead, they were often directly answerable to their territorial rulers, many of whom had turned saltpeter extraction into a princely prerogative.[512] For Jews, this opened up a field of activity that was relatively free of guild and social restrictions. What the profession required was good contacts with the authorities. If undertaken with skill, saltpeter production could earn a lot of money. For example, the Italian mining specialist and metallurgist Vannoccio Biringuccio (1480–1537)—who achieved fame as the author of an important work on this subject, *De la pirotechnia* (first published posthumously in 1540, with four editions to follow in the sixteenth century)—managed to get rich by obtaining a monopoly on saltpeter production.[513] One final point helps explain why Christian contemporaries believed Jews were particularly suited for saltpeter and gunpowder manufacture: the assumption that Jews were inherently hostile toward Christians and had already been supplying the Ottoman Empire with critical military technology.

These prejudices and expectations aside, was there really a *specific* Jewish know-how in this field? This question is more difficult to answer, although there is a great deal of evidence that knowledge about saltpeter production was widespread among Jews. This is particularly true with regard to Italy. In Umbria in the 1430s, a Jew named Musetto provided the gunpowder for the artillery of Città di Castello.[514] In Sicily there were Jews who, before their expulsion from the island in 1492, occupied key positions in the saltpeter trade. We also know of comparable activities in the Holy Roman Empire and Eastern Europe.[515] In the Ottoman Empire around 1600, three Jews were among the fifty-four people boiling saltpeter for the sultan.[516] Levantine Jews took up the manufacture of saltpeter and alum in mid-seventeenth-century Elba.[517] In southern Europe, Hebrew instructions for saltpeter manufacture also circulated outside the orbit of the royal courts.[518]

In most cases, Jewish know-how was not distinguishable from that of Christians. And it is doubtful whether it really was a Greek Jew who introduced gunpowder into German lands, as some scholars have asserted.[519] Although a Hebrew treatise on manufacturing gunpowder has come down to us from around 1500, this turns out to be a copy of the so-called *Feuerwerksbuch* (Fireworks Book) written by a Christian author.[520] The detailed description of saltpeter given by the noted Jewish physician David de Pomis in his dictionary *Tzemaḥ David* (1587) also contains nothing that goes beyond what Christians knew.[521] The remarks of Abraham Portaleone—who devoted an entire chapter in his encyclopedic work *Shiltei ha-Gibborim* (Shields of Heroes) to different types of "salts" and their application since biblical times—are mostly of antiquarian interest.[522] However, Portaleone also offered Hebrew instructions for operating a saltpeter pit.[523] A half century later, Baruch Spinoza was deeply preoccupied with saltpeter, although mostly as a reaction to Robert Boyle's experiments in England.[524]

The idea that Jews had special competence in saltpeter and gunpowder manufacture was clearly exaggerated, yet it continued to affect Christian views about this branch of the economy. There may be a psychological explanation for this. Ascribing a specific, even supernatural, expertise to Jews in this field helped Christians explain gunpowder's mysterious—and, in the eyes of some contemporaries, even diabolical—features. The widespread early modern legend about how the monk

Berthold Schwarz (Bertholdus Niger) invented gunpowder fulfilled a similar function. Independently of whether Schwarz ever actually existed (which is questionable), Protestants picked up the claim that he brought gunpowder into the world and linked it polemically with allegations of magic in the Catholic Church.[525] In reality, Jews' knowledge about saltpeter manufacturing was much greater than that of most monks. Still, this did not necessarily translate into *above average* technical skills.

The situation was different with respect to the trade in saltpeter. Here, Jewish merchants did indeed often benefit from extensive commercial networks and knowledge of several languages. We have examples of Jews trading in saltpeter and gunpowder from all over Europe, and occasionally even beyond. In the 1630s, the Portuguese Jew Benjamin Cohen supplied gunpowder to the leaders of religious brotherhoods in what is today Morocco.[526] As early as the mid-fifteenth century, the Ottoman sultan commissioned a Jew to deliver saltpeter for gunpowder production.[527] The key position the Jews occupied in the fifteenth-century Sicilian saltpeter trade has already been mentioned, and in 1492 a Sicilian Jew named Iuda Faccas even supplied saltpeter for the defense of Malta against the Turks.[528] There were comparable examples in the Holy Roman Empire as early as the fifteenth century. For example, Emperor Frederick III ordered Jews in his realm to deliver four hundred hundredweight of gunpowder in 1486 to support "our arduous war against the King of Hungary."[529] References to such deliveries by Jews, especially at the level of the empire's territorial rulers, increase in the sixteenth century.[530] The imperial city of Frankfurt bought saltpeter from Jews as early as the middle of the fifteenth century, and the city council judged its quality satisfactory.[531] There was also some demand for gunpowder among Jews themselves, even if it was not very great. In eastern Poland, fear of pogroms made it customary for Jews to keep shotguns in their homes, along with a sufficient supply of gunpowder.[532]

Although there were attempts to restrict or ban Jews trading in saltpeter and gunpowder in German lands, these efforts did not produce the desired outcome.[533] On the contrary, trading in gunpowder became a core business for the so-called court Jews. The formation of standing armies, especially during and after the Thirty Years War, played an important part in this development. The imperial court and war factor Samuel Oppenheimer, whose reputation rested not least on having procured large quantities of gunpowder from Holland and saltpeter from Bohemia, experienced a particularly rapid rise (see Chapter 2).[534] In Protestant regions, too, the authorities repeatedly used court Jews to provide their armies with equipment and to ensure gunpowder deliveries.[535] Joseph Süß Oppenheimer, the most famous court Jew of the eighteenth century (see Chapter 4), greatly impressed his patron, Duke Karl Alexander of Württemberg, by reforming saltpeter and gunpowder production in the duchy. Oppenheimer's reform proposals were partly implemented, and he even offered to produce some of the saltpeter himself.[536]

Did continuities concerning the Jewish trade in gunpowder go back to before the seventeenth century? We can now answer this question in the affirmative. While it is true that the radical structural and political upheavals caused by the Thirty Years War opened unprecedented opportunities for Jewish army suppliers, Jews were active in this profession as far back as the Late Middle Ages, and Colorni was one of these forerunners. His first attempt to produce saltpeter in Prague dates to 1593.[537] It was not without entrepreneurial risk. At the time, Bohemia was a center of saltpeter and gunpowder production, and the gunpowder manufactured there enjoyed a good reputation beyond the Holy Roman Empire.[538] As a result, Colorni had competitors, especially in the circles of the Prague alchemists, when he first asked imperial officials to issue a privilege for his method of producing saltpeter and gunpowder.[539] The court officials charged with examining Colorni's request expressed skepticism about the proposal from the "Italian Jew."[540] The emperor settled the issue by rewarding Colorni with a handsome sum of money.[541] However, Colorni continued his effort to solicit the emperor's support for commissions to manufacture gunpowder.[542]

Colorni's projects did not exist just on paper. By 1594, at the latest, he was actually operating a saltpeter hut in Prague.[543] In the meantime, the Long Turkish War had entered its second year, and the emperor's need for gunpowder grew steadily.[544] Credible reports were arriving from the Ottoman Empire about a massive upgrade of the Turkish army. The emperor had to convene an Imperial Diet for the summer of 1594 in an attempt to secure financial and military support from the territorial rulers of the empire.[545] For their part, the imperial authorities undertook measures to increase saltpeter production in Bohemia.[546] In light of this situation, the emperor—upon his arrival at the Imperial Diet in Regensburg—personally turned to Colorni and asked him to present a demonstration of his knowledge forthwith.[547] In return, Rudolf II arranged for Colorni to get the "requisite supplies."[548]

A few weeks later, Colorni presented two hundredweight of saltpeter out of his own stock, although the quality was not to the satisfaction of imperial officials.[549] He continued with the production, and soon high-level reports were arriving "that the Jew had a good supply of saltpeter."[550] Colorni apparently had an advocate in the jurist Bartholomäus Petz, a member of the imperial Aulic Council. In the 1580s, Petz had served as secretary to the imperial legation in Constantinople and later as imperial orator in the Ottoman Empire. This seasoned and well-traveled confidant of the emperor was open to Colorni's business ventures. But other imperial officials, especially those working for the custodian of the armory, disliked the "Saltpeter Jew."[551] These circles took offense at Colorni not least because he wanted to keep the option of selling his saltpeter on the free market. Even during wartime, he insisted on this option, especially since his initial investment had forced him into debt.[552] "He has become defiant enough," an imperial official noted after a conversation with Colorni in March 1595 ended with an altercation.[553] Ultimately, the emperor intervened and decided in favor of the "Italian Jew." Although Colorni was prohibited from selling his saltpeter abroad, he was given permission to "produce his outwork at the behest of the imperial chamber and receive a proper privilege for this."[554]

News about this positive turn in Colorni's saltpeter manufacturing venture in Prague quickly reached Italy. As early as May 1595, a ducal secretary reported back to Mantua that Colorni was highly regarded at the imperial court for his saltpeter production.[555] Colorni himself knew how to make the most of his momentum. While he had achieved what he wanted in Prague, he knew that this positive development could open up additional opportunities. For quite some time, he had been contemplating a return to Italy and his family. His success in the saltpeter and gunpowder business now offered him a springboard for this move, since both the Duke of Mantua and the Duke of Ferrara were eager to move into the front ranks of European military powers. Tellingly, Vincenzo I Gonzaga and Alfonso II d'Este were the only Italian princes who had answered imperial calls for military support against the Turks. Vincenzo even put himself at the head of military campaigns against the Turks three times—in 1595, 1597, and 1600. Colorni had good reason to interest the dukes of Mantua and Ferrara in his production method, and he sent samples of his saltpeter from Prague to Italy.[556]

At the court of the Este, Colorni's plans were crowned with success. Around 1597, apparently during a stay in Italy, he negotiated a privilege with the ducal munitions office (Ducale Munitione) that more or less guaranteed him a monopoly in the saltpeter business in the Duchy of Ferrara.[557] The office agreed to set up fully equipped production facilities in the three main cities of the duchy—Ferrara, Modena, and Reggio. In addition, the munitions office was to assume the costs for the initial operations, including pay for staff and for the procurement of firewood. Officials granted Colorni and his staff unrestricted permission to search for deposits of saltpeter at all public and private sites in the territory.[558] Under threat of fines, previous saltpeter and gunpowder producers were told to cooperate with Colorni.[559] In return, Colorni committed to delivering four hundred pounds of saltpeter to the munitions office each week.[560] He was permitted to sell his saltpeter and gunpowder to outside or private customers only with explicit approval from the authorities. The court compensated him for this restriction with both startup funding and a salary. We cannot know to what extent these plans paid off for both parties. Political events soon thwarted the project for good. With the death of Alfonso II in 1597, the duchy was plunged into a profound crisis. The following year, Ferrara was escheated to the pope. Under papal rule, granting a near-monopoly position to a Jew in such a sensitive economic area as saltpeter manufacture was hard to imagine.

This episode raises the question of what the saltpeter Colorni produced was actually all about. Previously unnoticed archival documents now allow us to paint a much fuller picture of Colorni's activities in saltpeter and gunpowder production. For instance, notarial deeds substantiate that he took his first steps in this field in Ferrara as early as the 1580s and that he was able to secure investments from wealthy fellow Jews.[561] In February 1585, Colorni and a Jew named Consiglio Carmi from Brescello entered into an agreement before a Christian notary about a partnership in the saltpeter and gunpowder business.[562] Specifically, the contract dealt with the manufacture of gunpowder for harquebuses and artillery guns.[563] There was a clear division of labor between the two parties. Colorni was to supply the technical know-how, and Carmi and his father the requisite money. Colorni needed these funds primarily to obtain privileges, conclude contracts, and defray travel costs. The agreement provided for Colorni to receive three-fourths of the profits from the business, and his investors only one-fourth. This unequal profit-sharing probably reflected the different risks taken by the business partners. Only Colorni was designated as the inventor, and only his name would be linked to transactions with the authorities. The Carmi family largely stayed in the background as a kind of silent partner. A document in Hebrew that is unfortunately not extant spelled out the agreement's precise details. We do know that the deal was sealed in the presence of two witnesses and Rabbi Abraham Basola.[564]

Who were Consiglio and Rafael Carmi, Colorni's Jewish business partners and investors? The answer to this question indicates that Colorni's "explosive" projects rested on a solid technical foundation. He had succeeded in obtaining the support of an Ashkenazic family as prestigious as it was financially strong.[565] Saul Rafael Carmi, whose son signed the deal before the notary in Ferrara, was one of the leading moneylenders in Lombardy. He had married a daughter of the rich Venetian Del Banco family. Saul Rafael also enjoyed a reputation as a scholar and political representative of Lombardy's Jewish community. The Carmi family maintained contacts with the leadings rabbis of the time, including Leon Modena and Menaḥem Azaria da Fano. The latter was executor of Saul Rafael's will following his death in 1591. The deceased even held the honorary title of a *Gaon*. His son Consiglio (Yekutiel) would later become one of the four official representatives of the Jewish community in Spanish Lombardy who negotiated with the authorities threatening to expel the Jews.

It is possible that family ties existed between the far-flung Colorni family from Mantua and the Carmis in Lombardy. In the Carmi family's partly preserved private correspondence from the 1570s, there is a reference to a "bridegroom from Colorno."[566] The specification "from Colorno" does not exclude the possibility that the bridegroom in question was a member of the Colorni family from Mantua. There were many variations in the way a surname was spelled at the time, including versions where the Italian particles "de" and "da" were inserted.[567] For example, in the 1570s Abramo Colorni was still signing his name as "Abram da Colorni [*sic*]," even though his family no longer had any ties to the small ancestral town of Colorno.[568] In any event, securing the support of the influential Carmi family was highly advantageous for Colorni. The family's willingness to invest reinforces our observation that there was constant interaction between (Jewish) economic life and the economy of secrets. The Carmi family undoubtedly knew that it was investing in a business characterized by secrecy. Colorni himself never left any doubt that his expertise in saltpeter and gunpowder had to do with knowledge of secrets. In his discussions with courts, Colorni was accustomed to talking about his ideas concerning saltpeter as "secreti."[569]

It is difficult for historians to reconstruct exactly what was concealed behind Colorni's "explosive" secret knowledge. The notary's document from 1585 does not allow us to infer how Colorni intended to produce the gunpowder. However, an undated instruction from him about how to manufacture gunpowder that has been preserved in the Este archives provides more information.[570] It indicates that Colorni used carbon, sulfur, and saltpeter ("salpetro raffinato") as the basis for his gunpowder. For "artillery gunpowder" he used a ratio of one part carbon and sulfur to four parts saltpeter. For harquebus gunpowder, he increased the saltpeter to six or seven parts, with carbon and sulfur, as usual, making up one part each. He argued that this type of gunpowder had to be "more powerful."

There is hardly any difference between this instruction and contemporary formulas that were already tried and tested. It is also clear that saltpeter was the most important raw material Colorni used in producing gunpowder. How, then, did he obtain the substantial amounts of saltpeter that were necessary? When Colorni rose to become the state-appointed saltpeter manufacturer for the Duchy of Ferrara in the late 1590s, his saltpeter projects basically rested on two foundations. To begin with, he relied on the traditional method for locating deposits of so-called wall saltpeter. Yet he knew how difficult this procedure could be. As we have seen, saltpeter men were often unpopular among the population, since their searches for saltpeter turned entire houses upside down. Colorni could not count on large-scale cooperation, especially as a Jew. It is telling, even if not entirely unusual for early modern entrepreneurs and inventors, that he and his staff were given express permission to carry weapons.[571]

Perhaps it was this experience that led Colorni to establish a second foundation for his saltpeter business by experimenting with the production of artificial saltpeter and even operating his own saltpeter landfills. It is quite possible that he gained additional know-how in saltpeter production during his time in Prague. Bohemia was a leading territory for saltpeter and gunpowder production, and the court in Prague gave Colorni an opportunity to work in the imperial laboratories. Older scholarship has asserted that he was preoccupied with the (downright impossible) production of saltpeter from out of air during his time in Prague.[572] However, there is no evidence for this thesis. It is true that a theory of "air saltpeter" existed at the time. It dated back to Paracelsus and was taken up by Colorni's Polish contemporary Michael Sendivogius and his followers.[573] However, there is no evidence, either in Prague or later in Stuttgart, that Colorni ever undertook to produce saltpeter merely out of the air. Rather, he claimed that he could produce it from *any* kind of soil. Thus, he held out the promise of "boiling good saltpeter from soil that had already been used once before, as well from the kind that is under the open sky and could be exposed to rain at any time."[574] The talk about rain made little sense within the context of traditional methods for manufacturing saltpeter, so it is possible that

Colorni was influenced by Sendivogius's theory of air saltpeter; the Polish alchemist regarded it as proven that invisible "air saltpeter" could find its way via rain into the earth, where it would lead to the growth of natural saltpeter.[575]

It is especially plausible to regard these ideas as influential because Sendivogius's career does intersect with Colorni's. The Polish alchemist was employed at the court of Rudolf II from 1593 onward, and, like Colorni, he would later spend time at the court of Württemberg. The question of specific influences by Sendivogius aside, it is evident that Colorni's plans took cues from alchemy. The notion that the earth's soil had the potential to repeatedly produce saltpeter had already been discussed by Paracelsus before it was popularized in the alchemical literature. Well into the seventeenth century, this theory enjoyed considerable popularity throughout Europe. In Colorni's own time, the noted mining expert Lazarus Ercker (1528–1594) wrote instructions for producing saltpeter in line with this theory. In England, such ideas were subject to intense discussion in the circle around the naturalist and reformer Samuel Hartlib (1600–1662), and it is possible that they stimulated the young Robert Boyle (1627–1691) to take an interest in experimental chemistry.[576] Boyle did indeed engage with these theories, even if critically. In his influential *The Sceptical Chymist*, he wrote, "[It] seems evident from that notable practice of the boylers of salt-petre, who unanimously observe . . . that if an earth pregnant with nitre be deprived, by the affusion of water, of all its true and dissoluble salt, yet the earth will after some years yeeld them again . . . Though I deny that some volatile nitre may by such earths be attracted (as they speak) out of air."[577]

Colorni was not the only contemporary who mulled over how to obtain saltpeter from conventional soil. It is quite doubtful whether setbacks in his experiments discouraged him. Like most alchemists at the time, he probably shared the view that if an experiment failed, either the setup had been faulty or the key writings had been misinterpreted.[578] Indeed, interest in the production of so-called earth saltpeter continued to be lively long after Colorni's time. Even if no breakthrough was achieved, the idea of earth saltpeter was not entirely off track; some historians of science today regard this theory as an "important step on the way to the discovery of oxygen."[579]

This brings us back to the question of what to make of Colorni's undertakings in the saltpeter industry. First, his activities in saltpeter and gunpowder manufacturing extended over a period of almost two decades, and the extant sources make clear that Colorni was able to produce significant quantities of saltpeter both in Prague and earlier in Ferrara—even if in the conventional manner, by clearing away wall saltpeter and operating saltpeter landfills. It was not farfetched for Colorni to claim, two years before his death, that he owed his expertise in this field to many years of studying the subject.[580] Second, Colorni was able to persuade members of the Jewish economic elite, such as the Carmi family, about the viability of his saltpeter and gunpowder projects and get them to offer financial backing early on. Third and finally, the Colorni family's undertakings in this field did not end with Abramo's death. Just a few months afterward, his son Simone (Samuel) Colorni contacted the Duke of Mantua and resumed his father's projects. Once again, there was talk about "different kinds of saltpeter and powders."[581] In continuing the family business, the son referred to his late father's "new inventions" and his ability to produce large quantities of saltpeter in a short period of time. However, he also proposed more conventional methods, including the operation of saltpeter landfills and the detection of wall saltpeter. To that end, he required workers and an official privilege from the authorities. A draft for such an authorization must have been enclosed with his petition; however, it is apparently no longer extant.

Quite apart from the question of whether the son succeeded in gaining a long-term foothold in saltpeter production, vivid recollections of Abramo Colorni's undertakings in this field seem to have remained alive in Mantua. Abraham Portaleone, who lived in Mantua at the time, devoted no fewer than three copious chapters to saltpeter manufacture in his 1612 Hebrew encyclopedia *Shiltei ha-Gibborim*. There, Portaleone writes, "Now the foreign word for the artificial salt that is obtained from the soil is salmistro, and it is used to produce the gunpowder with which warriors fill their firearms, namely the archibugi or moschettoni or artigleria, whenever they fire at enemies."[582] Portaleone's detailed exposition of how to produce "artificial salt" and operate a saltpeter pit could be an indication that he had discussed these matters with Abramo or Simone Colorni.[583] When it came to writing his chapters on armaments and artillery technology, Portaleone might also have relied on the Colorni family's expertise.[584] Portaleone does vaguely imply that his account drew on works "that were disseminated from hand to hand among all those who are interested in this science."[585] It is even possible that Colorni played a role in the Duke of Württemberg's decision to invite the physician Portaleone to Stuttgart in the late 1590s. But first, a momentous invitation would befall Colorni himself.

Projects, Protests, and a Feat

For Colorni, the years he spent at the imperial court were the pinnacle of his career. Hardly any Jew at that time was as close to the emperor of the Holy Roman Empire. Colorni got to know influential people at the Rudolphine court, lived in a house of his own, and had attendants assigned to him by the court. After a few setbacks, he also succeeded in getting his first book published and in gaining a foothold in saltpeter manufacturing. In the long run, however, Colorni was drawn back to Italy. After all, his family had remained behind in Mantua all those years. Occasionally, his son Simone visited him in Prague, as we know from letters. Yet there were also family responsibilities, such as attending to his daughter's marriage, that would normally have required the father to be back in Mantua.[586] We can see how much a leave of absence mattered to Colorni from a passage in his *Scotographia*, where he wove a plea to return home into his dedication to the emperor.[587] Intrigues at the imperial court might have contributed to these plans.[588] By the mid-1590s, the question of his return to Italy became more and more pressing.

There were now two additional reasons for this urgency. First, Colorni's project to publish a complete edition of his works in Prague had failed. He had made a major effort to obtain privileges for this edition in various Italian territories.[589] Although he was able to conduct the correspondence promoting his publication from out of the imperial court, problems emerged when it came to implementing the project. And this leads to the second factor, namely, that Colorni's experiences with printers in Prague had been disappointing. In 1592, work had begun in Prague on printing the *Scoto-*

graphia and another treatise, the *Arithmetica*.[590] In the end, the latter work never made it into print. The same is true for the *Chirofisionomia,* which Colorni also hoped to publish in Prague.[591] Originally, the decision to publish there must have been influenced by his realization that a work like the *Chirofisionomia* was unlikely to find favor in the eyes of the Inquisition in Italy.[592] It also became clear that Prague was not the ideal place, let alone the most suitable market, for printing works in Italian, especially since Colorni's writings also proved to be a typographical challenge. Just publishing the *Scotographia,* with its elaborate appendix of tables, had overtaxed the printer Johann Schumann and his assistants, leading to numerous mistakes.[593] Colorni was disheartened, and in a postscript he complained about the poor conditions that prevailed in Prague for printing Italian books.[594] In the Bohemian capital, only a few printing shops offered this service, among them the print shop of Schumann, an immigrant from German lands. When Schumann died in 1594, just a year after the publication of the *Scotographia,* Colorni's chances to print two additional books in Prague became even bleaker.[595] Schumann's printing shop, which his widow initially kept in business, was soon mired in financial troubles.[596]

These developments must have confirmed Colorni's belief that it would be best to find a Venetian printer, at least for those of his writings focusing on the art of engineering, meaning the *Euthimetria* and one other treatise (missing today) about different "instruments." With its outstanding printing shops, Venice was a suitable site for publishing these kinds of works, which included complicated figures and were also meant to appear in both Latin and Italian. Yet to supervise the printing of two such volumes from out of Prague proved too difficult and too expensive over the long run, which is why this project remained unrealized.[597] Colorni must have grasped that it would be increasingly difficult for him to publish his complete works if he did not return to Italy for good.

The main reason he wanted to return to Italy, however, was probably the looming political crisis in the Duchy of Ferrara. Officially, Colorni had remained a subject of Alfonso II d'Este and a member of the court of Ferrara throughout those years. He was also close to the Italian ambassadors at the imperial court. He undoubtedly knew about the impending reversion of Ferrara to the pope. In the course of the 1590s, it had become evident that Alfonso II would remain without an heir. It was just a matter of time before the duke's death would clear the way for the pope to stake his claim. Given this outlook, Colorni knew there were no long-term prospects for him in Ferrara. If he wanted to maintain his contacts in Italy and return home at some later date, he needed to act quickly.[598] In his letters from Prague, he increasingly tried to strengthen his ties with the Venetian authorities and especially with the court in Mantua. Soon, he was openly mentioning his wish to enter into service for the Gonzaga court and return to where his family lived.

Colorni's plans fell on fertile ground in Mantua, then ruled by Duke Vincenzo I, one of the most colorful princes of that period.[599] Residing in a labyrinthine palace and surrounded by almost eight hundred courtiers, Vincenzo cultivated outsized political ambitions and had an exorbitant craving for luxury.[600] The art-loving duke was also an impassioned alchemist who had a number of laboratories installed in the underground vaults of the Palazzo Te, just outside the city.[601] Long after his death, he was still remembered for his dissolute conduct, including his sexual intemperance. The character of the libertine duke in Giuseppe Verdi's opera *Rigoletto* (1851), set in Mantua, displays some of Vincenzo's traits. He had few scruples about intimidating the Jewish community in Mantua with occasional public executions, but he also frequently kept company with Jews in private, be it for business purposes or for theatrical productions at court. In 1594, the duke was even said to have been a guest at the house of the Jewish dancer and singer Isacchino Massarano.[602] For his part, Colorni had been invited into the company of the duke at Marmirolo as early as the 1580s. Vincenzo wanted to learn more about chiromancy from Colorni at that time, but by the 1590s Colorni's knowledge of military technology had become the priority. The duke, whose ambition for military adventures was well-known, had considerable interest in extracting saltpeter and manufacturing gunpowder. After all, Vincenzo had been the only Italian prince who complied with the imperial request to join the military campaign against the Turks—three times.[603] In Vincenzo's eyes, Colorni, who had already performed well as a young man in the service of the Gonzaga family, promised to be an asset to the court.[604] But there still was the matter of orchestrating his move to Mantua diplomatically. Despite existing marriage ties, there was a simmering rivalry between the houses of Este and Gonzaga.[605] Questions of diplomatic form were not the only reason why nearly two years elapsed between Colorni's departure from Prague in 1597 and his return to his hometown of Mantua.[606] These two years turned out to be the trickiest time of Colorni's life. He spent them in Stuttgart.

How did it happen that Colorni relocated to the duchy of Württemberg in southern Germany? Previously unknown documents about Colorni's time in Stuttgart cast new light on his time there, but they have not made reconstructing the background any easier. Quite the contrary. Let us begin with the facts: In December 1596, a letter from the Duke of Württemberg, Frederick I, reached the imperial court at Prague. In that letter, the duke asked the emperor to lend Colorni, "the great Jewish artificer" ("den großen Juden Künstler"), out to him for six weeks.[607] Shortly thereafter, the duke approached "the great Jew artificer from Ferrara" directly.[608] Before that, the duke had attained the approval of Alfonso II d'Este in Ferrara—and not a minute too soon, since shortly thereafter the Transylvanian Prince Sigismund Báthory (1572–1613), who had recently stayed at the imperial court in Prague, also put in a bid for Colorni's services.[609]

Yet machinations behind the invitation to Württemberg remain puzzling. One such possible intrigue later prompted Colorni himself to level serious accusations against a Jew named Rosso.[610] According to Colorni, Rosso had stirred up the Duke of Württemberg's hopes about the possibility of Colorni's appointment and then, using false information, obtained Colorni's release in Ferrara. As a reward for his placement services, this cunning Jew apparently tried blackmailing Colorni into sharing all of the income he would earn in Stuttgart. Since Colorni refused to engage in any such deals, the "astute and malevolent Jew" started spreading lies about Colorni in order to damage his reputation. And since it seems that Rosso intermittently intercepted letters, Colorni declared that he found out only late about the full extent of the intrigues.[611] Colorni ultimately put an end to these machinations by reporting them to the Duke of Württemberg; he also engaged the services of a lawyer.

This Rosso, for whom Colorni could not find a good word, remains an elusive figure for the historian. In any event, he was not the only Jew at this time who provided secretive mediation services between Bohemia, southern Germany, and Italy. Another such mediator, for example, was Seligmann von Brenz. On several occasions between 1596 and 1600, he served as a messenger between the imperial and Württemberg courts.[612] He also accompanied Colorni from Prague to Stuttgart in 1597.[613] Seligmann's activities were not confined to such jobs. Emperor Rudolf II availed himself of Seligmann's services for a variety of purposes; a mysterious Latin inscription on an imperial letter from this period mentions "the Jew Seligman, whose diligence in certain things has been proven."[614] In 1600, Seligmann was said to have acquired precious objects for the emperor in Venice, including "a large iron-framed mirror." For this purpose, Seligmann was given the handsome sum of 1,500 crowns, which the emperor authorized the Fuggers to disburse to the ambassador in Venice. Seligmann apparently received the money in Venice but then absconded without settling the bills, much to the emperor's annoyance. We have no record of how this affair ended, but it apparently cost Seligmann neither his head nor the emperor's trust.[615] He is probably the same Jew who maintained close ties with the powerful imperial *Kammerdiener* Philipp Lang. After a quarrel with Lang, Seligmann is said to have died in jail. When Lang fell from power and had to answer for himself a few years later, his relationship with Seligmann was the subject of an interrogation under torture. Lang's torturers accused him of obtaining the *Sigillum Salomonis*—a magic book—from "Seligman the Jew."[616]

It is possible to go a step farther and to speculate about whether Rosso and Seligmann were one and the same person.[617] But even if this were true, it would be hard to assess the extent to which Colorni's depiction of the events surrounding his appointment at Stuttgart is accurate. His reassignment from Prague to Stuttgart was accompanied by a variety of rumors, including the claim that Colorni had absconded from Prague dressed in peasant's clothes.[618] Nothing in the correspondence between the courts in Prague and Stuttgart indicates the truth or falsity of this accusation. But such allegations make it clear that Colorni did not lack envious opponents.

With all of this going on, relocating to Württemberg was a risky move for Colorni. In Stuttgart he could not count on powerful backers at court, as he had in Prague. Since the late fifteenth century, Jews had at best been tolerated in Württemberg as transients.[619] The Second *Regimentsordnung* of 1498, a ducal ordinance including prohibitions on Jewish trade and residence, even characterized Jews harshly as "these gnawing vermin" who were not to be tolerated in the duchy.[620] Well into the eighteenth century, the dukes of Württemberg adhered, by and large, to this *Regimentsordnung* restricting Jewish activity, which remained on the books until 1806. In some cases, the ordinance was applied with a special religious zeal. For example, Duke Christoph proposed to ban Jews from the entire Holy Roman Empire at the Imperial Diet in Augsburg in 1559.[621] The fact that even the famous "Commander of Jewry in the Holy Roman Empire" Josel von Rosheim had to undertake lengthy negotiations before he was allowed to travel through ducal territory shows how strictly the duchy implemented the *Regimentsordnung*.[622]

Colorni's appointment in 1597 was entirely due to the will of the reigning duke. To be sure, the duke was far from being a philosemite. Frederick I saw the Long Turkish War that broke out in 1593 as a "work of Jews."[623] However, he was interested in Kabbalah, and the exchange of Hebrew manuscripts was one subject of his correspondence with the emperor.[624] Yet the duke was not looking for a Jewish advisor on Kabbalistic or theological questions when he invited Colorni to Stuttgart in 1596. Frederick, who had acceded to the throne in 1593 and shared a passion for alchemy with Rudolf II, was much more interested in Colorni's talents as a saltpeter manufacturer. This is where the duke's true ambitions lay in the era of the Turkish war. There were even suspicions abroad that the duke wanted to put himself at the head of a Protestant army should it come to war with the Catholics.[625]

Frederick was interested in making rapid progress in gunpowder manufacturing, and he was prepared to pay handsomely for it. A polyglot well-versed in the natural sciences, he was regarded by his contemporaries as a learned but autocratic prince. Before acceding to the throne, he spent years traveling throughout Europe. Journeys to Denmark and Bohemia (1580), a diplomatic mission in Paris (1581), and a stay in the England of Elizabeth I (1592) had greatly broadened his horizons.[626] However, his reign was not characterized by diplomacy; instead, it was marked by tensions with the powerful Württembergian *Landschaft,* the legal body where representatives of the realm's various estates—cities, districts, and the Lutheran clergy—were organized. From the start of his reign, Frederick tried to subject economically backward Württemberg to a kind of proto-mercantilist modernization policy at a pace that sometimes appeared "downright hectic."[627] Infrastructure was to be extended, raw materials deposits developed, and new industries established. Although the Protestant Frederick largely pulled in the same direction as the strictly Lutheran *Landschaft* on religious issues, he alienated his subjects by trying to impose constitutional reforms in the spirit of early absolutism. The serious debts Frederick incurred, despite rising state revenues during the course of his reign, were an additional point of friction between the duke and the *Landschaft.* Salaries for the royal household and the duke's desire for luxury devoured large shares of the revenues, much to the *Landschaft*'s annoyance.[628] Unsurprisingly, Frederick found alchemists' promises that they could fill the state's coffers by producing gold particularly tempting, and he was generous in remunerating the many alchemists in his employ.[629]

Colorni arrived in Stuttgart early in 1597. The Württembergian *Landschaft* and burghers eyed his arrival with deep suspicion. In the unhurried town that was the capital of Württemberg, there were already misgivings about the numerous "Italian foreigners" serving in the ducal household. Frederick I occasionally even had to put his Württembergian subjects in their place when they tried to impede the work of his "artificers."[630] Undoubtedly, the arrival of an "Italian Jew," as the Stuttgart theologian Osiander soon began calling Colorni, was a special bone of contention for the local population. While their annoyance was still simmering, Colorni was able to take up his work without hindrance. In his letters to Mantua, he appeared highly satisfied with the salary of 25 gulden Frederick granted him. The duke also assigned him a house of his own that apparently would have satisfied even aristocratic requirements.[631] Colorni was full of praise for his new patron, who is said to have summoned him for a visit every day during his first few weeks at court.[632] Seven hundred people dined each day at the ducal palace in Stuttgart, Colorni reported back to Mantua.[633] The duke set up a saltpeter boiler for Colorni in the new hospital on the tournament fields, near today's Hospitalkirche, and the alchemist began to conduct his experiments.

By the autumn of 1597, word of Colorni's activities had spread throughout the duchy. The renowned Greek philology professor and humanist Martin Crusius (1526–1607) in Tübingen had long been following what transpired in the capital. In a diary entry from early November of that year, Crusius made a note of his concern that Jews and sorcerers would eventually take over the duchy.[634] The rumors circulating about the "great Jew artificer" invited just this kind of wild speculation. In mid-November, for example, Crusius received a report from his colleague, the Tübingen Hebraist Georg Weigenmaier (1555–1599), that was replete with obscure claims.[635] According to this account, Colorni knew how to make gold. In addition, he could transform water into wine and stones into loaves of bread. The Jew had even pulled a snake out of the pocket of his gown and thrown it onto the floor in the ducal castle, where it wound itself into a circle and finally transformed itself into a chain of pearls and precious stones. Some of the courtiers had tasted the wine and bread. However, the more irreproachable ones among them were incensed about the Jew's sorcery—although they kept silent out of fear of the duke. Colorni himself had denied that his arts were magic (μαγικα); he attributed them instead to Kabbalah (καβάλων).[636]

Whether Weigenmaier's colorful report corresponded with reality remains doubtful. Of course, it is possible that Colorni performed magic tricks at the Stuttgart court, as he had done earlier in his career. But we cannot know whether Weigenmaier really was a witness to these performances. In any event, this learned Hebraist, who was probably never closely acquainted with Jews at any point in his life, fashioned his remarks about Colorni using an imagery indebted to the Bible. The transformations of water, stones, and snakes are well-known biblical topoi, some taken from the story of Moses, that worked splendidly to undergird the image of the Jew as magus.[637] In addition, Garzoni's published account of Colorni's magic tricks—an account rich in superlatives—might have been available at Württemberg's state university in Tübingen. We do know that German-speaking Europe read Garzoni's *Piazza universale* long before it was first translated into German (in 1619).[638] Thus, anyone with skills in Italian could read Garzoni's vivid description of Colorni transforming a snake into a chain of precious stones—though even here it is hard to say whether this was a rhetorical gesture to the biblical topos or Garzoni's recollection of a trick he saw Colorni perform.[639] Crusius was all the more surprised, perhaps even disappointed, when he learned a few weeks later that Colorni had not actually come to Stuttgart to perform magic: "Of the Jew who is in Stuttgart it is said that he knows next to nothing about magic; just saltpeter," Crusius noted in his diary in 1598.[640]

Yet this conclusion was not the entire truth either. In reality, Colorni's business in Stuttgart went well beyond saltpeter manufacturing. We do not know what became of his initial promise to build a gun for Frederick I that, like the one already designed for the Este court, could fire several shots without reloading.[641] It also remains unclear whether Colorni actually ended up confiding the "secrets" he had dangled before the duke about how one could peer into the distance at night or transmit a message into any stronghold, even if the messenger were to be undressed.[642] At any rate, from Colorni's correspondence with the Gonzaga court it emerges that he was now also functioning as a mediator of knowledge and contacts across the Alps from out of Württemberg. Colorni even boasted of having revived the close contacts that had existed a century earlier between the Gonzaga family and the House of Württemberg.[643] From Stuttgart, Colorni's services included offering precious vases for sale, delivering musical instruments, and helping to hire musicians.[644] It is likely that he also engineered Duke Frederick's attempt to recruit Abraham Portaleone from Mantua in 1597.[645] The duke apparently valued Colorni's counsel from the outset. In 1597 news that Frederick I was highly satisfied with him spread as far as Ferrara.[646] Alfonso II extended Colorni's stay in Württemberg, originally planned at just six weeks, for an additional two months.[647]

It is quite likely that Colorni also advised the duke on economic policy. Frederick had cut Württemberg off from the Swabian imperial cities and was now trying to stimulate the economy by loosening the prohibition on Jews engaging in trade, in the face of bitter resistance from the *Landschaft*.[648] In the spring of 1598, a Jewish "consul" by the name of Maggino di Gabrielli and other merchants established a "Hebrew Orient Trading Company" in Stuttgart with the duke's approval.[649] Maggino, whom we briefly encountered in Chapter 4, was an entrepreneur who combined technological know-how, a knowledge of the arcane, and a distinct interest in experiments. In Italy, this Jewish inventor—who grew up in Venice—had obtained privileges for a special silk-manufacturing process, risen to become a glass producer on a grand scale, and also been engaged in the manufacture of oil, wax, and paper. In this capacity, Maggino did not hesitate to speak of his technological knowledge—borrowing from a topos widespread among alchemists—as an exclusive "gift of God." He apparently did have an interest in alchemy. What is more, he had already proven when he was barely thirty that he knew how to handle secrets at a political level. The Medici sent him on a delicate political mission to the Levant in 1592. For Maggino, entrepreneurial ambition and operating in the economy of secrets went hand in hand.

The Duke of Württemberg hoped for extensive earnings from the Hebrew Orient Trading Company's trade deals. However, for the duke's subjects and high-ranking personalities at court, Jewish merchants settling in Württemberg was the final straw. Tumultuous scenes erupted in Stuttgart. From the pulpit, the court chaplain ranted against the settlement of Jews; accusations of ritual murder began to circulate among the population. Initially, the duke tried to counter the protests with drastic measures that included ostracizing his court chaplain. Politically isolated, he eventually succumbed to pressure from his critics. He inserted restrictive stipulations into the Jewish merchants' charter. Maggino could only look on helplessly at these developments. Just three months later, he and his merchants left the duchy.

After Maggino's withdrawal, the situation for Colorni, who remained behind in Stuttgart as court alchemist, became increasingly precarious. In the spring of 1599, the Württemberg Diet demanded that the duke do a better job of managing the budget and exhorted him to end the admission of Jews to the duchy and to expel those remaining.[650] The Diet's resolution could have referred only to Colorni. The duke was also losing patience with Colorni, who had probably been involved in the Hebrew Orient Trading Company.[651] In addition, Vincenzo Gonzaga urged the duke in ever-stronger language to let Colorni return to Mantua, where "his work was needed."[652] Frederick finally decided to summon Colorni "to perform the promised experiment" in the saltpeter hut.[653] In the meantime, Colorni's home was placed under guard and an instruction was sent to the sentries at the city gates to prevent him from leaving the city. In addition, Frederick ordered that Colorni no longer be given anything "special to eat and drink" by the head of the court kitchen. This probably also affected any provisions of kosher food. From now on, Colorni would receive only the food intended for ordinary servants, although this did entitle him to three meals a day.[654] Colorni must have drawn his own conclusions about the tougher stance the duke was now taking. He knew that the ruler's wrath had already brought some alchemists to the gallows. In fact, Frederick holds a dubious record in the history of alchemy: no prince executed more alchemists than he did.[655]

In March 1599, Colorni managed to escape from Württemberg—quite a feat for a man who had already turned fifty-five. The mysterious getaway demonstrated his celebrated talent as an escape artist (*disprigionatore*), as he absconded with at least 4,000 gulden worth of honoraria that had already been paid out to him. On March 23, the mayor, court-appointed deputies, and a clerk of the ordnance inspected the almost empty home that Colorni had left behind.[656] The duke's thoughts turned immediately to revenge: Colorni should receive "just deserts for his malicious and highly criminal offense."[657] News of his escape spread through the duchy. Inquiries were even made in Frankfurt and Brandenburg, but he was long out of the country by the time the pace of the search picked up. In fact, Colorni had managed to return to Mantua, where the Gonzaga family protected him despite Frederick's numerous attempts at extradition.[658] The Duke of Mantua's wife, Eleonora, was especially committed to Colorni's welfare. True, the Este did briefly incarcerate him shortly after his return, since the new, politically weakened duke, Cesare d'Este, wanted to avoid any conflict with Württemberg over the Colorni affair and needed to demonstrate at least a symbolic willingness to cooperate. Shortly thereafter, however, Colorni was apparently released at the behest of Eleonora. But on 15 November 1599, as a free man in Mantua, he succumbed to a "fever," as it says in the city's register of deaths.[659] Whether Colorni was in fact the victim of poisoning at the behest of the Duke of Württemberg will probably have to remain an open question.[660]

Frederick I clung to his demand for punishment even after Colorni's death. Since the deceased could not be prosecuted, the son would take his place. The Württembergian duke did not even shy away from proposing a deal to help the Gonzaga family resolve a smoldering territorial dispute in exchange for extraditing Colorni's son.[661] However, Vincenzo Gonzaga steadfastly refused to extradite as long as there was no evidence of the son's involvement in the alleged criminal offenses. The Gonzaga really had no interest in an extradition in the first place, and the deportation issue ultimately fizzled out.

In the Footsteps of Daedalus

We could easily end this chapter with Colorni's dramatic return to Mantua and his unexpected death. But in doing so, we would miss an opportunity to frame his life story in the larger context of the phenomenon of Jewish professors of secrets. In the early modern economy of secrets, Abramo Colorni was by no means an isolated case. While he might have been an especially multifaceted Jewish professor of secrets, he was neither the first nor the last. We have seen that he had enemies and enviers. But Colorni's biography also illustrates the kind of acceptance and esteem Jews working in the economy of secrets could encounter. Decades after his death, Colorni's name was still not forgotten either in Christian or in Jewish circles.

As we have seen, the poet and diplomat Alessandro Tassoni held Colorni in high esteem; similarly, the Duke of Braunschweig-Lüneburg heaped praise on Colorni for his skills as a cryptographer. In the mid-seventeenth century, two Italian admirers—Francesco Rovai and Jacopo Gaddi—composed baroque eulogies in celebration of Colorni.[662] The poets praised him as a "famous engineer" who made every enemy afraid when he appeared.[663] Drawing on Garzoni's descriptions, they praised Colorni's inventions and war machines in elaborate verse.[664] The panegyric culminated in an idealization of the "Great Colorni," transfiguring him into a modern "Daedalus of Esperia" (Esperia being an archaic term for Italy).[665] The comparison of Colorni to the ancient Daedalus, whose technological achievements and inventions were the stuff of Greek mythology, was not without precedent. It was a familiar topos of early modern panegyrics to engineers.[666] Jews, too, employed this topos: in Colorni's lifetime, the Jewish scholar Angelo Alat(r)ini sang his praises as a "new Daedalus" ("o nuovo Dedalo, o, Colorni").[667] In a work about mirrors, Rafael Mirami, the Jewish physician from Ferrara and contemporary of Colorni, was also full of praise for the *Euthimetria*. He even called its author a "most ingenious engineer."[668]

After Colorni's death, commemoration of the Jewish Daedalus lived on well beyond the Italian Jewish community. For example, his name appeared in a book that caused a stir in both Jewish and Christian circles in the middle of the seventeenth century—*Esperanza de Israel* (1650) by Menasseh ben Israel (1604–1657).[669] The work revolves around the supposed discovery of the lost Ten Tribes of Israel in the New World. The author was a renowned Sephardic scholar and book printer living in Amsterdam whose Messianic enthusiasm became more intense under the effect of the Puritan revolution in England. Menasseh saw what looked like the impending resettlement of the Jews in England as a precondition for the arrival of the messianic age. Eventually, there were even negotiations between his representatives and Oliver Cromwell. For this reason, Menasseh was eager to invalidate common accusations against Jews. In *Esperanza de Israel*, he sketched out a kind of hall of fame of noted Jewish minds and their accomplishments. In the Spanish edition of the book, which was intended for Jewish readers, Menasseh mentioned Colorni between the famous Sephardic Abravanel family and the Ottoman Jew Salomo Ashkenazi (ca. 1520–1602). This situated Colorni in a circle of Jews who had achieved great renown at royal courts. Indeed, Menasseh seemed truly impressed by the esteem Colorni had enjoyed at various European courts.[670] For Christian readers, however, this aspect of Colorni's life was of lesser importance. They were more impressed by the list of his accomplishments as an inventor and natural philosopher. Here, the English translation of Menasseh's book, printed in 1652, is revealing. In this edition, designed for Christian readers, Menasseh places Colorni in a circle of Jewish natural philosophers and physicians—that is, among "the number of ours who are renowned by fame and learning."[671]

This leads us to an important question that I have only adumbrated thus far: What was Colorni's position within, and toward, contemporary Jewry? Although a popular *professore de' secreti* in the Christian world, was Colorni just a marginal figure in the Jewish community of his time? His arrest in Florence in the 1570s owing to quarrels with the head of the Jewish community there might confirm this impression at first glance. However, we have seen that the Florentine authorities later rescinded Colorni's banishment and that the extant sources do not cast a favorable light on the head of the local Jewish community. This episode certainly did not damage Colorni's reputation either among his contemporaries or in the Jewish community afterward. Instead, he had his share of reputable Jewish business partners, such as the Carmi family. He also had many Jewish eulogists, including Menasseh ben Israel. There is reason to doubt whether Colorni kept kosher at all times—least of all when he lived in Stuttgart, a city without any Jewish infrastructure for kashruth and where he was dining at the princely table at court.[672] Still, Colorni remained a Jew throughout his life even though he was urged to convert on several occasions.[673] His rootedness in the Jewish community also becomes clear from a reconstruction of his family background. His marriage to the daughter of the highly respected moneylender and scholar Yeḥiel Nissim da Pisa testifies to his reputation in Jewish circles. Bridegroom and father-in-law also may have shared common scholarly or even Kabbalistic interests. Furthermore, the inventory of his son's library shows that Colorni kept many Hebrew religious books in his house. Of course, owning Hebrew books was not at all unusual for Jews at the time.[674] In Colorni's case, however, it deserves special emphasis; the list makes it clear that both father and son were thoroughly acquainted with Jewish traditions and teachings.

The Colorni family from Mantua, which included Abramo's four cousins, did not belong to the economic elite of Italian Jews in the sixteenth and seventeenth centuries. Still, the family was held in high esteem, and its members played important roles inside the structures of Jewish self-government. For example, Abramo Colorni's father was a member of the Jewish delegation that tried to prevent the Council of Trent from burning Hebrew books. And in the year of Abramo Colorni's death (1599), his cousin Samuele Colorni held a high office in the Jewish community of Mantua.[675] Outside Mantua, too, the Colorni family was well-regarded in Jewish circles. An entry in the record book of the Jewish community at Verona from the first quarter of the seventeenth century lists members of the Colorni family from Mantua among the few Jews from outside who were allowed to be housed by the community in Verona.[676]

Abramo was no exception in the Colorni family. In the sixteenth and seventeenth centuries, other members of the family made a living in the marketplace of the rare and secret. For example, Isaaco da Colorni—apparently Abramo's cousin—supplied elaborate craftwork and precious stones to the Gonzaga family.[677] Abramo's nephew Giuseppe Colorni worked in the service of the Mantuan Duke Carlo II; he also procured paintings and art objects, occasionally from out of Geneva.[678] Around 1616, Lazzaro Colorni enjoyed enough of a reputation at the court of Ferrara to get the Duke of Este to intervene with the Gonzaga court in a Jewish marital matter.[679] A few years earlier, around 1600, a cousin of Abramo Colorni by the name of Salomone was involved in organizing several lavish productions by the Jewish theater ensemble at the court in Mantua.

Where prestige at the courts is concerned, though, it is Abramo Colorni's own son Simone who should be mentioned first—although this has been completely overlooked by previous scholarship. It has even been claimed that Abramo Colorni's only son was mentally handicapped and eked out a miserable existence.[680] This assumption rests on a statement made by the Duke of Mantua when he was attempting to prevent the son from being extradited to Württemberg. It was a tactical lie; Simone Colorni was not mentally handicapped in the slightest. In fact, he was extremely versatile and enterprising. While he did follow in his father's footsteps, he also enjoyed a reputation entirely in his own right. At the court in Mantua, he sported the literally dark byname Il Morino.[681]

Simone's date of birth is unknown, though we can conjecture that he was born in the 1570s. For years, Abramo took care to see that his son received instruction at the hands of a renowned teacher, Rabbi Angelo Alatini.[682] Alatini is known to posterity as the author of a pastoral comedy titled *I trionfi* (1575). His intellectual range—in particular, his knowledge of ancient literature—was formidable.[683] In a way, Simone was also schooled by his father. We have already seen that Simone was later able to demonstrate expertise in the manufacture of saltpeter. But from his father he also learned how to move about in the courtly world and in the economy of secrets. As a youth, Simone occasionally stayed with Abramo at the imperial court in Prague. From there, he delivered letters to the Duke of Mantua. Later, he also visited his father at the court in Stuttgart.[684] The skills Simone acquired early on about how to comport himself properly and conduct business at court certainly made a major contribution to his career. Although it is unclear in what year Simone officially entered into service for the Gonzaga family, we do know that, by the 1590s at the latest, Il Morino had become an indispensable procurer of information and objects of all kinds for the Gonzaga—and one who enjoyed the ducal family's trust.

Il Morino first appears in the Gonzaga family's correspondence in 1588, in connection with the purchase of a precious jewel in Venice.[685] He quickly acquired a reputation for his skill at appraising precious objects. The duke consulted him once as an expert on the credentials of a gem cutter and jeweler from out of town.[686] In 1591, on assignment from the Gonzaga court, Il Morino joined a nephew of the painter Titian to view the collection that had belonged to the late Cardinal Pietro Bembo (1470–1547), part of which was up for sale. He delivered drawings of ancient art works to the court.[687] He also played an important behind-the-scenes role in transferring Count Galeazzo Canossa's collection to Mantua in 1604. After lengthy negotiations with the count, the Gonzaga duke was inclined to acquire this important art collection. The price was high: in addition to getting a sum of almost 7,000 scudi, the count received the Cagliano fief in Monferrato along with the title of marchese.[688] As part of the exchange, several artworks of the first order came to Mantua, including *L'adorante*—one of the rare originals of a Hellenistic bronze statue, today in Berlin's Pergamon

Museum—along with a "certain antique Madonna" that happened to be no less than one painted by Raphael.[689] Il Morino was instrumental in transferring this valuable collection after he had already been involved in the negotiations.[690] Trading in precious stones, artworks, and luxury goods remained Simone Colorni's lifelong trademark, and his sphere of operations was not confined to Italy.[691] He also operated on occasion at the imperial court in Prague, where he had already established contacts during his father's lifetime. The Mantuan ambassador at the court in Prague was a special customer, buying gifts required for bribes, including precious stones, from Simone.[692]

In addition to trading in luxury goods, which required great discretion, Il Morino could also claim expertise in alchemy and arcane medicine. In 1595, he sent an ampoule containing a secret balsam to Mantua using a Jewish messenger from Venice.[693] In 1603, on assignment from an imperial alchemist in Prague, he delivered a case containing various "oils" that apparently included medicines.[694] Vincenzo Gonzaga greatly appreciated this delivery, and he soon ordered another casket with some of these oils.[695] Simone Colorni's product range also included one of the most coveted "secrets of nature" during that period: the unicorn, or rather the powder produced from its horn (see Chapter 2). The Mantuan ambassador at the imperial court was convinced that his life had been saved by prompt administration of Simone Colorni's unicorn powder following a nocturnal stroke.[696] The convalesced ambassador was not the only contemporary to trust and praise Il Morino. By backing Simone, the Gonzaga ducal family even risked tensions with the Duke of Württemberg when the latter demanded his extradition. Mantuan courtiers agreed that Duke Vincenzo had taken extraordinary measures when he personally intervened to prevent Simone Colorni's extradition.[697]

Who Was Abramo Colorni?

In the drafts to one of the most enigmatic works of modern literature, there is an entry that is as surprising as it is cryptic: "scotographia/-scribia," wrote James Joyce in one of the notebooks for his last great work, *Finnegans Wake*

(1939).⁶⁹⁸ Was this a coincidence, or did Joyce know about Abramo Colorni, the Jewish *professore de' secreti* whose 1593 treatise on cryptography was titled *Scotographia,* a neologism not found anywhere else? We do know that Joyce liked to take cues from Jewish history, as in *Ulysses,* a work containing various allusions to Jewish Renaissance mysticism.⁶⁹⁹ It is entirely plausible that Joyce learned of Colorni's work, or least its title, from the secondary literature or a library catalogue. After all, Joyce lived briefly in Italy after 1900. In the case of *Finnegans Wake,* the author's familiarity with the world of early modern Italy is strikingly revealed in the way the novel's basic setup is influenced by the philosophy of Giambattista Vico.⁷⁰⁰ Moreover, *Finnegans Wake* also contains a wide range of allusions to Judaism. One can read this equally witty and experimental opus, which has no plot in any conventional sense and uses words from almost seventy languages, as a "farced epistol to the hibruws" (Joyce's words)—a wordplay that borrows from the New Testament ("first epistle to the Hebrews").⁷⁰¹ If our hypothesis is correct, however, it does not necessarily mean Joyce was interested in Colorni as a Jew. If he came across the Mantuan Jew's cryptographic treatise, he was probably intrigued by the idea of a "dark writing," which is how the word "scotographia" would be translated. Symbolic imagery revolving around darkness and dreams plays an important role in *Finnegans Wake,* as Joyce himself acknowledged.⁷⁰² Joyce's interest in the concept of a "dark writing" has to be seen against this backdrop, even though he did not return to the term he had entered into his notebook when it came to putting the novel in writing. But even if the notebook entry was entirely coincidental, it is tempting to speculate about a link between Colorni, the *professore de' secreti* vaunted by contemporaries, and the very novel that has been called an unsurpassed literary "compilation of arcane materials."⁷⁰³

Secrecy and mastery of the arcane are keywords for understanding Colorni's biography. His career exhausted the entire spectrum of activities in the economy of secrets—from military inventions, to trading in curiosa and dealing with divinatory practices, to magic and card tricks. This could easily create the impression that Colorni chose his activities aimlessly and that he was indeed the kind of opportunistic charlatan that some historians suggest he was. Colorni is certainly not to be envied for his posthumous reputation in historical scholarship. This is not just because he has largely fallen into oblivion. (He is not even mentioned in the authoritative works on Jewish magic, alchemy, and esotericism.) When Colorni's biography actually does get mentioned, it is often written off as a curious episode.

We can distinguish three different approaches to Colorni in previous scholarship. First, there is local history research. Publications on Jewish history in Bohemia, and especially in Württemberg, depict Colorni simply as a magician or charlatan. As early as 1788, the German historian Friedrich Wilhelm Moser called him a "Cagliostro."[704] By contrast, a popular Stuttgart collection of tales from 1875 introduced the Jewish court alchemist Colorni under the distorted name "Calome" and launched the absurd rumor—not supported by any source—that Colorni had stolen a silver image of Jesus from the Spitalkirche.[705] It comes as no surprise that Colorni also appears in Lion Feuchtwanger's popular historical novel *Jud Süß* as a rather dubious character.[706] Even an otherwise commendable local history of the Jews in Stuttgart published in 1964 was still depicting Colorni as a magician.[707]

The second historiographic approach, prevalent in scholarship dealing with early modern Jewish history, is decidedly different. Here, Colorni is a Jewish Renaissance man, even a "Jewish Leonardo da Vinci."[708] To this category we can also add those studies in which individual details from Colorni's biography are (often anecdotally) taken out of context in order to prove that premodern Jews made major "contributions" to a variety of fields. At the beginning of the twentieth century, Colorni was praised as the purported Jewish father of the automatic rifle and as the inventor of all kinds of "useful things."[709] As a result of Garzoni's panegyric, Colorni even found a place in the category "Jews as shipbuilders."[710] From time to time, this idealization of Colorni led to him being co-opted in highly questionable ways. In the 1930s, when the situation of Jews in fascist Italy was deteriorating, the right-wing Jewish periodical *La nostra bandiera,* which openly sympathized with fascism, used an article about Colorni as a way of illustrating the contributions Jews had made to Italian culture.[711]

This uncritical view of Colorni goes back to the nineteenth century's *Wissenschaft des Judentums* (Science of Judaism). Among exponents of this scholarly movement, one finds cursory references to Colorni that marginalize his alchemical activities, an approach that started with the Colorni studies undertaken by Ferrara's Rabbi Giuseppe Jarè (1840-1915). The historically interested Rabbi Jarè himself had been indebted to the research agenda of the German *Wissenschaft des Judentums*. In Colorni he saw, above all, an eminent Italian.[712] By contrast, Italian patriotism was not the driving force behind German scholars' interest in Colorni. For the bibliographer and Orientalist Moritz Steinschneider—one of the most prominent minds of the *Wissenschaft des Judentums* in Germany—Colorni was first and foremost an exponent of the long history of "mathematics among the Jews."[713] Steinschneider placed Colorni in a group of Jewish intellectuals from sixteenth-century Italy who wrote about "scientific subjects" in an "independent" way "that Germany cannot boast prior to Mendelssohn, Jewish materials aside."[714] In this way, scholars rescued Colorni for the "prehistory" of the Haskalah. We owe a more balanced assessment of Colorni from that era to the Jewish scholar David Kaufmann, who noted in 1898 that Colorni "demonstrates, as if in a single picture, the versatility of the Italian Renaissance as architect, alchemist, and expert on Jewish literature"—even if this comment was made only in passing, and under the influence of Jacob Burckhardt's idealized conception of the Renaissance.[715]

A third and final historiographic approach has emerged in more recent accounts of Jewish history in Italy. It characterizes Colorni as a flamboyant adventurer or "half charlatan, half genius."[716] However, it is questionable whether these are more than catchy formulas that ultimately evade commitment to any particular view.

My portrait of Colorni has tried to follow none of these three historiographic traditions. In my opinion, Colorni was neither genius nor charlatan nor Jewish Leonardo. He envisioned himself first and foremost in the role of an early modern *professore de' secreti*, which he associated with a specific (Solomonic) ethos. This self-fashioning is reflected in his own writings. Contemporary sources also used the same language to discuss Colorni.

Indeed, nowhere in the sources from his time in Prague do we find a clear-cut professional designation for Colorni; officially, he operated neither as an alchemist nor as an engineer. The Venetian ambassador at the imperial court got to the heart of the matter when he reported back home that Colorni was esteemed and paid by the emperor as a person who "has many important secrets" ("provisionato dall'Imperatore come persona ch'ha molti secreti importanti").[717] This was also how the Medici court in Florence viewed things. When Colorni applied in 1592 to obtain a privilege from the Medici to publish his writings, a Florentine court official concluded, after consulting with the ambassador in Prague, that Colorni was a "very skilled man" who "knows various natural secrets and is therefore quite welcome by the Emperor."[718]

Even during all the years he was employed back in Italy, Colorni was more than just an engineer (the only official title that can be substantiated for his time at the court of Ferrara). He certainly did not see himself primarily or even exclusively as a magus either, even if he performed feats of magic in order to impress his public or his patrons throughout his life. One only needs to open his *Euthimetria* to find descriptions of engineering technology from his pen that are hardly compatible with the language of a magus. However, it would be just as misleading to believe that Colorni gradually transformed himself from a "serious naturalist" into a magus, whether out of opportunism or frustration. In reality, the two types of expertise frequently complemented each other and overlapped from the outset. While influences from occult thinking can be found in Colorni's understanding of mathematics, his magic was inseparable from his aspiration to the status of a *scientia*. The common thread running through these various skills was Colorni's ability to handle secrets.

Garzoni admired the versatility of Colorni's interests and skills early on. Yet he, too, acknowledged that the key to Colorni's mastery of so many different fields of knowledge was an overarching expertise in the economy of secrets. Colorni was, in Garzoni's words, a "master of secrets."[719] Seen in this light, Colorni's *Chirofisionomia* and *Scotographia* constituted two sides of the same coin. While the chiromancer attempts to decipher the secrets of the future and of a person's character from the shape and lines of the hand, the cryptographer tries to encode and decode the secrets of language. This becomes even more plausible when one considers that many contemporaries regarded the "reading" of physiognomic features as a special variant of the art of deciphering.[720]

The *professore de' secreti* Colorni was capable, in a figurative sense, of speaking several languages—including those of the engineer, the magus, and the courtier. But he also had to be careful to distance himself clearly from the roles he did not wish to play. One such role was that of the charlatan behaving like a marketplace barker, a type of character then widespread in Italy—and also performed by Jews.[721] Toward the end of his life Colorni himself remarked, with a certain self-assuredness, the he could never have won over so many esteemed patrons from the ranks of the high nobility if the arts he practiced had been based merely on lies and deception.[722] True, Colorni also had a good sense for theatricality, a skill often highly developed among charlatans who acted on the stage. But his knowledge amounted to more than that; in his eyes, it was an unequivocal gift of God, not a mere hodgepodge of secrets accidentally thrown together. Just like Della Porta, Colorni used the term "scienza" when he talked about his own knowledge and his arts.[723] The secrets he offered were ones he had extracted from nature by way of inquiry, some even by divine inspiration.[724] Colorni wanted a public that would marvel at his feats, but not one that was spellbound by superstition or that he needed to intimidate beforehand by using incantations. If Colorni wanted to avoid being associated with the devil and his arts, he did indeed need to insist he had acquired his knowledge in a natural and systematic way.

The role of professor of secrets came in handy here. The criteria for this relatively new profession had not been clearly defined, but there were models that could serve as examples—especially that of his contemporary Della Porta. It is not a coincidence that Colorni's career displays a number of features that recall Della Porta's life story. (It would also be interesting to find out what Della Porta knew about his Jewish colleague.) Both men published a cryptographic treatise, pleaded for a "scientific" form of natural magic, were intensely preoccupied with the practical application of mirrors, and took a similar approach to physiognomy and chiromancy. It is entirely possible that Della Porta and Colorni knew each other personally.[725] After all, the Neapolitan secrecy adept did maintain good contacts with the Este family—especially with Cardinal Luigi d'Este—during the late sixteenth century.

Colorni's career was undoubtedly shaped by influences from the Christian world. Ultimately, he depended on Christian princes for a major share of his jobs. For the whole of his career, Colorni benefited from the way the Christian world ascribed a distinctive mastery of the arcane to Jews. Does this mean that Colorni was merely a Jewish epigone of Della Porta? To put the question in exaggerated form: Were Jews like Colorni who made a living in the economy of secrets merely taking advantage of a niche conceded to them by Christian society? This is a critical question to which we shall return in the concluding chapter. But at this point, I believe it can already be answered in the negative. Colorni did not opt for the economy of secrets because he would have been blocked from a university path. On the contrary, he had attended the university in Ferrara and was very impressed with one of the Christian professors there. He could have obtained an academic degree in Ferrara or, under even easier conditions, in nearby Padua. It is also telling that Colorni's son followed unwaveringly in his father's footsteps and became, in his own right, a sought-after expert in the economy of secrets.

Abramo Colorni remained a Jew his entire life, and this was not an obstacle to his career path. On the contrary, it lent him credibility in the economy of secrets. However, he did not derive legitimation for his work as a professor of secrets from Christian imagination alone; he also drew legitimation from Jewish tradition itself. Of central importance here was the appeal to the biblical King Solomon. Colorni referred frequently to the fabled wise ruler. He cited King Solomon at critical junctures in his work, and he also enjoyed a reputation as translator of the *Clavicula Salomonis*—the very work that decisively shaped the image of the biblical king as a magus and secrecy adept. It is not surprising that Colorni saw the court in Prague as, in his own words, a modern reincarnation of the Solomonic world. At the pinnacle of this world, there was a ruler who, like Solomon, longed to acquire knowledge of all the world's secrets.

Colorni was not the only Jew during this era who saw King Solomon as a model for his own preoccupation with nature and its hidden secrets. This idealization and arcanization of King Solomon was also an attempt to fashion a competitive and distinctly Jewish alternative to the heathen figure of Hermes Trismegistos. For Colorni, King Solomon provided not only an opportunity for identification, but also for distinction. In the far-flung and complex early modern economy of secrets, the appeal to Solomon enabled Jews like Colorni to claim a special role as guardians of Solomonic knowledge that seemed genuine and promising.

SIX

The Culture and Crisis of Secrecy

THE EARLY MODERN ERA was the age of secrecy. No other period in European history has been marked by so profound a fascination with secrets and secret sciences. Among the myriads of arcana and *secreta* that populated the premodern cosmos, however, only a few demanded awe-struck contemplation or were inaccessible in everyday life. Quite the contrary, secrets were daily traded, exchanged, exhibited, recorded, or sometimes merely hinted at in a suggestive and deliberate way. This permanent circulation and communication of knowledge that was concealed but simultaneously useful formed the core of the economy of secrets. European Jews played a preeminent part in this economy, given their extremely small share of the total population.

What does this mean for the history of science and culture, not least from a Jewish perspective? First, we cannot adequately interpret Jews' major role in the economy of secrets using traditional historical narratives. This is true, for example, of the narrative about the "contribution" Jews made to "science." Second, there are also implications for our general understanding of that process which has often been described as the "Scientific Revolution." Did the persuasive power of epistemic paradigm shifts really blaze the trail for the "New Science," both in society as a whole and among a group like the Jews in particular? There were other fundamental and societal shifts that led to an erosion of the economy of secrets. My intention here is not to revisit the well-worn debate about the connection between religion and science—a debate that has focused primarily on certain religious and confessional groups, such as the Puritans and the Jesuits. Neither am I concerned with the much-discussed question of whether the rise of the New Science required pushing back against religion or, conversely, whether specific religious factors were actually conducive to science. In my opinion, we cannot answer these questions in any conclusive way. Instead, we must devote more attention to the broad array of opportunities that existed outside of those institutions that promoted the ideal of openly circulating knowledge. The picture that will emerge is one marked by both a pluralism of knowledge cultures and a complex entanglement of secrecy and openness.

Historiography and the "Contributory Narrative"

A great deal has been written on the question of whether, and to what extent, Jews contributed to the Scientific Revolution. This debate persists today. The German *Wissenschaft des Judentums* of the nineteenth and early twentieth centuries maintained that Jews' importance for the emergence of modern science was indisputable. Leading exponents of the *Wissenschaft des Judentums* went to great lengths to make their contemporaries, especially non-Jewish fellow Germans, aware of a spirit of research and a commitment to reason that were supposedly inherent to Judaism.[1] This discourse can be called the "contributory narrative."[2] It had a major effect on the field of Jewish history at large and led to what Raphael Patai aptly characterized as a decidedly "anti-alchemical approach of modern Jewish scholars."[3] Research about fields dismissed as peripheral or esoteric—such as alchemy, Kabbalah, and magic—hardly played a part in this reason-oriented approach to Jewish history. Around the turn of the twentieth century, the major bibliographer and Orientalist Moritz Steinschneider (1816–1907) proclaimed, in a verdict as one-sided as it seemed apodictic, that there had never been an appreciable Jewish contribution to alchemy at any time. Steinschneider saw alchemy as "nonsense" and argued that the "lack of alchemical writings among Jews" was one of Judaism's great achievements.[4] Even his younger contemporary Max Grunwald (1871–1953), who did not always keep in line with the *Wissenschaft des Judentums* and who helped to establish the new field of Jewish folklore studies, credited Maimonides in particular with having protected the "core of Judaism from every kind of superstitious excrescence." Grunwald consigned superstition and popular belief to the "periphery" of everyday Jewish life.[5]

Like many of their colleagues from the *Wissenschaft des Judentums*, Steinschneider and Grunwald overlooked what they did not want to see. For these historically well-versed, enlightened "citizens of Jewish faith," research into mystical and arcane practices among the Jews of bygone eras was highly suspect. Although their historical findings continue to be useful, the very titles of their works—*Mathematics among the Jews* or *The Jews as Inventors and Discoverers*, for example—clearly refer back to a time when scholars always had one eye on animosities against contemporary Jews. As a result, their studies were often apologetic or defensive in tone.[6] Tellingly, the groundwork for the systematic study of Kabbalah was laid from the 1920s onward by the Zionist-minded Gershom Scholem (1897–1982), who not only belonged to a younger generation but also viewed the project of a "German-Jewish symbiosis" with far fewer illusions. Scholem was also the first to address the connections between alchemy and Kabbalah at a scholarly level.[7] However, the first comprehensive study on magic in medieval and early modern Judaism was not published until 1939, with a book by the American Reform rabbi Joshua Trachtenberg. Trachtenberg described the variety of magical practices and attitudes that existed in Judaism, but he basically adhered to Steinschneider's apodictic assessment of alchemy. He maintained that "some [Jewish] physicians, in their experiments with chemistry, probably dabbled in alchemy also, but this branch of the magical [!] arts had in general very little currency among Jews."[8] In his monumental *Social and Religious History of the Jews*, Salo W. Baron arrived at a similar conclusion.[9] Even the most recent edition of the *Encyclopaedia Judaica* (2007) adopts the first (1971) edition's view that the number of Jewish alchemists was "relatively small."[10] A few years ago, an acknowledged expert on the Jewish history of science asked, in much the same spirit, why "alchemy [was] so marginal in Judaism"—as if research in this area had already made such headway that the question's underlying premise was beyond doubt.[11] To this day there has been only a single attempt at writing a history of Jewish alchemists—the 1994 study by the Hungarian Jewish folklorist Raphael Patai.[12] But his investigation, though rich in material, contains a number of inaccuracies—some of them quite substantial—and hasty generalizations.[13] Moreover, even Patai was unable to break away from the contributory narrative. In an attempt to refute the view that Jews were uninterested in alchemy, his study went so far as to include alchemists whose Jewish background is highly questionable or who had only shaky ties to Judaism.

But let us return to the notion that Jews embarked on the path of rational thinking and contributed to the formation of modern science whenever there was any social opening for them to do so. This contributory narrative hardly disappeared after 1933, when the *Wissenschaft des Judentums* came to an abrupt and brutal end in German-speaking Europe. The persistence of this narrative in the field of the history of science may also have something to do with the perceived need for a Jewish response to the influential Merton thesis, formulated in the 1930s by American sociologist Robert K. Merton under the influence of Max Weber. Historians of science had picked up and popularized this thesis, according to which the Puritans had particular affinities and dispositions for the Scientific Revolution.[14] Followers of Merton continue to insist that the thesis is much more subtle than it critics maintain.[15] And, indeed, Merton himself avoided any kind of strictly monocausal explanation. At the same time, it is undeniable that Merton's thesis developed a momentum all its own, initiating a large number of studies about the link between religion and the New Science. Soon enough, it attracted the attention of Catholic historians who tried to highlight Catholic, and especially Jesuit, involvement in science.[16] The persistent interest in whether religion promoted or inhibited the emergence of "science" in the early modern era also left an imprint on the agenda of Jewish history. As a result, historians of Jewish history have long neglected the importance of "pseudo-sciences" like alchemy, or even magic.

This is an irony of history. Robert K. Merton, originally Meyer R. Schkolnick, was the son of a poor Jewish family from Eastern Europe. He was a passionate magician in his youth, and he kept up the practice of magic throughout his life. As a young man, he borrowed from great magicians of the past the first and last names under which he would become known as one of the twentieth century's most important sociologists.[17] "Robert" was an homage to the acclaimed French magician Jean Eugène Robert-Houdin

(1805–1871), and "Merton" was inspired by the name of the legendary magus Merlin.

The Merton thesis constitutes an important factor behind the persistence of the contributory narrative, especially with regard to early modern Jewry. Examples of this tendency include the learned works of scholars such as Harry Friedenwald, Cecil Roth, Lewis S. Feuer, Moses A. Shulvass, and André Neher.[18] Unlike historians indebted to the *Wissenschaft des Judentums*—for whom "that which must not, can not be"—the British historian Cecil Roth did not conceal his budding skepticism.[19] He admitted that the "scientific" experiments he found among early modern Jews could hardly be described by using the categories of the emerging New Science. Roth concluded, with disillusionment, that the early modern figure of the Jewish charlatan had increasingly taken the place of the rational-minded Jewish intellectual of the Middle Ages. Roth titled an entire chapter on this subject "Physicians, Quacks, and Charlatans." His disillusionment should come as no surprise. For Roth, who was originally trained as a general historian, scientific activity among early modern Jews had to prove itself against the yardstick of seventeenth-century New Science as embodied by its heroes—Galileo, Bacon, Descartes—and institutions, especially academies and scientific societies.

In the 1980s, the Israeli historian Robert Bonfil, a resolute critic of Roth, pointed out the methodological dubiousness of measuring early modern Jewish history against the development and normative categories of Christian society.[20] However, even recent scholarship has a certain fixation on "big themes" from the Christian history of science—themes like the reception of Copernicanism. This fixation explains why there is a wealth of studies on the work of the Jewish author and astronomer David Gans (1541–1613)—a man who, even in the assessment of his most sympathetic biographer, was a scientist of rather modest scholarly stature.[21] By contrast, not a single satisfactory study, let alone one that is halfway systematic and comprehensive, exists about Jews in the mechanical arts, in technology transfer, or in the practice of alchemy.

Since these other forms of knowledge production flourished above all in early modern Italy, it is even more curious that they are almost completely ignored in a recent collection of articles devoted to the relationship between science and Judaism in Italy.[22] According to this edited volume, Jews made few contributions to the Scientific Revolution, as defined by figures such as Galileo, Descartes, Newton, and Leibniz. This diagnosis is followed by a dubious distinction between the Greco-analytical and Judeo-harmonizing conceptions of the world.[23] Judaism, we are told, preferred theoretical-abstract forms to experimental practices of knowledge; the introduction cites traditional Talmud study and the delayed entry of Jews into the industrial sector until the nineteenth century as reasons for this preference.[24] The last argument is particularly unconvincing. Although it is true that historians will not find Jews in premodern Christian guilds, there is hardly a branch of industry in which early modern Jews were not active. The manufacturing of glass, the development of military technology, the production of gunpowder, and the making of textiles and consumer goods—oil, soap, and sugar refining, for example—are just a few prominent examples.[25]

During the past two decades, the historian David Ruderman has offered a more nuanced view of the relationship between early modern science and Judaism. Ruderman focuses on Jewish physicians, medical students, and rabbis and on the ways these three specific groups reacted to the scientific upheavals of the early modern Christian world.[26] Especially in the case of Jewish medical students and physicians in Italy, Ruderman identifies a tension between traditional rabbinic teachings and the kind of knowledge acquired at Christian universities. He attributes this tension to incongruence—never overcome more than partially, even in the seventeenth century—between the methods of the New Science and traditional forms of Jewish learning.[27] In contrast to the Middle Ages, when renowned Jewish philosophers viewed the theoretical study of physics and metaphysics practically as a religious command compatible with faith, early modern rabbis formulated a more severe critique of fields of secular knowledge that threatened to contradict the fundamental doctrines of Judaism. However, rabbis did approve of a natural science restricted to empirical matters that would lead to the appreciation of the perfection of God's creation without challenging the tenets of Judaism.[28] Some historians have linked rabbinic approval of empiricism to a long-standing tradition whereby Jews resorted to direct perception and common sense as a way of refuting Christian mysteries—such as the Immaculate Conception and transubstantiation—that had been invoked against them for centuries.[29]

For many rabbis, empirical arguments clearly lost their appeal as soon as they threatened to turn against the teachings of Judaism. The study of (natural) science remained a double-edged sword, as Ruderman in particular has argued. This view also claims to explain why Jewish natural philosophers were "hardly the most prominent contributors to the scientific revolution," even though interest in the development of science was widespread.[30] Ruderman is not alone in concluding that "only a handful of Jews contributed substantially to science, and even these were primarily active in the field of medicine."[31] Alongside religious hurdles, scholars commonly cite the Jewish minority's social exclusion.[32] As we will see, however, neither the cessation of social barriers nor a triumph of the Haskalah, that is, of the Jewish Enlightenment movement, was solely responsible for the relatively late entry of Jews into modern science after 1800.

More recent contributions to the debate about the points of conflicts between early modern Judaism and the New Science do not depart significantly from this model. For instance, Hava Tirosh-Samuelson locates the reason for Jews' minimal contribution to the Scientific Revolution at the hermeneutic level, arguing that many Jews' traditional approach to nature was based on written texts, which exacerbated—if they did not entirely prevent—any transition to experimental and inductive epistemologies.[33] According to this explanation, it proved difficult for the Jewish "theology of nature" to converge with the emerging scientific method of the seventeenth century, since the prevailing view among Jewish naturalists was that natural phenomena were to be read as signs written in God's language. We are left with a picture of antagonism between a text-based Jewish epistemology that aimed primarily at harmonizing knowledge with faith, on one hand, and modern, scientific epistemology based on quantitative-experimental methods, on the other.[34]

Finally, there is the position of the late historian Amos Funkenstein. His studies of Jewish history were often unconventional. In this case, however, he opted for a relatively traditional explanation for why Jews did not develop "a sustained interest in the sciences during the scientific revolution."[35] Funkenstein's conception of "sciences" here is rather narrow and traditionally construed. For him, accepting heliocentrism is a major yardstick of "intellectual activity" in the field of natural science. His argument is based on the rather unconvincing premise that Jews "were remote from some centers of science, such as England and France."[36] The effects of Jews' supposed isolation from the centers of science were amplified by the intellectually defensive attitude of early modern Jews, for whom "every instance of intellectual activity beyond pure entertainment had to be linked to Jewish concerns."[37] Other historians have taken this argument one step farther, asserting that premodern Ashkenazi Jewry's rejection of science was "part and parcel of its intellectual being."[38]

The Economy of Secrets and the Plurality of Knowledge Cultures

The positions and arguments outlined here make it clear that scholars of Jewish history have dealt extensively with the relationship between religion and natural science. Moreover, they have frequently asked how Jewish activity in natural science related to the New Science and whether that relationship can be described using the categories of rejection or participation. But inquiring into this very linkage seems, in some respects, to make for a *question mal posée*. Tellingly, the editor of a recently published collection of articles devoted to the topic of Judaism and the sciences concedes, right in the introduction, that even the three articles examining the situation in Rudolphine Prague come to "conflicting conclusions" or, to put it more bluntly, arrive at completely different results.[39] But this should hardly come as a surprise. Limiting inquiry into the entire scope of Jewish natural science primarily to a single set of questions about Jewish interest in the New Science is bound to produce a distorted picture, for three reasons.

First, this way of posing the question tends to neglect important pieces of the broad historical record as revealed in extant sources. The Christian idea of a New Science, as it took shape from the seventeenth century onward, cannot be the only yardstick for interpreting all manifestations of Jewish activity in natural science, including in the economy of secrets. By focusing on the question of the "contribution" Jews made to "science," historians miss opportunities for investigating the full range of Jewish expertise in natural history, the occult, and technology, including the intersections of such knowledge with economic activity. As a result, early modern Jews' multifaceted expertise does not get studied as a phenomenon in its own right.

Second, there is the question of what scholars actually mean by the concept "New Science" in the first place. It is easier to invoke than to define. Indeed, scholars have used the term in very different ways.[40] Certainly, some of the arguments outlined above rest on an idealized image of how the early modern business of science was conducted in Christian society—an image inattentive to recent scholarship in the general history of science that has seriously questioned whether there actually was a linear, homogenous process warranting the designation "Scientific Revolution."[41] This does not mean that it would be proper to throw the concept of the New Science overboard entirely. Ultimately, no one can seriously overlook the gaping differences at the epistemological level between, say, Dee and Descartes or Della Porta and Galileo. Yet it is also necessary to stress that the New Science was just one of several knowledge cultures to choose from in the early modern era and that its position was not yet unchallenged.[42] While the New Science undoubtedly yielded many notable achievements, it cannot be cited as the sole explanation for that complex shift in priorities that occurred in the European knowledge economy as it made the transition to modernity. As Lorraine Daston and Katharine Park have demonstrated, for example, growing skepticism about wonders toward the end of the early modern period was not brought about primarily, much less solely, by the New Science.[43] A comparable picture also emerges for the economy of secrets. If we want to understand why the foundations of this economy began to erode after 1800, then we need to look for an answer at the level of society as a whole.

The third and final objection does not revolve so much around what defines the distinct knowledge cultures of the early modern era as it does around what connects them. In the 1960s, the influential, albeit controversial, British historian Frances Yates proposed a reassessment of the historical origins of the Scientific Revolution. Especially in her study of Giordano

Bruno, Yates took the view that Hermetic philosophy, with its idealized notion of the magus, paved the way for "modern science."[44] The Renaissance magus pioneered an active, experiment-oriented science that was trying to emancipate itself from the contemplative passivity of medieval science. Although Yates's thesis has been much discussed, and also severely criticized, strong evidence indicates that occult thought was not often sharply distinguished from science through the seventeenth century.[45] The best-known case is probably Isaac Newton's profound engagement with alchemical ideas. Francis Bacon also expressed interest, however ambivalently, in magic and alchemy.[46] Above all, there is the tradition of the *magia naturalis,* in which experiments and a preoccupation with physical forces and properties played an important role. This has even prompted some historians to argue that "science developed largely from a natural magic stripped of mysticism."[47]

In the field of Jewish history, too—and especially against the background of the Yates debate—scholarly interest in magical and occult knowledge among early modern Jews has increased, even if this interest is not always placed in a broader historiographic context. For example, scholars have noted that the works of Jewish natural philosophers like Yoḥanan Alemanno, Abraham Farissol, David de Pomis, and Abraham Yagel are rich in descriptions of strange animals, monsters, rare stones, and exotic plants.[48] Among some prominent Kabbalists, too, mystical-magical and naturalist-experimental interests are tightly interwoven.[49] In this light, David Ruderman has warned that early modern Jews' rather sluggish reception of Copernicus should not be the sole yardstick for measuring the intensity of their scientific activity.[50] Yet even he concludes that there was a growing tendency in the seventeenth century for Jewish authors to abandon their interest in the occult and mysticism in favor of the known and proven.[51] Granted, this might apply to the main group he examines—university-trained Jewish physicians—even if (as we have seen) a number of Jewish physicians in the sixteenth and seventeenth centuries demonstrated substantial knowledge in the fields of arcana and alchemy. At any rate, if one disregards the relatively small professional group of physicians who had academic training—a group that constituted not only an educational, but also often a social elite—the picture looks rather different. In fact, there is no evidence for any significant turn away from the broader economy of secrets well into the eighteenth century. The realm of the secret continued to provide a complex range of opportunities and to maintain its economic relevance.

In sum, historians today tend to see the complex and often occult character of early modern Jewish natural science in a more nuanced and unbiased way than their predecessors did only a few decades ago. Still, the question of how Jews reacted to the "challenge" posed by the New Science, or to what extent they were involved in it, continues to be a key issue in the study of early modern Jewish history.[52] This historiographic stalemate has caused the Jewish history of science to sometimes resemble, at the methodological level, one of the early modern era's most coveted objects—the *perpetuum mobile*. Constant repetition of the claim that early modern Jews barely contributed to the New Science is bound to perpetuate the question of what circumstances, incentives, or initial conditions were lacking.[53] This, in turn, has led scholars to focus on rabbinical discussions of science or on the works of a few individuals such as David Gans who were hardly representative.[54] It also leaves us in a methodological loop that has caused a number of historians to overlook other kinds of expertise, both broad and lucrative, that existed outside of the New Science. In fact, closed structures of patronage—and the economy of secrets as a whole—frequently represented a much more attractive market for traders in knowledge than did institutions committed, at least in theory, to openness.

There is also a discrepancy between normative texts and historical reality. Rabbinical writings showed relatively little interest in the New Science—if by this we mean Copernicus or the activities of the scientific academies—but that literary inattention did not necessarily translate into a lack of experimental or technological (arcane) expertise among Jews, or even among rabbis for that matter. Recall, for example, the late-sixteenth-century career of Clemente (Kalonimos) Pavia from Lodi, for whom there was no conflict among his roles as inventor, moneylender, and ordained rabbi. Pavia did not try to present his invention, a new type of water pump, at universities or among scholars. He and his two brothers, who helped him market his know-how, were not interested in impressing a learned public. Rather, they wanted courts and other affluent patrons to buy their technology—something they succeeded in doing. In such contexts, maintaining secrecy was more promising than open marketing or publication. This was also the case for Josef Ottolenghi (d. 1570), a rabbi from Cremona with a doctorate. Ottolenghi's rabbinical authority is well-attested: he ran a yeshiva and made a name for himself as an editor and publisher of Hebrew books.[55] Still, this did not prevent him from offering the Spanish king an undisclosed method for manufacturing steel and iron.[56] He also presented the Spanish court with a number of confidential projects in order to increase state revenues, and we know that at least one such project was adopted.[57]

It is not my intention to highlight such cases of technological or experimental knowledge merely as a better way to underpin the question of Judaism's relationship to the New Science. Nor am I arguing that the Jewish interest in secrets was solely the product of what has occasionally been called premodern "Jewish empiricism." While some early modern rabbis advocated an empirical conception of science, this endorsement alone can hardly explain a spectacular career like that of Abramo Colorni. First and foremost, we need to see the production, appropriation, and transfer of (secret) knowledge among early modern Jews within the larger context of the economy of secrets. In other words, early modern Jews could choose from a range of options for engaging with science that went beyond the simple categories of participation or rejection.[58]

In the same vein, we must adopt a conception about sites of knowledge that is broad enough to include courts, alchemical laboratories, armories, workshops, private collections and libraries, and general—though not necessarily public—spaces of sociability.[59] It is equally important to take into account the overarching shift in epistemological premises that occurred at the beginning of the modern era, namely, the increasingly tolerant attitude toward curiosity (*curiositas*), which had been deprecated for centuries in Christian Europe.[60] This change in attitude also affected contemporary Jews. Colorni, for example, explicitly saw himself as a "curious savant."[61]

At the level of society as a whole, the discovery—or rather rehabilitation—of curiosity marked an "epochal threshold," in Hans Blumenberg's words. This development was pivotal in laying the ground for the Scientific Revolution, or, to put it more cautiously, for a "revolution of knowledge."[62] Curiosity became a hallmark of the early modern knowledge economy in general and of the New Science in particular. But this hardly means that curiosity flourished only in institutions of open knowledge. The history of science has long underestimated the significance of aristocratic courts and the culture of curiosity fostered there.[63] This culture included the often-lavish chambers of curiosities owned by princes, as well as the equally ambitious cabinets of wonders maintained by private individuals. These collections became important sites for knowledge production.[64] Moreover, the New Science could not have taken shape without the involvement of those groups in society that both satisfied and fueled European curiosity by providing intermediary services for the procurement of information, material objects, and all other kinds of "useful knowledge" outside of open institutions. Among these intermediaries were merchants, whose importance for the Scientific Revolution has only recently been explored.[65]

The culture of *curiositas,* which made headway in the early modern era, required a permanent supply of goods. Indeed, among the most important driving forces behind curiosity in premodern Europe was trade in luxury goods, exotic objects, and out-of-the way information—in other words, goods that could never be entirely separated from the realm of secrecy, that were occasionally also explicitly characterized as secrets, and that owed their circulation not just to scientific interests. To be sure, curiosity did more than just reveal preexisting secrets; it also kept producing a constant stream of entirely new secrets.[66] The voyages of discovery and expeditions, undertaken primarily out of economic motives, are a case in point. These journeys soon also brought to light a virtually inexhaustible stream of knowledge as wondrous as it was mysterious.[67] Tellingly, the English virtuoso Joseph Glanvill (1636–1680), a member of the Royal Society, talked explicitly about an "America of secrets."[68] As late as the middle of the eighteenth century, Samuel Johnson's *Dictionary* was still defining a secret not only as "something studiously hidden," but also as "a thing unknown" and "something not yet discovered."[69]

"Trading in the marvelous," as Lorraine Daston has called it, was an inevitable byproduct of this flourishing curiosity, but it also contributed to that highly heterogeneous body of knowledge on which the exponents of the New Science drew.[70] True, they believed that the knowledge extracted from this quarry first had to be critically examined in order to comply with their own standards. But even as men of science subjected their wondrous finds to newfound scrutiny, they could not dispense with the services provided by brokers and procurers of information, objects, and curiosities. These early modern mediators and traders in knowledge were veritable "experts."[71] It was precisely this role at which many Jews excelled in the (knowledge) economy of early modern Europe.

Early modern Jews credibly promised to offer and procure an eclectic kind of knowledge encompassing many fields, chiefly by way of trading. Royal courts were among their customers, as were private individuals and scientific societies. It is fitting that many Jewish authors who wrote and talked about nature and its phenomena displayed an almost dazzling encyclopedism.[72] Admittedly, this could create the impression, at least for exponents of the New Science, that Jews' vast knowledge lacked—to use a single word, though an extremely important one—any "method."[73] But this hardly made Jews' services as mediators and traders in knowledge dispensable. Consider the case of the French savant Marin Mersenne (1588–1648), who did a great deal to popularize the ideas of the New Science in the seventeenth century.[74] Although he explicitly denied that Jews had a capacity for "method," his scholarly work often drew inspiration from the very same exotic objects and luxury goods in whose trade and provisioning early modern Jews were heavily involved.[75]

Only against this background can we do full justice to the role Jews played in the early modern knowledge economy. In studying this role, it is helpful to keep in mind what Joel Mokyr has said about "experts" in the premodern knowledge culture more generally: "The historical question is not whether engineers and artisans 'inspired' the scientific revolution or, conversely, whether the Industrial Revolution was 'caused' by science. It is whether practical men could have access to propositional knowledge that could serve as the epistemic base for the new techniques."[76]

Options and Utopias

It the context outlined here, it is particularly noteworthy that one of the first Jews granted admission into the illustrious Royal Society was, of all people, a Sephardic Jew "who traded in scientific intelligence."[77] This was Emanuel Mendes da Costa (1717–1791), who was elected to the Royal Society in 1747 and even held the office of a clerk between 1763 and 1767.[78] Starting in 1752, he was also a member of the Society of Antiquaries. Da Costa enjoyed a serious reputation for his expertise in some areas of human knowledge that were quite literally the most remote. He was a much-sought-after expert on the subject of Chinese Jews, among whom not a few Christians hoped to find the untainted original version of the Bible. Most of all, however, da Costa had acquired a reputation as a dealer in exotic fossils and as the author of *A Natural History of Fossils* (1757). One contemporary even called him the "Grand Monarch des Fossilistes." In order to buy up all his wondrous objects on the market—including fossils, seashells, and minerals—da Costa set up networks and contacts all over Europe. Nearly twenty-five hundred of his letters have been preserved to this day, and most of this correspondence revolves around the fossil trade. In his activities and business deals, da Costa benefited from their proximity to established "Jewish" occupations such as the trade in corals and diamonds, which his family also practiced. Da Costa personified, par excellence, the type of "expert" who dealt in knowledge of the wondrous and also in secrets of nature. His contemporaries already saw him more as an entrepreneur than as an example of that transfigured seventeenth-century ideal, the independent gentleman-virtuoso. After all, da Costa's life story contains some chapters, including his imprisonment for embezzlement and his final years living in utter impoverishment, that were hardly compatible with the code of honor of a gentleman-virtuoso. On the contrary, they remind us of the financial and entrepreneurial risks with which the trade in knowledge was inextricably linked.

Much of what has been said here about da Costa's trade in knowledge can also be applied to so-called court Jews on the Continent, who frequently distinguished themselves as suppliers of rare, exotic, and secret knowledge.[79] In his *Discorso circa il stato de gl'hebrei* (1638), a work much read in the Christian world, the Venetian rabbi Simone Luzzatto even declared that a prudent Christian government should tolerate Jews not least because Jewish merchants knew how to procure the most far-flung goods.[80] Moreover, there was one striking feature of the Jewish occupational structure that resulted in curiosity cabinets of a very special kind. The pawnbroking business that was widespread among Jews created veritable cabinets of wonders because of all the precious objects that accumulated in a pawnbroker's shop. Stored in the "vault" (*Gewölb*), to use the telling word of the time, these objects could be purchased by anyone if their original owners failed to redeem them.[81]

No less a personality than Francis Bacon, whom scholars have often depicted as one of the founding fathers of a modern, open science, reserved this role of knowledge mediator or expert for Jews when he wrote his utopian treatise *New Atlantis* (*Nova Atlantis*).[82] Although this treatise remained a fragment and was published only posthumously in 1627, it is by no means a work of secondary importance. In fact, it soon found large numbers of readers and went into multiple editions. Modern scholars have called the treatise a "futuristic picture of scientific research."[83]

Bacon embedded his utopian vision in a narrative framework. The protagonists are a group of European mariners who, following a daylong odyssey in the Pacific Ocean, arrive at the remote, previously unknown island of Bensalem.[84] In the course of their stay on the island, the guests acquire insights into the island's society and political-scientific life. In the eyes of the astonished Europeans, Bensalem proves to be an ideal society in which tolerance, hospitality, morality, and peace prevail. Above all, Bacon emphasizes the island's scientific achievements. Here, "Salomon's House," which Bacon describes as "the noblest foundation (as we think) that ever was upon the earth," plays a major role.[85] According to locals, the revered King Solamona founded this institution approximately nineteen hundred years earlier, and it exhibits features of "an Order or Society."[86]

It is run by the so-called Fathers and combines the entire spectrum of activities related to discovery and experiment under one roof. In addition to mining and medicine, these include a kind of premodern food chemistry as well as the development of industrial and military technology. The House is equipped with mechanical workshops and collections in mathematics and the natural sciences. Its purpose is "the knowledge of Causes, and secret motions of things; and the enlarging of the bounds of Human Empire, to the effecting of all things possible."[87]

Bacon's programmatic account of Salomon's House had considerable influence on the formation of the scientific enterprise during the seventeenth century; in the 1660s, it served as an important model when the Royal Society was founded in England.[88] Yet this does not mean that Salomon's House is committed to unconditional openness. Many of the scientific innovations discovered or developed there are actually kept secret from the public. If they are disclosed at all, it is first to the king and the senate. The House staff swears secrecy oaths, especially the twelve researchers who collect information about technologies and experiments on official missions abroad. Not only is scientific activity in Salomon's House closely intertwined with the interests of Bensalem's political leadership; it also crosses the line into industrial espionage. Salomon's House has an elitist character and betrays close ties to the theory of state arcana. The famous Baconian saying "knowledge is power" acquires a distinctly political dimension in this context.[89]

Interestingly, a Jewish merchant named Joabin plays a crucial role in establishing contact between the European guests and one of the Fathers of Salomon's House when this Father visits the city where the story takes place. Bacon draws a generally sympathetic portrait of the island's Jews. He even describes Joabin, who becomes friends with the first-person narrator, as a "good Jew."[90] Not only is Joabin a merchant, but he is also a "wise" man who is well-acquainted with Bensalem's society and customs and who gives the visitors a detailed report about the island.[91] He even says "that Moses by a secret cabala ordained the laws of Bensalem which they now use."[92] The European visitors are astonished to hear this account, which they regard merely as "Jewish dreams."[93] But their conclusion is rash and says little about the Jew's general credibility. After all, Bacon introduces Joabin as a "wise man, and learned, and of great policy, and excellently seen in the laws and customs of that nation."[94] Joabin would have known whereof he spoke.[95] Scholars have suspected that Joabin's cryptic statement concealed Bacon's implicit desire "to link the natural science utopia of 'Salomon's House' with a secret Kabbalah."[96] Whatever relationship the island's "secret cabala" may have had to the scientific activities of Salomon's House, we cannot overlook that Joabin is intimately acquainted with the island's (foundational) secrets. Modern scholars have been preoccupied with whether Bacon's characterization of Joabin indicated a positive or negative attitude toward Judaism.[97] Some have argued that the figure of Joabin reflected Bacon's own interest in Kabbalah or that it hinted at the chiliastic dimension of the utopia.[98] But these interpretations are speculative. Joabin's exact relationship to Salomon's House cannot be determined on the basis of Bacon's fragment, and the only thing we can say with certainty is that Bacon depicted Joabin as a mediator for contacts with Salomon's House.[99] While Joabin does not hold any official position in the differentiated hierarchy of Salomon's House, he serves in an "advisory, pioneer, or stimulating role."[100] In this capacity, he epitomizes the broad spectrum of opportunities available to Jews within the early modern knowledge economy. He also serves as a reminder that many more options were available than merely participation or rejection.

Some scholars have maintained that it was too risky, on political grounds, for Bacon to assign a Jew the role of an official employee or member of Salomon's House.[101] But this is a rash conclusion, especially since we still lack a comprehensive study about Bacon's relationship to Jews.[102] Nothing indicates that Bacon looked down on the role of the informal knowledge mediator and expert that he assigned to Joabin. In fact, the Jewish merchant is, with one exception, the only character in Bensalem that Bacon explicitly called "wise."[103] What is more, in Bacon's view an institution like Salomon's House, which relied on keeping certain knowledge secret, could not dispense with the services provided by Jews like Joabin.[104] Here, utopia and reality intersect. In light of Jews' real importance in the early modern economy of secrets, it was entirely plausible that a Jewish mediator like Joabin would enjoy the trust of an institution in which structures and spaces of secrecy were essential.

It might seem an irony of history that Bacon, often depicted as a forefather of open knowledge, discussed not only why secrecy was necessary, but also how such secret knowledge provided opportunities for Jews. On closer examination, however, his defense of secrecy is not as surprising as it might appear. In other works of his, as both a philosopher and a statesman, Bacon expressed sympathy for the concept of state secrets.[105] Moreover, both Bacon and many of his early followers believed there were secrets of nature, quite independently of whether they called for the open circulation of knowledge. Even leading minds of the eighteenth-century New Science maintained that certain natural phenomena were based on "occult qualities," as in the case of magnetism. Criticism was not directed so much against the idea that there were secrets of nature as against the belief that the occult qualities of objects could not be explained.[106] Bacon and his followers aimed to bring these occult properties to light using experimental methods and, as it were, wrest them from nature. Some scholars have even argued, with some exaggeration, that Bacon advocated "torturing" nature in order to elicit its secrets.[107] For our purposes, suffice it to say that Bacon's universal project of a "Great Instauration" required experts who, like Joabin, had a reputation for being able to deliver secrets and for knowing how to deal with them.

As a result, even in the age of the New Science, it was still more promising for Jews to assert their time-honored mastery of the arcane, whether real or ascribed, than to try becoming standard bearers for the new ideal of open knowledge. This was especially true given that the reality of New Science turned out to be more difficult than it was in Bacon's utopia. The emerging institutions of open knowledge were largely inaccessible to Jews, not least because the ideology of the open circulation of knowledge was hardly accompanied by social openness. In the Royal Society, for example, the "gentlemanly constitution of scientific truth" persisted for a long time.[108] The credibility of facts, especially facts obtained using experimental methods, was often linked to the experimenter's social position. Ideally, the scientist was a gentleman. Economic capital alone hardly translated into social capital. A contemporary English treatise tellingly describes Jews and merchants as the two groups that could hardly be expected to produce a proper gentleman.[109]

In reality, then, the idea of the open circulation of knowledge did not automatically lead to a permeable system of knowledge open to all.[110] Institutions of open knowledge were not characterized by social openness either in England or on the Continent. In fact, leading scientific societies in Europe, such as the Académie Royale in France, were marked by considerable social exclusivity. Jews were not the only victims of these restrictions.[111] And while the Royal Society, founded in London in 1660, promised to "freely admit . . . Men of different Religions, Countries, and Professions of Life," the first Jew was not admitted to its ranks until the beginning of the eighteenth century.[112]

Jews trying to enter into institutions of open knowledge, and specifically into learned scientific societies, faced considerable obstacles.[113] For a long time, only the medical faculties of some European, and especially Italian, universities offered Jews the opportunity to study.[114] In German-speaking Europe, this option was as good as nonexistent until well into the seventeenth century. Only in the eighteenth century did German universities gradually open up. Between 1706 and 1711, only about 150 Jewish students attended German universities. An enrollment jump in the last quarter of the eighteenth century brought the final number for the entire century to about 300.[115] Even in the era of "emancipation," career paths for Jews at universities remained restricted to the field of medicine.[116] Social discrimination against Jewish academics remained widespread.[117] In the nineteenth century, Jews often had to gain entry into scientific professions like modern medicine by way of special academic niches.[118]

There were many reasons why the economy of secrets and the role of the institutionally unattached expert remained attractive among Jews. It would be misleading, however, to think that the only Jews who "strayed" into the economy of secrets were the ones who failed at making the move into the universities. We have already seen, for example, how Abramo Colorni had a clear choice between the economy of secrets and the university, and how he opted for the path of a *professore de' secreti* without any apparent external pressure. Numerous additional examples cited above suggest that the appeal of the economy of secrets cannot be explained solely as a reaction to social discrimination that barred Jews from institutions of open knowledge. After all, Jews' exclusion from scientific societies and academies still left them the option to establish comparable institutions of their own. Even if Jews as a group never became prominent protagonists of the Scientific Revolution, Jewish Talmud Torah schools existed that were modeled on the idea of a "secular academy for higher learning," especially during the eighteenth century.[119] The school run by the broadly educated physician and rabbi Isaac Lampronti (1679-1756) in Ferrara, for example, issued publications that tried to emulate the bulletins of scientific academies.[120] In eighteenth-century England, a "Venetian Jew by the name of Servati now living in London" was said to have "a much finer and better laboratory than the Royal Society and the apothecaries, whose laboratories, especially those of the latter, [are] otherwise superb."[121] Jews therefore certainly had opportunities to adapt or imitate the institutional structures that were taking shape in Christian society.[122] Still, the economy of secrets remained no less attractive. To return to Bacon's utopia: one hardly needed to be an official member of Salomon's House in order to be respected and needed by it as an expert and mediator.

Arcana and Esteem in the Age of Enlightenment: Three Careers

One possible objection to this argument can be summed up in two words: the Enlightenment. On the Christian side of things, did not the Enlightenment cut the ground out from under the economy of secrets at the same time that, on the Jewish side, the Haskalah produced a new generation of open-minded Jews thirsting for education? In reality, things were not quite that simple. For example, one of the first Jews granted the opportunity to demonstrate his knowledge to the assembled professorate of the physics faculty at the prestigious University of Göttingen was, of all people, the Jewish magus and "supernatural philosopher" Jakob Philadelphia (ca. 1734-1797).[123] His presentation was witnessed by Heinrich Wilhelm Seyfried, editor of the journal *Berliner Peitsche,* who has left us a vivid account of his performance: "At the same time, Philadelphia proved that he was not inexperienced in physics. I still recall most vividly how, at a renowned university in the presence of the professors, he undertook the finest physical experiments with the greatest felicity; these very professors, these men with expertise in physics, did not hold back from giving Philadelphia their complete acclaim."[124]

Let us take a closer look at the biography of Jakob Philadelphia, the man who made appearances demonstrating his "physical, mechanical and optical arts" throughout Europe in the late eighteenth century.[125] Philadelphia has been largely forgotten, and most historians of German-Jewish history are not familiar with his name and life story.[126] To contemporaries, by contrast, this man who appeared "at almost all the courts of Europe with brilliant success" was well-known.[127] In fact, his name was still part of general knowledge even in the nineteenth century. He is immortalized in the works of several great German writers, including E. T. A. Hoffmann, Jean Paul, Heinrich Heine, Ludwig Börne, Heinrich von Kleist, C. F. D. Schubart, Georg Christoph Lichtenberg, Friedrich Schiller, and Johann Wolfgang von Goethe.[128] Goethe, who usually was not very sympathetic to Jews, even granted him a personal reception in Weimar.[129]

Philadelphia's early years remain an enigma. There is reason to believe he was born in 1734 to a Galician family and that he was originally called Jacob Meyer.[130] Philadelphia himself claimed he was born in Philadelphia, Pennsylvania. However, evidence indicates that his American birth was a mere legend and that he was actually born in the town of Wulfen, near Köthen. In any case, it is possible that his family emigrated to North America during Philadelphia's childhood. He first appeared as an "artist of mathematics" sometime in the 1760s in England, Ireland, Spain, and Portugal. Philadelphia himself also claimed (without any corroboration) that he had appeared before Empress Catherine II in Russia in 1771 and before Sultan Mustapha III in Constantinople in 1772. By contrast, his presentations in Vienna and Bratislava in 1774 are well-documented in the contemporary press. They may have opened up a major tour of Europe; at the very least, we know of appearances by the Jewish magus all over the Holy Roman Empire starting in the mid-1770s.

Philadelphia's career provides an impressive example of how the economy of secrets provided Jews with remarkable opportunities for employment and social recognition as late as the eighteenth century. Indeed, Philadelphia was more than just a talented magician and conjurer. He was also interested in natural phenomena while at the same time displaying skills as an adept entrepreneur. His career recalled the older tradition of the Jewish *professori de' secreti*. As it had done for many past masters of the arcane, the economy of secrets provided Philadelphia with an opportunity to forge contacts with royal courts and to pursue a decidedly mercantile agenda. In 1783, for example, he presented the Prussian court with a detailed plan for strengthening transatlantic trade with America, a project the cabinet minister in charge of commerce examined but ultimately rejected.[131]

One might interpret this rejection as a defeat for the Jewish magus, but the larger picture looks different. Philadelphia—who, according to the enthusiastic eighteenth-century poet Schubart, might have ended up burned at the stake as "the most abominable sorcerer" in an earlier era—proved adept at slipping through the close-meshed net of anti-Jewish prejudice and resentment over the course of a lifetime.[132] While Philadelphia's Jewish origin was known to most of his contemporaries, it was not used against him.[133] In a way, the Jewish magus, who served as the *parnas* (president) of his hometown's congregation for many years, was more successful at maintaining a Jewish identity in a largely Christian environment than were some contemporary *maskilim* (proponents of the Jewish Enlightenment). He was certainly spared anti-Jewish attacks to a much greater extent than his contemporary Moses Mendelssohn, the champion of reason-oriented Haskalah—and Mendelssohn, who might have encountered the magus at one of Philadelphia's appearances in Dessau, Berlin, or Potsdam, was probably aware of this. That does not mean that Mendelssohn felt any sympathy for Philadelphia. In general, he took a critical attitude toward the world of secrets, maintaining that Judaism had no knowledge of "such secrets as we must believe and not comprehend."[134] Clearly, the Jewish "Socrates from Berlin" would not have embarked on a career in the economy of secrets of the kind Philadelphia chose. He may even have been skeptical of the trade in secrets conducted by his contemporary and (purported) uncle, the court Jew and master alchemist Herz Wahl.[135] Unlike Wahl, Mendelssohn believed in the institutions of open knowledge. However, it is symptomatic that he was denied admittance to the Royal Academy of Sciences in Berlin. By contrast, Philadelphia was invited as a guest to the podium of a renowned university.

Careers like Philadelphia's were not isolated cases.[136] The magus, alchemist, and Kabbalist Samuel Jacob Ḥayyim Falk (ca. 1708-1782), Philadelphia's contemporary, had a career that was no less remarkable.[137] As with Philadelphia, there are different theories about Falk's background. It remains unclear whether he originally came from Bavaria or Podolia, or whether he actually spent his childhood in Galicia. What we do know is that Falk appeared as a Jewish magus and alchemist at a number of courts in the Holy Roman Empire by the 1730s, at the latest. His demonstrations caused such a stir that they were even banned in some territories. It is possible that these prohibitions motivated Falk to emigrate to England in the 1740s. In London, where he finally established residence, he continued to earn a living practicing all manner of arcane, and especially Kabbalistic, arts. Falk's reputation was widespread. Among Jews he was known as the "Ba'al Shem of London"—that is, as a man of miraculous talents.[138] According to some sources, Portuguese Jews even treated him like a ruler and priest.[139] Christians, too, repeatedly availed themselves of Falk's services. He liked to appear in a flowing robe and with a long beard.[140] The legendary Italian magus Cagliostro took lessons in the occult sciences from Falk in the 1770s.[141] In addition, aristocrats from all over Europe sought him out in London; his visitors included the Duke of Orléans, the Polish Prince Czartoryski, and the Marquise de la Croix.[142] In Freemasonic circles, Falk enjoyed a legendary reputation.[143]

We cannot say with certainty whether Falk himself linked his occult activities with a politically radical Freemasonic agenda.[144] Some contemporaries did indeed regard Falk's actual goals as "entirely political."[145] We are better informed about his involvement with alchemy. Contemporary travelogues by Christians mention a Jewish "Doctor Falk" who maintained an alchemical laboratory in London.[146] The Christian adventurer and Westphalian aristocrat Theodor Stephan Freiherr von Neuhoff (ca. 1694-1756), who was laying claim to the Corsican royal title at this time, even tried using Falk's alchemical experiments to produce the large sums of money he needed for his planned recapture of the throne.[147]

Life stories like those of Philadelphia and Falk might create the impression that Jewish participation in the economy of secrets during the eighteenth century was confined to a small circle of professional charlatans, while those Jews who were truly "scientific-minded" meticulously avoided this field. Not only would such a narrative be simplistic, but it would also bypass figures such as the Jewish physician Mordechai Gumbel Schnaber (1741–1797), who was known in England under the name of Gumpert Levison.[148] Born in Berlin to a family of rabbis, Levinson emigrated to London in the 1770s. There he took up the study of medicine with the famous surgeon John Hunter (1728–1793). By 1776 the Prussian Jew Levison had become a physician at the General Medical Asylum of the Duke of Portland.[149] Outside of medicine, Levison studied Newton's physics and the theories of the Swedish natural scientist Carl Linnaeus.[150] As a Jew writing treatises about religious philosophy, in turn, he attempted to define the relationship between science and Judaism.

Levison did not hesitate to defend Kabbalah against skeptics and was somewhat critical of Moses Mendelssohn's circle.[151] However, this does not mean he stood outside the Haskalah movement. Although he was no ordinary *maskil*, some of his positions, especially his efforts to spread knowledge and education, were certainly close to the Haskalah's program. In 1784 Levison even welcomed the founding of *Hame'assef*, the Hebrew journal devoted to promoting the Haskalah.[152] It testifies to the enduring appeal of the arcane that even the "enlightened" Levison, who was well-versed in the science of his day, maintained a strong interest in the economy of secrets. In London he was apparently in touch with Falk; at the same time, he translated parts of a work on alchemy into English.[153] In addition, he stayed for a time at the court of the Swedish King Gustav III in Stockholm. Not only was he appointed professor of medicine there, but he also started to construct an alchemical laboratory shortly after his arrival in 1780.[154] Levison's involvement with alchemy was not detrimental to his career. On the contrary: this expertise paved the way for his invitation to the court of the

Swedish king. The monarch even made Levison one of the first Jews honored with the title of "professor." Even though his collaboration with the Swedish court came to an end a few months later, Levison's life story highlights the professional opportunities available to Jews at the intersection of arcane science and courtly patronage as late as the eighteenth century.

The lives of Philadelphia, Falk, and their numerous Jewish epigones in the eighteenth century underscore how the premodern economy of secrets was just as attractive, especially to society's outsiders, as a system that propagated open knowledge. This does not mean that the economy of secrets was risk-free, especially for Jews. Among the drawbacks was the high degree of dependence on patronage structures, occasionally even from a single patron. Moreover, activities in the economy of secrets could, as we have seen, provide a target for anti-Jewish polemics.

At the same time, it would be misleading to say that the economy of secrets was detrimental to socialization. In this marketplace—conditioned as it was by Christian presuppositions on one hand and by the specific assets of secrecy on the other—remarkable opportunities were available to Jews well into the eighteenth century. Only from this perspective can we begin to answer the question recently posed by an astonished historian who wondered "how Jewish magicians and charlatans like Falk could leave a greater impact on the politics and culture of their times than the more sober and conventional of his Jewish contemporaries."[155]

The Waning of the Economy of Secrets in the Nineteenth Century

Historians have viewed the spread of an ideology of openness as a key factor for the Scientific Revolution's breakthrough.[156] There is no question that, at least within that particular knowledge culture often described as the New Science, the way knowledge circulated increasingly came to be oriented around an ideal of openness. Yet this does not imply that "closed systems of knowledge were incompatible with progress and liberty" (as one historian has argued), if it is even desirable to use such grand terms in the first place.[157] Jewish history allows us to make some general observations about the social function of secrets and secrecy at the time. Indeed, even outside of science, the institutions commonly associated with "openness" were not the only ones that enabled Jews to enter the civic world of the bourgeois era. Royal courts, with their predilection for the arcane, were no less important; they provided major opportunities, in the words of the historian Jacob Katz, for "neutral" or "semi-neutral meetings" between Jews and Christians where traditional prejudices could be overcome.[158] This also holds true for Freemasonry, a social setting in which the secret even functioned as a "culmination of the socialization process."[159] With Freemasonry in particular, it was irrelevant whether the secrets to which members were sworn actually existed. The philosopher Johann Gottlieb Fichte even noted in jest "that the greatest secret of the Freemasons is that they have none."[160] It was much more important that the *mode* of secrecy frequently proved genuinely promising for purposes of socialization. According to Wolfgang Hardtwig, "the secret society facilitated—and this seems paradoxical only at first glance—an expansion and intensification in communications, as well as a proliferation and acceleration in the exchange of ideas."[161] Even contemporary critics did not fail to notice this feature of the secret societies. As one critic admitted, "Arguably, the secret does not so much impede . . . the connectedness of all the members as it enlarges within the [secret] society everything that is binding and pleasant."[162]

There were Jewish Freemasons in the Netherlands and England as early as the first half of the eighteenth century. Although in reality Freemasonry did not always live up to its noble ideals, it did exercise considerable fascination over contemporary Jews.[163] Indeed, the secret societies proved to be one of the most important springboards for Jewish embourgeoisement. As late as 1858, the highly popular German-Jewish writer Berthold Auerbach was even calling Freemasonry the "ideal of society."[164] On the other hand, many critics of the secret societies saw intrinsic affinities between Freemasonry and Judaism. It was no coincidence that Pope Clemens XII (r. 1730–1740) called the Freemasonic lodges "synagogues of Satan."[165]

Since we have almost ventured beyond the threshold to the "bourgeois era," a possible objection becomes apparent: how to explain Jews' disproportionate participation in the sciences since the nineteenth century.

This much-discussed phenomenon, which is sometimes highlighted by referring to the number of Jewish Nobel Prize laureates, seems to contradict the argument that Jews were particularly attracted to the economy of secrets.

However, scholars have noted that Jewish "entry" into the sciences was a highly complex phenomenon whose dynamics have not yet been fully explored and that certainly cannot be explained with sweeping theories.[166] Moreover, it is hard to compare developments in the nineteenth century with the early modern situation because the general sociocultural parameters completely changed, for Jews even more so than for Christians.[167] Indeed, the fundamental differences between the ways that premodern and modern Jews practiced science cannot be overlooked. As David Ruderman has observed, key factors in this break are an unprecedented degree of political, cultural, and religious assimilation; the emergence of racial anti-Semitism; and a far-reaching transformation of the social, economic, and religious aspects of Jewish life.[168]

In light of these transformations, it would be rash to assume that the dawning of emancipation suddenly unleashed pent-up scientific energy that Jews had previously channeled into the economy of secrets. Such a view rests on a misguided teleological premise while also overlooking the discontinuity of events. We cannot compare the situation after 1800 with an earlier era in which the secret still occupied a firm place in everyday life, in science, and especially in the common worldview.[169] As we have seen, the rise of an ideology promoting open knowledge in the seventeenth century did not yet have a dramatic effect at the level of society as a whole. While the exponents of the New Science frequently invoked the ideal of open knowledge, it took a long time for that ideal to be implemented, and this process was not without challenges.[170] Bacon's vision of Salomon's House explicitly acknowledged the need for secrecy in certain fields. Even Robert Boyle, who was later celebrated as a pioneer of the new open science, occasionally resorted to codes and encryptions when recording the alchemical experiments he conducted in private.[171] There was a certain leeway for secrecy in the emerging domain of open knowledge, not least for the gentleman-virtuoso.[172] Well into the eighteenth century, the transition between open and secret forms of knowledge often remained quite fluid, and interactions were not unusual. As long as things remained this way, the economy of secrets did not contradict the New Science. Rather, these activities amounted to just one of several possible, and equally legitimate, ways to explore nature and its secrets.

As late as the Age of Enlightenment, the notion of secrecy was far from being mainly negative. The history of Freemasonry is a case in point. That Freemasonry, with its claim to promote the idea of people living together freely and in fraternal harmony, was enveloped by an aura as secretive as it was exclusive is one aspect of the "dialectic of Enlightenment."[173] Indeed, this fundamental tension between a universalist theory and a highly exclusive practice is a hallmark of Freemasonry. Historians should therefore hesitate before invoking a general "struggle of the Enlightenment against the secret."[174] What is true, however, is that certain Enlightenment thinkers began to raise fundamental moral objections against secrecy. In his powerful plea *What Is Enlightenment?*, Kant resolutely called upon each individual to "make *public use* of his reason in all matters"—which meant, for example, accounting for knowledge "before the entire reading public."[175] In Kant's view, any knowledge that evaded free and open examination by reason could no longer claim to be valid.[176]

But a "complete discrediting of secrecy" did not happen until the nineteenth century.[177] And this process did not happen abruptly, although there was a massive acceleration of "de-secretization" in the Western world over the course of the nineteenth century. The secret lost its cosmological status.[178] This also had to do with the gradual "disenchantment of the world," to use Max Weber's famous words.[179] However, it is important to stress that this increasing "de-secretization" was not solely the outcome of "the Enlightenment," of rationalization, or of the progressive promises associated with the institutions of open knowledge. The economy of secrets did not prove inevitably, and intrinsically, inferior to a system of open knowledge. Rather, as Georg Simmel already suspected, there was a far-reaching shift in socioeconomic, cultural, and mental parameters. A major role was played by the fact that "the individual has gained possibility of more complete privacy, since modern life has elaborated a technique for secretizing private matters of individuals, within the crowded conditions of great cities, possible in former times only by means of spatial separation."[180] According to Simmel, what was public became even more public, and what was private became even more private.[181] There is good reason to argue that the private sphere, too, has been turning increasingly public over the past few decades.[182] Openness has become the mantra of our time.

Of course, it would be ludicrous to maintain that there are no longer any secrets in public life. At the same time, we cannot overlook how secrecy no longer has a positive reputation in the normative discourses that shape our ideal of the public and of social interaction. One need only think of politics or science in this regard. In these areas, secrecy often runs up against suspicion, regulation, and supervision.[183] When we look at this wariness from a distance, we can clearly see how distinct the modern Western world's mistrust of secrecy really is. The research conducted by the ethnologist Beryl L. Bellman, who for many years has investigated the persistent political and social significance of secret societies in African countries, is instructive in this regard. Bellman observes a diametrically opposed attitude in the Western world: "The negative values normally attributed to secrecy come from the view that it is a kind of deviant or antisocial behavior. Secrecy is often associated with illegal or extralegal political groups that are either subversive or self-serving at the expense of the larger community, and with the subcultures involved with illicit drugs and alternative sexual lifestyles. When secrecy has been studied in bureaucratic settings such as business and government, it is still recognized as having bad implications."[184]

The secret does retain its validity in certain corners of the private sphere. We grant secrecy this much on paper—at least on the paper where democratic constitutions are inscribed. For example, the privacy of communications between patient and physician has been included in the catalogue of fundamental individual rights for some time now, not just recently. In our own era's public sphere, however, there is little room for a flourishing economy of secrets as in the early modern period. Today, secrecy understood as a maxim of personal conduct, which is what an early modern thinker like Gracián insisted it should be, is frowned upon as much as the arts of dissimulation and self-fashioning associated with secrecy. This development is correlated with the emergence of what the cultural critic Lionel Trilling has described as the ideas of sincerity and authenticity.[185]

While the twin concepts of the public and of openness rose to become central to bourgeois or civil society, both the place and (cosmological) status of the secret eroded within social life and its system of norms. An entry from a popular nineteenth-century German encyclopedia captures the full extent of this drastic change in attitudes: "The word 'secret' has by now been saddled with all the best people's curse. It is in secret that crime and treason are hatched, in secret where murder whets its daggers, where the newt and the serpent lie in wait for their victims, and in secret that the Inquisition celebrates its bloody orgies of execution, whereas it is in open daylight that honesty, conviction, and a free people all walk upright."[186]

Against the background of this kind of rhetoric, most Jews also began to turn away from the economy of secrets. As is so often the case when a minority adapts to the conventions of society's majority, many affirmed this change even more emphatically than their Christian contemporaries. The secret as a guiding principle vanished almost completely from Jewish thought well into the twentieth century. Its disappearance turned out to be especially salient in religious discourse, as Moshe Halbertal has observed: "The phenomenon that characterizes medieval Jewish thought—the preoccupation with Torah secrets and the use of the idea of the esoteric as a basic hermeneutic position—is completely absent from Jewish thought in the modern periods."[187] Halbertal is referring to Jewish thinkers such as Moses Mendelssohn, Hermann Cohen, and Martin Buber, but this list could easily be extended. This decline of the notion of secrecy within Judaism was more than just the long-term result of the rise of printing or of the "breakthrough" of the Enlightenment or Haskalah, as some have maintained.[188] After all, the economy of secrets did not lose its attractiveness for Jews, even well into the eighteenth century, despite the rhetoric of some *maskilim*.

This brings us back to our starting point: the massive entry of Jews into scientific professions after 1800. As we have seen, access to institutions of open knowledge was not the sole factor initiating the rise of Jewish interest in the sciences, especially since there were many places where institutional openness was actually slow in coming. The old mechanisms of exclusion and discrimination still functioned well into the twentieth century, especially at universities, and this impeded the entry of Jews into academic professions above all when it came to permanent appointments. We cannot explain Jews' turn away from the economy of secrets simply by deferring to factors like the "triumphal march" of open scientific institutions, the elimination of social hurdles, or the intrinsic persuasiveness of a paradigm shift in science. Rather, this phenomenon was to a significant extent also due to the general shift in attitudes toward open and secret knowledge that began on a massive scale in the nineteenth century. Secrecy became marginalized not only in science, but also in broad areas of public life. Tellingly, Jewish achievements in the economy of secrets were remembered, if at all, on the very margins of society, where secrecy was driven. One such niche, surrounded by an exotic aura, was the practice of magic—a field where Jews played a highly prominent role well into the twentieth century.[189] We still lack a detailed study of this Jewish involvement with magic in the modern world—an investigation that would also be a valuable contribution to recent scholarship exploring modernity and modern thought by asking what role they assign to magic.[190]

Outlook

The complex and dynamic relationship between open and secret knowledge began to erode in the nineteenth century. Not only did the secret lose its cosmological status, but it also acquired a highly negative connotation. It had indeed been "saddled with all the best people's curse." By contrast, premodern people did not see the realm of secrecy as a deficient mode of open knowledge. Even Bacon's famous words equating knowledge with power did not, at that time, necessarily refer only to open knowledge.

In many ways, this is no less true today. Where it exists, the realm of secrecy still creates structures of power all its own. What is more, it frequently revolves around strategies for acquiring and exercising power—as ethnological studies, in particular, suggest.[191] Modern people have certainly not unlearned how to avail themselves of secrets. What has been increasingly lost since the nineteenth century, however, is the artful handling of secrets. This entails more than just the simple options of either concealing or divulging, as the Jesuit and polymath Athanasius Kircher (1602–1680) noted. Kircher's career is itself a colorful example of how complex the premodern knowledge economy was, but his life also illustrates how artfully secrets were handled.[192] He was hardly the only contemporary to assume that the way one kept a secret could have a much greater effect than its actual disclosure.

Attitudes toward secrecy and openness are not an anthropological constant. They have varied across time and place.[193] In antiquity, we find relatively little interest in secrecy in the very field that is most associated with it today—the military.[194] Early modern Jewish history richly illustrates how the connotations associated with "openness" and "secrecy" can change over time. This is why historical scholarship cannot equate openness with progress and secrecy with regression. Rather, it is important to investigate the concrete and distinctive opportunities that the culture of secrecy once offered—and, where it persists, still offers—its protagonists.[195]

The idea that systems of knowledge must be as open as possible to guarantee participation by a broad range of society turns out to be more relative than absolute, as the case of early modern Jews makes clear. There are hardly any indications before 1800 that Jews were less attracted to the economy of secrets than they were to institutions of open knowledge. Moreover, the economy of secrets was capable of generating remarkable spaces for two-way interactions between a minority and the social majority while also providing distinct kinds of economic potential and social capital. Since it was embedded in the system of patronage, the economy of secrets provided Jews with considerable room to maneuver; like the patronage system itself, it was inextricably linked to structures of power.

The Jewish polyhistor, physician, and natural philosopher Joseph Salomon Delmedigo (1591–1655) recognized this. In fact, his case ties some of the core strands of this book together. Delmedigo, who grew up in Crete, had spent his youth studying mathematics, astronomy, and medicine at the University of Padua. He was even one of Galileo's students for a time. This fact alone was enough for many later scholars to treat Delmedigo as one of the few outstanding standard-bearers of the New Science among early modern Jews. Yet he did not endorse the New Science without reservations. Although he believed in Copernicanism, this did not prevent him from criticizing its exponents, or from challenging the Republic of Letters in general. Nor did it stop him from becoming seriously preoccupied, both in private and in his writings, with Kabbalah and alchemy. Delmedigo believed in the truths of Kabbalah even though he occasionally presented himself to the public, in the words of one scholar, as an "enlightened natural philosopher."[196] We know that Delmedigo's contemporaries valued his profound knowledge in the area of secrets, whether they were scientific or religious in nature. Delmedigo himself saw more opportunities for fame and wisdom in the economy of secrets than in a system where knowledge circulated openly.[197]

His book *Sefer Matzref la-Ḥokhmah,* which first appeared in his comprehensive two-part *Ta'alumot Ḥokhmah* (*Secrets of Wisdom;* Basel, 1629–1631), is illuminating in this regard.[198] In it Delmedigo praises not only experts in the mechanical arts—he refers, for example, to engineers—but also alchemists.[199] He deliberately includes Jewish experts in each of these fields and contrasts these kinds of experts and their useful knowledge with scholars he views as idle because they work only with their minds. Delmedigo's praise for the applied sciences as well as for alchemy and technology is a common thread running through all his writings—and this thematic uniformity is all the more remarkable given how the rest of his œuvre is riddled with inconsistencies.[200]

This line of argument was hardly unusual for its time. But there is more to the case of Delmedigo. Not only did he polemicize against a bookish conception of science that he deemed outmoded and too closely linked with Aristotle; he also described and legitimized a very real phenomenon among contemporary Jewry when he praised "experts" working in secret. When Delmedigo says that "they alone are worthy of being mentioned in front of kings," it reminds us about the substantial room for political and economic maneuvering that the economy of secrets opened up. Only in deeds and inventions deserving secrecy "can a man take pride because he has proved capable of achieving something great. That is why he, and not the one who poses grand questions and is petty-minded, will get to appear before kings."[201] As one of Delmedgio's twentieth-century biographers explains, "Whether these words were altogether meaningful to the Jews of the time and were meant for them in the first place is, of course, quite questionable."[202] We can now resolutely dispel these doubts and see Delmedigo's remarks, and early modern Jewish history overall, in a new light. It is true that each individual expert we have encountered possessed a different kind of knowledge. But they all shared certain features that, for Delmedigo and many others, made them wise: they appreciated what it meant to guard a secret (*sod*), they knew how to conceal their thoughts, and they understood how to keep silent.[203]

Throughout the early modern period, secret knowledge often led Jews into the realm of the *arcana imperii*—especially when they were in contact with political authorities or with the courts of the nobility. At these political centers of power, secret knowledge could turn into what Michel Foucault has called "power/knowledge."[204] A biblical verse that Abramo Colorni prominently cites in his *Scotographia* captures both his own career and the general opportunities available in the economy of secrets: "Wise men lay up knowledge: but the mouth of the foolish is near destruction" (Prov 10:14).[205]

In contemporary Western societies, frequently invoked categories like "the public" and "openness" are critical for shaping our ideals about how people should live together and how knowledge should be produced. As a result, we greatly underestimate the importance of secret forms of knowledge both in the premodern world and in contemporary non-Western societies. The early modern economy of secrets, which we have approached here from a Jewish perspective, highlights how the relationship between "secret" and "open" is subject to historical transformation. These categories themselves are not monolithic. Not only can the secret circulate in public unscathed, but it can also create specific kinds of publics—or, at least, meta-publics—by generating spaces of social interaction, zones of contact, and a dynamic market. By contrast, the universal appeal and applicability of openness are easier to assert than to prove. Today, we often regard the spaces and strategies for keeping secrets as dubious, at best. A sentence like "you have the right to remain silent" is usually uttered when the police take someone into custody. It may indeed be the case, as astute observers have noted, that our time is governed by a desire to know the "truth" more than any prior era was. But that is only one side of the coin. Confronted with all the demands for openness that we face daily, it is not enough to bemoan this situation while pinning one's hopes on, say, a legally guaranteed right to secrecy—or "protection of privacy," as we tend to call it. Rather, it is worthwhile to explore what advantages the early modern period actually had over ours: for early modern people, the secret was a *privilege* rather than just a *right*. Secrecy was an artful technique of the self that was worth guarding in its own right. We might benefit from (re)discovering secrecy as an opportunity for social interaction. At the beginning of the twenty-first century, when openness and disclosure are more than ever confused with sincerity and trust, this book will have achieved its goal if it has raised more questions than provided answers.

Acknowledgments

I have incurred many debts in writing this book as well as in the process of its translation. For advice, criticism, and support I thank David Armitage, Ivan Bergida, Mario Biagioli, Ann Blair, Emanuele Colorni, Bernard Cooperman, Natalie Zemon Davis, Joshua Eaton, Lucia Frattarelli Fischer, Anthony Grafton, Stefan Lang, Evelyn Lincoln, Wolf-Dieter Müller-Jahncke, Tara Nummedal, Alisha Rankin, Eileen Reeves, Monika Richarz, David B. Ruderman, Klaus Rürup, Shlomo Simonsohn, Barbara Staudinger, Manfred Staudinger, Gerhard F. Strasser, Joachim Telle, and Liliane Weissberg. Special thanks are due to Thomas Maissen and Gianfranco Miletto.

I also owe thanks to the staff at the various archives and libraries where I conducted my research. I am particularly obliged to Daniela Ferrari of the State Archive in Mantua, Laura Graziani Secchieri of the State Archive in Ferrara, and Herbert Hutterer of the Austrian State Archive in Vienna. At the Harvard Society of Fellows, I found the most felicitous, supportive, and intellectually stimulating setting a scholar can wish for. My sincere thanks to the Senior and Junior Fellows of the Society as well as to its administrators. I am particularly grateful to its chairman, Walter Gilbert.

Jeremiah Riemer has translated this book with great diligence while also accommodating my requests and suggestions. For this, and for many enjoyable conversations, I am much obliged to him. Jessie Dolch was an eagle-eyed copyeditor of the final draft. Jennifer Banks, my editor at Yale University Press, has supported this project from the very beginning and, together with Heather Gold, has expertly shepherded it through the publication process.

Finally, this translation is also a welcome opportunity to renew the book's dedication to my parents, with profound gratitude.

Notes

Chapter One. The Age of Secrecy

1. Fichte, *Vorlesungen über die Freimaurerei*, 213 (English ed., 194).
2. Mokyr, *Gifts of Athena*, 155–177.
3. Newman, "George Starkey"; Westerbarkey, *Das Geheimnis*, 171–173.
4. A by-now classic statement is Foucault, *Order of Things*, pt. 1.
5. Ginzburg, "High and Low"; Gestrich, *Absolutismus*, esp. ch. 2.
6. Luhmann, "Geheimnis," 103.
7. Assmann and Assmann, "Das Geheimnis und die Archäologie," 9.
8. Zedler, *Grosses vollständiges Universal-Lexicon*, s.v. "Arcanum."
9. Ibid.; see also G. Jüttner, "Arcanum," *LexMA*, 1:895. An especially noteworthy use of the term may be found in the petition presented by a burgher of Augsburg, Johann Heindl, to the Bavarian court around 1760. In the document Heindl makes the offer of an "Arcanum" in order to drive out "the terribly onerous vermin" from any room or "wallpaper." BayHStA, Generalregistratur Fasz. 1204, Nr. 130.
10. Reith, "Know-How."
11. Kugeler, "'Ehrenhafte Spione,'" esp. 136–137.
12. Zedler, *Grosses vollständiges Universal-Lexicon*, s.v. "Secretum." On books of secrets that contained these kind of *secreta*, see Eamon, *Science*, 112–120. See also Gentilcore, *Medical Charlatanism*, 359.
13. Eamon, *Science*, 54. On the continuity of this *secreta* concept in modified form in the seventeenth and eighteenth centuries, see the instructive study by Hutchison, "What Happened?"
14. "Sunt ergo secretorum tria prima genera: incognitum, quod tandem in lucem veniet: Cognitum paucis, quod maxime in precio est: & multis, quod evidentem causam non habent." Cardano, *De secretis*, 2:537–538.
15. On the subject of secrets and secrecy in rabbinical-talmudic contexts, see Wewers, *Geheimnis und Geheimhaltung*. With an emphasis on Kabbalah: Idel, "Secrecy, Binah and Derishah"; also Halbertal, *Concealment and Revelation*. See also Wolfson, "Murmuring Secrets." On secrecy in Jewish mysticism, also see the section below on alleged Jewish "mastery of the arcane."
16. This also applies mutatis mutandis to French (*secret/mystère*), Italian (*secreto/mistero*), and Spanish (*secreto/misterio*). See Gauger, "Geheimnis und Neugier," 22.

17. Ibid., 23.
18. Kant held the view that "[i]nvestigation into all forms of faith that relate to religion invariably runs across a *mystery* behind their inner nature, i.e. something *holy*, which can indeed be *cognized* by every individual, yet cannot be *professed* publicly, i.e. cannot be communicated universally." Kant explicitly distinguished between this "holy, mystery of religion (*mysterium*)" and the profusion of *arcana* and *secreta* (terms he used more narrowly than the present study): "There are mysteries that are hidden things of nature (*arcana*), and there are mysteries of politics (things kept secret, *secreta*); yet we *can* still become acquainted with either, inasmuch as they rest on empirical causes." See Kant, *Religion*, 140–141 (emphasis in original and translation).
19. Thus, the Kabbalistic idea of *tikkun* was occasionally understood as a "mandate for an active attempt to reform and improve the world." See Coudert, "Kabbalistic Messianism," 113–117 (quotation at 113). Scholem sees in practical Kabbalah above all a corpus of magical practices. In the usage of the Kabbalists, according to this view, "practical Kabbalah" would mean "simply magic, though practised by means which do not come under a religious ban." Scholem, *Major Trends*, 144. See also Gershom Scholem, "Kabbalah," in *EJ*, 11:588, 665–668.
20. Scholem, *Major Trends*, 26–28.
21. Idel, "Differing Conceptions," 169.
22. See Garzoni, *Il teatro* (1598), including the chapter about the Kabbalists (pp. 57–58) who "fanno professione d'una certa scienza eminente, à pochi nota, & che non solo appresso al volgo, incognita resta, ma anco in poco numero de' saggi manifesta ritrova." These matters were often "cose alte, & oscure, velate" (p. 57). See also the widely read *Discorso* (1638) of the Venetian rabbi Simone Luzzatto, who explained that rabbis were in charge of maintaining adherence to religious practices, while Kabbalists were responsible "per la misteriosa espositione della Scrittura." See Luzzatto, *Discorso*, 80v.
23. On the concept of "useful knowledge" popularized in recent history of science, see above all Mokyr, *Gifts*. See also the special issue of *History of Science* 45 (2007) about this topic, as well as Harrison, "Curiosity," 289. My use of the term "useful knowledge," which was coined especially with respect to the eighteenth century, differs from the original meaning in that I am referring not only to openly circulating knowledge, but also to secret knowledge.
24. Hölscher, *Öffentlichkeit*, 133; in general, see also Smith, *Business of Alchemy*.
25. Ferguson, *Bibliographical Notes*; Eamon, *Science*, esp. 4.
26. One could also adopt the terminology of Aleida and Jan Assmann, who distinguish between "substantial secrets" (which revolve around such abstract

phenomena such as love, death, the soul, origins, and time) and "strategic secrets." See Assmann and Assmann, "Erfindung des Geheimnisses," 7.
27. Grafton, "Der Magus," 11.
28. Hankins, "In Defence of Biography"; Szöllösi-Janze, "Lebens-Geschichte."
29. Szöllösi-Janze, "Lebens-Geschichte," 30.
30. This profession is characterized in Garzoni, *Piazza universale*, 1:241–243. On this phenomenon in general, see esp. Eamon, *Science*, ch. 4; now also, by way of a case study, Eamon, *Professor of Secrets*.
31. See, e.g., van Dülmen, *Geheimbund;* Reinalter, *Aufklärung;* Simonis, *Kunst des Geheimen*.
32. There are, however, a few useful collections of articles: Paravicini Bagliani, "Il segreto," Engel, Rang, Reichert, and Wunder, *Das Geheimnis;* Kaiser, "Pratiques du secret"; as well as the trilogy spanning several eras and edited by Assmann and Assmann, *Schleier und Schwelle*. Also covering several different eras is the introduction by Stuckrad, *Was ist Esoterik?*, which revolves primarily around questions from the history of ideas and religion. On the significance and function of secrets in different religions and cults of the ancient Mediterranean region, see Kippenberg and Stroumsa, *Secrecy and Concealment*. On the Middle Ages, primarily from the perspective of gender history, see Lochrie, *Covert Operations*. On the early modern era from the perspective of the history of ideas, see Hölscher, *Öffentlichkeit*. See also Gestrich, *Absolutismus*. Partly relevant, although focusing more on questions of the "public," is the edited volume by Melville and von Moos, *Das Öffentliche und das Private*. On forms of clandestinity in urban areas (with a focus on the period after 1800), see Aprile and Retaillaud-Bajac, *Clandestinités urbaines*. The relevant work on secrets from a historian of science is Eamon, *Science*. On "craft secrecy," see now also the contributions to Davids, "Openness and Secrecy"; as well as Long, *Openness, Secrecy, Authorship*. For literature on secret societies, see above n. 31.
33. A useful literature overview is provided by Spitznagel, Introduction to *Geheimnis und Geheimhaltung*.
34. For psychology, see Stok, *Geheimnis, Lüge und Missverständnis;* Spitznagel, *Geheimnis und Geheimhaltung;* for communication theory and linguistics, Westerbarkey, *Das Geheimnis;* Sievers, *Geheimnis und Geheimhaltung;* for ethnology, Bellman, *Language of Secrecy;* Luhrmann, "Magic of Secrecy"; and for religious studies, Wolfson, *Rending the Veil;* Kippenberg and Stroumsa, *Secrecy and Concealment;* Stuckrad, "Secrecy as Social Capital."
35. Simmel, "Sociology of Secrecy."
36. Ibid., 462.

37. Ibid., 461.
38. Ibid., 464.
39. Ibid., 462.
40. Hazelrigg, "Reexamination"; Petitat, *Secret et lien social*.
41. Schirrmeister, *Geheimnisse*, 35.
42. Voigts, *Das geheimnisvolle Verschwinden*, 57.
43. Westerbarkey, *Das Geheimnis*, 226.
44. Luhmann, "Geheimnis," 101.
45. Sievers, *Geheimnis und Geheimhaltung*, 30–34. See also Spitznagel, Introduction to *Geheimnis und Geheimnaltung*, 34.
46. Bok, *Secrets*, 9; similarly, from an ethnological perspective, see Bellman, *Language of Secrecy*, esp. 4.
47. Bok, *Secrets*, 5.
48. Voigts, *Verschwinden des Geheimnisses*, 57.
49. Schirrmeister, *Geheimnisse*, 31–33; Bellman, *Language of Secrecy*, 139, 144; on the "secret as communication mode," see also Sievers, *Geheimnis und Geheimhaltung*, esp. 24; Stuckrad, "Secrecy as Social Capital."
50. Simmel, "Sociology of Secrecy," 464.
51. Koselleck, *Critique and Crisis*, 72. Similar premises now guide an instructive study on political communication in sixteenth- and seventeenth-century Venice: de Vivo, *Information*, esp. 45.
52. Van Dülmen, *Geheimbund*, 116.
53. On this point, see Eis, "Von der Rede," 427–428; also Horchler, *Die Alchemie*, 49–54.
54. In seventeenth-century Spain, these so-called *arbitristas* (project makers) formed a kind of professional group that "bombarded" the government "with advice," according to Elliott, *Imperial Spain*, 300. On the project makers, see now also Lazardzig, "'Masque der Possibilität.'"
55. Recent literature on the "rise of public science" includes Stewart, *Rise of Public Science*. The claim about the dissemination of open knowledge is also made in Long, "Openness of Knowledge"; see also Eamon, *Science*, who concludes at the end of his study that "the ideology crafted in the Royal Society of science as public knowledge has become an integral part of the scientific ethos" (p. 356). See also Eamon, "From the Secrets of Nature."
56. Eamon, *Science*, esp. 54. On the secret sciences in Islam and their European reception, ibid., 39–45.
57. Ebeling, "'Geheimnis' und 'Geheimhaltung'"; see also Neugebauer-Wölk, "Esoterik."

58. On the exchange of secrets for other secrets, see e.g. Gentilcore, *Medical Charlatanism*, 363; see also Nummedal, *Alchemy and Authority*, 327; on additional nonmonetary objects of exchange, see also Newman, "George Starkey," 202.
59. As emphasized by Gentilcore (picking up on the Italian economic historian Gino Luzzatto), *Medical Charlatanism*, 274. Contemporary travelers in Venice frequently mentioned the "abundance of everything" ("abundantia omnium rerum"). See e.g. Fabri, *Evagatorium*, 3:431. On Venice as a central marketplace for all kinds of information, see Burke, "Early Modern Venice," and now also De Vivo, *Information*.
60. Barbierato, *Nella stanza dei circoli*. Rome has also occasionally been characterized as a "city of secrets." See Troncarelli, *La città dei segreti*.
61. Eamon, *Science*, 135, 194.
62. Gliozzi, "Sulla natura."
63. A useful overview of this literature may be found in Ferguson, *Bibliographical Notes*.
64. Eamon, *Science*, 54; Eamon, "From the Secrets of Nature," 338, also Hutchison, "What Happened?" On the normative canon of knowledge at universities during this era, see also Siraisi, *Medieval and Early Renaissance Medicine*, 70–77.
65. It should also be noted that the Aristotelian conception of the "occult properties" of numerous objects and phenomena of nature survived with some modifications; see Hutchison, "What Happened?"
66. Eamon, "'Secrets of Nature'," esp. 225.
67. Eamon, *Science*, 166.
68. Ibid., 253.
69. Strauss, *Persecution*, esp. 24.
70. Cipolla, "Diffusion."
71. Ibid., 47–48. See also Reith, "Know-How," 351–352.
72. Cipolla, "Diffusion," 48.
73. This was ten times the annual salary of the Spanish viceroy in Naples. Eamon, *Science*, 222.
74. Bachmann and Hofmeier, *Geheimnisse*, 192.
75. Biagioli, "From Prints to Patents," 164.
76. On Aldrovandi's interest in *secreta* literature, see Findlen, *Possessing Nature*, 212.
77. Burkardt, "Les secrets," 36.
78. Gentilcore, *Medical Charlatanism*, esp. 301–334.
79. Kodera, "Der Magus," 69.

80. "S'alcuno si volesse servire di tai nostri remedij mi trovara in Venetia a san Luca dove sempre saro pronto al servitio di tutto." Quoted in Eamon, *Science*, 397. On Fioravanti, see Camporesi, *Camminare il mondo*, and now also Eamon, *Professor of Secrets*.
81. Gentilcore, *Medical Charlatanism*, 363.
82. Ibid.; also Gentilcore, "'Charlatans, Mountebanks.'"
83. Ash, *Power, Knowledge, and Expertise*, 15; Eamon, *Science*, 222.
84. Greenblatt, *Renaissance Self-Fashioning*.
85. Gentilcore, *Medical Charlatanism*, 363.
86. Eamon, "Court."
87. Letter of 7 May 1610 from Padua to Belisario Vinta in Florence: "Io dei secreti particolari, tanto di utile, quanto di curiosità ed ammirazione, ne ho tanta copia, che la sola troppa abbondanza mi nuoce, ed ha sempre nociuto, perchè se io ne avessi avuto un solo, l'avrei stimato molto, e con quello facendomi innanzi potrei appresso qualche principe grande aver incontrata quella ventura, che finora non ho nè incontrata, nè ricercata." See Galileo, *Opere*, 6:97.
88. Quoted in Eamon, "Technology as Magic," 204.
89. Hutchison, "What Happened?"; Gestrich, *Absolutismus*, esp. 59; see also Vermeir, "Openness versus Secrecy."
90. Pico della Mirandola, *Oratio*, 68 (citing Aristotle).
91. Habermas, *Structural Transformation*.
92. Küster, *Vier Monarchien*.
93. I borrow the term "communicative forum" from ibid., esp. 473; see also Rau and Schwerhoff, "Öffentliche Räume," esp. 49.
94. This was already pointed out by Weber, *Wirtschaft und Gesellschaft*, 548; see also Hull, "Openness and Secrecy," as well as Bok, *Secrets*, 154, and Eamon, *Science*, 357; specifically with respect to political secrecy: Brunet, "Le langage du secret."
95. This point has been made succinctly by Shapin, "Science and the Public."
96. Bok, *Secrets*, 153; see also Schaffer and Shapin, *Leviathan and the Air-Pump*, 343.
97. For a detailed overview of this research, see the rubric "The 'Great Tradition' in the History of Science" in the annotated bibliography of Shapin, *Scientific Revolution*, 168–170.
98. Paradigm shift: Kuhn, *Structure of Scientific Revolutions*. For a fuller discussion, see below, ch. 6.
99. On the popularity of Hermetism and the *magia naturalis* in the Enlightenment era, see esp. Debus, *Chemistry*, ch. 1, esp. 16.

NOTES TO PAGES 18-21

100. Maxwell-Stuart, *Occult*, 1-3.
101. Hölscher, *Öffentlichkeit*, 7.
102. Gestrich, *Absolutismus*, esp. 44; Simonis, *Kunst des Geheimen*.
103. Henkel and Schöne, *Emblemata*.
104. Maxwell-Stuart, *Occult*, 1-3; Gestrich, *Absolutismus*, 43. In a Protestant context: Trepp, *Glückseligkeit*, 44, 52.
105. Eamon, *Science*, 3.
106. Anonymous, "Itziger Hang zu Geheimnissen."
107. Van Dülmen, *Geheimbund*, 116; see also Simonis, *Kunst des Geheimen*.
108. The research literature on this field is vast. A useful introduction is provided by the chapters and selective bibliography (pp. 203-220) in Reinalter, *Aufklärung*. See also Neugebauer-Wölk, *Esoterische Bünde;* also Neugebauer-Wölk, "Arkanwelten."
109. Gestrich, *Absolutismus*, 250. Gestrich's study, influenced in its theoretical outlook by Luhmann, remains the most penetrating work on this subject.
110. Hölscher, *Öffentlichkeit*, 8.
111. Gestrich, *Absolutismus*, 34.
112. Foucault, *Security*.
113. Ibid., 275.
114. Couto, "Spying," 276. On the discrepancy between the ideal and reality of policy concerning secrets of state (in a Venetian context), see De Vivo, *Information*, esp. 4.
115. Münkler, *Im Namen des Staates*, 285.
116. Stolleis, *Arcana imperii*, 33. On the formation of the "Geheimer Rat" (Privy Council) in particular, see Oestreich, "Das persönliche Regiment"; for the diplomatic context, see Carter, *Secret Diplomacy*.
117. Hölscher, *Öffentlichkeit*, 132.
118. Gestrich, *Absolutismus*, 35.
119. Ibid.
120. Ibid., 41.
121. Ibid., 35 and ch. 2.
122. Kantorowicz, "Mysteries of State."
123. Gestrich, *Absolutismus*, 55.
124. Stolleis, *Arcana imperii;* Hölscher, *Öffentlichkeit*, 131.
125. Habermas, *Structural Transformation*, 52.
126. Münkler, *Im Namen des Staates*, 285.
127. Danneberg, "Aufrichtigkeit," 46.
128. Gracián, *Art of Worldly Wisdom*, no. 160: "Profound secrecy has some of the lustre of the divine."

129. Ibid., no. 3; see also variations of the same sentiment in nos. 98, 179, and 237. (In the standard English edition of Gracián, translator Joseph Jacobs uses the wording "play with *the* cards on the table" [emphasis added] in maxim no. 3.)
130. Certaldo, *Libro di buoni costumi*, 88; Brant, *Narrenschiff*, ch. 51.
131. De Vivo, *Information*, 40–45; Le Person, "Les 'practiques' du secret."
132. Luhmann, "Geheimnis," 118.
133. Reith, "Know-How," 372.
134. Ibid., 372–373.
135. Ibid., passim. See also Müller, *Fürstenhof*, 61.
136. Extensive collections of petitions submitted by project makers may be found in various archives across Europe. For the Habsburg court: ÖStA, Hofkammerarchiv, Verschiedene Vorschläge; for the Este: ASMo, ASE, Invenzioni, progetti, scoperte; for the Wittelsbach dukes: BayHStA, Generalregistratur, Fasz. 1204, Nr. 130.
137. Roth, *Jews in the Renaissance*, x.
138. For a fuller discussion, see below ch. 6.
139. Steinschneider, "Mathematik," 90.
140. Liechtenstein, "Ein eigenhändiger Brief," 392.
141. Carlebach, "Attribution of Secrecy," esp. 115–117. Now also Heil, *"Gottesfeinde–Menschenfeinde."*
142. Carlebach, "Attribution," 117; Heil, *"Gottesfeinde–Menschenfeinde."*
143. Sennett, *Flesh and Stone*, 247.
144. On this point, ibid., ch. 7.
145. See Carlebach, "Attribution," 122.
146. Heil, *"Gottesfeinde–Menschenfeinde,"* 376–387. See also Carlebach, "Attribution," 119–120.
147. Carlebach, "Attribution," 125–128.
148. Marlowe, *Jew of Malta*. See e.g. the passages "Be true and secret" (2.3); "then now be secret" (3.4); "if we two be secret" (4.1).
149. "[L]a Natione Hebrea dispersa, e disseminata per il mondo, priva d'alcun capo di protetione, con pronta flessibilità si dispone sempre in conformità de Publici comandi," is how Rabbi Luzzatto put it in his *Discorso*, fol. 22r; see also ibid., ch. 5 in general.
150. Melamed, "Legitimating Myth."
151. See Ruderman, *Kabbalah*, 3: "From his perspective, the religious obligation of Jews to comprehend the natural world was merely a contemporary manifestation and extension of the special bond between the religious and the occult that had existed in Judaism since its inception."

152. Idel, "Secrecy," 342. This secret knowledge was occasionally even elevated into an aspect of Jewish pride; on this point, see Lachter, "Spreading Secrets," esp. 136–137.
153. Halbertal, *Concealment and Revelation*. Halbertal speaks of the "use of the medium of secrecy in order to absorb and introduce new theologies into the heart of Judaism" (pp. 138–140).
154. Ibid., 140, and ch. 16 in general.
155. Scholem, *Major Trends,* remains essential reading on Kabbalah. Since Scholem's day, admittedly, the field of Jewish mysticism has become a branch of scholarly research all its own of bewildering complexity. Some of Scholem's arguments are now viewed more critically or with greater nuance. It would go beyond the framework of the present study to detail these controversies. Some facets of the overall phenomenon of Kabbalah, including Christian Kabbalah and practical Kabbalah, are treated below (with references to additional literature). A detailed overview and bibliography with additional literature on the development and state of research on Kabbalah and on the discussion about Scholem may be found in the entry "Kabbalah" written by Moshe Idel in *EJ*, 11:586–692.
156. Coudert, "Kabbalistic Messianism," 115.
157. Knorr von Rosenroth, *Kabbala denudata*. On the early modern metaphor of the "palace of secrets," see Kenny, *Palace*.
158. A good introduction is still Secret, *Les kabbalistes chrétiens*. See also Kilcher, *Sprachtheorie*.
159. Kluge, *Etymologisches Wörterbuch,* s.v. "Kabale."
160. See Davis, "Fame and Secrecy," esp. 68.
161. Now also Ruspio, *La nazione portoghese,* 67.
162. One historian of the crypto-Jews in early modern Spain even talks about the secret as one of the "éléments fondateurs de l'existence marrane." See Muchnik, "Du secret," 31.
163. Balletti, *Gli ebrei,* 81.
164. Siegmund, *Medici State,* 105.
165. Diedrichs, *Das Ma'assebuch,* 517–524, quotation at 519.
166. Sonne, "Avnei Bonim," 160.
167. Bonfil, *Jewish Life,* 90–91.
168. Israel, *European Jewry,* 139–140.
169. Schiavi, "Gli ebrei," 506. On the importance of this trade among Jews, see also Sandri and Alazraki, *Arte e vita ebraica,* 15.
170. Sogliani, "La repubblica e il ducato," 62.
171. *Gonzaga/Venice* I, doc. 330.

172. *Gonzaga/Milan,* doc. 684.
173. *Gonzaga/Rome,* doc. 239.
174. "[Hanno] gusto che si trattasse con loro con ogni segretezza." See *Gonzaga/Venice II,* doc. 1074.
175. Pagis, "Baroque Trends."
176. Jütte, "Rotwelsch," 136.
177. "[L]a cognitione che hanno delle lingue & delle lettere Greche, Arabiche, Caldee & Hebraiche. Nelle quali lingue . . . hanno scritto li principali Autori della Medicina, & Filosofia naturale, & dell'Astrologia: scienze tutte congiunte alla Medicina." Nicolay, *Le navigationi,* bk. 3, ch. 13:99.
178. Quoted in Stern, *Documents of Performance,* 53. Emphasis is mine.
179. Ps.-Roger Bacon, *Mirror of alchimy,* 77. This treatise went through various editions in the early modern period. On its authorship and popularity, see Schütt, *Auf der Suche,* 280–282.
180. Cappel, *Arcanum punctationis revelatum.*
181. Pico della Mirandola, *Heptaplus.* See Ansani, "Giovanni Pico Della Mirandola's Language," and now also Black, *Pico's Heptaplus.*
182. Pico della Mirandola, *Heptaplus,* 374–376: "Firma est sententia omnium veterum, quam ut indubiam uno ore confirmant, omnium artium, omnis sapientiae et divinae et humanae, integram cognitionem in quinque libris mosaicae legis includi; dissimulatam autem et occultatam in litteris ipsis quibus dictiones legis contextae sunt. . . . At, vocabulis resolutis, elementa eadem divulsa si capiamus et iuxta regulas, quas ipsi tradunt, quae de eis conflari dictiones possunt rite coagmentemus, futurum dicunt ut elucescant nobis, si simus capaces occlusae sapientiae, mira de rebus multis sapientissima dogmata, et si in tota hoc fiat lege, tum demum ex elementorum hac quae rite statuatur et positione et nexu erui in lucem omnem doctrinam secretaque omnium liberalium disciplinarium."
183. See e.g. von Stuckrad, *Esoterik,* 126. See also, in general, Zinguer, *L'Hébreu.*
184. Wakefield, *On the Three Languages,* 83: "At haec lingua divitias suas dissimulat, et flores dulcesque fructus in sinu habet, non ostentat. Quid plura? In recessu plus retinet unde detineat, quam praefert in fronte unde capiat bracteatisque Alcibiadis Silenis est simillima. Quorum simulacra extrinsecus erant hispido ore, tetro et aspernabili, verum intus plena gemmarum supellectilis rarae et praeciosae."
185. Thus, in the 1480s, the Dominican monk Felix Fabri wrote about the Jewish tour guide who was hired by his traveling group: "quasi occulte ducente nos Judaeo, qui dixit, quod quaedam occulta nobis vellet ostendere." Fabri, *Evagatorium,* 2:125.

186. Simonis, *Kunst des Geheimen*, 371; and in general ibid., 371–405.
187. Gentilcore, *Medical Charlatanism*, 329.
188. Patai, *Jewish Alchemists*, 599.
189. Ibid., 11; Bernard Suler, "Alchemy," in *EJ*, 1:599–600; Trachtenberg, *Devil*, 73–74. Similar beliefs were widespread in the Islamic world: Ullmann, *Die Natur- und Geheimwissenschaften*, 187–188. On the interconnection between late ancient and Jewish myths about the origin of alchemy, see Idel, "Origin of Alchemy."
190. Will-Erich Peuckert, "Jude, Jüdin," in *HdA*, 4:810.
191. Patai, *Jewish Alchemists*, 233; Hoheisl, "Christus," esp. 71; Suler, "Alchemy," in *EJ*, 1:599.
192. Idel, foreword to Trachtenberg, *Jewish Magic*, xvi. On Kabbalah and alchemy, see also Ruderman, *Kabbalah*.
193. The manuscript is located today in the Moussaieff Collection in Jerusalem. See Bos, "Hayyim Vital's 'Practical Kabbalah.'" See also Patai, *Jewish Alchemists*, 340–364.
194. Scholem, "Alchemie und Kabbala"; Schwarz, *Cabbalà;* Patai, *Jewish Alchemists*, 152–169; Coudert, "Kabbalistic Messianism," 116.
195. Suler, "Alchemy," in *EJ*, 1:600.
196. Patai, *Jewish Alchemists*, 11; Ansani, "Giovanni Pico Della Mirandola's Language," 95.
197. Patai, *Jewish Alchemists*, 10. See also Steinschneider, "Pseudo-Juden."
198. Scholem, "Alchemie und Kabbala," 28.
199. Park, *Secrets of Women*, esp. 82–91.
200. This is the main subject of Park's *Secrets of Women*. I am grateful to Katharine Park for a stimulating discussion about the questions raised in her book.
201. Ariosto, *Il Negromante*.
202. Vasoli speaks of Iachelino as a "figura molto familiare alla società italiana del tempo." See Vasoli, "Gli astri," 129.
203. "Per certo, questa è pur gran confidenzia, / Che mastro Iachelino ha in se medesimo, / Che mal sapendo leggere e mal scrivere, / Faccia professïone [*sic*] di filosofo, / D'alchimista, di medico, di astrologo, / Di mago, e di scongiurator di spiriti." 2.1.526–531.
204. "Or è Giovanni, or Piero; quando fingesi / Greco, quando d'Egitto, quando d'Africa; / Et è, per dire il ver, giudeo d'origine, / Di quei che fur cacciati di Castilia. / Sarebbe lungo a contar quanti nobili, / Quanti plebei, quante donne, quanti uomini / Ha giuntati e rubati." 2.1.549–555.
205. Corrigan, foreword to *Two Renaissance Plays*, 7.

206. For a biography of Latis and information on his astronomical and astrological writings, see esp. Goldschmidt, "Bonetto de Latis." On Latis as an astrologist, see also Bonfil, *Rabbis*, 78.
207. Nummedal, *Alchemy*, 152; Burkardt, "Les secrets," 35.
208. "Habuerunt quoque conflatoria subterranea, ubi alchimie operam dederunt." Quoted in Straus, *Urkunden*, doc. 1040.
209. Bernhard Karle, "Alchemie," in *HdA*, 1:254; see also Roth, "Abramo Colorni," 157.
210. Martin Luther, *Tischreden* (no. 5567) in Luther, *Werke*, 5:246. The translation used here is by Hazlitt.
211. Trachtenberg, *Devil*; Hsia, *Myth of Ritual Murder*.
212. On this, see Bachmann and Hofmeier, *Geheimnisse der Alchemie*, esp. 9–13.
213. Nummedal, *Alchemy*, 18; Moran, "German Prince-Practitioners," 273. On women and alchemy, see Rankin, "Becoming an Expert Practitioner," 52.
214. Kallfelz, "Der zyprische Alchimist Marco Bragadin," 480.
215. In the minutes of a conversation Bragadino had with the Venetian authorities (1589), it is reported "che hora alle librarie non si trovava più alcun libro di alchemia et che molti soffiavano et questa potrebbe esser la causa che diversi si impoveririano consumando il suo." Quoted in Striedinger, *Der Goldmacher Marco Bragadino*, doc. 298 (p. 267).
216. Nummedal, *Alchemy*, 12.
217. Ibid.
218. Smith, "Alchemy as a Language of Mediation"; see also Trevor-Roper, *Princes and Artists*, esp. 99.
219. Newman, "From Alchemy to 'Chymistry,'" 498.
220. "[I]tem Guilielmus Varignana, Judaeus quantum apparet, vir magnae eruditionis," as Hermann Conring wrote in his *In universam artem medicam introductio* (1654). Quoted in Ferguson, *Bibliographical Notes*, 209.
221. On this treatise and its reception, see Gundolf Keil, "Secretum secretorum," in *LexMA*, 7:1662–1663; Keil, "Secretum secretorum," in *VerfLex*, 8:993–1013; also Bachmann and Hofmeier, *Geheimnisse*, 31–32; Trachtenberg, *Devil*, 63.

Chapter Two. Masters of the Arcane and Their Métiers

1. Claus Priesner and Karin Figala, "Vorwort," in *LexAlch*, 9.
2. Nummedal, *Alchemy and Authority*, 14.
3. See esp. Patai, *Jewish Alchemists*; Scholem, "Alchemie und Kabbala."

4. See the detailed and critical reviews of Patai's book by Gad Freudenthal in *Isis* 86 (1995): 318–319 and by Y. Tzvi Langermann in the *Journal of the American Oriental Society* 116 (1996): 792–793.
5. Patai, *Jewish Alchemists*, 235; Patai, "Sephardic Alchemists," 240.
6. "[P]ossis et valeas artem alquimie ubique terrarum nostrarum experiri, et quod de arte ipsa persenseris ad plenum probare per experientiam et liberaliter exercere." Quoted in Rubió y Lluch, *Documents per l'historia*, 2:346.
7. Patai, *Jewish Alchemists*, 236; Patai, "Sephardic Alchemists," 240.
8. "[C]um christianis, judeis aut sarracenis qui cum eis in dictis operibus voluerint interesse." Quoted in Rubió y Lluch, *Documents per l'historia*, 1:319.
9. Mentgen, "Jewish Alchemists in Central Europe."
10. Bachmann and Hofmeier, *Geheimnisse der Alchemie*, 15.
11. As early as the fourteenth century, the alchemist Nicolas Flamel is said to have received an alchemical treatise from a Jew. Although it is true that Jews were passing on alchemical knowledge in this period, this particular report probably belongs to the realm of legend. See Didier Kahn, "Flamel, Nicolas," in *LexAlch*, 136–138.
12. The only surviving manuscript is preserved in the university library at Heidelberg (cpg 597). On the manuscript and its content, see Horchler, *Alchemie*, 146–150, and Eis, "Alchymey teuczsch," 12.
13. "[S]o he should take three of the best of the arts he commands—ones that he regards and names as the best, or three that we prefer most—and teach them to us well and properly, and he shall vow and promise under oath that he has taught them to us completely and properly." Quoted in Eis, "Alchymey teuczsch," 12.
14. "[So t]hat the art stays only with our heirs and our lords and masters at Leuchtenberg and Hals and does not go any further." Quoted in ibid., 12.
15. Ibid.
16. Gershom Scholem, "Kabbalah," in *EJ*, 11:587, 591.
17. Mentgen, "Jewish Alchemists," 346–347.
18. *GJ* 3.1:605.
19. Mentgen, "Jewish Alchemists," 348.
20. Baader, "Zur Criminaljustiz der Nürnberger," 356.
21. Mentgen, "Jewish Alchemists," 349.
22. Sirat, *History of Jewish Philosophy*, 227–228.
23. For more on Nelle, see the section on the Rudolphine court in Chapter 5.
24. Ries, "Juden als herrschaftliche Funktionsträger," 304.
25. Ries, *Jüdisches Leben in Niedersachsen*, 382.

26. Ibid.; the Aaron mentioned here is probably identical with the alchemist of the same name mentioned by Nummedal, *Alchemy and Authority*, 235.
27. Rhamm, *Die betrüglichen Goldmacher*, 109. This also explains the existence of a 1576 letter of safe-conduct issued by Duke Julius of Brunswick-Wolfenbüttel for Aaron Goldschmidt, which gives the Jew a right to residence for any length of time. The document is mentioned in Ries, *Jüdisches Leben*, 165.
28. Nummedal, *Alchemy and Authority*, 102–103.
29. See the document in Patai, *Jewish Alchemists*, 269.
30. On Sephardic physicians and alchemy, see Studemund-Halévy, "Sefardische Residenten," 163–164.
31. On Texeira, see esp. Studemund-Halévy, *Biographisches Lexikon*, 791–795.
32. Studemund-Halévy, "Sefardische Residenten," 163.
33. Studemund-Halévy, *Biographisches Lexikon*, 232–235.
34. Moreno-Carvalho, "Newly Discovered Letter," 73–76.
35. Studemund-Halévy, *Biographisches Lexikon*, 234.
36. This treatise can be found in his *Anacephaleoses da Monarchia Luzitana* (Lisbon, 1624). See Studemund-Halévy, "Sefardische Residenten," 164.
37. On his biography, see Studemund-Halévy, *Biographisches Lexikon*, 660–662; also Patai, *Jewish Alchemists*, 437–446.
38. Gestrich, *Absolutismus und Öffentlichkeit*, 83–85.
39. Patai, *Jewish Alchemists*, 437–446; Studemund-Halévy, "Sefardische Residenten," 164.
40. "Ein Jüdischer Brief / Mesahab genannt / von der Alchimie und Kunst Gold zu machen," in Schudt, *Jüdische Merckwürdigkeiten*, 327–339 (no. 11 of the appendix "Documenta und Schrifften").
41. Hannemann, *Ovum hermetico-paracelsico-trismegistum*.
42. Güdemann, *Geschichte des Erziehungswesens*, 3:156; skeptically on this point: Scholem, "Alchemie und Kabbala," 60.
43. Brann, *Geschichte der Juden in Schlesien*, 155.
44. On his alchemical interests, see Barzilay, *Yoseph Shlomo Delmedigo*, 261.
45. Wischnitzer, *History of Jewish Crafts*, 135.
46. Bos, "Hayyim Vital's 'Practical Kabbalah.'" On the date, see ibid., 56.
47. The episode is described in Reuveni's diary; Aescoly, *Sippur David ha-Reuveni*, 19.
48. Portaleone, *De auro dialogi tres*. See also Kottek, "Jews between Profane and Sacred Science"; Miletto, *Glauben und Wissen*, 245–259; Patai, *Jewish Alchemists*, 379–380.
49. Patai, *Jewish Alchemists*, 365–375.

50. Scholem, "Alchemie und Kabbala," 72; see also Tocci, who nevertheless inclines, on the whole, toward underestimating the significance of the phenomenon: Tocci, "Dottrine 'ermetiche' tra gli ebrei."
51. Segre, *Jews in Piedmont*, vol. 1, docs. 608, 732, 738, 748.
52. Ibid., doc. 495.
53. Mentgen, "Jewish Alchemists," 350–351.
54. Modena, *Autobiography*, 108–109.
55. For Modena's report on his joint experiments in the years 1602–1603, ibid., 102, 168.
56. *Gonzaga/Venice* I, doc. 85. The name of the Jew is not named in this source.
57. According to an anonymous *Vita Sendivogii* from the late sixteenth century, printed in Maxwell-Stuart, *Occult*, 213.
58. Modena, *Autobiography*, 79.
59. Urbani and Zazzu, *Jews in Genoa*, vol. 1, doc. 540.
60. Ibid., doc. 553.
61. On Jews and medical arcana, see the relevant section later in this chapter.
62. E.g., Güdemann, *Geschichte des Erziehungswesens*, 1:69, 312–313.
63. Horchler, *Alchemie*, 278–280.
64. Newman and Principe, "Alchemy vs. Chemistry."
65. Nacaman's petition of 16 May 1630, ASV, Senato Terra, filza 315.
66. Report of the Provveditori alla Iustizia Vecchia and the Cinque Savi alla Mercanzia of 10 June 1630, ASV, Senato Terra, filza 315.
67. Karin Figala, "Quecksilber," in *LexAlch*, 295–300; Claus Priesner, "Zinnober," in *LexAlch*, 378–379.
68. Privilege of the Senate from 13 June 1630, ASV, Senato Terra, filza 315. On this privilege and on the history of the company, so far we have only Berveglieri, *Inventori stranieri*, 104–111.
69. Calabi, Camerino, and Concina, *La città degli ebrei*, 57.
70. Ibid., 63.
71. Privilege of the Senate from 13 June 1630, ASV, Senato Terra, filza 315.
72. Privilege of the Senate (1660), ASV, Senato Terra, filza 673.
73. Berveglieri, *Inventori stranieri*, 104–105. On the general suspicion of the Ufficiali al Cattaver that the Jews were claiming too many, or unjustified, privileges, see Pullan, *Jews of Europe*, 152.
74. "[M]olto fondo per li fornelli e per le macine [*sic*]." Sarfatti's petition of 3 February 1660, ASV, Senato Terra, filza 673; and ibid.: "il rischio del fuoco, senza il quale non possono correggersi li ingredienti velenosi."
75. Privilege of the Senate from 13 March 1660, ASV Senato Terra, filza 673.

76. On a few of these exceptions, especially for physicians, see Ravid, "New Light on the Ghetti," 149–176.
77. Berveglieri, *Inventori stranieri*, 106.
78. Ibid.
79. Balletti, *Gli ebrei*, 165.
80. Frattarelli Fischer, *Vivere fuori dal Ghetto*, 156.
81. Berveglieri, *Inventori stranieri*, 109.
82. Thus, the Magistrato alle Artiglierie stated in 1759: "[I]l segreto di fare il solimato e il precipitato, inserviente il primo a molti usi della medecina, della chirurgia e al lavoro degli orefici, non è comune a tutte le nazioni, ma credesi conosciuto solamente in Olanda e in Turchia." Quoted in ibid., 107.
83. Ibid., 108–111.
84. Patai, "Sephardic Alchemists," 244.
85. Hölscher, *Öffentlichkeit und Geheimnis*, 132.
86. Telle, "Paracelsus als Alchemiker," 159. Also Debus, *Chemistry*, ch. II, esp. 187.
87. E.g., Horchler, "Alchemie in der deutschen Literatur," 311.
88. Quoted in Telle, "Paracelsus als Alchemiker," 159; also Weeks, *Paracelsus*, 153.
89. "Arcanum," in Zedler, *Grosses vollständiges Universal-Lexicon*, 2:1182.
90. Hortzitz, *Der "Judenarzt,"* 20; Jütte, "Zur Funktion," 175.
91. "Auf Kräuter und Steine versteht sich der Jude besonders." Goethe, *Reineke Fuchs*, in *Werke*, 2:392. The translation used here is that of Alexander Rogers.
92. Olivieri, "Il medico ebreo," 456.
93. At the end of his autobiography, Modena lists twenty-six activities with which he earned money during his lifetime. The list includes the ones mentioned here. See Modena, *Autobiography*, 162.
94. Cecil Roth and Leah Bornstein-Makovetsky, "Ashkenazi, Solomon," in *EJ*, 2:577–578; Arbel, *Trading Nations*, 78–86.
95. Olivieri, "Il medico ebreo," 450–452.
96. Schudt, *Jüdische Merckwürdigkeiten*, bk. VI, 389.
97. Fugger, *Korrespondenz*, II/2, docs. 3211, 3226, 3236.
98. Biblioteca Nazionale Marciana, It., III. 10 (ms. 5003). And see the short description of this manuscript in Frati and Segarizzi, *Catalogo*, 1:312–313.
99. Biblioteca Nazionale Marciana, It., III. 10 (ms. 5003), fols. 29r, 30r, 73v–75r.
100. Marcus, *Jew in the Medieval World*, 399–400.
101. Cooperman, "Trade and Settlement," 163; Roth, *Jews in the Renaissance*, 48–49; Siegmund, *Medici State*, 230.

102. The privilege speaks of "l'arte di fabbricare le paste di muschio, et ambra." Printed in Ferrari, "La cancelleria gonzaghesca," 310. Ongaro also arranged deliveries of basic commodities and luxury items to the court in Mantua. *L'Elenco dei beni*, nos. 1827, 1830, 1882, 2581; also *Gonzaga/Florence*, doc. 353.
103. Toaff, *Il prestigiatore di Dio*, 38–39.
104. Treue, "Zur Geschichte jüdischer Ärzte," 179.
105. Ruderman, *Kabbalah*; for German-speaking Europe: Zinger, "'Natural' and 'Unnatural' Causes," 127–155.
106. Treue, "Zur Geschichte jüdischer Ärzte."
107. Barbierato, *Nella stanza dei circoli*, 176.
108. Written communication from William Eamon to the author, 23 February 2009.
109. On Jewish physicians as astrologers, see Friedenwald, *Jewish Luminaries*, 11–12. On rabbis as astrologers, see Bonfil, *Rabbis and Jewish Communities*, 78.
110. On astrology in Judaism, see esp. Leicht, *Astrologumena Judaica*; also Trachtenberg, *Jewish Magic and Superstition*, ch. 16.
111. Schiavi, "Gli ebrei," 504.
112. Preto, *I servizi segreti*, 484.
113. Esp. Trachtenberg, *Devil and the Jews*, ch. 7.
114. See the dubious verdict against a Jew named Mosse [*sic*] who was burned in Regensburg for mixing poisons because "he taught a number of persons [in Regensburg] how to make evil poisons and took money for this, and also requested things from pharmacies useful to this undertaking." Quoted in Straus, *Urkunden und Aktenstücke*, doc. 140.
115. Ritzmann, "Judenmord," 101–130.
116. Trachtenberg, *Devil and the Jews*, 97; Ritzmann, "Judenmord," 109; Glanz, *Geschichte des niederen jüdischen Volkes*, 48.
117. See the concluding section of this chapter.
118. On the spread of poisoning among the rulers of Italy during the Renaissance, see Lewin, *Die Gifte in der Weltgeschichte*, 288–324, and esp. on Venice: 322–324; on Venice as "patria dei veleni," see Preto, *Servizi segreti*, 361–374.
119. Preto, *Servizi segreti*, 364.
120. Lamanskij, *Secrets d'état de Venise*, 818.
121. Lewis, "Privilege Granted," 563; Babinger, "Ja'qûb-Pascha"; Preto, *Servizi segreti*, 308; Gentilcore, *Medical Charlatanism*, 297.
122. See the edition of the relevant Venetian documents in Babinger, "Ja'qûb-Pascha."

123. Lamanskij, *Secrets d'état*, doc. 20; Jacoby, "Un agent juif," 75; Babinger, "Ja'qûb-Pascha," 254–258; Preto, *Servizi segreti*, 308.
124. Babinger, "Ja'qûb-Pascha," 254.
125. Lamanskij, *Secrets d'état*, doc. 44.
126. Burdelez, "Role of Ragusan Jews," 194.
127. "Memoriale di Abraam Colorni," ASMo, ASE, Ingegneri, b. 2. This undated petition, written for Cesare d'Este, is unpublished. For more on this proposal, see also the undated letter of Abramo Colorni to Cesare d'Este and his undated *memoriale* for the Republic of Venice, printed in J-1891, 48–49. Exactly what Colorni envisioned cannot be said with absolute certainty. Presumably, he was thinking of producing weapons that would emit poisonous vapors. Colorni was not the only contemporary who took interest in weapons of this kind: as early as around 1500, Leonardo da Vinci, too, was preoccupied with these kinds of ideas. In the sixteenth and seventeenth centuries, mercury and arsenic fumes came to be regarded as especially suitable to this purpose. See Lewin, *Gifte in der Weltgeschichte*, 93–96; on weapons impregnated with poison, ibid., 571–574.
128. Preto, *Servizi segreti*, 368.
129. Chayim Cohen, "Poison," in *EJ*, 16:283–284.
130. Heil, *Vorstellung von jüdischer Weltverschwörung*, 395–397.
131. Quoted in ibid., 396.
132. Patai, *Jewish Alchemists*, 408; Jābir ibn Hayyān, *Buch der Gifte*, 4. See also Ullmann, *Natur- und Geheimwissenschaften*, 208.
133. Maimonides, *Treatise on Poisons*.
134. Patai, *Jewish Alchemists*, 354; Bos, "Hayyim Vital's 'Practical Kabbalah,'" 94.
135. On the use of sublimate by the Venetian authorities, see Preto, *Servizi segreti*, 364. On the general importance of sublimate as a poison at the time, see Lewin, *Gifte in der Weltgeschichte*, 252. The mercury compound indicated here should not be confused with the equally poisonous arsenic sublimate that was occasionally likewise called "sublimate," as in the writings of the sixteenth-century Sephardic physician Amatus Lusitanus. See Lewin, *Gifte in der Weltgeschichte*, 418. In any case, the Jewish manufacturers in Venice knew about how poisonous the substance was, as can be gathered from the documents in ASV, Senato Terra, filza 673.
136. On cinnabar as a poison, see Cardano, *De venenis libri tres*, 312. From the perspective of modern medicine: Lewin, *Gifte und Vergiftung*, 260.
137. Frattarelli, *Vivere fuori*, 156; Balletti, *Gli ebrei*, 165.
138. Navarrini, "La guerra chimica."

139. See e.g. the story told in Jābir ibn Hayyān, *Buch der Gifte,* 144; Lewin, *Gifte in der Weltgeschichte,* 533–547; Preto, *Servizi segreti,* 314.
140. Preto, *Servizi segreti,* 301–327; Cooperman, "Trade and Settlement," 69.
141. Preto, *Servizi segreti,* 314.
142. See Marlowe's portrait of the "Jew of Malta" as a well poisoner: Marlowe, *Jew of Malta,* 2.3.
143. Lamanskij, *Secrets d'état,* doc. 19, and pp. 78, 460.
144. Burdelez, "Role of Ragusan Jews," 194.
145. Preto, *Servizi segreti,* 318–320.
146. Köhn, "Dimensionen," esp. 317–319.
147. Kahn, *Codebreakers,* esp. 108.
148. Pesic, "Secrets," 675.
149. Kugeler, "Geheimnis," 139, 147; see also Thompson and Padover, *Secret Diplomacy,* esp. 253–263; on the rise of the ambassadorial system in general: Mattingly, *Renaissance Diplomacy.*
150. See esp. Wagner, "Studien," 11:156–189; 12:1–29; 13:8–44; Meister, *Anfänge;* Meister, *Die Geheimschrift;* and Kahn, *Codebreakers,* esp. chs. 3 and 4; also Couto, "Spying," as well as Kranz and Oberschelp, *Mechanisches Memorieren.* The terminology I use relies on the glossary of "fundamental cryptological terms" in Strasser, *Lingua Universalis,* 16–18.
151. Bonfil, *Jewish Life,* including the chapter "The Importance of Letter Writing," 234–237. See also the pertinent contributions in Menache, *Communication.*
152. Ofer, "Methods," 55.
153. Landau and Wachstein, *Jüdische Privatbriefe,* 60.
154. Shulvass, *Jews in the World of the Renaissance,* 175; Cassuto, *Gli ebrei,* 226.
155. On his biography, see Tovia Preschel and Abraham David, "Porto, Abraham Menahem," in *EJ,* 16:406; see also Sonne, "Avnei Bonim le-Toldot," esp. 147.
156. Busi, "Il succo dei favi," 53, n. 30; also Sonne, "Avnei Bonim le-Toldot," 177. Busi notes that only one copy of the book has been preserved. It is located in the Biblioteca Palatina in Parma, and I was not able to examine it.
157. Ofer, "Methods of Encoding," 56–57.
158. See Chapter 3.
159. Bos, "Hayyim Vital's 'Practical Kabbalah,'" 99.
160. Portaleone, *Heldenschilde,* 389.
161. Della Porta, *Magiae naturalis,* 62–64; see also Macrakis, "Ancient Imprints."
162. Preto, *Servizi segreti,* 251.
163. Ibid., 281.
164. Calendar of State Papers (Venice), vol. 4, doc. 658.

165. Ibid. xxvi.
166. Ibid., doc. 658.
167. Ibid., xxvi.
168. Ibid., docs. 715, 682, 864.
169. Ibid., docs. 682, 715, 726, 864.
170. The relevant Talmudic passages are compiled in Wewers, *Geheimnis*, 24.
171. Kottek, "Jews between Profane and Sacred Science," 112.
172. Brann, *Trithemius*, 205. On the Jewish side, this includes Archevolti's *Arugat ha-Bosem* (Venice, 1602) and Portaleone's *Shiltei ha-Gibborim* (Mantua, 1612).
173. Samsonow, "Hehler des Sinns," 283; Kahn, *Codebreakers*, 91–92.
174. Gershom Scholem, "Kabbalah," in *EJ*, 11:597.
175. Godfrey Edmond Silverman, "Vigenère, Blaise de," in *EJ*, 20:525; see also Secret, *Les kabbalistes chrétiens*, 203–207.
176. Strasser, *Lingua Universalis;* also Katz, *Philo-Semitism*, esp. 43–88, 233.
177. Burdelez, "Role of Ragusan Jews," 193.
178. See e.g. the case of a certain Laudadio Levi, who served the Gonzagas but spoke too carelessly about his code's key (*zifara*) and therefore landed in jail. Balletti, *Gli ebrei*, 164.
179. Jedlicki, *Die entartete Welt*, 217.
180. Fritz, *"Eine Rotte,"* 361–364.
181. D'Argens, *Jewish Spy*. On the author and his attitude toward Judaism, see Israel, "Philosophy," esp. 176–177.
182. New editions came out, for example, in London (1744 and 1765/1766) and in Dublin (1753).
183. Diplomats: Kugeler, "'Ehrenhafte Spione,'" 128.
184. Couto, "Spying," 293.
185. Jütte, "Jewish Consuls."
186. Quoted in Treue, "Zur Geschichte jüdischer Ärzte," 188.
187. Letter of the Court War Council to the Hofkammer from 1681, quoted in Buchberger, "Zwischen Kreuz und Halbmond," 69.
188. Cooperman, "Trade and Settlement," 69. On the exaggeration, Preto, *Servizi segreti*, 481–485.
189. De Vivo, *Information*, 90.
190. Preto, *Servizi segreti*, 481.
191. Ibid., 484.
192. I thank Dr. Anne-Simone Knöfel, who has been doing research on the history of the "Secret Expedition" of Count Brühl, for drawing my attention to this episode.

193. Buchberger, "Zwischen Kreuz und Halbmond," 71.
194. Preto, *Servizi segreti*, 484.
195. Burke, "Early Modern Venice," 393.
196. Israel, *European Jewry*, 136–137.
197. Stern, *Court Jew*, 9–10.
198. *GJ* 3.1:584; Mentgen, "Jewish Alchemists," 346–347.
199. Jacoby, "Un agent juif."
200. Balletti, *Gli ebrei*, 163.
201. Buchberger, "Zwischen Kreuz und Halbmond," 69–70. On Höschl in particular, see also Buchberger, "Lebl Höschl."
202. "[E]ssendo proprio dell'Ebreo d'esser segreto, non è nobile in questa città, che non habbia un Ebreo confidente, che lo serve in diverse occorrenze, nè Ebreo, che non habbia un Gentilhuomo Procuratore, anzi in molte case non si tiene allo Ebreo la portiera." Quoted in Lamanskij, *Secrets d'état*, 702.
203. "[H]anno gran familiarità gli Ebrei mercanti e riguardevoli con i Christiani nobili." Giulio Morosini, *Via della fede* (1683), quoted in Ravid, "Between the Myth," 164.
204. Alexandre-Toussaint Limojon de Saint-Didier, *The City and Republick of Venice* (1672–1674, English ed. 1699), quoted in Ravid, "Travel Accounts," 131.
205. John Clenche, *A Tour in France and Italy, Made by an English Gentleman* (1675), quoted in Ravid, "Travel Accounts," 130.
206. "Maximilian Misson, *A New Voyage to Italy* (1688, English ed. 1739), quoted in Ravid, "Travel Accounts," 133.
207. Schudt, *Jüdische Merckwürdigkeiten*, bk. 6, 226; see also ibid., 160. Schudt's source was apparently the *Histoire des religions de tous les royaumes du monde* (1676), by Jean Jovet.
208. Cozzi, *Giustizia 'contaminata.'*
209. De Vivo, *Information*, 92–93.
210. Preto, *Servizi segreti*, 43; De Vivo, *Information*, 74.
211. Balletti, *Gli ebrei*, 127–129.
212. Zimmer, *Jewish Synods*, 156 (source appendix).
213. Biagioli, "From Prints to Patents," 167. On the early modern patent system, see also Frumkin, "Early History."
214. Biagioli, "Patent Republic," esp. 1137–1138.
215. Berveglieri, *Inventori stranieri*, 20.
216. Biagioli, "From Prints to Patents," 157.
217. Marika Keblusek, "Keeping It Secret"; Eamon, *Science*, 88.
218. Eamon, "Technology as Magic," esp. 186.

219. On the history of the engineering profession, see Galluzzi, *Renaissance Engineers;* Galluzzi, *Leonardo;* Parsons, *Engineers;* Gille, *Engineers;* Biral and Morachiello, *Immagini dell'ingegnere;* Grafton, *Leon Battista Alberti;* Brusatin, "La macchina"; K.-H. Ludwig, "Ingenieur," in *LexMA,* 5:417-418.
220. Gouk, "Natural Philosophy," 235; see also Eamon, "Technology as Magic."
221. Galluzzi, *Renaissance Engineers,* 26.
222. Grafton, *Leon Battista Alberti,* 119. In general, see also White, "Medical Astrologers."
223. Eamon, "Court," 31; Moran, *Alchemical World,* 173; Long, "Power," 40.
224. On Foucault's investigations into the linkage between science and power in the formation of the modern state, see esp. Foucault, *Security, Territory, Population.*
225. Simonsohn, "Considerazioni introduttive," 328. There is also a discussion of this topic, using Tuscany as a case, in Cooperman, "Trade and Settlement," 185-194; see also Roth, *Jews in the Renaissance,* esp. 237, and Toaff, *Il prestigiatore,* 19-20. On Jews as technical experts in late medieval German-speaking Europe, see the brief remarks in Toch, "Economic Activities," 208.
226. Berveglieri, *Inventori stranieri,* 42.
227. Rabkin, "Interfacce multiple," 5.
228. Lopez and Raymond, *Medieval Trade,* doc. 49 (Siena 1445); Simonsohn, *Jews in Sicily,* vol. 7, doc. 4999 (Sicily 1487); vol. 8, doc. 5306 (Sicily 1490); Segre, *Jews in Piedmont,* vol. 1, doc. 1141 (Savoy 1573); *GJ* 3.1:606 (fifteenth-century Goslar); ibid., 3.3:2146 (regarding lead works in the Duchy of Berg managed by a Jew, 1516); Grunebaum, "Les juifs d'Orient," 125 (in general on the Ottoman Empire).
229. Toch, "Economic Activities," 208; see also *GJ* 3.3:2146.
230. For the case of the imperial city of Frankfurt: *Regesten I* (Andernacht), doc. 2997 (a Jew who knows about mills tries to get an audience with the council; 1498), doc. 3264 (a Jew offers to build a mill for the council; 1502), doc. 3854 (mention of a Jewish mill maker; 1513), and doc. 3858 (the council negotiates with the Jew Schmul about building a mill; 1513). In 1426, in turn, the Nuremberg Council hired a Jewish mill builder, see *GJ* 3.3:2146.
231. *GJ* 3.3:2146.
232. Schlundt, *"Und hat sich das ertz,"* 14-17, 29, 36-37, 242-245. I thank Gerd Mentgen for bringing this reference to my attention.
233. *GJ* 3.1:606.
234. Luzzatto, "Ricordi storici," 531; Roth, "Abramo Colorni," 147.
235. Olivieri, "Il medico ebreo," 451, 456.

236. Preto, *Servizi segreti,* 159.
237. Privilege of the Senate from 12 August 1634, ASV, Senato Terra, filza 373.
238. "Ho fabricato l'edificio fuori della Città, sebene in luoco ritirato, però per necessità a molti aperto, et palese." Petition of Daniel Israel Perez from 15 January 1635, ASV, Senato Terra, filza 373.
239. Senate resolution from 9 May 1635, ASV, Senato Terra, filza 373.
240. Report to the Doge from 2 March 1635 and 15 March 1635, ASV, Senato Terra, filza 373.
241. Berveglieri, *Inventori stranieri,* 115–116.
242. ASMn, AG, Liber dei decreti, vol. 56, fol. 242v. This privilege from 15 April 1636 was issued for his "inventione facile per portar acque da fiumi a campi, e levarle."
243. Shulvass, *Jews in the World of the Renaissance,* 146.
244. Balletti, *Gli ebrei,* 54.
245. Leoni, "Alcuni esempi," 91; Leoni, "Per una storia," 156.
246. Roth, *Jews in the Renaissance,* 237. On this "Isach de Noyone ebreo," see Simonsohn, *Jews in the Duchy of Milan,* vol. 1, doc. 18. This document deals with the defamation of the engineer by a Christian contemporary. It is questionable to what extent the accusation expressed there, that Isaac was a swindler, is accurate.
247. Bonetti, *Gli ebrei,* 11.
248. Simonsohn, *Jews in the Duchy of Milan,* vol. 1, docs. 332, 404, 418.
249. Campori, *Gli architetti,* 43.
250. Simonsohn, *History of the Jews in the Duchy of Mantua,* 270.
251. Simonsohn, *Jews in the Duchy of Milan,* vol. 1, doc. 1344.
252. Ginsburger, *Les juifs et l'art militaire.*
253. Biale, *Power and Powerlessness,* 72–77.
254. See esp. Litt, "Juden und Waffen," as well as the other contributions to that volume.
255. *Regesten I* (Andernacht), doc. 1039.
256. *GJ* 3.3:2146.
257. Among Italian Jews, the surname Colonia itself does not necessarily point to an origin in Cologne. It could also refer to Cologna Veneta (see Colorni, "Cognomi ebraici italiani," 72). In this case, however, the sources explicitly characterize Abralino as an "inzignero ebreo thodesco" [*sic*].
258. Simonsohn, *Jews in the Duchy of Milan,* vol. 1, doc. 1042.
259. Wischnitzer, *History of Jewish Crafts,* 212.
260. Poliakov, *Jewish Bankers,* 114.

261. Veinstein, "Note," 90.
262. Simonsohn, *Jews in Sicily*, vol. 4, doc. 2274.
263. Ibid., vol. 5, doc. 2656.
264. A source from 1467 speaks of him as "mastru di artiglirii zoe pulviri, bombardi et altri magisterii," cf. ibid., vol. 6, doc. 3698. As late as 1482 he is characterized in an exchange of letters by the authorities as quite useful for "lu armamentu per larti et speculacioni di ingegnu ki teni." Vol. 7, doc. 4637, also doc. 4578 (for 1481).
265. His responsibilities are outlined in 1481 as "mastru bombardiere a rafinari salinitru, gubernari, mectiri in ordini li bombardi, spingardi, passavolanti et quilli parari et sparari." Ibid., vol. 7, doc. 4578. An additional Jewish "mastru di artigliaria" not otherwise specified by name from this period is mentioned in the same source.
266. Ibid., vol. 8, doc. 5241; vol. 7, doc. 5201.
267. Wischnitzer, *History of Jewish Crafts*, 143.
268. See Chapter 5.
269. "La natione hebrea . . . fù celebre appresso tutte le genti a lei coetanee in quanto al maneggio dell'Arme," according to Luzzatto, *Discorso*, fol. 73v. And see comparable remarks in Portaleone, *Heldenschilde*, esp. chs. 40–43. On Portaleone, see also Miletto, "Bibel als Handbuch."
270. Fabri, *Evagatorium in Terrae Sanctae*, 3:187.
271. Veinstein, "Note," 91.
272. Take, for example, the case of Samuel Pallache, who delivered weapons from the Netherlands to Morocco in the 1630s. See García-Arenal and Wiegers, *Man of Three Worlds*, esp. 73. See also a 1408 document from Ferrara that speaks of a Jew who sold "certi arnesi ed armi" to a Christian. The purchase price was 96 lire. See Franceschini, *Presenza ebraica*, doc. 150. For late medieval Ashkenazic Jewry, see Toch, *Economic Activities*, 208.
273. Ries, *Jüdisches Leben*, 407. I am grateful to Dr. Ries for additional information about this source.
274. Ibid., 405.
275. Jersch-Wenzel and Rürup, *Quellen*, 4:229.
276. Ginsburger, *Les juifs et l'art militaire*, 165.
277. Ibid., 162.
278. Thus, for instance, the moneylender Vitale Sacerdote in 1573 delivered various kinds of weapons ("morrioni e archibusi") for the army of the Duke of Savoy. See Segre, *Jews in Piedmont*, vol. 1, doc. 1104.
279. Stern, *Court Jew*, ch. 1 ("The Court Jew as Commissary").

280. Israel, *European Jewry*, ch. 6. On the significance of powder deliveries for the formation of court Jewry, see García-Arenal and Wiegers, *Man of Three Worlds*, 130.
281. Stern, *Court Jew*, ch. 1; Schwarzfuchs, "Les Juifs de Cour," 390; Israel, *European Jewry*, 124–126.
282. Stern, *Court Jew*, 22.
283. Ibid., 29.
284. Schwarz, "Ein Wiener Donaubrückenprojekt"; Gelber, "An umbakanter briv."
285. Schwarz, "Ein Wiener Donaubrückenprojekt," 80.
286. Petition of Mendel Isaak to Emperor Rudolf II, 4 July 1589: "[B]ecause I am indeed skilled in the matter and have had such work done for the late King Batory in Poland, namely ships and pontoons in Russia and Moscow on large flowing waters, as he was waging war with the Muscovites, therefore I also wanted to undertake this, and I am aware that I need workers for this and that I will have to instruct them well." Reprinted in ibid., doc. 1.
287. Report of the Hofkammer of 1 July 1589, ibid., doc. 2.
288. Petition of Mendel Isaak to Emperor Rudolf II (end of 1589), ibid., doc. 7.
289. This emerges from documents that N. Gelber published in 1937. See Gelber, "An umbakanter briv."
290. Schwarz, "Ein Wiener Donaubrückenprojekt," 84.
291. ÖStA, Hofkammerarchiv, Verschiedene Vorschläge, Nr. 81 (1589).
292. Segre, "Gli ebrei lombardi," 93; and see Simonsohn, *Jews in the Duchy of Milan*, vol. 3, doc. 4118.
293. Segre, "Gli ebrei lombardi," 87.
294. Simonsohn, *History of the Jews in the Duchy of Mantua*, 270.
295. Rabbi: Bonfil, *Rabbis and Jewish Communities*, 122 (following the unpublished *Pinkas Kehilla kedosha be-Casale* [Casale Monferrato]). Moneylender: see below, Chapter 6. The moneylending activities are attested for the first time in 1592; see Colorni, "La corrispondenza," 685.
296. Simonsohn, *Jews in the Duchy of Milan*, vol. 3, docs. 4255, 4257, 4310, 4316, 4414.
297. For Tuscany: Cooperman, "Trade and Settlement," 185–194; for Mantua: Simonsohn, *History of the Jews in the Duchy of Mantua*, 270, 280; for Venice: Berveglieri, *Inventori stranieri*, esp. 88–89.
298. The case of saltpeter production is treated in greater detail in Chapter 5.
299. Cooperman, "Trade and Settlement," 190–191.
300. Cassuto, *Gli ebrei*, 194 and docs. 59, 60.

301. "Et mi pare che ad ogni modo doviate tirarli al servitio vostro, perchè simile occasione non si trovono ogni giorno." Quoted in ibid., doc. 59.
302. "[N]e facessi qualche prova, et se havessino come dicono qualche secreto intrattenerli." Quoted in Cassuto, *Gli ebrei*, doc. 60; see also Wischnitzer, *History of Jewish Crafts*, 143.
303. "[H]avendo io per acquistare molti secreti peregrinato il mondo, et anco speso del mio havere, e la miglior parte de miei anni." Petition of Salamon Navarro from 11 December 1590, ASV, Senato Terra, filza 119. Presumably, this secrecy maven was Salamon di Lazzaro Navarro, a Jew from Livorno who collaborated in the 1590s with the Jewish inventor Maggino di Gabrielli and was primarily active in textile manufacture—another reminder that figures like Salamon Navarro should not be hastily branded as charlatans. On this Salamon from Livorno, see Bemporad, *Maggino di Gabriello*, 26, 96, 262.
304. For comparable cases, see Gentilcore, *Medical Charlatanism*, 362.
305. Petition of Salomon da Bassano from 6 February 1591, ASV, Senato Terra, filza 119.
306. Petition of Simon di Roman from 6 February 1591, ASV, Senato Terra, filza 119.
307. On the profession of the *sensali* (also: *sanseri*), who, in addition to trading in goods, acted as brokers, see de Vivo, *Information*, 108–109.
308. Striedinger, *Der Goldmacher Marco Bragadino*, 108.
309. Camporesi, *Il pane selvaggio*.
310. Della Porta, *Magiae naturalis*, 93–96.
311. See e.g. the report of the *Provveditori e sopraproveditori alla biave* from 11 February 1591, ASV, Senato Terra, filza 119.
312. All of the petitions are in ASV, Senato Terra, filza 119.
313. Cooperman, "Trade and Settlement," 1.
314. Roth, "Note on the Astronomers."
315. Israel, *European Jewry*, 180.
316. Sonne, "Shemona Michtavim," 145.
317. Delmedigo, *Sefer Matzref la-Ḥokhma*, 49.
318. "Being young I studied Physicke, and began / to practise first upon the Italian; / . . . And after that was I an Engineere, / and in the warres, twixt France and Germanie, / Under pretence of helping Charles the fifth, / Slew friend and enemy with my strategems." Marlowe, *Jew of Malta*, 2.3.
319. Freeman, "Source."
320. Ethel Seaton assumes that Marlowe was well informed about the situation and the milieu of Sephardic (crypto-)Jews at the Elizabethan court owing to his espionage work. Seaton, "Fresh Sources." Bawcutt even sees in the fig-

ure of Barabas the portrait of the famous Sephardic Jew Joseph Nasi, the Duke of Naxos. Bawcutt, "Introduction," 5–9.

321. Since I did not have access to the French edition, I quote from the Italian edition: Nicolay, *Le navigationi,* 142: "I quali [the marranos] con gran pregiudicio, & danno della Christianità, hanno insegnate al Turco molte inventioni, artificij, & machine di guerra; come il fare l'artegliaria gli archibugi, la polve da cannone, le palle e l'altre arme."

322. Ha-Cohen, *Vale of Tears,* 115; Gábor Ágoston, *Guns,* 45.

323. Dubnow, *Weltgeschichte,* 6:19; Cahnman, "Role and Significance," xxii.

324. Ágoston, *Guns,* 45; Veinstein, "Note," 89; Israel, *Diasporas,* 53–54; Cooperman, "Trade and Settlement," 54. Less skeptical, by contrast, is Glick, "Moriscos and Marranos," 113–125.

325. The animus against Jews that Nicolay expressed in his *Navigationi et viaggi* is plainly evident, e.g., in bk. IV, ch. 16 (p. 145).

326. Veinstein, "Note," 89.

327. Ágoston, *Guns,* 42–46.

328. Ibid., 45–46.

329. Ibid., 65.

330. Ibid., 46.

331. Braude, "Rise and Fall," 232.

332. Aescoly, *Sippur David ha-Reuveni.*

333. Bacci, *L'alicorno,* 18.

334. Ibid., 51.

335. The classic study on the history of ideas about the unicorn is Shepard, *Lore.* See also Manzonetto, *Storia di un alicorno,* and Daston and Park, *Wonders,* esp. 74–75.

336. Manzonetto, *Storia di un alicorno,* 75–78.

337. Bacci, *L'alicorno,* 71, 75; also Shepard, *Lore,* 119.

338. Hermann Güntert, "Einhorn," in *HdA,* 2:709.

339. See Bauer and Haupt, *Kunstkammerinventar,* 4.

340. Manzonetto, *Storia di un alicorno.*

341. Morselli, "'Il più grande edificio'" 131.

342. Franchini et al., *La scienza,* 118.

343. Shepard, *Lore,* 114.

344. *Gonzaga/Venice* II, doc. 116.

345. Manzonetto, *Storia di un alicorno,* 7.

346. Shepard, *Lore,* esp. 30; Hermann Güntert, "Einhorn," in *HdA,* 2:710.

347. "Segreti di Levante." Thus in a 1592 letter from the Mantuan correspondent in Ancona to Duke Vincenzo Gonzaga, see *Gonzaga/Rome,* doc. 164.

348. The animals mentioned were "lupi cervieri di levante." See *Gonzaga/Venice* II, docs. 25–27.
349. Reggiep Bey from Tripolis to Ferdinando II de' Medici, ASF, Medico del principato, 1082, fol. 645, 10 May 1662. I quote this source from the digital Medici Archive Project (www.medici.org), doc. ID 17814.
350. Jütte, "Jewish Consuls."
351. Bacci, *L'alicorno*, 55.
352. H. Brandenburg, "Einhorn," in *RAC*, 4:841, 843; also Shepard, *Lore*, 136.
353. Cecil Roth, "Abenaes, Solomon," in *EJ*, 1:249–250; see also Wolf, "Jews in Elizabethan England," esp. 24–29.
354. Pullan, *Jews of Europe*, 186.
355. Roth, "Abenaes," in *EJ*, 1:249–250.
356. Also Shepard, *Lore*, 118.
357. Brandenburg, "Einhorn," in *RCA*, 849–851.
358. E.g., Num 23:22; Deut 33:17; Pss 22:22; 29:6, 92:11; Job 39:9–12. On postbiblical sources about the *re'em* and its physical appearance, also see Ginzberg, *Legends*. Bible scholars today tend to identify the term *re'em* with a wild buffalo or wild bull. Hellenistic Jews, by contrast, associated the *re'em* with the rhinoceros. Even in the Vulgate, the term is translated as "rhinoceros" in Latin. Over the centuries, the interpretation of the *re'em* as a unicorn gained in credibility for both Jews and Christians. Luther generally saw the *re'em* as a unicorn. See Güntert, "Einhorn," in *HdA*, 711; Brandenburg, "Einhorn," in *RCA*, 845–846.
359. Ginzberg, *Legends*, 1:688.
360. Bacci, *L'alicorno*, 31.
361. Houghton Library, Harvard University (call no. 525.73.186).
362. For talmudic mentions of a (legendary) creature with a horn, see esp. *b. Shabbat* 28b and *b. Avodah Zarah* 8a.
363. Metzger and Metzger, *Jewish Life*, 26–27.
364. Horowitz, "Odd Couples," 250.
365. *Regesten II* (Andernacht), docs. 2908, 3510, 3578.
366. De Pomis, *Tzemah David*, 20, 190. And see Shepard, *Lore*, 117.
367. Ruderman, "Unicorns," esp. 352. Portaleone's remarks are now available in a carefully edited German edition: Portaleone, *Heldenschilde*, ch. 53.
368. Zimmels, *Magicians*, 230.
369. Ruderman, "Unicorns."
370. *Gonzaga/Prague*, doc. 1080.
371. Ruderman, "Unicorns," 347. The tradition of interpreting the unicorn in heroic terms (even if no longer in the way Yagel did this) might explain why, as

late as the nineteenth century, this animal was depicted in the family coat of arms of the powerful Rothschild banking family. See Horowitz, "Odd Couples," 251.
372. Ruderman, "Unicorns," 355.

Chapter Three. Zones of Interaction

1. For late antiquity: Veltri, *Magie und Halakha;* Blau, *Das altjüdische Zauberwesen;* see also the literature listed in Ruderman, *Jewish Thought,* 380–382. For the early modern era: Idel, "Magical and Neoplatonic Interpretations"; Idel, "Jewish Magic"; Ruderman, *Kabbalah;* Grözinger and Dan, *Mysticism, Magic and Kabbalah;* Grözinger, "Jüdische Wundermänner in Deutschland."
2. Guggenheim, "Meeting on the Road," 134–136; similarly: Glanz, *Geschichte des niederen jüdischen Volkes,* 48–49.
3. Idel, "Jewish Magic," 86.
4. Ibid., 85; see also Kieckhefer, "Did Magic Have a Renaissance?," 210.
5. Trachtenberg, *Devil and the Jews;* Trachtenberg, *Jewish Magic and Superstition,* ch. 1; Hsia, *Myth of Ritual Murder,* esp. 6; Barbierato, *Nella stanza dei circoli,* esp. 305; Kieckhefer, *Forbidden Rites,* 115; Güdemann, *Geschichte des Erziehungswesens,* 3:153–155; Will-Erich Peuckert, "Jude, Jüdin," in *HdA,* 4:811–817.
6. For England: Katz, *Philo-Semitism,* 4.
7. Barbierato, *Nella stanza dei circoli,* 305; Garin, "L'umanesimo italiano e la cultura ebraica"; Thorndike, *History of Magic,* 1:450–461; Glanz, *Geschichte des niederen jüdischen Volkes,* 48–49. On the idea of Moses as a Hermetic magus, widespread among Jews and Christians: Idel, "Hermeticism and Judaism," 67.
8. The research literature on early modern magic in general is vast. For a bibliographical overview, see Vasoli, *Magia e scienza,* 295–303. Thorndike's *History of Magic* remains a standard work in this field.
9. Thomas, *Religion and the Decline of Magic,* esp. 761–762.
10. Eamon, "Technology as Magic," 197. On *magia naturalis* in general: Peuckert, *Gabalia;* Stuckrad, *Was ist Esoterik?,* 100–113.
11. Malinowski, *Magic, Science and Religion.*
12. Idel, "Jewish Magic," 98.
13. Ibid.
14. On the myth of the golem, see esp. Idel, *Der Golem.*
15. According to this account, a certain Rabbi Moses melted down a wax figure representing the bishop, which caused the bishop's death. Brann, *Trithemius*

and Magical Theology, 58. Similar legends, told with a certain schadenfreude, were recorded in the popular Yiddish *Mayse-Bukh* (first published 1602).

16. The idea of "zones of interaction" takes cues from the field of postcolonial studies; see esp. Bhabha, *Location of Culture.* For an attempt to apply such concepts to the field of early modern Jewish history, see now also Israel et al., *Interstizi.*
17. Modena, *History of the Rites,* 223–224.
18. Vogelstein and Rieger, *Geschichte der Juden in Rom,* 2:185.
19. Pullan, *Jews of Europe,* 73, 77.
20. Aikema, *Pietro della Vecchia.*
21. Patai, *Jewish Alchemists,* 523.
22. Geographical boundaries: Borchardt even compares the boom in magic, which crossed linguistic and political boundaries during the Renaissance, with the phenomenon of humanism. Borchardt, "Magus as Renaissance Man." Social distinctions: this has been vividly demonstrated by Barbierato, *Nella stanza dei circoli,* e.g. 289.
23. Ibid., 113–115.
24. Milani, "Indovini ebrei." See also Pullan, *Jews of Europe,* 161; Ioly Zorattini, "Jews, Crypto-Jews and the Inquisition," 114.
25. Balletti, *Gli ebrei e gli Estensi,* 141.
26. Barbierato, *Nella stanza dei circoli,* 313–327.
27. Sennett, *Flesh and Stone,* 237; Barbierato, *Nella stanza dei circoli,* 313–327.
28. Milani, "Indovini ebrei," 211.
29. Thus, there was a tradition in which the character of Rübezahl (the mountain spirit of folklore) was regarded as a Jewish magician from Venice. Peuckert, "Jüdin," in *HdA* 4:812.
30. Barbierato, *Nella stanza dei circoli,* 304.
31. Milani, "Indovini ebrei," 212.
32. Ibid., 210.
33. Barbierato, *Nella stanza dei circoli,* 309.
34. Modena, *Autobiography,* 162. The estate he left behind included thirteen books and manuscripts with occult content. Adelman, "Leon Modena," 40–41.
35. Pullan, *Jews of Europe,* 90.
36. Barbierato, *Nella stanza dei circoli,* 309.
37. Ibid.; Biondi, "Gli ebrei e l'inquisizione," 277, 284.
38. Cassuto, *Gli ebrei a Firenze,* 273.
39. Italy: Aron-Beller, *Jews on Trial,* esp. 22.
40. Goethe, "Dichtung und Wahrheit," in *Werke,* 9:149–150.

41. *Regesten I* (Andernacht), doc. 2405.
42. This is also true with respect to Jewish mysticism: Idel, "Le passage de l'intelligence," esp. 168–175.
43. Idel, "Differing Conceptions," 168.
44. Ruderman, *Kabbalah;* Tirosh-Samuelson, "Theology of Nature," 559; there is now a case study about the noted Sephardic Jew Giuseppe Attias (1672–1739) in Livorno, in whose library were numerous magical writings by Christian authors: Frattarelli Fischer, *Vivere fuori dal Ghetto,* 319.
45. Idel, "Hermeticism and Judaism;" see also Kottek, "Jews between Profane and Sacred," 115.
46. Barbierato, *Nella stanza dei circoli,* 283.
47. Toaff, *Il prestigiatore di Dio,* 236–237.
48. On the Kabbalah as a zone of contact for Jews and Christians, see Ruderman, *Jewish Enlightenment,* 160 (with additional literature).
49. Delumeau, *Le mystère Campanella,* 47–48, 53.
50. Modena, *Autobiography,* 108–109.
51. ASMo, ASE, Ebrei, b. 23b. Altogether, three undated letters by Sasson to the court have been preserved.
52. Barbierato, *Nella stanza dei circoli,* 172. See now also Goldberg, *Jews and Magic.*
53. See Tirosh-Samuelson, "Theology of Nature," 550.
54. On this brief report by Isaac Katz, see Efron, "Common Goods," 236; Veltri, "Yehuda Löw," 205.
55. Gans, *Tzemaḥ David,* 145.
56. Erzherzog Maximilian to Philipp Lang, 14 July 1603, HHStA, Familienarchiv, Lang-Akten, Karton 1, fol. 22r: "We had heard of the Jerusalemite Jew [as well as of another unknown person]; also, where to find them. But because they insisted that we should not talk about them and also because they do not want to reveal themselves to everybody, we promised to keep this secret. But since His Majesty the Emperor wishes that we lead the negotiations with them, we will look for ways to fulfill His Majesty's order." Later on the letter mentions the metal antimony. On the occult interests of the archduke in general, see Evans, *Rudolf II,* 62.
57. Aescoly, *Sippur David ha-Reuveni,* e.g. 22, 42, 67.
58. Stollberg-Rilinger, "Das Verschwinden des Geheimnisses," 229.
59. On the history of this method, see Couto, "Spying in the Ottoman Empire," 292–294; Burke, "Early Modern Venice," 394. This method was occasionally also called the "Cicero method," since Cicero was said to have used these kinds of substitutions in his letters: Strasser, *Lingua Universalis,* 23–25.

60. All details according to Arbel, *Trading Nations*, 151.
61. Bakhtin, *Rabelais and His World*.
62. Valvasor, *Die Ehre dess Hertzogthums Crain*, pt. 3, bk. XI, 93–94.
63. On Jews and magic mirrors, see also Chapter 5.

Chapter Four. Trading in Secrets and Economic Life

1. Smith, *Business of Alchemy*; Nummedal, *Alchemy and Authority*, esp. 13, 73; Nummedal, "Practical Alchemy"; Krampl, "Diplomaten," 156.
2. Striedinger, *Der Goldmacher Marco Bragadino*, esp. 19.
3. Redlich, "Der deutsche fürstliche Unternehmer."
4. During, *Modern Enchantments*, 1.
5. Roper, *Oedipus*, 128.
6. Grössing and Stuhlhofer, "Versuch einer Deutung"; Stierlin, *Astrologie und Herrschaft*; Grafton, "Girolamo Cardano," esp. 183; Grafton, *Cardano's Cosmos*.
7. Nummedal, *Alchemy and Authority*, 73; Krampl, "Diplomaten."
8. Nummedal, *Alchemy and Authority*, 73, 91–94.
9. Smith, *Business of Alchemy*.
10. Stern, *Court Jew*, 244–245.
11. As in, e.g., Patai, *Jewish Alchemists*, e.g. 5, 520.
12. Consider the case of the Udine-born physician Salomo Ashkenazi (ca. 1520–1602), who initially worked as a doctor for the Polish king and later for the Ottoman sultan. Ashkenazi, who owned several ships and was active in both the medical and diplomatic fields, built an extensive trade network that extended from Crete across Italy to Poland. See Arbel, *Trading Nations*, 78–86.
13. Nummedal, *Alchemy and Authority*, 86–89.
14. Patai, *Jewish Alchemists*, 174.
15. Ackermann, "Münzmeister Lippold," 11.
16. See the confession in ibid., 93 (doc. 7).
17. Segre, *Gli ebrei*, esp. 24.
18. Simonsohn, *Jews in the Duchy of Milan*, 1:xxxi, doc. 3135.
19. Ibid., doc. 3622.
20. Roth, "Joseph Nasi"; for a summary of the events in Savoy, see also Segre, *Jews in Piedmont*, 1:liv–lvi.
21. Roth, "Joseph Nasi," 467.
22. Ibid.
23. Segre, *Jews in Piedmont*, docs. 1104, 1141.
24. Segre, *Jews in the Duchy of Milan*, docs. 3903, 4087.

25. Ibid., doc. 4118; Segre, *Gli ebrei lombardi,* 93.
26. Segre, *Gli ebrei lombardi,* 87.
27. Simonsohn, *Jews in the Duchy of Milan,* doc. 4414.
28. Cohen and Mann, "Melding Worlds," 111; and see 181 (catalogue section).
29. This could well have been a sapphire, a gem that was linked to the biblical term *sapir* and was therefore shrouded in a certain mystique. For the payment: Haupt, "Kaiser Rudolf II," doc. 1734.
30. *Gonzaga/Prague,* doc. 1005.
31. Ibid., docs. 1008, 1012, 1026.
32. *Gonzaga/Venice* II, doc. 126. This could have been the engineer named Giovanni Sigismondo Fristh [*sic*], whose arrival in Mantua is announced shortly thereafter. Ibid., doc. 131. No additional information could be obtained about this engineer.
33. The quotations are from Friedenwald, *Jews and Medicine,* 1:53, and Münster, "L'Enarratio brevis."
34. Frattarelli Fischer, *Vivere fuori dal Ghetto,* 90.
35. *Gonzaga/Venice* II, docs. 182, 185, 186, 210.
36. Milano, "Un'azienda di banchieri."
37. Cardano, *De venenis libri tres,* 313. Lewin also points out that cantharides were already used as a poison in premodern times. On this usage from the perspective of modern medicine, see Lewin, *Gifte und Vergiftung,* 986–989.
38. ÖStA, Hofkammerarchiv, Verschiedene Vorschläge, Nr. 122. There is information on Levi as a banker in Mantua in Simonsohn, *History of the Jews in the Duchy of Mantua,* 232, 790–791.
39. "[S]ecreto d'avere modo et via de fare Agumentare ogn['] anno un utile che rendera tanto che sarà Bastante per tutti li spesi del suo stato." ASMo, ASE, Invenzioni, progetti, scoperte, b. 1 (two undated petitions [1609]).
40. All of the following information on this, unless otherwise specified, is taken from Jütte, "Handel, Wissenstransfer und Netzwerke"; on Maggino, see also Toaff, *Il prestigiatore di Dio,* 91–131, and Liscia Bemporad, *Maggino di Gabriello.*
41. Lincoln, "Jew and the Worms," esp. 92.
42. On this overlap, see esp. the relevant chapters in Ganzenmüller, *Beiträge.*
43. ASR, Collezione dei bandi, vol. 7.
44. Di Gabrielli, *Dialoghi,* 2.
45. Jütte, "Handel, Wissenstransfer und Netzwerke," 272–273.
46. Frattarelli Fischer, *Vivere fuori dal Ghetto,* 98.
47. Di Gabrielli, *Dialoghi.*
48. Lincoln, "Jew and the Worms," 96.

49. In his treatise, talk of his secrets is ubiquitous. See e.g. the unpaginated letter of dedication to the pope, Di Gabrielli, *Dialoghi*, and in addition: 7, 11, 12, 16, 17, 59, 61, 64, 67, 83, 90, 91.
50. Maggino to Frederick I, 31 March 1598, HStAS, A 56 Bü 10, fol. 20r.
51. "[The] art God gave Me, that I . . . never revealed." Maggino to Frederick I, 15 June 1598, HStAS, A 56 Bü 10, fol. 38r.
52. Jütte, "Abramo Colorni," 456–460.
53. Biondi, "Gli ebrei."
54. Ibid., 277, 284.
55. "Noi . . . hebrei quando sentiamo nominare il Santo Ufficio habiamo paura." Quoted in ibid., 276.
56. Gentilcore, *Medical Charlatanism*, 298, 329.
57. His Jewish origin is asserted, albeit without any proof, in Stonehill, *Jewish Contribution*, 93. I was unable to find additional reliable information about Isacchi.
58. Isacchi, *Inventioni*.
59. All of the details on this case are according to Rhamm, *Die betrüglichen Goldmacher*, esp. 19, 75.
60. Quoted in ibid., 117.
61. Dante Alighieri, *Divine Comedy, Inferno*, Canto 29.
62. Nummedal, *Alchemy and Authority*, esp. 62.
63. On Luther's generally critical position on alchemy, see Klingner, *Luther und der deutsche Volksaberglaube*, 109–111.
64. Luther to Joachim II, Elector of Brandenburg, 9 March 1545, in Luther, *Werke*, 11:49–52.
65. Liechtenstein, "Ein eigenhändiger Brief."
66. A number of more recent studies have been devoted to Luther's anti-Judaism, which intensified during the course of his life. Suffice it to refer to Oberman, *Wurzeln des Antisemitismus*, esp. ch. 3. Additional literature is mentioned in Joseph E. Heller and B. Mordechai Ansbacher, "Luther, Martin," in *EJ*, 13:271–272.
67. On the connections between alchemy and coinage, see also Müller-Jahncke and Telle, "Numismatik und Alchemie," esp. 229–230, 261.
68. See now esp. Trawnicek, *Münzjuden*, 72, who speaks of an "Arkancharakter des Münzwesens"; see also Haasis, *Joseph Süß Oppenheimer*, 128, 132.
69. On Jews as moneyers in the Middle Ages, see Wenninger, "Juden als Münzmeister." This study also touches on the situation in the early modern period; see 135, 137. On the significance of dealing in and delivery of coins for early modern court Jews, see esp. Stern, *Court Jew*, ch. 6.

70. Sandri and Alazraki, *Arte e vita ebraica*, 17; Schlundt, "Und hat sich das ertz," ch. 2.
71. Battenberg, *Die Juden in Deutschland*, 96.
72. Israel, *European Jewry*, 172.
73. Stern, *Jud Süß*, 116–117.
74. Schudt, *Jüdische Merckwürdigkeiten*, bk. VI, 210.
75. Goer, "Monetäre Thematik," esp. 126–130, 136–139, 146–158; see also Gerber, *Jud Süß*, 68–69, 93, 96, 359.
76. Breuer, "Die Hofjuden," 111; Gömmel, "Hofjuden und Wirtschaft," 62; see also Stern, *Court Jew*, ch. 6.
77. On his grandfather's and family's wealth, see Ries, *Jüdisches Leben*, 417–418.
78. Ibid., 119.
79. Nummedal, *Alchemy and Authority*, 102–103.
80. Ries, *Jüdisches Leben*, 405.
81. Ibid., 120.
82. On the history of this aristocratic family and its interests in natural science and alchemy, see Annemarie Enneper, "Rosenberg," in *NDB*, 22:57–58; see also Evans, *Rudolf II*, 140–143.
83. Göller, "Abhängigkeit und Chance," 280–286.
84. Löwenstein, *Quellen*, doc. 2121.
85. On his biography, see esp. Stern, *Jud Süß*; Haasis, *Joseph Süß Oppenheimer*. On Oppenheimer in the eyes of his contemporaries, see Gerber, *Jud Süß*.
86. Wolf, "Joseph Süß Oppenheimer" [1981], 94; see also Wolf, "Joseph Süß Oppenheimer" [1983].
87. Wolf, "Joseph Süß Oppenheimer" [1981], 94.
88. Wolf, "Joseph Süß Oppenheimer" [1983], 223.
89. Ibid.
90. Ibid., 226.
91. Ibid., 228.
92. Ibid., 239.
93. One preserved coin may be found today in the Hessisches Landesmuseum Darmstadt, Inv.-Nr. 18090. See the picture in Wolf, "Joseph Süß Oppenheimer" [1981], 98.
94. Ibid., 102. I can now corroborate Wolf's assumption that this transcription was an alchemical allusion. The motto *occulta patebunt* is in fact a quotation from a remark attributed to Hermes Trismegistos concerning the philosopher's stone as circulated, for instance, in the frequently published and translated alchemical book by the Frenchman Alexandre-Toussaint Limojon de Saint-Didier. There it says: "The same *Philosopher* [viz. Hermes Trismegistos] does

still more particularly take Notice of the Nativity of this admirable Stone, when he says: "*The King shall come out of the Fire, and shall rejoice in his Marriage, and the hidden Things shall be laid open. [Rex ab igne veniet, ac conjugio gaudebit, & occulta patebunt.]*" See Limojon de Saint-Didier, *Hermetical Triumph*, 121 (emphasis in original).

95. Wolf, "Joseph Süß Oppenheimer" [1983], 254.
96. Stern, *Jud Süß*, ch. 8; Haasis, *Joseph Süß Oppenheimer*, 126–151.
97. Haasis, *Joseph Süß Oppenheimer*, 131.
98. Duke Karl Alexander to Oppenheimer, undated letter (presumably 1734/1735), quoted in Emberger and Kretzschmar, *Die Quellen sprechen lassen*, 55, source 12 (with picture on 56). On this source, see also ibid., 115.
99. Stern, *Jud Süß*, 106, 142.
100. Ibid., 14.
101. On this, see (with additional bibliographical references) Emberger and Kretzschmar, *Die Quelle sprechen lassen*.
102. Nummedal, *Alchemy and Authority*, 156.
103. Quoted in Hofacker, *Alchemie am Hof*, 23.
104. This is all the more surprising since some of Oppenheimer's biographers are aware of the fact of Honauer's execution, see e.g. Stern, *Jud Süß*, 175; Elwenspoek, *Jud Süß Oppenheimer*, 169. On the different stages of Oppenheimer's execution, see (in general) esp. Haasis, *Joseph Süß Oppenheimer*, 441–448. In her authoritative work on the reception history of the Oppenheimer case, Gerber does mention the previous history of the gallows in two places (*Jud Süß*, 261, 477). However, she sees the figure of the alchemist merely as an "intermediate link between swindling at court and swindling or robbery on the street" (477), thus overlooking how the analogy between court Jew and alchemist constituted an independent contemporary discourse that was already present in Luther's writings.
105. Haasis, *Joseph Süß Oppenheimer*, 389–391.
106. In Gerber's study alone, seven contemporary pamphlets or broadsheets that compare Honauer and Süß are listed (without even touching on the issue of later reprints): *Jud Süß*, esp. 477. These are (1) Anon., "Curieuser [*sic*] Nachrichten aus dem Reich der Beschnittenen," pt. 2 (Frankfurt am Main/Leipzig, 1738), 77, pt. 4 (Nuremberg, 1738), 64–69; (2) Anon., "Ausführliche Beschreibung des Eisernen Galgens . . . ," n.p, n.d. [1738]; (3) Anon., "Wahrhaffte Vorstellung und Ausführliche Beschreibung des Eisernen Galgens," n.p., n.d. [1738]; (4) Anon., "Kurtze Erzaehlung von dem vonhero an dem Eisern Galgen gefangenen Goldmacher und dessen Anhang," n.p., n.d. (with different

reprints); (5) Johannes Andreas Mattsperger, "Wahrhafftige Abbildung Des Bey Stuttgard erbauten eysenen Galgens," Mahler am mittlern Lech, n.d.; (6) Anon., "Eigentliche Abbildung und Beschreibung / wie der bekannte Jud / Joseph Süß Oppenheimer [. . .]," engraving, n.p., n.d. (table 12); (7) Elias Baeck, "Wahrhaffte, und nach der Natur accurat Gezeichnete Abbildung, des Juden Süß," engraving, Augsburg, around 1738 (table 8). In addition, a manuscript in the Stuttgart Landesbibliothek (Süssiana, Cod. hist. fol. 348) includes a fictitious conversation in the netherworld between Honauer and Oppenheimer (Gerber, *Jud Süß*, 592).

107. Anon., "Eigentliche Abbildung und Beschreibung" / wie der bekannte Jud / Joseph Süß Oppenheimer . . . ," engraving, n.p., n.d., reproduced in Emberger and Kretzschmar, *Die Quellen sprechen lassen*, 8 (and see Gerber, *Jud Süß*, table 12).

108. The caption to the alchemist's portrait reads: "The Georg Honauer depicted here, a native of Moravia, who passed himself off as a great man and wanted to make gold from iron and . . . duped Fridrich Duke of Würtenberg out of several millions, was first hanged on this newly erected iron gallows on 2 April 1597." Untitled engraving, n.p., n.d. [1738], quoted in Emberger and Kretzschmar, *Die Quellen sprechen lassen*, 9 (ill.); see also Gerber, *Jud Süß*, table 3.

109. Otto, "Alchimisten und Goldmacher," 52.

110. Stern, *Jud Süß*, 170.

111. Opinion of the Special Court, 9 January 1738, HStAS, A 48/14, Bü 12 (emphasis mine). I am profoundly grateful to Dr. Gudrun Emberger (Gotha), who shared this unpublished source with me. The alchemists mentioned in the source are Petrus Montanus and Hans Heinrich von Mühlenfels, who, like their colleague Honauer, were executed during the reign of Duke Frederick I. Not mentioned in the document is the execution of the alchemist Hans Heinrich Nüschler (1601), which also happened under Frederick's reign.

112. Gerber, *Jud Süß*, esp. 27–28.

113. Moser, "Der Fürst," 249.

114. For all subsequent information about the history of the Wahl family I am relying, unless otherwise specified, on the excellent study undertaken by Dieter Blinn: "Die Hofjuden Herz und Saul Wahl."

115. Quoted in ibid., 319.

116. Ibid., 325.

117. Nummedal, *Alchemy and Authority*, 104–109.

118. Blinn, "Die Hofjuden," 312.

119. See Hartung, "Johann Joachim Becher," 276–284.
120. Quoted in Blinn, "Die Hofjuden," 312.
121. Quoted in ibid., 315.
122. Quoted in ibid., 330.

Chapter Five. Abramo Colorni, Professor of Secrets

1. The first study of Colorni's life and work was undertaken by the Ferrarese rabbi Giuseppe Jarè. This very short biography, published on the occasion of a wedding and therefore with a low print run, dates to the mid-1870s: Jarè, *Abramo Colorni* [1874]. At the beginning of the 1890s Jarè revisited the topic after having continually compiled new sources, especially of Italian provenance. This sixty-page study, which includes an extensive appendix with documents (some of which were already published in 1874), appeared as a booklet as well as in the third volume of the *Atti della deputazione ferrarese di storia patria* (1891). Henceforth I refer to the booklet edition: Jarè, *Abramo Colorni* [1891]. The booklet pagination differs from that of the *Atti* edition. Since the documents published by Jarè are hereafter cited according to date, however, this pagination difference does not matter much. Archival sources that were published in the 1891 study will be cited, as a rule, following Jarè's edition—even in instances where I had access to the originals. Conversely, references using an archival record number mean that the corresponding source was not known to Jarè. In 1953 the British historian Cecil Roth republished a thumbnail biography of Colorni that he produced in the 1920s and is largely based on Jarès's research: Roth, "Amazing Abraham Colorni" (Roth, "Abramo Colorni, geniale inventore mantovano"). A short biographical sketch may also be found in Simonsohn, *History of the Jews in the Duchy of Mantua,* 704–705. See also Colorni, "Genealogia," esp. 644–645. The *Jewish Encyclopedia* (New York, 1901–1906) contains an entry by I. Broydé about Colorni (4:179). In the fifth volume of the *Encyclopaedia Judaica,* published in Berlin in 1930, Umberto Cassuto was responsible for the entry on Colorni (632). The *Universal Jewish Encyclopedia* (New York, 1941) likewise has an entry on Colorni, although its author can no longer be identified (3:305–306). By contrast, both the *Jüdisches Lexikon* (Berlin, 1928–1934) and the first and second editions of the authoritative *Encyclopaedia Judaica* (*EJ*) (1971 and 2007, respectively) have no entry on Colorni. But there is a good overview in Carlo Colombero's entry on Colorni in the *DBI* (27:466–468). Nothing new is added in Adler, "Abraham Colorni." My own earlier essay "Abramo Colorni, jüdischer Hofalchemist" focuses primarily on the

Württemberg years (and is partly superseded by the present study.) A recent publication is Toaff, *Il prestigiatore di Dio*. Although I became aware of this study only shortly before completing the German edition of this book, Toaff's study could still be taken into account. His book is more of a popular science biography of Colorni presenting some new, if rather speculative, theses. Toaff relies primarily on the sources compiled by Jarè and on the two Colorni manuscripts in the HAB Wolfenbüttel. He does not take into account most of the Italian archival sources I used for this book—such as those from the archives of the Gonzaga, Este, and Medici. Nor does he draw on sources from the Habsburg archives, such as those I present later in this chapter.

2. Among the most prominent members of the family in the twentieth century was the recently deceased legal historian Vittore Colorni (1912–2005), who also published major studies on the history of Italian Jewry. It was also Vittore Colorni who masterfully reconstructed his ancestors' family tree. See Colorni, "Genealogia."

3. Simonsohn, *History of the Jews in the Duchy of Mantua*, 264.

4. Ibid. 416.

5. On financial quarrels between the the stepmother and Abramo after the father's death, see ASMn, AN, b. 1250 bis, 170/171; also: Registrazioni notarili, a. 1577, fol. 740v–741v.

6. "Nella honorata scienza delle mecaniche, alle quali sin da pueritia sete stato sempre particolarmente inclinato." Garzoni, *Piazza universale*, 1:20.

7. Garzoni reported that Colorni was "disciplinato per la nativa cura de' parenti al par d'ogn'altro soggetto politico e civile." Ibid., 18.

8. On premodern sources mentioning Jews as fencers, see Wenninger, "Von jüdischen Rittern," 52.

9. Modena, *History of the Rites*, 213–214.

10. Thus, for example, at different places in Colorni's *Euthimetria*.

11. Colorni from Prague to Alfonso II d'Este, 30 August 1588 (*J-1891*, 27).

12. This list was available to the historian Shlomo Simonsohn in the 1950s. See Simonsohn, "Sefarim ve-Sifriyot." Unfortunately, Simonsohn only touches on the document, which apparently listed only religious writings in Hebrew. Despite intensive efforts I was unable to find this list of Abramo Colorni in the collections of the Archivio israelitico di Mantova. On the Mantuan book lists in general, see Baruchson-Arbib, *La culture livresque*.

13. AIM, filza 9, no. 125. An edition of this list is in Jütte, "Abramo Colorni," 496–498.

14. For examples, see the section below on Colorni's *Chirofisionomia*.

15. See some of the words in German and Czech ("lingua Boema") used in Colorni, *Scotographia overo,* I.1.
16. Here I follow Eleazar Gutwirth, who has urged paying more attention to aspects of self-fashioning in research on Jews at royal courts. Gutwirth, "Jews and Courts," 5.
17. Alessandro Janovitz from the Politecnico di Milano intends to write a study on the place of Colorni's *Euthimetria* and *Scotographia* in the history of technology and mathematics.
18. For a comparison of the Este and Gonzaga courts: Venturi, "Mantova e Ferrara." On the marriage policy and its implications for the ducal collections, see Morselli, "Este e Gonzaga."
19. On Mantua: Simonsohn, *Jews in the Duchy of Mantua;* Ferrara: Balletti, *Gli ebrei.* For an overview on Ferrara, see also Muzzarelli, "Ferrara"; in addition, see Franceschini, *Presenza ebraica;* Pesaro, *Memorie storiche;* Leoni, "Per una storia."
20. Simonsohn, *History of the Jews in the Duchy of Mantua,* 196–317.
21. Harrán, *Salamone Rossi;* Beecher, "Leone de' Sommi and Jewish Theatre"; Simonsohn, *History of the Jews in the Duchy of Mantua,* 656–677.
22. See esp. Miletto, "Teaching Program."
23. ASMn, AN, b. 1250 bis, 170/171. Here David Provenzali is mentioned in connection with the financial settlement that Colorni and his stepmother concluded after the death of the father in 1577. From these documents it also emerges that the year of Provenzali's death, which was previously unknown to scholars, must have fallen in the period after 1577.
24. Busi, "Il laboratorio."
25. A source from 1601, for example, documents Jews trading in salt from the salterns of Cervia. See *Gonzaga/Prague,* doc. 819.
26. Grafton, *Leon Battista Alberti,* 321. For more details on the ambitious building and landscaping projects of Alfonso II, see Ceccarelli, *La città di Alcina.*
27. Regarding Ferrara, there is an extensive collection of pertinent documents under the rubric *Ingegneri* in the ASMo, ASE.
28. "Sovente . . . ho sentito disputare all'eccelente medico et filosofo raro veramente nella età nostra, il signor Antonio Maria Parolinni [sic], leggendo l'anatomia qui nel studio di Ferrara." *Chirofisionomia,* fol. 37v. Parolini is also mentioned as a teacher in fols. 144v. and 195r.
29. The surname is also encountered under the variant of Parolari. Parolini's tractate on the plague appeared under the title *Trattato della peste dell'eccellentissimo Antonio Maria Parolini medico Ferrarese* (Ferrara: Suzzi, 1630). On his life

and works, see Pardi, *Lo studio,* 163; Borsetti Ferranti Bolani, *Historia almi Ferrariae gymnasii,* 2:183-184; Ughi, *Dizionario storico,* 98-99.

30. This is the case, in particular, for the *Chirofisionomia.*
31. As in a letter from Frederick I of Württemberg to Vincenzo Gonzaga, 30 January 1597, ASMn, AG, b. 517. My thanks to Gianfranco Miletto for this reference.
32. Franceschini, "Privilegi dottorali." On individual cases of Jewish students in Ferrara before 1559, see Colorni, "Spigolature su Obadià Sforno."
33. Franceschini, "Privilegi dottorali."
34. "Colendissimo Precettore Eccellentissimo Filosofo & Medico il Sig. Antonio Maria Parolini," according to Mirami in the letter of dedication (n.p.) to his *Compendiosa.*
35. Ibid.
36. Findlen, "Formation of a Scientific Community," 370.
37. Findlen, *Possessing Nature,* 252.
38. Ibid., 9.
39. Pardi, *Lo studio,* 164-165.
40. Mirami, *Compendiosa Introduttione,* n.p.
41. Colorni to Francesco Gonzaga, n.p., n.d. (before 9 October 1572), ASF, Mediceo del Principato, 580, fol. 80r-v. Also as doc. 44 in Barocchi and Bertelà, *Collezionismo mediceo.*
42. So far I have not been able to find any information about the exact nature of Colorni's affilation with the Gonzaga of Novellara. There is no information to be found about this in Bodo and Tonini, *Archivi.* It is nonetheless conceivable that Colorni held some kind of official office, such as court engineer. A Jewish court physician at the Novellara court is attested for the period in question (the 1570s). See Fabbrici, "Alcune considerazioni," 51.
43. Francesco Gonzaga to Francesco de' Medici, 9 October 1572. The letter of recommendation is likewise in ASF, Mediceo del Principato, 580, fol. 79r-v. A reprint (smoothed over orthographically) may be found in Barocchi and Bertelà, *Collezionismo mediceo* in the note to doc. 44.
44. Whether Leonardo's letter remained a draft is still a subject of scholarly discussion. For a thorough treatment of this document, see Gille, *Engineers of the Renaissance,* 124-126. For sketches of the corresponding bridges in Leonardo's *Codex Atlanticus,* see Galluzzi, *Renaissance Engineers,* 58 and ill. 52.
45. Bernardoni, "Le artiglierie."
46. See esp. Viganò, *Architetti e ingegneri militari italiani.*
47. Grafton, "Der Magus," 21.
48. Ibid., 22.

49. This emerges clearly from Colorni's *Euthimetria*.
50. On the dissemination of Kyeser's *Bellifortis* well beyond German-speaking Europe, see Makkai, "De Taccola à Veranzio," esp. 339.
51. Garzoni likewise states that Colorni had already been in service to several other princes before being hired in Ferrara: "Ecco che voi havete servito molti principi . . . " See Garzoni, *Piazza universale*, 1:19.
52. Colorni from Stuttgart to Aderbale Manerbio, 5 January 1598, ASMn, AG, b. 475, fols. 527r–534r.
53. See e.g. Chledowski, *Der Hof von Ferrara*, 310–335.
54. Cattini and Romani, "Le corti parallele," 72.
55. On the court of Ferrara under Alfonso, see Chledowski, *Der Hof von Ferrara*, esp. 310–335; Solerti, *Ferrara e la corte estense;* Bentini and Spezzaferro, *L'impresa di Alfonso II*. On the structure of the court, see also Guerzoni, "Administration of the Este Courts." On the development of the Este court and territory since the Renaissance in general, see Bentini, *Gli Este a Ferrara;* also Papagno and Quondam, *La corte e lo spazio*.
56. See Mirami, *Compendiosa Introduttione*, preface, n.p. See also the address that Garzoni uses several years later in *Piazza universale* (1:16): "A M[aestro] Abramo Colorni Mantoano di natione Hebreo, ingegniero del Serenissimo di Ferrara."
57. This conjecture about a link tying Colorni to the Mesola project was first articulated in Ricci, *Storia dell'architettura in Italia*, 3:176. See also *J-1874*, 7. D'Arco even calls Colorni an "architect," although without additional evidence: D'Arco, *Delle arti*, 2:180. I do not rule out the possibility that Colorni was indeed involved in building projects. By no means, however, was this his main field: for this reason, too, I prefer "engineer" as the professional designation for Colorni at this time. See also Toaff, *Il prestigiatore di Dio*, 82–85. On the Mesola project in general, see Ceccarelli, *La città di Alcina*.
58. Chledowski, *Der Hof von Ferrara*, 310. At the Este court there was also a traditional interest in astrology. On this point, see Vasoli, "Gli astri e la corte."
59. Burattelli, "Gli ebrei di Mantova," 157. The family member in question is Salomone Colorni. I identify him as Abramo's cousin, on the basis of evidence in Colorni, "Genealogia," 648 (although there is no mention there of any participation in theatrical productions).
60. Colorni's expertise in this field was also valued at the Savoy court, where in 1581 there is talk of business dealings with "alcune medaglie." See a letter of Jacob II of Savoy-Nemours to Alfonso II d'Este, 4 May 1581 (*J-1891*, 22). Whether Colorni also had ancient Jewish coins (or ones regarded as such) for sale is not known, but it is entirely conceivable in light of the contemporary

interest in "Jewish coins." On the interest in these coins at that time, see e.g. Jaffé, "Peiresc," esp. 309.
61. Furlotti, "Ambasciatori," 324.
62. Garzoni talks about the "anticaglie, delle quali è ripieno compitamente in Ferrara lo studio vostro sì raro," see *Piazza universale*, 1:20. See in addition ibid., 2:1115. The important Jewish scholar Azaria de' Rossi, author of the controversial *Me'or Einayim*, was likewise a connoisseur of antique coins, which were presented to him by a Jewish benefactor in Mantua. See Shulvass, *Jews in the World of the Renaissance*, 188. It is entirely possible that Colorni was a middleman in this business.
63. Chledowski, *Der Hof von Ferrara*, 423. On the extensive antique collection of the Este, see also Corradini, "Le raccolte estensi di antichità."
64. Busi, "Seismic History," 475-476.
65. Garzoni, *Piazza universale*, 1:19-20.
66. "Arcobusi, che da una canna sola sparano quattro, o cinque arcobusate a un tratto."Ibid., 20.
67. Grunwald, "Die Juden als Erfinder und Entdecker."
68. See *J-1891*, 8.
69. Secreto particolare for Frederick I of Württemberg [ca. 1597], HStAS, A 47 Bü 3, Fasz. 11.
70. Colombero, "Colorni," 467. In this context, special attention should be given to a remark made by Alessandro Tassoni, a contemporary who was well-acquainted with the Este court and also knew Colorni. In his *Pensieri* (1612) Tassoni mentions an unnamed "[A]rchitetto del duca Alfonso II di Ferrara, il quale fece due mila archibugi che, caricati una volta sola, fanno dieci tiri seguiti a colpo sicuro." See Tassoni, *Pensieri*, bk. X, ch. 26, 934.
71. Niederkorn, "Wunderwaffen," 348. Colombero ("Colorni," 467) points out that comparable experiments had already been made in the 1570s in Milan.
72. White, "Medical Astrologers," 303.
73. See Leonardo's sketches in the *Codex Atlanticus*, fol. 56v-a, reproduced in Parsons, *Engineers*, 60.
74. Isacchi, *Inventioni di Gio*.
75. Quoted in Jähns, *Geschichte der Kriegswissenschaften*, 1:663.
76. Solerti, *Ferrara e la corte estense*, 19.
77. Niederkorn, "Wunderwaffen," 346.
78. Ibid., 346-347.
79. Ibid., 347.
80. Ibid.

81. He talks about "machine et Inventionj . . . pertinenti alla Guerra." See his "Provisioni et ordini da osservarsi nel negotio de salnitri" in ASMo, ASE, Ingegneri, b. 2.
82. "Memoriale di Abraam Colorni" [undated, for Cesare d'Este], ASMo, ASE, Ingegneri, b. 2. This petition is unpublished. On this project, see also an undated letter of Abramo Colorni to Cesare d'Este as well as an undated Memoriale by Colorni for the Republic of Venice, reprinted in *J-1891*, 48–49. On weapons like these during the early modern period, also see the section on Jews and poisons in Chapter 2).
83. "Ho provato di sapere da lui un segreto," thus Jacob II of Savoy-Nemours to Alfonso II d'Este, 4 May 1581 (*J-1891*, 22).
84. Francesco Gonzaga to Francesco de' Medici, 9 October 1572, ASF, Mediceo del Principato, 580, fol. 79r.
85. Simonsohn, *Jews in the Duchy of Milan*, doc. 3896; Toaff, *Il prestigiatore di Dio*, 251.
86. He was not allowed, however, to leave his lodgings after the time at which the ghetto was closed. See the "licentia à Abram Colorni hebreo ferrarese" of 12 February 1587, ASV, Ufficiali al Cattaver, b. 243, fol. 65r.
87. Ravid, "New Light on the Ghetti," esp. 161.
88. See a letter on the matter of *Scotographia* from Colorni to the Venetian ambassador in Prague [December 1591] in *J-1891*, 33–34, as well as a completely undated *Memoriale* on weapons technology, ibid., 49. In my own research in Vienna, I also found a previously unknown exposé by Colorni on "alcune inventioni, et stratageme di molto valore in tempo di Guerra." This document and Colorni's related letter of 21 November 1592 deal with cryptography and with gunpowder and saltpeter production. See HHStA, Staatenabteilung, Italien, Venedig, Dispacci di Germania 19, fols. 316r–321r.
89. Thus, the Venetian ambassador Giovanni Dolfin, who was a declared skeptic about the "miraculous arts" ("scienze miracolose") at the Rudolphine court, forwarded several of Colorni's petitions revolving around secret projects to the Venetian authorities. See esp. a letter by Dolfin of 8 December 1592 in HHStA, Staatenabteilung, Italien, Venedig, Dispacci di Germania 19, fol. 316r. See also a letter by Dolfin from 10 December 1591 in *J-1891*, 33.
90. See the prefaces to Colorni's unpublished *Euthimetria* (MS Wolfenbüttel). Among the writers (whom I cannot identify more specifically) of odes to Colorni are Francesco Zorli, Francesco Maselli, and a certain "Signor Cinthio." See also Tassoni, *Pensieri*, bk. X, ch. 18, 892. On the mention of Colorni in Tassoni's book, see also below.
91. Garzoni, *Piazza universale*, 1:16–22.

92. On Garzoni's œuvre, see the useful overview in Cherchi, *Enciclopedismo;* see also Battafarano, *Tomaso Garzoni.* On the *Piazza universale* in particular, see esp. McClure, *Culture of Profession;* Rossi, "Strukturelle Eigenschaften"; Kimmel, "La Piazza Universale."
93. In the foreword to the edition of the *Piazza universale* used here, Bronzini assumes that there were at least fifteen Italian editions through the year 1665. Rossi counts twenty-five Italian editions through 1675. See Rossi, "Strukturelle Eigenschaften," 349. Kimmel mentions twenty-seven Italian editions (apparently for the entire seventeenth century); see Kimmel, "La Piazza Universale," 1.
94. Battafarano, "L'opera di Tomaso Garzoni," 35-79. See also Kimmel, who substantiates German editions for 1619, 1626, 1641, and 1659 (all printed in Frankfurt am Main). Kimmel, "La Piazza Universale," 2.
95. Battafarano, "L'opera di Tomaso Garzoni."
96. See Kimmel, "La Piazza Universale," 68.
97. "[Il] vostro nome celebre hormai per tutte le parti d'Italia." Garzoni, *Piazza universale,* 1:17.
98. Ibid., 18.
99. Ibid., esp. 17-19. Also in his preface to Colorni's "Chirofisionomia" (MS Wolfenbüttel, n.d.), Garzoni alludes to a possible baptism and the "via della salute."
100. Thus the interpretation in McClure, *Culture of Profession,* 83.
101. See e.g. Garzoni's detailed chapter "De' cabalisti" (Discorso 29) in the *Piazza universale.*
102. "Risposta alla soprascritta lettera fatta dal molto Reverendo Padre Predicatore Don Tomaso da Bagnacavallo" [1588] as preface to the "Chirofisionomia" (MS Wolfenbüttel, n.p.).
103. Garzoni, *Piazza universale,* 1:17.
104. This emerges from one of the printed marginal comments that may be found for the first time in the second edition of the *Piazza universale* (1587). Here mention is made of a *vita* written by Garzoni in which "tutte queste cose sono esplicate meglio." *Piazza universale,* appendix, 2:1205.
105. Garzoni, *La sinagoga de gl'ignoranti,* 202.
106. Mirami, *Compendiosa Introduttione,* 45.
107. Colorni, "Genealogia," 645.
108. See the archival findings in Toaff, *Il prestigiatore di Dio,* 33-34.
109. Luzzati, *La casa dell'ebreo,* 257.
110. As evident from the family tree in Colorni, "Genealogia," 650.
111. On Yeḥiel Nissim da Pisa, see Guetta, "Religious Life." There is considerable research on Yeḥiel. For additional literature, see also Luzzati, "Prestito

ebraico e studenti ebrei all'università di Pisa" in Luzzati, *La casa dell'ebreo*, 118. On the family: Menachem Artom and Aron Leoni, "Pisa, da (family)," in *EJ*, 16:184–185, as well as Kaufmann, "Ein Jahrhundert," 2:257–276.

112. Aescoly, *Sippur David ha-Reuveni*.

113. See Siegmund, *Medici State*, 356. Siegmund includes the da Pisa family among the financial "super elite" of Tuscan Jews at that time. For marriages of da Pisa family members, a dowry was typically more than 1,000 scudi, in other words, approximately the same order of magnitude as among the local nobility.

114. The prominent physician and scholar Azaria de' Rossi, for example, made several acquisitions from these collections after Yeḥiel's death. See Kaufmann, "Zur Geschichte der Kämpfe," 86.

115. All particulars here following Siegmund, *Medici State*, 280, 215. In the legal documents cited by Siegmund, there is mention only of one "Abramo di Salamone da Mantova." I am grateful to Stefanie Siegmund for sharing this piece of information. That the person in question really was Abramo Colorni emerges from an annotation in the files of the Nove conservatori del Contado (ASF, Nove conservatori del Contado, filza 16, fol. 12). There, mention is made of "Abramo da colorna [sic] hebreo." Many thanks to Lucia Frattarelli Fischer for pointing to this source.

116. The sources mention a "bagno comune ordinato nel ghetto delli hebrei." See Siegmund, *Medici State*, 515.

117. See ibid., 367.

118. Francesco Gonzaga to Francesco de' Medici, 9 October 1572, ASF, Mediceo del Principato, 580, fol. 79r–v.

119. Ibid., where the talk is of "spiedi e spade secrete." More than a decade later, Garzoni mentions Colorni's "cortelli damaschini col marizzo perfettissimo di vostra inventione." *Piazza universale*, 1:21. It can indeed be shown that, several years later (1598), Colorni sent a parcel with weapons like this to the imperial court. See the letter Colorni sent from Stuttgart to Aderbale Manerbio in Prague, 8 February 1598, ASMn, AG, b. 475, fols. 436r–438r.

120. Jacob II of Savoy-Nemours to Alfonso II d'Este, 4 May 1581 (*J-1891*, 22).

121. One classic example is Veranzio, *Machinae novae*. On the early modern art of engineering, see also "Military and Civilian Technology" in Chapter 2.

122. Knobloch, *L'art de la guerre*, 207. Also very critical on the feasibility of many mechanical inventions is Gille, *Engineers*, 12.

123. On the transmission of the Wolfenbüttel manuscript, see below. To my knowledge, the only substantive approaches to the work so far have been the re-

marks made by Toaff, *Il prestigiatore di Dio*, 54–62, along with the brief sketch in Reeves, *Galileo's Glassworks*, 86–88.
124. *Euthimetria*, fol. 12v.
125. Quoted in Troitzsch, "Erfinder," 444.
126. Garzoni, *Piazza universale*, 1:21.
127. Bonavilla and Marchi, *Dizionario etimologico*. In this dictionary's entry on "Eutimetria/Euthimetria" (3:248), it says: "Nome che alcuni geometri danno a quella parte della geometria che risguarda semplicemente le linee rette."
128. Cardano, *Operatione della linea*.
129. *Euthimetria*, bk. 4.
130. Ibid., bk. 1., pts. 1–2.
131. On the functioning of premodern odometers, see also Bürger, "Physikalische Unterhaltungen" (with illustrations).
132. "Questi strumenti da mostrare in una carrozza da campagna quante miglia si fanno e che tempo ci corre Abram Colornio [sic] ebreo ha professato di saperli fare a' di nostri," thus Tassoni, *Pensieri*, bk. X, ch. 18, 892.
133. HAB Wolfenbüttel, Cod.-Guelf. 14.8. Aug. 4°. The manuscript begins with sonnets by various Italian poets and a table of contents. For a brief description, see Heinemann, *Die Handschriften*, 182.
134. See the Privilege of Duke of Guglielmo from 1580 (*J-1891*, 21).
135. ASF, Pratica segreta, filza 73, fol. 155r-v; also filza 189, fol. 189r-v [1592].
136. Latin edition: Note (by Colorni?) n.p., n.d. [1592], ASF, Auditore delle riformagioni, filza 18, fol. 954r.
137. On the science of measuring and the related field of cartography in early modern Europe, see Bennett, "Mechanical Arts," 686–693.
138. See also the favorable remarks about the *Euthimetria* in Mirami's *Compendiosa Introduttione*, esp. 45. On contemporaries' interest in optical instruments, especially for measuring distances, see esp. Reeves, *Galileo's Glassworks*.
139. For he owned a copy of Mirami's *Compendiosa Introduttione*. See Pavone, *Introduzione al pensiero*, 2:373.
140. Reeves, "Occult Sympathies and Antipathies," 103.
141. The "profondissime Tavole Mathematiche" are only mentioned by Garzoni (*Piazza universale*, 1:21).
142. Report of the Tuscan official entrusted with the assessment, 27 February 1592, ASF, Auditore delle riformagioni, filza 18, fol. 953r.
143. "Instrumenti, che oltre all'operationi sopradette sono atti a ciascun effetto pertinente alla Prospettiva, astrologia, et alla fabrica delli horologij solari." ASF, Auditore delle riformagioni, filza 18, fol. 953r.

144. Note (by Colorni) n.p., n.d. [1592], ASF, Auditore delle riformagioni, filza 18, fol. 954r.
145. This was Steinschneider's assumption, who claimed the young Colorni as a representative of "mathematics among the Jews." See Steinschneider, "Mathematik bei den Juden," 1:88–99, 2:193; 3:300–301.
146. Zetterberg, "Mistaking"; Breger, "Mathematik und Religion"; Holländer, "Mathesis und Magie"; see also Debus, *Chemistry,* ch. 4, esp. 7–12.
147. Cardano, *De secretis,* 543.
148. *Euthimetria,* fol. 12v.
149. Biagioli, "Social Status," 47.
150. Ash, *Power, Knowledge, and Expertise,* 179.
151. Quoted in Burke, *Social History,* 84. The quotation from Wallis has been checked against the original and appears here in a slightly expanded version.
152. Biagioli, "Social Status," esp. 46; Voss, "Between the Cannon and the Book."
153. Zetterberg, "Mistaking," 86, 91.
154. Breger, "Mathematik und Religion."
155. A useful introduction is Harkness, *John Dee's Conversations.*
156. Ash, *Power, Knowledge, and Expertise,* 179.
157. Zetterberg, "Mistaking," 87–90.
158. Ibid.; see also Holländer, "Mathesis und Magie," esp. 35.
159. See esp. Cipolla, "Diffusion." On this topic, see "Military and Civilian Technology" in Chapter 2.
160. There are mathematical elaborations, for example, in his 1593 treatise on cryptography, *Scotographia,* where one of their objectives is to legitimate this "dark writing."
161. Zetterberg, "Mistaking," 85.
162. See his allusion to measuring the "torre del Domo di Ferrara" in the *Euthimetria,* fol. 198v.
163. Harrán, *Salamone Rossi.* See also Simonsohn, *History of the Jews in the Duchy of Mantua,* 669–677.
164. Solerti, *Ferrara,* 54–55.
165. Biagioli, *Galileo,* 163.
166. Ibid., 167.
167. "Mia opinione nell'arte di riguardare i segni della mano." *Chirofisionomia,* dedication to Vincenzo I Gonzaga, n.p.
168. Ibid.: "In quel giorno nel quale ritrovandomi io nella sua corte in famigliare collegio con alcuni de suoi gentil' huomini alla presenza di Vostra Altezza in Marmiruolo [*sic!*] mentre andavamo come per ischerzo a guisa di Chiromanti i segni della mano considerando, io sembrassi per aventura di essere di cotal

professione intendente, onde se indusse l'Altezza Vostra di farmi quell commandamento."
169. Ibid.: "Ho imitato l'obedienza del Santissimo Abram."
170. Sabattini, *Bibliografia*, 20.
171. Aquilecchia, "Appunti," 212.
172. Orbaan, "La Roma," 297.
173. "Non erano ancor dannati e prohibiti i libri." From *Chirofisionomia*, dedication to Vincenzo I Gonzaga, n.p.
174. My dating of the first draft draws on the fact that in the second edition of the *Piazza universale* (1587) Garzoni is already mentioning the *Chirofisionomia*. See Garzoni, *Piazza universale*, 1:21.
175. Ibid. This assessment is along the same lines as the critique that Garzoni had already expressed a few years earlier about what he saw as dubious charlatans in the field of chiromancy and metoposcopy: Garzoni, *Il teatro* [1583], 108r–v.
176. Garzoni, Preface to "Chirofisionomia," n.p.
177. Bishop Ferdinando Davila to Vincenzo I Gonzaga, 1 December 1595, ASMn, AG, b. 1527, fols. 482r–484v. Colorni is not mentioned by name in this letter. But it emerges clearly from the context that he is the man meant by the reference to the "Ebbreo in Praga." A partial reprint may also be found in *Gonzaga/Venice* II, doc. 302, although Colorni is not identified in this document by the editor.
178. On this phenomenon, see Porter, *Windows of the Soul;* Sabattini, *Bibliografia;* Clarke, "Metoposcopy"; Aquilecchia, "In facie."
179. Porter, *Windows of the Soul*, 269.
180. Ibid., ch. 6.
181. See e.g. Clarke, "Metoposcopy."
182. Thomas, *Religion*, 283.
183. For the case of a Catholic priest owning physiognomic literature (later confiscated by the Inquisition), see Barbierato, *Nella stanza dei circoli*, 172. On a seventeenth-century Lutheran theologian who was an enthusiastic chiromancer, see Trepp, "Von der Glückseligkeit," 107.
184. Benjamin, "Theses," 264.
185. This was certainly known even in Benjamin's time. Ludwig Blau had already pointed out that there was no such thing as a general prohibition against fortune-telling in Judaism. See Blau, *Das altjüdische Zauberwesen*, 3.
186. Idel, "Differing Conceptions," 170; Ruderman, *Kabbalah*, 132–135.
187. On the Hebrew terminology, see Gershom Scholem, "Chiromancy," in *EJ*, 4:652–654.

188. Today in the Palazzo Chiericati in Vicenza. See also Aikema, *Pietro della Vecchia*, no. 166.
189. Simonsohn, *Jews in the Duchy of Milan*, doc. 3663.
190. Scholem, *Major Trends*, 48.
191. Ibid., 160.
192. Scholem, "Chiromancy," in *EJ*, 653.
193. Modena, *Autobiography*, 111; Modena, *Leo Modenas Briefe und Schriftstücke*, 83.
194. Barzilay, *Yoseph Shlomo Delmedigo*, 261.
195. Lehmann, "A Livornese 'Port Jew'," 63; on Attias, see also Salah, *La république des lettres*, 49.
196. Biagioli, *Galileo*, esp. 5.
197. *Chirofisionomia*, HAB Wolfenbüttel, Cod.-Guelf. 4.9. Aug. 4°. Nothing is known about the provenance of this manuscript. See Heinemann, *Handschriften*, II, 4:123; Lewinsky, "Alcuni manoscritti." An additional manuscript of the *Chirofisionomia* is located in the David Kaufmann collection that is today part of the library of the Hungarian Academy of Sciences in Budapest. The Budapest copy could not be consulted during the research for this book. It was, however, inspected at the turn of the twentieth century by Jarè and described by him in a brief note: Jarè, "La chiriofisionomia." According to this note, the Budapest manuscript contains, in connection with Garzoni's letter, a few poems by Claudius Ancantherus, who was known to be a physician at the Rudolphine imperial court. This could indicate a provenance for the manuscript from Prague. On the Budapest manuscript, see also Weisz, *Katalog*, No. 257.
198. See what amounts to only cursory information in Jarè, "La chiriofisionomia"; as well as Toaff, *Il prestigiatore di Dio*, 72–82. Since the *Chirofisionomia* was never published, the work is missing from Sabattini's bibliography of printed literature on chiromancy.
199. *Chirofisionomia*, fol. 24v.
200. Della Porta, *Della Chirofisonomia*.
201. On the work's dissemination, see also the aforementioned letter from Bishop Ferdinando Davila to Vincenzo I Gonzaga, 1 December 1595, ASMn, AG, b. 1527, fols. 482r–484v.
202. Trabucco, "Lo sconosciuto autografo," 283.
203. Ibid., 282.
204. This, at least, is what Colorni reports in a letter, converted into a preface, to the "Molto Reverendo Padre Predicatore Don Tomaso [Garzoni] da Bagnacavallo Canonico Regollare," in the *Chirofisionomia*, n.p.

205. Ibid., fols. 213r–214r. Various passages in Bellonci, *Segreti,* discuss the political confusion surrounding the duke's virility.
206. On this, see Ruderman, "Introduction." See also Simonsohn, "Sefarim ve-Sifriyot"; also Baruchson-Arbib, *La culture livresque.*
207. On this, see Weinberg, "Beautiful Soul."
208. Luisa Cozzi, "La formazione culturale e religiosa," xxxiv.
209. Ibid., xlviii.
210. Reeves, *Galileo's Glassworks,* 89.
211. Isa 3:9. In the Vulgate (to which Colorni refers) it says: "Agnitio vultus eorum respondit eis et peccatum suum quasi Sodomae praedicaverunt nec absconderunt vae animae eorum quoniam reddita sunt eis mala." Colorni's comment on this: "Il Profetta Isaia . . . mostra d'esser Fisionomico et di vedere i peccati de gli huomini sculti nel viso loro quando dice nel cap.o 3.o." *Chirofisionomia,* fol. 23r.
212. Scholem, *Major Trends,* 48.
213. *Chirofisionomia,* fol. 29v. Colorni's Jewish contemporary, the physician and encyclopedist Abraham Portaleone, valued this work. See Portaleone, *Heldenschilde,* 1:352.
214. "Tholomeo Prencipe delli Astrologhi et vero osservatore dei moti celesti." *Chirofisionomia,* fol. 221v.
215. See ibid., esp. ch. 11, fols. 64v–72v.
216. Ibid., fols. 37v, 40v.
217. Portaleone, *Heldenschilde,* 1:352.
218. Ibid., ch. 38.
219. " . . . che non si deve sciocamente essere pronto in giudicare d'un effetto o d'un accidente solamente per un segno o due che nella mano appaiono, ma conviene essere diligente investigatore di tutti i fonti de i quali ne sono insegnati dalla filosofia, parte dalla medicina, parte dall'Astrologia." *Chirofisionomia,* fol. 107r.
220. Ibid., dedication letter to Vincenzo I Gonzaga, n.p.
221. *Chirofisionomia,* fol. 9v. Tricasso: See e.g. Tricasso, *Enarratio pulcherrima principorum Chyromantiae,* Cocles: The chiromancer in question was Bartolomeo della Rocca, known as Cocles. This author's work was especially good at addressing clients from all strata of society. The evidence for this includes editions with very different features. A small-sized edition for less well-to-do buyers was, for example, the 1555 edition *Physiognomiae & chiromantiae compendium.* A lavishly outfitted large edition, by contrast, is the 1517 *Chyromantie ac physionomie Anastasis.* Pseudo-Geber: Colorni writes "Algebre." Presumably he refers to *De la geomantia / dell'eccel. filosofo Gioanni* [sic]

Geber . . . con una brevissima chiromantica phisionomia (Venedig: Rapirio, 1552), which I have not had the opportunity to view. Cf. Sabattini, *Bibliografia*, 45.

222. This is treated in the second chapter of the *Chirofisionomia*, esp. fols. 14v-24v.

223. Porter, *Windows of the Soul*, 96.

224. Physiognomy, chiromancy, and astrology "non debb'essere in tutto probata nè in tutto dannata se non per quelle superstitioni et vanità che hanno inserto alcuni indegni veramente del nome di scientiati." *Chirofisionomia*, fol. 21r.

225. In fact, on closer examination, the *Chirofisionomia* even exhibits similarities in substance with Tricasso's work. See Tricasso, *Tricassi Cerasariensis Mantuani*.

226. Della Porta, *De hum. physiognomonia*.

227. Della Porta, *Della Chirofisonomia*, 5 (editor's foreword). In the recently discovered autograph of this treatise by Della Porta, there is no indication that the author himself intended to give his work the title *Chirofisonomia*. See Trabucco, "Lo sconosciuto autografo," esp. 282.

228. Porter, *Windows of the Soul*, 169.

229. See, in general, Eamon, *Science*, 214. Della Porta even maintained, "Doctrina mea non est, sed veterum scriptorum studiis nobilitata." See Della Porta, *De hum. physiognomonia*, dedicatory letter to Cardinal d'Este, n.p.

230. "Chiromantia astrologica prorsus vana & illicita, scientiae nomen non meretur," thus Del Rio, *Disquisitionum magicarum*, bk. III, ch. 3, 263.

231. This was the assessment of Bishop Ferdinando Davila in a letter to Vincenzo I Gonzaga, 1 December 1595, ASMn, AG, b. 1527, fols. 482r-484v.

232. See Del Rio, *Disquisitionum magicarum:* "Physica Chiromantia licita est, & physiognomiae pars, & ideo de illa idem quod de hac iudicium. . . . Ratio est, quia per lineas & partes manus, considerat ipsam corporis temperiem, & ex temperie corporis probabiliter indagat animae propensiones, hanc probat artem Aristoteles" (bk. III, ch. 3, 263).

233. Trabucco, "Lo sconosciuto autografo," 284-288.

234. Ibid., 291-295.

235. On Della Porta's concept of *scienza*, see Kodera, "Der Magus."

236. "Tutta la magia naturale sarebbe un' fumo quando non havesse il fondamento delle proportionji dei numeri e delle linee, et dei pesi." *Euthimetria*, fol. 12v.

237. Wis 11:21 (Vulgate; translation from King James Version, 11:20). Garzoni also took up this verse and attested that Colorni's inventions rested on the harmonic triad of *proportione, peso,* and *misura. Piazza universale*, 1:20.

238. Naredi-Rainer, *Architektur und Harmonie*, 20.

239. Garzoni, *Piazza universale*, 21–22.
240. Garzoni, *Il serraglio*.
241. Garzoni, *La sinagoga*, 202.
242. Garzoni, *Il serraglio*, 226.
243. Ibid., 225.
244. "[C]ome è parso più mesi sono agli occhi miei," thus Garzoni, *Piazza universale*, 1:21; Garzoni, *Il serraglio*, 226.
245. Garzoni, *Piazza universale*, 1:21.
246. Yagel, *Valley of Vision*, 39, 92. Card games were generally quite popular during the Renaissance, not least among Italian Jews. See e.g. Shulvass, *Jews in the World of the Renaissance*, 178.
247. Blau, *Das altjüdische Zauberwesen*; Veltri, *Magie und Halakha*; see also Trachtenberg, who points out that, for some rabbis, the "method" of magic counted for more than the outcome: Trachtenberg, *Jewish Magic*, esp. 19–22.
248. Blau, *Das altjüdische Zauberwesen*, 3.
249. Ibid., 20.
250. Ruderman, *Kabbalah*, 102.
251. On the family relationship, see above. On Yeḥiel's interest in magic, see Guetta, "Religious Life," 93–94.
252. Grözinger, "Jüdische Wundermänner."
253. Thomas, *Religion and the Decline of Magic*, 318.
254. During, *Modern Enchantments*, 79.
255. Ibid., 75; Daniel, *Magic*, 133.
256. Colorni from Prague to Alfonso II d'Este, 29 November 1588 (*J-1891*, 30): "[Rudolf II] mi vene a dire che lo Scotto facea vedere certe imagine in un specchio et che ciò gli parea cosa molto miracolosa, onde io risposi che mi dava l'animo di trovare più bella via di quella." On Scotto's tricks with magic mirrors, see Bechtold, "Hieronymus Scotus," 110. Toaff, by contrast, tends to identify the "Scotto" mentioned here by Colorni with the alchemist Edward Kelley, who was also working at the court in Prague during the late 1580s; see Toaff, *Il prestigiatore di Dio*, 159. In light of the fact that Girolamo Scotto, in contrast to Kelley, was a well-known figure at Italian courts at that time, it is more plausible that Colorni had him, and not the Englishman, in mind. On Colorni's own magic mirrors for Rudolf II, see below.
257. The present biographical sketch is based, unless otherwise indicated, on what is thus far the most persuasive biographical investigation by Bechtold, "Hieronymus Scotus."
258. Striedinger, *Goldmacher Marco Bragadino*, 279.

259. De Nolhac and Solerti, *Il viaggio di Enrico III*, 236.
260. "Summam creatae ac naturalis sapientiae perfectionem, ac veluti supremum arcanarum scientiarium apicem, hoc est, facultatem res miras & inusitatas, ratione quadam occulta & aliis ignota, perficiendi." Schott, *Optica*, 10.
261. Kieckhefer, "Did Magic Have a Renaissance?" 207. See also Kodera, "Der Magus und die Stripperinnen," 60; Peuckert, *Gabalia;* Rossi, Introduction to *La magia naturale*, 7–36.
262. Burton and Grandy, *Magic, Mystery and Science*, 39.
263. Eamon, *Science*, 209.
264. "Et perche io gli hò dato la parola di tacere i modi, sol posso dire in generale, che quasi tutte queste sono industrie di mani meschiate con accortezza d'ingegno, & con audacia di animo, & di parole, e ingaggi suppositij destratamente operati, i quali son mirabili, perche s'ignorano i modi" Garzoni, *Il serraglio*, 226.
265. Garzoni, *Piazza universale*, 1:21.
266. Ibid.: "Quello che possede la natural magia compitamente."
267. See also Hsia, *Myth of Ritual Murder*, 6.
268. Trachtenberg, *Devil*, 72.
269. D'Esaguy, "Commentaires," 227.
270. Simonsohn, *History of the Jews in the Duchy of Mantua*, 33.
271. Leicht, *Astrologumena Judaica*, 355; and on the *Clavicula Salomonis* in general: 343–356.
272. On the dissemination and effect of this corpus of texts in the early modern period, see the fine study by Barbierato, *Nella stanza dei circoli*. On the dissemination in German-speaking Europe in particular, see the rather brief remarks in Heimo Reinitzer and Gisela Kornrumpf, "Salomonische Schriften [C]," in *VerfLex*, 11:1367–1368.
273. Mathiesen, "Key of Solomon."
274. Ibid., 3.
275. Boudet and Véronèse, "Le secret," 106.
276. Reeves, "Occult Sympathies," 103.
277. As in a sermon in Siena from 1425. Cited in Ben-Aryeh Debby, *Renaissance Florence*, 102.
278. Barbierato, *Nella stanza dei circoli*, 6.
279. Boudet and Véronèse, "Le secret," 109; Åkerman, "Queen Christina's Latin Sefer-ha-Raziel Manuscript."
280. Thorndike, *History of Magic*, 6:147; Barbierato, *Nella stanza dei circoli*, 37.
281. Quoted in Kopp, *Die Alchemie*, 2:244.
282. Reeves, *Occult Sympathies*, 108.

283. Mathiesen, "Key of Solomon," 3.
284. Ibid.
285. Boudet and Véronèse, "Le secret," 102.
286. Åkerman, "Queen Christina's Latin Sefer-ha-Raziel Manuscript," esp. 21.
287. Boudet and Véronèse, "Le secret," 102.
288. Leicht, *Astrologumena Judaica*, 343.
289. Mathiesen, "Key of Solomon," 5.
290. Ibid., 3.
291. Leicht, *Astrologumena Judaica*, 355; Mathiesen, "Key of Solomon," 6; Boudet and Véronèse, "Le secret," 106; Rohrbacher-Sticker, "Mafteah Shelomoh"; Rohrbacher-Sticker, "Hebrew Manuscript"; Steinschneider, *Die hebräischen Übersetzungen*, 938. In 1914 Hermann Gollancz published, admittedly with assumptions that were not entirely accurate, the facsimile of a manuscript of the *Clavicula Salomonis* apparently from the seventeenth century: Gollancz, *Sepher Maphteah Shelomo*.
292. Barbierato, *Nella stanza dei circoli*, 41.
293. Ibid., 42.
294. Leicht, *Astrologumena Judaica*, 344; Rohrbacher-Sticker, "Mafteah Shelomoh," 265.
295. See the inventory in Girolla, "La biblioteca," 68.
296. Leicht, *Astrologumena Judaica*, 344.
297. BL, King's 288; Sloane Ms. 3091; Harley Ms. 3981.
298. Kieckhefer, *Forbidden Rites*, 122.
299. See a collection of *Clavicula* manuscripts and additional (Solomonic) magic literature in the section Astronomia, Astrologia, Magia of ASMo, ASE, b. 5 and 6.
300. Torijano, *Solomon the Esoteric King*, 230.
301. Gentile and Gilly, *Marsilio Ficino*, 228.
302. On this, see esp. Miletto, *Glauben und Wissen*.
303. 1 Chr 22:14; 29:2; 2 Chr 1:15; 1 Kgs 10:2. See also Bernard Suler, "Alchemy," in *EJ*, 1:600; Ginzberg, *Legends of the Jews*, 2:977.
304. Torijano, *Solomon*; Trachtenberg, *Devil*, 63–64.
305. Thus Rabbi Jacob ben David Provenzali in a letter from 1490, see Patai, *Jewish Alchemists*, 337. Whether the writer of this letter believed what he was writing is disputed. See Scholem, "Alchemie und Kabbala," 72–73.
306. Diedrichs, *Das Ma'assebuch*, 558–564; quotation on p. 563.
307. A fundamental work on this is Miletto, *Glauben und Wissen*.
308. See Ps 25:14; see also Prov 3:32. On the early modern interpretation of these verses, in which Solomon is regarded as someone initiated into the "secret,"

see Zedler, *Grosses vollständiges Universal-Lexicon,* s.v. "Geheimnis des HErrn."
309. Bennett and Mandelbrote, *Garden,* esp. 135–156, 144. Webster, *Great Instauration,* 327.
310. For more details on Salomon's house and Bacon's utopia, see Chapter 6.
311. Bennett and Mandelbrote, *Garden,* 144.
312. Thus Webster, *Great Instauration,* 327.
313. On the meaning of the temple in general, see Naredi-Rainer, *Salomos Tempel;* Rosenau, *Vision of the Temple;* Bennett and Mandelbrote, *Garden,* esp. 135–156; on the Jewish tradition in particular, see Miletto, *Glaube und Wissen.*
314. *Scotographia,* dedicatory letter to the emperor, n.p. Rudolf: Mout, "Hermes Trismegistos Germaniae."
315. Stephen Powle to Sir Francis Walsingham, 20 February 1588 (Venice), in *Calendar of State Papers Foreign,* 21/1:514. At the Spanish court of Philip II, too, there was great concern about the capture of Maximilian. See the diary of Khevenhüller, the imperial ambassador to Philip II: *Geheimes Tagebuch,* 167.
316. *Nuntiaturberichte aus Deutschland,* II/2:lxvii.
317. Ibid., cviii.
318. "[U]n giudeo che si dicea saper trarre di prigione quasi miracolosamente," it says in an instruction from Alfonso II to his ambassador at the imperial court, Ascanio Giraldini, 29 March 1588 (*J-1891,* 23). This document, under the title "Estratto sopra il disprigionatore per opera d'Abraham Colorno" [1588], may also be found in ASMo, ASE, Ingegneri, b. 2.
319. Garzoni, *Piazza universale,* 1:19. There is a very theatrical discussion there about dungeons "dalle quali con tanta facilità, rompendo i ferri, spezzando le porte, disserrando i gangheri, sbuccando i parieti, et portando via chatene, et ceppi, vi liberate a vostro piacere."
320. "L'hebreo che pretende saper disprigionare," thus Ascanio Giraldini to Alfonso II d'Este, 19 April 1588 (*J-1891,* 25).
321. Rohrbacher-Sticker, "Hebrew Manuscript," 132.
322. For an example from the Jewish literature, see Bos, "Hayyim Vital's 'Practical Kabbalah'," 67.
323. Ascanio Giraldini to Alfonso II d'Este, 10 May 1588 (*J-1891,* 25). Toaff's claim that Colorni first arrived in Prague in May 1589 is farfetched. See Toaff, *Il prestigiatore di Dio,* 137, 252.
324. Editions: Nothing is found, for example, in Dee, *Diaries;* Spampanato, *Documenti;* Pucci, *Lettere;* Dačický z Heslova, *Paměti.*

325. Hausenblasová, *Der Hof Kaiser Rudolfs II*, 97; Zimmer, "Praga caput regni," 289. The number of alchemists is put at fifty in a 1603 letter from the Mantuan resident Aderbale Manerbio to Vincenzo I Gonzaga, see *Gonzaga/Prague*, doc. 945.
326. I am grateful to Manfred Staudinger for sharing his knowledge on the collections from the Rudolphine era. His advice and Internet portal (www.documenta.rudolphina.org) provided crucial support during my search for the needles in the haystack. Likewise a helpful starting point was the collection of (summarized) documents in Gröbl and Haupt, *Kaiser Rudolf II*, 8/9 (2006/2007): 207–353; also 10 (2008): 229–399. It is entirely possible that additional documents on Colorni are located in the Hofkammer archives. The history of documents from the Rudolphine period, however, is not favorable to any systematic investigation. In the twentieth century these collections were twice (after World War I and World War II) torn from the context in which they were originally transmitted. Today, therefore, the files are spread out in different archives in Vienna and Prague. My spot checks in the Czech National Archives and the Archives of the Prague Castle proved futile. I am grateful to Dr. Lenka Matušiková (National Archives Prague) and Dr. Martin Halata (Archives of the Prague Castle) for their support in sounding out the Prague collections.
327. There are now a large number of studies about Rudolf and his court. A classic is Evans, *Rudolf II*. In addition: Hausenblasová, *Der Hof Kaiser Rudolfs II*; Zimmer, *Praga caput regni;* Konečný, *Rudolf II;* Fučíková, *Rudolf II and Prague;* Fučíková, *Prag um 1600;* Kaufmann, *L'école de Prague;* Kaufmann, *Mastery of Nature;* Trevor-Roper, *Princes and Artists*, 85–125.
328. Zimmer, *Praga caput regni*, 289–290.
329. On the arcane activies, see Evans, *Rudolf II*, esp. chs. 6 and 7; Mout, "Hermes Trismegistos Germaniae"; Gouk, *Natural Philosophy;* Hubicki, "Rudolf II." More in the style of popular history is Marshall, *Magic Circle*.
330. Other adepts from the Bohemian nobility are mentioned by Julian Paulus, "Rudolph II," in *LexAlch*, 309.
331. A testament to this approach is the study, replete with errors, by Bolton, *Follies of Science*.
332. Evans, *Rudolf II*, esp. 74.
333. Smith, "Alchemy as a Language of Mediation"; see also Trevor-Roper, *Princes and Artists*, 99.
334. Hausenblasová, *Der Hof Kaiser Rudolfs II*, 114–118; Trevor-Roper, *Princes and Artists*, 99.

335. On interest in the Kabbalah, see esp. Evans, *Rudolf II*, 90–91, 236–239.
336. In any event, Kepler, who lived in Graz at the time, was in the picture about the alchemical activities at the court of his native Württemberg, not least by way of letters from his former Tübingen professor Martin Crusius: Kepler, *Gesammelte Werke*, 13:121. Crusius, for his part, occasionally devoted diary entries to the Colorni case at the court in Stuttgart.
337. Ascanio Giraldini to Alfonso II d'Este, 21 June 1588 (*J-1891*, 26).
338. Ascanio Giraldini to Alfonso II d'Este, 7 June 1588 (*J-1891*, 26).
339. Ascanio Giraldini to Alfonso II d'Este, 19 July 1588 (*J-1891*, 26).
340. Ascanio Giraldini to Alfonso II d'Este, 9 August 1588 (*J-1891*, 27).
341. The person in question was Mendel Isaak from either Crakow or Vienna, the same man whose Danube bridge project was discussed in Chapter 2. On the services rendered by Mendel to the Habsburgs, see Gelber, "An umbakanter briv." See esp. Mendel's letter to the emperor about the situation in Poland from 16 January 1589 (ibid., 404–405).
342. "L'Hebreo nostro se ne sta qui allegramente," Ascanio Giraldini reported to Alfonso II d'Este on 9 August 1588 (*J-1891*, 27).
343. Ascanio Giraldini to Alfonso II d'Este, 30 August 1588 (*J-1891*, 27).
344. Colorni to Alfonso II d'Este, 28 November 1588 (*J-1891*, 28).
345. HHStA, Familienarchiv, Karton 103, fol. 267r: undated and unsigned report "how [the emperor] can bring about the payment, for the Oriental diamond and other wares purchased in Vienna by Abraham the Jew, of several thousands of *thalers* within a fortnight feasibly and in a legitimate manner." See also Voltelini, "Urkunden und Regesten," doc. 12602.
346. Simone Colorni to Conte Marcello Donato, 17 June 1588, ASMn, AG, b. 1520, fol. 792r. See also *Gonzaga/Venice* II, doc. 13.
347. Colorni to Alfonso II d'Este, 28 November 1588 and 29 November 1588 (*J-1891*, 27–31).
348. Boström, "Philipp Hainhofer," 570.
349. See e.g. the respective chapters in Della Porta, *Magiae naturalis;* also: Birelli, *Alchimia Nova*, bk. IX, chs. 39–44.
350. On the construction and relativity of evidence in general in this era, see esp. Shapin, *Social History*.
351. Santi, "Per una storia," esp. 238–240.
352. Peuckert, *Gabalia*, 205–216; Santi, "Per una storia," 245.
353. Thus Schudt with reference to the *Mayse-Bukh:* Schudt, *Jüdische Merckwürdigkeiten*, bk. 6, ch. 31. The corresponding tale may indeed be found in the *Ma'assebuch* (ed. Diederichs), 517.

354. See also Chapter 3. Additional examples of magic mirrors in early modern magical literature among Jews are in Grunwald, "Aus Hausapotheke und Hexenküche," 83. Delmedigo, a Jewish student of Galileo, described different kinds of mirrors from a technical perspective in Hebrew. See Barzilay, *Yoseph Shlomo Delmedigo,* 145. A few years earlier (1582), the Jewish physician Rafael Mirami published an introduction to the "art of mirrors," in *Compendiosa Introduttione.*
355. Colorni to Alfonso II d'Este, 29 November 1588 (*J-1891,* 31).
356. Rudolf II to Alfonso II d'Este, 21 September 1589. Published in Pace, *Divi Rudolphi imperatoris,* 131. The original letter seems to be no longer extant (in the archives in neither Vienna nor Modena); it also remained unknown to Jarè.
357. Chledowski, *Der Hof von Ferrara,* 312–314; Quirini Popławska, "Aus den polnisch-habsburgisch-toskanischen Verbindungen," esp. 255.
358. See *Nuntiaturberichte aus Deutschland,* II/3:414.
359. See above for details on this.
360. Chledowski, *Der Hof von Ferrara,* 312.
361. See e.g. *List and Analysis of State Papers,* 3:431.
362. Khevenhüller, *Geheimes Tagebuch,* 167.
363. *Nuntiaturberichte aus Deutschland,* II/3:556.
364. Zimmer, "Die Gonzaga und der Prager Hof Kaiser Rudolf II: Historischer Überblick," 18; Zimmer, "Die Gonzaga und der Prager Hof Kaiser Rudolf II: Kunsthistorische Fragmente," 210.
365. This entire correspondence is located today in the Archivio Gonzaga of the ASMn.
366. Roth, "Un consorzio ebraico mantovano." On the confidentiality of this mission, see esp. 498.
367. On this war and its challenges for the emperor, see esp. Niederkorn, *Die europäischen Mächte.*
368. Ambassador Giovanni Dolfin to the Doge, 8 December 1592, HHStA, Staatenabteilung, Italien, Venedig, Dispacci di Germania 19, fol. 317r.
369. On Rumpf, see Hausenblasová, *Der Hof Kaiser Rudolfs II,* 67.
370. Archduke Matthias awarded the title of court physician to the "Medicinae et Philosophiae Doctor" Moses Lucerna in 1595. See HHStA, Familienarchiv, Karton 99. Following his appointment by Matthias, Lucerna was primarily active in Vienna. Previously he had worked for several years as personal physician to the administrator of the Teutonic Order in Mergentheim and as the "Italian" physician in the Jewish quarter of Frankfurt am Main. See *Regesten*

I (Andernacht), docs. 2103, 2196, 2206, 2223, 2252, 2392, 2394, 2408, 2526. See, in addition, Treue, "Zur Geschichte jüdischer Ärzte," 157, 160, 169-170.

371. These poems may be found in the Budapest *Chirifisionomia* manuscript from the Kaufmann collection. See Jarè, "La Chiriofisionomia," 28. The Wolfenbüttel manuscript does not contain these poems.

372. More specifially, the ambassadors from Mantua, Ferrara, and Florence.

373. Colorni to Aderbale Manerbio, 8 February 1598, ASMn, AG, b. 475, fols. 436r-438r. See a similar letter from Colorni to Manerbio [?], 29 March 1598, ibid., fols. 486r-v.

374. Klein, *Wohltat und Hochverrat,* 53-58. On the situation of Prague Jews under Rudolf II, see also Evans, *Rudolf II,* 236-242.

375. For a critical reappraisal, see also Veltri, "'Ohne Recht und Gerechtigkeit.'"

376. Klein, *Wohltat und Hochverrat;* Veltri, "'Ohne Recht und Gerechtigkeit.'"

377. Cohen and Mann, "Melding Worlds," 111. See also 181 (catalogue section of Cohen and Mann, *From Court Jews to the Rothschilds*).

378. Janáček, "Les Italiens à Prague," 21.

379. Efron, "Common Goods," 246; Ruth Kestenberg-Gladstein, "Bassevi of Treuenberg (Treuenburg), Jacob," in *EJ,* 3:208-209.

380. Sherwin, *Mystical Theology;* Veltri, "Yehuda Löw."

381. Ruderman, *Jewish Thought,* 10-11, 54-99. Useful, although with a tendency to harmonize, are the following: Efron, "Irenism"; Efron, "Jews and Natural Philosophy"; Neher, *Jewish Thought.*

382. For more details on this, see Chapter 3.

383. Veltri, "Jüdische Einstellungen"; Sherwin, *Mystical Theology,* 180-182.

384. On the location of Colorni's house in Prague and his relation to the local Jewish community, there is a testimony from a Prague Jew named Salomon, who was asked about Colorni's past during an interrogation in Württemberg in 1598: "He [Salomon] was a poor schoolmaster, had earlier resided in Prague, but is now for several months no longer there, and he had certainly . . . known the escaped Jew [Colorni], for the latter had lived in Prague in a little house outside of the Jewish quarter." The *Obervogt* (bailiff) of Göppingen to Frederick I von Württemberg, 5 September 1599, HStAS, A 47 Bü 3, Fasz. 12. The remarks by the Jew Salomon portray Colorni, in rather unflattering words, as an outsider who also never showed up in synagogue in Prague. The reliability of these assertions, however, is questionable: the testimony was not made freely and was probably intended from the outset to meet the expectations of the officials from Württemberg. For more details on this source, see below.

385. Evans, *Rudolf II,* 241.

386. We have only fragmentary information about Giraldini, who was entrusted by Alfonso with delicate diplomatic missions (including negotiations in 1574 concerning the Polish crown). He was born in Siena and converted in the 1550s. Still, his Jewish origins were not forgotten, and there is a 1579 document from the court of Ferrara referring to him as "Ascanio, che è stato ebreo." See Solerti, *Ferrara e la corte estense*, 46. The poet Torquato Tasso, championed by the Este, likewise made remarks along these lines about Giraldini. See Toaff, *Il prestigiatore di Dio*, 138. There also circulated derogatory remarks about Giraldini as someone who was "born as Jew in Siena and baptized as an ass." See Chledowski, *Der Hof von Ferrara*, 328. Information about the place of his conversion is conflicting: a pamphlet mentioned by Solerti (*Ferrara e la corte estense*, 46) seems to suggest that Giraldini was baptized in Macerata.

387. See the study, rich in material but tendentious, by Hurter, *Philipp Lang*, 210. The trial files and Lang's confiscated correspondence are located today in the HHStA, Familienarchiv, Lang-Akten, Kartons 1–8.

388. All particulars on Gans here following Feuer, "Francis Bacon and the Jews." See also Efron, "Jews and Natural Philosophy," 16.

389. Diary entry from 28 February 1585, quoted in Casaubon, *A true & faithful relation*, 382. See also Dee, *Diaries of John Dee*, 173.

390. For now, see esp. Evans, *Rudolf II*, 209; Scholem, "Alchemie und Kabbala," 74–76; Ferguson, *Bibliotheca Chemica*, 1:204, 306; 2:231.

391. Evans, *Rudolf II*, 209.

392. Colorni, "La corrispondenza," 805. Evans's assumption that "Delle" was the alchemist's name and "Nelle" the family name (*Rudolf II*, 209) seems unlikely.

393. Telle, *Paracelsus im Gedicht*, 267.

394. Printed fragments of Nelle's rhyming verse may be found, for example, in *Keren Happuch*, 73–74, 105–107.

395. Quoted in Telle, *Paracelsus im Gedicht*, 78. This partial edition (77–78; appendix, 267) is based on a manuscript that is located today in Hamburg's Staats- und Universitätsbibliothek (Cod. alch. 651, fols. 47–65). It is apparently a copy by the alchemist Benedictus Nicolaus Petraeus.

396. Paracelsus: Evans, *Rudolf II*, 209; discourse: printed as part of Puli, *Centrum Naturae Concentratum*, 39–48; art of smelting and philosophical meditations: Falkenstein, *Beschreibung*, 413; sublimation: this is an alchemical manuscript (seventeenth century) from the library of the Tournai episcopal seminar (Séminaire Cod. 138). See Faider and van Sint Jan, *Catalogues des manuscrits*, 6:287.

397. Ferguson, *Bibliotheca Chemica*, 1:306; Scholem, "Alchemie und Kabbala," 74.

398. The theory that Nelle was a Polish Jew by the name of Minelle apparently goes back, without closer substantiation, to David Kaufmann. See Jarè, "La Chiriofisionomia," 28. See also Roth, "Abramo Colorni," 157.
399. Also skeptical about the conversion: Scholem, "Alchemie und Kabbala," 76.
400. These records are today in the Prague City Archives. For a description, see Janáček, "Les Italiens à Prague," 21.
401. Thus *Keren Happuch,* 73–74, 105–107.
402. Quoted in Evans, *Rudolf II,* 209.
403. Ibid.
404. Brann, *Geschichte der Juden in Schlesien,* 154.
405. On the Rosenberg family and Reichenstein, see Evans, *Rudolf II,* 216.
406. "Mardocheus Nelle, Judaeus, wonnedt zu Crakkauw in pollenn anno 1573." Quoted in Scholem, "Alchemie und Kabbala," 75.
407. Falkenstein, *Beschreibung,* 10.
408. In the 1880s, the manuscript was found in an archive in Dresden and partly transcribed by U. Schneider. However, the alchemical section in particular was omitted by the editor, since he believed that "the alchemical and Kabbalistic bombast it uses ... only amounts to nonsense [!]." See Schneider, "'Eine merkwürdige Prophezeihung [sic]'"; quotation on p. 370.
409. Barclay, *Euphormionis Lusinini Satyricon.*
410. Ibid., ix and Appendix A.
411. Ibid., xvi.
412. The historical models for the figures in the satire can be identified on the basis of contemporary readers' accounts. Ibid., Appendix B (359–378).
413. Trevor-Roper, *Princes and Artists,* 121.
414. "Illis Aquilius per internuncios imperat; ipse plusquam Assyriorum Principum solitudine inclusus, otiosam majestatem ineptissima gravitate damnavit." Barclay, *Euphormionis Lusinini Satyricon,* 318.
415. Ibid., 320. Trifartitus: apparently Barclay meant the landgrave Count Georg Ludwig von Leuchtenberg, see ibid., Appendix B, S. 375.
416. "Contulit se in scientiarium amabilem locum." Ibid., 330.
417. "Nec mora, nescio quis linteo purissimo praecinctus, ad Aquilium intravit, vitroque purissimo exiguum liquorem hilarissima fronte ostendit. Aquilius, quicquid erat, crepitu manuum collaudans, examinare coepit ad lucem, & cum homine suavissime loqui. Cum a Trifartito quaererem, quisnam esset tam illustris familiaritatis homo? Hebraeus, inquit, Aquilianis artibus praefectus, quo nemo gratiosior in regia vivit." Ibid., 328.
418. "Any trusted Jewish advisor-alchemist of Rudolf will do," according to the modern editor, ibid., Appendix B, 369.

419. Ibid.
420. Ibid.
421. Stieve, "Lang, Philipp," in *ADB*, 17:617. Stieve links this rumor to the persona of the previously mentioned, supposedly baptized *Kammerdiener* Philipp Lang.
422. The original Latin text of the address is reprinted in *Nuntiaturberichte aus Deutschland*, II/3:77–78 (n. 3).
423. The letter literally speaks of "ea infinita virginum et mulierum stupra et magicas incantantiones ac praestigia, quibus cum suo Iudaeo Halo dat operam, impatientes nonnumquam aures offendere" (quoted in ibid., 78). The term "Halo" remains unclear to me. Nonetheless, the identification of this Jew with Colorni is beyond doubt (see above). Might this be a case of a transcription error ("Halo" instead of "Italo") made in the Vatican manuscript consulted by the editors of the *Nuntiaturberichte?* The latter spelling would make more sense and is, in any event, a verifiable variant of the Latin adjective "Italicus."
424. "[V]ien à dire che non passa mai giorno che non consumi molt'hore con un hebreo mandatogli dal signor Duca di Ferrara, il qual hebreo è Dottore di quest'arte [viz. magic]," thus Giulio Strozzi to Vincenzo I Gonzaga, Prague, 14 November 1589, ASMn, AG, b. 464, fol. 268r (see also *Gonzaga/Prague*, doc. 338).
425. *Gonzaga/Prague*, docs. 338, 360, 362.
426. *Nuntiaturberichte aus Deutschland*, II/3:41.
427. Ibid., xxi.
428. Colorni, *Scotographia*. I used the copy in the HAB Wolfenbüttel while also consulting the copy in the Bavarian State Library in Munich. The work may be found in a number of additional libraries and collections worldwide. Suffice it to mention the copy in the Mendelsohn Collection at the University of Pennsylvania (see Galland, *Historical and Analytical Bibliography*, 45) and the copy from the collection of Count Giacomo Manzoni (1816–1889), see *Bibliotheca Manzoniana*, 144. On the smaller pocket edition, see below.
429. Mantua: Colorni to Guidobuon de Guidoboni, 10 November 1592 (*J-1891*, 35); Venice: HHStA, Staatenabteilung, Italien, Venedig, Dispacci di Germania, vol. 19, fols. 316r–321r [1592]; as well as Giovanni Dolfin to the Doge, 10 December 1591 (*J-1891*, 33); Florence: ASF, Pratica segreta, filza 73, fol. 155r–v; as well as filza 189, fol. 189r–v [1592]; also Auditore delle riformagioni, filza 18, fols. 953r–954r.
430. On the pocket edition, see Toaff, *Il prestigiatore di Dio*, 172, 267. In Czech libraries, there are supposed to be both quarto and duodecimo editions in Latin. I have personally never seen a Latin copy and am relying here on the

information provided in Petra Večeřová's study about the publications of the Schumann printing company. See Večeřová, *Šumanská tiskárna*, 133–134, 166–167.

431. Thus, for example, Colorni does not appear in David Kahn's comprehensive history of cryptography: Kahn, *Codebreakers*. Even Sacco does not mention Colorni in his downright patriotic history of cryptography in sixteenth- and seventeenth-century Italy: Sacco, *Un primato italiano*, 45. Thus far the only substantive discussion of the *Scotographia*, albeit relatively brief and not always quite accurate, is Jaffe, *Story of O*, 97–105. Rather cursory, too, is the treatment in Toaff, *Il prestigiatore di Dio*, 168–174. A recent study of the Schumann printing company deals only with typographical matters: Večeřová, *Šumanská tiskárna*, 133–134, 166–167.

432. Selenus, *Cryptomenytices*, 185–245.

433. Strasser, "Die kryptographische Sammlung," 83. On the effect and reception of the duke's treatise, see Strasser, "Geheimschrift," esp. 182, 191. See also Strasser, "Noblest Cryptologist."

434. Thus, for example, the duke commended the "modi uti nec inelegantes, ità digni observatione non oscitanti: Quos Modos debemus Abramo Colorno Hebraeo Mantuano." See Selenus, *Cryptomenytices*, 185.

435. Ibid. On Seghetus's biography, see Odlozilik, "Thomas Seget"; Favaro, "Dall'Album amicorum di Tommaso Segett."

436. "Colornus," in Zedler, *Grosses vollständiges Universal-Lexicon*, 6:758.

437. *Scotographia*, instructions on use of the volume, n.p.

438. "[P]erche essendo questa inuentione trouata principalmente per benefitio delle cose di stato, et seruitio particolare de Principi." *Scotographia*, Bii–v.

439. See e.g. the comprehensive contemporary collection of cipher keys and manuscript tractates in ASMn, AG, b. 423–425 [Cifre sciolte, cifre in libri].

440. "Et in somma tutte quelle nationi sotto l'imperio e dominio di Polonia, Suetia, tedesche e simile, e con cantoni de Suizzeri trovo che in profession di cifre non hanno alcun senso ne valore perche come trovanno lettere di cifre le abrugiano e stracciano," thus Matteo Argenti in his cipher book, not published during his lifetime. Quoted in Meister, *Die Geheimschrift*, 115.

441. *Scotographia*, bk. I, ch. 10 ("Discorso intorno à gl'avvertimenti, che sono atti per diciferare le cifre senza contracifra").

442. Especially since Italian and French royal courts at this time were already employing specialists in deciphering. On this, see e.g. Pesic, "Secrets, Symbols, and Systems."

443. "Perche è di nostra intentione che questa fatica sia comune à ciascuna natione." *Scotographia*, Biii–r/v.

444. A detailed discussion about the reasons for and implications of his decision may be found in bk. I, ch. 1.
445. Kahn, *Codebreakers*, 114.
446. *Scotographia*, Bii–v: "Proferrire ogni sorte di parole in qual si uoglia lingua, & non solo à quelle, che si scriuono con caratterj latini, ma nelle pellegrine, & barbare ancora."
447. Ibid.: "Se ben sia data alla stampa, può ciascuno fuor di pericolo scriuere in uarie maniere à suoi confidenti."
448. Ibid., bk. I., ch. 6.
449. Kahn, *Codebreakers*, 145.
450. *Scotographia*, bk. I, ch. 3.
451. Ibid., bk. I, ch. 6.
452. Ibid., bk. I., ch. 7 ("Modo d'occultare i ragionamenti, col mezzo de caratteri dell'abaco").
453. See *Scotographia*, fol. 8r.
454. Ibid., fol. 11v: "Debba abbondantemente bastare in assicurarcj, che ingegno humano (ancorche sia fatto perito di queste nostre inventioni . . .) non sarà mai bastante di scoprire li segreti, scritti di tal sorte, fuor che con la corrispondente contracifra."
455. Ibid., fol. 13v: "Quelli, che sono occupati, in varij negotij, [et] quelli . . . che gli conviene scrivere molte lettere."
456. For additional ways in which Alberti influenced Colorni, see Jaffe, *Story of O*, 99.
457. Brann, *Trithemius and Magical Theology*, esp. 180.
458. Shumaker, *Natural Magic*, 132.
459. Wagner, "Studien," 11 (1886): 184.
460. Ibid., 183.
461. Della Porta, *Magiae naturalis* [1558], 62–64; Wagner, "Studien," (12) 1887: 19.
462. Portaleone, *Heldenschilde*, ch. 42, 389.
463. "Per mandar in un Campo o fortezza una lettera, che non sia trovata d'alcuno, ancora ch'il portator di essa passasse pel mezzo de gli inimici, e che fosse spogliato nudo . . . ancor che fosse forzato a dirlo." Undated "secreto particolare" for Frederick I of Württemberg [ca. 1597], HStAS, A 47 Bü 3, Fasz. 11.
464. It is possible that Colorni, like Gustavaus Selenus after him, took cues from Polyaenus's *Stratagematum libri octo*, published by Isaac Casaubon a few years earlier (Leiden, 1589). On this source, see Strasser, "Die kryptographische Sammlung," 91.

465. From a Jewish perspective, this method certainly would have been the most problematic in terms of Halakha. See Lev 19:28 ("Ye shall not make any cuttings in your flesh for the dead, nor print any marks upon you").

466. *Scotographia*, Bv.

467. Ibid., fol. 13v: "Fondato sopra fondamenti reali, fisici, & Mathematici."

468. It is telling that as late as the nineteenth century the biographer Julius Fürst was still referring to Colorni's work as *Steganographia* (*Bibliotheca Judaica*, 1:184). In a short nineteenth-century article about Colorni, De Rossi too called the *Scotographia* a steganography: De Rossi, *Historisches Wörterbuch*, 85.

469. Strasser, "Die kryptographische Sammlung," 92.

470. This observation in Jaffe, *Story of O*, 105.

471. See, in general, Bachmann and Hofmeier, *Geheimnisse der Alchemie*, 11–13; Principe, "Robert Boyle's Alchemical Secrecy"; Eamon, *Science*, 357. On the close relationship between alchemy and cryptography in the sixteenth century, see also Brann, *Trithemius*, 180.

472. See e.g. the remarks of his English contemporary, the poet and clergyman John Donne (1572–1631), about the Kabbalists: for him they were "the Anatomists of words, and have a Theologicall Alchimy to draw soveraigne tinctures and spirits from plain and grosse literall matter, observe in every variety some great mystick signification." Quoted in Katz, *Philo-Semitism*, 79.

473. Kahn, *Codebreakers*, 91–92.

474. Della Porta, *De furtivis literarum*, 18. I refer here to the London edition, which is a pirated copy.

475. *Scotographia*, bk. I, ch. 1.

476. The motto is clearly visible on an unnumbered page inserted between the frontispiece and the letter of dedication.

477. Jaffe, *Story of O*, 108.

478. Della Porta, *De furtivis literarum*, 134.

479. Kahn, *Codebreakers*, 133.

480. Ofer, "Methods of Encoding," 56.

481. The papal nuncio reported to the Curia, "che volendo l'imperatore far prova nella sua camera di certa inventione di polvere, prese in un subito il foco et offese leggiermente nel viso S. Mtà, facendole più danno in abbrugiar le ciglia et peli della barba che nella carne." Letter of 25 March 1591, in *Nuntiaturberichte*, II/3:290. See also the report of the Venetian ambassador Giovanni Dolfin to the Doge and Senate, Prague, 26 March 1591, in *Calendar of State Papers* (Venice), 8: 535. See likewise *Gonzaga/Prague*, doc. 388.

482. Hubicki, "Rudolf II," esp. 299.

483. Niederkorn, *Die europäischen Mächte*.

484. There is still no comprehensive study about saltpeter production during the Late Middle Ages or early modern period. But see De Vries, "Sites," 311. The best overview remains Thiele's study, although it only touches tangentially on the questions of cultural history while focusing primarily on France and Germany: *Salpeterwirtschaft und Salpeterpolitik*. See also the entry "Salpeter" by Rainer Leng, *LexMA*, 7:1318, and the corresponding entry by Lawrence Principe, *LexAlch*, 318–319. For additional literature, see also the note below.

485. See the relevant sections of the economic policy agenda outlined by the English physician and natural scientist Benjamin Worsley (1618–1673) in the 1640s. Reprinted in Webster, *Great Instauration*, 539–546. See also Szydło, *Alchemy of Michael Sendivogius*, 130.

486. Nummedal, *Alchemy and Authority*, esp. 139–141.

487. Horchler, *Die Alchemie*, 273–274.

488. Hall, *Weapons and Warfare*, 67. De Vries assumes a proportion of 75 percent saltpeter and 12.5 percent each of sulfur and carbon ("Sites," 310).

489. Rossi, *Philosophy, Technology, and the Arts*, 82.

490. Weyer, *Graf Wolfgang II. von Hohenlohe*, esp. 328–330.

491. Schmidtchen, *Bombarden*, 162; Hall, *Weapons and Warfare*, 74; see also the overview in De Vries, "Sites," 310–312.

492. Thiele, *Salpeterwirtschaft*, 3, 199, 202.

493. Schmidtchen, *Bombarden*, 178; see also Singer, "On a 16th Century Cartoon."

494. Debus, *Chemistry*, ch. 9, esp. 46; Moran, *Distilling Knowledge*, 38; Szydło, *Water*.

495. Szydło, *Water*, xiv and, in detail, chs. 6 and 7. Johann Rudolph Glauber (1604–1670) was still of the opinion that the Hermetic literature contained explanations about the qualities of saltpeter. See Debus, *Chemistry*, ch. 9, 59.

496. Newman, "From Alchemy to 'Chymistry,'" 514.

497. Hall, *Weapons and Warfare*, 75. This was true, for example, for Kyeser (ca. 1405), Biringuccio (1540), Agricola (1556), and Ercker (1574).

498. Thiele, *Salpeterwirtschaft*, 59–61, 108.

499. The letter from 30 July 1515 and an additional letter of recommendation from the cardinal on the same day are reprinted in Cassuto, *Gli ebrei a Firenze*, docs. 59, 60.

500. Roth, "Forced Baptisms," 243.

501. Patai's argument, according to which Abraham Eleazar was a real historical character, remains dubious. See Patai, *Jewish Alchemists*, 238–257.

502. Schütt, *Auf der Suche nach dem Stein der Weisen*, 467.

503. See e.g. Schudt, *Jüdische Merckwürdigkeiten*, bk. 6, ch. 20, 166. On the Jewish side, see de Pomis, *Tzemaḥ David*, 105–106.

504. Schudt cites Hannemann's *Ovum hermetico-paracelsico-trismegistum* (1694); see Schudt, *Jüdische Merckwürdigkeiten*, 335 (Documenta und Schrifften). The verse from Deuteronomy is 29:22 in the Masoretic Text but 29:23 in both the Vulgate and the (original) King James Version quoted here.
505. "La natione hebrea . . . fù celebre appresso tutte le genti a lei coetanee in quanto al maneggio dell'Arme," thus Luzzatto, *Discorso*, fol. 73v. See also Portaleone, *Heldenschilde*, chs. 40–43.
506. Schudt, *Jüdische Merckwürdigkeiten*, 335 (Documenta und Schrifften)
507. Ibid., bk. 6, ch. 20, 166. Here, too, the reference is to Jer 2:22.
508. Hall, *Weapons and Warfare*, 76.
509. Prague: Schreckenberg, *Die Juden in der Kunst Europas*, 335; Frankfurt: *Regesten I* (Andernacht), doc. 4230.
510. Schreckenberg, *Juden in der Kunst Europas*, 335 (with illustration).
511. Webster, *Great Instauration*, 377.
512. Thiele, *Salpeterwirtschaft*, ch. 5 and esp. 115, 198, 212.
513. Moran, *Distilling Knowledge*, 39; on the profitability of the saltpeter industry, see also De Vries, "Sites," 311.
514. Toaff, *Love, Work, and Death*, 205.
515. Toch, "Economic Activities," 208. On Jewish gunpowder manufacturers in Silesia in the late sixteenth century: Brann, *Geschichte der Juden in Schlesien*, 154. See also the source on the Jewish gunpowder maker Samuel von Wertheim (1588) in *Regesten I* (Andernacht), doc. 3031.
516. Veinstein, "Note," 91.
517. Fischer, *Vivere fuori dal Ghetto*, 157.
518. See the formula of the Kabbalist Ḥayyim Vital in an unpublished manuscript (after 1610). On this, see Bos, "Hayyim Vital's 'Practical Kabbalah,'" 106.
519. This speculation has originated from an Augsburg source from 1353. See Krauss, "Wer hat das Schießpulver nach Deutschland gebracht?," 159.
520. Ginsburger, "Les juifs et l'art militaire," 157; on the *Feuerwerksbuch* in general, see also Long, *Openness, Secrecy, Authorship*, 117–120.
521. De Pomis, *Tzemaḥ David*, 105–106.
522. Portaleone, *Heldenschilde*, ch. 76.
523. Ibid., 661–662.
524. See Spinoza's letters to Heinrich Oldenburg, the secretary of the Royal Society in London, in Spinoza, *Briefwechsel*, no. 6 (1662) and no. 13 (1663).
525. Singer, "On a 16th Century Cartoon."
526. García-Arenal and Wiegers, *Man of Three Worlds*, 38.
527. Veinstein, "Une communauté ottomane," 797.

528. Sicilian saltpeter trade: Simonsohn, *Jews in Sicily*, e.g. doc. 3691 (delivery for the viceroy, 1466); doc. 3708 (ditto); doc. 3839 (a Jew loads twenty-two barrels of saltpeter onto ships, Palermo 1469); doc. 3906; doc. 5306 (in 1490 a Jew receives permission to search for saltpeter deposits throughout the Kingdom of Sicily); doc. 5394 (in 1491 two Jews load saltpeter for export onto Venetian ships in the port of Palermo); docs. 5874–5875 (notarized private saltpeter sale to a Christian, Palermo 1416); doc. 5896 (Palermo 1444). On Faccas: doc. 5552.

529. Straus, *Urkunden und Aktenstücke*, doc. 556.

530. For Hesse, see e.g. Löwenstein, *Quellen*, doc. 3365; for Lower Saxony, see Ries, *Jüdisches Leben*, 405, 419.

531. *Regesten I* (Andernacht), docs. 925, 3031.

532. Biale, *Power and Powerlessness*, 74.

533. Especially noteworthy is the patent granted by Charles VI on 17 March 1727 permitting the "sale of powder and saltpeter-nitre alla minuta alone to authorized Christian merchants" and "consequently [excluding] all Jews entirely from this, not only under threat of punishment for contraband, but also, according to the evidence of the circumstances, under penalty of body and life." This ordinance was confirmed in 1742. See Pribram, *Urkunden und Akten*, 1:320. See also a similar decree from 1807, ibid., 2:134, as well as a Hofkammer decree of 12 December 1832 in which trade in saltpeter from Lombardy is banned for Jews. Ibid., 2:458.

534. Stern, *Court Jew*, ch. 1; Schwarzfuchs, "Les Juifs de Cour," esp. 390; Israel, *European Jewry*, 124–126.

535. See also Israel, *European Jewry*, 126–128.

536. Stern, *Jud Süß*, 52–56; Haasis, *Joseph Süß Oppenheimer*, 153–154. See also Oppenheimer's petition to the duke in the matter of saltpeter and gunpowder making [1734], printed in the appendix to Stern's study, doc. 20.

537. ÖStA, HKA, HFÖ Bd. 467-E, fol. 99r; Bd. 469-R, fol. 118r, fol. 130v. See also a letter by Colorni from Prague to Vincenzo I Gonzaga dated 12 July 1593. Here Colorni mentions certain "business transactions" in the field of munitions procurement that the emperor had assigned him ("alcuni negotij, che per bisogno della monitione [il Imperatore] mi commando"). ASMn, AG, b. 467, fol. 415r (= *J-1891*, 38).

538. In contrast to gunpowder production in Strasbourg, Nuremberg, and Sweden, it was the case in Bohemia that "la polvere di Boemia è piu lustra e piu netta," according to Tommaso Contarini, *Relazione di Germania* [1596], in Firpo, *Relazioni di ambasciatori veneti al senato*, 3:212.

539. ÖStA, HKA, HFÖ Bd. 469-R, fol. 161v.
540. ÖStA, HKA, HFÖ Bd. 467-E, fol. 99r; Bd. 469-R, fol. 161v. In German it was called the proposal of the "Wellischen Juden"—"wellisch" ("welsch" today) referring to a southern foreigner.
541. The books of the court treasury office mention an "honorarium" ("gnaden gelt") of 350 thalers. ÖStA, HKA, HFÖ, Hofzahlamtsbücher, Bd. 44, fol. 452v. This honorarium is higher than the sum that the emperor had authorized to be paid a few years earlier (1588) as a gratuity to the philosopher Giordano Bruno (300 thalers). On Bruno's stay at the court in Prague, see Evans, *Rudolf II*, 229–230.
542. ÖStA, HKA, HFÖ Bd. 475-E, fol. 19v.
543. Isaac Pfendler to the Hofkammer, 31 August 1594. ÖStA, HKA, HFÖ Rote Nr. 64.
544. "The head of the armory reports that there is a great shortage of supply and need for saltpeter," thus Isaac Pfendler to the Hofkammer, 3 September 1594. ÖStA, HKA, HFÖ Rote Nr. 64.
545. Müller, "Die Verdienste Zacharias Geizkoflers," esp. 257.
546. Sometimes several orders per day were issued regarding the procurement of saltpeter. Thus, for example, on 16 August a directive was issued "to purchase the saltpeter available in Prague and the cities in Bohemia" as well as a separate instruction to Isaac Pfendler for saltpeter purchases. See ÖStA, HKA, HFÖ Gedenkbücher [böhmische Reihe] Bd. 324, fols. 208v–209v.
547. Rudolf II to the Bohemian Chamber, 6 July 1594. ÖStA, HKA, HFÖ Gedenkbücher [böhmische Reihe] Bd. 324, fols. 184v–185r. Reprinted in Bondy and Dworsky, *Zur Geschichte der Juden*, doc. 901. The source collection compiled by Bondy and Dworsky contains no additional sources on Colorni.
548. ÖStA, HKA, HFÖ Bd. 479-R, fol. 184r.
549. "The Jew Abraham Colorni has also made two hundredweight saltpeter. I saw it, but I did not particularly like it (to the extent I understand the matter), for it is rather brownish . . . and black which indicates that it has too much lye," thus Isaac Pfendler to the Hofkammer, 3 September 1594, ÖStA, HKA, HFÖ Rote Nr. 64.
550. ÖStA, HKA, HFÖ Bd. 484-E, fol. 28r.
551. See also Colorni's letter to Vincenzo I Gonzaga of 12 July 1593 (*J-1891*, 38).
552. Isaac Pfendler to the Hofkammer, 17 March 1595 [Note]. ÖStA, HKA, HFÖ Rote Nr. 65.
553. Isaac Pfendler to the Hofkammer, 17 March 1595. ÖStA, HKA, HFÖ Rote Nr. 65.

554. Isaac Pfendler to the Hofkammer, 17 March 1595 [Note]. ÖStA, HKA, HFÖ Rote Nr. 65. I have been unable to locate this privilege. My search in HH-StA, Reichshofrat, Gratialia und Feudalia, turned up nothing.

555. "Non le taccio ch'egli qui è tenuto che vaglia qualche cosa, massime in suggetto de' salnitri," thus Guido Avellani to the ducal councilor Tullio Petrozzani, 9 May 1595, ASMn, AG, b. 469, fol. 155r-v (only partly in *Gonzaga/Prague*, doc. 490).

556. Guido Avellani to Tullio Petrozzani, 9 May 1595, ASMn, AG, b. 469, fol. 155r-v.

557. "Capitoli convenuti fra la Ducal[e] Munitione et M. Abraham Colorni intorno al far salnitri, et fabbricar polve[re] di arcobugio nello stato di S. Altezza Serenissima." Undated and unpaginated manuscript [1597?], ASMo, ASE, Ingegneri, b. 2 (earlier drafts may be found in the same collection).

558. Ibid.: "Che sia concesso al detto M. Abraham assoluta podestà ò a suoi agenti di poter ad ogni suo piacere mandar per tutto lo stato nei luoghi tanto pubblici, come particolari à spazzare il salnitro nei muri et scorticare e cavare ancora la terra atta produrne senza però danneggiar ne gli edifici ne i padroni."

559. Ibid.: "Che tutti quei che havran[no] ad isercitar l'arte de' salnitri ò della Polve[re] siano obbligati ad accordarsi con M. Abraham il quale sia però tenuto à dar prima parte di cotal accomodamento a chi sarà diputato sovraintendente alle munitioni [*sic*] acciò non vegna fatto aggravio ad alcuno."

560. Ibid.: "Che il medesimo M. Abraham sia tenuto di consignar ogni settimana a chi sarà diputato dalla Munitione lire quattrocento di salnitro della sudetta qualità, et bontà."

561. ASFe, Archivio Notarile Antico, Notaio Antonio Colorni, matr. 715, p. 39s (schede 1585).

562. Acting as notary here was a certain Antonio Colorni. The identical surname of the notary and client is apparently a coincidence. In any event, Antonio Colorni was not a (baptized) relative of Abramo Colorni. Instead, the notary was a member of Ferrara's aristocratic and Catholic Colorni family, whose ancestors, like Abramo's, had once lived in the tiny town of Colorno. On the distinction between these two families, see Colorni, "Genealogia," 639.

563. "Conventionem et societatem in negocio salnitri et pulveris vulgariter nuncupatum da arcobugio et da artiglieria." ASFe, Archivio Notarile Antico, Notaio Antonio Colorni, matr. 715, p. 39s (schede 1585).

564. Abraham Basola's biographical data remain unknown. He is briefly mentioned in the *Jewish Encyclopedia* (1901–1906), where it is said he was active primarily in Cremona. See Castiglione and von Günzburg, "Basilea," 2:576.

565. All information about the Carmi family according to Horowitz, "I Carmi di Cremona."
566. Boksenboim, *Iggerot Beit Carmi,* doc. 53.
567. See Colorni, "Genealogia," 639.
568. See a letter from Colorni to Francesco Gonzaga, n.p., n.d. [before 9 October 1572], ASF, Mediceo del Principato, 580, fol. 80r-v.
569. See the "Provisioni et ordini da osservarsi nel negotio de salnitri et Polvere per poterlo condurre con gl'utili et vantaggi trovatj per Abram Colorni hebreo mantovano" [1597?], ASMo, ASE, Ingegneri, b. 2. See also Colorni's undated "Secreto particolare" for Frederick I of Württemberg [ca. 1597], HStAS, A 47 Bü 3, Fasz. 11.
570. The undated document is titled "Scrittura di messer Abram" (*J-1891,* 50–53).
571. "Che possa . . . portar in tutti i luoghi dello stato ogni sorte d'armi, tanto da diffesa quanto da offesa, etiam gli archibugi di misura[,] permettendosi la medesima licenza a gli officiali principiali del negotio." See "Capitoli convenuti fra la Ducal[e] Munitione et M. Abraham Colorni," ASMo, ASE, Ingegneri, b. 2.
572. Hubicki, "Rudolf II," 299. Hubicki refers to the Jewish alchemist under the distorted name "Calorni" and mentions him only marginally.
573. Debus, *Chemistry,* ch. 9; Szydło, *Water;* Szydło, "Alchemy of Michael Sendivogius"; Porto, "Michael Sendivogius."
574. Frederick I von Württemberg to Kammerrat (Chamber Councilor) Rößlin, 22 August 1598, HStAS, A 56 Bü 3, Fasz. 12. See also Colorni's undated "Secreto particolare" for Frederick I of Württemberg [ca. 1597]: "Modo di fabricare salnitro in gran quantità e con brevità di tempo e con vantaggio di qual si voglia terra, in tutti i luoghi o coperto o vero discoperto . . . e questo senza incommodar i popoli e senza guastimento degli alloggiamenti."
575. This theory is described concisely in Newman, *Gehennical Fire,* 87–89. See also Thiele, *Salpeterwirtschaft,* 15.
576. Webster, *Great Instauration,* 377–380; Porto, "Michael Sendivogius," esp. 11, 15.
577. Quoted in Porto, "Michael Sendivogius," 16.
578. Schütt, *Auf der Suche,* 474.
579. Thus, e.g., Hofacker, *Alchemie am Hof,* 34.
580. "Provisioni et ordini da osservarsi nel negotio de salnitri et Polvere," ASMo, ASE, Ingegneri, b. 2.
581. Samuel [Simone] Colorni to Vincenzo I Gonzaga, 28 January 1600, ASMn, AG, b. 2680.

582. Portaleone, *Heldenschilde,* 658.
583. In his *Shiltei ha-Gibborim,* however, Portaleone does not mention Colorni by name.
584. Portaleone, *Heldenschilde,* esp. ch. 42 ("How to produce powder for large catapults").
585. Ibid., ch. 43, 404.
586. Colorni to Vincenzo I Gonzaga, 12 July 1593 (*J-1981,* 37–38).
587. "Darmi grata licenza, accio ch'io poßi [*sic*] andare à rivedere le cose mie famigliari, per le quali, sono tuttavia in grauj pensieri," thus Colorni in the *Scotographia,* letter of dedication to the emperor, n.p.
588. Toaff, *Il prestigiatore di Dio,* 187.
589. Mantua: Colorni to Guidobuon de Guidoboni, 10 November 1592 (*J-1891,* 35); Venice: HHStA, Staatenabteilung, Italien, Venedig, Dispacci di Germania, 19: fols. 316r–321r [1592]; as well as Giovanni Dolfin to the Doge, 10 December 1591 (*J-1891,* 33); Florence: ASF, Pratica segreta, filza 73, fol. 155r–v; as well as filza 189, fol. 189r–v [1592]; and Auditore delle riformagioni, filza 18, fols. 953r–954r.
590. "Il libro della Scotographia, et di Arithmetica si stampano al presente qui in praga," it says in a note [by Colorni?] n.p., n.d. [1592], ASF, Auditore delle riformagioni, filza 18, fol. 954r.
591. In any event, I was unable to verify works with this title, even under the assumption that they appeared anonymously, in the authoritative online catalogues or in the relevant published bibliographies.
592. The suspicion that one could only publish a work like the *Chirofisionomia* in "questa libertà di spirito et di stampe di Germania" was articulated in 1595 by Bishop Ferdinando Davila in a letter to Vincenzo I Gonzaga, 1 December 1595, ASMn, AG, b. 1527, fols. 482r–484v.
593. See Colorni's list of errata (*Scotographia,* n.p.). See also the handwritten corrections made anonymously in the copy of the HAB Wolfenbüttel (perhaps made by no less than Duke August of Braunschweig-Lüneburg).
594. The reader would have to "scusare il luogo, & gl'operanti, che sono totalmente inesperti della lingua Italiana," thus Colorni, *Scotographia,* fol. 16v.
595. On the history of this printing company (and the *Scotographia*), see Večeřová, *Šumanská tiskárna,* esp. 131–134.
596. Ibid., 256.
597. Here, too, online catalogues and the relevant published bibliographies were consulted to no avail.
598. Colorni to Aderbale Manerbio, 8 February 1598, ASMn, AG, b. 475, hier fol. 436r.

599. On the court at Mantua in the sixteenth century, see Morselli, *Gonzaga*. See also the excellent multivolume edition of the correspondence of the Mantuan court (published under the title *Le collezioni Gonzaga*). Additional literature is mentioned above.

600. Court: See the calculations in Cattini and Romani, "Le corti parallele," 70. See also Rebecchini, *Private Collectors in Mantua*, 39; on Vincenzo: Bellonci, *Segreti dei Gonzaga*; on his need for luxury, see also Piccinelli, "Le facies del collezionismo artistico."

601. Ferrari, "La cancelleria gonzaghesca," 310.

602. Harrán, *Salamone Rossi*, 30–31.

603. On Vincenzo's military ambition and his Turkish campaigns in a pan-European context, see Niederkorn, *Die europäischen Mächte*, 425–435.

604. On the illustrious circle of engineers employed at the Gonzaga court, see Carpeggiani, "Ingegneri a Mantova"; and Bertolotti, *Architetti, ingegneri e matematici*.

605. Bellonci, *Segreti dei Gonzaga*, 125. See also Contarini, "Relazione di Mantova" [1588], in Segarizzi, *Relazioni degli ambasciatori veneti*, 1:84.

606. "Servitore ordinario stipendiato da S. A.," it says about Colorni in a letter from Eleonora Gonzaga to Cesare d'Este, 6 July 1599 (*J-1891*, 57).

607. Frederick I of Württemberg to Emperor Rudolf II, 22 December 1596, HStAS, A 47 Bü 3, Fasz. 11.

608. Ibid.

609. Frederick I of Württemberg to Alfonso II d'Este, 30 January 1597, ASMo, ASE, Carteggio principi esteri, Württemberg, b. 1604/30. The same day, Frederick also turned to Vincenzo Gonzaga in this matter. In the letter to Mantua, Colorni is also characterized as a "Medico e philosopho clarissimo." ASMn, AG, b. 517; Marco Antonio Ricci to Alfonso II d'Este, 7 July 1597 (*J-1891*, 39–40); Sigismund Báthory to Alfonso II d'Este (ibid., 40).

610. Colorni to Aderbale Manerbio, 8 February 1598, ASMn, AG, b. 475, fols. 436r–438r; also esp. Colorni to Aderbale Manerbio, 5 May 1598, ASMn, AG, b. 475, fols. 527r–534r. I refer to the latter letter in what follows. Although, in these letters to Manerbio, all kinds of negative adjectives are heaped on the Jewish machinator, he is not mentioned by name. He must have been identical with that "fraudolente hebreo Rosso" mentioned in a letter by Colorni to Vincenzo I Gonzaga from 27 January 1598 (*J-1891*, 41).

611. In a postscript from 29 March 1598 Colorni urged his Prague correspondent Aderbale Manerbio to stop sending letters to Stuttgart and to direct them instead to the "maestro della posta di Ganzstat." The place in question was apparently Cannstatt, not far from Stuttgart. ASMn, AG, b. 475, 486r–v.

612. See the mentions in the correspondence between Emperor Rudolf II and Frederick I of Württemberg in HHStA, Familienkorrespondenz, Schachtel 4. A "pass for the Jew Seligmann from Brenz for traveling to Prague" may be found in HStAS A 47 Bü 3, Fasz. 11. In 1600 he is mentioned in the sources as the bearer of a letter from the emperor, HStAS A 56 Bü 12. See also Hahn, *Erinnerungen und Zeugnisse*, 205.
613. Colorni to Vincenzo I Gonzaga, 27 January 1598 (*J-1891*, 41).
614. Zimerman, "Urkunden, Acten und Regesten," xv–lxxxiv, doc. 4660.
615. Ibid., doc. 4678.
616. See the study, tendentious but with an appendix rich in source material, by Hurter, *Philipp Lang*, 210.
617. But see also Toaff, who identifies Rosso, even if merely on the basis of one source from Jarè, with a certain Salomon Roques (Roces, Rocca) from Verona or Ferrara. Toaff, *Il prestigiatore di Dio*, 223.
618. In a letter to Manerbio from 8 February 1598, Colorni mentioned that the deceitful Jew Rosso had disseminated this lie in Prague. ASMn, AG, b. 475, fols. 436r–438r. And, in fact, rumors of this kind were soon circulating, at least among Prague's Jews. In the course of subsequent investigations against Colorni, a traveling Jew named Salomon from Prague reported in 1599 during an interrogation by officials from Württemberg: "[Colorni was] a reckless fellow, was regarded among the Jewish community as a mere artist, but with all his art he has used nothing more than deceit, and even proffered to his Imperial Majesty that he could make saltpeter and powder which will cost His Imperial Majesty a lot, but he the Jew had created only little of use, ultimately he escaped Prague in peasant's clothes, so nobody knew whither he had gone." See the report of the bailiff of Göppingen to Frederick I of Württemberg, 5 September 1599, HStAS, A 47 Bü 3, Fasz. 12. I already indicated above that one should treat these unflattering assertions about Colorni with caution, since Salomon's testimony here was not made of his own free will. This Jew who had been subjected to an interrogation had good reason to accommodate the Württemberg authorities in his testimomy. Salomon was, after all, planning to travel through Württemberg territory, and at the end of September 1599, probably on his way back, he was subjected to another interrogation, this time in Vaihingen. See the report of the bailiff of Vaihingen to Frederick I of Württemberg, 29 September 1599, HStAS, A 47 Bü 3, Fasz. 12.
619. See the last will and testament of Duke Eberhard im Bart [1492/1496] in Reyscher, *Vollständige . . . Sammlung*, 2:9. On policy toward Jews in early modern Württemberg, see Lang, *Ausgrenzung und Koexistenz*.

620. Reyscher, *Vollständige . . . Sammlung*, 2:23.
621. Pfaff, "Die früheren Verhältnisse,"172.
622. HStAS, A 56 U 15.
623. Sauer, *Herzog Friedrich*, 245.
624. Frederick I, for example, wrote to the emperor on 2 September 1600 about a "Hebrew book that is supposed to be in my hands." HHStA, Familienkorrespondenz, Schachtel 4.
625. Contarini, *Relazione di Germania* [1596], in Firpo, *Relazioni di ambasciatori veneti*, 3:213.
626. See esp. Sauer, *Herzog Friedrich I*.
627. Hofacker, *Alchemie am Hof*, 10.
628. Fleischhauer, *Renaissance in Württemberg*, 271–273.
629. Hofacker, *Alchemie am Hof;* Günzler, "Herzog Friedrich."
630. Fleischhauer, *Renaissance in Württemberg*, 273.
631. Colorni to Aderbale Manerbio, 8 February 1598, ASMn, AG, b. 475, fols. 436r–438r.
632. Colorni to Aderbale Manerbio, 5 May 1598, ASMn, AG, b. 475, fols. 527r–534r.
633. Colorni to Vincenzo I Gonzaga, 27 January 1598 (*J-1891*, 42). See also Colorni to Aderbale Manerbio, 8 February 1598, ASMn, AG, b. 475, fol. 436r–438r. This number was not exaggerated. For the year 1607, the historian Paul Sauer counts a total of 513 regular members at the court of Frederick I. See Sauer, *Herzog Friedrich I*, 125. By way of comparison: the court at Mantua had approximately 800 members under Vincenzo I.
634. Crusius, *Diarium*, entry from 9 November 1597 (1:407). I am grateful to Peter Mommsen for assistance in translating Greek passages in the Crusius diaries.
635. Ibid., entry from 13 November 1597 (1:409).
636. On 13 December 1597 Crusius noted again that there was a Hebrew in Stuttgart who was a "stone-to-bread-maker" (the original has the Greek word), ibid., 1:421.
637. On the popularity of this topos in early modern discourses about magic, see also During, *Modern Enchantments*, 4. During sees one reason for this popularity in the possibility of associating the magician Moses with Hermes Trismegistos, often depicted with snakes.
638. Battafarano, "L'opera di Tomaso Garzoni," 35.
639. Garzoni, *Piazza universale*, 1:21.
640. Crusius, *Diarium,* marginalia on the entry from 1 January 1598 (2:1). The original wording is: "Iudaeus, qui Stutg. est, dicitur nihil admodum μαγικον scire: allein mit Salpeter."

641. Undated "Secreto particolare" for Frederick I of Württemberg [ca. 1597], HStAS, A 47 Bü 3, Fasz. 11.
642. Ibid.
643. "Et se dio mi concede vita spero di fortificar . . . la amicitia talmente che in ogni tempo se ne potra sperare ogni bene," thus Colorni to Vincenzo I Gonzaga, 27 January 1598 (*J-1891*, 41).
644. Colorni to Vincenzo I Gonzaga, 27 January 1598 (*J-1891*, 42); Colorni from Stuttgart to Vincenzo I Gonzaga, 16 June 1598 (*J-1891*, 43).
645. Jarè mentions this without any indicating information about sources (*J-1874*, 12).
646. See two thank-you letters from Frederick I of Württemberg to Alfonso II d'Este from 8 May and 29 August 1597, ASMo, ASE, Carteggio principi esteri, Württemberg, b. 1604/30.
647. Alfonso II d'Este to Colorni, 14 October 1597 (*J-1891*, 41).
648. Sauer, *Herzog Friedrich I*, 225.
649. All of the information on this episode is taken, unless otherwise indicated, from: Jütte, "Abramo Colorni." See also Lang, *Ausgrenzung und Koexistenz*, 112–136.
650. The Landtag to Frederick I of Württemberg, 16 March 1599, in Adam, *Württembergische Landtagsakten*, 2:150.
651. At court the failure of the trading company and Colorni's fruitless efforts were conceived as two sides of the same coin. A detailed report about the trading company written in the summer of 1598 by the ducal councilor Buwinckhausen was combined with a report about the activity of the Jewish court alchemist—even though these were two different affairs. On the back of the document there is this revealing note: "Report regarding the Consul Jew and Abram Colorno," HStAS, A 47 Bü 3, Fasz. 12.
652. "Per bisogno che havemo dell'opera sua," thus Vincenzo I Gonzaga to Frederick I of Württemberg, 20 November 1598 (*J-1891*, 54).
653. Frederick I of Württemberg to Kammerrat Rößlin, 22 August 1598, HStAS, A 56 Bü 3, Fasz. 12.
654. Ibid.
655. Kopp, *Die Alchemie*, 1:181.
656. Inventory list of the saltpeter hut, 23 March 1599, HStAS, A 47 Bü 3, Fasz. 12.
657. Frederick I of Württemberg to the bailiff of Burgau County, 24 March 1599, HStAS, A 47 Bü 3, Fasz. 12.
658. The related correspondence between the Duke of Mantua and the Duke of Württemberg is reprinted in *J-1891*, sections XIV and XV. The efforts at

getting Colorni extradited are also partly documented in HStAS, A 47 Bü 3, Fasz. 12.

659. This is what is recorded in Mantua's *registri necrologici*. See Simonsohn, *History of the Jews in the Duchy of Mantua*, 705.

660. Toaff raises this possibility: *Il prestigiatore di Dio*, 224-225.

661. Frederick I of Württemberg to Vincenzo I Gonzaga, 29 May 1600 (*J-1891*, 59).

662. Gaddi, *Adlocutiones et elogia exemplaria*, 167-173. On Gaddi's biography, see Fabio Tarzia, "Gaddi, Jacopo," in *DBI*, 51:159-160.

663. Gaddi, *Adlocutiones et elogia exemplaria*, 170.

664. Ibid.: "Ei del Germano orgoglio / Frangea lo scoglio, e in macchine guerriere / Chiuso, inerme vincea l'armate schiere. / Spinger al Ciel potea le balze alpestri / Da mine aprendo i sotterranei lampi, / Strugger Cittadi, e campi / Farle alberghi di belve ermi, e silvestri."

665. Ibid., 169.

666. See e.g. Troitzsch, "Erfinder, Forscher und Projektemacher," 452. See also Kris and Kurz, *Die Legende vom Künstler*, 94-96.

667. In a poem prefacing the *Euthimetria*, fol. 5r.

668. Mirami, *Compendiosa Introduttione*, preface, n.p. See also ibid., 45, where Colorni is praised as a "raro ingeniero della età nostra." Thus far there is no substantial research on Mirami and his work. See only the brief mentions in Moritz Steinschneider, "Mathematik bei den Juden," in *MGWJ* 6 (1906): 729-753; Friedenwald, *Jewish Luminaries*, 114. On Mirami's *Compendiosa Introduttione alla prima parte della specularia* in particular, see the remarks in Toaff, *Il prestigiatore di Dio*, 50-52; Reeves, *Galileo's Glassworks*, 36-38; and Pavone, *Introduzione al pensiero*, 2:373-375. I could not find any evidence of Mirami in sources on the history of the Jews in Ferrara and Italy. Franceschini, an expert on the Jewish community of Ferrara, knows him only as the author of the *Compendiosa Introduttione;* see Franceschini, "Privilegi dottorali." To be sure, the *Compendiosa Introduttione* is not Mirami's only work. We also have evidence of him as the author of an unpublished manuscript about calculating the calendar (titled *Informationi intorno alle rivolutioni del tempo*): Antonelli, *Indice dei manoscritti*, 190.

669. Menasseh ben Israel, *Esperanza de Israel*.

670. "En quanta estimacion vivio entre varios Principes de Italia, Abraham Colorni, consta de aquella Epistola que le dirigió Thomas Garzoni, en la su Piazza vniversal del mondo." Ibid., 103.

671. Menasseh ben Israel, *Hope of Israel*, 155.

672. Also skeptical on this point is Toaff, *Il prestigiatore di Dio*, 196.

673. Garzoni, *Piazza universale,* esp. 17-19. See likewise Garzoni's preface to the *Chirofisionomia* (MS Wolfenbüttel, n.p.). In the 1570s Francesco Gonzaga of Novellara had also hastily presumed that it would be easy to convert the Jewish engineer to Christianity ("facilmente lo fara Christ[iano] che serà pur un guadagnare un'Anima"). ASF, Mediceo del Principato, 580, fol. 79r.
674. See Simonsohn, "Sefarim ve-Sifriyot"; Baruchson-Arbib, *La culture livresque.*
675. Levi, "Famosi," 609. My identification of this Samuele (Simone) as Abramo's cousin is based on the genealogical material in Colorni, "Genealogia," 646-647.
676. More specifically, they were allowed to live in the house of a certain Gumprecht. See Boksenboim, *Pinkas Kahal Verona,* 3:120.
677. Colorni, "Genealogia," 648; *Gonzaga/Venice* II, doc. 606.
678. Bertolotti, *Artisti,* 163; Simonsohn, *History of the Jews in the Duchy of Mantua,* 656; Colorni, "Genealogia," 649.
679. Morselli, "Este e Gonzaga," doc. 4. The Lazzaro in question is not mentioned in Colorni, "Genealogia."
680. Toaff, *Il prestigiatore di Dio,* e.g. 33, 54, 202. Toaff's assertion that there are very few sources on Simone Colorni (ibid., 277) is not tenable. In fact, the findings from the ASMn presented here seem to be merely the tip of the iceberg.
681. He is encountered in the sources both under the name Samuele and (more frequently) under the name Simone. On the correspondence of these names among Italian Jews, see Colorni, "La corrispondenza," 675, 783-785, and on the Simone Colorni in particular, see Colorni, "Genealogia," 645. The Simone Colorni in question here—Abramo Colorni's son—should not be confused with Simone di Moise, a relative active in the money business, who likewise lived in Mantua. On relatives in the Colorni family, see Colorni, "Genealogia," 646.
682. From unpublished documents in the ASMo it emerges that this instruction was given between the (Jewish calendar) years 5342 (1582 CE) and 5346 (1586 CE). ASMo, ASE, Ingegneri, b. 2. Abramo's repeated failure to pay the teacher, however, eventually led to a legal quarrel.
683. See Melzi, "Una commedia." As late as 1611, incidentally, Leon Modena was making an effort to publish Alatini's *Trionfi;* see Modena, *Autobiography,* 126.
684. Frederick I of Württemberg to Vincenzo I Gonzaga, 6 May 1598 (*J-1891,* 53).
685. *Gonzaga/Venice* II, doc. 13.
686. This is mentioned in passing by Ferrari, "La cancelleria gonzaghesca," 309-310. Presumably, "messer Simone ebreo" who is mentioned in 1608 in

connection with jewelry deals in Venice is also identical with Il Morino; see *Gonzaga/Florence,* doc. 492.
687. *Gonzaga/Venice* II, docs. 106, 115, 117.
688. Ibid., 49.
689. Ibid. A photo of *L'adorante* may be found in Jestaz, "Bronzo e bronzetti nella collezione Gonzaga," 318.
690. *Gonzaga/Venice* II, docs. 677, 681.
691. Ibid., doc. 645 (jewels from Venice); doc. 1031 (painting); doc. 1036 (maiolica). See also Bertolotti, *Figuli, fonditori e scultori,* 44.
692. *Gonzaga/Prague,* doc. 923.
693. *Gonzaga/Venice* II, doc. 235.
694. *Gonzaga/Prague,* doc. 945.
695. On this, and on the practical difficulties in completing the job, see ibid., docs. 948, 950, 953, 967.
696. Ibid., doc. 1080.
697. Thus, a court offical wrote that "A[ltezza] S[ua] . . . in questo riguardo ha fatto meraviglie per rispetto di M. Morino." Ferrando Pessia to Vincenzo I Gonzaga, 14 March 1600, ASMn, AG, b. 2680. Simone Colorni was, to be sure, arrested once more in Mantua that same year at the insistence of the Duke of Württemberg. As we have seen, the matter of extradition ultimately fizzled out.
698. See Ferrer, "Wondrous Devices in the Dark," 424, 434.
699. See Campanini, "A Neglected Source," 109–110.
700. On this, see Crispi, Slote, and van Hulle, Introduction to *How Joyce Wrote Finnegans Wake,* 19, 22.
701. Joyce, *Finnegans Wake,* 228. On this, see also Bishop, Introduction, viii. Bishop points out that Joyce is likewise conjuring up associations with "highbrows" as well as the barroom atmosphere of the toast "to the high brews."
702. Ferrer, "Wondrous Devices in the Dark"; Bishop, Introduction, esp. xiv–xvi.
703. Bishop, Introduction, viii.
704. Moser, "Der Fürst," 249.
705. Nick, *Stuttgarter Chronik,* 217. The method, announced by Nick in the foreword, to "adjust [the sources] to my purpose," is evident here. In fact, most of the citations from sources related to Colorni are completely fictitious.
706. Feuchtwanger, *Jud Süß,* 158.
707. Zelzer, *Weg und Schicksal,* 18.
708. Baron, *Social and Religious History,* 12:80; Adler, "Abraham Colorni," 16.

709. This is mentioned, e.g. in Grunwald, "Die Juden als Erfinder und Entdecker." See also the entry "Abraham Colorni," in Wininger, *Große Jüdische National-Biographie,* 1:586–587. Colorni becomes an "important scholar" in the Yiddish treatment by Sziper, "Geszichte fun idiszer teater-kunst un drame," 38; see also Steinschneider, "Mathematik bei den Juden," 1 (1905): 88–89; 2 (1905): 193; 3 (1905): 300–301.
710. Grunwald, *Hamburgs deutsche Juden,* 216.
711. "L'ingegnere e arcanista Colorna [sic]," in *La nostra bandiera* of 1 February 1937. I take the reference to this article, which I was unable to view, from Anon., "Abramo Colorni," in Landman, *Universal Jewish Encyclopedia,* 3:305–306. On the Jewish-fascist journal *La nostra bandiera* in general, see Stille, "Italian Jewish-Fascist Editor."
712. *J-1891,* 6. Jarè was not alone in Italy with his pride in Colorni; see e.g. Ravenna, Review of *Abramo Colorni.*
713. Steinschneider, "Mathematik bei den Juden," esp. 1 (1905): 88–89.
714. Steinschneider, "Allgemeine Einführung," 748.
715. Kaufmann, "Leone de Sommi Portaleone," 297–298.
716. Simonsohn, *History of the Jews in the Duchy of Mantua,* 650. Toaff makes the adventurous aspects of Colorni's life story the center of interest, beginning with his book's subtitle: *Il prestigiatore di Dio: Avventure e miracoli di un alchimista ebreo nelle corti del Rinascimento.*
717. Giovanni Dolfin to the Doge, 10 December 1591 (*J-1891,* 33).
718. "Io non ho visto quest'opere, ma pare siano per esser grate à virtuosi, et l'Ambasciatore di corte cesarea mi fa fede, che quest'huomo sia molto virtuoso, et habbia cognitione di varij secreti naturali, et . . . sia assai accetto all Imperatore al quale fu mandato gia dal Duca di Ferrara." Report from 27 February 1592, ASF, Auditore delle riformagioni, filza 18, fol. 953r–v.
719. "Potete andare altiero sì d'esser l'unico al mondo secretario di natura, et mastro di secreti pellegrini et rari," thus Garzoni, *Piazza universale,* 1:21.
720. "Learn how to *decipher* [descifrar] a face and spell out the soul in the features," according to the recommendation, for example, of Gracián, *Art of Worldly Wisdom,* no. 273 (emphasis added).
721. See esp. Gentilcore, *Medical Charlatanism.*
722. "[S]'io fossi huomo, ch'io andassi con bugie, et simulationi, che non si può già credere, ch'io havessi tenuti per Padroni cosi lungo tempo cosi gran Principi, et cosi Nobili intelletti," thus Colorni to Aderbale Manerbio, 5 May 1598, ASMn, AG, b. 475, fol. 528r.
723. See Kodera, "Der Magus und die Stripperinnen."

724. "L'inventioni, et Secreti di qualche valore, che il Signor Iddio mi ha concesso di sapere investigare et trovare di proprio giuditio," thus Colorni to Giovanni Dolfin, 21 November 1592, HHStA, Staatenabteilung, Italien, Venedig, Dispacci di Germania 19, fol. 319r.
725. This does not, of course, exclude the possibility that there might have been a certain competition between Colorni and Della Porta, as Eileen Reeves suspects. Reeves, *Galileo's Glassworks*, 71.

Chapter Six. The Culture and Crisis of Secrecy

1. On this, see also Brenner, *Prophets of the Past,* esp. 151–155.
2. See also Cohen and Cohen, *Jewish Contribution.*
3. Patai, *Jewish Alchemists,* 9.
4. Steinschneider, "Pseudo-Juden," 42. See also Trachtenberg, *Jewish Magic,* 304.
5. Grunwald, "Aus Hausapotheke und Hexenküche," 4.
6. To name just a few: Birnbaum and Heppner, *Juden als Erfinder;* Grunwald, "Die Juden als Erfinder"; Theilhaber, *Schicksal und Leistung;* Roth, *Jewish Contribution,* esp. the chapter "Scientific Progress" (146–166).
7. Scholem, "Alchemie und Kabbala."
8. Trachtenberg, *Jewish Magic,* 304. Trachtenberg later repeated this assertion in his study on the accusation of sorcery against Jews. See Trachtenberg, *Devil,* 72–73.
9. Baron, *Social and Religious History,* 8:223, 225.
10. Bernard Suler, "Alchemy," in *EJ,* 1:601: "The number of Jews who practiced the art of alchemy was apparently relatively small; however, the state of knowledge on this point is incomplete."
11. Freudenthal, Review of *The Jewish Alchemists.*
12. Patai, *Jewish Alchemists.*
13. See the detailed and critical reviews of Patai's study by Freudenthal and by Langermann.
14. Merton, *Science, Technology and Society.* Shapin details the reception of the Merton thesis among historians in *The Scientific Revolution,* 195–196. See also Trepp, *Von der Glückseligkeit.*
15. Shapin, "Understanding the Merton Thesis." For a recent and well-taken critique of the Merton thesis, see Cook, *Matters of Exchange,* 82–84.
16. For a summary of this, see Shapin, *Scientific Revolution,* esp. 197–198.
17. See Calhoun, "Robert K. Merton Remembered."
18. Friedenwald, *Jews and Medicine;* Friedenwald, "Jewish Luminaries"; Roth, *Jews in the Renaissance;* Roth, *Jewish Contribution;* Feuer, "Scientific Revo-

lution"; Shulvass, *Jews in the World of the Renaissance*; Neher, *Jewish Thought;* Neher, "Gli ebrei e la rivoluzione copernicana."
19. Roth, *Jews in the Renaissance.*
20. Bonfil, *Jewish Life in Renaissance Italy,* esp. 42.
21. "In today's universities we would place him among the technical assistants . . . Neither in Jewish studies nor in the general sciences was David Gans more than a modest workman," according to Neher, *Jewish Thought,* 13.
22. Di Meo, *Cultura ebraica.*
23. Israel, "È esistita una 'scienza ebraica' in Italia?"
24. Rabkin, "Interfacce multiple." See also, e.g., Feuer's "Scientific Revolution," which makes use of similar arguments, esp. 300–304. To be sure, Feuer concedes that there were a few "advocates of the scientific standpoint" among the ranks of premodern Jews, but on the whole he sees religion and Talmud study before 1800 as posing almost insurmountable obstacles to the advent of science. "Ghetto Judaism" was even, in his opinion, "contaminated with strong ingredients of masochist asceticism."
25. For Italy in general, see Bonfil, *Jewish Life,* 93–94. A differentiated picture of the Jewish occupational structure in the medieval Holy Roman Empire is provided by Toch, "Economic Activities"; Toch, "Die wirtschaftliche Tätigkeit"; for the early modern period, see esp. Battenberg, *Die Juden in Deutschland,* 94–97.
26. See esp. Ruderman, *Jewish Thought.* See also by Ruderman, *Kabbalah;* "Contemporary Science"; "Language of Science"; and "Impact of Science."
27. Ruderman, "Impact of Science," 434.
28. Ruderman, "Jewish Thought," esp. 11, 222. See also Ruderman, *Kabbalah,* 73; also Veltri, "Science and Religious Hermeneutics," esp. 134; also Veltri, "Jüdische Einstellungen."
29. Feuer, "Bacon and the Jews," 21. A more differentiated picture in Lasker, *Jewish Philosophical Polemics,* esp. 10. On the use of scientific arguments to counter Christian polemics as late as the end of the early modern period, see Richarz, *Der Eintritt der Juden,* 10.
30. Ruderman, "Language of Science," 188.
31. Ruderman, *Jewish Thought,* 12.
32. Ibid., 372.
33. Tirosh-Samuelson, "Theology of Nature," 535.
34. Ibid., esp. 561.
35. Funkenstein, *Perceptions,* 211.

36. Ibid., 216. The view that the Netherlands and Italy were not leading sites of the New Science is easy to rebut. On the Netherlands, see esp. Cook, *Matters of Exchange;* on Italy, see e.g. Findlen, "Formation of a Scientific Community."
37. Funkenstein, *Perceptions,* 211. See also the critique of Funkenstein in Ruderman, *Jewish Thought,* 371. According to Ruderman, Funkenstein was "certainly wrong to view Judaism as less tolerant or enthusiastic than Christianity in validating the autonomous pursuit of the sciences."
38. Reiner, "Attitude of Ashkenazi Society."
39. Efron, Introduction.
40. Daston and Park, *Wonders,* 329-333.
41. See esp. Shapin, *Scientific Revolution,* 1.
42. Vickers, Introduction, esp. 30. I do, however, have some reservations about some of the theses Vickers attaches to this general proposition.
43. Daston and Park, *Wonders,* 329-331.
44. Yates, *Giordano Bruno.*
45. For a critical take, see esp. Vickers, Introduction. There is a comprehensive bibliographic overview on the controversy about the Yates thesis in Brann, *Trithemius and Magical Theology,* 255-256.
46. Grafton, *Cardano's Cosmos,* 165; Eamon, *Science,* 288.
47. Shumaker, *Natural Magic,* 38. See also Webster, *From Paracelsus to Newton,* esp. 2, 57.
48. Ruderman, "Impact of Science," 429.
49. Ruderman, *Kabbalah;* see also Ruderman, "Language of Science," 184.
50. Ruderman, "Impact of Science," 426.
51. Ibid., 429.
52. Even Ruderman is concerned with explaining how "scientific thought and activity were a central concern of early modern Jewish culture." See Ruderman, *Jewish Thought,* 13.
53. The titles of scholarly articles on this subject are a good indicator: Langermann, "Was There No Science in Ashkenaz?"; and see also the title of the special issue of the *Jahrbuch des Simon-Dubnow-Institut* devoted to this subject—"Science and Philosophy in Early Modern Ashkenazic Culture: Rejection, Toleration, and Appropriation"—which conspicuously makes use of polarizing categories.
54. This is even true of the innovative study by Mokyr, which takes a more conventional stance in its sections dealing with Jewish history. See Mokyr, *Gifts of Athena,* e.g. 64, 290.
55. See Giorgio Romano, "Ottolenghi, Joseph ben Nathan," in *EJ,* 15:519; see also Simonsohn, *Jews in the Duchy of Milan,* 1:xxxix.

56. Simonsohn, *Jews in the Duchy of Milan,* doc. 3453.
57. See ibid., docs. 3423, 3467, 3516.
58. In my view, the distinction between Jews as "consumers" or "contributors," as used by Moshe Idel with regard to the Renaissance, allows little room for the necessary differentiation. See Idel, "Differing Conceptions," 140. A more nuanced approach is taken by Cantor, who compares the scientific activities of two minorities in England (Jews and Quakers) for the period between 1650 and 1900. See Cantor, *Quakers, Jews, and Science,* ch. 5, esp. 159.
59. Long, *Openness, Secrecy, Authorship,* 249.
60. The classic treatment is Blumenberg, *Der Prozeß der theoretischen Neugierde;* see also Ginzburg, "High and Low," esp. 38; Daston, "Neugierde"; Daston and Park, *Wonders;* Krüger, *Curiositas;* Harrison, "Curiosity"; Dauphiné, "La curiosité poétique"; Eamon, *Science,* esp. 314–318.
61. "Curioso intelletto": Colorni, *Scotographia,* letter of dedication to the emperor, n.p.
62. Mokyr, *Gifts of Athena.* See also Berg, "Genesis," 124–125.
63. Moran, *Patronage and Institutions;* Moran, "Alchemical World"; by way of summary also Moran, "Courts and Academies"; Galluzzi, "Il mecenatismo mediceo"; Biagioli, *Galileo;* Kaufmann, "Empiricism and Community," esp. 411. See also the *Micrologus* special issue *I saperi nelle corti.* Briefly on the meaning of the courts for the "Scientific Revolution," see also Shapin, *Scientific Revolution,* 126.
64. Kaufmann, "From Mastery of the World"; Bredekamp, *Antikensehnsucht;* Findlen, *Possessing Nature.*
65. Smith and Findlen, *Merchants and Marvels;* Cook, *Matters of Exchange;* Trepp, *Von der Glückseligkeit,* esp. 399–400.
66. Assmann and Assmann, "Die Erfindung des Geheimnisses," 7.
67. Shapin, *Scientific Revolution,* 19.
68. Eamon, *Science,* 273.
69. Johnson, *A Dictionary of the English Language,* 2:1776. Retrieved online at http://johnsonsdictionaryonline.com/?page_id=7070&i=1776. This definition seems to take cues from earlier traditions: Cardano, for example, had a similar view (as we have seen above).
70. Daston, "Neugierde," 45. On the Royal Society's intensive engagement with exotic knowledge, see Eamon, *Science,* 299; see likewise Daston and Park, *Wonders,* 231–240. On the significance of curiosity for the acquisition of "useful knowledge," see also Harrison, "Curiosity," esp. 289.
71. Ash, *Power, Knowledge, and Expertise;* Mokyr, *Gifts of Athena,* esp. 57.

72. Miletto, *Glauben und Wissen;* see also Ruderman, "At the Intersection of Cultures," esp. 19; on the significance of Jews in particular for the procurement of rare texts, see Efron, "Common Goods," 238.
73. "Method was meant to be all," as emphasized by Shapin, *Scientific Revolution,* 90. See also McMullin, "Openness and Secrecy in Science," 17.
74. Ornstein, *Role of Scientific Societies,* 140.
75. "Cet espece de gens sont fort ignorans et n'ont le plus souvent nulle methode en ce qu'ils donnent, s'il y a quelque chose de bon," according to Mersenne in a letter to André Rivet from 17 September 1632, reprinted in Mersenne, *Correspondance,* 329; Daston, "Neugierde," 302.
76. Mokyr, *Gifts of Athena,* 65.
77. Cantor, *Quakers, Jews, and Science,* 171.
78. All details on da Costa are taken from Cantor, *Quakers, Jews, and Science,* esp. 123 and 170–172.
79. On this, see above, esp. Chapter 4. See also Israel, *European Jewry,* 144; Stern, *Court Jew,* esp. 41.
80. Luzzatto, *Discorso,* ch. 5.
81. See e.g. Glückel von Hameln, *Die Memoiren,* 208–210.
82. An example of the "transfiguration" of Bacon by scholars: Dobbs, "From the Secrecy of Alchemy," 89.
83. Heinisch, *Der utopische Staat,* 217. "The general public were probably more familiar with [this work] than with any of Bacon's more philosophical writings," according to Webster, *Great Instauration,* 249. A useful introduction to this work by Bacon is also provided in Sargent, "Bacon as an Advocate," esp. 152–164.
84. Bacon, *New Atlantis,* in *Works,* 3:120–166.
85. Ibid., 145.
86. Ibid.
87. Ibid., 156.
88. See e.g. Bennett and Mandelbrote, *Garden,* 144; Prior, "Bacon's Man of Science," 348.
89. Weinberger, "Science and Rule in Bacon's Utopia," 870. Moody Prior, by contrast, is too idealistic in viewing the staff of Salomon's House more like scientists who are "above the state." Prior, "Bacon's Man of Science," 368; Ash, *Power, Knowledge, and Expertise,* 207–209.
90. Bacon, *New Atlantis,* 153.
91. Ibid. 151.
92. Ibid.
93. Ibid.

94. Ibid.
95. See also Niewöhner, "Natur-Wissenschaft und Gotteserkenntnis," 83.
96. Ibid.
97. Menascè, "Presenza ebraica nell'utopia"; Yates, "Science, Salvation, and the Cabala"; Feuer, "Francis Bacon and the Jews."
98. Yates, "Science, Salvation, and the Cabala."
99. Feuer, "Francis Bacon and the Jews," 2.
100. Ibid., 20; Menascè, "Presenza ebraica nell'utopia," 704.
101. Feuer, "Francis Bacon and the Jews," 19.
102. Katz's statement that "the connection between Bacon and the Jews has not yet been fully appreciated" remains valid. Katz, *Philo-Semitism*, 25.
103. Bacon, *New Atlantis*, 151; see also Weinberger, "Science and Rule," 881.
104. On this, see also Ash, *Power, Knowledge, and Expertise*, 209.
105. Bacon, *The Advancement of Learning*, in *Works*, 3:473-474: "Concerning Government, it is a part of knowledge secret and retired." See also his *Essays or Counsels Civil and Moral*, in *Works*, 6:377-517, specifically Essay VI ("Of Simulation and Dissimulation"). See also Essay XX ("Of Counsel"), esp. 425.
106. Hutchison, "What Happened?"
107. Merchant, "'Violence of Impediments,'" 748; see also Eamon, *Science*, 299. On this debate in general: Merchant, "Secrets of Nature"; also Vickers, "Francis Bacon, Feminist Historiography"; Pesic, "Proteus Rebound"; Pesic, "Wrestling with Proteus."
108. Steven Shapin, *Social History of Truth*, xi.
109. "[One ought] not account him a gentleman, which is onely descended of noble bloud, in power great, in iewels rich, in furniture fine, in attendants brave: for all these are found in Merchant and Iewes. But to be a perfect Gentleman is to bee measured in his words, liberall in giuing, sober in diet, honest in liuing, tender in pardoning, and valiant in fighting," according to Richard Gainsford, *The Rich Cabinet Furnished with Varieties of Excellent Discriptions, Exquisite Characters, Witty Discourses, and Delightfull Histories* (London, 1616), quoted in Shapin, *Social History of Truth*, 62.
110. Martin, "Natural Philosophy and Its Public Concerns," 105-109.
111. Long, *Openness, Secrecy, Authorship*, 248; Shapin, *Scientific Revolution*, 123.
112. Thus Thomas Sprat's *The History of the Royal Society* (London, 1667), quoted in Cantor, *Quakers, Jews, and Science*, 104. First Jew: ibid., 106.
113. Bonfil, "Accademie rabbiniche."
114. Ruderman, *Jewish Thought*, 372. On Jewish students at other Italian universities such as Pisa, Perugia, or Bologna, see Colorni, "Sull'ammissibilità."

115. Toury, "Der Eintritt der Juden ins deutsche Bürgertum," 181. See also Richarz, *Der Eintritt der Juden*.
116. Richarz, *Der Eintritt der Juden;* Wolff, "Antijudaismus"; William W. Brickman, "Universities," in *EJ*, 20:406–409.
117. Richarz, *Der Eintritt der Juden*, esp. 164–172.
118. Volkov, "Soziale Ursachen," esp. 158–161.
119. Ruderman, "Contemporary Science and Jewish Law," 212.
120. Ibid.
121. Schudt, *Jüdische Merckwürdigkeiten*, bk. VI, 403. I could not find any additional information about this Venetian Jew Servati (Sarfatti?). His name is absent from Koren, *Jewish Physicians*.
122. See also Bonfil, "Accademie rabbiniche."
123. Georg Christoph Lichtenberg to Georg Heinrich Hollenberg from 9 January 1777. See Lichtenberg, *Schriften und Briefe*, 4:290.
124. Quoted in Joost, *Georg Christoph Lichtenberg*, 6.
125. As in a petition of 1790 to the city council of Groningen. Quoted in ibid., 12.
126. Accordingly, only a few studies deal with the man and his career. See esp. ibid.; Buchberger, "Jüdische Taschenspieler"; Heymann, "Der Erzmagier Philadelphia"; Sachse, "Jacob Philadelphia"; and my own study, which I have drawn upon here: Jütte, "Haskala und Hokuspokus."
127. Buchberger, "Jüdische Taschenspieler," 151.
128. For detailed bibliographical information, see Jütte, "Haskala und Hokuspokus"; see also Ebstein, "Jacob Philadelphia," 22–28.
129. Goethe, *Tagebücher*, I/2:427.
130. All additional biographical details, unless otherwise noted, according to Jütte, "Haskala und Hokuspokus."
131. Geiger, "Jacob Philadelphia."
132. Quoted in Ebstein, "Jacob Philadelphia," 24.
133. For more details, see Jütte, "Haskala und Hokuspokus," 42–49.
134. Mendelssohn, "Gegenbetrachtungen über Bonnets Palingenesie," in *Gesammelte Schriften*, 7:95.
135. See Chapter 4.
136. Even a generation after Philadelphia's death, there is evidence of Jewish magicians who were clearly modeling themselves after this master. See Jütte, "Haskala und Hokuspokus," 48. As late as the eighteenth century there were also sectarian groups and individuals who were not part of (rabbinical) Judaism but nonetheless highlighted their knowledge of a supposedly Jewish magic. See Maciejko, "Sabbatian Charlatans."

137. On his biography, see esp. Schuchard, "Dr. Samuel Jacob Falk"; Schuchard, "Lord George Gordon"; Ruderman, *Jewish Enlightenment*, 159–169; Roth, "King and the Kabbalist"; Patai, *Jewish Alchemists*, 455–462; Scholem, "Alchemie und Kabbala," 105–106. I was unable to obtain the volume by Michal Oron, *Mi-Ba'al Shed le-Va'al Shem: Shemu'el Falk, ha-Ba'al Shem mi-London* (Jerusalem, 2002).
138. On the phenomenon and the popularity of these kinds of allegedly miracle-working rabbis, see also Grözinger, "Jüdische Wundermänner."
139. Patai, *Jewish Alchemists*, 461.
140. Roth, "King and the Kabbalist," 142.
141. Schuchard, "Lord George Gordon," 207.
142. Ibid., 206.
143. Ruderman, *Jewish Enlightenment*, 164.
144. This opinion e.g. in Schuchard, "Lord George Gordon"; Schuchard, "Dr. Samuel Jacob Falk"; a critical perspective on the political dimension of Falk's activities is offered by Ruderman, *Jewish Enlightenment*, 159–169.
145. See Schuchard, "Lord George Gordon," 209.
146. Patai, *Jewish Alchemists*, 462; Schuchard, "Lord George Gordon," 205.
147. On this episode, see esp. Roth, "King and the Kabbalist," 152–156.
148. On his life, see esp. Schoeps, "Gumpertz Levison"; Graupe, "Mordechai Shnaber-Levison"; Ruderman, *Jewish Thought*, 332–368.
149. Ruderman, *Jewish Thought*, 345–346.
150. Ibid., 350.
151. Graupe, "Mordechai Shnaber-Levison," 19.
152. Ibid.
153. Schuchard, "Dr. Samuel Jacob Falk," 216. It was a work titled *System öfver Alchemien* by the Swede August Nordenskjöld, with whom Levison was also privately acquainted. See Schoeps, "Gumpertz Levison," 153.
154. Ruderman, *Jewish Thought*, 348.
155. Ruderman, *Jewish Enlightenment*, 168.
156. The literature on this subject is vast. I take the term "ideology of openness in science" from Eamon, "From the Secrets of Nature," 333. See also e.g. Long, *Openness, Secrecy, Authorship*, esp. 247; Larry Stewart, *Rise of Public Science*; Rossi, "Bacon's Idea of Science."
157. Eamon, "From the Secrets of Nature," 347.
158. Still fundamental reading on the subject is Katz, *Jews and Freemasons*; for additional literature, see also Anonymous, "Freemasons," in *EJ*, 7:228–230. On the concept of the "neutral" and "semineutral society," see also Katz, *Out of the Ghetto*, ch. 4.

159. Schrader, "Zur sozialen Funktion," 180; on the central importance of the secret for the eighteenth century's secret societies, see also Hardtwig, "Eliteanspruch," esp. 64, 84.
160. Fichte, *Vorlesungen über die Freimaurerei*, 173.
161. Hardtwig, "Eliteanspruch," 74. See also Simonis, *Die Kunst des Geheimen*, esp. 26–27.
162. Biester, "Antwort an Herrn Professor Garve," 81.
163. See also Schuchard, "Lord George Gordon," esp. 189; Ruderman, *Jewish Enlightenment*, 151.
164. Quoted in Glasenapp and Horch, *Ghettoliteratur*, I/1:179. In light of such statements, one is less inclined to share Katz's skepticism regarding the importance of Freemasonry for Jews—a research field he himself had founded. See Katz, *Out of the Ghetto*, 44–47.
165. Westerbarkey, *Das Geheimnis*, 152. On the history of the supposed cooperation and alliance between these two groups, see above all Katz, *Jews and Freemasons*, esp. chs. 10–12 and 15.
166. Ruderman, *Jewish Thought*, 13. See also Volkov, "Soziale Ursachen."
167. Ruderman, *Jewish Thought*, 341.
168. Ibid.
169. Hölscher, *Öffentlichkeit und Geheimnis*, 44.
170. See Shapin, "Science and the Public," 996; see also Golinski, "A Noble Spectacle," esp. 30, and Galison, "Buildings and the Subject of Science," 5.
171. Principe, "Robert Boyle's Alchemical Secrecy."
172. Shapin, *A Social History of Truth*, 105–106.
173. Habermas, *Structural Transformation*, 34–36.
174. Voigts, *Das geheimnisvolle Verschwinden des Geheimnisses*, 29.
175. Kant, "What Is Enlightenment," in *Basic Writings*, 136–137 (emphasis in original).
176. See also Simonis, *Kunst des Geheimen*, 13.
177. Gestrich, *Absolutismus und Öffentlichkeit*, 36; See also Hölscher, *Öffentlichkeit und Geheimnis*, e.g. 154; also Groethuysen, *Origines de l'esprit bourgeois*, 1:116, 190.
178. Niklas Luhmann, "Geheimnis, Zeit und Ewigkeit," 118.
179. See the classic study by Thomas, *Religion and the Decline of Magic*.
180. Simmel, "Das Geheimnis," 413. Translation slightly modified.
181. Ibid. Also relevant, if historically somewhat simplistic, is Habermas, *Structural Transformation*.
182. Reichert, "Neue Formen," esp. 17. See also Hölscher, *Öffentlichkeit und Geheimnis*, 170; Bok, *Secrets*, 305; Voigts, *Das geheimnisvolle Verschwinden*.

183. See also Max Weber's observations on the function of the official secret in bureaucratic contexts: Weber, *Wirtschaft und Gesellschaft*, 572–573, 855.
184. Bellman, *Language of Secrecy*, 4.
185. Trilling, *Sincerity and Authenticity*.
186. *Meyers Neues Konversationslexikon für alle Stände* (1848), quoted in Hölscher, *Öffentlichkeit und Geheimnis*, 128.
187. Halbertal, *Concealment and Revelation*, 140.
188. Ibid., 140–141. Manfred Voigts likewise assumes that as early as "during the Enlightenment, the secret had to have its sting removed in Judaism too." As examples he cites Moses Mendelssohn and Salomon Maimon. See Voigts, *Das geheimnisvolle Verschwinden*, 63.
189. Dammann alone presents more than sixty prominent careers (starting in the late eighteenth century). Dammann, *Die Juden in der Zauberkunst*. Buchberger even speaks of a "preeminence of Jews in magic." See Buchberger, "Jüdische Taschenspieler," 174. For the context, see also Otte, *Jewish Identities*.
190. Cues can be taken from During, *Modern Enchantments;* as well as Meyer and Pels, *Magic and Modernity*.
191. Luhrmann, "Magic of Secrecy," esp. 161. See also, from a sociological perspective, Schirrmeister, *Geheimnisse*, 49.
192. Malcolm, "Private and Public Knowledge," esp. 305.
193. Bellman, *Language of Secrecy;* Davids, "Openness or Secrecy?"; Long, *Openness, Secrecy, Authorship*, esp. 245.
194. Long and Roland, "Military Secrecy."
195. See also Long, *Openness, Secrecy, Authorship*, 7.
196. Ruderman, *Jewish Thought*, 118–152, esp. 129, 146.
197. Ibid., 155.
198. Delmedigo, *Sefer Matzref la-Ḥokhma*.
199. Ibid., ch. 7.
200. See Barzilay, *Yoseph Shlomo Delmedigo*, 98, 135, 139, 258.
201. Delmedigo, *Sefer Matzref la-Ḥokhma*, ch. 7:49.
202. Barzilay, *Yoseph Shlomo Delmedigo*, 139.
203. This according to a letter written by Delmedigo that was also included in the work *Ta'alumot Chochma*. See the original Hebrew passage quoted in Barzilay, *Yoseph Shlomo Delmedigo*, 116.
204. For Foucault's investigations into the entanglement of knowledge and power during the formation of the modern state, see esp. Foucault, *Security, Territory, Population*.
205. Colorni, *Scotographia*, fol. 8r.

Bibliography

Abbreviations

ADB	*Allgemeine Deutsche Biographie.* 56 vols. Leipzig: Duncker & Humblot, 1875-1912.
DBI	*Dizionario biografico degli italiani.* Rome: Istituto della Enciclopedia italiana, 1960–.
EJ	*Encyclopaedia Judaica.* 2nd ed. 22 vols. Detroit: Macmillan, 2007.
GJ	*Germania Judaica.* 3 vols. Tübingen: Mohr, 1963-2003.
Gonzaga/ [Place name]	*Le collezioni Gonzaga.* 11 vols. Milan: Silvana, 2000-2006 (see the bibliography for individual volumes, s.v. *Il carteggio*).
HdA	*Handwörterbuch des deutschen Aberglaubens.* 3rd ed. 10 vols. Berlin: De Gruyter, 2000.
J-1874	Giuseppe Jarè, *Abramo Colorni: Ingegnero mantovano del secolo XVI: Cenni con documenti inediti.* Mantua: Balbiani, 1874.
J-1891	Giuseppe Jarè, *Abramo Colorni. Ingegnere di Alfonso d'Este: Nuove ricerche.* Ferrara: Premiate Tipografia Sociale, 1891.
LexAlch	Claus Priesner and Karin Figala, eds. *Alchemie: Lexikon einer hermetischen Wissenschaft.* Munich: C. H. Beck, 1998.
LexMA	*Lexikon des Mittelalters.* 10 vols. Munich: Artemis, 1977-1999.
MGWJ	*Monatsschrift für Geschichte und Wissenschaft des Judentums.*
NDB	*Neue Deutsche Biographie.* Berlin: Duncker & Humblot, 1953–.
RAC	*Reallexikon für Antike und Christentum.* Stuttgart: Hiersemann, 1950–.
Regesten I (Andernacht)	Dietrich Andernacht, ed. *Regesten zur Geschichte der Juden in der Reichsstadt Frankfurt am Main von 1401-1519.* 4 vols. Hanover: Hahn, 1996-2006.
Regesten II (Andernacht)	Dietrich Andernacht, *Regesten zur Geschichte der Juden in der Reichsstadt Frankfurt am Main von 1520-1616,* 2 vols. Hanover: Hahn, 2007.
VerfLex	*Die deutsche Literatur des Mittelalters: Verfasserlexikon.* 14 vols. Berlin: De Gruyter, 1978-2008.

Manuscript Sources

Ferrara, Archivio di Stato (ASFe)

Archivio Notarile Antico, Notaio Antonio Colorni, matr. 715, p. 39s (schede 1585)

Florenz, Archivio di Stato (ASF)

Mediceo del Principato, 580
Pratica segreta, filza 73; 189
Auditore delle riformagioni, filza 18

London, British Library (BL)

Add. 10862
Harley 3981
King's 288
Sloane 3091

Mantua, Archivio di Stato (ASMn)

Archivio Gonzaga (AG):
b. 423; 424; 425; 464; 467; 469; 475; 517; 1520; 1527; 2680
Liber dei decreti, vol. 56
Archivio notarile (AN):
b. 1250 bis
Indici della registrazione notarile, a. 1570–1600
Registrazioni notarili, a. 1577

Mantua, Archivio israelitico (AIM)

Filza 9

Modena, Archivio di Stato (ASMo)

Archivio segreto estense (ASE):
Astronomia, Astrologia, Magia, b. 3; 4; 5; 6
Carteggio principi esteri, Württemberg, b. 1604/30
Ebrei, b. 23b
Ingegneri, b. 2
Invenzioni, progetti, scoperte, b. 1

Munich, Bayerisches Hauptstaatsarchiv (BayHStA)

Generalregistratur Fasz. 1204, no. 130

Rome, Archivio di Stato (ASR)

Collezione dei bandi, vol. 7 (1588–1590)

Stuttgart, Hauptstaatsarchiv (HStAS)

A 47 Bü 3, Fasz. 11; 12
A 56 Bü 10, Fasz. 11; 12
A 56 U 15

Venice, Archivio di Stato (ASV)

Ufficiali al Cattaver, b. 243
Senato Terra, filza 119; 315, 373; 673

Venice, Biblioteca Nazionale Marciana

It., III. 10 (MS 5003) (Anon., [Libro di] Segreti d'arti diverse)

Vienna, Haus-, Hof-, und Staatsarchiv (HHStA)

Familienarchiv, Lang-Akten, Kartons 1–8
Familienarchiv, Karton 99; 103
Familienkorrespondenz, Schachtel 4 (Rudolf II)
Reichshofrat, Gratialia und Feudalia, Privilegia varii generis
Staatenabteilung, Italien, Kleine Staaten, Fasz. 10 (Ferrara)
Staatenabteilung, Italien, Venedig, Dispacci di Germania, vol. 19 (1592)

Vienna, Österreichisches Staatsarchiv (ÖStA)

Gedenkbücher, Böhmische Reihe, vol. 324
Gedenkbücher, Österreichische Reihe, vol. 156
Gedenkbücher, Österreichische und böhmische Reihe, Indices, a. 1587–1597
Hofkammerarchiv (HKA):
Hoffinanz Österreich (HFÖ), Rote Nr. 64; 65
Hoffinanzprotokolle, vols. 467-E; 469-R; 475-E; 479-R; 484-E
Hofzahlamtsbücher, vol. 44
Hofzahlamtsbücher, Indices, a. 1587–1597
Verschiedene Vorschläge, nos. 15; 81; 122

Wolfenbüttel, Herzog August Bibliothek (HAB)

Cod.-Guelf. 4.9. Aug. 4°
Nova Chirofisionomia / e censura contra tutte le superstitiose vanità che in tali suggetti sono state da molti trattate, nella quale si mostra et insegna, quello che più veramente et ragionamente per fondamenti cavati dalla / Theologia, Filosofia, e Medicina credere si possa o debba, e tutto chiaramente e utilmente Opera d'Abramo Colorni Hebreo Mantovano.

Cod.-Guelf. 14.8. Aug. 4°
Euthimetria / d'Abramo Colorni Hebreo Mantovano / Ridotta in facilissima pratica, et divisa in sei libri, nel primo s'insegna di misurare giustamente il viaggio fatto in carroccia, et in nave, / Nel secondo / Di misurare terreni assai più facilmente, et con minor travaglio che con le pertiche ò canne, / et nel terzo/ Di misurar con la vista ogni sorte di distantie, Altezze, et profundità con un modo agevole da metter in picciol disegno la pianta d'un paese et di livellare il pendio per condur Acque, nel 4 [sic!] si mostra un piacevolissimo modo da poter misurar con la vista tutte le sopradette misure co'l mezzo d'un specchio, e tutto senza travaglio de numeri ma con nove maniere facilissime, et inventioni de istromenti ritrovati da esso autore.

Printed Primary Sources

Adam, Albert Eugen, ed. *Württembergische Landtagsakten, zweite Reihe.* 3 vols. Stuttgart: Kohlhammer, 1910–1919.

Aescoly, Aaron Zeev, ed. *Sippur David ha-Reuveni.* 2nd ed. Jerusalem: Mossad Bialik, 1993.

Andernacht, Dietrich. *Regesten zur Geschichte der Juden in der Reichsstadt Frankfurt am Main von 1520–1616.* 2 vols. Hanover: Hahn, 2007.

———. *Regesten zur Geschichte der Juden in der Reichsstadt Frankfurt am Main von 1401–1519.* 4 vols. Hanover: Hahn, 1996–2006.

Anonymous. "Itziger Hang zu Geheimnissen." *Berlinische Monatsschrift* (2) 1785: 478–479.

Ariosto, Ludovico. *Il Negromante.* In *Tutte le opere di Ludovico Ariosto,* edited by Cesare Segre, 4:448–542. Verona: Mondadori, 1974.

Bacci, Andrea. *L'alicorno: Discorso dell'eccellente medico, et filosofo M. Andrea Bacci: nel quale si tratta della natura dell'Alicorno, & delle sue virtù Eccellentiβime.* Florence: Marescotti, 1573.

Bacon, Francis. *Works.* Edited by James Spedding, Robert Leslie Ellis, and Douglas Denon Heath. 14 vols. London: Longman, 1861–1879.

Barclay, John. *Euphormionis Lusinini Satyricon.* Edited by David A. Fleming. Nieuwkoop: De Graaf, 1973.

Barocchi, Paola, and Giovanna Gaeta Bertelà, eds. *Collezionismo mediceo—Cosimo I, Francesco I e il Cardinale Ferdinando: Documenti, 1540-1587.* Modena: Panini, 1993.

Bauer, Rotraud, and Herbert Haupt, eds. *Das Kunstkammerinventar Kaiser Rudolfs II., 1607-1611.* In *Jahrbuch der Kunsthistorischen Sammlungen in Wien* 72 (1976).

Biester, Johann Erich. "Antwort an Herrn Professor Garve, über vorstehenden Aufsatz." *Berlinische Monatsschrift* 2 (1785): 68-90.

Birelli, Giambattista. *Alchimia Nova: Das ist die güldene Kunst oder aller Künsten Gebärerin . . . Von allerley alchimistischen unnd metallischen Geschäfften, Wässern unnd Oelen. . . .* Frankfurt am Main: Hoffman, 1603.

Boksenboim, Yacov, ed. *Iggerot Beit Carmi, Cremona 1570-1577.* Tel Aviv: Tel Aviv University, 1983.

———, ed. *Pinkas Kahal Verona.* 3 vols. Tel Aviv: Tel Aviv University, 1989-1990.

Bondy, Gottlieb, and Franz Dworsky, eds. *Zur Geschichte der Juden in Böhmen, Mähren und Schlesien von 906 bis 1620.* 2 vols. Prague: Bondy, 1906.

Borsetti Ferranti Bolani, Ferrante. *Historia almi Ferrariae gymnasii.* 2 vols. Ferrara: Pomatelli, 1735.

Brant, Sebastian. *Das Narrenschiff.* Edited by Adam Walther Strobel. Quedlinburg: Basse, 1839.

Calendar of State Papers and Manuscripts Relating to English Affairs, Existing in the Archives and Collections of Venice, and in Other Libraries of Northern Italy. 38 vols. London: Longman, 1864-1947.

Calendar of State Papers Foreign. 28 vols. London: Longman, 1861-1950.

Cappel, Louis. *Arcanum punctationis revelatum, sive De punctorum vocalium & accentuum apud Hebræos vera & germana antiquitate diatriba.* Leiden: Maire, 1624.

Cardano, Girolamo. *De secretis.* In *Opera omnia*, 2:537-551.

———. *De venenis libri tres.* In *Opera omnia*, 7:275-355.

———. *Opera omnia.* Edited by C. Spon. Lyon: Huguetan and Ravaud, 1663. Reprint, Stuttgart–Bad Cannstatt: Frommann, 1966.

———. *Operatione della linea.* In *Opera omnia*, 4:602-620.

Casaubon, Meric. *A true & faithful relation of what passed for many yeers between Dr. John Dee . . . and some spirits tending . . . to a general alteration of most states and kingdomes in the world. . . .* London: Maxwell, 1659.

Certaldo, Paolo da. *Libro di buoni costumi*. Edited by Alfredo Schiaffini. Florence: Le Monnier, 1945.

Colorni, Abramo. *Scotographia overo, scienza di scrivere oscuro, facilissima & sicurissima, per qual si voglia lingua; le cui diverse inventioni divisi in tre libri, serviranno in più modi, & per Cifra & per Contracifra: Le quali, se ben saranno communi a tutti, potranno nondimeno usarsi da ogn'uno, senza pericolo d'essere inteso da altri, che dal proprio corrispondente. . . . Con Privilegio di quasi tutti i Potentati Christiani*. Prague: Sciuman, 1593.

Crusius, Martin. *Diarium Martini Crusii*. Edited by Wilhelm Göz and Ernst Conrad. 2 vols. Tübingen: Laupp, 1927–1931.

D'Argens, Jean-Baptiste de Boyer. *The Jewish spy: Being a philosophical, historical and critical correspondence by letters which lately pass'd between certain Jews in Turkey, Italy, France*. 5 vols. London: Browne & Hett, 1739–1740.

Dačický z Heslova, Mikuláš. *Paměti*. Edited by Ant. Rezek. 2 vols. Prague: Nákladem Matice České, 1878–1880.

Dante Alighieri. *The Divine Comedy*. Translated by Allen Mandelbaum. London: Campbell, 1995.

de Pomis, David. *Tzemaḥ David: Dittionario novo hebraico molto copioso, decciarato in tre lingue: Con bellissime annotationi, e con l'indice latine, e volgare, de tutti li suoi significati*. Venice: Gara, 1587.

Dee, John. *The Diaries of John Dee*. Edited by Edward Fenton. Oxfordshire: Day Books, 1998.

Del Rio, Martin. *Disquisitionum magicarum libri sex, quibus continetur accurata curiosarum artium et vanarum superstitionum confutation, utilis theologis, iurisconsultus, medicis, philologis*. Lyon: Pillehotte, 1612.

Della Porta, Giovan Battista. *De furtivis literarum notis: vulgo de ziferis libri IIII*. London: Wolphius, 1591.

———. *De hum. physiognomonia* [sic]. Vico Equense: Cacchius, 1576.

———. *Della Chirofisonomia, overo, di quella parte della humana fisonomia che si appartiene alla mano, libri due*. Naples: Bulifon, 1677.

———. *Magiae naturalis libri XX*. Naples: Salvianus, 1589.

———. *Magiae naturalis sive de miraculis rerum naturalium libri IIII*. Naples: Cancer, 1558.

Della Rocca, Bartolomeo [Cocles, pseud.]. *Barptolomaei [sic] Coclitis Bononiensis naturalis philosophiae ac medicinae doctoris physiognomiae & chiromantiae compendium*. Strasbourg: Machaeropeus, 1555.

———. *Bartholomei Coclitis Chyromantie ac physionomie Anastasis*. Bologna: De Benedictis 1517.

Delmedigo, Joseph Salomon. *Sefer Matzref la-Ḥokhma*. Jerusalem, [1980?].

Descartes, René. *The Philosophical Writings*. Translated by John Cottingham et al. 3 vols. Cambridge: Cambridge University Press, 1984-1991.

Di Gabrielli, Maggino. *Dialoghi di M. Magino Gabrielli hebreo venetiano sopra l'utili sue inventioni circa la seta: Ne' quali anche si dimostrano in vaghe Figure Historiati tutti gl'essercitij, & instrumenti, che nell'Arte della Seta si ricercano*. Rome: Gigliotti, 1588.

Diederichs Ulf, ed. *Das Ma'assebuch, seine Entstehung und Quellengeschichte*. Munich: DTV, 2003.

Fabri, Felix. *Fratris Felicis Fabri Evagatorium in Terrae Sanctae, Arabiae et Egypti peregrinationem*. Edited by Konrad Dietrich Hassler. 3 vols. Stuttgart: Literarischer Verein, 1843-1849.

Fichte, Johann Gottlieb. *Vorlesungen über die Freimaurerei*. In *Ausgewählte politische Schriften*, edited by Zwi Batscha and Richard Saage, 169-216. Frankfurt am Main: Suhrkamp, 1977. Translated in Roscoe Pound, *Masonic Addresses and Writing of Roscoe Pound* (New York: Macoy, 1953).

Firpo, Luigi, ed. *Relazioni di ambasciatori veneti al Senato*. 14 vols. Turin: Bottega d'Erasmo, 1965.

Franceschini, Adriano. *Presenza ebraica a Ferrara: Testimonianze archivistiche fino al 1492*. Florence: Olschki, 2007.

Fugger, Hans. *Die Korrespondenz Hans Fuggers von 1566 bis 1594: Regesten der Kopierbücher aus dem Fuggerarchiv*. Edited by Christl Karnehm. 3 vols. Munich: Kommission für Bayerische Landesgeschichte, 2003.

Gaddi, Jacopo. *Adlocutiones et Elogia Exemplaria, Cabalistica, Oratoria, Mixta, Sepulcralia*. Florence: Nestei, 1636.

Galilei, Galileo. *Le Opere di Galileo Galilei*. Edited by Eugenio Albèri. 15 vols. Florence: Società Editrice Fiorentina, 1842-1856.

Gans, David. *Tzemaḥ David*. Edited by Mordechai Breuer. Jerusalem: Magnes, 1983.

Garzoni, Tomaso. *Il serraglio de gli stupori del mondo*. Edited by Paolo Cherchi. Russi: Vaca, 2004.

———. *Il teatro de' vari e diversi cervelli mondani*. Venice: Zanfretti, 1583.

———. *Il teatro de' vari e diversi cervelli mondani*. Venice: Zoppini, 1598.

———. *La piazza universale di tutte le professioni del mondo*. Edited by Giovanni Battista Bronzini. 2 vols. Florence: Olschki, 1996.

———. *La sinagoga de gl'ignoranti*. Venice: Somasco, 1589.

Glückel von Hameln. *Die Memoiren der Glückel von Hameln*. Translated by Bertha Pappenheim. Vienna: Meyer und Pappenheim, 1910.

Goethe, Johann Wolfgang von. *Tagebücher: Historisch-kritische Ausgabe*. Edited by Jochen Golz. Stuttgart: Metzler, 1995-.

———. *Werke: Hamburger Ausgabe.* Edited by Erich Trunz. 14 vols. Munich: C. H. Beck, 1998.
Gollancz, Hermann, ed. *Sepher Maphteah Shelomo: An Exact Facsimile of an Original Book of Magic in Hebrew.* London: Oxford University Press, 1914.
Gracián, Baltasar. *The Art of Worldly Wisdom.* Translated by Joseph Jacobs. London: Macmillan, 1904.
Ha-Cohen, Joseph. *The Vale of Tears.* Translated by Harry S. May. The Hague: Nijhoff, 1971.
Hannemann, Johann Ludwig. *Ovum hermetico-paracelsico-trismegistum.* Frankfurt am Main: Knoch, 1694.
Il carteggio tra Bologna, Parma, Piacenza e Mantova, 1563–1634. Edited by Barbara Furlotti. Vol. 4 of *Le collezioni Gonzaga.* Milan: Silvana, 2000.
Il carteggio tra Firenze e Mantova, 1554–1626. Edited by Roberta Piccinelli. Vol. 3 of *Le collezioni Gonzaga.* Milan: Silvana, 2000.
Il carteggio tra la corte cesarea e Mantova, 1559–1636. Edited by Elena Venturini. Vol. 5 of *Le collezioni Gonzaga.* Milan: Silvana, 2002.
Il carteggio tra Milano e Mantova, 1563–1634. Edited by Roberta Piccinelli. Vol. 6 of *Le collezioni Gonzaga.* Milan: Silvana, 2003.
Il carteggio tra Roma e Mantova, 1587–1612. Edited by Barbara Furlotti. Vol. 9 of *Le collezioni Gonzaga.* Milan: Silvana, 2003.
Il carteggio tra Venezia e Mantova, 1563–1587. Edited by Daniela Sogliani. Vol. 8 of *Le collezioni Gonzaga.* Milan: Silvana, 2003.
Il carteggio tra Venezia e Mantova, 1588–1612. Edited by Michaela Sermidi. Vol. 10 of *Le collezioni Gonzaga.* Milan: Silvana, 2003.
Isacchi, Giovanni Battista. *Inventioni di Gio. Battista Isacchi da Reggio nelle quali si manifestano varij secreti & utili avisi a persone di guerra e per i tempi di piacere.* Parma: Viotto, 1579.
Jābir ibn Hayyān. *Das Buch der Gifte des Ǧābir ibn Hayyān: Arabischer Text in Faksimile (HS. Taymūr, tibb. 393, Kairo).* Translated and edited by Alfred Siggel. Wiesbaden: Steiner, 1958.
Jersch-Wenzel, Stefi, and Reinhard Rürup, eds. *Quellen zur Geschichte der Juden in den Archiven der neuen Bundesländer.* 6 vols. Munich: Saur, 1996–2000.
Joyce, James. *Finnegans Wake.* London: Penguin, 1999.
Kant, Immanuel. *Basic Writings of Immanuel Kant.* Edited by Allan W. Wood. New York: Random House, 2001.
———. *Religion within the Boundaries of Mere Reason and Other Writings.* Translated by Allen W. Wood and George di Giovanni. Cambridge: Cambridge University Press, 1998.

Kepler, Johannes. *Gesammelte Werke*. Munich: C. H. Beck, 1938–.
Keren Happuch, Posaunen Eliae des Künstlers, oder Teutsches Fegfeuer der Scheide-Kunst, Worinnen nebst den Neu-gierigisten und grössesten Geheimnüssen für Augen gestellet. . . . Hamburg: Libernickel, 1702.
Khevenhüller, Hans. *Hans Khevenhüller, kaiserlicher Botschafter bei Philipp II: Geheimes Tagebuch, 1548–1605*. Edited by Georg Khevenhüller-Metsch. Graz: Akademische Druck- und Verlagsanstalt, 1971.
Knorr von Rosenroth, Christian. *Kabbala denudata seu, Doctrina Hebraeorum transcendentalis et metaphysica atque theologica*. 2 vols. Sulzbach: Lichtenthaler, 1677–1684.
L'elenco dei beni del 1626–1627. Edited by Rafaella Morselli. Vol. 2 of *Le collezioni Gonzaga*. Milan: Silvana, 2000.
Landau, Alfred, and Bernhard Wachstein, eds. *Jüdische Privatbriefe aus dem Jahre 1619*. Vienna: Braumüller, 1911.
Lichtenberg, Georg Christoph. *Schriften und Briefe*. Edited by Wolfgang Promies. 4 vols. Frankfurt am Main: Zweitausendeins, 1998.
Limojon de Saint-Didier, Alexandre-Toussaint. *The Hermetical Triumph: Or, The Victorious Philosophical Stone. A Treatise more compleat and more intelligible than any has been yet, concerning The Hermetical Magistery*. London: Hanet, 1723.
List and Analysis of State Papers, Foreign Series: Elizabeth I. 7 vols. London: H. M. Stationery Office, 1964–2000.
Löwenstein, Uta, ed. *Quellen zur Geschichte der Juden im Hessischen Staatsarchiv Marburg, 1267–1600*. 3 vols. Wiesbaden: Kommission für die Geschichte der Juden in Hessen, 1989.
Luther, Martin. *Werke: Kritische Gesamtausgabe: Weimarer Ausgabe*. Weimar: Böhlau, 1883–.
Luzzatto, Simone. *Discorso circa il stato de gl'hebrei: Et in particolar dimoranti nell'inclita città di Venetia*. Venice: Calleoni, 1638. Reprint, Bologna: Forni, 1976.
Maimonides, Moses. *Treatise on Poisons and Their Antidotes*. Edited by Suessman Muntner. Philadelphia: Lippincott, 1966.
Marlowe, Christopher. *The Jew of Malta*. Vol. 4 of *The Complete Works of Christopher Marlowe*, edited by Roma Gill. Oxford: Oxford University Press, 1995.
Menasseh ben Israel. *Esperanza de Israel*. Edited by Santiago Perez Junquera. Madrid: Perez Junquera, 1881.
———. *The Hope of Israel*. Edited by Henry Méchoulan and Gérard Nahon. Oxford: Oxford University Press, 1987.

Mendelssohn, Moses. *Gesammelte Schriften: Jubiläumsausgabe*. 24 vols. Stuttgart-Bad Cannstatt: Frommann, 1971–.

Mersenne, Marin. *Correspondance du P. Marin Mersenne*. Edited by Paul Tannery and Cornélis de Waard. 17 vols. Paris: CNRS, 1933–1988.

Mirami, Rafael. *Compendiosa Introduttione alla prima parte della specularia, cioè della Scienza de gli specchi: Opera nova, nella quale brevemente e con facil modo si discorre in torno agli Specchi e si rende la cagione, di tutti i loro miracolosi effetti: Composta da Rafael Mirami Hebreo Fisico, e Matematico*. Ferrara: Heirs of Rossi & Tortorino, 1582.

Modena, Leon. *The Autobiography of a Seventeenth-Century Venetian Rabbi: Leon Modena's Life of Judah*. Edited and translated by Mark R. Cohen. Princeton: Princeton University Press, 1988.

———. *The History of the Rites, Customes, and Manner of Life, of the Present Jews throughout the World*. Translated by Edmund Chilmead. London: J.L., 1650.

———. *Leo Modenas Briefe und Schriftstücke: Ein Beitrag zur Geschichte der Juden in Italien und zur Geschichte des hebräischen Privatstiles*. Edited by Ludwig Blau. Strasbourg: Trübner, 1907.

Nicolay, Nicolas de. *Le navigationi et viaggi fatti nella Turchia di Nicolo de Nicolai . . . Cameriere, & Geografo ordinario del Re di Francia*. Venice: Ziletti, 1580.

Nuntiaturberichte aus Deutschland nebst ergänzenden Aktenstücken, 1585 (1584)–1590. 2 vols. Paderborn: Schöningh, 1895–1919.

Pace, Bernardino Comite de, ed. *Divi Rudolphi imperatoris, Caesaris Augusti epistolae ineditae desumptae ex codice manu exarato caesaeo classis jur. civ. LXXVII*. Vienna: Kurzböck, 1771.

Pico della Mirandola, Giovanni. *Heptaplus*. Edited by Eugenio Garin. Florence: Vallecchi, 1942.

———. *Oratio de hominis dignitate*. Edited by Gerd von der Gönna. Stuttgart: Reclam, 2009.

Portaleone, Abraham. *De auro dialogi tres: In quibus non solum de Auri in re Medica facultate, verum etiam de specifica eius, & cæterarum rerum forma, ac duplici potestate, qua mixtis in omnibus illa operatur, copiose disputatur*. Venice: Porta, 1584.

———. *Die Heldenschilde*. Translated and edited by Gianfranco Miletto. 2 vols. Frankfurt am Main: Lang, 2002.

Pribram, Alfred F., ed. *Urkunden und Akten zur Geschichte der Juden in Wien*. 2 vols. Vienna: Braumüller, 1918.

Ps.-Roger Bacon. *The mirror of alchimy, composed by the thrice-famous and learned fryer, Roger Bachon, sometimes fellow of Martin Colledge*. . . . London: Olive, 1597.

Pucci, Francesco. *Lettere, documenti e testimonianze*. Edited by Luigi Firpo and Renato Piattoli. 2 vols. Florence: Olschki, 1955-1959.

Puli, Ali [pseud.]. *Centrum Naturae Concentratum: Oder: Ein Tractat von dem wiedergebohrenen Saltz: Insgesamt und eigendlich genandt: Der Weisen Stein*. In *Quadratum alchymisticum: Das ist: Vier auserlesene rare Tractätgen vom Stein der Weisen*. Hamburg: Liebezeit, 1705.

Reyscher, August Ludwig, ed. *Vollständige, historisch und kritische bearbeitete Sammlung der württembergischen Gesetze*. 19 vols. Stuttgart: Cotta, 1828-1851.

Rubió y Lluch, Antonio, ed. *Documents per l'historia de la cultura catalana mig-eval*. 2 vols. Barcelona: Institut d'Estudis Catalans, 1908-1921.

Schott, Caspar. *Optica*. Vol. 1 of *Magia Universalis Naturae Et Artis, Sive Recondita naturalium & artificialium rerum scientia*. . . . Würzburg: Schönwetter, 1658.

Schudt, Johann Jacob. *Jüdische Merckwürdigkeiten . . . Was sich Curieuses und denckwürdiges in den neuern Zeiten bey einigen Jahrhunderten mit denen in alle IV. Theile der Welt sonderlich durch Teutschland zerstreuten Juden zugetragen*. . . . Frankfurt am Main, 1714. Reprint, Berlin: Lamm, 1922, 4 vols.

Segarizzi, Arnaldo, ed. *Relazioni degli ambasciatori veneti al senato*. 2 vols. Bari: Laterza, 1912-1913.

Segre, Renata, ed. *The Jews in Piedmont*. 3 vols. Jerusalem: Israel Academy of Sciences and Humanities, 1986-1990.

Selenus, Gustavus. *Cryptomenytices et cryptographiae libri IX in quibus planißima steganographiae à Johanne Trithemio . . . olim conscripta, enodatio traditur*. Lüneburg: Stern, 1624.

Simonsohn, Shlomo, ed. *The Jews in Sicily*. 9 vols. Leiden: Brill, 1997-2006.

———, ed. *The Jews in the Duchy of Milan*. 4 vols. Jerusalem: Israel Academy of Sciences and Humanities, 1982-1986.

Spampanato, Vincenzo, ed. *Documenti della vita di Giordano Bruno*. Florence: Olschki, 1933.

Spinoza, Baruch de. *Briefwechsel*. Edited by Carl Gebhardt and Manfred Walther. Vol. 6 of *Sämtliche Werke*, edited by Carl Gebhardt. 2nd ed. Hamburg: Meiner, 1977.

Straus, Raphael, ed. *Urkunden und Aktenstücke zur Geschichte der Juden in Regensburg, 1453-1738*. Munich: C. H. Beck, 1960.

Tassoni, Alessandro. *Pensieri e scritti preparatori.* Edited by Pietro Puliatti. Modena: Panini, 1986.
Tricasso, Patricio. *Tricassi Cerasariensis Mantuani enarratio pulcherrima principorum Chyromantiae . . . Eiusdem Tricassi Mantuani opus chyromanticum absolutißimum. . . .* Nuremberg: Montanus & Neuberus, 1560.
Urbani, Rossana, and Guido Nathan Zazzu, eds. *The Jews in Genoa.* 2 vols. Leiden: Brill, 1999.
Valvasor, Johann Weichard. *Die Ehre dess Hertzogthums Crain.* Ljubljana, 1689. Reprint, Munich: Trofenik, 1971.
Veranzio, Fausto. *Machinae novae Fausti Verantii Siceni cum declaratione Latina, Italica, Hispanica, Gallica et Germanica.* Venice, 1595. Reprint, Zagreb: Novi Liber, 1993.
Voltelini, Hans von, ed. "Urkunden und Regesten aus dem k.u.k. Haus-, Hof- und Staatsarchiv in Wien." *Jahrbuch der kunsthistorischen Sammlungen des Allerhöchsten Kaiserhauses* 15 (1894): 49–179.
Wakefield, Robert. *On the Three Languages.* Edited and translated by Gareth Lloyd Jones. Binghamton: SUNY Press, 1989.
Yagel, Abraham. *A Valley of Vision: The Heavenly Journey of Abraham ben Hananiah Yagel.* Edited and translated by David B. Ruderman. Philadelphia: University of Pennsylvania Press, 1990.
Zedler, Johann Heinrich, ed. *Grosses vollständiges Universal-Lexicon aller Wissenschafften und Künste, welche bißhero durch menschlichen Verstand und Witz erfunden und verbessert worden. . . .* 68 vols. Halle: Zedler, 1731–1754.
Zimerman, Heinrich, ed. "Urkunden, Acten und Regesten aus dem Archiv des k. k. Ministeriums des Innern." *Jahrbuch der kunsthistorischen Sammlungen des Allerhöchsten Kaiserhauses* 7 (1888): xv–lxxxiv.

Secondary Sources

Ackermann, Aaron. "Münzmeister Lippold: Ein Beitrag zur Kultur- und Sittengeschichte des Mittelalters." *Jahrbuch der Jüdisch-Literarischen Gesellschaft* 7 (1909): 1–112.
Adelman, Howard E. "Leon Modena: The Autobiography and the Man." In *The Autobiography of a Seventeenth-Century Venetian Rabbi: Leon Modena's Life of Judah,* edited by Mark R. Cohen, 19–49. Princeton: Princeton University Press, 1988.
Adler, Joseph. "Abraham Colorni: An Uncommon Jew in the Italian Renaissance." *Midstream: A Monthly Jewish Review* 32 (1996): 16–18.

Ágoston, Gábor. *Guns for the Sultan: Military Power and the Weapons Industry in the Ottoman Empire.* Cambridge: Cambridge University Press, 2005.

Aikema, Bernard. *Pietro della Vecchia and the Heritage of the Renaissance in Venice.* Florence: Istituto universitario olandese di storia dell'arte, 1990.

Åkerman, Susanna. "Queen Christina's Latin Sefer-ha-Raziel Manuscript." In *Judaeo-Christian Intellectual Culture in the Seventeenth Century: A Celebration of the Library of Narcissus Marsh, 1638–1713,* edited by Allison P. Coudert, Sarah Hutton, Richard H. Popkin, and Gordon M. Weiner, 13–25. Dordrecht: Kluwer Academic, 1999.

Ansani, Antonella. "Giovanni Pico Della Mirandola's Language of Magic." In *L'Hébreu au temps de la Renaissance,* edited by Ilana Zinguer, 89–104. Leiden: Brill, 1992.

Antonelli, Giuseppe. *Indice dei manoscritti della Civica Biblioteca di Ferrara.* Ferrara: Taddei, 1884.

Aprile, Sylvie, and Emmanuelle Retaillaud-Bajac, eds. *Clandestinités urbaines: Les citadins et les territoires du secret, XVIe–XXe.* Rennes: Presses Universitaires de Rennes, 2008.

Aquilecchia, Giovanni. "'In facie prudentis relucet sapientia': Appunti sulla letteratura metoposcopica tra Cinque e Seicento." In *Giovan Battista Della Porta nell'Europa del suo tempo,* edited by Maurizio Torrini, 199–228. Napoli: Guida, 1990.

Arbel, Benjamin. *Trading Nations: Jews and Venetians in the Early Modern Eastern Mediterranean.* Leiden: Brill, 1995.

Aron-Beller, Katherine. *Jews on Trial: The Papal Inquisition in Modena, 1598–1638.* Manchester: Manchester University Press, 2011.

Ash, Eric H. *Power, Knowledge, and Expertise in Elizabethan England.* Baltimore: Johns Hopkins University Press, 2004.

Assmann, Aleida, and Jan Assmann. "Das Geheimnis und die Archäologie der literarischen Kommunikation: Einführende Bemerkungen." In Assmann and Assmann, eds., *Geheimnis und Öffentlichkeit.* 7–16.

———. "Die Erfindung des Geheimnisses durch die Neugier." In Assmann and Assmann, eds., *Geheimnis und Neugierde,* 14–28.

———, eds. *Geheimnis und Neugierde.* Vol. 3 of *Schleier und Schwelle.* Munich: Fink, 1999.

———, eds. *Geheimnis und Offenbarung.* Vol. 2 of *Schleier und Schwelle.* Munich: Fink, 1998.

———, eds. *Geheimnis und Öffentlichkeit.* Vol. 1 of *Schleier und Schwelle.* Munich: Fink 1997.

Baader, Jos. "Zur Criminaljustiz der Nürnberger." *Anzeiger für Kunde der deutschen Vorzeit* 9 (1862): 364–365.

———. "Zur Geschichte der Alchemie oder Goldmacherkunst." *Anzeiger für Kunde der deutschen Vorzeit* 10 (1863): 356–358.

Babinger, Franz. "Ja'qûb-Pascha, ein Leibarzt Mehmed's II: Leben und Schicksale des Maestro Jacopo aus Gaeta." In *Aufsätze und Abhandlungen zur Geschichte Südosteuropas und der Levante*, 2:240–262. Munich: Trofenik, 1966.

Bachmann, Manuel, and Thomas Hofmeier. *Geheimnisse der Alchemie*. Basel: Schwabe, 1999.

Bakhtin, Michail. *Rabelais and His World*. Cambridge, MA: MIT Press, 1968.

Balletti, Andrea. *Gli ebrei e gli Estensi*. Reggio Emilia: Anonima Poligrafica Emiliana, 1930.

Barbierato, Federico. *Nella stanza dei circoli: Clavicula Salomonis e libri di magia a Venezia nei secoli XVII e XVIII*. Milan: Bonnard, 2002.

Baron, Salo Wittmayer. *A Social and Religious History of the Jews*. 2nd ed. 18 vols. Philadelphia: Jewish Publication Society of America, 1952–1983.

Baruchson-Arbib, Shiffra. *La culture livresque des juifs d'Italie à la fin de la Renaissance*. Paris: CNRS, 2001.

Barzilay, Isaac. *Yoseph Shlomo Delmedigo (Yashar of Candia): His Life, Works and Times*. Leiden: Brill, 1974.

Battafarano, Italo Michele. "L'opera di Tomaso Garzoni nella cultura tedesca." In *Tomaso Garzoni: Uno zingaro in convento*, 35–79. Ravenna: Longo, 1990.

———, ed. *Tomaso Garzoni: Polyhistorismus und Interkulturalität in der frühen Neuzeit*. Bern: Lang, 1991.

Battenberg, J. Friedrich. *Die Juden in Deutschland vom 16. bis zum Ende des 18. Jahrhunderts*. Munich: Oldenbourg, 2001.

Bawcutt, N. W. Introduction to *The Jew of Malta,* by Christopher Marlowe, 1–57. Edited by N. W. Bawcutt. Manchester: Manchester University Press, 1978.

Bechtold, A. "Hieronymus Scotus." *Archiv für Medaillen- und Plaketten-Kunde* 4 (1923/1924): 103–118.

Beecher, Donald. "Leone de' Sommi and Jewish Theatre in Renaissance Mantua." *Renaissance and Reformation* 17 (1993): 5–19.

Bellman, Beryl L. *The Language of Secrecy: Symbols and Metaphors in Poro Ritual*. New Brunswick: Rutgers University Press, 1984.

Bellonci, Maria. *Segreti dei Gonzaga*. Florence: Mondadori, 1966.

Ben-Aryeh Debby, Nirit. *Renaissance Florence in the Rhetoric of Two Popular Preachers: Giovanni Dominici, 1356–1419, and Bernardino da Siena, 1380–1444*. Turnhout: Brepols, 2001.

Benjamin, Walter. "Theses on the Philosophy of History." In *Illuminations*, 251–261. Translated by Harry Zohn. New York: Schocken, 1968.
Bennett, Jim. "The Mechanical Arts." In *Early Modern Science*, edited by Katharine Park and Lorraine Daston, 673–695. Vol. 3 of *The Cambridge History of Science*, edited by David C. Lindberg and Ronald L. Numbers. Cambridge: Cambridge University Press, 2006.
Bennett, Jim, and Scott Mandelbrote, eds. *The Garden, the Ark, the Tower, the Temple: Biblical Metaphors of Knowledge in Early Modern Europe*. Oxford: Museum of the History of Science, 1998.
Bentini, Jadranka, ed. *Gli Este a Ferrara: Una corte nel Rinascimento*. Milan: Silvana, 2004.
Bentini, Jadranka, and Luigi Spezzaferro, eds. *L'impresa di Alfonso II: Saggi e documenti sulla produzione artistica a Ferrara nel secondo Cinquecento*. Bologna: Nuova Alfa, 1987.
Berg, Maxine. "The Genesis of 'Useful Knowledge.'" *History of Science* 45 (2007): 123–133.
Bernardoni, Andrea. "Le artiglierie come oggetto di riflessione scientifica degli ingegneri del Rinascimento." *Quaderni storici* 130 (2009): 35–65.
Bertolotti, Antonio. *Architetti, ingegneri e matematici in relazione coi Gonzaga signori di Mantova nei secoli XV, XVI e XVII*. Genoa: Tipografia del R. Istituto Sordo-Muti, 1885. Reprint, Bologna: Forni, 1971.
———. *Artisti in relazione coi Gonzaga duchi di Mantova nei secoli XVI e XVII*. Modena: Vincenzi, 1885.
———. *Figuli, fonditori e scultori in relazione con la corte di Mantova nei secoli XV, XVI, XVII*. Milan: Prato, 1890. Reprint, Bologna: Forni, 1977.
Berveglieri, Roberto. *Inventori stranieri a Venezia, 1474–1788: Importazione di tecnologia e circolazione di tecnici, artigiani, inventori*. Venice: Istituto veneto di scienze, lettere ed arti, 1995.
Bhabha, Homi K. *The Location of Culture*. London: Routledge, 2000.
Biagioli, Mario. "From Prints to Patents: Living on Instruments in Early Modern Europe." *History of Science* 44 (2006): 139–186.
———. *Galileo, Courtier: The Practice of Science in the Culture of Absolutism*. Chicago: University of Chicago Press, 1993.
———. "Patent Republic: Representing Inventions, Constructing Rights and Authors." *Social Research* 73 (2006): 1129–1172.
———. "The Social Status of Italian Mathematicians, 1450–1600." *History of Science* 27 (1989): 41–95.
Biale, David. *Power and Powerlessness in Jewish History*. New York: Schocken Books, 1986.

Bibliotheca Manzoniana: Catalogue de la bibliothèque de feu M. le comte Jacques Manzoni. Città di Castello: Lapi, 1892.

Biondi, Albano. "Gli ebrei e l'inquisizione negli stati estensi." In *L'inquisizione e gli ebrei in Italia,* edited by Michele Luzzati, 265–285. Rome: Laterza, 1994.

Biral, Alessandro, and Paolo Morachiello, eds. *Immagini dell'ingegnere tra Quattro e Settecento: Filosofo, Soldato, Politecnico.* Milan: Angeli, 1985.

Birnbaum, Nathan, and Ernst Heppner. *Juden als Erfinder und Entdecker.* Berlin: Welt-Verlag, 1913.

Bishop, John. Introduction to *Finnegans Wake,* by James Joyce, vii–xxv. London: Penguin, 1999.

Black, Crofton. *Pico's Heptaplus and Biblical Hermeneutics.* Leiden: Brill, 2006.

Blau, Ludwig. *Das altjüdische Zauberwesen.* 2nd ed. Berlin: Lamm, 1914.

Blinn, Dieter. "'Man will ja nichts als Ihnen zu dienen, und das bisgen Ehre'— Die Hofjuden Herz und Saul Wahl im Fürstentum Pfalz-Zweibrücken." In *Hofjuden—Ökonomie und Interkulturalität: Die jüdische Wirtschaftselite im 18. Jahrhundert,* edited by Rotraud Ries and J. Friedrich Battenberg, 307–331. Hamburg: Christians Verlag, 2002.

Blumenberg, Hans. *Der Prozeß der theoretischen Neugierde.* Frankfurt am Main: Suhrkamp, 1973.

Bodo, Simona, and Caterina Tonini, eds. *Archivi per il collezionismo dei Gonzaga di Novellara.* Modena: Panini, 1997.

Bok, Sissela. *Secrets: On the Ethics of Concealment and Revelation.* New York: Vintage, 1989.

Bolton, Henry Carrington. *The Follies of Science at the Court of Rudolph II, 1576–1612.* Milwaukee: Pharmaceutical Review Publishing, 1904.

Bonavilla, Aquilino, and Marco Aurelio Marchi. *Dizionario etimologico di tutti i vocaboli usati nelle scienze, arti e mestieri che traggono origine dal greco.* Milan: Pirola, 1819.

Bonetti, Carlo. *Gli ebrei a Cremona, 1278–1630.* Cremona: Forni, 1917.

Bonfil, Robert. "Accademie rabbiniche e presenza ebraica nelle università." In *Dal Rinascimento alle riforme religiose,* edited by Gian Paolo Brizzi and Jacques Verger, 133–151. Vol. 2 of *Le Università dell'Europa.* Milan: Silvana, 1991.

———. *Jewish Life in Renaissance Italy.* Berkeley: University of California Press, 1994.

———. *Rabbis and Jewish Communities in Renaissance Italy.* London: Littman Library of Jewish Civilization, 1993.

Borchardt, Frank L. "The Magus as Renaissance Man." *Sixteenth Century Journal* 21 (1990): 57–76.

Bos, Gerrit. "Hayyim Vital's 'Practical Kabbalah and Alchemy': A 17th-Century Book of Secrets." *Journal of Jewish Thought and Philosophy* 4 (1994): 55–112.

Boström, Hans-Olof. "Philipp Hainhofer: Seine Kunstkammer und seine Kunstschränke." In *Macrocosmos in Microcosmo: Die Welt in der Stube: Zur Geschichte des Sammelns, 1450 bis 1800*, edited by Andreas Grote, 555–580. Opladen: Leske & Budrich, 1994.

Boudet, Jean Patrice, and Julien Véronèse. "Le secret dans la magie rituelle médiévale." *Micrologus: Natura, scienze e società medievali* 14 (2006): 101–150.

Brann, Marcus. *Geschichte der Juden in Schlesien*. Jahres-Berichte des jüdisch-theologischen Seminars Fraenckel'scher Stiftung, 5. Breslau: Schatzky, 1910.

Brann, Noel L. *Trithemius and Magical Theology: A Chapter in the Controversy over Occult Studies in Early Modern Europe*. Albany: SUNY Press, 1999.

Braude, Benjamin. "The Rise and Fall of Salonica Woolens, 1500–1650: Technology Transfer and Western Competition." In *Jews, Christians, and Muslims in the Mediterranean World after 1492*, edited by Alisa Meyuhas Ginio, 216–236. London: Cass, 1992.

Bredekamp, Horst. *Antikensehnsucht und Maschinenglauben: Die Geschichte der Kunstkammer und die Zukunft der Kunstgeschichte*. Berlin: Wagenbach, 1993.

Breger, Herbert. "Mathematik und Religion in der frühen Neuzeit." *Berichte zur Wissenschaftsgeschichte* 18 (1995): 151–160.

Brenner, Michael. *Prophets of the Past: Interpretations of Jewish History*. Translated by Steven Rendall. Princeton: Princeton University Press, 2010.

Breuer, Mordechai. "Die Hofjuden." In *Tradition und Aufklärung, 1600–1780*, edited by Michael A. Meyer and Michael Brenner, 106–125. Vol. 1 of *Deutsch-jüdische Geschichte in der Neuzeit*. Munich: C. H. Beck, 2000.

Brunet, Jean-Paul Brunet. "Le langage du secret: Des mots pour (ne pas) le dire." *Les cahiers de la sécurité intérieure* 30 (1997): 87–101.

Brusatin, Manlio. "La macchina come soggetto d'arte." In *Scienza e tecnica nella culture e nella società dal Rinascimento a oggi*, edited by Gianni Michelin, 31–77. Turin: Einaudi, 1980.

Buchberger, Reinhard. "Jüdische Taschenspieler, kabbalistische Zauberformeln: Jakob Philadelphia und die jüdischen Zauberkünstler im Wien der Aufklärung." In *Rare Künste: Zur Kultur- und Mediengeschichte der Zauberkunst*, edited by Brigitte Felderer and Ernst Strouhal, 151–166. Vienna: Springer, 2007.

———. "Lebl Höschl von Wien und Ofen: Kaufmann, Hofjude und Spion des Kaisers." In *Hofjuden und Landjuden: Jüdische Leben in der Frühen Neuzeit*, edited by Sabine Hödl, Peter Rauscher, and Barbara Staudinger, 217–250. Berlin: Philo, 2004.

———. "Zwischen Kreuz und Halbmond: Jüdische Spione im Zeitalter der Türkenkriege." In *Nicht in einem Bett: Juden und Christen in Mittelalter und Frühneuzeit*. Special issue, *Juden in Mitteleuropa* (2005): 66–71.

Burattelli, Claudia. "Gli ebrei di Mantova e il teatro di corte." In *Spettacoli di corte a Mantova tra Cinque e Seicento*, 141–188. Florence: Le Lettere, 1999.

Burdelez, Ivana. "The Role of Ragusan Jews in the History of the Mediterranean Countries." In *Jews, Christians, and Muslims in the Mediterranean World after 1492*, edited by Alisa Meyuhas Ginio, 190–197. London: Cass, 1992.

Bürger, Wolfgang. "Physikalische Unterhaltungen." *Spektrum der Wissenschaft* 2 (February 2004): 102–103.

Burkardt, Albrecht. "Les secrets de magie et d'alchimie à Florence à la fin du XVIe siècle: Circulation et pratiques d'appropriation à travers une étude de cas." In Aprile and Retaillaud-Bajac, eds., *Clandestinités urbaines*, 35–51.

Burke, Peter. "Early Modern Venice as a Center of Information and Communication." In *Venice Reconsidered: The History and Civilization of an Italian City-State, 1297–1797*, edited by John Martin and Dennis Romano, 389–419. Baltimore: Johns Hopkins University Press, 2000.

———. *A Social History of Knowledge: From Gutenberg to Diderot*. Cambridge: Polity, 2000.

Burton, Dan, and David Grandy, eds. *Magic, Mystery and Science: The Occult in Western Civilization*. Bloomington: Indiana University Press, 2004.

Busi, Giulio. "Il laboratorio cabbalistico mantovano." In *L'enigma dell'ebraico nel Rinascimento*, 99–128. Turin: Aragno, 2007.

———. "Il succo dei favi: Influssi italiani nella letteratura ebraica del Rinascimento." In *L'enigma dell'ebraico nel Rinascimento*, 47–56. Turin: Aragno, 2007.

———. "The Seismic History of Italy in the Hebrew Sources." *Annali di Geofisica* 38 (1995): 473–478.

Cahnman, Werner J. "Role and Significance of the Jewish Artisan Class" In *A History of Jewish Crafts and Guilds*, by Mark Wischnitzer, xiii–xxvii. New York: David, 1965.

Calabi, Donatella, Ugo Camerino, and Ennio Concina. *La città degli ebrei: Il Ghetto di Venezia, architettura e urbanistica*. Venice: Albrizzi, 1996.

Calhoun, Craig. "Robert K. Merton Remembered." *Footnotes: Newsletter of the American Sociological Association* 31, no. 3 (2003). http://www.asanet.org/footnotes/mar03/indextwo.html.

Campanini, Saverio. "A Neglected Source Concerning Asher Lemmlein and Paride da Ceresara: Agostino Giustiniani." *European Journal of Jewish Studies* 2 (2008): 89–110.

Camporesi, Piero. *Camminare il mondo: Vita e avventure di Leonardo Fioravanti, medico del Cinquecento*. Milan: Garzanti, 1997.

———. *Il pane selvaggio*. 2nd ed. Bologna: Il mulino, 1983.

Campori, Giuseppe. *Gli architetti e gl'ingegneri civili e militari degli Estensi dal secolo XIII al XVI*. Modena: Vincenzi, 1882.

Cantor, Geoffrey. *Quakers, Jews, and Science: Religious Responses to Modernity and the Sciences in Britain, 1650–1900*. Oxford: Oxford University Press, 2005.

Carlebach, Elisheva. "Attribution of Secrecy and Perceptions of Jewry." *Jewish Social Studies* 3 (1996): 115–136.

Carpeggiani, Paolo. "Ingegneri a Mantova tra XVI et XVII secolo." In *Giambattista Aleotti e gli ingegneri del Rinascimento,* edited by Alessandra Fiocca, 269–292. Florence: Olschki, 1998.

Carter, Charles Howard. *The Secret Diplomacy of the Habsburgs, 1598–1625*. New York: Columbia University Press, 1964.

Cassuto, Umberto. *Gli ebrei a Firenze nell'età del Rinascimento*. Florence: Galletti & Cocci, 1918.

Cattini, Marco, and Marzio Romani. "Le corti parallele: Per una tipologia delle corti padane dal XIII als XVI secolo." In *La corte e lo spazio: Ferrara estense,* edited by Giuseppe Papagno and Amedeo Quondam, 47–82. Rome: Bulzoni, 1982.

Ceccarelli, Francesco. *La città di Alcina: Architettura e politica alle foci del Po nel tardo Cinquecento*. Bologna: Il mulino, 1998.

Cherchi, Paolo. *Enciclopedismo e politica della riscrittura: Tommaso Garzoni*. Pisa: Pacini, 1980.

Chledowski, Casimir von. *Der Hof von Ferrara*. Translated by Rosa Schapire. Munich: Müller, 1919.

Cipolla, Carlo M. "The Diffusion of Innovations in Early Modern Europe." *Comparative Studies in Society and History* 14 (1972): 46–52.

Clarke, Angus G. "Metoposcopy: An Art to Find the Mind's Construction in the Forehead." In *Astrology, Science and Society: Historical Essays,* edited by Patrick Curry, 171–195. Woodbridge: Suffolk, 1987.

Cohen, Jeremy, and Richard I. Cohen, eds. *The Jewish Contribution to Civilization: Reassessing an Idea*. Oxford: Littman Library of Jewish Civilization, 2008.

Cohen, Richard I., and Vivian B. Mann. "Melding Worlds: Court Jews and the Arts of the Baroque." In *From Court Jews to the Rothschilds: Art, Patronage, and Power, 1600–1800,* 97–123. Munich: Prestel, 1996.

Colombero, Carlo. "Abramo Colorni." In *Dizionario biografico degli Italiani*, 27:466–468. Rome: Istituto della Enciclopedia italiana, 1982.

Colorni, Vittore. "Cognomi ebraici italiani a base toponomastica straniera." In *Judaica Minora: Saggi sulla storia dell'ebraismo italiano dall'antichità all'età moderna: Nuove Ricerche*, 65–83. Milan: Giuffrè, 1991.

———. "Genealogia della famiglia Colorni, 1477–1977." In *Judaica Minora: Saggi sulla storia dell'ebraismo italiano dall'antichità all'età moderna*, 637–660. Milan: Giuffrè, 1983.

———. "La corrispondenza fra nomi ebraici e nomi locali nella prassi dell'ebraismo italiano." In *Judaica Minora: Saggi sulla storia dell'ebraismo italiano dall'antichità all'età moderna*, 681–826. Milan: Giuffrè, 1983.

———. "Spigolature su Obadià Sforno: La sua laurea a Ferrara e la quasi ignota edizione della sua opera 'Or 'amim' nella versione latina." In *Judaica Minora: Saggi sulla storia dell'ebraismo italiano dall'antichità all'età moderna*, 461–472. Milan: Giuffrè, 1983.

———. "Sull'ammissibilità degli ebrei alla laurea anteriormente al secolo XIX." In *Judaica Minora: Saggi sulla storia dell'ebraismo italiano dall'antichità all'età moderna*, 473–489. Milan: Giuffrè, 1983.

Cook, Harold J. *Matters of Exchange: Commerce, Medicine, and Science in the Dutch Golden Age*. New Haven: Yale University Press, 2007.

Cooperman, Bernard Dov. "Trade and Settlement: The Establishment and Early Development of the Jewish Communities in Leghorn and Pisa, 1591–1626." Ph.D. diss., Harvard University, 1976.

Corradini, Elena. "Le raccolte estensi di antichità: Primi contributi documentari." In *L'impresa di Alfonso II: Saggi e documenti sulla produzione artistica a Ferrara nel secondo Cinquecento*, edited by Jadranka Bentini and Luigi Spezzaferro, 163–192. Bologna: Nuova Alfa, 1987.

Corrigan, Beatrice. *Two Renaissance Plays: Il Negromante and Sofonisba*. Manchester: Manchester University Press, 1975.

Coudert, Allison P. "Kabbalistic Messianism versus Kabbalistic Enlightenment." In *Jewish Messianism in the Early Modern World*, edited by Matt D. Goldish and Richard H. Popkin, 107–124. Dordrecht: Kluwer Academic, 2001.

Couto, Dejanirah. "Spying in the Ottoman Empire: Sixteenth-Century Encrypted Correspondence." In *Correspondence and Cultural Exchange in Early Modern Europe, 1400–1700*, edited by Francisco Bethencourt and Florike Egmond, 274–312. Vol. 3 of *Cultural Exchange in Early Modern Europe*, edited by Robert Muchembled and William Monter. Cambridge: Cambridge University Press, 2007.

Cozzi, Gaetano. *Giustizia "contaminata": Vicende giudiziarie di nobili ed ebrei nella Venezia del Seicento.* Venice: Marsilio, 1996.

Cozzi, Luisa. "La formazione culturale e religiosa e la maturazione filosofica e politco-giuridica nei 'Pensieri' di Paolo Sarpi." In *Pensieri naturali, metafisici e matematici*, by Paolo Sarpi, xxv-lxxxviii. Milan: Ricciardi, 1996.

Crispi, Luca, Sam Slote, and Dirk van Hulle. Introduction to *How Joyce Wrote Finnegans Wake: A Chapter-by-Chapter Genetic Guide*, edited by Luca Crispi and Sam Slote, 3-48. Madison: University of Wisconsin Press, 2007.

D'Arco, Carlo. *Delle arti e degli artefici di Mantova: Notizie raccolte ed illustrate con disegni e con documenti.* 2 vols. Mantua: Agazzi, 1857. Reprint, Bologna: Forni, 1975.

D'Esaguy, Augusto. "Commentaires à la vie et à l'œuvre du Dr. Elie Montalto." In *Mélanges d'histoire de la médecine hébraïque: Études choisies de la Revue d'Histoire de la Médecine Hébraïque, 1948-1985*, edited by Gad Freudenthal and Samuel Kottek, 223-235. Leiden: Brill, 2003.

Dammann, Günther. *Die Juden in der Zauberkunst: Jüdische Zauberkünstler: Eine Biographiensammlung.* 2nd ed. Berlin: Günther Dammann, 1933.

Daniel, Noel, ed. *Magic, 1400s-1950s.* Cologne: Taschen, 2009.

Danneberg, Lutz. "Aufrichtigkeit und Verstellung im 17. Jahrhundert: Dissimulatio, simulatio und Lügen als debitum morale und sociale." In *Die Kunst der Aufrichtigkeit im 17. Jahrhundert*, edited by Claudia Benthien and Steffen Martus, 45-92. Tübingen: Niemeyer, 2006.

Daston, Lorraine. "Neugierde als Empfindung und Epistemologie in der frühmodernen Wissenschaft." In *Macrocosmos in Microcosmo: Die Welt in der Stube: Zur Geschichte des Sammelns, 1450 bis 1800*, edited by Andreas Grote, 35-59. Opladen: Leske & Budrich, 1994.

Daston, Lorraine, and Katharine Park. *Wonders and the Order of Nature.* New York: Zone Books, 1998.

Dauphiné, James. "La curiosité poétique pour les sciences et les métiers." In *Crises et essors nouveaux, 1560-1610*, edited by Tibor Klaniczay, Eva Kushner, and Paul Chavy, 427-436. Vol. 4 of *L'Époque de la Renaissance, 1400-1600.* Amsterdam: Benjamins, 2000.

Davids, Karel, ed. "Openness and Secrecy in Early Modern Science." Special issue, *Early Science and Medicine* 10, no. 3 (2005).

———. "Openness or Secrecy? Industrial Espionage in the Dutch Republic." *Journal of European Economic History* 24 (1995): 333-348.

Davis, Joseph. "Ashkenazic Rationalism and Midrashic Natural History: Responses to the New Science in the Works of Rabbi Yom Tov Lipmann Heller, 1578-1654." *Science in Context* 10 (1997): 605-626.

Davis, Natalie Zemon. "Fame and Secrecy: Leon Modena's 'Life' as an Early Modern Autobiography." In *The Autobiography of a Seventeenth-Century Venetian Rabbi: Leon Modena's Life of Judah*. Edited by Mark R. Cohen, 50–70. Princeton: Princeton University Press, 1988.

De Nolhac, Pier, and Angelo Solerti. *Il viaggio di Enrico III in Italia, re di Francia e le feste a Venezia, Mantova e Torino*. Rome: Roux, 1890.

De Rossi, Giovanni Bernardo. *Historisches Wörterbuch der jüdischen Schriftsteller und ihrer Werke*. Bautzen: Reichel, 1839–1846. Reprint, Amsterdam: Philo Press, 1967.

De Vivo, Filippo. *Information and Communication in Venice: Rethinking Early Modern Politics*. Oxford: Oxford University Press, 2007.

De Vries, Kelly. "Sites of Military Science and Technology." In *Early Modern Science*, edited by Katharine Park and Lorraine Daston, 306–319. Vol. 3 of *The Cambridge History of Science*, edited by David C. Lindberg and Ronald L. Numbers. Cambridge: Cambridge University Press, 2006.

Debus, Allen G. *Chemistry, Alchemy and the New Philosophy, 1550–1700: Studies in the History of Science and Medicine*. London: Variorum, 1987.

Delumeau, Jean. *Le mystère Campanella*. Paris: Fayard, 2008.

Di Meo, Antonio, ed. *Cultura ebraica e cultura scientifica in Italia*. Rome: Editori riuniti, 1994.

Dobbs, B. J. T. "From the Secrecy of Alchemy to the Openness of Chemistry." In *Solomon's House Revisited: The Organization and Institutionalization of Science*, edited by Tore Frängsmyr, 75–94. Canton: Science History Publications, 1990.

Dubnow, Simon. *Weltgeschichte des jüdischen Volkes*. 10 vols. Berlin: Jüdischer Verlag, 1925–1929.

Dülmen, Richard van. *Der Geheimbund der Illuminaten: Darstellung, Analyse, Dokumentation*. Stuttgart–Bad Cannstatt: Frommann, 1975.

Dülmen, Richard van, and Sina Rauschenbach, eds. *Macht des Wissens: Die Entstehung der modernen Wissensgesellschaft*. Cologne: Böhlau, 2004.

During, Simon. *Modern Enchantments: The Cultural Power of Secular Magic*. Cambridge, MA: Harvard University Press, 2002.

Eamon, William. "Court, Academy, and Printing House: Patronage and Scientific Careers in Late Renaissance Italy." In *Patronage and Institutions: Science, Technology, and Medicine at the European Court, 1500–1750*, edited by Bruce T. Moran, 25–50. Rochester: Boydell, 1991.

———. "From the Secrets of Nature to Public Knowledge." In *Reappraisals of the Scientific Revolution*, edited by David C. Lindberg and Robert S. Westman, 332–365. Cambridge: Cambridge University Press, 1990.

———. *The Professor of Secrets: Mystery, Medicine, and Alchemy in Renaissance Italy*. Washington, DC: National Geographic, 2010.

———. *Science and the Secrets of Nature: Books of Secrets in Medieval and Early Modern Culture*. Princeton: Princeton University Press, 1994.

———. "The 'Secrets of Nature' and the Moral Economy of Early Modern Science." *Il segreto: Micrologus: Natura, scienze e società medievali* 14 (2006): 215–235.

———. "Technology as Magic in the Late Middle Ages and the Renaissance." *Janus* 70 (1983): 171–212.

Ebeling, Florian. "'Geheimnis' und 'Geheimhaltung' in den Hermetica der Frühen Neuzeit." In *Antike Weisheit und kulturelle Praxis Hermetismus in der Frühen Neuzeit*, edited by Anne-Charlott Trepp and Hartmut Lehmann, 63–80. Göttingen: Vandenhoeck & Ruprecht, 2001.

Ebstein, Erich. "Jacob Philadelphia in seinen Beziehungen zu Goethe, Lichtenberg und Schiller." *Zeitschrift für Bücherfreunde* 3 (1911): 22–28.

Efron, Noah J. "Common Goods: Jewish and Christian Householder Cultures in Early Modern Prague." In *Peace and Negotiation: Strategies for Coexistence in the Middle Ages and the Renaissance*, edited by Diane Wolfthal, 233–255. Turnhout: Brepols, 2000.

———. Introduction to "Judaism and the Sciences," edited by Noah J. Efron and Snait Gissis. Special issue, *Science in Context* 10 (1997): 527–528.

———. "Irenism and Natural Philosophy in Rudolfine Prague: The Case of David Gans." *Science in Context* 10 (1997): 627–649.

———. "'Our forefathers did not tell us': Jews and Natural Philosophy in Rudolfine Prague." *Endeavour* 26 (2002): 15–18.

Eis, Gerhard. "Alchymey teuczsch." *Ostbairische Grenzmarken* 1 (1957): 11–16.

———. "Von der Rede und dem Schweigen der Alchemisten." *Deutsche Vierteljahrsschrift für Literaturwissenschaft und Geistesgeschichte* 25 (1951): 415–435.

Elliott, John H. *Imperial Spain, 1469–1716*. London: Pelican, 1970.

Elwenspoek, Curt. *Jud Süß Oppenheimer: Der große Finanzier und galante Abenteurer des 18. Jahrhunderts*. Stuttgart: Süddeutsches Verlagshaus, 1926.

Emberger, Gudrun, and Robert Kretzschmar, eds. *Die Quellen sprechen lassen: Der Kriminalprozess gegen Joseph Süß Oppenheimer, 1737/1738*. Stuttgart: Kohlhammer, 2009.

Engel, Gisela, Brita Rang, Klaus Reichert, and Heike Wunder, eds. *Das Geheimnis am Beginn der europäischen Moderne*. Frankfurt am Main: Klostermann, 2002.

Evans, Robert J. W. *Rudolf II and His World: A Study in Intellectual History, 1576–1612*. London: Thames and Hudson, 1997.

Fabbrici, Gabriele. "Alcune considerazioni sulle fonti documentarie e sulla storia delle comunità ebraiche di Modena e Carpi, secoli XIV–XVIII." In *Le comunità ebraiche a Modena e a Carpi: Dal medioevo all'età contemporanea*, edited by Franco Bonilauri and Vincenza Maugeri, 51–65. Florence: Giuntina, 1999.

Faider, Paul, and Pierre van Sint Jan. *Catalogue des manuscrits conservés à Tournai (bibliothèque de la ville et du Séminaire)*. Vol. 6 of *Catalogue général des manuscrits des bibliothèques de Belgique*. Gembloux: Duculot, 1950.

Falkenstein, Karl. *Beschreibung der Königlichen Öffentlichen Bibliothek zu Dresden*. Dresden: Walther'sche Hofbuchhandlung, 1839.

Favaro, Antonio. "Dall'Album amicorum di Tommaso Segett." *Atti e memorie della accademia di scienze lettere ed arti in Padova* 6 (1889): 57–62.

Ferguson, John. *Bibliographical Notes on Histories of Inventions and Books of Secrets*. Glasgow: Glasgow University Press, 1883. Reprint, Staten Island: Pober, 1998.

———. *Bibliotheca Chemica: A Catalogue of the Alchemical, Chemical and Pharmaceutical Books in the Collection of the Late James Young of Kelly and Durris*. 2 vols. Glasgow: Maclehose and Sons, 1906.

Ferrari, Daniela. "La cancelleria gonzaghesca tra Cinque e Seicento: Carriere e strategie parentali dei duchi." In *L'esercizio del collezionismo*, edited by Raffaella Morselli, 297–318. Vol. 1 of *Gonzaga: La celeste galleria*. Milan: Skira, 2002.

Ferrer, Daniel. "Wondrous Devices in the Dark." In *How Joyce Wrote Finnegans Wake: A Chapter-by-Chapter Genetic Guide*, edited by Luca Crispi and Sam Slote, 410–435. Madison: University of Wisconsin Press, 2007.

Feuchtwanger, Lion. *Jud Süß*. Vol. 1 of *Gesammelte Werke in Einzelbänden*. Berlin: Aufbau Verlag, 1991.

Feuer, Lewis S. "Francis Bacon and the Jews: Who Was the Jew in the New Atlantis?" *Jewish Historical Studies* 29 (1982–1986): 1–25.

———. "The Scientific Revolution among the Jews." In *The Scientific Intellectual: The Psychological and Sociological Origins of Modern Science*, 297–318. New York: Basic Books, 1963.

Findlen, Paula. "The Formation of a Scientific Community: Natural History in Sixteenth-Century Italy." In *Natural Particulars: Nature and the Disciplines in Renaissance Europe*, edited by Anthony Grafton and Nancy Siraisi, 369–400. Cambridge, MA: MIT Press, 1999.

———. *Possessing Nature: Museums, Collecting, and Scientific Culture in Early Modern Italy.* Berkeley: University of California Press, 1994.
Fleischhauer, Werner. *Renaissance im Herzogtum Württemberg.* Stuttgart: Kohlhammer, 1971.
Foucault, Michel. *The Order of Things: An Archaeology of the Human Sciences.* New York: Pantheon, 1971.
———. *Security, Territory, Population: Lectures at the Collège de France, 1977–78.* Edited by Michel Senellart. Translated by Graham Burchell. New York: Palgrave Macmillan, 2007.
Franceschini, Adriano. "Privilegi dottorali concessi ad ebrei a Ferrara nel sec. XVI." In *Spigolature archivistiche prime,* 163–194. Atti e memorie della deputazione provinciale ferrarese di storia patria 19. Ferrara: SATE, 1975.
Franchini, Dario A., et al. *La scienza a corte: Collezionismo eclettico, natura e immagine a Mantova fra Rinascimento e Manierismo.* Rome: Bulzoni, 1979.
Frati, Carlo, and A. Segarizzi. *Catalogo dei codici Marciani italiani.* 2 vols. Modena: Ferraguti, 1909.
Frattarelli Fischer, Lucia. *Vivere fuori dal Ghetto: Ebrei a Pisa e Livorno, secoli XVI–XVIII.* Turin: Zamorani, 2008.
Freeman, Arthur. "A Source for the 'Jew of Malta.'" *Notes and Queries* 207 (1962): 139–141.
Freudenthal, Gad. Review of *The Jewish Alchemists,* by Raphael Patai. *Isis* 86 (1995): 318–319.
———, ed. "Science and Philosophy in Early Modern Ashkenazic Culture: Rejection, Toleration, and Appropriation." Special issue, *Jahrbuch des Simon-Dubnow-Instituts* 8 (2009).
Friedenwald, Harry. *Jewish Luminaries in Medical History and a Catalogue of Works Bearing on the Subject of the Jews and Medicine from the Private Library of Harry Friedenwald.* Baltimore: Johns Hopkins University Press, 1944.
———. *The Jews and Medicine: Essays.* 2 vols. New York: Ktav Publishing House, 1967.
Fritz, Gerhard. *"Eine Rotte von allerhandt rauberischem Gesindt": Öffentliche Sicherheit in Südwestdeutschland vom Ende des Dreißigjährigen Krieges bis zum Ende des Alten Reiches.* Ostfildern: Thorbecke, 2004.
Frumkin, Maximilian. "Early History of Patents for Invention." *Transactions of the Newcomen Society for the Study of the History of Engineering and Technology* 26 (1947–1949): 47–56.
Fučíková, Eliška, ed. *Prag um 1600: Beiträge zur Kunst und Kultur am Hofe Rudolfs II.* Freren: Luca Verlag, 1988.

———, ed. *Rudolf II and Prague: The Court and the City*. London: Thames and Hudson, 1997.

Funkenstein, Amos. *Perceptions of Jewish History*. Berkeley: University of California Press, 1993.

Furlotti, Barbara. "Ambasciatori, nobili, religiosi, mercanti e artisti: Alcune considerazioni sugli intermediari d'arte gonzagheschi." In *L'esercizio del collezionismo*, edited by Raffaella Morselli, 319–328. Vol. 1 of *Gonzaga: La celeste galleria*. Milan: Skira, 2002.

———. "I Gonzaga e la corte papale: Protagonisti e comparse 'in questo teatro del mondo che così viene chiamato Roma.'" In *Il carteggio tra Roma e Mantova, 1587–1612*, 13–104. Vol. 9 of *Le collezioni Gonzaga*. Milan: Silvana, 2003.

Fürst, Julius. *Bibliotheca Judaica*. 3 vols. Leipzig: Engelmann, 1849–1863. Reprint, Hildesheim: Olms, 1960.

Galison, Peter. "Buildings and the Subject of Science." In *The Architecture of Science*, edited by Peter Galison and Emily Thompson, 1–25. Cambridge, MA: MIT Press, 1999.

Galland, Joseph S. *An Historical and Analytical Bibliography of the Literature of Cryptology*. Evanston: Northwestern University, 1945.

Galluzzi, Paolo. "Il mecenatismo mediceo e le scienze." In *Idee, instituzioni, scienza ed arti nella Firenza dei Medici*, edited by Cesare Vasoli, 189–215. Florence: Giunti-Martello, 1980.

———, ed. *Leonardo da Vinci: Engineer and Architect*. Montreal: Montreal Museum of Fine Arts, 1987.

———. *Renaissance Engineers: From Brunelleschi to Leonardo da Vinci*. Florence: Istituto e Museo di Storia della Scienza, 1996.

Ganzenmüller, Wilhelm. *Beiträge zur Geschichte der Technologie und der Alchemie*. Weinheim: Verlag Chemie, 1956.

García-Arenal, Mercedes, and Gerard Wiegers. *A Man of Three Worlds: Samuel Pallache, a Moroccan Jew in Catholic and Protestant Europe*. Baltimore: Johns Hopkins University Press, 2003.

Garin, Eugenio. "L'umanesimo italiano e la cultura ebraica." In *Gli ebrei in Italia: Dall'alto Medioevo all'età dei ghetto*, edited by Corrado Vivanti, 361–383. Turin: Einaudi, 1996.

Gauger, Hans-Martin. "Geheimnis und Neugier—in der Sprache." In Assmann and Assmann, eds., *Geheimnis und Neugierde*, 14–28.

Geiger, Ludwig. "Jacob Philadelphia and Frederick the Great." *Publications of the American Jewish Historical Society* 16 (1907): 85–94.

Gelber, N. "An umbakanter briv fun Mendl Itskhok fun Kroke tsum keyzer Rudolf II." *Yivo Bleter* 11 (1937): 401–405.

Gentilcore, David. "'Charlatans, Mountebanks and Other Similar People': The Regulation and Role of Itinerant Practitioners in Early Modern Italy." *Social History* 20 (1995): 297–314.

———. *Medical Charlatanism in Early Modern Italy.* Oxford: Oxford University Press, 2006.

Gentile, Sebastiano, and Carlos Gilly. *Marsilio Ficino e il ritorno di Ermete Trismegisto.* Florence: Centro Di, 1999.

Gerber, Barbara. *Jud Süß: Aufstieg und Fall im frühen 18. Jahrhundert: Ein Beitrag zur Historischen Antisemitismus- und Rezeptionsforschung.* Hamburg: Christians Verlag, 1990.

Gestrich, Andreas. *Absolutismus und Öffentlichkeit: Politische Kommunikation in Deutschland zu Beginn des 18. Jahrhunderts.* Göttingen: Vandenhoeck & Ruprecht, 1994.

Gille, Bertrand. *Engineers of the Renaissance.* Cambridge, MA: MIT Press, 1966.

Ginsburger, Moses. "Les juifs et l'art militaire au moyen-âge." *Revue des études juives* 88 (1929): 156–166.

Ginzberg, Louis. *Legends of the Jews.* 2 vols. Philadelphia: Jewish Publication Society, 2003.

Ginzburg, Carlo. "High and Low: The Theme of Forbidden Knowledge in the Sixteenth and Seventeenth Centuries." *Past and Present* 73 (1976): 28–41.

Girolla, Pia. "La biblioteca di Francesco Gonzaga secondo l'inventario del 1407." *Atti e memorie della Reale accademia virgiliana di Mantova* 14–16 (1923): 30–72.

Glanz, Rudolf. *Geschichte des niederen jüdischen Volkes in Deutschland: Eine Studie über historisches Gaunertum, Bettelwesen und Vagantentum.* New York: Waldon, 1968.

Glasenapp, Gabriele von, and Hans Otto Horch. *Ghettoliteratur: Eine Dokumentation zur deutsch-jüdischen Literaturgeschichte des 19. und frühen 20. Jahrhunderts.* 2 vols. Tübingen: Niemeyer, 2005.

Glick, Thomas F. "Moriscos and Marranos as Agents of Technological Diffusion." *History of Technology* 17 (1995): 113–125.

Gliozzi, Mario. "Sulla natura dell' 'Accademia de' Secreti' di Giovan Battista Porta." *Archives internationales d'histoire des sciences* 3 (1950): 536–541.

Goer, Michael. "'Gelt ist also ein kostlich Werth': Monetäre Thematik, kommunikative Funktion und Gestaltungsmittel illustrierter Flugblätter im 30 jährigen Krieg." Ph.D. diss., University of Tübingen, 1981.

Goldberg, Edward L. *Jews and Magic in Medici Florence: The Secret World of Benedetto Blanis.* Toronto: University of Toronto Press, 2011.

Goldschmidt, Daniel. "Bonetto de Latis e i suoi scritti latini e italiani." In *Scritti in memoria di Enzo Sereni: Saggi sull'ebraismo romano*, edited by Daniel Carpi, Attilio Milano, and Umberto Nahon, 88–94. Jerusalem: Mossad Shelomoh Me'ir, 1970.

Golinski, Jan V. "A Noble Spectacle: Phosphorus and the Public Cultures of Science in the Early Royal Society." *Isis* 80 (1989): 11–39.

Göller, Andreas. "Abhängigkeit und Chance—jüdisches Leben im Umfeld des Trierer Stiftsadels: Feivelmann von St. Paulin und die Familie Kratz von Scharfenstein." In *Beziehungsnetze aschkenasischer Juden während des Mittelalters und der frühen Neuzeit*, edited by Jörg R. Müller, 275–288. Hanover: Hahn, 2008.

Gömmel, Rainer. "Hofjuden und Wirtschaft im Merkantilismus." In *Hofjuden—Ökonomie und Interkulturalität: Die jüdische Wirtschaftselite im 18. Jahrhundert*, edited by Rotraud Ries and J. Friedrich Battenberg, 59–65. Hamburg: Christians Verlag, 2002.

Gouk, Penelope. "Natural Philosophy and Natural Magic." In Fučíková, ed., *Rudolf II and Prague*, 231–237.

Grafton, Anthony. *Cardano's Cosmos: The Worlds and Works of a Renaissance Astrologer*. Cambridge, MA: Harvard University Press, 1999.

———. "Der Magus und seine Geschichte(n)." In *Der Magus: Seine Ursprünge und seine Geschichte in verschiedenen Kulturen*, edited by Anthony Grafton and Moshe Idel, 1–26. Berlin: Akademie Verlag, 2001.

———. "Girolamo Cardano oder: der gelehrte Astrologe." In *Zwischen Narretei und Weisheit: Biographische Skizzen und Konturen alter Gelehrsamkeit*, edited by Gerald Hartung and Wolf Peter Klein, 179–191. Hildesheim: Olms, 1997.

———. *Leon Battista Alberti: Baumeister der Renaissance*. Berlin: Berlin Verlag, 2002.

Graupe, Heinz Moshe. "Mordechai Shnaber-Levison: The Life, Works and Thought of a Haskalah Outsider." *Leo Baeck Institute Yearbook* 41 (1996): 3–20.

Greenblatt, Stephen. *Renaissance Self-Fashioning: From More to Shakespeare*. Chicago: University of Chicago Press, 1980.

Gröbl, Lydia, and Herbert Haupt. "Kaiser Rudolf II: Kunst, Kultur und Wissenschaft im Spiegel der Hoffinanz, 1576–1595." *Jahrbuch des Kunsthistorischen Museums Wien* 8/9 (2006/2007): 207–353.

Groethuysen, Bernhard. *Origines de l'esprit bourgeois en France: L'Église et la bourgeoisie*. Paris: Gallimard, 1927.

Grössing, Helmuth, and Franz Stuhlhofer. "Versuch einer Deutung der Rolle der Astrologie in den persönlichen und politischen Entscheidungen einiger

Habsburger des Spätmittelalters." *Anzeiger der Österreichischen Akademie der Wissenschaften, Philosophisch-Historische Klasse* 17 (1980): 267–283.
Grözinger, Karl Erich. "Jüdische Wundermänner in Deutschland." In *Judentum im deutschen Sprachraum,* 190–221. Frankfurt am Main: Suhrkamp, 1991.
Grözinger, Karl Erich, and Joseph Dan, eds. *Mysticism, Magic and Kabbalah in Ashkenazi Judaism.* New York: De Gruyter, 1995.
Grunebaum, Paul. "Les juifs d'Orient d'après les géographes et les voyageurs." *Revue des études juives* 27 (1893): 121–135.
Grunwald, Max. "Aus Hausapotheke und Hexenküche." *Mitteilungen der Gesellschaft für jüdische Volkskunde* 3 (1900): 1–87.
———. "Die Juden als Erfinder und Entdecker." *Ost und West* 9 (1913): 755–756.
———. *Hamburgs deutsche Juden bis zur Auflösung der Dreigemeinden, 1811.* Hamburg: Janssen, 1904.
———. *Juden als Rheder [sic] und Seefahrer.* Berlin: Poppelauer, 1902.
Güdemann, Moritz. *Geschichte des Erziehungswesens und der Cultur der abendländischen Juden während des Mittelalters und der neueren Zeit.* 3 vols. Vienna: Hölder, 1880–1888.
Guerzoni, Guido. "The Administration of the Este Courts in the XV–XVII Century." *Micrologus: Natura, Scienze e Società Medievali* 16 (2008): 537–567.
Guetta, Alessandro. "Religious Life and Jewish Erudition in Pisa: Yehiel Nissim da Pisa and the Crisis of Aristotelism." In Ruderman and Veltri, eds., *Cultural Intermediaries,* 86–108.
Guggenheim, Yacov. "Meeting on the Road: Encounters between German Jews and Christians on the Margins of Society." In *In and Out of the Ghetto: Jewish-Gentile Relations in Late Medieval and Early Modern Germany,* edited by R. Po-chia Hsia and Hartmut Lehmann, 125–136. Cambridge: Cambridge University Press, 1995.
Günzler [sic]. "Herzog Friedrich und seine Hof-Alchymisten." *Würtembergische [sic] Jahrbücher für vaterländische Geschichte, Geographie, Statistik und Topographie* 1 (1829): 216–233.
Gutwirth, Eleazar. "Jews and Courts: An Introduction." *Jewish History* 21 (2007): 1–13.
Haasis, Hellmut G. *Joseph Süß Oppenheimer, genannt Jud Süß: Finanzier, Freidenker, Justizopfer.* Reinbek: Rowohlt, 1998.
Habermas, Jürgen. *The Structural Transformation of the Public Sphere: An Inquiry into a Category of Bourgeois Society.* Translated by Thomas Burger. Cambridge, MA: MIT Press, 1991.
Hahn, Joachim. *Erinnerungen und Zeugnisse jüdischer Geschichte in Baden-Württemberg.* Stuttgart: Theiss, 1988.

Halbertal, Moshe. *Concealment and Revelation: Esotericism in Jewish Thought and Its Philosophical Implications*. Princeton: Princeton University Press, 2007.
Hall, Bert S. *Weapons and Warfare in Renaissance Europe: Gunpowder, Technology, and Tactics*. Baltimore: Johns Hopkins University Press, 1997.
Hankins, Thomas L. "In Defence of Biography: The Use of Biography in the History of Science." *History of Science* 17 (1979): 1–16.
Hardtwig, Wolfgang. "Eliteanspruch und Geheimnis in den Geheimgesellschaften des 18. Jahrhunderts." In *Aufklärung und Geheimgesellschaften: Zur politischen Funktion und Sozialstruktur der Freimaurerlogen im 18. Jahrhundert*, edited by Helmut Reinalter, 63–86. Munich: Oldenbourg, 1989.
Harkness, Deborah E. *John Dee's Conversations with Angels: Cabala, Alchemy, and the End of Nature*. Cambridge: Cambridge University Press, 1999.
Harrán, Don. *Salamone Rossi: Jewish Musician in Late Renaissance Mantua*. Oxford: Oxford University Press, 2003.
Harrison, Peter. "Curiosity, Forbidden Knowledge, and the Reformation of Natural Philosophy in Early Modern England." *Isis* 92 (2001): 265–290.
Hartung, Gerald. "Johann Joachim Becher oder: Die Projekte und Konzepte eines närrischen Gelehrten." In *Zwischen Narretei und Weisheit: Biographische Skizzen und Konturen alter Gelehrsamkeit*, edited by Gerald Hartung and Wolf Peter Klein, 262–287. Hildesheim: Olms, 1997.
Haupt, Herbert. "Kaiser Rudolf II: Kunst, Kultur und Wissenschaft im Spiegel der Hoffinanz, 1596–1612." *Jahrbuch des Kunsthistorischen Museums Wien* 10 (2008): 229–399.
Hausenblasová, Jaroslava. *Der Hof Kaiser Rudolfs II: Eine Edition der Hofstaatsverzeichnisse, 1576–1612*. Prague: Artefactum, 2002.
Hazelrigg, Lawrence E. "A Reexamination of Simmel's 'The Secret and the Secret Society': Nine Propositions." *Social Forces* 47 (1969): 323–330.
Heil, Johannes. *"Gottesfeinde–Menschenfeinde": Die Vorstellung von jüdischer Weltverschwörung, 13. bis 16. Jahrhundert*. Essen: Klartext, 2006.
Heinemann, Otto von. *Die Handschriften der herzoglichen Bibliothek zu Wolfenbüttel: Zweite Abtheilung*. 5 vols. Wolfenbüttel: Zwissler, 1890–1903.
Heinisch, Klaus J. *Der utopische Staat*. Reinbek: Rowohlt, 1960.
Henkel, Arthur, and Albrecht Schöne. *Emblemata: Handbuch zur Sinnbildkunst des 16. und 17. Jahrhunderts*. Stuttgart: Metzler, 1996.
Heymann, Fritz. "Der Erzmagier Philadelphia." In *Der Chevalier von Geldern: Eine Chronik der Abenteuer der Juden*, 360–383. Cologne: Melzer, 1963.

Hofacker, Hans-Georg. " . . . *sonderliche hohe Künste und vortreffliche Geheimnis": Alchemie am Hof Herzog Friedrichs I. von Württemberg, 1593-1608.* Stuttgart: Wegrahistorik-Verlag, 1993.

Hoheisl, Karl. "Christus und der philosophische Stein: Alchemie als über- und nichtchristlicher Heilsweg." In *Die Alchemie in der europäischen Kultur- und Wissenschaftsgeschichte,* edited by Christoph Meinel, 61–84. Wiesbaden: Harrassowitz, 1986.

Holländer, Hans. "Mathesis und Magie: Täuschungsbedarf und Erkenntnisfortschritt im 18. Jahrhundert." In *Rare Künste: Zur Kultur- und Mediengeschichte der Zauberkunst,* edited by Brigitte Felderer and Ernst Strouhal, 33–54. Vienna: Springer, 2007.

Hölscher, Lucian. *Öffentlichkeit und Geheimnis: Eine begriffsgeschichtliche Untersuchung zur Entstehung der Öffentlichkeit in der frühen Neuzeit.* Stuttgart: Klett-Cotta, 1979.

Horchler, Michael. *Die Alchemie in der deutschen Literatur des Mittelalters: Ein Forschungsbericht über die deutsche alchemistische Fachliteratur des ausgehenden Mittelalters.* Baden-Baden: Deutscher Wissenschafts-Verlag, 2005.

Horowitz, Elliott. "I Carmi di Cremona: Una famiglia di banchieri ashkenaziti nella prima età moderna." *Zakhor* 3 (1999): 155–170.

———. "Odd Couples: The Eagle and the Hare, the Lion and the Unicorn." *Jewish Studies Quarterly* 11 (2004): 243–258.

Hortzitz, Nicoline. *Der "Judenarzt": Historische und sprachliche Untersuchungen zur Diskriminierung eines Berufsstands in der frühen Neuzeit.* Heidelberg: Winter, 1994.

Hsia, R. Po-chia. *The Myth of Ritual Murder: Jews and Magic in Reformation Germany.* New Haven: Yale University Press, 1988.

Hubicki, Włodzimierz. "Rudolf II. und die Alchimisten." In *Actes du IXe congrès international d'histoire des sciences: Barcelona-Madrid, 1–7 septembre,* 296–302. Barcelona: Associacion para la historia de la ciencia espanola, 1960.

Hull, David. "Openness and Secrecy in Science: Their Origins and Limitations." *Science, Technology and Human Values* 10 (1985): 4–13.

Hurter, Friedrich. *Philipp Lang. Kammerdiener Kaiser Rudolphs II: Eine Criminal-Geschichte aus dem Anfang des siebenzehnten Jahrhunderts: Aus archivalischen Acten gezogen durch Friedrich Hurter.* Schaffhausen: Hurter, 1851.

Hutchison, Keith. "What Happened to Occult Qualities in the Scientific Revolution?" *Isis* 73 (1982): 233–253.

I saperi nelle corti. Special issue, *Micrologus: Natura, Scienze e Società Medievali* 16 (2008).

Idel, Moshe. *Der Golem: Jüdische magische und mystische Traditionen des künstlichen Anthropoiden.* Frankfurt am Main: Suhrkamp, 2007.

———. "Differing Conceptions of Kabbalah in the Early 17th Century." In *Jewish Thought in the Seventeenth Century,* edited by Isadore Twersky and Bernard Septimus, 137–200. Cambridge, MA: Harvard University Press, 1987.

———. Foreword to *Jewish Magic and Superstition: A Study in Folk Religion,* by Joshua Trachtenberg, ix–xxv. Philadelphia: University of Pennsylvania Press, 2004.

———. "Hermeticism and Judaism." In *Hermeticism and the Renaissance: Intellectual History and the Occult in Early Modern Europe,* edited by Ingrid Merkel and Allen Debus, 59–76. London: Folger Shakespeare Library, 1998.

———. "Jewish Magic from the Renaissance Period to Early Modern Hasidism." In *Religion, Science, and Magic in Concert and in Conflict,* edited by Jacob Neusner, Ernest S. Frerichs, and Paul Virgil McCracken Flesher, 82–117. New York: Oxford University Press, 1989.

———. "Le passage de l'intelligence: L'influence intellectuelle des juifs." In *Le passage d'Israël,* edited by Shmuel Trigano, 155–176. Vol. 3 of *La société juive à travers l'histoire.* Paris: Fayard, 1993.

———. "The Magical and Neoplatonic Interpretations of the Kabbalah in the Renaissance." In *Essential Papers on Jewish Culture in Renaissance and Baroque Italy,* edited by David B. Ruderman, 107–169. New York: New York University Press, 1992.

———. "The Origin of Alchemy according to Zosimos and a Hebrew Parallel." *Revue des études juives* 145 (1986): 117–124.

———. "Secrecy, Binah and Derishah." In *Secrecy and Concealment: Studies in the History of Mediterranean and Near Eastern Religions,* edited by Hans G. Kippenberg and Guy Stroumsa, 311–343. Leiden: Brill, 1995.

Ioly Zorattini, Pier Cesare. "Jews, Crypto-Jews and the Inquisition." In *The Jews of Early Modern Venice,* edited by Robert C. Davis and Benjamin Ravid, 97–116. Baltimore: Johns Hopkins University Press, 2001.

Israel, Giorgio. "È esistita una 'scienza ebraica' in Italia?" In *Cultura ebraica e cultura scientifica in Italia,* edited by Antonio Di Meo, 29–52. Rome: Editori riuniti, 1994.

Israel, Jonathan I. *Diasporas within a Diaspora: Jews, Crypto-Jews and the World of Maritime Empires, 1540–1740.* Leiden: Brill, 2002.

———. *European Jewry in the Age of Mercantilism, 1550–1750.* Oxford: Oxford University Press, 1985.

———. "Philosophy, Deism, and the Early Jewish Enlightenment, 1655–1740." In *The Dutch Intersection: The Jews and the Netherlands in Modern History*, edited by Yosef Kaplan, 173–202. Leiden: Brill, 2008.

Israel, Uwe, et al., eds. *Interstizi: Culture ebraico-cristiane a Venezia e nei suoi domini dal Medioevo all'età moderna*. Rome: Edizioni di storia e letteratura, 2010.

Jacoby, David. "Un agent juif au service de Venise: David Mavrogonato de Candie." *Thesaurismata* 9 (1972): 68–96.

Jaffé, David. "Peiresc—Wissenschaftlicher Betrieb in einem Raritäten-Kabinett." In *Macrocosmos in Microcosmo: Die Welt in der Stube: Zur Geschichte des Sammelns, 1450 bis 1800*, edited by Andreas Grote, 302–322. Opladen: Leske & Budrich, 1994.

Jaffe, Michele Sharon. *The Story of O: Prostitutes and Other Good-for-Nothings in the Renaissance*. Cambridge, MA: Harvard University Press, 1999.

Jähns, Max. *Geschichte der Kriegswissenschaften, vornehmlich in Deutschland*. 3 vols. Munich: Oldenbourg, 1889.

Janáček, Josef. "Les Italiens à Prague à l'époque précédant la bataille de la Montagne Blanche, 1526–1620." *Historica: Les sciences historiques en Tchécoslovaquie* 23 (1983): 5–45.

Jarè, Giuseppe. *Abramo Colorni: Ingegnere di Alfonso d'Este: Nuove ricerche*. Ferrara: Premiate Tipografia Sociale, 1891. Also published in *Atti della deputazione ferrarese di storia patria* (1891): 257–317.

———. *Abramo Colorni: Ingegnero mantovano del secolo XVI: Cenni con documenti inediti*. Mantua: Balbiani, 1874.

———. "La chiriofisionomia [sic] di Abramo Colorni." *Rivista Israelitica* 2 (1905): 25–28.

Jedlicki, Jerzy. *Die entartete Welt: Die Kritiker der Moderne, ihre Ängste und Urteile*. Frankfurt am Main: Suhrkamp, 2007.

Jestaz, Bertrand. "Bronzo e bronzetti nella collezione Gonzaga." In *Le raccolte*, edited by Raffaella Morselli, 313–329. Vol. 2 of *Gonzaga: La celeste galleria*. Milan: Skira, 2002.

Joost, Ulrich. *Georg Christoph Lichtenberg: "Avertissement" gegen Jakob Philadelphia 1777: Faksimile des Erstdrucks*. Darmstadt, 2004.

Jütte, Daniel. "Abramo Colorni, jüdischer Hofalchemist Herzog Friedrichs I., und die hebräische Handelskompanie des Maggino Gabrielli in Württemberg am Ende des 16. Jahrhunderts: Ein biographischer und methodologischer Beitrag zur jüdischen Wissenschaftsgeschichte." *Aschkenas* 15 (2005): 435–498.

———. "Handel, Wissenstransfer und Netzwerke: Eine Fallstudie zu Grenzen und Möglichkeiten unternehmerischen Handelns unter Juden zwischen

Reich, Italien und Levante um 1600." *Vierteljahrschrift für Sozial- und Wirtschaftsgeschichte* 95 (2008): 263-290.

———. "Haskala und Hokuspokus: Die Biographie Jakob Philadelphias (ca. 1734-1797) und ihre Implikationen für die deutsch-jüdische Geschichte." *BIOS: Zeitschrift für Biographieforschung, Oral History und Lebensverlaufsanalysen* 20 (2007): 40-51.

———. "The Jewish Consuls in the Mediterranean and Holy Roman Empire during the Early Modern Period: A Study in Economic and Diplomatic Networks, 1500-1800." In *Cosmopolitan Networks in Commerce and Society, 1660-1914*, edited by Andreas Gestrich and Margrit Schulte Beerbühl, 153-186. London: German Historical Institute, 2011.

Jütte, Robert. "Rotwelsch—die Sprache der Bettler und Gauner." In *Das Buch der Vaganten: Spieler, Huren, Leutbetrüger*, edited by Heiner Boehncke and Rolf Johannsmeier, 133-143. Cologne: Prometh, 1987.

———. "Zur Funktion und sozialen Stellung jüdischer 'gelehrter' Ärzte im spätmittelalterlichen und frühneuzeitlichen Deutschland." In *Gelehrte im Reich: Zur Sozial- und Wirkungsgeschichte akademischer Eliten des 14. bis 16. Jahrhunderts*, edited by Rainer Christoph Schwinges, 159-179. Berlin: Duncker & Humblot, 1996.

Kahn, David. *The Codebreakers: The Story of Secret Writing*. New York: Scribner, 1996.

Kaiser, Wolfgang. "Pratiques du secret." *Rives méditerranéennes* 17 (2004): 7-10.

Kallfelz, Hatto. "Der zyprische Alchimist Marco Bragadin und eine Florentiner Gesandtschaft in Bayern im Jahre 1590." *Zeitschrift für bayerische Landesgeschichte* 31 (1968): 475-500.

Kantorowicz, Ernst H. "Mysteries of State: An Absolutist Concept and Its Late Mediaeval Origins." *Harvard Theological Review* 48 (1955): 65-91.

Katz, David S. *Philo-Semitism and the Readmission of the Jews to England, 1603-1655*. Oxford: Clarendon, 1982.

Katz, Jacob. *Jews and Freemasons in Europe, 1723-1939*. Cambridge, MA: Harvard University Press, 1970.

———. *Out of the Ghetto: The Social Background of Jewish Emancipation, 1770-1870*. Cambridge, MA: Harvard University Press, 1973.

Kaufmann, David. "Ein Jahrhundert aus der Geschichte der Familie Jechiel von Pisas." In *Gesammelte Schriften*, edited by Markus Brann, 2:257-276. Frankfurt am Main: Kauffmann, 1910.

———. "Leone de Sommi Portaleone, der Dramatiker und Synagogengründer von Mantua." *Allgemeine Zeitung des Judentums*, June 24, 1898.

———. "Zur Geschichte der Kämpfe Asarja deï Rossis." In *Gesammelte Schriften,* edited by Markus Brann, 3:83-95. Frankfurt am Main: Kauffmann, 1910.

Kaufmann, Thomas DaCosta. "Empiricism and Community in Early Modern Science: Some Comments on Baths, Plants, and Courts." In *Natural Particulars: Nature and the Disciplines in Renaissance Europe,* edited by Anthony Grafton and Nancy Siraisi, 401-417. Cambridge, MA: MIT Press, 1999.

———. "From Mastery of the World to Mastery of Nature: The Kunstkammer, Politics, and Science." In *The Mastery of Nature: Aspects of Art, Science, and Humanism in the Renaissance,* 174-194. Princeton: Princeton University Press, 1993.

———. *L'école de Prague: La peinture à la cour de Rodolphe II.* Paris: Flammarion, 1985.

———. *The Mastery of Nature: Aspects of Art, Science, and Humanism in the Renaissance.* Princeton: Princeton University Press, 1993.

Keblusek, Marika. "Keeping It Secret: The Identity and Status of an Early Modern Inventor." *History of Science* 43 (2005): 37-56.

Kenny, Neil. *The Palace of Secrets: Béroalde de Verville and Renaissance Conceptions of Knowledge.* Oxford: Oxford University Press, 1991.

Kieckhefer, Richard. "Did Magic Have a Renaissance? An Historiographic Question Revisited." In *Magic and the Classical Tradition,* edited by Charles Burnett and W. F. Ryan, 199-212. London: Warburg Institute, 2006.

———. *Forbidden Rites: A Necromancer's Manual of the Fifteenth Century.* Stroud: Sutton, 1997.

Kilcher, Andreas. *Die Sprachtheorie der Kabbala als ästhetisches Paradigma: Die Konstruktion einer ästhetischen Kabbala seit der Frühen Neuzeit.* Stuttgart: Metzler, 1998.

Kimmel, Lore. "'La Piazza Universale di tutte le professioni del Mondo' (1585) von Thomaso [sic] Garzoni und die spanische Übersetzung und Umarbeitung in 'Plaza Universal de todas ciencias y artes' (1615) von Christóbal Suarez de Figueroa." Ph.D. diss., Ludwig Maximilians University Munich, 1968.

Kippenberg, Hans G., and Guy Stroumsa, eds. *Secrecy and Concealment: Studies in the History of Mediterranean and Near Eastern Religions.* Leiden: Brill, 1995.

Klein, Birgit E. *Wohltat und Hochverrat: Kurfürst Ernst von Köln, Juda bar Chajjim und die Juden im Alten Reich.* Hildesheim: Olms, 2003.

Klingner, Erich. *Luther und der deutsche Volksaberglaube.* Berlin: Mayer & Müller, 1912.

Kluge, Friedrich. *Etymologisches Wörterbuch der deutschen Sprache.* Berlin: De Gruyter, 1967.

Knobloch, Eberhard, ed. *L'art de la guerre: Machines et stratagèmes de Taccola, ingénieur de la Renaissance.* Paris: Gallimard, 1992.

Kodera, Sergius. "Der Magus und die Stripperinnen: Giambattista della Portas indiskrete Renaissancemagie." In *Rare Künste: Zur Kultur- und Mediengeschichte der Zauberkunst,* edited by Brigitte Felderer and Ernst Strouhal, 55-77. Vienna: Springer, 2007.

Köhn, Rolf. "Dimensionen und Funktionen des Öffentlichen und Privaten in der mittelalterlichen Korrespondenz." In *Das Öffentliche und Private in der Vormoderne,* edited by Gert Melville and Peter von Moos, 309-357. Cologne: Böhlau, 1998.

Konečný, Lubomír, ed. *Rudolf II, Prague and the World: Papers from the International Conference Prague, 2-4 September 1997.* Prague: Artefactum, 1998.

Kopp, Hermann. *Die Alchemie in älterer und neuerer Zeit: Ein Beitrag zur Kulturgeschichte.* 2 vols. Heidelberg: Winter, 1886. Reprint, Hildesheim: Olms, 1962.

Koren, Nathan. *Jewish Physicians: A Biographical Index.* Jerusalem: Israel Universities Press, 1973.

Koselleck, Reinhart. *Critique and Crisis: Enlightenment and the Pathogenesis of Modern Society.* Cambridge, MA: MIT Press, 1988.

Kottek, Samuel S. "Jews between Profane and Sacred Science in Renaissance Italy: The Case of Abraham Portaleone." In *Religious Confessions and the Sciences in the Sixteenth Century,* edited by Jürgen Helm and Annette Winkelmann, 108-118. Leiden: Brill, 2001.

Krampl, Ulrike. "Diplomaten, Kaufleute und ein Mann 'obskurer' Herkunft: Alchemie und ihre Netzwerke im Paris des frühen 18. Jahrhunderts." In *Nützliche Netzwerke und korrupte Seilschaften,* edited by Arne Karsten and Hillard von Thiessen, 137-162. Göttingen: Vandenhoeck & Ruprecht, 2006.

Kranz, Horst, and Walter Oberschelp. *Mechanisches Memorieren und Chiffrieren um 1430: Johannes Fontanas "Tractatus de instrumentis artis memorie."* Stuttgart: Steiner, 2009.

Krauss, Samuel. "Wer hat das Schießpulver nach Deutschland gebracht?" *Neue jüdische Monatshefte* 3 (1919): 250-253.

Kris, Ernst, and Otto Kurz. *Die Legende vom Künstler: Ein geschichtlicher Versuch.* Frankfurt am Main: Suhrkamp, 1995.

Krüger, Klaus, ed. *Curiositas: Welterfahrung und ästhetische Neugierde in Mittelalter und früher Neuzeit.* Göttingen: Wallstein, 2002.

Kugeler, Heidrun. "'Ehrenhafte Spione': Geheimnis, Verstellung und Offenheit in der Diplomatie des 17. Jahrhunderts." In *Die Kunst der Aufrichtigkeit im*

17. Jahrhundert, edited by Claudia Benthien and Steffen Martus, 127–148. Tübingen: Niemeyer, 2006.

Kuhn, Thomas S. *The Structure of Scientific Revolutions.* Chicago: University of Chicago Press, 1996.

Küster, Sebastian. *Vier Monarchien, vier Öffentlichkeiten: Kommunikation um die Schlacht bei Dettingen.* Münster: Lit, 2004.

Lachter, Hartley. "Spreading Secrets: Kabbalah and Esotericism in Isaac ibn Sahula's Meshal ha-kadmoni." *Jewish Quarterly Review* 100 (2010): 111–138.

Lamanskij, Vladimir Ivanovič. *Secrets d'état de Venise: Documents, extraits, notices et études servant à éclaircir les rapports de la Seigneurie avec les Grecs, les Slaves et la Porte ottomane, à la fin du XVe et au XVIe siècle.* Zapiski Istoriko-filologicheskago fakul'teta Imperatorskago S.-Peterburgskago universiteta 12. Saint Petersburg: Imprimerie de l'Académie imperiale des sciences, 1884.

Landman, Isaac, ed. *The Universal Jewish Encyclopedia.* 10 vols. New York: Universal Jewish Encyclopedia, 1939–1943.

Lang, Stefan. *Ausgrenzung und Koexistenz: Judenpolitik und jüdisches Leben in Württemberg und im "Land zu Schwaben," 1492–1650.* Ostfildern: Thorbecke, 2008.

Langermann, Y. Tzvi. Review of *The Jewish Alchemists,* by Raphael Patai. *Journal of the American Oriental Society* 116 (1996): 792–793.

———. "Was There No Science in Ashkenaz? The Ashkenazic Reception of Some Early-Medieval Hebrew Scientific Texts." *Jahrbuch des Simon-Dubnow-Instituts* 8 (2009): 67–92.

Lasker, Daniel J. *Jewish Philosophical Polemics against Christianity in the Middle Ages.* New York: Ktav Publishing House, 1977.

Lazardzig, Jan. "'Masque der Possibilität': Experiment und Spektakel barocker Projektemacherei." In *Spektakuläre Experimente: Praktiken der Evidenzproduktion im 17. Jahrhundert,* edited by Helmar Schramm, Ludgar Schwarte, and Jan Lazardzig, 176–212. Berlin: De Gruyter, 2006.

Le Person, Xavier. "Les 'practiques' du secret au temps de Henri III." *Rives méditerranéennes* 17 (2004): 11–36.

Lehmann, Matthias B. "A Livornese 'Port Jew' and the Sephardim of the Ottoman Empire." *Jewish Social Studies* 11 (2005): 51–76.

Leicht, Reimund. *Astrologumena Judaica: Untersuchungen zur Geschichte der astrologischen Literatur der Juden.* Tübingen: Mohr Siebeck, 2006.

Leoni, Aron di Leone. "Alcuni esempi di quotidiana imprenditorialità tra Ferrara, Ancona e Venezia nel XVI secolo." *Zakhor: Rivista di storia degli ebrei d'Italia* 4 (2000): 57–114.

———. "Per una storia della nazione tedesca di Ferrara nel Cinquecento." *Rassegna mensile di Israel* 62 (1996): 137–166.
Levi, Isaia. "Famosi." *Il vessillo israelitico* 53 (1905): 608–610.
Lewin, Louis. *Die Gifte in der Weltgeschichte: Toxikologische allgemeinverständliche Untersuchungen der historischen Quellen.* Hildesheim: Gerstenberg, 1984.
———. *Gifte und Vergiftung: Handbuch der Toxikologie.* Berlin: Stilke, 1929.
Lewinsky, A. "Alcuni manoscritti italiani nella biblioteca ducale di Wolfenbüttel." *Rivista israelitica* 1 (1904): 236–237.
Lewis, Bernard. "The Privilege Granted by Mehmed II to His Physician." *Bulletin of the School of Oriental and African Studies* 14 (1952): 550–563.
Liechtenstein, Richard. "Ein eigenhändiger Brief Dr. Martin Luthers an den Kurfürsten Joachim II. von Brandenburg." *Allgemeine Zeitung des Judentums*, August 17, 1906, p. 392.
Lincoln, Evelyn. "The Jew and the Worms: Portraits and Patronage in a Sixteenth-Century How-To Manual." *Word & Image* 19 (2003): 86–99.
Liscia Bemporad, Dora. *Maggino di Gabriello "Hebreo Venetiano": I Dialoghi sopra l'utili sue inventioni circa la seta.* Florence: Edifir, 2010.
Litt, Stefan. "Juden und Waffen im 16. und 17. Jahrhundert—Anmerkungen zu einem Alltagsphänomen." *Aschkenas* 13 (2003): 83–92.
Lochrie, Karma. *Covert Operations: The Medieval Uses of Secrecy.* Philadelphia: University of Pennsylvania Press, 1999.
Long, Pamela O. "The Openness of Knowledge: An Ideal and Its Context in 16th-Century Writings on Mining and Metallurgy." *Technology and Culture* 32 (1991): 318–355.
———. *Openness, Secrecy, Authorship: Technical Arts and the Culture of Knowledge from Antiquity to the Renaissance.* Baltimore: Johns Hopkins University Press, 2001.
———. "Power, Patronage, and the Authorship of Ars: From Mechanical Know-How to Mechanical Knowledge in the Last Scribal Age." *Isis* 88 (1997): 1–41.
Long, Pamela O., and Alex Roland. "Military Secrecy in Antiquity and Early Medieval Europe: A Critical Reassessment." *History and Technology* 11 (1994): 259–290.
Lopez, Robert S., and Irving W. Raymond, eds. *Medieval Trade in the Mediterranean World: Illustrative Documents.* New York: Columbia University Press, 1955.
Luhmann, Niklas. "Geheimnis, Zeit und Ewigkeit." In *Reden und Schweigen*, by Niklas Luhmann and Peter Fuchs, 101–138. Frankfurt am Main: Suhrkamp, 1992.

Luhrmann, T. M. "The Magic of Secrecy." *Ethos* 17 (1989): 131–165.
Luzzati, Michele. *La casa dell'ebreo: Saggi sugli ebrei a Pisa e in Toscana nel medioevo e nel Rinascimento.* Pisa: Nistri-Lischi, 1985.
Luzzatto, Leone. "Ricordi storici." *Il Vessillo israelitico* 54 (1906): 530–532.
Maciejko, Pawel. "Sabbatian Charlatans: The First Jewish Cosmopolitans." *European Review of History* 17 (2010): 361–378.
Macrakis, Kristie. "Ancient Imprints: Fear and the Origins of Secret Writing." *Endeavour* 33 (2009): 24–28.
Makkai, Laszlo. "De Taccola à Veranzio: L'ingénieur de la Renaissance en Hongrie." In *Mélanges en l'honneur de Fernand Braudel,* 1:337–347. Toulouse: Privat, 1973.
Malcolm, Noel. "Private and Public Knowledge: Kircher, Esotericism, and the Republic of Letters." In *Athanasius Kircher: The Last Man Who Knew Everything,* edited by Paula Findlen, 297–308. New York: Routledge, 2004.
Malinowski, Bronisław. *Magic, Science and Religion, and Other Essays.* Garden City: Doubleday, 1954.
Manzonetto, Flora. *Storia di un alicorno tra Venezia e Istanbul.* Venice: Centro internazionale della Grafica, 1989.
Marcus, Jacob R. *The Jew in the Medieval World: A Source Book, 315–1791.* Cleveland: Median Books, 1961.
Marshall, Peter. *The Magic Circle of Rudolf II: Alchemy and Astrology in Renaissance Prague.* New York: Walter, 2006.
Martin, Julian. "Natural Philosophy and Its Public Concerns." In *Science, Culture and Popular Belief in Renaissance Europe,* edited by Stephen Pumfrey, Paolo L. Rossi, and Maurice Slawinski, 100–118. Manchester: Manchester University Press, 1991.
Mathiesen, Robert. "The Key of Solomon: Towards a Typology of the Manuscripts." *Societas Magica Newsletter* 17 (2007): 1–9.
Mattingly, Garrett. *Renaissance Diplomacy.* London: Penguin, 1973.
Maxwell-Stuart, P. G., ed. *The Occult in Early Modern Europe: A Documentary History.* London: Macmillan, 1999.
McClure, George W. *The Culture of Profession in Late Renaissance Italy.* Toronto: University of Toronto Press, 2004.
McMullin, Ernan. "Openness and Secrecy in Science: Some Notes on Early History." *Science, Technology and Human Values* 10 (1985): 14–23.
Meister, Aloys. *Die Anfänge der modernen diplomatischen Geheimschrift: Beiträge zur Geschichte der italienischen Kryptographie des XV. Jahrhunderts:* Paderborn: Schöningh, 1902.

———. *Die Geheimschrift im Dienste der päpstlichen Kurie: Von ihren Anfängen bis zum Ende des XVI. Jahrhunderts.* Paderborn: Schöningh, 1906.

Melamed, Abraham. "A Legitimating Myth: Ashkenazic Thinkers on the Purported Jewish Origins of Philosophy and Science." *Jahrbuch des Simon-Dubnow-Instituts* 8 (2009): 299–315.

Melville, Gert, and Peter von Moos, eds. *Das Öffentliche und das Private in der Vormoderne.* Cologne: Böhlau, 1998.

Melzi, Robert C. "Una commedia rinascimentale di Angelo Alatini: 'I trionfi.'" *Italia: Studie e ricerche sulla storia, la cultura e la letteratura degli ebrei d'Italia* 13–15 (2001): 343–356.

Menache, Sophia, ed. *Communication in the Jewish Diaspora: The Pre-Modern World.* Leiden: Brill, 1995.

Menascè, Esther. "Presenza ebraica nell'utopia baconiana della New Atlantis." *Rassegna mensile di Israel* 39 (1973): 682–712.

Mentgen, Gerd. "Jewish Alchemists in Central Europe in the Later Middle Ages: Some New Sources." *Aleph* 9 (2009): 345–352.

Merchant, Carolyn. "Secrets of Nature: The Bacon Debates Revisited." *Journal of the History of Ideas* 69 (2008): 147–162.

———. "'The Violence of Impediments': Francis Bacon and the Origins of Experimentation." *Isis* 99 (2008): 731–760.

Merton, Robert K. *Science, Technology and Society in Seventeenth Century England.* New York: Fertig, 1970.

Metzger, Thérèse, and Mendel Metzger. *Jewish Life in the Middle Ages: Illuminated Hebrew Manuscripts of the Thirteenth to the Sixteenth Centuries.* New York: Alpine Fine Arts Collection, 1982.

Meyer, Birgit, and Peter Pels, eds. *Magic and Modernity: Interfaces of Revelation and Concealment.* Stanford: Stanford University Press, 2003.

Michelini Tocci, Franco. "Dottrine 'ermetiche' tra gli ebrei in Italia fino al Cinquecento." In *Italia judaica: Atti del I convegno internazionale,* edited by the Commissione mista per la storia e la cultura degli ebrei in Italia, 287–301. Rome: Ministero per i beni culturali e ambientali, 1983.

Milani, Marisa. "Indovini ebrei e streghe cristiane nella Venezia dell'ultimo '500." *Lares* 53 (1987): 207–213.

Milano, Attilio. "Un'azienda di banchieri e provveditori ebrei alla corte dei Gonzaga Nevers nel Seicento." *Rassegna mensile di Israel* 28 (1962): 180–202.

Miletto, Gianfranco. "Die Bibel als Handbuch der Kriegskunst nach der Interpretation Abraham ben David Portaleones." In *An der Schwelle zur Moderne: Juden in der Renaissance,* edited by Giuseppe Veltri and Annette Winkelmann, 78–89. Leiden: Brill, 2003.

———. *Glauben und Wissen im Zeitalter der Reformation: Der Salomonische Tempel bei Abraham ben David Portaleone, 1542–1612*. Berlin: De Gruyter, 2004.

———. "The Teaching Program of David ben Abraham and His Son Abraham Provenzali in Its Historical-Cultural Context." In Ruderman and Veltri, eds., *Cultural Intermediaries*, 126–148.

Mokyr, Joel. *The Gifts of Athena: Historical Origins of the Knowledge Economy*. Princeton: Princeton University Press, 2002.

Moran, Bruce T. *The Alchemical World of the German Court: Occult Philosophy and Chemical Medicine in the Circle of Moritz of Hessen, 1572–1632*. Stuttgart: Steiner, 1991.

———. "Courts and Academies." In *Early Modern Science*, edited by Katharine Park and Lorraine Daston, 251–271. Vol. 3 of *The Cambridge History of Science*, edited by David C. Lindberg and Ronald L. Numbers. Cambridge: Cambridge University Press, 2006.

———. *Distilling Knowledge: Alchemy, Chemistry, and the Scientific Revolution*. Cambridge: Harvard University Press, 2005.

———. "German Prince-Practitioners: Aspects in the Development of Courtly Science, Technology, and Procedures in the Renaissance." In *Technology and Culture* 22 (1981): 253–274.

———, ed. *Patronage and Institutions: Science, Technology, and Medicine at the European Court, 1500–1750*. Rochester: Boydell, 1991.

Moreno-Carvalho, Francisco. "A Newly Discovered Letter by Galileo Galilei: Contacts between Galileo and Jacob Rosales (Manoel Bocarro Francês), a Seventeenth-Century Jewish Scientist and Sebastianist." *Aleph* 2 (2002): 59–91.

Morselli, Raffaella. "Este e Gonzaga: 'Piccolo' e grande collezionismo di due famiglie amiche tra Cinquecento e Seicento." In *Sovrane passioni: Studi sul collezionismo estense*, edited by Jadranka Bentini, 37–90. Milan: Motta, 1998.

———, ed. *Gonzaga: La celeste galleria*. 2 vols. Milan: Skira, 2002.

———. "'Il più grande edificio principesco del mondo': Storia e fortuna delle collezioni ducali da Guglielmo Gonzaga al sacco di Mantova." In *L'elenco dei beni del 1626–1627*, 35–173. Vol. 2 of *Le collezioni Gonzaga*. Milan: Silvana, 2000.

Moser, Friedrich Wilhelm. "Der Fürst zwischen seinem Hofprediger und Cabinets-Juden." *Patriotisches Archiv für Deutschland* 9 (1788): 245–286.

Mout, M. E. H. N. "Hermes Trismegistos Germaniae: Rudolf II en de arcane wetenschappen." *Leids Kunsthistorisch Jaarboek* 1 (1982): 161–189.

Muchnik, Natalia. "Du secret imposé à la clandestinité revendiquée: Les communautés cryptojudaïsantes madrilènes face à l'Inquisition, XVIᵉ–XVIIIᵉ siècle." In Aprile and Retaillaud-Bajac, eds., *Clandestinités urbaines*, 23–34.

Müller, Johannes. "Die Verdienste Zacharias Geizkoflers um die Beschaffung der Geldmittel für den Türkenkrieg Kaiser Rudolfs II." *Mittheilungen des Instituts für Oesterreichische Geschichtsforschung* 21 (1900): 251–304.

Müller, Rainer A. *Der Fürstenhof in der Frühen Neuzeit.* Munich: Oldenbourg, 2004.

Müller-Jahncke, Wolf-Dieter, and Joachim Telle. "Numismatik und Alchemie: Mitteilungen zu Münzen des 17. und 18. Jahrhunderts." In *Die Alchemie in der europäischen Kultur- und Wissenschaftsgeschichte*, edited by Christoph Meinel, 229–275. Wiesbaden: Harrassowitz, 1986.

Münkler, Herfried. *Im Namen des Staates: Die Begründung der Staatsraison in der Frühen Neuzeit.* Frankfurt am Main: Fischer, 1987.

Münster, Ladislao. "L'Enarratio brevis de senum affectibus de David de Pomis, le plus grand médecin israélite en Italie au XVIᵉ siècle." In *Mélanges d'histoire de la médecine hébraïque: Études choisies de la Revue d'Histoire de la Médecine Hébraïque, 1948–1985*, edited by Gad Freudenthal and Samuel Kottek, 161–181. Leiden: Brill, 2003.

Muzzarelli, Maria Giuseppina. "Ferrara, ovvero un porto placido e sicuro tra XV e XVI secolo." In *Vita e cultura ebraica nello stato estense*, edited by Euride Fregni and Mauro Perani, 235–257. Nonantola: Comune di Nonantola, 1993.

Naredi-Rainer, Paul von. *Architektur und Harmonie: Zahl, Maß und Proportion in der abendländischen Baukunst.* Cologne: DuMont, 1982.

———. *Salomos Tempel und das Abendland: Monumentale Folgen historischer Irrtümer.* Cologne: Dumont, 1994.

Navarrini, Roberto. "La guerra chimica di Vincenzo Gonzaga." *Civiltà mantovana* 4 (1969): 43–47.

Neher, André. "Gli ebrei e la rivoluzione copernicana." *Rassegna mensile di Israel* 39 (1973): 552–562.

———. *Jewish Thought and the Scientific Revolution of the Sixteenth Century: David Gans, 1541–1613 and His Times.* Oxford: Oxford University Press, 1986.

Neugebauer-Wölk, Monika. "Arkanwelten im 18. Jahrhundert: Zur Struktur des Politischen im Kontext von Aufklärung und frühmoderner Staatlichkeit." *Aufklärung: Interdisziplinäres Jahrbuch zur Erforschung des 18. Jahrhunderts und seiner Wirkungsgeschichte* 15 (2003): 7–65.

---. "Esoterik in der Frühen Neuzeit: Zum Paradigma der Religionsgeschichte zwischen Mittelalter und Moderne." *Zeitschrift für Historische Forschung* 27 (2000): 321-364.

---. *Esoterische Bünde und bürgerliche Gesellschaft: Entwicklungslinien zur modernen Welt im Geheimbundwesen des 18. Jahrhunderts.* Göttingen: Wallstein, 1995.

Newman, William R. "From Alchemy to 'Chymistry.'" In *Early Modern Science,* edited by Katharine Park and Lorraine Daston, 497-517. Vol. 3 of *The Cambridge History of Science,* edited by David C. Lindberg and Ronald L. Numbers. Cambridge: Cambridge University Press, 2006.

---. *Gehennical Fire: The Lives of George Starkey, an American Alchemist in the Scientific Revolution.* Cambridge, MA: Harvard University Press, 1994.

---. "George Starkey and the Selling of Secrets." In *Samuel Hartlib and Universal Reformation: Studies in Intellectual Communication,* edited by Mark Greengrass, Michael Leslie, and Timothy Raylor, 193-210. Cambridge: Cambridge University Press, 1994.

Newman, William R., and Lawrence M. Principe. "Alchemy vs. Chemistry: The Etymological Origins of a Historiographic Mistake." *Early Science and Medicine* 3 (1998): 32-65.

Nick, Friedrich. *Stuttgarter Chronik und Sagenbuch: Eine Sammlung denkwürdiger Begebenheiten, Geschichten und Sagen der Stadt Stuttgart und ihrer Gemarkung.* Stuttgart: Gutzkow, 1875.

Niederkorn, Jan Paul. *Die europäischen Mächte und der "Lange Türkenkrieg" Kaiser Rudolfs II., 1593-1606.* Vienna: Verlag der Österreichischen Akademie der Wissenschaften, 1993.

---. "Wunderwaffen für die Türkenabwehr: Herzog Alfonso II. von Ferrara und der 'Lange Türkenkrieg' Kaiser Rudolfs II." *Römische Historische Mitteilungen* 29 (1987): 338-349.

Niewöhner, Friedrich. "Natur-Wissenschaft und Gotteserkenntnis: Das jüdische Modell." *Berichte zur Wissenschaftsgeschichte* 18 (1995): 79-84.

Nummedal, Tara. *Alchemy and Authority in the Holy Roman Empire.* Chicago: University of Chicago Press, 2007.

---. "Practical Alchemy and Commercial Exchange in the Holy Roman Empire." In *Merchants and Marvels: Commerce, Science and Art in Early Modern Europe,* edited by Pamela H. Smith and Paula Findlen, 201-222. New York: Routledge, 2002.

Oberman, Heiko A. *Wurzeln des Antisemitismus: Christenangst und Judenplage im Zeitalter von Humanismus und Reformation.* Berlin: Severin und Siedler, 1981.

Odlozilik, Otakar. "Thomas Seget: A Scottish Friend of Szymon Szymonowicz." *Polish Review* 11 (1966): 3–39.
Oestreich, Gerhard. "Das persönliche Regiment der deutschen Fürsten am Beginn der Neuzeit." In *Geist und Gestalt des frühmodernen Staates: Ausgewählte Aufsätze*, 201–234. Berlin: Duncker & Humblot, 1969.
Ofer, Yosef. "Methods of Encoding in Samuel de Archevolti's Arugat ha-Bosem." *European Journal of Jewish Studies* 2 (2008): 45–63.
Olivieri, Achille. "Il medico ebreo nella Venezia del Quattrocento e Cinquecento." In *Gli ebrei a Venezia, secoli XIV–XVIII: Atti del convegno internazionale organizzato dall'Istituto di storia della società e dello stato veneziano della Fondazione Giorgio Cini . . . 5–10 giugno 1983*, edited by Gaetano Cozzi, 449–468. Milan: Edizioni Comunità, 1987.
Orbaan, J. A. F. "La Roma di Sisto V negli Avvisi." *Archivio della R. società romana di storia patria* 33 (1910): 277–312.
Orfali, Kristina. "The Rise and Fall of the Swedish Model." In *Riddles of Identity in Modern Times*, edited by Antoine Prost and Gérard Vincent, 417–449. Vol. 5 of *A History of Private Life*, edited by Philippe Ariès and Georges Duby. Cambridge, MA: Harvard University Press, 1991.
Ornstein, Martha. *The Role of Scientific Societies in the Seventeenth Century*. Chicago: University of Chicago Press, 1938.
Otte, Marline. *Jewish Identities in German Popular Entertainment, 1890–1933*. Cambridge: Cambridge University Press, 2006.
Otto, Eduard. "Alchimisten und Goldmacher an deutschen Fürstenhöfen: Mitteilungen aus dem Thesaurus Pictuarum der Darmstädter Hofbibliothek." *Zeitschrift für Kulturgeschichte* 6 (1899): 46–66.
Pagis, Dan. "Baroque Trends in Italian Hebrew Poetry as Reflected in an Unknown Genre." In *Italia Judaica: Atti del II convegno internazionale*, edited by the Commissione mista per la storia e la cultura degli ebrei in Italia, 263–277. Rome: Ufficio centrale per i beni archivistici, 1986.
Papagno, Giuseppe, and Amedeo Quondam, eds. *La corte e lo spazio: Ferrara estense*. 3 vols. Rome: Bulzoni, 1982.
Paravicini Bagliani, Agostino, ed. "Il segreto." Special issue, *Micrologus: Natura, scienze e società medievali* 14 (2006).
Pardi, Giuseppe. *Lo studio di Ferrara nei secoli XV e XVI*. Ferrara: Zuffi, 1903.
Park, Katharine. *Secrets of Women: Gender, Generation, and the Origins of Human Dissection*. New York: Zone Books, 2006.
Parsons, William Barclay. *Engineers and Engineering in the Renaissance*. Cambridge, MA: MIT Press, 1968.

Patai, Raphael. *The Jewish Alchemists: A History and Source Book.* Princeton: Princeton University Press, 1994.

———. "Sephardic Alchemists." In *From Iberia to Diaspora: Studies in Sephardic History and Culture,* edited by Yehuda K. Stillman and Norman A. Stillman, 235–244. Leiden: Brill, 1999.

Pavone, Mario. *Introduzione al pensiero di Giovanni Battista Hodierna: Filosofo, matematico e astronomo dei primi Gattopardi.* 2 vols. Modica: SETIM, 1981–1982.

Pesaro, Abramo. *Memorie storiche sulla comunità israelitica ferrarese.* Ferrara: Tipografia Sociale, 1878. Reprint, Bologna: Forni, 1986.

Pesic, Peter. "Proteus Rebound: Reconsidering the 'Torture of Nature.'" *Isis* 99 (2008): 304–317.

———. "Secrets, Symbols, and Systems: Parallels between Cryptanalysis and Algebra, 1580–1700." *Isis* 88 (1997): 674–692.

———. "Wrestling with Proteus: Francis Bacon and the 'Torture' of Nature." *Isis* 90 (1999): 81–94.

Petitat, André, ed. *Secret et lien social: Actes du Colloque Secret et société, Université de Lausanne.* Paris: L'Harmattan, 2000.

Peuckert, Will-Erich. *Gabalia: Ein Versuch zur Geschichte der magia naturalis im 16. bis 18. Jahrhundert.* Berlin: Schmidt, 1967.

Pfaff, Karl. "Die früheren Verhältnisse und Schicksale der Juden in Württemberg." *Württembergische Jahrbücher für vaterländische Geschichte, Geographie, Statistik und Topographie* 2 (1857): 157–198.

Piccinelli, Roberta. "Le facies del collezionismo artistico di Vincenzo Gonzaga." In *L'esercizio del collezionismo,* edited by Raffaella Morselli, 341–348. Vol. 1 of *Gonzaga: La celeste galeria.* Milan: Skira, 2002.

Poliakov, Léon. *Jewish Bankers and the Holy See: From the Thirteenth to the Seventeenth Century.* London: Routledge & Paul, 1977.

Porter, Martin. *Windows of the Soul: Physiognomy in European Culture, 1470–1780.* Oxford: Oxford University Press, 2005.

Porto, Paulo Alves. "Michael Sendivogius on Nitre and the Preparation of the Philosopher's Stone." *Ambix* 48 (2001): 1–16.

Preto, Paolo. *I servizi segreti di Venezia.* Milan: Il Saggiatore, 1994.

Principe, Lawrence M. "Robert Boyle's Alchemical Secrecy: Codes, Ciphers and Concealment." *Ambix* 39 (1992): 63–74.

Prior, Moody E. "Bacon's Man of Science." *Journal of the History of Ideas* 15 (1954): 348–370.

Pullan, Brian. *The Jews of Europe and the Inquisition of Venice, 1550–1670.* Oxford: Basil Blackwell, 1983.

Quirini Popławska, Danuta. "Aus den polnisch-habsburgisch-toskanischen Verbindungen: Die Prager Episode des Jahres 1589." In *Prag um 1600: Beiträge zur Kunst und Kultur am Hofe Rudolfs II.*, edited by Eliška Fučíková, 254–260. Freren: Luca Verlag, 1988.

Rabkin, Yakov M. "Interfacce multiple: Scienza contemporanea ed esperienza ebraica." In *Cultura ebraica e cultura scientifica in Italia*, edited by Antonio Di Meo, 3–27. Rome: Editori riuniti, 1994.

Rankin, Alisha. "Becoming an Expert Practitioner: Court Experimentalism and the Medical Skills of Anna of Saxony, 1532–1585." *Isis* 98 (2007): 23–53.

Rau, Susanne, and Gerd Schwerhoff. "Öffentliche Räume in der Frühen Neuzeit: Überlegungen zu Leitbegriffen und Themen eines Forschungsfeldes." In *Zwischen Gotteshaus und Taverne: Öffentliche Räume in Spätmittelalter und Früher Neuzeit*, 11–52. Cologne: Böhlau, 2004.

Ravenna, Leone. Review of *Abramo Colorni: Ingegnero mantovano del secolo XVI*, by Giuseppe Jarè. *Il vessillo israelitico* 40 (1892): 38–41.

Ravid, Benjamin. "Between the Myth of Venice and the Lachrymose Conception of Jewish History: The Case of the Jews of Venice." In *The Jews of Italy: Memory and Identity*, edited by Bernard D. Cooperman and Barbara Garvin, 151–192. Bethesda: University Press of Maryland, 2000.

———. "New Light on the Ghetti of Venice." In *Shlomo Simonsohn Jubilee Volume: Studies on the History of the Jews in the Middle Ages and Renaissance Period*, edited by Daniel Carpi et al., 149–176. Tel Aviv: Tel Aviv University, 1993.

———. "Travel Accounts of the Jews of Venice and Their Ghetto." In *Between History and Literature: Studies in Honor of Isaac Barzilay*, edited by Stanley Nash, 118–150. Tel Aviv: Ha-Kibuts ha-me'uchad, 1997.

Rebecchini, Guido. *Private Collectors in Mantua, 1500–1630*. Rome: Storia e letteratura, 2002.

Redlich, Fritz. "Der deutsche fürstliche Unternehmer: Eine typische Erscheinung des 16. Jahrhunderts." *Tradition: Zeitschrift für Firmengeschichte und Unternehmerbiographie* 1 (1958): 17–32.

Reeves, Eileen. *Galileo's Glassworks: The Telescope and the Mirror*. Cambridge, MA: Harvard University Press, 2008.

———. "Occult Sympathies and Antipathies: The Case of Early Modern Magnetism." In *Wissensideale und Wissenskulturen in der frühen Neuzeit: Ideals and Cultures of Knowledge in Early Modern Europe*, edited by Wolfgang Detel and Claus Zittel, 97–114. Berlin: Akademie Verlag, 2002.

Reichert, Klaus. "Neue Formen des Geheimen am Beginn der Moderne." In *Das Geheimnis am Beginn der europäischen Moderne*, edited by Gisela Engel,

Brita Rang, Klaus Reichert, and Heike Wunder, 12–20. Frankfurt am Main: Klostermann, 2002.

Reinalter, Helmut, ed. *Aufklärung und Geheimgesellschaften: Zur politischen Funktion und Sozialstruktur der Freimaurerlogen im 18. Jahrhundert.* Munich: Oldenbourg, 1989.

Reiner, Elchanan. "The Attitude of Ashkenazi Society to the New Science in the Sixteenth Century." *Science in Context* 10 (1997): 589–603.

Reith, Reinhold. "Know-How, Technologietransfer und die Arcana artis im Mitteleuropa der Frühen Neuzeit." *Early Science and Medicine* 10 (2005): 349–377.

Rhamm, Albert. *Die betrüglichen Goldmacher am Hofe des Herzogs Julius von Braunschweig: Nach den Proceßakten dargestellt.* Wolfenbüttel: Zwissler, 1883.

Ricci, Amico. *Storia dell'architettura in Italia dal secolo IV al XVIII.* Modena: Regio-Ducal camera, 1857–1859.

Richarz, Monika. *Der Eintritt der Juden in die akademischen Berufe: Jüdische Studenten und Akademiker in Deutschland, 1678–1848.* Tübingen: Mohr, 1974.

Ries, Rotraud. "Juden als herrschaftliche Funktionsträger." In *Höfe und Residenzen im spätmittelalterlichen Reich: Bilder und Begriffe,* edited by Werner Paravicini, 1:303–307. Ostfildern: Thorbecke, 2005.

———. *Jüdisches Leben in Niedersachsen im 15. und 16. Jahrhundert.* Hanover: Hahn, 1994.

Ritzmann, Iris. "Judenmord als Folge des 'Schwarzen Todes': Ein medizinhistorischer Mythos?" *Medizin, Gesellschaft und Geschichte* 17 (1998): 101–130.

Rohrbacher-Sticker, Claudia. "A Hebrew Manuscript of Clavicula Salomonis." *British Library Journal* 21 (1995): 128–136.

———. "Mafteah Shelomoh: A New Acquisition of the British Library." *Jewish Studies Quarterly* 1 (1993/1994): 263–270.

Roper, Lyndal. *Oedipus and the Devil: Witchcraft, Sexuality, and Religion in Early Modern Europe.* London: Routledge, 1994.

Rosenau, Helen. *Vision of the Temple: The Image of the Temple of Jerusalem in Judaism and Christianity.* London: Oresko Books, 1979.

Rossi, Massimiliano. "Strukturelle Eigenschaften und Modelle in der moralischen Enzyklopädie des Tommaso Garzoni, 1549–1589." In *Macrocosmos in Microcosmo: Die Welt in der Stube: Zur Geschichte des Sammelns, 1450 bis 1800,* edited by Andreas Grote, 349–370. Opladen: Leske & Budrich, 1994.

Rossi, Paolo. "Bacon's Idea of Science." In *The Cambridge Companion to Bacon*, edited by Markku Peltonen, 25–46. Cambridge: Cambridge University Press, 1996.

———. Introduction to *La magia naturale nel Rinascimento: Testi di Agrippa, Cardano, Fludd*, 7–36. Turin: UTET, 1989.

———. *Philosophy, Technology, and the Arts in the Early Modern Era*. New York: Harper & Row, 1970.

Roth, Cecil. "Abramo Colorni, geniale inventore mantovano." *Rassegna mensile di Israel* 9 (1934): 147–158.

———. "The Amazing Abraham Colorni." In *Personalities and Events in Jewish History*, 296–304. Philadelphia: Jewish Publication Society of America, 1953.

———. "Forced Baptisms in Italy." In *Gleanings: Essays in Jewish History, Letters and Art*, 240–263. New York: Hermon Press, 1967.

———. *The Jewish Contribution to Civilisation*. 3rd ed. London: East and West Library, 1956.

———. *The Jews in the Renaissance*. Philadelphia: Jewish Publication Society of America, 1959.

———. "Joseph Nasi, Duke of Naxos, and the Counts of Savoy." *Jewish Quarterly Review* 57 (1967): 460–472.

———. "The King and the Kabbalist." In *Essays and Portraits in Anglo-Jewish History*, 139–164. Philadelphia: Jewish Publication Society of America, 1962.

———. "A Note on the Astronomers of the Vecinho Family." In *Gleanings: Essays in Jewish History, Letters and Art*, 174–178. New York: Hermon Press, 1967.

———. "Un consorzio ebraico mantovano e l'elezione al trono di Polonia nel 1587." In *Rassegna mensile di Israel* 28 (1962): 494–499.

Ruderman, David B. "At the Intersection of Cultures: The Historical Legacy of Italian Jewry." In *Gardens and Ghettos: The Art of Jewish Life in Italy*, edited by Vivian B. Mann, 1–23. Berkeley: University of California Press, 1989.

———. "Contemporary Science and Jewish Law in the Eyes of Isaac Lampronti of Ferrara and Some of His Contemporaries." *Jewish History* 6 (1992): 211–224.

———. "The Impact of Science on Jewish Culture and Society in Venice (with Special Reference to Jewish Graduates of Padua's Medical School)." *Gli ebrei a Venezia, secoli XIV–XVIII: Atti del convegno internazionale organizzato dall'Istituto di storia della società e dello stato veneziano della Fondazione Giorgio Cini, . . . , 5-10 giugno 1983*, edited by Gaetano Cozzi, 417–448. Milan: Edizioni Comunità, 1987.

---. Introduction to Ruderman and Veltri, eds., *Cultural Intermediaries*, 1–23.

---. *Jewish Enlightenment in an English Key: Anglo-Jewry's Construction of Modern Jewish Thought*. Princeton: Princeton University Press, 2000.

---. *Jewish Thought and Scientific Discovery in Early Modern Europe*. New Haven: Yale University Press, 1995.

---. *Kabbalah, Magic and Science: The Cultural Universe of a Sixteenth-Century Jewish Physician*. Cambridge: Harvard University Press, 1988.

---. "The Language of Science as the Language of Faith: An Aspect of Italian Jewish Thought in the Seventeenth and Eighteenth Centuries." In *Shlomo Simonsohn Jubilee Volume: Studies on the History of the Jews in the Middle Ages and Renaissance Period*, edited by Daniel Carpi et al., 177–189. Tel Aviv: Tel Aviv University, 1993.

---. "Unicorns, Great Beasts and the Marvelous Variety of Things in Nature in the Thought of Abraham b. Hananiah Yagel." In *Jewish Thought in the Seventeenth Century*, edited by Isadore Twersky and Bernard Septimus, 343–364. Cambridge, MA: Harvard University Press, 1987.

---. *A Valley of Vision: The Heavenly Journey of Abraham ben Hananiah Yagel*. Philadelphia: University of Pennsylvania Press, 1990.

Ruderman, David B., and Giuseppe Veltri, eds. *Cultural Intermediaries: Jewish Intellectuals in Early Modern Italy*. Philadelphia: University of Pennsylvania Press, 2004.

Ruspio, Federica. *La nazione portoghese: Ebrei ponentini e nuovi cristiani a Venezia*. Turin: Zamorani, 2007.

Sabattini, Gino. *Bibliografia di opere antiche e moderne di chiromanzia e sulla chiromanzia*. Reggio Emilia: Nironi & Prandi, 1946.

Sacco, Luigi. *Un primato italiano: La crittografia nei secoli XV e XVI*. Rome: Instituto storico e di cultura dell'arma del Genio, 1958.

Sachse, Julius. "Jacob Philadelphia, Mystic and Physicist." *Publications of the American Jewish Historical Society* 16 (1907): 73–83.

Salah, Asher. *La république des lettres: Rabbins, écrivains et médecins juifs en Italie au XVIIIe siècle*. Leiden: Brill, 2007.

Samsonow, Elisabeth von. "Die Hehler des Sinns: Zum Verhältnis von Kabbala und Secret Service." In Assmann and Assmann, eds., *Geheimnis und Öffentlichkeit*, 280–290.

Sandri, M. G., and Paolo Alazraki. *Arte e vita ebraica a Venezia, 1516–1797*. Florence: Sansoni, 1971.

Santi, Francesco. "Per una storia degli specchi magici." *Micrologus: Natura, scienze e società medievali* 14 (2006): 237–257.

Sargent, Rose-Mary. "Bacon as an Advocate for Cooperative Scientific Research." In *The Cambridge Companion to Bacon,* edited by Markku Peltonen, 146–171. Cambridge: Cambridge University Press, 1996.

Sauer, Paul. *Herzog Friedrich I. von Württemberg, 1557–1608: Ungestümer Reformer und weltgewandter Autokrat.* Munich: DVA, 2003.

Schaffer, Simon, and Steven Shapin. *Leviathan and the Air-Pump: Hobbes, Boyle, and the Experimental Life.* Princeton: Princeton University Press, 1985.

Schiavi, Luigi Arnaldo. "Gli ebrei in Venezia e nelle sue colonie: Appunti storici su documenti editi ed inediti." *Nuova antologia,* 3rd ser., 47 (1893): 485–519.

Schirrmeister, Claudia. *Geheimnisse: Über die Ambivalenz von Wissen und Nicht-Wissen.* Wiesbaden: Deutscher Universitäts-Verlag, 2004.

Schlundt, Rainer. *"Und hat sich das ertz wol erzaiget": Nordpfälzer Bergbau der Herzöge von Zweibrücken-Veldenz im 15. und 16 Jahrhundert.* Speyer: Pfälzische Gesellschaft zur Förderung der Wissenschaften, 1982.

Schmidtchen, Volker. *Bombarden, Befestigungen, Büchsenmeister: Von den ersten Mauerbrechern des Spätmittelalters zur Belagerungsartillerie der Renaissance: Eine Studie zur Entwicklung der Militärtechnik.* Düsseldorf: Droste, 1977.

Schneider, Ulrich. "Eine merkwürdige Prophezeihung [sic]." *Im neuen Reich: Wochenschrift für das Leben des deutschen Volkes in Staat, Wissenschaft und Kunst* 11 (1881): 369–376.

Schoeps, Hans Joachim. "Gumpertz Levison: Leben und Werk eines gelehrten Abenteurers des 18. Jahrhunderts." *Zeitschrift für Religions- und Geistesgeschichte* 4 (1952): 150–161.

Scholem, Gershom. "Alchemie und Kabbala." In *Judaica IV,* edited by Rolf Tiedemann, 19–128. Frankfurt am Main: Suhrkamp, 1984.

———. *Major Trends in Jewish Mysticism.* New York: Schocken Books, 1995.

Schrader, Fred E. "Zur sozialen Funktion von Geheimgesellschaften im Frankreich zwischen Ancient Régime und Revolution." In Assmann and Assmann, eds., *Geheimnis und Öffentlichkeit,* 179–193.

Schreckenberg, Heinz. *Die Juden in der Kunst Europas: Ein historischer Bildatlas.* Göttingen: Vandenhoeck & Ruprecht, 1996.

Schuchard, Marsha Keith. "Dr. Samuel Jacob Falk: A Sabbatian Adventurer in the Masonic Underground." In *Jewish Messianism in the Early Modern World,* edited by Matt D. Goldish and Richard H. Popkin, 203–226. Dordrecht: Kluwer, 2001.

———. "Lord George Gordon and Cabalistic Freemasonry: Beating Jacobite Swords into Jacobin Ploughshares." In *Secret Conversions to Judaism in*

Early Modern Europe, edited by Martin Mulsow and Richard H. Popkin, 183–231. Leiden: Brill, 2004.
Schütt, Hans-Werner. *Auf der Suche nach dem Stein der Weisen: Die Geschichte der Alchemie.* Munich: C. H. Beck, 2000.
Schwarz, Arturo. *Cabbalà e alchimia: Saggio sugli archetipi comuni.* Milan: Garzanti, 2004.
Schwarz, Ignaz. "Ein Wiener Donaubrückenprojekt aus dem XVI. Jahrhundert." *Jahrbuch für Landeskunde von Niederösterreich* 12 (1913): 78–100.
Schwarzfuchs, Simon. "Les Juifs de Cour." In *Le passage d'Israël,* edited by Shmuel Trigano, 383–405. Vol. 3 of *La société juive à travers l'histoire.* Paris: Fayard, 1993.
Seaton, Ethel. "Fresh Sources for Marlowe." *Review of English Studies* 5 (1929): 385–401.
Secret, François. *Les kabbalistes chrétiens de la Renaissance.* Paris: Dunod, 1964.
Segre, Renata. *Gli ebrei lombardi nell'età spagnola: Storia di un'espulsione: Memoria.* Memorie dell'Accademia delle scienze di Torino 28. Turin: Accademia delle scienze, 1973.
Sennett, Richard. *Flesh and Stone: The Body and the City in Western Civilization.* New York: Norton, 1996.
Sermidi, Michaela. "Vanità, lusso, arte e scienza: Il collezionismo omnivoro di Vicenzo I Gonzaga a Venezia." In *Il carteggio tra Venezia e Mantova, 1588–1612,* 13–72. Vol. 10 of *Le collezioni Gonzaga.* Milan: Silvana, 2003.
Shapin, Steven. "Science and the Public." In *Companion to the History of Modern Science,* edited by Robert Cecil Olby, Geoffrey N. Cantor, and John Rufus Roderick Christie, 990–1007. London: Routledge, 1990.
———. *The Scientific Revolution.* Chicago: University of Chicago Press, 1996.
———. *A Social History of Truth: Civility and Science in Seventeenth-Century England.* Chicago: University of Chicago Press, 1994.
———. "Understanding the Merton Thesis." *Isis* 79 (1988): 594–605.
Shepard, Odell. *The Lore of the Unicorn.* New York: Barnes & Noble, 1967.
Sherwin, Byron L. *Mystical Theology and Social Dissent: The Life and Works of Judah Loew of Prague.* London: Associated University Presses, 1982.
Shulvass, Moses A. *The Jews in the World of the Renaissance.* Leiden: Brill, 1973.
Shumaker, Wayne. *Natural Magic and Modern Science: Four Treatises, 1590–1657.* Binghamton: Center for Medieval and Early Renaissance Studies, 1989.
Siegmund, Stefanie B. *The Medici State and the Ghetto of Florence: The Construction of an Early Modern Jewish Community.* Stanford: Stanford University Press, 2006.

Sievers, Burkhard. *Geheimnis und Geheimhaltung in sozialen Systemen.* Opladen: Westdeutscher Verlag, 1974.
Simmel, Georg. "Das Geheimnis und die geheime Gesellschaft." In *Soziologie. Untersuchungen über die Formen der Vergesellschaftung,* 383–455. Vol. 11 of *Gesamtausgabe,* edited by Otthein Rammstedt. Frankfurt am Main: Suhrkamp, 1992. Translated by Albion Small as "The Sociology of Secrecy and of Secret Societies." *American Journal of Sociology* 11 (1906): 441–498.
Simonis, Linda. *Die Kunst des Geheimen: Esoterische Kommunikation und ästhetische Darstellung im 18. Jahrhundert.* Heidelberg: Winter, 2002.
Simonsohn, Shlomo. "Considerazioni introduttive." In *Gli ebrei a Venezia, secoli XIV–XVIII: Atti del convegno internazionale organizzato dall'Istituto di storia della società e dello stato veneziano della Fondazione Giorgio Cini, Venezia, . . . , 5–10 giugno 1983,* edited by Gaetano Cozzi, 323–332. Milan: Edizioni Comunità, 1987.
———. *History of the Jews in the Duchy of Mantua.* Jerusalem: Kiryath Sepher, 1977.
———. "Sefarim ve-Sifriyot shel Yehudei Mantova, 1595." *Kiryat Sefer* 37 (1961/1962): 103–122.
Singer, Dorothea Waley. "On a 16th Century Cartoon Concerning the Devilish Weapon of Gunpowder: Some Medieval Reactions to Guns and Gunpowder." *Ambix* 7 (1959): 25–33.
Siraisi, Nancy G. *Medieval and Early Renaissance Medicine: An Introduction to Knowledge and Practice.* Chicago: University of Chicago Press, 1990.
Sirat, Colette. *A History of Jewish Philosophy in the Middle Ages.* Cambridge: Cambridge University Press, 1990.
Smith, Pamela H. "Alchemy as a Language of Mediation at the Habsburg Court." *Isis* 85 (1994): 1–25.
———. *The Business of Alchemy: Science and Culture in the Holy Roman Empire.* Princeton: Princeton University Press, 1994.
Smith, Pamela H., and Paula Findlen. "Commerce and the Representation of Nature in Art and Science." In *Merchants and Marvels: Commerce, Science and Art in Early Modern Europe,* 1–25. New York: Routledge, 2002.
———, eds. *Merchants and Marvels: Commerce, Science and Art in Early Modern Europe.* New York: Routledge, 2002.
Sogliani, Daniela. "La repubblica e il ducato: Rapporti culturali e artistici tra la Serenissima e Mantova negli anni di Guglielmo Gonzaga." In *Il carteggio tra Venezia e Mantova, 1563–1587,* 15–81. Vol. 8 of *Le collezioni Gonzaga.* Milan: Silvana, 2003.

Solerti, Angelo. *Ferrara e la corte estense nella seconda metà del secolo decimosesto.* Città di Castello: Lapi, 1891.
Sonne, Isaiah. "Avnei Bonim le-Toldot ha-Yehudim be-Verona." *Kobez al Jad* 3 (1940): 145–183.
———. "Shemona Michtavim mi-Ferrara min ha-Me'a ha-shesh essre." *Zion: A Quarterly for Research in Jewish History* 14 (1952): 148–156.
Spitznagel, Albert, ed. *Geheimnis und Geheimhaltung: Erscheinungsformen—Funktionen—Konsequenzen.* Göttingen: Hogrefe, 1998.
———. Introduction to *Geheimnis und Geheimhaltung: Erscheinungsformen—Funktionen—Konsequenzen,* 19–51. Göttingen: Hogrefe, 1998.
Steinschneider, Moritz. "Allgemeine Einführung in die jüdische Literatur des Mittelalters." *Jewish Quarterly Review* 16 (1904): 734–764.
———. *Die hebräischen Übersetzungen des Mittelalters und die Juden als Dolmetscher.* Berlin: Kommissionverlag des bibliographischen Bureaus, 1893. Reprint, Graz: Akademische Druck- und Verlagsanstalt, 1956.
———. "Mathematik bei den Juden." *MGWJ* 1 (1905): 78–95; 2 (1905): 193–204; 3 (1905): 300–314.
———. "Pseudo-Juden und zweifelhafte Autoren." *MGWJ* 1 (1893): 39–48.
Stern, Selma. *The Court Jew: A Contribution to the History of the Period of Absolutism in Europe.* Translated by Ralph Weiman. New Brunswick: Transaction Press, 1986.
———. *Jud Süß: Ein Beitrag zur deutschen und zur jüdischen Geschichte.* Berlin: Akademie Verlag, 1929.
Stern, Tiffany. *Documents of Performance in Early Modern England.* Cambridge: Cambridge University Press, 2009.
Stewart, Larry. "Experimental Spaces and the Knowledge Economy." *History of Science* 45 (2007): 155–177.
———. *The Rise of Public Science: Rhetoric, Technology, and Natural Philosophy in Newtonian Britain, 1660–1750.* Cambridge: Cambridge University Press, 1992.
Stierlin, Henri. *Astrologie und Herrschaft: Von Platon bis Newton.* Frankfurt am Main: Athenäum-Verlag, 1988.
Stille, Alexander. "An Italian Jewish-Fascist Editor: Ettore Ovazza and La Nostra Bandiera." In *Why Didn't the Press Shout? American and International Journalism during the Holocaust,* edited by Robert Moses Shapiro, 317–331. New York: Yeshiva University Press, 2003.
Stok, Wilhelm. *Geheimnis, Lüge und Mißverständnis: Eine beziehungswissenschaftliche Untersuchung.* Kölner Vierteljahrshefte für Soziologie, Ergänzungsheft 2. Munich: Duncker & Humblot, 1929.

Stollberg-Rilinger, Barbara. "Das Verschwinden des Geheimnisses: Einleitende Bemerkungen." In *Das Geheimnis am Beginn der europäischen Moderne*, edited by Gisela Engel, Brita Rang, Klaus Reichert, and Heike Wunder, 229-233. Frankfurt am Main: Klostermann, 2002.

Stolleis, Michael. *Arcana imperii und Ratio status: Bemerkungen zur politischen Theorie des frühen 17. Jahrhunderts*. Göttingen: Vandenhoeck & Ruprecht, 1980.

Stonehill, C. A. *The Jewish Contribution to Civilization*. With a Preface by Stefan Zweig. Birmingham: Juckes, 1940.

Strasser, Gerhard F. "Die kryptographische Sammlung Herzog Augusts: Vom Quellenmaterial für seine 'Cryptomenytices' zu einem Schwerpunkt in seiner Bibliothek." *Wolfenbütteler Beiträge* 5 (1982): 83-121.

———. "Geheimschrift." In *Sammler, Fürst, Gelehrter: Herzog August zu Braunschweig und Lüneburg 1579-1666*, edited by Paul Raabe, 181-191. Braunschweig: Limbach, 1979.

———. *Lingua Universalis: Kryptologie und Theorie der Universalsprachen im 16. und 17. Jahrhundert*. Wiesbaden: Harrassowitz, 1988.

———. "The Noblest Cryptologist: Duke August the Younger of Brunswick-Luneburg (Gustavus Selenus) and His Cryptological Activities." *Cryptologia* 7 (1983): 193-217.

Strauss, Leo. *Persecution and the Art of Writing*. Chicago: University of Chicago Press, 1988.

Striedinger, Ivo. *Der Goldmacher Marco Bragadino: Archivkundliche Studie zur Kulturgeschichte des 16. Jahrhunderts*. Munich: Ackermann, 1928.

Stuckrad, Kocku von. "Secrecy as Social Capital." In *Constructing Tradition: Means and Myths of Transmission in Western Esotericism*, edited by Andreas B. Kilcher, 239-252. Leiden: Brill, 2010.

———. *Was ist Esoterik? Kleine Geschichte des geheimen Wissens*. Munich: C. H. Beck, 2004.

Studemund-Halévy, Michael. *Biographisches Lexikon der Hamburger Sefarden: Die Grabinschriften des Portugiesenfriedhofs an der Königstraße in Hamburg-Altona*. Hamburg: Christians Verlag, 2000.

———. "'Es residieren in Hamburg Minister fremder Mächte'—Sefardische Residenten in Hamburg." In *Hofjuden—Ökonomie und Interkulturalität: Die jüdische Wirtschaftselite im 18. Jahrhundert*, edited by Rotraud Ries and J. Friedrich Battenberg, 154-176. Hamburg: Christians Verlag, 2002.

Sziper, Ignacy. *Geszichte fun idiszer teater-kunst un drame*. Warsaw: Kultur-lige, 1923.

Szöllösi-Janze, Margit. "Lebens-Geschichte—Wissenschafts-Geschichte: Vom Nutzen der Biographie für Geschichtswissenschaft und Wissenschaftsgeschichte." *Berichte zur Wissenschaftsgeschichte* 23 (2000): 17–35.

Szydło, Zbigniew. "The Alchemy of Michael Sendivogius: His Central Nitre Theory." *Ambix* 40 (1993), 129–146.

———. *Water Which Does Not Wet Hands: The Alchemy of Michael Sendivogius.* Warsaw: Polish Academy of Sciences, 1994.

Telle, Joachim. "Paracelsus als Alchemiker." In *Paracelsus und Salzburg: Vorträge bei den internationalen Kongressen in Salzburg und Badgastein anlässlich des Paracelsus-Jahres 1993*, edited by Heinz Dopsch and Peter F. Kramml, 157–172. Salzburg: Gesellschaft für Salzburger Landeskunde, 1994.

———. *Paracelsus im Gedicht: Theophrastus von Hohenheim in der Poesie des 16. bis 21. Jahrhunderts.* Hürtgenwald: Pressler, 2008.

Theilhaber, Felix A. *Schicksal und Leistung: Juden in der deutschen Forschung und Technik.* Berlin: Welt-Verlag, 1931.

Thiele, Ottomar. *Salpeterwirtschaft und Salpeterpolitik: Eine volkswirtschaftliche Studie über das ehemalige europäische Salpeterwesen.* Tübingen: Laupp, 1905.

Thomas, Keith. *Religion and the Decline of Magic: Studies in Popular Beliefs in Sixteenth- and Seventeenth-Century England.* London: Weidenfeld and Nicolson, 1973.

Thompson, James Westfall, and Saul K. Padover. *Secret Diplomacy: Espionage and Cryptography, 1500–1815.* New York: Ungar, 1963.

Thorndike, Lynn. *A History of Magic and Experimental Science.* 8 vols. New York: Columbia University Press, 1964–1966.

Tirosh-Samuelson, Hava. "Theology of Nature in Sixteenth-Century Italian Jewish Philosophy." *Science in Context* 10 (1997): 529–570.

Toaff, Ariel. *Il prestigiatore di Dio: Avventure e miracoli di un alchimista ebreo nelle corti del Rinascimento.* Milan: Rizzoli, 2010.

———. *Love, Work, and Death: Jewish Life in Medieval Umbria.* Translated by Judith Landry. London: Littman Library, 1996.

Toch, Michael. "Die wirtschaftliche Tätigkeit." In *GJ* 3:2139–2164.

———. "Economic Activities of German Jews in the Middle Ages." In *Wirtschaftsgeschichte der mittelalterlichen Juden: Fragen und Einschätzungen*, edited by Michael Toch, 181–210. Munich: Oldenbourg, 2008.

Torijano, Pablo A. *Solomon the Esoteric King: From King to Magus, Development of a Tradition.* Leiden: Brill, 2002.

Toury, Jacob. "Der Eintritt der Juden ins deutsche Bürgertum." In *Das Judentum in der Deutschen Umwelt, 1800–1850: Studien zur Frühgeschichte der*

Emanzipation, edited by Hans Liebeschütz and Arnold Paucker, 139–242. Tübingen: Mohr, 1977.

Trabucco, Oreste. "Lo sconosciuto autografo della Chirofisonomia di G. B. Della Porta." *Bruniana & Campanelliana* 1 (1995): 273–295.

Trachtenberg, Joshua. *The Devil and the Jews: The Medieval Conception of the Jew and Its Relation to Modern Anti-Semitism.* Philadelphia: Jewish Publication Society of America, 1983.

———. *Jewish Magic and Superstition: A Study in Folk Religion.* New York: Behrman's Jewish Book House, 1939.

Trawnicek, Peter. *Münzjuden unter Ferdinand II. nach den Akten des Hofkammerarchivs in Wien.* Kiel: Solivagus, 2010.

Trepp, Anne-Charlott. *Von der Glückseligkeit alles zu wissen: Die Erforschung der Natur als religiöse Praxis in der Frühen Neuzeit.* Frankfurt am Main: Campus, 2009.

Treue, Wolfgang. "'Verehrt und angespien': Zur Geschichte jüdischer Ärzte in Aschkenas von den Anfängen bis zur Akademisierung." *Würzburger medizinhistorische Mitteilungen* 21 (2002): 139–203.

Trevor-Roper, Hugh. *Princes and Artists: Patronage and Ideology at Four Habsburg Courts, 1517–1633.* London: Thames and Hudson, 1976.

Trilling, Lionel. *Sincerity and Authenticity.* London: Oxford University Press, 1974.

Troitzsch, Ulrich. "Erfinder, Forscher und Projektemacher: Der Aufstieg der praktischen Wissenschaften." In *Macht des Wissens: Die Entstehung der modernen Wissensgesellschaft,* edited by Richard van Dülmen and Sina Rauschenbach, 439–464. Cologne: Böhlau, 2004.

Troncarelli, Fabio, ed. *La città dei segreti: Magia, astrologia e cultura esoterica a Roma, XV–XVIII.* Milan: Angeli, 1985.

Ughi, Luigi. *Dizionario storico degli uomini illustri ferraresi nella pieta, nelle arti, e nelle scienze colle loro opera, o fatti principali.* Ferrara: Rinaldi, 1804.

Ullmann, Manfred. *Die Natur- und Geheimwissenschaften im Islam.* Leiden: Brill, 1972.

Vasoli, Cesare. "Gli astri e la corte: L'astrologia a Ferrara nell'età ariostesca." In *La cultura delle corti,* 129–158. Bologna: Capelli, 1980.

———, ed. *Magia e scienza nella civiltà umanistica.* Bologna: Il mulino, 1976.

Večeřová, Petra. *Šumanská tiskárna, 1585–1628.* Prague: Scriptorium, 2002.

Veinstein, Gilles. "Note sur les transferts technologiques des séfarades dans l'empire ottoman." In *1492: L'expulsion des juifs d'Espagne,* edited by Roland Goetschel, 83–92. Paris: Maisonneuve et Larose, 1995.

———. "Une communauté ottoman: Les juifs d'Avlonya (Valona) dans la deuxième moitié du XVIe siècle." In *Gli ebrei a Venezia, secoli XIV–XVIII: Atti del convegno internazionale organizzato dall'Istituto di storia della società e dello stato veneziano della Fondazione Giorgio Cini, . . . , 5–10 giugno 1983*, edited by Gaetano Cozzi, 781–828. Milan: Edizioni Comunità, 1987.

Veltri, Giuseppe. "Jüdische Einstellungen zu den Wissenschaften im 16. und 17. Jahrhundert: Das Prinzip der praktisch-empirischen Anwendbarkeit." In *Judentum zwischen Tradition und Moderne*, edited by Gerd Biegel and Michael Graetz, 149–159. Heidelberg: Winter, 2002.

———. *Magie und Halakha: Ansätze zu einem empirischen Wissenschaftsbegriff im spätantiken und frühmittelalterlichen Judentum*. Tübingen: Mohr, 1997.

———. "'Ohne Recht und Gerechtigkeit': Rudolf II. und sein Bankier Markus Meyzl." In *An der Schwelle zur Moderne: Juden in der Renaissance*, edited by Giuseppe Veltri and Annette Winkelmann, 233–255. Leiden: Brill, 2003.

———. "Science and Religious Hermeneutics: The 'Philosophy' of Rabbi Loew of Prague." In *Religious Confessions and the Sciences in the Sixteenth Century*, edited by Jürgen Helm and Annette Winkelmann, 119–135. Leiden: Brill, 2001.

———. "Yehuda Löw oder: der hohe Rabbi von Prag als Philosoph des Judentums." In *Zwischen Narretei und Weisheit: Biographische Skizzen und Konturen alter Gelehrsamkeit*, edited by Gerald Hartung and Wolf Peter Klein, 192–218. Hildesheim: Olms, 1997.

Venturi, Gianni. "Mantova e Ferrara: Due corti al tramonto: Un esempio di geografia cultura." In *L'esercizio del collezionismo*, edited by Raffaella Morselli, 213–229. Vol. 1 of *Gonzaga: La celeste galleria*. Milan: Skira, 2002.

Vermeir, Koen. "Openness versus Secrecy: Some Historical and Conceptual Issues." Paper presented at the conference States of Secrecy, Harvard University, Cambridge, MA, 11 April 2009.

Vickers, Brian. "Francis Bacon, Feminist Historiography, and the Dominion of Nature." *Journal of the History of Ideas* 69 (2008): 117–141.

———. Introduction to *Occult and Scientific Mentalities in the Renaissance*, 1–55. Cambridge: Cambridge University Press, 1984.

Viganò, Marino. *Architetti e ingegneri militari italiani all'estero dal XV al XVIII secolo*. 2 vols. Livorno: Sillabe, 1994–1999.

Vogelstein, Hermann, and Paul Rieger. *Geschichte der Juden in Rom*. 2 vols. Berlin: Mayer & Müller, 1895.

Voigts, Manfred. *Das geheimnisvolle Verschwinden des Geheimnisses: Ein Versuch*. Vienna: Passagen, 1995.

Volkov, Shulamit. "Soziale Ursachen des jüdischen Erfolgs in der Wissenschaft." In *Antisemitismus als kultureller Code: Zehn Essays*, 146–165. Munich: C. H. Beck, 2000.

Voss, Mary J. "Between the Cannon and the Book: Mathematicians and Military Culture in Sixteenth-Century Italy." Ph.D. diss., Johns Hopkins University, 1994.

Wagner, F. "Studien zu einer Lehre von der Geheimschrift." *Archivalische Zeitschrift* 11 (1886): 156–189; 12 (1887): 1–29; 13 (1888): 8–44.

Weber, Max. *Wirtschaft und Gesellschaft: Grundriß der verstehenden Soziologie*. Edited by Johannes Winckelmann. Tübingen: Mohr, 1985.

Webster, Charles. *From Paracelsus to Newton: Magic and the Making of Modern Science*. Cambridge: Cambridge University Press, 1982.

———. *The Great Instauration: Science, Medicine and Reform, 1626–1660*. London: Duckworth, 1975.

Weinberg, Joanna. "The Beautiful Soul: Azariah de' Rossi's Search for Truth." In Ruderman and Veltri, eds., *Cultural Intermediaries*, 109–126.

Weinberger, J. "Science and Rule in Bacon's Utopia: An Introduction to the Reading of the New Atlantis." *American Political Science Review* 70 (1976): 865–885.

Weisz, Max. *Katalog der hebräischen Handschriften und Bücher des Professors Dr. David Kaufmann s.A.* Frankfurt am Main: Kaufmann, 1906.

Wenninger, Markus J. "Juden als Münzmeister, Zollpächter und fürstliche Finanzbeamte im mittelalterlichen Aschkenas." In *Wirtschaftsgeschichte der mittelalterlichen Juden: Fragen und Einschätzungen*, edited by Michael Toch, 121–138. Munich: Oldenbourg, 2008.

———. "Von jüdischen Rittern und anderen waffentragenden Juden im mittelalterlichen Deutschland." *Aschkenas* 13 (2003): 35–82.

Westerbarkey, Joachim. *Das Geheimnis: Zur funktionalen Ambivalenz von Kommunikationsstrukturen*. Opladen: Westdeutscher Verlag, 1991.

Wewers, Gerd A. *Geheimnis und Geheimhaltung im rabbinischen Judentum*. Berlin: De Gruyter, 1975.

Weyer, Jost. *Graf Wolfgang II. von Hohenlohe und die Alchemie: Alchemistische Studien in Schloß Weikersheim, 1587–1610*. Sigmaringen: Thorbecke, 1992.

White, Lynn. "Medical Astrologers and Late Medieval Technology." *Viator: Medieval and Renaissance Studies* 6 (1975): 295–308.

Wininger, Salomon. *Große jüdische National-Biographie*. 7 vols. Cernăuti: Orient, 1925–1936.

Wischnitzer, Mark. *A History of Jewish Crafts and Guilds*. New York: David, 1965.

Wolf, Jürgen Rainer. "Joseph Süß Oppenheimer ('Jud Süß') und die Darmstädter Goldmünze: Ein Beitrag zur hessen-darmstädtischen Finanzpolitik unter Landgraf Ernst Ludwig." In *Neunhundert Jahre Geschichte der Juden in Hessen: Beiträge zum politischen, wirtschaftlichen und kulturellen Leben*, edited by the Kommission für die Geschichte der Juden in Hessen, 214-261. Wiesbaden: Kommission für die Geschichte der Juden in Hessen, 1983.

———. "Joseph Süß Oppenheimer ('Jud Süß') und die Darmstädter Goldmünzprägung unter Landgraf Ernst Ludwig." *Numismatisches Nachrichtenblatt* 30 (1981): 93-106.

Wolf, Lucien. "Jews in Elizabethan England." *Transactions of the Jewish Historical Society of England* 11 (1928): 1-91.

Wolff, Eberhard. "Antijudaismus als Teil der Judenemanzipation: Die Auseinandersetzung des Göttinger Geburtshelfers Friedrich Benjamin Osiander mit seinem Schüler Joseph Jacob Gumprecht um 1800." *Medizin, Gesellschaft und Geschichte* 17 (1998): 57-100.

Wolfson, Elliot R. "Murmuring Secrets: Eroticism and Esotericism in Medieval Kabbalah." In *Hidden Intercourse: Eros and Sexuality in the History of Western Esotericism*, edited by Wouter J. Hanegraaff and Jeffrey J. Kripal, 65-109. Leiden: Brill, 2008.

———, ed. *Rending the Veil: Concealment and Secrecy in the History of Religions.* New York: Seven Bridges, 1999.

Yates, Frances A. *Giordano Bruno and the Hermetic Tradition.* London: Routledge, 1991.

———. "Science, Salvation, and the Cabala." *New York Review of Books*, 27 May 1976.

Zelzer, Maria. *Weg und Schicksal der Stuttgarter Juden.* Stuttgart: Klett, 1964.

Zetterberg, J. Peter. "The Mistaking of 'the Mathematicks' for Magic in Tudor and Stuart England." *Sixteenth Century Journal* 11 (1980): 83-97.

Zimmels, Hirsch Jakob. *Magicians, Theologians and Doctors: Studies in Folkmedicine and Folk-lore as Reflected in the Rabbinical Responsa, 12th-19th Centuries.* London: Goldston, 1952.

Zimmer, Eric. *Jewish Synods in Germany during the Late Middle Ages, 1286-1603.* New York: Yeshiva University Press, 1978.

Zimmer, Jürgen. "Die Gonzaga und der Prager Hof Kaiser Rudolf II: Historischer Überblick." In *Rudolf II, Prague and the World: Papers from the International Conference Prague, 2-4 September, 1997*, edited by Lubomír Konečný, 16-23. Prague: Artefactum, 1998.

———. "Die Gonzaga und der Prager Hof Kaiser Rudolf II: Kunsthistorische Fragmente." *Umění* 46 (1998): 207-221.

———. "Praga caput regni: Kulturaustausch zur Zeit Kaiser Rudolfs II." In *Krakau, Prag und Wien: Funktionen von Metropolen im frühmodernen Staat,* edited by Marina Dmitrieva and Karen Lambrecht, 283–297. Stuttgart: Steiner, 2000.

Zinger, Nimrod. "'Who Knows What the Cause Is?': 'Natural' and 'Unnatural' Causes for Illness in the Writings of Ba'alei Shem, Doctors and Patients among German Jews in the Eighteenth Century." In *The Jewish Body: Corporeality, Society, and Identity in the Renaissance and Early Modern Period,* edited by Maria Diemling and Giuseppe Veltri, 27–155. Leiden: Brill, 2009.

Zinguer, Ilana, ed. *L'Hébreu au temps de la Renaissance.* Leiden: Brill, 1992.

Index

Aachen, Hans von, 163
Aaron (Jewish sorcerer), 157
Abenaes, Salomon, 81, 82
abortifacients, 52
Abraham de Ragusa, 71
Abraham Eleazar, 187–88
Abralino de Colonia, 70
Abramo da Cremona, 69
Abravanel, Leon, 51
Abravanel, Yehuda. *See* Ebreo, Leone
Académie Royale, 243
Accademia de' Secreti, 12
Achino, Magister, 69
Adalbert of Hamburg, Archbishop, 38
Adam of Bremen, 38
Agricola, Georgius, 5
Agrippa, 89, 90
Alatini, Angelo, 212; *I trionfi*, 215
Alberti, Leon Battista, 57, 121, 125, 135, 180–81
alchemy, 5, 11, 12, 17, 22, 23, 30–49, 54, 86, 90–91, 94–114, 117, 125–26, 160, 172–74, 175, 182–83, 198, 202, 209, 216, 225, 226–27, 228, 247–49, 257; executions of practitioners, 109–11, 210; fraud and, 102–3; medicine and, 3, 95, 98–99, 226; practical vs. transmutational, 46; royal courts and, 40, 41, 72, 163–65, 184–86, 205, 206, 210; saltpeter use, 185, 186–87, 192, 198; science and, 233. *See also* gold
Aldrovandi, Ulisse, 15
Alemanno, Yoḥanan, 85, 153, 233
Alexander VI, Pope, 33
Alfonso, King of Aragon and Sicily, 71
Alfonso II d'Este, Duke of Ferrara, 125, 127–29, 162, 305n70; Colorni and, 167–69, 201–2, 203, 208; death of, 194; lack of heir of, 128, 168, 202; war against Turks and, 194
ammonium, 188–89
Anatoli, Jacob, 40
Ancantherus, Claudius, 170
Annals of Hirsau, 86
Ansbach, Margrave of, 154
antidotes. *See* poisons and antidotes
anti-Judaism, 32, 33, 86, 191, 205, 209–10, 246, 249; alleged magical skills and, 156; Christian fantasies and, 23, 24; Luther and, 104, 111; Marlowe play as exemplar of, 24, 77–78; Menasseh rebuttals to, 212–13; poisoned well rumors and, 24, 52, 55–56; Scientific Revolution and, 230, 243, 255; secrecy as strategy against, 26–28; spy stereotype and, 60–61; stench charges and, 188–89. *See also* expulsion of Jews
anti-Semitism (racial), 1, 251
aphrodisiacs, 51, 89, 99
Aragon, 38, 71
arcana, 3–8, 17–36, 49–56, 89, 225, 242–49, 252; cryptography and, 56–60; economic life and, 94–115; Jewish mastery of, 7–8, 22–36, 172–75, 242–43; Kabbalah and, 25–26; women and, 32, 50
arcana imperii. *See* state arcana
Archevolti, Samuel, *Arugat ha-Bosem*, 58, 184
Arcimboldo, Giuseppe, 163
Argenti, Matteo, 178
argutia, concept of, 28

415

Ariosto, Ludovico, 145; *Il negromante,* 32–33
Aristotle, 3, 12, 25, 36, 145, 150, 151, 257; *Physiognomonica,* 147
arsenic fumes, 270n127
art collections, 215–16
Ashkenazi, Salomo, 49–50, 294n12
Ashkenazi Jews, 26, 38, 41, 68, 70, 82, 170, 195, 231
astrology, 25, 28, 51, 66, 90, 109, 137, 143; chiromancy and, 150; Colorni defense of, 119, 145, 147, 149; mathematics linked with, 138; risks associated with, 33
Attias, David, *La Güerta de Oro,* 144
Attias, Giuseppe, 293n44
Auerbach, Berthold, 250
August, Duke of Braunschweig-Lüneburg, 178
August I, Elector of Saxony, 80, 174
Augustine, *De Civitate Dei,* 146
Avicenna, 146
Azaria de Fano, Menaḥem, 195

Bacci, Andrea, 79; *L'alicorno,* 79, 82
Bacon, Francis, 150, 255; *New Atlantis* (*Nova Atlantis*), 161, 239–42, 244, 251
Bacon, Roger, 152, 228, 233; *Mirror of Alchimy,* 29
Baden, Margrave of, 72
Bakhtin, Michael, 93
Barclay, John, *Euphormionis Lusinini Satyricon,* 174–76
Baron, Salo W., *Social and Religious History of the Jews,* 226
Barozzi, Francesco, 87–88
Basola, Abraham, 195
Bassano, Salomon da, 76
Bassevi, Jacob and Samuel, 171
Bavaria, Duke of, 177
Becher, Johann Joachim, 5, 95, 113
Bembo, Pietro Cardinal, 215
Benjamin, Walter, 143

Bensalem (ideal society), 239–42
Bernardino da Siena, 157
Bettini, Simone, 69
Biagioli, Mario, 65, 140
Bible, 25, 31, 42, 146, 147, 183, 188, 217, 238, 259; condemnation of magic, 153; cryptography and, 184; measurement and, 151; on miraculous transformations, 207, 208; poisons mentioned in, 54; rabbinical fourfold meaning of, 29; *re'em*-unicorn association, 82, 83, 290n358; science vs., 171; search for hidden meanings in, 29–30; on secrets, 160–61; as warfare handbook, 71–72. *See also* Solomon, King
biological warfare, 55, 56
Biringuccio, Vannoccio, *De la pirotechnia,* 189
black magic. *See under* magic
Blanis, Benedetto, 91
Blumenberg, Hans, 236
Bok, Sissela, 10
Bonetto de Latis, 33
Bonfil, Robert, 228
book burning, 117, 214
Book of Poisons (Arabic), 54–55
Book of Wisdom (apocrypha), 151
Borgia, Cesare, 71
botany, 122, 123
Boyer d'Argens, Jean-Baptiste de, *Lettres Juives,* 66–67
Boyle, Robert, 190, 251; *The Skeptical Chymist,* 198
Bragadino, Marco, 34–35, 76, 154
Brahe, Tycho, 164
Brandenburg, Elector of, 104
Brant, Sebastian, *The Ship of Fools,* 21
Braunschweig-Lüneburg, Dukes of, 178, 211
Braunschweig-Wolfenbüttel, Duchy of, 102, 106, 276n27
bridges, 72–74, 124, 134, 320n341

Brugnaleschi, Valeria, 88
Brühl, Heinrich von, Count, 62
Bruno, Giordano, 164, 232–33
Buber, Martin, 254
Buch von kaiserlichen Kriegsrechten, 127–28
Burckhardt, Jacob, 219
Buzalini, Isachi, 45

cabal (term derivation), 25
Cagliostro, 218, 247
Calcagnino, Guido, Count, 168
Calenberg, Duke of, 105
Caliman (Venetian Jew), 89
Calonimos, Davide, 51
Cammeo, Abraham di, 44
Campanella, Tommaso, 16, 90; *The City of the Sun,* 148
Camporesi, Piero, 76
canals, 68, 73, 124
Canossa, Galeazzo, Count, 215
Capsali, Eliya, 78
Caracosa (Saracosa) Samuel, 38
Cardano, Girolamo, 14, 59, 135; *De rerum varietate,* 181; *De secritis,* 3–4, 14; *De subtilitate,* 181
Cardoso, Isaac, 83
card tricks, 152, 153, 154, 166
Carlebach, Elisheva, 23–24
Carlo II, Duke of Mantua, 214
Carmi, Consiglio, 195, 196, 213
Carmi, Rafael, 195–96, 213
Castro, Abraham, 43
Catherine II, Empress of Russia, 245
Catholic Church, 20, 21, 23, 26, 86–88, 100, 102, 120, 122, 191; alchemy and, 33, 103; chiromancy and, 141, 142, 143, 150; Colorni clerical friendships, 116, 130–31, 140–42; *Index librorum prohibitorum,* 148, 157; magic and, 90, 155, 156, 157; Scientific Revolution and, 227. *See also* Inquisition; papacy

Cattaneo, Giovanni, 62
Certaldo, Paolo da, *Book of Good Manners,* 21
Cervi, David, 27, 81, 98
Challo, Marco, 51
charlatans, 15–16, 102, 141, 146, 149, 166, 221, 228, 248
chemicals, 75, 99, 130
chemical weapons, 55, 56
chemistry, 45–48, 49, 88, 89, 106, 114, 198; poisons and, 52–56
Chinese Jews, 238
chiromancy, 5, 117, 119, 140–48, 220–21; "natural" vs. "false," 148–50
Christian IV, Duke of Palatinate-Zweibrücken, 112, 113–15
Christian IV, King of Denmark, 188
Christina, Queen of Sweden, 41
Christoph, Duke of Württemberg, 205
cinnabar, 46, 55
ciphers. *See* cryptography
Cipolla, Carlo, 13, 14
circumcision, 23, 26
Città di Castello, 190
Clapmarius, Arnold, 19; *De Arcanis Rerumpublicarum,* 19
Clausburg, Ludwig Cramer von, 95
Clavicula Salomonis, 78, 101, 156–62; Colorni translation of, 158–59, 162, 222
Clement VII, Pope, 80
Clement XII, Pope, 250
Clenche, John, 64
Cocles. *See* Rocca, Bartolomeo della
codes. *See* cryptography
Cohen, Benjamin, 191
Cohen, Hermann, 254
Cohen, Joseph ha-, 78
coinage, 45, 67, 96, 104–9, 171, 304–5nn60, 61
Cologne, Archbishop of, 154

Colorni, Abramo, 54, 69–70, 116–223, 235; background and family of, 6, 117–20, 123–24, 131–33, 196, 199–200, 202, 213–14; biographical significance of, 211–23; Christian and Jewish admirers of, 117, 118, 130–31, 133, 134, 184, 222; contemporary view of, 152, 212–23; core of reputation of, 152–61; cryptographic system of, 57, 59, 117, 119, 129, 177–84, 211, 217, 221; death of, 211, 214; earliest extant source on, 123–24; intellectual range of, 145–46; Jewish business partners of, 195–96, 213; Jewish devotion of, 116–17, 149, 183, 213, 222; linguistic proficiency of, 118–19; magic practice and, 152–61, 207, 220; mathematical secrets and, 134–35, 151, 152, 166; miracles alleged to, 207; patrons of (*see* Este family; Gonzaga family; Rudolph II; Stuttgart court); as *professore de' secreti*, 5–6, 7, 13, 116–17, 119, 129, 130, 145–46, 149, 154, 160, 161, 208, 211–22, 243–44; as "Saltpeter Jew," 71, 185, 192–200, 205, 207, 208, 210; self-fashioning of, 123–24, 151, 221; Venetian reputation of, 129–30, 201; works: 119; *Arithmetica*, 136, 201; *Chirofisionomia*, 119, 121, 140, 144, 145–49, 150, 151, 170, 201, 220–21; *Clavicula* translation, 158–59, 162, 222; *Euthimetria*, 119, 134–38, 151, 201, 220; *Scotographia*, 57, 119, 177–84, 200–201, 216, 217, 220–21, 259; *Tavole mathematiche* (lost), 135, 136
Colorni, Colomba (daughter), 132
Colorni, Diamante (stepmother), 117
Colorni, Gentile (mother), 117
Colorni, Giuseppe (nephew), 214
Colorni, Isaaco da (cousin), 214
Colorni, Lazzaro (cousin), 214
Colorni, Salomone (cousin), 214
Colorni, Salomone (father), 117

Colorni, Samuele (cousin), 214
Colorni, Simone (Il Morino) (son), 6, 83, 132, 166, 199, 200, 211–16, 222
Colorni, Violante (first wife), 131–32, 212
Colorni, Vittore, 301n2
Conegliano, Israel, 51
confidentiality, 27, 66
Coniano, Joel Abram, 89
Constantinople. *See* Ottoman Empire
Conti, Gauya (Gaiuczu), 71
converted Jews, 23–24, 26, 30, 59, 63, 71, 142, 171–72, 173, 187; *conversos*, 26, 81; practice of alchemy and magic by, 102–3
Copernicanism, 171, 228, 233, 234, 257
copper trade, 104–5
correspondence, 9, 57, 179
Cosimo I, Grand Duke of Tuscany, 81
cosmetics, 50
Costa, Emanuel Mendes da, 238–39; *A Natural History of Fossils*, 238
Council of Trent, 117, 122, 214
counterfeiting, 33, 103, 105, 110
Counter-Reformation, 120, 131
court Jews, 40–41, 42, 121, 170–71, 175, 214, 248, 249; as alchemists, 107–15; discreet secrecy and, 169, 239; gunpowder trade and, 191–92; Luther's warning against, 104, 111; moneyer office and, 95–96, 104, 105; Oppenheimer's importance as, 73, 106–11, 192; spying by, 62, 63
crane apparatus, 124, 126
Cremona, 33, 69, 143
Croix, Marquise de la, 247
Croll, Oswald, 164
Cromwell, Oliver, 212
Crusius, Martin, 207, 208
cryptography, 5, 9–10, 17, 36, 56–60, 117, 119, 129, 161, 177–84, 211, 217, 221; Jewish codes and, 26–27, 59, 60, 63, 91–92; polyalphabetic method, 180; Talmudic origins, 58

crypto-Jews, 26, 122–23
curiosities, cabinet of, 80, 166, 236, 239
curiosity, 235–37
Czartoryski, Prince of Poland, 247

Daedalus of Esperia, 212
Dalmatia, 56, 69
Dante, 183; *Divine Comedy,* 118; *Inferno,* 103
Danube bridge project, 73–74, 320n341
Da Pisa, Yeḥiel Nissim, 6, 132–33, 153, 213
Daston, Lorraine, 232, 237
Dee, John, 138, 139, 164, 172, 232
Del Banco family, 195
Della Porta, Giovan Battista, 12, 13, 14, 15, 59, 86, 136, 155, 183, 221, 232; *De furtivis literarum notis,* 181; *Della chirofisonomia,* 144–45, 149–51; *Magia naturalis,* 14, 76, 181
Dellavolta, Manuello, 63
Delle, Martinus de. *See* Nelle, Mardochaeus de
Delmedigo, Joseph Salomon, 43, 77, 144, 256–58; *Sefer Matzref la-Ḥokhmah,* 256
desalinization project, 73, 97
Descartes, René, 228, 229, 232
Deus absconditus (hidden God), 20
devil, 155, 186, 188, 190, 221
Digges, Thomas, 136
diplomacy, 57, 61, 204
disprigionare (secret of escaping), 159, 162
divination, 18, 139–41, 143
Dolfin, Giovanni, 306n89
Dominican order, 90
Donne, John, 328n472
Dresden Palace, 22, 41
Dülmen, Richard van, 11
dyes, 45, 114

Eamon, William, 13
economic life, 2, 5–7, 94–115. *See also specific aspects*

Elbe River, 73
Eleonora, Duchess of Mantua, 210, 211
Elizabeth I, Queen of England, 138, 206
emblems, 18, 28
empiricism, 235
encryption. *See* cryptography
Encyclopaedia Judaica, 226
engineering, 5, 73, 117, 119, 124–26, 133, 134, 138, 152, 160, 201, 220, 221; Jewish expertise in, 66–70, 121, 257; military (*see* weapons); panegyrics to, 212
England, 14, 77–78, 81, 150, 160–61, 172, 212, 247–48; encryption and, 58–59; Jewish Freemasons, 250; Jewish scientists, 244, 248; mathematics and, 137–38, 139; saltpeter production ideas, 198
Enlightenment, 5–6, 11, 18, 61, 157, 254; arcana and, 244–49, 252
Enlightenment, Jewish. *See* Haskalah
entrepreneurs, 27, 94–95, 99, 101, 115, 238
Ercker, Lazarus, 41, 106, 198
Ernest d'Or (gold coin), 108
Ernst Ludwig, Landgrave of Hesse-Darmstadt, 107–8
esotericism, 25, 101
espionage, 36, 60–65, 91–92, 97
Este, Alfonso d.' *See* Alfonso II d'Este
Este, Cesare d,' 128, 168, 210
Este, Leonello d,' Marquis of Ferrara, 69
Este, Luigi d,' Cardinal, 222
Este family, 26, 48, 63, 89, 91, 101, 119–23, 221; Colorni ties with, 69–70, 119–20, 123, 125, 126–30, 132, 135, 139, 140, 153, 159, 162, 168–69, 178, 194–97, 199, 201–2, 208, 210–11, 214, 220; employment of engineers, 121, 126; Gonzaga rivalry with, 203; tolerance toward Jews of, 120–22; weapons technology and, 128–29, 196. *See also* Ferrara, Duchy of

excrement, 188–89
executions, 109–11, 210
exotic animals, 81
expert knowledge, 67, 255, 257–58
explosive devices, 116, 184–200
expulsion of Jews, 33–34, 63, 71, 74, 78, 97, 190, 196; Este resettlement of, 120; magical prevention of, 86

Faccas, Iuda, 191
faith healers, 32
Falk, Samuel Jacob Ḥayyim (Ba'al Shem of London), 247–48, 249
false messiahs, 86
Fano, Salomon, 83
Farissol, Abraham, 233
Fattorino, Gabriele, 132
Faulhaber, Johann, *Ingenieurs Schul*, 135
Feifel (Jewish physician), 61
Feivelmann (Jewish moneylender), 106
fencing, 117–18, 140
Ferdinand II, Holy Roman Emperor, 171
Ferdinand III, Holy Roman Emperor, 42
Ferdinando, Grand Duke of Tuscany, 77, 98–99
Ferrara (city), 94
Ferrara, Duchy of: papal takeover of, 128, 168, 194, 201–2. *See also* Este family; University of Ferrara
Ferrara, Duke of. *See* Alfonso II d'Este
fertilizers, 114, 185
Feuchtwanger, Lion, *Jud Süß*, 218
Feuer, Lewis S., 228
Feuerwerksbuch (Fireworks Book), 190
Fichte, Johann Gottlieb, 1, 250
Ficino, Marsilio, 145, 155
Fideli, Ercole de' (Salomone da Sesso), 71
finance. *See* money business
Fioravanti, Leonardo, 15, 51
firearms. *See* gunpowder; weapons
Florence, 91, 123, 133, 178, 213
flour, 75–76

Foa, Abraham, 43–44
food preservation, 185
fortune telling. *See* astrology; chiromancy; divination
fossils, 238
Foucault, Michel, 19, 67, 258
France, 78, 114, 156, 157, 243
Frankfurt, 70, 82, 189, 191; "rabbinical conspiracy" (1603), 170
Frederick I, Duke of Württemberg, 101, 182, 200, 202, 205–11, 214, 216, 299n111
Frederick II, Holy Roman Emperor, 41
Frederick III, Holy Roman Emperor, 191
Frederick IV, Duke of Tyrol, 39, 64
Freemasonry, 1, 10–11, 18, 114, 247, 250, 252
Friedenwald, Harry, 228
Fugger family, 50, 204
Funkenstein, Amos, 230–31

Gabrieli, Gaspare, 123
Gaddi, Jacopo, 211–12
Gaeta, Jacopo da (Ya'qūb Pasha), 53
Galen, 145, 147
Galileo, 16, 42, 136, 140, 144, 178, 228, 229, 232, 256
Gans, David, 171, 172, 228, 234
Gans, Joachim (Gaunse), 172
Garzoni, Tomaso, 118, 130–31, 141–42, 155–56; on Colorni's skills, 152, 162, 207–8, 211, 218, 220; works of: *Chirofisionomia*, 142; *Piazza universale*, 126–27, 130, 131, 142, 152, 155–56, 162, 208; *Serraglio de gli stupori del mondo*, 131; *La sinagoga de gl'ignoranti*, 131
Gauyu (Gaudiu), 71
gems, 131, 215, 216; conjuring up of, 154; trade in, 27, 98, 109, 166

Gerosolimitano, Domenico, 54
Gervasius, Julius, 187–88
Giacomoa la Mantilara, 90
Ginsburger, Moses, 70
Gionatavo, Salomon, 99
Giraldini, Ascanio, 172
Glanvill, Joseph, 236
glassmaking, 3, 99–100, 136, 209, 229
Gnosticism, 25
Goethe, Johann Wolfgang von, 49, 89, 157, 245
gold: alchemy and, 34, 37, 41, 42, 45, 94, 99, 101, 107–14, 206, 207; coinage and, 108, 195; extraction experiments, 112–14; saltpeter and transmutation to, 187
Goldschmidt, Aaron, 40–41
golem legend, 86, 91, 171
Gonzaga, Francesco, Count of Novellara, 123–24, 129, 134
Gonzaga, Margherita, 125
Gonzaga, Vincenzo. *See* Vincenzo I Gonzaga
Gonzaga family, 51, 69, 80, 83, 98, 99, 117, 154, 158, 176; Colorni ties with, 119–24, 130, 136, 140–41, 146, 153, 159, 169, 178, 193, 194, 199, 200–203, 208, 210–11, 213–16; Este rivalry with, 203; tolerance of Jews by, 120–21, 140; witchcraft punishment and, 156. *See also* Mantua, Duchy of
Gottschalk (alchemist), 41, 105–6
government secrets. *See* state arcana
Gracián, Baltasar, 253; *Art of Worldly Wisdom*, 21
Grafton, Anthony, 6, 124–25
Grechetto, Isac, 75
Grunwald, Max, 225–26; *Mathematics among the Jews*, 226
guilds, 3, 70, 189
gunpowder, 71, 95, 98, 184–200, 202, 205, 229

guns. *See* weapons
Guothild, Frau, 54
Gustav III, King of Sweden, 248–49
Gustavus Adolphus, King of Sweden, 166–67

Habermas, Jürgen, 16
Habsburgs, 63, 73–75, 161–63, 165. *See also* Holy Roman Empire
Halbertal, Moshe, 25, 254
Hals, Salman von, 62–63. *See also* Teublein, Salman
Hamann, Johann Georg, 30
Hamburg, 41, 42, 113
Hame'assef (Journal), 248
Hannemann, Johann Ludwig, 43
Hardtwig, Wolfgang, 250
harquebus, 69–70, 72, 127, 128–29
Hartlib, Samuel, 198
Haskalah, 230, 244, 246, 248, 254
Hebrew Bible. *See* Bible
Hebrew language, 23, 25–31, 60, 82, 91, 102, 118, 146, 183, 190; alchemical manuscripts, 37, 43, 54; arcane dimension of, 28–31; codes based on, 58, 63, 184; magic book, 157, 158–59; poison terminology, 54; "power words," 31
Hebrew Orient Trading Company, 209, 210
Heine, Heinrich, 244
Henry VIII, King of England, 58–59
herbalists, 32, 50
Herder, Johann Gottfried, 30
Hermes Trismegistos, 151, 159, 223, 297n94
Hermetic tradition, 12, 90, 151, 157, 187, 233
Hildesheim, 40–41, 72
Hippocrates, 145
Hodierna, Giovanni Battista, 136
Hoffmann, E.T.A., 245

Holyday, Barten, 28
Holy Roman Empire, 67, 70, 73, 96, 101, 104, 162, 176–78, 190, 191, 200, 205, 245; gunpowder trade, 192–93; Jewish alchemists, 38–41, 247; largest Jewish community, 170. *See also* Long Turkish War; Rudolf II
Honauer, Jörg, 109–11
horoscopes, 109
Höschl, Lebl, 63
humanism, 23, 292n22
Hunter, John, 248
hydraulics, 68–69, 74–75, 77
hygiene, 188

Iachelino (fictional), 32–33
iatrochemistry, 49
Idel, Moshe, 25, 31
Illuminati, 11, 18
Immaculate Conception, 230
impotence, 99, 145
India, 80–81, 186
Industrial Revolution, 237–38
Inquisition, 26, 34, 41, 64, 89, 118, 187, 201; chiromancy ban, 150–51; secrecy of, 254; trials of alleged magi, 87, 88, 101–2, 156, 157
intellectual property, 65, 66
inventions, 65–69, 73, 74–75, 97–98, 99, 102, 117, 124–25, 127, 135, 152, 166, 212, 213; modern era's three most important, 185
invisible messages, 58, 59, 181–82
iron gallows, 11, 109, 110, 111
iron trade, 104–5
iron works, 114
Isaac of Noyon (Magister Achino), 69
Isaak, Mendel, 72–73, 320n341
Isacchi, Giovanni Battista, 102, 127
Isidore of Seville, 146
Islamic world, 11, 31, 53, 54–55, 70–71. *See also* Ottoman Empire

Israel, Jonathan, 72–73
Israelites, 24–25, 71, 183, 188, 212

Jābir ibn Ḥayyān, 54–55
Jacob of Pforzheim, 72
Jarè, Giuseppe, 219, 312n197; *Abramo Colorni*, 300n1
Jesuits, 21, 224, 227, 256
jewels. *See* gems
Jewish calendar, 136
Jewish converts. *See* converted Jews
Jewish emancipation, 27, 243, 251
Jewish Enlightenment. *See* Haskalah
Jewish folklore studies, 225, 226
Jewish mysticism. *See* Kabbalah; occult
Jewish Renaissance, 217, 218
Joabin (fictional), 240–42
Joachim II, Elector of Brandenburg, 95, 96
John I, King of Aragon, 38
Johnson, Samuel, *Dictionary,* 236–37
Joyce, James *Finnegan's Wake,* 216–17; *Ulysses,* 217
Judaism: *arcana Dei,* 4; "contributory narrative" of, 225, 228; Joyce allusions to, 217; literacy's importance to, 57; New Science vs. fundamental forms of, 229; seventeenth-century writings about, 24; theoretical abstract forms and, 229. *See also* anti-Judaism
Judgment Day, 138
"Jud Süß." *See* Oppenheimer, Joseph Süß
Julius II, Pope, 33
Julius, Duke of Braunschweig-Wolfenbüttel, 106, 276n27

Kabbala denudata, frontispiece of, 25
Kabbalah, 4–6, 51, 58–60, 90, 132, 138, 147, 153, 213, 233, 241, 247, 257; alchemy and, 43, 207, 226; "alchemy of words" and, 183; Christian interest in, 5, 25, 29, 30, 31, 59–60, 131, 164, 205;

court Jews and, 95; cryptography and, 183; defense of, 248; fortune telling and, 143–44; Mantua as center of, 120; post-1920s study of, 226; secrets of, 5, 25–26, 89, 109
Kahn, David, 326n431
Kant, Immanuel, 4–5, 264n18; *What Is Enlightenment?,* 252
Karl Alexander, Duke of Württemberg, 108–11, 192
Kassel, Landgrave of, 40
Kassel, Sammel von, 68
Katz, Jacob, 250
Kaufmann, David, 219
Kelley, Edward, 164
Kepler, Johannes, 164, 178, 320n336
Kircher, Athanasius, 155, 256
Kleist, Heinrich von, 245
knowledge. *See* open knowledge; secret knowledge
knowledge culture, 231–44, 249; definitions of, 232–33; experts and, 67, 237, 255, 257–58; sites of, 235. *See also* Scientific Revolution
knowledge economy, 2, 11–12, 232, 235–39, 256
Koselleck, Reinhart, 10–11
Kunstbüchlein (unpublished books), 50
Kyeser, Conrad, 125, 127; *Bellifortis,* 127

Lampronti, Isaac, 244
Lang, Philipp, 172, 175, 204
Lateran Palace, 100
Latin language, 119, 157, 158, 174, 179
Lattis, Fortunio, 75
Lavater, Johann Caspar, 149
lead, 48, 106
Leibniz, Gottfried Wilhelm, 113, 229
lenses, 136
Leo X, Pope, 33
Leonardo da Vinci, 55, 124–25, 127, 138, 218, 219, 280n127

Leone Ebreo (Yehuda Abravanel), 146–47; *Dialoghi d'amore,* 146
letter-writing, 9, 57, 179
Leuchtenberg, Landgrave of, 38, 39
Levant, 28, 46, 50, 60, 71, 77, 81, 101, 190
Levi, Giacob, 61–62
Levi, Iseppe Prospero, 99
Levi, Josef, 69
Levi, Salomone di Vita, 27
Levison, Gumpert, 248–49
Lichtenberg, Georg Christoph, 245
lies, sociology of, 9
Lilith, conjuring spirit of, 101
Lima, Angelo (Mordecai Baruch), 81
Limojon de Saint-Didier, Alexandre-Touissant, 297n94
Linnaeus, Carl, 248
Lippold (Jewish mint master), 95–96
Lipsius, Justus, 178
Livorno, 97, 101, 144
Llull, Ramon, 89
Lodi, 74–75, 97, 98
Loew ben Bezalel, Judah (the Maharal), 91, 92, 171
Lombardy, 75, 96, 97, 129, 195, 196
Long Turkish War, 74, 169, 184–85, 192–93, 194, 202, 205
Lorraine, Duke of, 176–77
"Lorraine Address to Sixtus V" (forgery), 176–77
Lucerna, Moses, 170, 321–22n370
Luhmann, Niklas, 2, 9, 21
Lunardi, Abraham, 49
Luria, Isaac, 143–44
Lusitanus, Amatus, 83, 122–23, 280n135
Luther, Martin, 23, 104, 111, 290n358
Luzzatto, Simone, 265n22; *Discorso circa il stato de gl'hebrei,* 239

Machiavelli, Niccolò, 20–21, 56
machine gun, 127
machine technology, 119, 126, 134–36

Maddalena the Greek, 90
Mafteach Shelomo (magic book), 158
Maggino di Gabrielli, 99–100, 209;
  Dialoghi sopra l'utili sue inventioni circa la seta, 100
magia naturalis, 151, 154, 156, 182, 233; definition of, 155
magic, 5, 6, 18, 22, 83–93, 117, 132, 152–61, 172, 176, 191, 207–8, 220, 227, 233, 249; alchemy as, 32–33, 34; Ba'al Shem and, 247; black vs. white, 34, 139, 153, 155, 156, 159; engineers linked with, 66, 67; entrepreneur potential and, 94; first "do-it-yourself" tricks book, 152; Inquisition trials and, 87, 88, 101–2, 156, 157; mathematics linked with, 138, 139; science as form of, 16, 221, 333; unicorn properties of, 80. *See also* occult
magic mirrors, 93, 166–67
magnetism, 3, 242
magus. *See* magic
Maharal. *See* Loew ben Bezalel, Judah
Maier, Michael, 164
Maimon, Salomon, 353n188
Maimonides, 32, 40, 146, 225–26;
  Tractatus de venenis, 55
Mainz, Bishop of, 26
Mainz, Elector of, 113
Malinowski, Bronisław, 86
Malta, 191
Mantino, Graziadio, 68
Mantino, Jacob, 59
Mantua, Duchy of, 43, 50–51, 54, 81, 98, 99, 176, 177; artworks and, 215; Colorni family and, 117, 119–20; Colorni's return to, 210–11; employment of engineers, 69, 70, 121; flourishing Jewish life, 120–21, 140, 202; theatrical productions, 126. *See also* Gonzaga family
Mantua, Duke of. *See* Vincenzo I Gonzaga

manufacturing, 14, 114, 209, 229; secrecy and, 21–22. *See also* patents
Mariano di Jacopo. *See* Taccola
Markus, Josias, 102–3
Marlowe, Christopher, 24; *The Jew of Malta,* 24, 77–78
Marmirolo castle, 140–41
Marranos, 120
maskilim, 246
Masonic order. *See* Freemasonry
Massarano, Isacchino, 202
mathematics, 5, 117, 135–39, 140, 151, 152, 166
Matthias, Archduke, 321n370
matzo, 34
Mavrogonato, David, 63
Maximilian, Archduke of Austria, 92, 161–62, 165, 167
Mayse-Bukh (1602), 26, 160, 292n15
measurement, 135, 136, 139, 151
Medici, Giulio de' Cardinal, 75, 187
Medici, Lorenzo de,' 75, 187
Medici family, 16, 26, 91, 100–101, 123, 129, 133, 134, 136, 140, 144, 209, 220
medicine, 28, 33, 36, 57, 121–23, 146–48, 160, 188, 213, 216, 229, 230, 248; alchemy and, 3, 41–44, 95, 98–99, 226; antiquity and, 145, 147, 150; arcana and, 3, 19, 36, 49–56, 89; astrology and, 51; Jewish students of, 122, 243; magic linked with, 90, 156; Scientific Revolution and, 233–34; unicorn horn use as, 52, 80–81, 82, 83
Mehmet II, Sultan, 53
Menahem (Magister Menaym Judaeus), 38
Menasseh ben Israel, *Esperanza de Israel,* 212–13
Mendelssohn, Moses, 112, 219, 246–47, 248, 254, 353n188
Mendes, Alvaro. *See* Abenaes, Salomon
mercantile activity, 27, 72, 117, 239, 243; alchemy and, 94, 95, 98, 99–100;

arcana and, 94–115, 245; curiosity and, 236; espionage and, 61, 63; Jewish networks of, 54, 191; trade secrets and, 21–22
mercury compounds, 46, 48, 55
Merlin (legendary magus), 228
Merton, Robert K., 227–28
Merton thesis, 227, 228
messianism, 43, 82, 86, 212
metallurgy, 72, 95–96, 104, 106–7, 182, 185. *See also* gold
metoposcopy, 143
Meyer, Jacob. *See* Philadelphia, Jakob
Meyzl, Mordechai, 98, 170–71, 175
Me-zahab (biblical), 42
midwives, 32
Milan, 53, 69
Milan, Duke of, 44, 69, 70
military technology. *See* gunpowder; warfare; weapons
mineral salts, 75
mining, 67, 185
"miracle rabbis," 86
Mirami, Rafael, 122, 123, 131, 212
Mirowitz, Leobel, 74
mirrors, 135, 136, 146, 181, 212, 221; magic, 93, 166–67
Misson, Maximilian, 64
Modena (city), 194
Modena, Duchy of, 44, 55, 123, 168
Modena, Duke of, 54, 99
Modena, Leon, 44, 49, 86, 89, 90, 118, 144, 146, 195
Modena, Mordecai (son), 44, 90–91
Modena, Shemaia (uncle), 44
Mokyr, Joel, 237
Molcho, Salomon, 86
money business, 1–2, 6, 27, 51, 95–98, 120–21, 238; treatise on, 132
moneyer, office of, 95–96, 104, 105
Monferrat, Margrave of, 69
Montalto, Eliahu, 156

Montanus, Petrus, 299n111
Montecatini, Antonio, 123
Monteverdi, Claudio, 169
Morino, Il. *See* Colorni, Simone
Morosini, Giulio, 63
Moser, Friedrich Wilhelm, 111, 218
Moses (biblical), 29, 31, 71, 207–8, 240
Moses Israel of Thessaloniki, 187
Moyses of Mühlhausen, 70
Mühlenfels, Hans Heinrich von, 111
munitions. *See* weapons
Münzjuden, 105
Muslims. *See* Islamic world
Mussafia, Binyamin, 42–43, 188; *Mezahab Epistola*, 42–43
Mustapha III, Sultan, 245
mystery, 4, 5, 21, 30, 230
mysticism, 20, 28–29, 51, 217. *See also* Kabbalah

Naples, 41, 51; academy of secrets, 12
natural history, 122, 123, 232. *See also* secrets of nature
natural philosophy, 12, 28, 123, 147, 213, 230, 233
Navarro, Salamon, 75–76
Neher, André, 228
Nelle, Mardochaeus de, 172–74
Neoplatonism, 25, 151
Netherlands, 28, 192, 250
Neuhoff, Theodor Stephan Freiherr von, 247–48
Newman, William R., 35
Newton, Isaac, 229, 233, 248
Nice, 53–54, 96
Nicholas of Cusa, *Dialogus de Deo abscondito*, 20
Nicolay, Nicolas de, *Quatre premiers livres de navigations*, 78, 79
Nobel Prize laureates, 251
North American expeditions, 172

Nuremberg, 39, 40, 68
Nüschler, Hans Heinrich, 299n111

occult, 3, 4, 17–18, 22, 35, 51, 90, 98, 163–64, 232–34, 247; Hebrew language and, 28–29, 30, 31, 60, 102; as "science," 18, 233, 234, 242; Venetian ghetto as marketplace for, 88–89
odometer, 135
ointments, secret recipes, 50–51
Ongaro, Manuele, 50–51
open knowledge, 11, 13, 17, 242–43, 249–59
"open" secrets, 9, 16
Oppenheimer, Joseph Süß, 106–11, 192
Orléans, Duke of, 247
Osiander, Lucas, 206
Ottolenghi, Josef, 235
Ottoman Empire, 28, 43, 48–56, 58, 67, 81, 83, 123, 128, 187; Jewish military expertise and, 72, 78–79, 189; Jewish saltpeter trade and, 190, 191; Jewish spying for, 61, 63, 91. *See also* Long Turkish War
oxygen, discovery of, 187–88, 198

Pacification Treaty (1589), 165
Padua, 30, 122, 222, 256
Pagis, Dan, 28
Palatinate-Zweibrücken, 112, 113–15
Pallache, Samuel, 286n272
palmistry. *See* chiromancy
papacy, 26, 33, 97, 100, 128, 141, 176–79
Papal States, 87, 141; Ferrara reversion to, 168, 194, 201–2
Paracelsus, 3, 31, 49, 167, 173, 197, 198
PaRDeS (acronym), 29
Park, Katharine, 232
Parolini, Antonio Maria, 121, 122
Pasciuto, Daniel ("The Prophet"), 69
Patai, Raphael, 35, 49, 226–27
patents, 65–66, 67, 68, 69, 75, 99
Pavia brothers, 74–75, 97–98, 234–35

pawnbroking, 2, 239
Perez, Daniel Israel, 68–69
perfumes, 50
Pergamon Museum (Berlin), 215–16
Peter IV, King of Aragon, 38
Petrarch, 183
Petrus, Mundanus, 111
Petz, Bartholomäus, 193
Philadelphia, Jakob, 244–47, 248, 249
Philip II, King of Spain, 74–75, 96, 97, 318n315
philosopher's stone, 95, 113, 297n94
physicians. *See* medicine
physiognomy, 140, 142–44, 147–50, 221
Piazza universale, 126–27, 130, 131
Pico della Mirandola, Giovanni, 16, 29, 30, 85
Pietro d'Abano, 152
plague, 50, 52, 54, 56, 121
Plato, 145, 147–48, 152
Plotinus, 152
pogroms, 52, 191
poisons and antidotes, 52–56, 75, 83, 99, 280n127
Poland, 43, 44, 70, 73, 74, 191, 197; disputed Crown of, 161–62, 165, 168, 169
polyalphabetic method, 180
Pomis, David de, 83, 98–99, 190, 233; *Tzemaḥ David,* 190
porcelain manufacture, 22
Portaleone, Abraham, 83, 148, 181–83, 208; *De auro dialogi tres,* 43; *Shiltei ha-Gibborim,* 58, 190, 199–200
Portland, Duke of, 248
Porto, Abraham Menaḥem, 57–58; *Zafnet Paneaḥ,* 58
Portuguese Jews, 26, 27
Prague, 106, 170–71, 189; imperial court (*see* Rudolf II); Maharal and, 91, 92, 171; print shops, 201–2; saltpeter from, 188, 189, 192, 197, 199
Prague Ḥoshen, 98, 170

prestidigitators, 153
Preto, Paolo, 62
Prévost, Jean, *La Première Partie es subtiles et plaisantes inventions*, 153
printing, 12, 14, 185, 254
privacy, right of, 9, 252–53, 259
professore de' secreti, 12, 13, 15, 51, 119, 145–46, 149, 154, 155, 160, 161; models for, 221–22, 246 (*see also under* Colorni, Abramo)
Protestants, 23, 146, 191, 192, 205, 206, 209
Provenzali, David, 120
Psalms, 183
Pseudo-Albertus Magnus, 89
Pseudo-Aristotle, 12, 36, 145, 147
Pseudo-Geber, 148
Pseudo-Paracelsus, 167
pseudo-sciences. *See* alchemy; magic
Ptolemy, 147
public, 254; early modern concept of, 16–17, 21; specific kinds of, 258
public life, secrets vs. open, 253
publishing of secrets, 13–17
Puritans, 212, 224, 227

rabbinic tradition, 25, 29, 30, 57–58, 86, 89, 153; Scientific Revolution vs., 229–30, 234–35
Rafael, Marco, 58–59
Raleigh, Sir Walter, 172
Ravatoso, Samuel, 71
re'em (biblical), 82, 83, 290n358
Regensburg, 34, 39
Reggio, 88, 94, 102, 128, 168, 194
Reuchlin, Johannes, 30
Reuveni, David, 43, 79, 132
Rhine River gold, 113
rhinoceros, 83
riddle poems, 28
ritual baths, 67
ritual murder, 24, 209
Roanoke colony, 172

Robert-Houdin, Jean-Eugène, 227–28
Rocca, Bartolomeo della (Cocles), 148, 149, 313n221
rocket design, 127
Rome, 70–71, 75, 99, 100
Roper, Lyndal, 94
Rosales, Jacob, 41–42; *Anotaçam crisopeia* (*On the Art of Making Gold*), 42
Rosenberg, Peter Wok von, 106
Rosenberg family, 106, 173–74
Rosheim, Josel von, 205
Rosicrucians, 18, 114
Rossi, Azariah de,' 305n62; *Me'or 'Enayim*, 146
Rossi, Salamone, 120
Rosso (Jewish mediator), 203–4
Roth, Cecil, 22–23, 228; "Amazing Abraham Colorni," 300n1
Rothschild family, 291n371
Rotwelsch (argot), 60
Rovai, Francesco, 211–12
Royal Academy of Sciences (Berlin), 247
Royal Society (London), 93, 236, 238, 240, 242, 243, 244
Rübezahl (rain spirit), 292n29
Ruderman, David, 229, 230, 233, 251
Rudolf II, Holy Roman Emperor, 33, 83, 98, 106, 128–29, 138, 150, 204, 205, 231; alchemists and, 35, 41, 72, 163, 164, 184–86; cabinet of curiosities of, 80; Colorni as court favorite of, 110, 118, 119, 144, 145, 154, 161–77, 193, 197–201, 203, 220; Colorni's son and, 215, 216; cryptology and, 178–79; gunpowder needs and, 192–93; Jewish arcana and, 172–75; Maharal meeting with, 91; papal charges against, 176–77; passion for occult of, 163–64; Prague court as intellectual/artistic center, 163–64, 169, 222; roman à clef about, 174–75; technology and, 72–73

Rumpf, Wolfgang, 170
Ruscelli, Girolamo, *Secreti del reverendo donno Alessio piemontese*, 13

Sacerdote, Simone, 97
Sacerdote, Vitale, 96, 97, 280n278
Saint-Didier, Limojon de, 63–64
Salman of Hals. *See* Teublein, Salman
Salman the Mining Master, 68, 69
Salomon, Michel Angelo, 56
Salomone da Sesso (Ercole de' Fideli), 71
Salomone da Zara, 56
Salomon of Piove, 53
Salomon's House, 239–40, 241, 244, 251
saltpeter, 44, 71, 75, 184–92, 208; historical development of, 185; Jewish specific knowledge of, 189–91; manufacture of artificial, 186, 189–91, 197–98, 205, 207, 210, 215; natural formation of, 186, 197, 198; unpleasant odors from, 188–89; uses/trade in, 191–92. *See also* gunpowder
Saluzzo, Margravine of, 44
Sanguineti, Isaac, 101–2
Sarfatti, Abram, 48
Sarfatti, Nacaman, 46–48, 130
Sarfatti family, 46–48, 55, 75
Sarpi, Paolo, 146
Saruk, Ḥayyim, 58, 91
Sasso, Salomone da. *See* Fideli, Ercole d'
Sasson, Abraham, 91
Savorgnano, Mario, 59
Savoy, Duchy of, 77, 96, 97, 304n60
Savoy-Nemours, Duke of, 129, 134
Schiller, Friedrich, 245
Schkolnick, Meyer R. *See* Merton, Robert K.
Schnaber, Mordecai Gumbel. *See* Levison, Gumpert
Scholem, Gershom, 5, 226
Schott, Caspar, 155
Schubart, C.F.D., 245, 246

Schudt, Johann Jacob, 24, 42, 50, 64, 188
Schumann, Johann, 177, 201
Schwarz, Berthold (Bertholdus Niger), 191
Science: biblical supremacy to, 171; Colorni's defense of, 149, 221; premodern vs. modern Jews and, 6, 226, 251
Scientific Revolution, 7, 11, 16, 18, 224–59; from a Christian perspective, 228, 231–32; continuation of arcane practices and, 22; curiosity as basis for, 236–37; Delmedigo as Jewish standard-bearer for, 256–57; Jews and, 17, 224–34, 242–43, 250–51, 254–57; meaning of "New Science" and, 232; openness ideology and, 17, 249, 251; reassessed historical origins of, 232–33; social position and, 242–43
Scotto, Girolamo (Hieronymus Scotus), 153–54, 155
scrap metal trade, 104–5
secreta literature, 14–16, 35–36, 50, 51, 90, 102, 148
"Secret Expedition," 62
secret ink. *See* invisible messages
secret knowledge, 3, 8, 17, 25–26, 32, 242; mystery s, 4. *See also* open knowledge
secret languages, 27–28
secret messages, 181–82
secret societies, 8, 11, 18, 250, 253. *See also* Freemasonry
secrets of nature, 4, 7, 12, 18, 19, 79–84, 160, 163, 164, 216, 221, 234, 242; Kabbalah as key to, 25
secrets of state. *See* state arcana
Secretum secretorum (pseudo-Aristotle), 12, 36, 145
secret writing, 58–59
Sefer Raziel, 157
Sefer Yossipon, 82
Seghetus, Thomas, 178

Segre, Abraham, 44–45
Selenus, Gustavus (pseud.), 178
Seligmann (Jewish physician), 40
Seligmann von Brenz, 204
Sendivogius, Michael, 44, 164, 197, 198
Sennett, Richard, 23, 88
Sephardic Jews, 26, 28, 72, 91, 122, 212, 238; alchemy practice, 37–38, 41–44, 46; renowned families, 212; settlement in Italy, 96–97; technological expertise, 77, 78
Servati (Venetian Jew), 244
Seyfried, Heinrich Wilhelm, 244–45
Sforza, Caterina, 50
Sforza, Francesco, 53, 69
Sforza, Lodovico, 124
Shulvass, Moses A., 228
Sicily, 71, 190, 191
Sigillum Salomonis (magic book), 204
Sigismund, Archduke of Austria, 40
Sigismund Báthory, Prince of Transylvania, 203
Sigismund Vasa, Prince of Sweden, 161–62
silk mills, 13–14, 99, 100, 209
silver, 105, 114
Simeon of Mainz, 167
Siminto, Magister, 71
Simmel, Georg, 8–9, 10, 252, 253; "Das Geheimnis und die geheime Gesellschaft," 8–9
Simon di Roman, 76
Simonsohn, Shlomo, 67
Sixtus V, Pope, 99, 100, 141, 176–77
Smith, Pamela, 164
soap, 50
Society of Antiquaries, 238
Society of Mines Royal, 172
sociology, 8–9, 10, 227
Solomon, King, 32, 151, 158, 159–61, 183, 184, 219, 222–23
Solon, 146, 156, 180

Sömmering, Philipp, 102–3
Sommi, Leone de,' 120, 169
sorcery, 23, 86, 88, 90, 155, 156, 207; economic/political overlap with, 94
Spain, 43, 71, 74–75, 96; *conversos,* 26, 81; expulsion of Jews from, 78, 97, 120; Jewish spies for, 60
Spanish Armada (1588), 81
Spanish fly, 99
Spinoza, Baruch, 190
spying. *See* espionage
standing armies, 72, 191–92
state arcana, 66–67, 94, 97–98, 99, 161–77, 253, 258, 259; coinage as, 104; cryptography and, 56–60; factors in, 19–22; poison use and, 53–54, 55; Salomon's House and, 240; technology and, 13–14
steganography, 9–10
Steinschneider, Moritz, 219, 225–26
Stephen Báthory, King of Poland, 73
Stern, Selma, 72, 109
Strasser, Gerhard, 182
Strauss, Leo, 13
Stuttgart court, 197; Colorni's stay at, 111, 164, 200, 203–11, 214, 218. *See also* Württemberg, Duchy of
sublimate, 182, 280n135; mecuric chloride, 46, 55, 75
sulfur, 106
sundial, 166
superstitions, 88, 142, 149, 154, 221, 226
Sweden, 41, 161–62, 166–67, 248–49
Switzerland, 96
Symuel, Perret, 44
syphilis treatment, 90

Taccola (Mariano di Jacopo), 66, 125
Tacitus, 19
talismans, 80
Talmud, 59, 82, 184, 229, 244
Tartaglia, 125

Tasso, Torquato, 125
Tassoni, Alessandro, 130, 211; *Pensieri*, 135, 305n70
technology, 36, 65-79, 94, 97, 228, 232; as state secret, 13-14
telescope invention, 136
Telle, Joachim, 173
Ten Tribes of Israel, 212
Terentius, Marcus, 146
Teublein, Salman (Salomon), 38, 39, 62-63
Texeira, Manoel, 41
textiles, 114, 185, 229; patents, 75
theater, 15, 66, 126, 214
Thirty Years' War, 72-73, 171, 192
Thomas, Keith, 143, 153
Thomas Aquinas, *Summa contra Gentiles*, 146
tikkun, 264n19
Timolione (Venetian Jew), 44
Tirosh-Samuelson, Hava, 230
Titian, 215
Torah, 171, 244; secrets of, 25, 84, 143, 254
Trachtenberg, Joshua, 226
trade. *See* mercantile activity
Trani, Moses, 83
transmutation. *See* alchemy; gold
Treuenberg, Jacob von (Jacob Bassevi), 171
Tricasso, 148, 149
Trier, 68, 86, 101, 106
Trieste, 61
Trilling, Lionel, 254
Trismosin, Salomon, *Aureum vellus*, 41
Trithemius, Johannes, 57, 89, 178; Ave Maria method, 183-84; *Polygraphiae libri sex*, 181; *Steganographia*, 181, 182
Tübingen, 207, 208
Turks. *See* Ottoman Empire
Tuscany, 37, 48, 50, 55, 75, 132, 133, 136
Tuscany, Grand Duke of, 81

Ulm, Josep von, 68
Umbria, 190
unicorn, 36, 52, 79-84, 216; miraculous goblet, 81
universities, 12-13, 229; Jews and, 122, 243-44, 255
University of Ferrara, 121, 122, 123, 222
University of Göttingen, 244-45
University of Padua, 122, 222, 256
University of Tübingen, 207-8
University of Wittenberg, 102
Uraltes Chymisches Werck (1735), 187-88
Ursi, Giuseppe (Iosef d'Orso Tedesco), 133
usus et fabrica books, 14, 100
utopianism, 148, 161, 239-42, 244

Valchus (Jewish physician), 53
Valvasor, Johann Weichard, 93, 167
Varignana, Guglielmo, *Secreta sublimia ad varios curandos morbos*, 35-36
Varro, 146
Vecchia, Pietro della, 87, 143
Vegetius, 146
Venice, 12-13, 27, 30, 46-65, 88-89, 93, 96-97, 129, 130, 157, 167, 169-70, 177, 204, 215; alchemy practice, 34-35, 44, 46, 98; biological warfare, 55-56; chemical industry, 46-48; cipher messages, 58, 59; Colorni ties with, 129-30, 201, 220; famine (1590), 75-77; Inquisition, 187; intellectual/technical activity, 65-69, 101; Jewish magic, 87-91; Jewish medicine, 49-50, 51, 53, 54, 98; Jewish poison expertise, 53-56, 75; Jewish spying for, 60-65, 91; unicorn horn possession, 80
Vergil, 183
Verona, 45, 57, 214
Vico, Giambattista, 217
Vienna, 57, 73-74, 95, 156, 245; expulsion of Jews from, 63

Vigenère, Blaise de, 59–60
Vincenzo I Gonzaga, Duke of Mantua, 27, 55, 75, 120, 140–41, 142, 145, 156, 158, 159, 169, 199, 210; character and conduct of, 202–3; Long Turkish War and, 194, 202; refusal to extradite Colorni's son, 211, 214, 216
Vita, Levi di, 98
Vital, Ḥayyim, 31, 55, 58; *Kabbala ma'asit ve-Alkimiyya*, 31, 43
vitriol, 6
Vitruvius, 66, 135, 151
Voltaire, 157
voyages of discovery, 172, 236

Wahl, Saul (son), 113–15
Wahl Dessauer, Herz (father), 112–13, 114, 115, 246
Wakefield, Robert, 30
Wallis, John, 137–38
warfare, 127–28; astrology and, 66; Bible on, 71; chemical and biological, 54, 55; cryptographic messages, 58; standing armies, 72, 191–92
water clock, 124
water projects, 74–75
weapons, 12, 66, 67, 102, 124–29, 208, 212, 218, 229; artillery, 78–79, 98, 124, 200; cannon, 79, 125; harquebus, 69–70, 72, 127, 128–29; Jewish expertise/manufacture of, 54, 69–72, 187, 189; poisoned, 54, 55, 56, 280n127; repeating firearms, 124, 127–29; saltpeter uses, 185, 186, 187. *See also* gunpowder
Weber, Max, 227, 252

Weigenmaier, Georg, 207
Welling, Georg von, *Opus magocabbalisticum et theologicum*, 157
well poisoning, charges of, 24, 52, 55–57
Westerbarkey, Joachim, 9
wheelchair, 134
white magic. See *magia naturalis*
Wissenschaft des Judentums, 23, 219, 225–26, 227, 228
witchcraft, 87, 156, 186
Wolfenbüttel, 42, 102–3, 163; ducal library of, 135–36
women, experts in secrets, 32, 50
Württemberg, Duchy of, 198; Jewish alchemists, 41, 101, 108–10; status of Jews, 205, 209–10. *See also* Stuttgart court
Württemberg, Duke of. *See* Frederick I; Karl Alexander
Würzburg, Bishop of, 154

Yagel, Abraham, 25, 83–84, 152, 153, 233; *Beit Ya'ar ha-Levanon*, 83
Yates, Frances, 232–33
Yeniche (itinerants' language), 60
Yiddish language, 26, 63

Zacharias (Jewish alchemist), 43
Zacuti (Jewish poisoner), 54
Zalfaldi, Nataniel, 48
Zevi, Shabbetai, 86
Zohar, 143
Zonca, Vittorio, 13–14; *Nuovo teatro di machine et edificii*, 13
Zweibrücken, 112, 113, 115